Advance Praise

Pain and Passion joyfully recreates the colourful cast of characters –
and the chaos – that made Stampede Wrestling so much fun.

> – Greg Oliver, author, *The Pro Wrestling Hall of Fame: The Canadians*

Pain and Passion is an awesome book. I couldn't put the book down and
would rank it with any wrestling book ever written. Brutally honest ...
neither exploitive nor apologetic about the subject.... The depth of getting
into so many of the key personalities and stories is amazing. Stampede
Wrestling may have never been the biggest wrestling promotion in the
world, but it very well may have been the most interesting.

> – Dave Meltzer, editor, *Wrestling Observer*

Heath McCoy's *Pain and Passion* drags the reader out of the squared
circle for a piledriving peek at the characters of Stampede Wrestling.
Warts-and-all stories are spooled out in an engaging and unflinching
manner – rich with detail, ripe with deceit. A ring-a-ding-dong-dandy
about a true Calgary institution.

> – Scott Cruickshank, *Calgary Herald*

Pain and Passion

The History of Stampede Wrestling

Heath McCoy

CANWEST BOOKS

Published by CanWest Books Inc.
A subsidiary of CanWest MediaWorks Publications Inc.
1450 Don Mills Road
Toronto, ON
Canada, M3B 2X7

Library and Archives Canada Cataloguing in Publication

McCoy, Heath, 1970–

    Pain and passion : the history of Stampede Wrestling / Heath McCoy.

ISBN 0-9736719-8-X

    1. Stampede Wrestling – History. 2. Hart family. 3. Wrestling
promoters – Alberta – Calgary – History. 4. Wrestling – Alberta-
Calgary – History. I. Title.

GV1198.15.A2M33 2005   796.812'097123'38   C2005-905309-7

Cover and Interior Design by Peter Ross/Counterpunch
Edited by Judy Phillips
Proofread by Susan Johnson
Prepress by Emerson Group
Cover Photography by Bob Leonard
Heath McCoy's Photo by Ted Jacob/Calgary Herald
Printed and Bound in Canada by Transcontinental

First Edition

10 9 8 7 6 5 4 3 2 1

To Grampa, because I've always loved watching wrestling with you; Gramma for not making us change the channel; and to Mom and Dad, who were the best parents a kid could have (despite your lousy rules).

And to my wife, Tamara. No one knows how much personal pain and passion went into this book like you do. Thanks for getting me through it. I love you.

Contents

Acknowledgments

All told, I conducted close to sixty interviews while researching for this book. I also relied heavily on certain organizations and sources. Many of these were invaluable to me, and there would be no *Pain and Passion* without them. I would like to thank the following:

Members of the Hart family including Bret, Bruce, and Smith Hart, and in particular Keith, Ross, and Alison Hart, who went above and beyond in terms of their openness and availability to me. Nattie Neidhart belongs in this category too. While writing, I was struck by her warmth and encouragement. I'm rooting for you, Nattie.

Another key assist came from Bob Leonard, the Stampede Wrestling photographer for over three decades. Bob has an almost photographic recall of the good old days. Luckily, he's a hell of a nice man and was willing to share those tales with me, even when I hounded him on an almost daily basis.

Calgary's Glenbow Museum was a veritable goldmine, giving me access to its extensive Hart family collection. Special thanks to archivist Tonia Fanella. She had a real appreciation for the human element and the historical importance of the Stampede Wrestling story, and it was great working with her.

I'm also grateful to wrestling journalists David Meltzer of the *Wrestling Observer Newsletter* and Greg Oliver of the Slam! Wrestling website. Their amazing work over the years answered countless questions for me. A number of books were also of great value, including Marsha Erb's *Stu Hart: Lord of the Ring*; Martha Hart's *Broken Harts: The Life and Death of Owen Hart*;

Diana Hart's *Under the Mat*; and Tom "Dynamite Kid" Billington's *Pure Dynamite. Sex, Lies, and Headlocks*, by Shaun Assael and Mike Mooneyham was also superb when it came to understanding the WWE.

Thanks to the *Calgary Herald* for its resources, and for giving me time off to tackle this project. A tip of the hat to publisher Peter Menzies, who supported the book from the start; Steve Jenkinson; and Shelley Youngblut, editor of the *Herald*'s in-house magazine, *Swerve*. A story I wrote for Shelley last December, on the great villains of Stampede Wrestling, netted me a Western Canadian Magazine Award and it gave me confidence that I was on to something special with this book.

As for Ryan Kellough over at Global TV Calgary, who made me an incredible tape of old matches that captured the Stampede Wrestling spirit perfectly – you're awesome! Thanks also to news anchor Gord Gillies for his help.

Further acknowledgements go to Michelle Billington, Bad News Allen, Dan Kroffat, Nomi Whalen, Leo Burke, Lorrie Mills, Ben Bassarab, the Cuban Assassin, Chris Benoit, Archie Gouldie, John Helton, Bob Lueck, Honky Tonk Wayne, Phil Klein, Alberta premier Ralph Klein, Les Thornton, Bud Osborne, Angelo Mosca, Gerry Morrow, Gama Singh, Jock and Diana Osler, Don Leo Jonathon, Glenn Ruhl, George Scott, Mike Shaw, Frank Sisson, Tor Kamata, Paul "The Butcher" Vachon, Abdullah the Butcher, Mlad Elzein, John Dolin, Kate Krestow, and Trevor Korsrud.

I can't forget the people at CanWest Books who worked so hard to make this book see the light of day – on time. Thanks to Carole-Ann Hayes, Leah Campbell, and Tracy Nixon, and, at Counterpunch, Peter Ross.

Finally, a big hug for you, Mags, for always encouraging me when this project seemed impossible (and thanks to Paul for the scotch)!

A special thanks to my editor, Judy Phillips, who came to the table late, cleaned up a daunting mess at an insanely crushing crunch time, and dealt with me when I acted like one of J.R. Foley's maniacal minions.

Introduction

When I was eleven years old, I wanted to be Dynamite Kid. Even when he was one of the bad guys, committing heinous acts against my other idol, Bret Hart, I secretly worshipped the tough, cocky Englishman who moved with the agility of Spider-Man in the wrestling ring.

In the early 1980s, I watched *Stampede Wrestling* religiously, glued to the TV every Saturday afternoon in the living room of my Saskatoon home. When the show was over, I'd snatch my little brother and re-enact the matches, with him as my crash test dummy. Poor kid. In the schoolyard, my friends and I played Stampede Wrestling at recess, pretending to be the stars of the Calgary-based promotion, imitating the down-home play-by-plays of announcer Ed Whalen as we hammered on each other. "Off those ropes! Look out, Nellie! It's a malfunction at the junction!"

I was the runt of my class then, neither good at nor particularly taken with most sports. Comic books were my passion, which never makes one the most popular kid in school. But where wrestling was concerned, I bonded with my classmates. All the boys were hooked on the wild brawls and zany theatre-meets-sports soap opera that the famed Hart family concocted each week. And pro wrestling was perfectly in keeping with my love of comic books. The Hart boys, Dynamite Kid, Davey Boy Smith – they were like superheroes come to life.

Every so often, my dad and my grandpa took me to the Monday night matches too, when Stampede Wrestling came to the Saskatoon Arena. Grandpa had been watching wrestling since the 1950s and he was still a big fan. When things got too far out or bloody, Gramps would assure me the action was fake, though he didn't seem to believe that himself when he'd howl with indignation at the villains' wicked ways: "That son-of-a-bitch is cheating!"

For several generations on the Canadian Prairies, Stu Hart's Stampede Wrestling was an institution: a staple of the pop culture diet for hundreds of thousands of fans. But the show's influence was far more than just regional. In the late 1980s, it was broadcast across the country on TSN (The Sports Network). Over the decades, bootleg tapes of *Stampede Wrestling* were broadcast in up to thirty countries around the world. Some of the most famous wrestlers of all time emerged from the promotion, from Gene Kiniski and Superstar Billy Graham (Hulk Hogan's forefather) to Bret and Owen Hart, the British Bulldogs, and current superstar Chris Benoit. From its remote neck of the woods in Western Canada, Stampede Wrestling helped shape the wrestling world into the multimillion-dollar mega-industry it is today.

Even though the modern mat game has become too flash-over-substance for my liking – dominated as it is by Vince McMahon's media colossus, the WWE (World Wrestling Entertainment) – I'm still a wrestling fan. Wrestling has always had a crude, trashy nature. It's part of the fun, and I don't share the opinion of the legions of critics (including the Hart family) who blast the WWE on moral grounds. Yes, McMahon has upped the trash-ante with bottom-feeding gimmicks, beer-guzzling anti-heroes, overt sexual innuendo, and a bevy of half-naked women he tries to pass off as wrestlers. But to me, the spectacle is not that far removed from the typical heavy metal concert, and I love a good heavy metal concert.

But I do think the game has lost something special, and I miss the heyday of Stampede Wrestling. There was something so pure about the product. Yes, it was showbiz too. Character-driven, with predetermined matches, of course Stampede Wrestling was contrived. But not nearly like the WWE is today. WWE has become the wrestling equivalent of the most bloated arena rock concert. It's a slick, larger-than-life dose of maximum, big-budget entertainment. But it has also gotten too predictable, over-the-top to the point of ridiculousness, and far too showy for its own good. The WWE is so bogged down by the frills that it has lost its heart.

Stampede Wrestling, on the other hand, had a real honky-tonk spirit. Low-budget, down-and-dirty production that it was, with weekly brawls in barn-like arenas across the West, it was all heart. It is like the difference between the Rolling Stones of today, with their perfectly choreographed extravaganzas, and the raw, dynamic blues-rock band the Stones used to be.

On paper, the WWE offers more bang for the buck, while Stampede Wrestling could be a rather sloppy, low-rent affair. But the latter felt a lot more genuine, and when Stampede was on a roll, it produced some of the greatest pro wrestling in the history of the game. The wild matches. The kooky angles. The spectacular performers. Stampede Wrestling had it all.

As it was a Prairie production, not rooted in the big media centres of Montreal or Toronto, the Stampede Wrestling story was never chronicled in the way it deserved to be. I felt that was a shame. The promotion was a cultural institution in the West, and its influence was felt across the pro wrestling world. From the action in the ring to the captivating behind-the-scenes story that propelled that action, I see the Stampede Wrestling story as a wild and woolly, rock 'n' roll saga. It's a comedy and a tragedy all at once. Over fifty years in the making, it's a largely undocumented chapter in the history of Canadian pop culture. It needed to be documented, and that's what I've set out to do here.

I quickly came to realize that I wasn't merely telling a story about wrestling for wrestling fans. Rather, I was telling a touching human tale about the people in the extraordinary Stampede Wrestling world and the family that grew up at the helm of the crazy business, for better and for worse.

This book doesn't pull any punches in the telling of this history, but it is meant as a tribute to those characters and the wonderfully deranged drama they created. As ol' Ed Whalen liked to say, in his own hokey but lovable way, it made for a real "ring-a-ding-dong dandy."

Heath McCoy
Calgary 2005

Chapter one

Mutiny and the Sinking of Stampede Wrestling

It was *Lord of the Flies* on steroids. But unlike little boys with spears stranded on a deserted island, this scene featured overgrown hulks – Stampede wrestlers – armed with crushing muscle power and driven wild by the scent of blood, like a school of sharks. As in the classic novel, they had turned on one of their own.

Bruce Hart, thirty-nine, the son of famed wrestling promoter Stu Hart, looked out on the lynch mob surrounding the vehicle in which he had locked himself for safety. There was no talking his way out of this jam. He felt a sharp, throbbing ache in his freshly busted jaw. Outside the van – which earlier that day had hauled the mob to this arena parking lot in Yellowknife (or Hay River, depending on who recalls the incident) – the wrestlers circled hungrily. The wildest of the lot were stoked on steroids, booze, and various drugs, from painkillers to cocaine. They hammered on the windows, kicking and violently rocking the vehicle, taunting their prey, challenging him to come out and play.

Bruce, paralyzed with fear next to his panicked assistant, the hapless Bob Johnson, a family friend and wrestling cling-on, knew he was in for one mother of a beating. As the booker and boss's son, he was the acting chief on this wrestling tour, but there was no way he was going to step out of the van. He had been around wrestlers all his life, and he knew full well he was past the point of restoring order.

Opposite page: Another gonzo night behind the scenes in Stampede Wrestling: Dynamite Kid and Duke Myers get crazy, early 1980s. Top: While his impact on Stampede Wrestling was primarily felt as a trainer, booker, and producer of the TV show, Ross Hart also stepped into the ring occasionally. Here, he gives Drago Zhivago an abdominal stretch, 1980s.

These goons had travelled over a thousand miles, coming from Calgary. For a good portion of the trip, eighteen of them had been packed like gigantic slabs of beef in one van, with no air conditioning, in the sweltering summer heat. It was a nightmare for everybody involved, Bruce thought, but at the moment there was nothing to be done about it. Instead of trying to make the best of a bad situation, those bastards were lashing out, looking for someone to blame. He couldn't believe things had descended into such ugliness, into this cheap, hell ride to the middle of nowhere, where the freaks had taken over the circus.

His father's Calgary-based wrestling promotion, Stampede Wrestling, had been a western Canadian institution since 1948, forty-one years ago. The television show had been syndicated across North America and, thanks to bootleg tapes, had been seen in as many as thirty countries. Wrestling fans from around the globe knew about Stampede Wrestling. It had spawned some of the biggest wrestling stars in the world. Bruce's own brother Bret Hart was one of them. The famed British Bulldogs, Dynamite Kid and Davey Boy Smith, former tag team champions of the world, were another two. Ironically, it was the Bulldogs leading this mutiny.

Such was the wrestling business that you could be on top one day – a face on network TV, a main event star in the biggest arenas in the world – and the next day you were back in the shithouse, trudging along on tours like this one. In a matter of months, the Bulldogs had gone from first-class flights to this garbage run through the Northwest Territories, and they weren't happy about it.

Tom Billington – Dynamite Kid – was at the forefront of the attack. He was volatile, malicious, the loosest canon of the bunch. Billington was seconded by his steroid-raging cousin, the 245-pound Davey Boy Smith. It's not clear who rounded out the mob that descended on the van, though the Stampede Wrestling roster at the time included a young Chris Benoit, who is today one of the biggest wrestling stars in the world; former football player Lethal Larry Cameron; "The Angel of Death" Dave Sheldon; Johnny Smith; Ron Ritchie; and Goldie Rogers. Some of them may have looked on in horror, helpless as the scene unfolded.

Bruce believes some of the wrestlers were sympathetic to his plight, but they weren't willing to chance becoming targets themselves. "Usually [the gang would] pick up on whoever was the weak one in the herd and all the hyenas would jump on him and start ripping at him, tearing him apart until he snapped and cracked," remembers Benoit of his early days on the road as a Stampede wrestler.

Dynamite knocked threateningly on the driver's window and demanded Bruce roll it down. "[He] looked scared to death," Billington recalls in his autobiography *Pure Dynamite*. Bruce had good reason to be petrified. It was only a matter of time before the blood-thirsty Dynamite Kid came crashing through the glass.

It never happened. Someone had called the police. Bruce welcomed the shrill whine of their sirens that pierced the night. "They told Dynamite to cool it and he started threatening them," Bruce says. "He told them to fuck off. He was drunk, disorderly, stoned. He was almost trying to lead a riot [against the police]." As the RCMP restrained Dynamite, Bruce and Johnson got out of the van and headed for the hospital, where Bruce's jaw was wired shut. "That was a trip to remember," Bruce says bitterly. "Kind of like the *Titanic*."

What fuelled this ugly mutiny? What caused these men to lash out so violently against the boss's son? The answer is impossible to grasp without a taste of the filth these wrestlers wallowed in on their journey.

The Stampede Wrestling circuit had always been a harsh road. For over four decades, the revolving-door roster would do the loop, week after never-ending week. There was the Friday night show in Calgary for the TV taping. Then it was off to Edmonton, Saskatoon, Regina, Lethbridge, Red Deer, one night after another, sleazy motel to sleazy motel, and then back to Calgary to do it all again. Somehow they would squeeze in the smaller centres, too. Taber, Swift Current, Milk River, Tisdale, various Indian reservations, any gopher hole across the Prairies would do – wherever paying, screaming, fist-shaking wrestling fans were to be found. Cancelling shows was not an option. There could be a blinding blizzard. The roads could be glare ice. The junky van could be falling apart on the highway. It didn't matter. You made the shows or you weren't paid.

And every few months, the loop veered out, touching down in centres across British Columbia and Manitoba. The northern territories – Alaska, Montana, Washington – they were hit as well at one time or another. During the late 1980s, Stampede Wrestling was broadcast across Canada on TSN, The Sports Network, and the Harts decided to take advantage of that, increasingly venturing outside the regular Saskatchewan-Alberta loop. That's why, in the summer of 1989, Bruce had booked this cursed trip to the Northwest Territories.

Mlad Elzein, who was performing as the evil Arab wrestling manager Abu Wizal, had missed this particular trek, but he knows exactly what would have happened and why: "I'm not proud to say it, but we were a bunch of junkies back then. [We took] pain pills, marijuana, cocaine, anything we could get our hands on. Tommy was into pill-popping. I can't even imagine all the pills him and Davey took."

No one remembers how many towns were hit or how many days they had been on the road, but everyone remembers the trip as one long, foul ordeal. At first, there had been two vans. The villains, or heels, generally rode together, the so-called good guys travelling in the "babyface" van. Some of the seats were torn and broken, wobbling in their bases. There were holes in the floor. In one van, the liner had been ripped from the ceiling. The cabs reeked with the rotten smell of body odour and sweat, stale beer, and cigarettes, the odd belch or fart fired into the mix for comedic relief. Somebody had also pissed in the back of one of the wagons.

And the farther north the caravan travelled, the more uninviting the roads. "These big semis would come up from behind and you'd have to pull over and let them by. Then you'd wait for all the dust to settle down," Johnson remembers. "You'd be travelling along and all of a sudden that's the end of the road. There's a lake there. You'd have to wait a half hour for the barge to come along and take you across.... Then you'd travel another fifty kilometres and hit another lake and you'd wait for the next barge."

Bruce Hart remembers obscenely fat bumblebees and the kamikaze horseflies splattered on the windshield, and the deer, antelope, and porcupines that sauntered onto the road. "There were buffaloes up there that looked like they were on steroids," he says. "They'd roam around the highway not yielding to anyone. They'd stroll across the road and give you this look like, 'Ahh, fuck you. I'll let you go when I feel like it.'"

Dynamite Kid and Davey Boy Smith had only recently returned to the Stampede Wrestling circuit after a phenomenal four-year run in the World Wrestling Federation (WWF). Its WrestleMania was considered the Super Bowl of the wrestling world, and the Bulldogs had appeared on three of the cards. In one, in which they won the WWF World Tag Team titles, heavy metal star Ozzy Osbourne stood in their corner. For that single match, the British Bulldogs were paid $20,000 each.

They had children's toys made of their likenesses. They were on posters, collector's cards, and all manner of merchandising. They made more money then they ever thought they'd see in their lives, enough that Dynamite was able to pay cash for a $220,000 eighteen-acre ranch outside Calgary for him and his wife. And as they had become stars of network television, the

Bulldogs appeared in public service announcements, preaching, hypocritically, to the kiddies about the virtues of clean living. They even made a guest appearance on the hit TV action series *The A-Team*.

These were but a few of the perks to be had when you were two of the top stars in the WWF. That organization, run by Vince McMahon Jr., had changed the face of professional wrestling. For decades, the North American wrestling scene had been divided into multiple territories, such as Stu Hart's western Canadian promotion. Each promoter had his own slice of land, his own kingdom as it were, and he controlled the wrestling cards in that territory. While they did swap talent, and occasionally do co-promotions, it was rare that promoters crossed into each other's territory. When that did happen, it usually provoked a territorial war and the aggressor would find himself blacklisted in the industry.

But McMahon didn't follow the rules. Instead, he finagled a national presence for himself on network TV and in the world of pay-per-view. He defied the territorial boundaries, booking shows in every territory across the country, poaching each organization's top talents while he was at it. McMahon orchestrated high-profile tie-ins with the rock world via Cyndi Lauper and MTV. He boasted the superhero-like Hulk Hogan as his top champion, a megastar who crossed over to the mainstream when he appeared in *Rocky* III with Sylvester Stallone.

McMahon epitomized the flash-over-substance '80s. It was a decade in which a Hollywood star became president of the United States, the marketing images in a rock video became more important than the music, and blockbuster movies reigned supreme. It was a decade punctuated by unparalleled corporate greed, a time tailor-made for a figure like McMahon, and he prospered, turning his father's Connecticut- and New York–based territory into a global multimedia empire that brought professional wrestling to the masses in a way that Stu Hart never dreamed possible. The WWF was impossible to compete with. The old wrestling territories seemed like small potatoes next to its big-budget cartoon flash. As their fans abandoned them, the territories toppled one after another.

Despite its superb talent roster and loyal fan base, Stampede Wrestling had also fallen on hard times financially. Stu Hart was considering selling the business in 1984 when Vince McMahon came along, looking to break into the western Canadian market. Rather than fighting what was probably a losing battle – with its grassroots production values and single camera TV tapings, how could Stampede hope to compete? – Stu sold McMahon the promoting rights to his territory. The deal called for Stu to be paid $100,000 a

Abdullah the Butcher (left) and the Dynamite
Kid during a tour of Japan, early 1980s.

year for ten years, plus 10 percent of the gate from all house shows in Calgary and Edmonton. Stu, in turn, would give McMahon his TV spots across Western Canada.[1] Another stipulation was that McMahon hire the top talents of Stampede Wrestling, including Stu's son Bret Hart, his sons-in-law Jim Neidhart and Davey Boy Smith, and Dynamite Kid.

Cousins Dynamite and Davey had been Stampede Wrestling icons during the early 1980s. Dynamite, who came from the poor English coal mining town of Wigan, had been wrestling since he was a teenager. It was Bruce Hart who brought him to Calgary in 1978 when he was only nineteen years old. At first, Stu was reluctant, believing the kid – who then stood five-foot-eight and weighed no more than 170 pounds – to be a runt. Surely he'd be squashed by the hulks of the wrestling game.

But Dynamite soon turned the promotion, which was doing lukewarm business in the late 1970s, on its head. Nobody had seen moves like his, and the fans were excited again. This little runt was a draw, bringing folks back into the arenas by the hundreds. A fearless acrobat, he launched himself across the ring when hit, making his opponents look like supermen. When he was bounced off the ropes or given a simple hip toss, he flew like a crash-test dummy shot from a cannon. On the offensive, he sprang at his foes like a panther.

Dynamite was genuinely tough, too. Even though the outcomes of bouts were generally predetermined and the punches pulled, it wasn't uncommon for the boys to get rough with each other. Despite his size, Dynamite quickly made it clear that he could hold his own. He was fast, strong, and prone to sharp, violent outbursts. He had a complex about his size, an insecurity he carried like a demon on his shoulder, and when he felt slighted in any way, when the trigger was pulled on his temper, Dynamite was someone to be feared. He loved being feared. Being "a hard man," as the Brits call it, was everything to Dynamite. "Win, lose, or draw," he used to boast; he'd never back down from anybody. Once he discovered steroids, eventually bulking up to almost 230 pounds, he became more volatile and dangerous than ever.

Davey Boy Smith, from Manchester, arrived in Calgary in 1981. Four years younger than Dynamite, he worshiped his cousin and tried to emulate him in every way. Although he lacked Dynamite's mean streak, fearlessness, and talent for innovation, Smith was an exceptionally gifted athlete and his star power was obvious. Pin-up-boy handsome with a warm look in his eyes, Davey Boy became a favourite with the female fans. They cried when the bad guys beat on him. He could fly almost as high as Dynamite, too, and once he got on steroids, or "the juice" as the boys called it, he developed a massive build that Dynamite, to his chagrin, could never match.

While Dynamite and Davey Boy had been cast as bitter foes throughout most of their Stampede run, McMahon recreated them as a team, the British Bulldogs, and their hard, fast, acrobatic style left spectators awestruck. But the dream soon crumbled. First, Dynamite's high-impact style caught up with him, and he ruptured two discs in his back. The Bulldogs were forced to drop their title belts. It was the beginning of a steady physical decline that would eventually end Dynamite's revolutionary career.

To make matters worse, the Bulldogs' were living at a punishing pace, wrestling well over three hundred nights a year, never taking time off to let their injuries heal. On the road, they partied like decadent rock stars – nightly booze binges, some of the wrestlers smoking crack cocaine after the matches.[2] Along with his regular intake of steroids – up to 1,200 milligrams of testosterone injected into his buttocks daily[3] – Dynamite was becoming increasingly reliant on a number of addictive substances. Of his WWF years, he writes: "A normal working day for me was: speed to wake me up in the morning to catch an early flight, Valium to make me sleep on the plane, Percoset just before the match, then we'd wrestle, hit the beer, and the cocaine, until the early hours, before taking another Valium to put me to sleep at night."[4]

The Bulldogs became notorious in WWF dressing rooms for their malicious pranks. Dynamite had long been fond of slipping Ex-Lax into the wrestlers' coffee, often causing them to have embarrassing accidents just about the time they hit the ring. Wayne Farris, who wrestled in both Stampede Wrestling and the WWF as a sleazy Elvis wannabe named the Honky Tonk Man, says the Bulldogs once slipped a sleeping pill into wrestler Outback Jack's drink. They then shaved off all his hair, including his eyebrows, stripped him naked, and stuck him in an elevator, sending him down to the hotel lobby.

"I seen him terrorize people," Honky Tonk says of his experiences with Dynamite in the WWF dressing room. One day, a French Canadian wrestler named Jacques Rougeau Jr. blamed Dynamite when he found his clothing in tatters after a match. Dynamite swore he was innocent and attacked Rougeau later that evening, sucker-punching him while he was playing cards in the dressing room. Weeks later, in retaliation, Jacques and his brother Raymond blind-sided Dynamite, who claims Jacques was wearing a pair of brass knuckles. Dynamite lost four teeth and his mouth was torn to shreds.[5] "He got exactly what he deserved," says Honky Tonk. Although McMahon tried to patch things up, Dynamite was always on bad terms with the WWF after that incident, and it wasn't long before the Bulldogs left the organization.

Meanwhile, back in Calgary, the Harts were running Stampede Wrestling again, having revived the promotion in 1985. Surprisingly, the WWF juggernaut had encountered a backlash in Alberta. The group's early live events in the province proved to be a financial disappointment. Fans had turned away in droves at least in part out of loyalty to the local wrestling they missed so much.[6] McMahon, who wasn't making money in the territory, wanted out of his agreement with Stu, saying it wasn't feasible for him. He told Stu he was free to start up Stampede Wrestling again. Stu agreed to the new deal, and Stampede Wrestling was back in business.

After the Bulldogs left the WWF, it was natural that they return to Stampede Wrestling. But Dynamite was no longer the same man who had once set the promotion ablaze. He couldn't get over his loss to Rougeau. He couldn't accept that another man had beaten him down, that he might be lesser in the eyes of his boys. His reputation as the hardest man in the ring had been compromised. Somebody had stood up against his tyranny and won. It preyed on Dynamite, eating away at his pride like acid, driving him nearly insane with bitterness.

"After the incident with Rougeau, I think Tommy felt the need to reclaim his invincibility," says Ross Hart, another son of Stu who worked behind the scenes training and doing TV production. "Suddenly, he didn't feel like the toughest guy on the block anymore."

Ego-bruised and drug-crazed, Dynamite returned to Stampede Wrestling in the early part of 1989 on the condition that he become head booker for the territory. Working with the promoter, the booker formulates the show's storylines and determines the outcome of the matches. Who will get the big push and win a title belt? Who will wrestle babyface and who will wrestle heel? The booker calls all these shots, and Dynamite wanted the gig.

Bruce Hart had been the main booker since Stampede reopened in the fall of '85, but Stu sensed it was time for a change. At his best, Bruce was a fantastic ideas man, years ahead of his time. Corrupt referees. Rebellious heroes who were borderline villains. Creepy monster heels who were in league with the forces of the occult. These concepts would all make the WWF millions of dollars in the years to come, and Bruce was beating them to the punch on it. The fans loved the twisted angles Bruce dreamed up.

But Stu disagreed with the way his son managed the business. The wrestlers found Bruce manipulative and backstabbing. They didn't like the way he played dressing room politics. Bruce had his favourites, the wrestlers claimed, and he held grudges, too. You'd be his chosen star one day, destined for the main event matches. But if you didn't suck up to him, or if you fell on his bad side, your character would founder. Of course, this is a common complaint against bookers in the wrestling world. The booker is the man calling the shots, and it's a rare booker who makes everyone in the dressing room happy.

Another concern Stu had about Bruce was that he couldn't bring order to the road. Wrestlers had always partied, fought, and screwed their way around the circuit; they always played crazy ribs on one another. Under Bruce's watch, though, the situation often bordered on chaos.

But in the eyes of the boys, Bruce's greatest sin was his ego, using his power as the booker to cast himself as one of the promotion's top heroes. He was always putting himself over as a champion babyface, constantly trumping the biggest, baddest heels. Bruce was five-foot-nine and probably less then 200 pounds (though he was billed as being 212), and his physique was nothing special. Many of the boys took exception to having to be beaten by Bruce match after match. This punk didn't look the part of a champion, they grumbled, arguing that it was bad for business. How could the fans buy into it?

Stu often shared such reservations about Bruce, according to wrestler Gama Singh. "Stu hated that Bruce always had five or six heels in the corner [of the ring] and they all had weapons and Bruce would go into that corner and beat the hell out of these guys." Stu didn't think it was believable coming from Bruce. Stu was passionate that the action inside the ring look real. The fans had to buy into every move. However, it's not uncommon for bookers who also wrestle to cast themselves as stars. And it's hard to deny that the fans loved Bruce. Even though his ring skills didn't come close to those of Dynamite Kid, he was a solid performer who knew how to work a crowd. That didn't matter to the wrestlers, who griped that the only reason he had got where he was in the game was because he was the boss's brat. So Stu relieved Bruce of his booking duties and when Dynamite, swinging his star clout, demanded the job, he got it.

But according to Ross Hart, Dynamite's booking was disastrous. "He was awful," Ross says. "He was a great wrestler, a great performer, but his booking concepts were terrible. It was just a lot of gimmicks – let's have a cage match, let's have a street match – and it was quite often built around ill-conceived storylines. Storylines need to be developed over a period of time and, with Tommy, he was just hot-shotting, trying to do these things instantaneously. You might attract fans for a while, but then there's nothing to follow it with, and a lot of the matches were poorly received."

In April, Dynamite took a month off to wrestle in Japan. When he returned, he found that Stu had handed the reins back to Bruce. "Dynamite wasn't the performer he had been, at that point," Ross says. "He wasn't making the effort anymore and he was pretty battered up with all his injuries. He was never the same after his back surgery. I think he was having trouble coming to terms with the reality that his career was spiralling downward. Then he got the slap in the face of being replaced as a booker, the commander, by Bruce.... I don't think Tommy could accept that.... He basically plotted and established the first mutiny he could."

Bruce Hart was taking his turn driving on the Yellowknife trek. A Japanese wrestler who went by the name of Sumu Hara was riding shotgun, while Dynamite, Davey Boy, and the other wrestlers partied in the back.

"Me and this Japanese guy were the only guys in that van who were not completely plastered," Bruce says. "Everyone else was drunk or stoned. Dynamite came up and he kept trying to offer me a beer. I don't mind having a beer, but not while I'm driving, so I said 'No, it's okay.' But he started getting insistent ... which was immediately a tip-off to me. They were getting almost belligerent and obnoxious about it, so finally, for a peaceful co-existence, I said okay. I faked drinking it a bit and then passed it to the Japanese guy."

As Bruce had suspected, the beer was spiked. That was clear when the gang pulled over for gas in Fox Creek, about two and a half hours northwest of Edmonton, and Sumu Hara was "so fucked up he literally couldn't crawl out of the van." Bruce turned to Dynamite and Davey and snapped, "I'm driving, you imbeciles! If I had drunk that beer, what the hell do you think would've happened? This is a two-lane stretch of highway. We could've hit a semi head-on!" "They just gave me this fuck-you type of look," Bruce says.

About an hour later, the van blew its engine, forcing all eighteen wrestlers to squeeze together in the second van, their travel cases perched on their knees. As the summer heat rose to scorching temperatures, so too did the tension. The van began to feel like an oven. Bruce, having taken his turn at the wheel, climbed into Johnson's Thunderbird, hoping to lighten the load in the van. On the bright side, Bruce says, that night's show in Yellowknife was stellar.

The next evening, as Bruce remembers, the tour hit Hay River, a town of thirty-five hundred, a couple of hours' drive southwest of Yellowknife. Bruce had to arrive early for a radio interview he had scheduled to promote the night's match. Again he caught a ride with Johnson. He invited several of the wrestlers to ride with him, but nobody wanted to get up earlier than they had to.

The trouble began that evening. The show was supposed to kick off at 7:30 PM, but none of the other wrestlers had arrived except the ring veteran Bulldog Bob Brown and his nephew, Kerry Brown, who had driven up on their own. Irate, Bruce started the show almost half an hour late, squaring off against the chunky 275-pounder Kerry Brown. Bruce and Kerry fought for forty-five minutes – "way too long for an opening match," Bruce says. "Luckily, this was a virgin crowd and they were fairly tolerant." After stalling for a time, Bruce hit the ring again, this time with Bulldog Bob. "I came up with this bogus pretext where he said I cheated to beat Kerry or some bullshit," Bruce says.

When the others finally arrived, Bruce stormed into the dressing room. Bruce says he confronted Dynamite for being late, which Dynamite took exception to. Dynamite claims he encountered a cocky Hart "grinning like a Cheshire cat," taking pleasure in how awful the road trip had been for those in the van.[7] Drunken Dynamite threw an iron fist, belting Bruce in the jaw. Bruce claims Davey Boy followed up the assault with a headbutt to the teeth. Pandemonium ensued as Bruce went down, the wrestlers gathering around like frenzied gorillas. They wanted blood.

Dynamite stormed toward the ring to wrestle his match. On the way, he swung a punch at Johnson, who was acting as ring announcer, clocking him in front of the fans. After the match, Dynamite returned to the dressing room for another stab at Bruce. That's when Bruce and Johnson dashed to the van and locked themselves inside.

It's still not clear exactly why the wrestlers were so late arriving that evening. Dynamite claimed that a rock hit the van's windshield, smashing it out, and that the van got another flat tire. Bruce doesn't buy it. He heard another story from some of the more innocent wrestlers on the trip. "They were all drinking and fucking around in Yellowknife that night, and they didn't leave until at least 5 PM," Bruce says. "They had been chasing whatever women were up there, and finally they set off all hammered. About forty miles outside of town, Dynamite got this brilliant idea to give them an excuse for being late and he kicked the windshield out of the van.... So the big excuse was that a rock hit the windshield.... The whole thing blew up in their faces though, 'cause now they're riding along and getting pelted by these bees and horseflies."

When the van blew its tire, the motley crew was out of luck. The boys had thrown out the spare to make room in the cab. Bruce thinks they may have hitchhiked into Hay River. "I couldn't believe that adults would actually do things this stupid," Bruce says of the whole sordid scene.

When word of the absurd misadventure reached Stu Hart in Calgary, he was disgusted. Once he could have dealt with this anarchy, but at the age of seventy-four, he just didn't have it in him. He hadn't signed up for this when he broke into pro wrestling in the mid-1940s. It was no longer the game he loved. Steroids and a pharmacy of other drugs had ruined the business. Stu had dealt with his share of wild men – egos, tempers, the boozers, the losers – but things had come unglued. Each week there was a crisis.

His wife Helen – his pretty little "Tiger Belle" – certainly wasn't up to it anymore, either. This type of nonsense was sapping her strength. She had never wanted to be in this lousy business to begin with, but she had been Stu's partner for forty years. She had balanced the books, signed the cheques, dealt with irate wrestlers, social misfits, so many crazies. She charmed them all, too. She could charm anybody. But lately, she was just tired. Every day, she begged Stu to get out of the business.

That certainly seemed like the best idea. Despite the kinks behind the scenes, Stampede Wrestling remained a quality product, and with the success of its graduates on the world stage it was more renowned than ever. Raw and rough, it was a treat for the pro wrestling lover. And yet, it was losing its battle with the glamour and glitz of the WWF. Every time Stampede developed a big name, that son of a bitch McMahon snatched him for his own increasingly bloated show. The Bulldogs, Bad News Allen, Honky Tonk Man, even Stu's own sons Bret and Owen – all of them had done stints in the WWF.

The WWF wasn't the paradise it was made out to be, as far as Stu was concerned. It didn't necessarily make one's career. Owen, his youngest son, was already planning to leave McMahon. That kid could fly like Dynamite and he could wrestle a good meat-and-potatoes technical match down on the mat with the best of them. And he had a lot of charisma. In many ways, he was the best wrestler of all the Hart sons. He was an instant sensation in Stampede Wrestling. But he was young, competing with the world's biggest talents in the WWF, and McMahon wasn't about to push him as a main event star until he proved himself at the bottom of the card. Fair enough. Owen would have to work his way to the top like everybody else.

But McMahon dressed Owen up with another one of his cockamamie concepts. They made him a masked wrestler called the Blue Blazer, a superhero who came to the ring in a goofy feathered cape. It was as cheesy as could be, and the fans knew it. Their response to the Blue Blazer was lukewarm, and if you weren't exciting the fans, you had little chance of working your way up to the main event. Disillusioned, Owen had given his notice. Maybe he could be persuaded to return to Stampede Wrestling for one more glorious run before Stu put the business to bed altogether.

That's right. It was time to end this. Since starting up the business again in 1985, he had been losing sickening amounts of money – about $1 million – trying to keep this flagging business alive. Helen was afraid they were going to lose their Calgary mansion, their only remaining asset.

The year before, Helen had been happy that he had sold the business to the WWF, after a lifetime of taking financial risks with this roller coaster wrestling game. But then the deal fell through, and that goddamned Bruce, he just couldn't let it lie. And truth be told, a part of Stu missed the action. Wrestling was in his blood. Helen was his life, his soul; he loved her passionately from the first day he met her. But wrestling was his mistress. He couldn't resist one more fling. Now he wished he had stuck to his guns. His mistress had become nothing but trouble, and she was bringing the family to ruin. Stu wanted out.

His son Bret – who had been a tag team champion with that wild son-in-law Jim Neidhart, wrestling as The Hart Foundation – was getting a huge push in the WWF as a singles star. Owen, he had a bright future ahead of him, too, whether he wanted to wrestle or not. His wedding was only days away, to the headstrong Martha Patterson, who he had been dating since high school. But the fiasco in the Northwest Territories had managed to poison even that. Dynamite Kid, considered one of the family, had been invited to Owen's wedding – until his attack on Bruce. Bruce, who was to be Owen's best man, said he wouldn't appear at the wedding if Dynamite attended. How do you break such news to a time bomb like Dynamite Kid? Especially when you need him to work the next series of matches?

Yet another wrestling-related headache. But there would be no more. Stu Hart started making plans to pull the plug on Stampede Wrestling. And this time he damn well would.

Chapter two

Superman of the Prairies: Young Stu Hart

The Stampede Wrestling story begins, and many believe it should end, with Stewart Edward Hart. Stu. His story is the stuff of legends, cut from the rugged, red-blooded mythology of the Wild West. Define what it means to be tough – in the two-fisted traditions of John Wayne or a 1940s comic book hero – and in Stu Hart you have the realization of that all-but-extinct ideal. A rock-hard, square-jawed man up to any physical challenge; a tireless worker; a pillar of strict moral fibre (even though he made his name in a morally ambiguous world); a virile stud bull who fathered twelve children, many of them chiselled physical specimens in their own right; a man who was never seen to shed a tear, no matter the crushing crises, because men don't cry.

Stu Hart was forged in steel. A superman of the Prairies. But he was no antiquated macho brute. Here too was a man who cooked for his children, mended their clothes, cared for them when they were ill, and got them off to school each and every day. Stu Hart was a gentleman who unashamedly fostered his maternal instincts while his wife handled the business end of the family business, taking care of the finances, the advertising, and the bookkeeping. Not so strange now, perhaps, but very much so in the 1950s.

The Stu Hart saga began on May 3, 1915, when the wrestling legend was born in a small farm on the southern edge of Saskatoon. The Canadian Prairies were North America's final frontier, the last unsettled strip of the Wild West. The Canadian government invited homesteaders, for a $10 title fee, to

A finely chiselled Stu Hart, an amateur wrestling champion in 1936. Stu made this beaded belt himself, one of his many domestic skills.

settle a quarter section of land; as long as they built homes and harvested the land, it was theirs. The idea of building a new life and owning land attracted people from across North America and Europe. They made their way to the Prairies, often with little money or resources.

The homesteaders soon found that the promised land was one of many hardships. The summers were hot and dry, the winters deathly cold. They needed a team of horses and oxen to pull their plows, to break into the hard virgin soil so they could seed each field by hand. Often their wheat was hit by frost, frozen before it was ripe.

Stu's father, Edward – born in 1881 in Bruce County, Ontario, near what is today Peterborough – was a small boy when his father John decided to move the family west. With his wife, born Fannie Sargeant, and eight children, the Harts settled in Brandon, Manitoba, to live with Fannie's parents on the Sargeant farm.

With the West being settled and towns springing up across the Prairies, John, a carpenter, knew there would be an abundance of work. His plans were shattered when he was caught in a blizzard and forced to walk twenty miles to shelter. He died of pneumonia a few weeks later. Without John's income, Fannie struggled to make ends meet. Edward dropped out of school to do his part. He was instilled with the notion that the world was a harsh, bleak place where one had to perpetually work, struggling for the good life.

Raised in a strict Baptist household, Edward came to embrace religion, firmly believing that the most important thing a man could have was his honour and standing with the Lord. Edward learned the butcher's trade, though he also worked as a farmhand and a logger as he restlessly criss-crossed the West making a living. In his mid-twenties, he found himself in Saskatoon, where he met Elizabeth Stewart.

Elizabeth, a teacher, was born in 1878 and raised in Bismarck, North Dakota, where her father Donald Stewart had immigrated from Scotland with his English wife, Elizabeth Curtis. A scrappy, high-minded settler, Donald served as a territorial legislator in Bismarck until he became fed up with politics and moved his family to a farm in the newly established Canadian province of Saskatchewan.

When Elizabeth met Edward, she was impressed by the handsome man's proud, stoic stance and his tireless work ethic. She was also drawn to his stubborn self-righteousness, which reminded her of her father. Later, when Edward's unyielding nature brought hardship on their family, she may have seen things differently, although, in true pioneer spirit, it was always in her character to persevere rather than complain.

Elizabeth and Edward were married in 1907, living on the Stewart farm on the outskirts of Saskatoon, where they started their family. They had two daughters, Sylvester and Edrie, before Stu came into the world. From the moment Stu learned to walk, his father had indoctrinated him into the grind of farm life and the never-ending chores that came with it. Under the no-nonsense Edward, Stu's upbringing was sadly fun-free. When he fashioned a ball out of string and rags, his father confiscated it, telling him that the farm was a place for work, not play.

Edward toiled away over the years as a farmhand and, for a short time, as a firefighter in Saskatoon, but he had to quit the job because he refused to work Sundays. Not content to live with his in-laws, he was always working toward harvesting his own tract of land. He made his move when Stu was in first grade, moving the family to a farm in Forgan, Saskatchewan, near the Alberta border. The clay-hardened land there failed to yield much of a crop, and it was a trial to keep the children and livestock fed.

When Stu was nine years old, his father signed an agreement to take possession of a crop share near Tofield, Alberta, forty miles east of Edmonton. There, as a tenant farmer, he was to give a part of each crop as rent. He was to claim the land on May 1, 1925, but when he returned to Forgan, he fell ill, as did his family and much of the town, stricken with an outbreak of whooping cough and scarlet fever. It took the family nearly two months to recover. When at last they did, the Harts had to transport two horses, a wagon full of their possessions, and about twenty cows fifty miles to the Rosetown, Saskatchewan, train station, camping in ditches along the way. When they finally made the train, Stu rode in the cattle car so that he could sell fresh milk at each stop. The trip took about two weeks. In taped interviews with Calgary's Glenbow Museum, Stu remembered it all as a terrific adventure – until the train stopped in Tofield.

It was July 1. The Harts were a full two months late, establishing what was to become a family trait for tardiness. They had not even herded the livestock off the boxcar when they learned the land had been sold in Edward's absence to James Jobb, owner of the local dry-goods store. Soon Edward and Jobb were embroiled in a heated faceoff. Jobb had already begun to clear the land and he was not about to leave. Edward refused to back down. He bought two nine-by-six foot canvas tents, led his family and livestock to the land, and set up camp by the dirt road outside the farm fence. The parents slept in one tent while Stu shared the other with his sisters, sleeping on mattresses of pine bows stuffed in gunny sacks.

Day after day, Edward appeared in court with his signed contract for the

Top left: Baby Stu Hart, 1915.

Top right: Stu's parents, Edward and Elizabeth Hart.

Bottom: Helen Hart as a baby with her parents, Harry and Ellie Smith, in Long Beach, New York, 1924.

sale of the land, fighting to regain the farm. Jobb launched a countersuit to have the Harts evicted and, as the courts proved painfully slow, the store owner took heart when summer turned to fall and then to the cruel Prairie winter – when temperatures plunge to frightening lows of twenty-five, thirty, even forty degrees below zero Celsius; when winds whip mercilessly at frostbitten skin; when snow falls knee-deep. Surely such conditions would have his hated squatters fleeing for their lives, Jobb thought. But it wasn't to be. Instead, Edward forced the family to dig in.

On the harshest nights, winds blew with such fierceness that they threatened to tear the tents apart. The wind penetrated the canvas, chilling those inside to the bone. Stu had no one to warm himself next to, as did his mother and father and his two sisters, so he huddled up with his dog. The falling snow piled up on the tent tops, threatening to collapse the shelters. Stu often got up in the middle of the night to brush the snow away.

Each evening, Elizabeth stood over an open fire and a wood-burning stove to prepare whatever food the family could find – rabbits, gophers, birds – any animal Stu could take down with his slingshot. His father helped out whenever he could, but often he was in Edmonton, meeting with his lawyer. At bedtime, Elizabeth heated rocks by the fire and put them in gunny sacks to lay at the children's feet. Even so, most mornings Stu woke up with his toes frozen stiff inside his boots. His morning regiment did nothing to warm him up. Before school, he and his sisters had to milk twenty cows. Stu's hands got so cold that he would bury them as deeply as he could into the folds of the cows' udders to keep warm.[1]

It's little wonder Stu and his sisters looked forward to the warmth of the Tofield school five miles away, which they rode to on horseback. But school proved harsh, too. It was no secret that the Harts were poor and living off the land, and Stu's classmates and even his teachers often treated him with disdain. He was also berated because he was left-handed, which was seen as a form of deviance. Forced to work with his right hand, Stu became ambidextrous. "I pitch fastball with this hand and I punch with this one," he would later say.

Remarkably, Stu never painted his family as despairing throughout this time when the world must have seemed so wicked. According to Marsha Erb, who wrote Stu's biography, *Stu Hart: Lord of the Ring*, nobody bickered. If Elizabeth ever rebelled against Edward's obstinacy in placing his vendetta over his family's welfare, Stu was not privy to it. None of them questioned Edward's wisdom. On warmer nights, the family sat around the fire and listened to Edward play his harmonica. They had each other and no one else. Stu formed two characteristics in these conditions that he would carry throughout his life: he learned to be patient and hardworking, calmly slogging his way through any tragedy no matter how devastating, and he learned to suppress his feelings.[2]

In late 1926, after the family had endured two winters in their tents, the court ruled in Edward's favour. Almost immediately he built a nine-foot-square cabin on the property. But he was soon presented with a bill for back taxes on the land which he could not pay. Jobb, said Stu, was "lying in the grass," and slithered in, picking up the land in the judicial sale. Edward resumed his conflict with Jobb. It was back to the tents for the Harts. Back to the same horrible standoff.

By the end of 1928, the RCMP interceded, arresting Edward and sentencing him to six months in prison for "trespassing on his own land," as Stu saw it. The authorities also came to the school in Tofield and took custody of the children. The humiliation in Stu's voice three-quarters of a century later is clear as he described being led away in front of his classmates. The three children and their mother were put on a train bound for Edmonton, under the care of the Salvation Army.

In Tofield, the RCMP burned what little the family owned: the tents they lived in for more than three years, the log cabin, and their few belongings, including pictures and keepsakes. It was all gone. "They burnt it all right down to the ground," Stu remembered. More than seventy years later, his hurt was unmistakable and profound.

The angry hotel manager cuffed Stu sharply upside his head. The blow stung, but the mean jab at Stu's pride stung more. "When [Stu] was eighty-eight years old, he was still remembering that like it happened yesterday," says his daughter Alison Hart. "He'd say, 'He cuffed me, that son of a bitch. He had no right to cuff me.'" The Salvation Army had placed Stu and his sisters at an Edmonton hotel. On the day they arrived, Stu turned on the bathtub taps to run a bath. Having little experience with modern amenities, he promptly forgot about them. The tub soon overflowed, and water leaked down to the lobby. The hotel manager stormed in to scold the dirty vagabond children he had been forced to house.

Within a few weeks, the Harts were reunited, after Edward's lawyer argued Edward out of jail. The family moved into a tiny house in Edmonton's Bonnie Doon district, southeast of downtown. Most of the city's streets were still unpaved, and when it rained, cars frequently got stuck in the mud. Virginia Lorenz, a young girl who lived across the street from the Harts, remembers Edward coming out with his horses to help pull the cars out of the muck.

Virginia never liked Edward, though. "Oh, he was a bastard," she says. "Everybody disliked him. I don't know where he practised his religion but he was so bad with it, it was Satanic, almost.... And he was the boss.... You read about it in old English books, about how the old man would treat his family like slaves.... His ego was as big as all get out." Virginia also recalls Edward being "smart as a whip" and a "wheeler-dealer," always trying to talk his way out of paying his rent on the land. He was constantly busy, she says, but never seemed to accomplish much. "He would build something and work on it like crazy. Then the whole thing would fall down when he was finished."

But in Edmonton, Stu found a way to assert his independence from his father. Indeed, his life began in Edmonton, because that's where he became an athlete. In 1929, the provincial capital was in its infancy, its population under seventy-five thousand. Other than work, there wasn't much to do. Like many kids, Stu spent time at the local YMCA participating in the free activities offered. He was most fascinated by wrestling. For weeks, he watched young wrestlers twisting and stretching each other, inflicting pain on the grungy mats. Before long, the boys took notice of him and, always looking for fresh meat to pound, they invited him to try his hand at the world's oldest sport.

Stu stepped onto the mat with one of the grapplers and, after a short back and forth tussle, his opponent had him tied up in one excruciating hold after another. His head was pushed between his knees and down his chest until he could have kissed his belly button, until he thought his neck might break; his elbows were twisted behind his head until he feared his shoulders would pop from their sockets; his legs were pulled apart and he could feel his groin muscles about to tear and burst. He fought to break free, but with his neck so compromised – it felt like it had been stretched several inches – with his face buried in his stomach, he was struggling to breathe. He was beginning to black out. It was the exact routine Stu would one day master and inflict on countless victims, wrestlers and otherwise, one he described in interview after interview with relish.

When his opponent finally let him go, Stu rolled off the mat. He was dizzy, his eyes were bloodshot, and he could barely hold his head up for the throbbing in his neck. It was a torturous experience, the kind that has scared many away from wrestling forever. But Stu was smitten with the art of grappling, instinctively recognizing that this ritual was how you paid your dues, how you toughened up. He was addicted. Wrestling is a science, a chess game in which two warriors countermove, each hold leading to the other. The art is in turning one's own momentum against him, all in the name of tangling your man up and forcing him down before he could do the same to you. It was poetry.

For Stu, who had been made to feel so degraded growing up, wrestling, if you could master it, was the ultimate form of empowerment. "I was a stretching post for them," he later said of his early experiences, "but I longed for the day when I could tie them into knots. When that day came, I could walk down the street knowing anyone within my eyesight, I could have 'em for lunch."[3]

Stu eagerly returned for more, absorbing unreal doses of punishment. Within a few years, he was able to hold his own with the best of the grapplers. But he was never deterred by the pain. He was drawn to it. He learned from it. Throughout this time, Stu rarely met a sport he could not master. He tackled football, hockey, baseball, soccer, cricket, and lacrosse with gusto, playing on every team he could. But life during the Great Depression couldn't be only about sports – you had to do your share to make ends meet.

Canada's economy had been crippled by the stock market crash of 1929. Those who still had jobs were barely making enough to survive. A report released by the federal Department of Labour in 1933, in the midst of the Depression, suggested that a family needed between $1,200 and $1,500 a year to maintain the "minimum standard of decency." At that time, 60 percent of men and 82 percent of women made less than $1,000 a year. Parents often found it difficult to keep their children in school because they needed them to work. Stu managed to stay in school, but he did his part working as a newspaper carrier. During his school lunch hour, he sold copies of the *Edmonton Journal* at the train station. He made more money selling the *Edmonton Liberator* though, which was published by J.J. Maloney, head of the Ku Klux Klan's Alberta branch.

The paper was full of propaganda directed against Roman Catholics, French Canadians, and the federal government's immigration policy – potent stuff during the bitter Depression, when people were looking for scapegoats. Stu filled his bicycle basket with copies of the newspaper and sold them on the streets on Saturday afternoons. "They sold like hotcakes," he remembered. Stu's schedule was relentless, but he managed to complete high school and then two years of post-secondary education in business.

The young grappler was sixteen when he got his first taste of professional wrestling, attending a match in Edmonton that featured Jack Taylor, the British Empire Wrestling champion who hailed from Regina. "I'm not sure how I got into the matches," Stu told the Glenbow Museum. "I probably sneaked in."

Taylor, who was fighting East Indian wrestler Tiger Duhlea that night, was Canada's biggest pro wrestling star and Stu marvelled at his skills in the ring, his tremendous strength, and his muscular twenty-inch neck.[4] Professional wrestling had not yet strayed far from its classical roots. There was still great emphasis on submission holds, takedowns, and the kind of mat-bound combat Stu encountered at the YMCA. But there was also a theatrical aspect that thrilled Stu. He loved the heated pre-match banter and the way it electrified the howling, fist-shaking crowd. He was dazzled by the flashier moves – the drop kicks, body slams, and flying mares – executed over the thirty-minute bout. When Taylor had his arm raised in victory, Stu had found a new hero. That day, he considered becoming a pro wrestler. But at the time, he had the more dignified dream of making Canada's Olympic wrestling team.

Stu focused on this goal throughout his early adult life, and he trained relentlessly, living on a strict diet of vitamin E, wheat germ, cod liver oil, raw egg, meat, and peanut butter. He detested smoking and seldom touched alcohol. By the time he was in his early twenties, Stu had taken Virginia's brother, Al Oeming, under his wing, and they worked out together, along with a clique of bodybuilders, in the Oeming's basement.

Virginia remembers her mother being tormented by the sound of the men huffing and puffing and snorting in the basement. "It was worse than a pig pen," she says. "But they had a wrestling mat on the floor and the area was walled off with white sheets. There was a full-length mirror, barbells, and skipping ropes, and these guys would really go to town on their pumpitude. It was a scream.... That area in the basement was considered the inner sanctum. It was taboo for anybody in the family to go down there."

Eventually, Stu became a powerful, lantern-jawed specimen, standing just over five-foot-ten with a fighting weight of 191 pounds. He had the finely sculpted body of a classical Greek statue. Stu was also carving out a smashing career as an amateur wrestler, winning both the city and provincial championships and then a silver medal in the 1937 Dominion Games, wrestling as a middleweight. In 1938, he qualified for the British Empire Games in Melbourne, Australia, but the city of Edmonton lacked the funds to send him. He was able to get to the Canadian National Wrestling Championships in Vancouver in 1939, however, where he emerged as the country's Light Heavyweight champion, which qualified him for the 1940 Olympic Games, scheduled for Helsinki, Finland.

But amateur wrestling did not pay the bills and throughout those early years, Stu worked tirelessly. He worked as a bouncer in Calgary, cut cord in Yellowknife, and coached wrestling at the University of Alberta. He also put his considerable football skills to work and, in 1938 and 1939, played with the Canadian Football League's Edmonton Eskimos. Even in football, though, wrestling was his ticket. When at first the coach, Bob Fritz, said he couldn't use Stu, the young grappler challenged him to a workout on the mat to prove how powerful he was. It's one of Stu's favourite stories. He stretched Fritz until "he just lay on the mat vomiting," the Hart patriarch told the *Calgary Herald* in 1991. "After that, I played sixty minutes a game."[5] Stu usually played centre, but he is also remembered as a strong blocker and, when playing tackle, was particularly punishing.

During the Second World War, which Canada joined in 1939, Stu worked in aircraft repair as a sheet-metal worker at Edmonton's Northwest Industries. He considered enlisting, but he was determined to realize his Olympic dream. He never would: both the 1940 and 1944 Olympics were cancelled because of the war.

Stu's athletic career was nearly snuffed out, along with his life, on Christmas Eve, 1941. Following a long day at work repairing damaged aircraft shells, Stu was bicycling home down Jasper Avenue. He looked forward to spending a quiet Christmas with his family. They were still going through a tough time following the death of Stu's mother two years earlier. Elizabeth had been suffering from diabetes but she kept it a secret, fearing the medical bills would send the family back to the wilderness they endured in the '20s. When she eventually wound up in the hospital, it was too late to save her. Stu was always tormented by this because, at that point, he was financially stable enough to have helped his mother. Meanwhile, his sister Sylvester moved to British Columbia and cut off ties with the family. Edrie lived with their father, Edward, until Edrie died in the 1950s. Edward lived to be ninety-two, moving from job to job and never really getting on anywhere because of his stubborn ways. He never gave up his farming dream, either. And he never understood what Stu saw in these pointless sports endeavours of his when one could live the life of a farmer, close to nature and close to God.

But Stu respected his father just the same and was looking forward to spending Christmas with the old man when he heard the shrill siren of a fire truck behind him. As he started to pull over on his bicycle, a careless motorist bolted across First Avenue into the path of the truck. The engine swerved to miss the car. Brakes were pressed to the metal and tires screamed as the truck skidded out of control. Stu was hit and flew thirty feet, crashing end over end across the pavement with his bike.

Lying in the street, he heard a woman comment, "So young to die," and then she fainted, slumping down on top of Stu's shattered body. Stu had broken his elbows and thumbs, and his spine was injured. Only his muscular frame saved him from becoming crippled. His skin was shaved away across much of his body from road burn.[6] Still, he would rise to fight another day.

Stu spent several months recuperating in Edmonton's Royal Alexandra Hospital. It was spring when he had a visit from Al Oeming, who had been drafted into the armed forces. The day Oeming began his training, Stu decided to enlist as well. Stu's athleticism made him a hot commodity in the navy but, curiously, not as a warrior. Instead, he was put to work as an athletic director in charge of the navy's sports teams. It was thought that a thoroughbred like Stu could boost the morale of the soldiers and even the Canadian people, who had already suffered many losses in the war. Before his accident, Stu had captained a popular baseball team of sheet-metal workers in Edmonton called Hart's All-Stars. The All-Stars were reformed as the Canadian navy's baseball team. Its goal was to stop the unstoppable, undefeated U.S. team – an elite group composed in part of former professional ball players. In the fall of 1942, Hart's All-Stars accomplished its mission and beat the Americans.

Hoping to see some action, Stu eventually applied for service on a base in Cornwallis, Nova Scotia. But instead of being sent to the battlefront, he wound up entertaining the troops in wrestling exhibitions. On leave sometime in 1943, he and a friend visited New York City. There, in a café, Stu met the man who would change his life.

Joseph "Toots" Mondt noticed Stu's thick tree-trunk neck and approached, asking him if he was a wrestler. Stu took one look at Mondt's gnarled cauliflower ears and knew he was looking at a seasoned pro. Mondt, it turned out, was the most powerful wrestling promoter in America. In his late fifties when Stu met him, Mondt was, in fact, one of the most influential men in the history of the sport, instrumental in taking professional wrestling from its carnival roots in the early part of the twentieth century to the arenas of the world by the 1920s and '30s. Mondt helped pioneer the concepts that continue to define pro wrestling: larger-than-life characters, predetermined matches, dramatic storylines – all of it sold as the real deal in order to pack the arenas.

In this muscular, good-looking Prairie boy, Mondt saw cash potential. In Mondt, Stu saw opportunity. Their bond was cemented by Stu being from Canada, home of Jack Taylor. Taylor had been promoted in New York by Farmer Burns, who had given Mondt his break in the business, and Toots automatically associated Stu with his respected colleague. Mondt wanted

Stu on a wrestling program within the next week. But Stu had his commitments to the navy. Mondt was persistent. He gave Stu his business card and assured him he would have work for him whenever he called.

Even though the war ended in 1945, the navy, wanting to hang on to its athletic showpiece, did not discharge Stu until 1946. When he eventually landed in New York, Stu hit the ground running. Accounts of his early pro matches rave about the expertly executed headlocks, drop kicks, and body slams which, more often than not, resulted in victories for Hart, the Canadian sensation. In one match, reported in a New York newspaper, Stu emerged the winner of an elimination tournament in which he "crushed" four opponents, including former world champion Texas Babe Sharkey.[7]

Stu adapted quickly to the crude, unsportsmanlike tactics of the pro circuit. The fists, eye gouges, hair pulling – Stu could take it and serve it back with interest. In one memorable bout, held in the Bronx Winter Gardens, Stu bested the despised grappler Abe Stein. When Stu's hand was raised in victory, Abe attacked Hart, nearly causing a riot in the arena as fans charged the ring shouting anti-Semitic slurs at Stein. Stu didn't need the fans' help. In a newspaper picture, Stu has Stein down on the mat, tied up tight. In the background, a police officer restrains one angry patron, who looks ready to lay the boots to Stu's foe.

Stu faced a lot of "old crowbars," as he called them: hardened brawlers, veterans who liked nothing better than to give the younger, better-looking wrestlers a good beating. "We had quite a few of the bodybuilders," Stu told the Glenbow Museum with a chuckle. "They were kind of dandies. They had nice bodies and some of them were in love with their countenance. They were pretty looking men and the old heels liked to scratch them across the face. I'd see them looking at themselves in the mirror, seeing how badly they'd been messed up."

At first, Stu was seen as one of the pretty boys. Tall, dark, and handsome, with a build that could put movie idols to shame, Stu made a big splash with the female fans, who often covered him with kisses as he made his way to the ring. If not for his skills, his opponents would have made hamburger meat out of him, matches predetermined or not. "They were just old destroyers that would grab you in a side headlock and hang on like it was their last breath," Stu said. "They'd drag you down so you couldn't fall smart. You'd look like a bum. Then they'd maul you."[8]

Stu took plenty of cheap shots and was rudely inducted into Cauliflower Alley, as the wrestlers called it. The crusty old brutes would grab his ears and fold them, squeezing them and trying to rip them off his head. Bubbles of blood formed in the ears, eventually calcifying. The broken cartilage thickened and twisted. Veteran wrestlers wear their cauliflower ears as badges of honour pinned to their skulls, and Stu Hart was no exception. As an old man, he loved to have people touch his mangled ears, which were brittle as bone.

During his year and a half stint in New York, and then through his career as a full-time wrestler, which lasted until the 1960s, Stu earned his place working against the biggest legends in the business, including Frank Sexton, Earl McCready, Killer Kowalski, Verne Gagne, Nature Boy Buddy Rogers, Whipper Billy Watson, Gene Kiniski, Pat O'Connor, and Lou Thesz. He travelled across North America, performing everywhere from rundown theatres to that most coveted of all wrestling venues, Madison Square Garden.

But for whatever reason – possibly because he emphasized the art of genuine, scientific wrestling over performing – Stu never caught on as the champs did. Mondt never gave him the push that would have put him in that top bracket of the business where he could earn the big bucks. Stu's $90 a week wasn't bad, though. Money like that went a long way when you could buy a new Chevrolet for about $800.[9]

Stu's New York studio apartment at 137 Amsterdam Avenue, rented for $12 a month, was big enough that he could share it with fellow wrestlers Sandor Kovacs and James Blears. And with the massive rat that came up the toilet one day and camped by the trash can. Kovacs and Blears reacted like a couple of elephants spooked by a mouse. Stu rattled the garbage bag, fleshed out the rodent, and then pounced on it with both feet. The flattened beast was unceremoniously tossed out the window to the alley below.[10]

Like Stu, Kovacs and Blears would make their mark as wrestling promoters, with Kovacs running a territory in Vancouver and Blears, in Hawaii. During their time off, Stu and his roommates often headed to Coney Island to work on their tans. In the summer of 1946, fellow wrestler Paul Boesch lured his friends to Long Beach, where he worked as a lifeguard, promising to introduce them to Harry J. Smith, a retired Olympic track star. He also mentioned that Smith had five beautiful daughters who often hung out at the beach. The Prairie superman was to meet his Tiger Belle.

Helen Smith had it all. She was petite and as elegant as a china doll, with long, painted-red finger nails. But the gorgeous brunette was much more than a pretty face. She was clever. She carried herself with dignity. She had been high school valedictorian and planned to go to university and become an English teacher. For now, she had a good job working as a secretary for

Top: The future Helen Hart, then Helen Smith, in 1945. Stu always said his lovely wife looked like Rita Hayworth.

Middle: Stu wrestling Eddie King in New York in 1948, preparing to twist the man into a human pretzel.

Bottom: Helen Smith at Long Beach, New York, 1948. Helen is posed with Stu's friends, wrestlers Sandor Kovacs (left) and Lord Jan Bleers (right).

the Long Beach School Board. With that job she had supported her family through hard times. The twenty-two-year-old had the undying respect of her four little sisters. But none looked up to her so much as her youngest sister, the pixyish Diana. "Helen was on a pedestal," Diana says. "Girlie was her nickname. We had a three-bedroom house and she had her own room. My parents had their room and the four of us were in the other one. She was the first born and she was just so smart. Brilliant. She read a lot and she had to have her own room. I was never jealous of her.... I thought the world of her."

Diana fondly remembers the day the Smith girls met Stu Hart. "I remember [Helen] was lying there on the sand and I fixed her hair," says Diana. "She was so pretty. She had beautiful, naturally curly hair...."

When Paul Boesch introduced the three well-built wrestlers to the Smith girls, the jocks made a fine impression. "These gentlemen were so nice," Diana says. "I thought Stu had a British accent. He sounded so refined.... And Stu was smitten, I guess." Stu thought Helen looked like movie star Rita Hayworth, and he was charmed by her classy demeanour. She was nothing like the low-rent ring rats, the wrestling groupies, he was accustomed to.

Later that day, the wrestlers walked the Smith girls home, and Stu met Helen's father, Harry, who had been a member of the 1912 Olympic track team in Stockholm, Sweden. Harry was also a former long-distance and middle-distance state champion, and he had run the Boston Marathon each year for ten years straight. Stu was fascinated by Harry and the two athletes clicked immediately.

Helen wasn't quite as enamoured with the muscular Canadian wrestler. He was handsome and polite, but not her type. Wrestling wasn't for her. She was looking for a man of sophistication and had a number of suitors. She had a passion for dancing and wanted to be swept off her feet by a prince, a man she could samba with.[11]

Nevertheless, Stu and his buddies returned to Long Beach whenever possible that summer. "That was a very happy time," says Diana. "They were always coming to the beach and sending me out for hot dogs. It was fun and festive. They had a portable radio and I don't remember a day of rain. I remember them going in the ocean and, boy, Stu could really swim.... I loved those guys. They were so nice to me, and when you're little, you're so boy crazy. I had it all figured out. There were three guys for my three sisters and, in my mind, it was so perfect."

But it took a while for Stu and Helen to become an item, says Diana. "They never dated that I can remember until [Helen] brought him home to meet my mother. That day I do remember," she giggles. Stu, sporting a golden tan, showed up in a stylish green velvet shirt with a rose tucked behind his ear. He wanted to impress Ellie Smith. But Helen's mother would never be impressed by a professional wrestler, and a farm boy from Western Canada at that. "She had a problem with every one of her sons-in-law," says Stu's daughter Alison. "She was just a fresh Greek woman." It seems an apt description for Stu's feisty soon-to-be mother-in-law. Ellie was born in the Greek town of Mesologi, moving with her parents to the United States when she was a baby. Diana says her mother was proud of her Greek heritage, "but she wanted to be an American.... She never allowed her five girls to get pierced ears because it was very foreign. Only foreigners had their ears pierced in those days."

To Ellie, who placed a premium on wealth, class, and the finer things in life, America was the land of opportunity. When she married the Olympic athlete of Irish descent she probably felt she was on the right track. Harry Smith was a somebody, a man of impressive social standing. When his athletic career ended, he became a sports columnist for the *New York Tribune*. He then turned to carving out a nice living for himself in real estate. But the Smiths had fallen on hard times after the stock market crash of 1929. Their troubles were compounded a few years later when Harry was the victim of a hit-and-run accident, which put him out of work for a number of years.

Ellie hoped that her first-born daughter would marry a doctor or a lawyer. This Canadian wrestler wouldn't do, and while Helen and Stu were dating, Ellie tried to talk her daughter into ending it. Stu played into Ellie's hands a few times. On their first formal date, he took Helen to one of his matches in which he was slammed and stomped. Upset, Helen fled the arena. Stu caught up to her and explained that he was having fun and she shouldn't worry. Stu was none too smooth when it came to the courtship ritual, but somehow the big Alberta lug began charming the New York princess.

When summer ended, Stu began travelling across North America on wrestling tours, keeping in touch with Helen through letters. The passion in them is undeniable. In one of Stu's, the eternal optimist reveals his soft side, even expressing fear when a letter from Helen arrives late: "I thought I had lost my last friend when I had not heard from you. A letter from you gave me a new lease on life.... [It was] just what I needed to give me that added push.... My courage is renewed again."

A letter from Helen is full of longing, hinting of sexual desire. "The fellow Pat dated the other night called for her here and he wore a Scotch plaid scarf just like yours, and it really gave me an electric shock just to see it," Helen wrote. "It reminded me of you. There are a number of things that remind me of you, Stu, especially songs. You know music is synonymous with emotions for me and emotions are synonymous with you.... One of the girls is waiting for me to join her and go over to the club. I am tired of the club.... I am lonely, even with all these people around.... I just want to come home to you.... I love you."

When Stu and Helen were finally reunited, it was inevitable they marry. "The wedding was supposed to be on December 26 but we had a huge blizzard and in our little community everything stopped," says Diana. "There was so much snow. We couldn't even get to the church.... So the wedding was delayed until New Year's Eve, 1947. And even then it was a small wedding. People couldn't make it because of the snow." In true Hart fashion, Stu showed up twenty minutes late for the big event.

The plan was to leave New York after the ceremony. Stu was taking his new bride to their new home, a trailer park in Great Falls, Montana. From there he would wrestle and book matches for promoters Larry Tillman and Jerry Meeker, who ran a territory that extended from the U.S. Pacific Northwest to Western Canada. Stu was gradually making his way home to the Prairies.

A trailer park in Montana! Wrestling matches in a frozen wasteland! And where was this Western Canada, anyway? Three thousand miles away. Would they live like Eskimos? Heartbroken and deeply offended, Ellie Smith would always resent Stu for stealing Helen away to such a godforsaken place and introducing her to the ugly world of pro wrestling.

Nevertheless, after they were married, Stu and Helen followed the snowplow out of Long Beach in Stu's blue Dodge. Their honeymoon was less than romantic. First, Helen's grandmother, who didn't speak a word of English, had to be dropped off at her home in the Bronx. That was followed by a whirlwind road trip to Alberta to meet Stu's family, before the next wrestling match in Montana. There was work to be done and no time to waste.

Years later, Helen immortalized the moment in a humorous autobiographical piece she wrote titled *Harts and Cauliflowers*: "Twenty-four years ago we were married in a blizzard. I've been snowed under ever since."

Chapter three

Raising Harts: the Early Years

She may have been a princess, but Helen Hart could be bloody tough when she needed to be. That was never clearer than the evening in 1949 when she shattered every bone in her face on the teak dashboard of Stu's car.

Stu and Helen, who had left their infant son, Smith, with a sitter, were returning to their Great Falls trailer after a wrestling match. The couple was cruising along a quiet road in northern Montana when a car ran a stop sign straight into their path. In her autobiography, *Under the Mat*, Diana Hart, Stu and Helen's youngest daughter, claims the driver of the other vehicle was a woman escaped from a mental institution, making her getaway in a stolen car.[1]

Stu was unharmed save a few scrapes and bruises, but Helen, pregnant with their second child, was nearly killed, slamming headfirst into the dashboard. Stu never forgot his amazement as Helen, numb with shock, took out a notebook and calmly began recording the details of the accident for the insurance claim while they awaited the ambulance.[2]

Her skull was fractured, her teeth were shattered, her jaw was broken, and her nose and cheek bones had to be completely reconstructed. She also wound up in a body cast. But the physical agony was nothing compared with the anguish Helen felt when the doctors told her that her unborn child had little chance of survival. But she wasn't going to give up on her baby. When the doctors tried to give her painkillers to ease the hellish ache that tore across her crushed face, she refused to take them, believing they would hurt the baby's chances.

Stu and Helen on their honeymoon, in 1948, during a stop in Calgary.

Receiving the news in New York, the Smith family, who would care for little Smith for nearly two years, was grief stricken. Helen's sister Diana heard that as her sister's pregnant belly swelled, the doctors had to keep resetting her body cast, making it ever larger. But everybody feared the effort was in vain.

It seemed a miracle then when on January 13, 1950, Helen gave birth to Bruce Hart. From that moment, there was a special bond between the mother and her blue-eyed baby boy whose beautiful blond hair reminded her of her father's. "Bruce was definitely mother's fair-haired one," says Keith, the couple's third son, who was born the following year. "She spoiled him right from the start."

Stu would have liked to have been by his wife's side throughout her ordeal, which included several surgeries for facial reconstruction, but he had to take care of business to pay the medical bills. He had recently begun his own wrestling promotion in Edmonton, and Larry Tillman and Jerry Meeker, who controlled wrestling across most of Western Canada, were less than thrilled. They took advantage of any opportunity to oust Stu. Control over Alberta's pro wrestling scene was in a state of a flux, and other would-be promoters were also sniffing around, eager to take over.

"He had to promote his business or walk away from it," says Keith. "He had it all lined up, and there were all these vultures waiting to scoop it from him.... He had to leave my mom in the hospital for months, and that's when she had Bruce."

Stu had started his Edmonton operation, Klondike Wrestling, in 1948 while working for Tillman and Meeker as a wrestler and booker. When it came to Alberta, Tillman and Meeker had been neglecting the capital city. Stu was contacted by Edmonton's mayor and its police chief, who wanted to get a locally run wrestling promotion started. They convinced Stu that as a homegrown sports hero who had made a name for himself in the Big Apple, he was the man to do it.

With his friend Al Oeming as co-promoter, Stu began running shows out of Edmonton.* While working with Oeming, Stu continued to wrestle from his base in Great Falls.

Klondike Wrestling was a hit, with Stu bringing in such notables as world champion Orville Brown and Saskatchewan grappler Earl McCready, who had wrestled at the 1928 Olympic Games in Amsterdam. Other colour-

*After a short career in wrestling, Oeming went on to be a prominent zoologist, opening up the Alberta Game Farm in 1959.

ful characters in the early days of Klondike Wrestling included Chief Thunderbird, the hated local boys Ray and Bud Osborne, Dave Ruhl; "Logger" Jack MacDonald, Rube and Jim "Riot Call" Wright, and Al "Mr. Murder" Mills from Camrose, Alberta, who teamed up with his ugly brother, Tiny. Tiny, whose stringy, shoulder-length hair was seen as shocking in the 1940s, would rake his sweaty mane over his face like a dirty caveman.

Stu's solo promoting venture was becoming so successful that it was causing a major rift between him and the Great Falls promoters, Tillman and Meeker. They began worrying, rightfully so, that Stu's promotion could establish itself across Alberta. When their Calgary co-promoter, Darby Melnick, beat a man in a brawl behind a restaurant so badly that it looked as if he might be charged with manslaughter, Tillman bought out Melnick's share and moved to Calgary to fortify the Alberta territory, hoping to prevent Stu's expansion.[3]

Tillman tried to muscle and connive his way into Edmonton as a co-promoter for Klondike Wrestling, but Stu would not be bullied. He tried to buy Stu out, but the paltry sum he offered was more of an insult than anything. When Stu wouldn't budge, Tillman countered by refusing to book Hart for any Calgary bouts.

Finally, in May 1951, Tillman was fed up and sold the Calgary territory to Stu for $50,000. It wasn't a bargain, but Stu saw potential in the territory, and he made enough money in Edmonton that he was able to put $10,000 down and pay the rest in instalments over the next six months. "My dad did the honourable thing there, because I think he could've just run [Tillman] out of the city," says Ross Hart.

When Stu bought the Calgary territory, he kept the existing company names for business purposes. On paper, the organization was called the Foothills Athletic Club. The name on billboards was Big Time Wrestling.

Stu's opening night in Calgary was explosive. He brought in French Canadian strongman Paul Baillargeon, who, using a sling, lifted an 1,800-pound horse and carried it up a ladder, to the amazement of the crowd jammed into the Stampede Corral on the Calgary Stampede grounds.

Calgary was exactly what Stu was looking for. A base for his expanding business and a home for his expanding family. By the end of the summer, Stu had acquired a mansion on the outskirts of the city, which would gain fame as "Hart House." That made it official. The Harts were first and foremost Calgarians, forever to be associated with the city. And Big Time, later to be called Stampede Wrestling, would become a central part of Calgary's culture for nearly four decades.

Top: Stu hanging a lickin' on wrestler Carl Greg, Regina, 1951.

Bottom: Stu and Helen with wrestler Ted Christy in Calgary, 1955.

For years, Calgary played second fiddle to the capital city of Edmonton, home not only to the provincial government but also to a university and a large airport. But by the early 1950s, Calgary was coming into its own, taking its place as the business centre of Alberta's oil boom. In doing so, the plucky little ranching town in the foothills stepped up, in its own scrappy way, determined to bark with the big dogs.

Between 1944 and 1964, Calgary's population grew from 97,000 to 295,000. During that time, writes historian Mike Maunder, a distinct identity emerged. It was a Cowtown. A city of oil barons and Stetsons. A land of feisty entrepreneurs. It was home of the Calgary Stampede, which was becoming larger and more famous by the year. But despite its new money, Calgary clung to its image as a down-to-earth city of hard-working cowboys. "The men who emerged in the new Calgary were not timid branch-plant operators but fierce, go-for-broke, rough-and-tumble gamblers," writes Maunder. "The new spirit went directly back to the ranchmen of the frontier."[4] These were folks who liked to see a good fight; folks Stu could sell wrestling to.

In many ways, Stu was in the right place at the right time, thinks Tonia Fanella, an archivist at Calgary's Glenbow Museum, which in 2005 organized a tribute to the Hart patriarch, one of several Albertans honoured in the museum's "Mavericks" display. "Calgary wasn't always as cosmopolitan as it is today," Fanella says. "There was a lingering small town mentality.... This was a young city when Stu started up.... You didn't have the wealth of big-city attractions you do now. Stu came along at the right time and filled a void."

When Big Time Wrestling emerged in the 1950s, there was no Calgary Flames hockey team to rally around. Any sort of nightlife was scarce. Calgary's skiing craze had yet to take off. Kids didn't have video games, computers, and home entertainment systems to fill their time. Wrestling matches became the number one form of entertainment for many a family. In no time, the Friday night fights were a big draw, with Stu and company often selling out the Victoria Pavilion on the Stampede grounds, a two-thousand-capacity venue that looked and smelled like a barn. When he had a really hot ticket on his hands, Stu took the action to the Corral, where he could cram in up to seven thousand fans.

As well as the cast of Klondike crushers, Stu brought in such international wrestling stars as Gorgeous George, Whipper Billy Watson, Yukon Eric, and the vicious Killer Kowalski (who had torn off Yukon Eric's ear in a Montreal match). Stu's promotion became so hot that gradually he began to expand his territory throughout Alberta and Saskatchewan and into British Columbia, Montana, and Washington.

While Stu was off establishing the business, disturbing issues were taking root in his young family – issues that would fester and grow over the years and profoundly affect the promotion. According to Keith, Helen's accident was perhaps the pivotal moment in the family's evolution. The bond between Helen and Bruce, forged when she almost lost her baby, was powerful, and Bruce would eventually benefit from this relationship. From the start, Bruce had both his mother's creative flair and his father's ambition. Jock Osler, who married Helen's sister Diana, remembers his nephew being a serious young man. "I remember having conversations with Bruce when he was just a kid about what he was going to do," says the former *Calgary Herald* journalist and press secretary for Progressive Conservative prime minister Joe Clark. "He wanted to be a very serious sort of person and make his mark in life and what not. He was a very sensitive kid, too, and he lacked confidence."

By the time he was an adult, Bruce's all-consuming ambition was to take over the family business when his father was ready to retire. But his wild, over-the-top ideas would not always find favour with conservative, old-fashioned Stu. They butted heads over direction when it came to violence in the ring, and the development of characters and storylines. Stu also took exception to the ways in which Bruce did business and dealt with the talent.

If there was one person in the world who could change Stu's mind when he had it set, it was Helen. According to Keith, Bruce knew this, and when he wanted his way, particularly where the wrestling business was concerned, he would work on his mother. He could usually sway her. "[He'd] put pressure on my mom, to put pressure on my dad," Keith explains.

The eldest Hart child, Smith, was also affected by Helen's accident. Smith was not yet one year old when he was sent to New York to live with Helen's family. For almost two years, he was showered with love and affection. Gramma Smith, or Gaga as the Hart kids called her, grew particularly attached to her first grandchild, and indulged him. Among Smith's earliest memories is of throwing spaghetti at the walls in Gaga's house. Rather than the cuff to the head he would get if he pulled that stunt around his father, the boy's behaviour earned him nothing but adoring laughs and love in the Smith home.[5] "When we finally got the family back together," Keith says, "Smith was a spoiled little monster who, I think, had a deep-rooted hatred for my dad, who took him from this place where he [could do anything]."

The general consensus on Smith is that he's something of a harmless rascal, out for a good time and an easy ride in life. Most people seem to get a kick out of the big lug, and deep down, his family members say, he has a good, kind heart. He never made his mark in the wrestling business, though he would dabble on the mat in the 1970s. His presence was most greatly felt behind the scenes of the business, which often led to trouble as he tried to alter the program against his father's wishes.

Smith's irresponsible character later manifested itself in various ways, including fathering four children with four women. His daughter, Satanya Ecstasy Hart, was, according to brother Ross, named in defiance of God. Smith met Satanya's mother, a stunning young woman named Maria Rosado, when he was wrestling in Puerto Rico in the 1970s. Maria and Smith lived in Hart House until the late 1980s, when she and Smith separated. According to Diana Hart, Rosado suffered from schizophrenia; her drug use compounded her problems, and she grew increasingly erratic. One of her favourite tricks was to strip naked and stand on the balcony of the Hart home, waving at passing airplanes.[6] Maria eventually died of pneumonia.

The mother of Smith's son Chad, an HIV-infected woman named Zo Amber Lee Beattie, had a history of prostitution and hard-drug abuse, said Smith in a *Calgary Herald* interview in 1999, the year of Beattie's death. In the *Herald* piece, which reported on Smith's fight for custody of his child, the eldest Hart son was frank about meeting Beattie when he was in his mid-thirties and she was a teenage runaway.[7] A few years later, a tumultuous relationship began and, in the mid-'90s, the couple had a child.

Smith, who lived with his parents until they died, was definitely the black sheep of the family. How could he have been anything but a letdown for stoic, hard-working Stu, who had pulled himself up from abject poverty? It's a joke among many former Stampede wrestlers that Stu's nickname for his oldest son was Shed, short for Shithead. "Smith gave my parents so many hardships," says Ross. "My dad almost disowned him. He let him live at the house, but [after a while,] he wouldn't let him have anything to do with running the shows."

The Oslers defend Smith. "He's an intelligent kid, but he's a little bent," says Jock. "He just has a different way than most people." Diana adds: "Maybe if [Stu and Helen] had encouraged him…. But who had the time?" Keith, though, pulls no punches: "Both of my parents realized they missed the boat with Smith, but instead of putting him out and making him fend for himself, they sheltered him," he says.

Keith, born in 1952, assumed the stereotypical role of the responsible elder sibling when neither of his older brothers fit the bill. He had a successful career working for his father before embarking on a career as a firefighter. Keith would also work as a school teacher, like brothers Bruce and Ross, and in 1993 he ran (unsuccessfully) as a Liberal candidate for the Alberta provincial legislature.

Stu and Helen's romantic, passionate love eventually brought twelve children into the world, with Helen pregnant nearly every year from the time they were married until 1965, and the birth of Owen. Helen used to joke that every time her husband hung his pants on the bedpost, she got pregnant. She once wrote: "We found ourselves producing progeny at an embarrassing rate and couldn't seem to kick the habit, ultimately demonstrating … that it takes only one and one, both insane, to make twelve."

The rest of the brood came to include Wayne, later a Stampede Wrestling referee; Ross, who helped with training and with production of the TV show; and Bret and Owen, who became world famous in the WWF. Another son, Dean, now dead, would have little to do with the business.

The Harts' four striking daughters also became connected to the wrestling business. Ellie (Elizabeth) married wrestler Jim "The Anvil" Neidhart; Alison married wrestler Ben Bassarab; and Georgia married B.J. Annis, who dabbled in wrestling and owned BJ's Gym, where many of the wrestlers trained. The youngest daughter, Diana, married "The British Bulldog" Davey Boy Smith.

In 2001, Diana wrote a scandalous, legal-minefield of a book about the Harts called *Under the Mat*, exposing the family's dirty laundry. It was pulled from the shelves when Owen's widow Martha threatened a libel suit, taking exception to the way she and Owen were portrayed. Both Bret and Bruce also denounced the book as a distorted account. But not all of Diana's book can be written off as mere fiction. Some of what she wrote is corroborated, such as her wild story – much of which is confirmed by the Hart siblings and in Marsha Erb's Stu Hart biography – about her brother Dean, the fifth Hart son, born in 1954.

Perhaps the best looking of the sons, with flowing chestnut locks; seductive eyes; and smooth, Mediterranean features, Dean was fiery. Even though Dean was the smallest of the brothers at only five-foot-eight and 160 pounds, Bret says he looked up to him. "He was always a scrapper," Bret told *WWF Magazine*. "He showed me how important it was to defend yourself and not let others bully you."[8]

Dean used his entrepreneurial flair to start an auto body business in downtown Calgary, where the trendy Eau Claire Market stands today. He also owned a landscaping company. As well, Dean promoted rock concerts at Clearwater Beach, a 160-acre man-made sandbar just west of Calgary on the Elbow River, which Stu bought in 1964. Stu turned Clearwater into a summer destination, renting out camping spots and operating concessions stands on the beach. Dean's Clearwater concerts were horribly mismanaged. At one, riots on the property cost Stu thousands of dollars.[9] (Stu also got in trouble with the Calgary Board of Health, which deemed the water at Clearwater unsafe. By the mid-1970s, he sold the area, at a huge financial loss.)

Diana describes her brother as being "smooth with older women." He borrowed their cars and persuaded them to lend him money for his business schemes. "He was a con artist in some ways," says Ross.

In 1978, Dean was hit by a bus in downtown Calgary. The accident damaged his kidneys. To deal with the pain, he began smoking marijuana.[10] Shortly after, Dean moved to Hawaii, where he got mixed up with the Samoan mafia. The extent of his involvement with the criminals is unclear. But it is known that, perhaps unwittingly, he wound up transporting for the mob boxes containing weapons. Later, the gangsters, who were facing murder charges, believed Dean was planning to testify against them.[11] In 1981, Dean fled Hawaii and returned to the safety of Calgary, but eventually returned to Hawaii, thinking the situation had blown over. According to Diana Hart, his enemies caught up with him and nearly beat him to death.[12]

Defeated, Dean returned to Calgary, where he tried be a part of Stampede Wrestling behind the scenes. He was bitter having to take a backseat role to his brothers, who had by this time carved positions for themselves in the family business. In 1990, at the age of thirty-six, Dean died of Bright's disease, a kidney dysfunction.

With skeletons like this in the closet, and the very public family feuds of recent years, the Hart clan is often perceived as a white-trash pack of brutes. But that's not entirely fair. For the most part, the Harts are a warm and thoughtful, if eccentric, family. They're intelligent and creative people. Many in the family are civic-minded (a number of them helped Alberta premier Ralph Klein during his 2004 election campaign) and support countless charities. They're a sensitive, passionate bunch, fiercely proud of their family legacy.

But there's a fine line between pride and ego, and sometimes over the years, the Harts have crossed that line. This has affected relations within the family. "Being in the same industry bred a competitive environment in which jealousy and backstabbing ran rampant," writes Martha Hart in her Owen Hart biography, *Broken Harts*. "[That] was a real shame given they had all grown up being taught to stick up for one another."[13]

Pride also affected the family's outlook on the world. "I don't know if it was a false sense of security ..." Owen said in the documentary *Wrestling with Shadows*, "[but] we had this [self-] image like, 'We're the Harts and we're invincible.'"[14]

It's fitting then that the invincible family grew up in a veritable fortress. Hart House, the Victorian mansion described by more than one wrestler as an Addams Family home, perched in the hills of southwest Calgary. A million screams were heard from its basement's training facility, known as the Dungeon; the world-famous lair that launched countless wrestling careers. This hub of circus-like activity was the foundation on which Stu built his business and raised his constantly swelling family.

Perhaps it was the ultimate form of personal redemption for those formative years spent in that tent on the cruel Prairies. Could that explain Stu Hart's love for such grandiose, eccentric displays of wealth as Hart House? Or was it just another step in the realization of Stu's ambitious vision? After all, if one was going to carve out an empire in the violent, cartoonish world of pro wrestling, didn't one need an equally over-the-top base of operations? A fortress from which to launch the army of battling bruisers who were going to enthrall the people of Western Canada. That's what Stu needed, and that's what he found in the summer of 1951 when he responded to a classified ad in the *Calgary Herald* stating that the Patterson home was up for sale.

The eight-thousand-square-foot red-brick mansion had a rich history long before the Harts came to it. It was built in 1905 by Edward Henry Crandell, a brick and masonry baron who had come from Ontario in 1899. Crandell raised his family in the sprawling three-storey, twenty-room estate located seven miles from what was then downtown. When his children had grown and left home, he leased the building to the Red Cross to use as an orphanage. One of Crandell's sons eventually returned and raised his own family there. When the brick business collapsed during the Depression, the place was sold to Judge H.S. Patterson. By 1951, Patterson, too, had decided to sell.

That's when Stu Hart arrived. The house on the hill, proudly overlooking the booming oil town, immediately appealed to Stu. He thought it regal. He loved the brick pillars at the entrance to the property and the winding driveway. The three chimneys and brick verandas in both the front and back gave it presence, Stu thought, as did the elegant staircase with its lovely oak railing. There were two master bedrooms, each with a fireplace. The hardwood floors made up for the frozen soil Stu once slept on. And from the moment he saw the dingy concrete basement, he could picture the homemade gym he would have there.

The property included a coach house, joined to the mansion by a small greenhouse covered with vines and climbing roses.[15] Thirty acres of lush grasslands surrounded the mansion. Perfectly manicured flowerbeds filled the yard. Stu bought the house for $25,000. It never occurred to him that Helen, still recovering from her accident, would not be as excited as he was about it. Typically, her pessimism offset Stu's boundless optimism and, when she was taken to the house several weeks later, she didn't like what she saw. The place reminded her of a seedy, old hotel.[16] It was tacky. A bit creepy, too, looming above the city like a haunted castle.

But Stu was not discouraged. He set out fulfilling his vision for Hart House, making it homey yet opulent in his odd-duck way. The high ceilings were adorned with gold-leaf trim. For $500 each, he purchased six chandeliers that once adorned Edmonton's luxurious Hotel MacDonald, christening each with a woman's name. He laid Persian carpets in the living room and hung fine lace curtains. He bought a long rosewood table for the dining room and a sleek leather sofa for the study to complement the antique glass bookcases. Inside the cases sat a collection of hardcover classic novels and eleven volumes of encyclopedias, most of them "unviolated," Helen joked.

But much of this elegance was to be offset by the veritable ark-load of animals that had the run of the house. Over the years, visiting journalists would give flabbergasted reports of cats curled up in punch bowls, Rottweilers slobbering on the torn antique furniture, the smell of cat urine emanating from the rugs and the pee-stiffened curtains. Then there was Terrible Ted, the wrestling grizzly bear that slept under the porch. Young Bret Hart liked to stand on the porch and let ice cream drip onto his feet so that the bear licked his toes clean from in-between the floorboards.[17] Helen had a run-in with Ted when Stu locked him in the basement without telling her. She had gone downstairs to do laundry, only to find the bear grunting at her in the dark. Frightened out of her wits, she stormed out of the mansion, threatening to leave the madhouse for good.[18]

The Hart children contributed to the home's less than immaculate state. Helen used to say that every room in the mansion was a rumpus room. Even though the family had maids to help out, the Hart matriarch was probably only half kidding when she told a reporter in 1990, "The place hasn't been dusted since 1973."[19]

For a family of such sturdy stock, dinner was always a production. Stu encouraged hearty eating, even when business was poor. He wouldn't tolerate a scrap of food going to waste. Stu was head chef and proud of his industrial-strength kitchen, stocked with stainless steel appliances often culled from defunct Calgary restaurants. Each Sunday evening, the family gathered in the dining room for a lavish feast. This was where the family politics often took shape. It was here the children formed alliances, teasing each other mercilessly and listening to Stu's many stories. It was a tradition that survived in one form or another until the Harts sold the house in 2004. Stu's strange associates were constantly on hand at the Sunday dinners, invited without anybody thinking twice. In Bret's words, this included "an endless and ever changing assortment of freaks, musclemen, midgets, giants, and tough guys."[20]

Truth be told, über-manly Stu was a regular Mr. Mom. When the newspapers wrote about the family during the 1950s and '60s, Helen played the part of the doyenne, but in her autobiographical writings she admitted her domestic shortcomings. "The familiar mother-of-a-large-brood prototype is a tranquil, generously proportioned woman, complete with comfortable chuckle, capable hands, infinite wisdom, and a propensity for baking oatmeal cookies," she writes. "I hate to let people down, but this is not me.... When it comes to my boiled rutabagas, my unsegregated wash loads and my extemporaneous housework, it may well be said that I have passed this way in vain."[21]

Helen never met a sewing machine she liked, either. Fortunately, Stu turned out to be handy with one. He mended the children's clothes as well as stitching up torn wrestling mats. And the man who made giants beg for mercy in the ring proved to have a tender touch where his Tiger Belle was concerned, giving Helen beauty salon treatments – from manicuring her nails (which were always perfect) to curling her hair – in their bedroom. Stu never thought of it as a chore but as a rare slice of intimate time for him and his wife.

Helen did her part in the office, looking after the business end of the wrestling biz. By the 1970s, the sexual revolution had crept its way into the macho cowboy culture of Calgary and the arrangement was slightly more acceptable than it had been in the previous decades. But even then, Stu seemed embarrassed – though he was no doubt playing it up – when the family was profiled in *The Albertan* for a 1977 article about men helping around the house.

In the cheeky piece, Stu is shown wearing an apron and vacuuming, while Helen sits with a coffee, reading the newspaper. "I ... I ... I'm in something of a compromising position here," Stu told the reporter. "You see, I need a typist, a receptionist to field my calls, a payroll clerk, somebody to handle the bookkeeping and bank deposits and to look after the advertising for my wrestling cards. So I've got this little feminist of mine up in the office and that means I have to go down and do some of the cooking. I make the breakfast and get the kids off to school."[22]

But Helen was much more than just a glorified secretary. She was Stu's equal partner in the business, making financial decisions and co-signing

Top: Stu, Helen, and their brood at the Hart family's Sunday dinner, 1961. The fourth girl on the left making a face at the boy on the far right is Ellie. The little boy is Bret Hart. According to Alison Hart, their rivalry goes back a long time.

Bottom: The Hart children sit on an unidentified wrestler, who has his head on one crate and his feet on another. He has just been hypnotized by Reveen the Impossiblist, who told him his body was as stiff as a board.

the cheques. Perhaps her greatest role was as the resident diplomat, snake charmer, and, when things got really out of control, lion tamer. "She was on the front lines dealing with the wrestlers," Ross says. "When they phoned to find out where they were booked, she'd take the call, and she developed a rapport with them. A lot of them she never even met, but she was on the phone with them constantly. She would charm them and that made the business easier for my dad, because they loved my mom. So with Archie "The Stomper" Gouldie or Abdullah the Butcher, who could be really temperamental and hard to deal with about money or the development of their characters, she would smooth things over and it would be a nice bridge for them to cross before they had to talk to my dad."

Alison Hart aptly describes her parents' relationship as "tag team parenting and tag team business partners." It was an arrangement frowned upon by Stu's father, Edward. If Helen's mother disapproved of Stu, Stu's father was equally unhappy with his son's choice of wife. "My grandfather wanted my dad to marry a nice, stout farm girl," Alison says. "He wanted a woman to be out there milking the cows. Stu came along with this New York City girl who would never have had anything to do with an outhouse! She wouldn't go near one … and my grandfather thought that was just awful. He thought, 'Stu, you've got to take control! A woman doesn't have a say! You're the man!'… My poor father was caught in the middle of that tug-of-war."

Both Stu and Helen worked around the clock. Stu, in particular, was a workhorse who could function without much sleep. His schedule was unreal, especially in the early days when he was still active in the ring and was regularly on the road with the wrestlers as they did the weekly loop through Alberta and Saskatchewan. After wrestling a full match, he sorted out the gate money, helped take down the ring, and put out any fires that needed extinguishing. Then, instead of hitting the hotel pub or the next town with his colleagues, Stu raced home, arriving on his doorstep in the early hours of the morning to catch an hour or two of sleep, if he was lucky, before it was time to get the children to school.

"He was up before six, farm hours all the way," Keith says. "He always had hot porridge on the table. He'd milk the cows every morning, strain the milk. He fed us the same rolled oats and cracked wheat he fed the cows. He'd get eggs from the chickens." When it was discovered that eldest daughter Ellie was allergic to cow's milk, Stu bought a goat, which he milked every morning.

The frantic pace sometimes got the better of him. Stu was constantly late getting the children to school. That didn't make life easy for the Hart kids, and their teachers could be hard on them, sometimes going so far as to mock their father's profession. Alison remembers Stu falling asleep during a parent-teacher meeting. "I remember seeing my poor dad crammed into one of those little kid desks. All the other parents were wide awake, and there he was, sleeping away. I understood, though. I remember looking at him and thinking, 'He's tired. He's had a long day. Let him rest.'"

In the early days of Big Time Wrestling, life seemed idyllic to the Hart children. Keith recalls his father coming home from lucrative wrestling tours bearing gifts. "He'd have toys for the boys, chocolates for my mom.... He'd buy a brand new Cadillac every year, and he'd always keep the old ones and let the wrestlers drive them on the tours. He had his suits tailor-made. Raw silk. Shark skin. I remember being about seven and one of the wrestlers, this big Mexican called The Mighty Ursus, would pick us up in my dad's Cadillac. We'd drive around and everybody would be waving. We were true celebrities."

Keith remembers his mother and father being friendly with a rather highbrow crowd in those days. "My mom and dad hobnobbed with people like Peter Lougheed [later premier of Alberta] and all the 'blue-eyed sheiks' [oil tycoons]. They were very suave and sophisticated." But even in those early years, Keith knew there was something that set the Harts apart from other kids, rich or poor. "Growing up with the wrestling business was like growing up with a big four-ring circus in your backyard," he says. "We had bears and we had brutes. Who else had that?"

Jock Osler says it was ingrained in the Hart children from an early age that they were special. "This was Fortress Hart. 'We are the Harts and you're not.' That's what they lived by," he says. Bruce Hart confirmed as much in a 1993 interview with *WWF Magazine*: "Wrestling is the divine right of kings in this family. Others are born with silver spoons in their mouths. We were born with silver turnbuckles in ours."[23]

Chapter four

The Dungeon

While the kitchen, dining room, and office were all important arteries of Hart House, the real guts of the operation was in the grey, dimly lit bowels of the mansion. The heart of Stampede Wrestling beat in the Dungeon, constantly pumping fresh, vital blood into the show even as it rejected that which was unfit.

Nobody seems to remember who gave the name to Stu's basement gymnasium, but anybody who spent any quality time down there came to realize how fitting the brutal title was. And no trip through the Hart House is complete without a long look at Stu's lair. There were two ways to access the Dungeon. The first was at the side of the house, just off the back porch. A narrow set of concrete stairs, slippery with ice in winter, led to the door, which never seemed to be locked, even when nobody was at home. If the Harts weren't such a physical threat, it's certain that somebody would have pulled up in a rig and robbed the place blind. The second access was inside the house, near the kitchen: a steep iron-grate staircase, appropriately intimidating considering what awaited those who made the descent.

The clothes washer and dryer could be found down in the grungy concrete bunker, along with a rumbling furnace room housing an old-style incinerator. A concrete shower stall, the tiles encrusted with years of mildew and grime, came in handy after sweaty workouts. Diana Hart's autobiography contains a vivid description of the young Hart children standing

Archie "The Stomper" Gouldie and Bret Hart slug it out in a bloody chain match, 1983.

naked in an "assembly line," waiting for their brief date with the high-powered showerhead. As told by Diana, the experience sounds like a jailhouse hose-down: "The shower ... has so much force it feels like it's ripping your skin off," she writes. "The spray is so forceful and fine it's like sharp quills piercing you."[1]

In later years, an ancient treadmill sat beside the shower, supplied by wrestler and Hart son-in-law Jim Neidhart. Nothing like the sleek treadmills of today, this tank-like machine had a two-foot-wide conveyor belt, the tread made of twine and sandpaper for traction, that ran over rumbling steel rollers. Neidhart used it when he had played football for the Oakland Raiders and had it shipped to the Hart House in the 1980s. The family loved it, especially Stu, who ran on it every day well into his seventies.

But the room that counted the most was the Dungeon. Spread on the floor was an all-too-thinly padded wrestling mat, seventeen by seventeen feet, its borders reinforced with wood planks, steel weights, and a barbell to keep it from sliding. The mat, perhaps once white, over the years had become a putrid yellow-grey, stained with the various bodily fluids it had soaked up, from sweat and blood to snot and vomit. Nobody can remember a time it had been washed.

The wood-panelled walls were frequently in a state of disrepair, cracked and splintered from lumbering muscled bodies and craniums being slammed into them. The ceiling was so low that the taller wrestlers frequently smashed through it with their heads and feet as they learned how to take high falls, body slams, and bumps. Eventually, the metal pipes became exposed, and a few times grapplers broke through those as well.

At the Dungeon entrance, just off the mat, was Stu's gym, equipped with benches, barbells, and dumbbells – up to 600 pounds' worth. The weights, which Stu had custom-designed, had the Hart name engraved in the iron. Over the years, most of these weights would go missing. Back when most people had never laid eyes on a simple Universal weight machine – common in every high school gym today – Stu's gym had a row of homemade weight-and-pulley contraptions, primitive by today's standards but effective when it came to building rock-hard muscles.

Once a week, the Hart patriarch went down to the Dungeon with the talent and any wannabe wrestlers trying to break into the show: play time was on. Stu taught the boys how to wrestle the way he had learned at the Edmonton YMCA. He stretched them – locking them in submission holds and bending and twisting them until they screamed, cried, and vomited, thinking they were going to die. Many simply blacked out.

Bruce Hart launches a knee drop on Tom Stanton from the top turnbuckle, early 1980s.

Up to the 1970s, Stampede Wrestling closed down for six weeks or so each summer. The angles – the twists and turns in the storylines – would build up during the year to an exciting climax at the Calgary Stampede in mid-July. That's when all the feuds came to a head in an explosion of grudge matches. Stu paid top dollar to get the world's biggest wrestlers in his ring, from Whipper Billy Watson and Killer Kowalski in the 1950s to Harley Race and the six-foot-eleven, 500-pound Andre the Giant in the 1970s. He also brought in such boxing heroes as Jack Dempsey, Joe Louis, and Rocky Marciano to promote the shows and act as guest referees.

During those six summer weeks, many of the wrestlers moved on to other promotions, forcing Stu to build a new roster. To that end, he began recruiting a new batch of rookies. The group usually consisted of local tough guys, amateur wrestlers, bodybuilders, police officers, and even CFL players looking to make some bucks during the off-season. Often these types showed up with the condescending attitude that wrestling was nothing but a cheap scam, a ticket to easy money. Stu liked nothing better than to teach these punks a painful lesson in respect.

At first, Stu toyed with the new recruit, feeling him out, casually flipping him through holds, each one more painful than the last, until the wannabe grappler was hopelessly tied up on the mat. Then Stu smothered his opponent, pinching the nose and mouth with his huge mitts until the man couldn't breathe. Panic would set in. The legs would begin to kick. Stu gave him a gasp of air, then cut off his breathing again.

Stu's favourite move was known as the college ride. "That's the old pro educating you about respect in the ring," says trusted family friend Greg Everett, who was stretched on many occasions. "He stuck my chin down my chest, which pulls from the base of your tailbone all the way up your back to the tip of your head. You're blacking out at this point, going in and out of consciousness, and at the same time he'd be pulling your legs apart. He'd be ripping your whole groin apart and you could feel the little sinews snapping, like pins pricking. Your left arm would be pulled so far behind your head it felt like your shoulder was going to break.... Yeah, you were in a whole mess of pain."

Most men wound up crawling out of the Dungeon humiliated, whimpering like hobbled dogs. Those who returned won Stu's respect, and he set about teaching them the secrets of the business, moulding them into Stampede wrestlers.

Growing up, the Hart kids got their kicks watching these men strut into the house like proud warriors. They speculated among themselves as to who would pass the test and who would be reduced to a bawling infant. The young Harts sat in the living room and listened with cruel amusement as the tortured screams rose through the air vents. Little Owen Hart once tape-recorded the sounds, which, as an adult, he later played for WWF wrestlers enthralled by Stu's legend. Alison describes the sounds on the tape: "He's saying to him, almost tenderly, 'Don't cry. You'll be all right.' The guy's crying, screaming, begging for mercy. Stu goes, 'All right, now. I'll take your leg and … this might hurt a bit … C'mon now, have some goddamn dignity. Be a man."

It's no wonder that, as Smith Hart told WWF *Magazine*, "It wasn't at all strange to look out the window of your room and watch some guy in nothing but wrestling trunks, howling and running from the basement in the snow. Or [you'd see] Dad walking one of his students around the property after he had blacked out."[2]

Alison says she viewed these scenes as "Dad getting some exercise.… I had no attachment to the victim. Even when I was dating them." Stu loved luring his daughters' boyfriends into the Dungeon. "When the boys came to the house to pick us up, Dad would look at their arms and necks and ask them if they liked wrestling," Alison recalls. "If the boys said they did, Dad took them down to the Dungeon.… They never asked us out again."

Retired wrestler Bud Osborne trained in the Dungeon during the 1950s. He remembers Stu laying a brutal beating on a man who had insulted him. "There was this cocky little Greek and he had run into Stu in the [grocery store] one day. He kind of poked him in the belly and told him he was getting a little flabby. That was a very stupid thing to do. Stu told him he looked like he could make a million [in the ring] and he invited him down to the Dungeon for a tryout. Stu almost killed him. The guy told me later he saw his whole life flash before his eyes just before he passed out."

Jock Osler remembers when he first became friendly with Stu in the 1950s, while a cub reporter at the *Calgary Herald*. Osler was introduced to the promoter by sports columnist Johnny Hopkins, who used to moonlight for Stu, ghostwriting the wrestling programs. Occasionally, *Herald* reporters accompanied Hopkins to Hart House. After a while, the reporters asked the inevitable question: "Is wrestling fake?" By way of explanation, Stu gave the hapless scraps a friendly invitation to the Dungeon. "He'd indulge them for a while," says Osler, who saw many a stretching – something he wisely avoided. "He'd go along with whatever they wanted to do to him. Then, all of a sudden, he'd tie 'em up in knots and make 'em squeal.… He loved that."

If anybody crossed Stu anywhere near the Dungeon, God help them. Bret Hart recalls the night some fool kid tried to steal a Cadillac from the Harts'

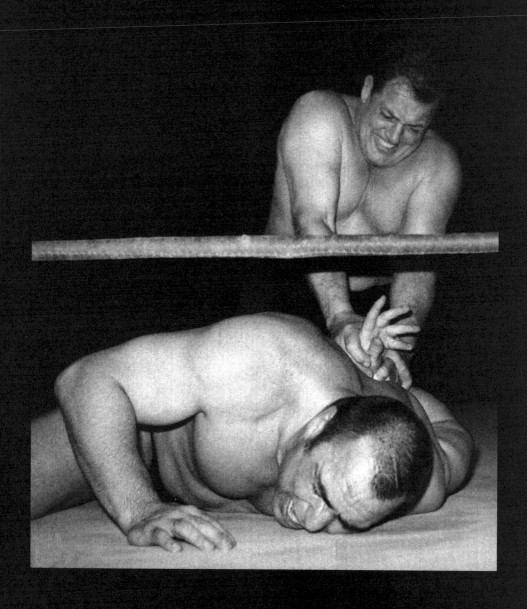

The teacher and pupil, years later. Stu pins
Archie "The Stomper" Gouldie to the mat
with a vicious hammerlock. Stu often said
that Gouldie was the most accomplished
professional wrestler he ever trained in the
Dungeon, early 1970s.

yard. But the snow on the driveway was too thick and the car got stuck. Before the kid knew it, Stu had snatched him up and hauled him into the Dungeon. Rather than call the cops, the wrestler disciplined the kid himself with a bit of mat-bound torture, then phoned his parents. Stu later learned the kid was from a poor family and gave him a job as an usher at the wrestling matches.[3]

There are countless stories of Stu taking such liberties, right up to his final years. The stories are most often funny, but they are also disturbing. For all his good and noble qualities, Stu had a sadistic side. Stretching wannabe wrestlers was one thing. If that's the way a grappler had to pay his dues, so be it. Wrestling was not for the meek. But when it came to punishing average joes, curious reporters, and teens trying to date his daughters, something was definitely amiss with the Hart patriarch's behaviour.

Many have come to the conclusion that Stu was a bully, abusing his physical power. "I thought it was bullshit," says ex-wrestler Ben Bassarab, who married Alison Hart. "He never once said to a guy, 'Listen, I'm going to take you downstairs and put you in a hold and hurt you. I'm not going to let you go. The more you scream and kick, the more I'm going to put the pressure on you' ... that's not teaching. To me, that's bullying."

The late Lou Thesz, believed by many to be the greatest wrestler of all time, was also critical of Stu's methods. According to wrestling journalist David Meltzer, Thesz claimed that "Stu was great at demonstrating holds on willing participants and those without wrestling training, but not in getting the top guys in them."[4]

The Hart boys reject the notion that their dad was a bully. Stu stretched people to make them appreciate wrestling, Bret says. Bruce argues that the cutting-edge wrestlers who emerged from the Dungeon – the Hart boys, Archie "The Stomper" Gouldie, Rick Martel, Brian Pillman, Chris Benoit, Lance Storm, and Chris Jericho to name a few – were all moulded in large part by Stu's methods. They paid their dues by going through the hell of the Dungeon and, in turn, "they gave the business their best."[5]

At one point or another, Stu gave all his eight sons the full Dungeon experience. As a boy, Owen was deathly afraid of his father. In the documentary *Wrestling with Shadows*, Bret talks about going to school with blood-shot eyes because his father had put him in a hold the night before, squeezing him until the blood vessels in his eyes burst.[6] It is difficult to hear such stories and not think Stu abusive. But none of the sons viewed him that way. Getting stretched by their father, says Keith, "was an honour." He recalls his father locking him in holds and putting so much pressure on his nose that it bled. "I know he broke my nose a few times, playing around," Keith says.

"I remember being on the bottom, and the only way I could get out is if I got slippery enough that I could slip out. I deliberately drooled on myself, so I was slippery as an eel. I'd get out for a second. Then he'd catch me by the hair and drag me back in.... He was aware of everything he was doing. I think he thought it was good for me."

Greg Everett, who worked as a referee for a time, describes the Dungeon experience as "medieval torture." "It's a bizarre right of passage, liked an honour badge," says Everett. "I trusted [Stu] 100 percent. But you realized that, at any time during the proceedings ... he could break your neck. He could kill you easily." Indeed, nothing describes the Dungeon experience like the battle-scarred testimonials of the men who did their tours of duty down there.

"Stu was unbelievably vicious," says Archie "The Stomper" Gouldie. "I was about nineteen the first time I went down there [in the early 1960s]. I watched him take these big linemen from the Calgary Stampeders who wanted to wrestle, they'd come down and train, and, Lord have mercy, you learned to respect him. He just believed that if you were going to be a wrestler, this was the way to start. His way or no way."

"Cowboy" Dan Kroffat paints a vivid, terrifying picture of his time in the Dungeon. "I came to train with Stu in the summer of 1969," Kroffat recalls. "He had about twenty of us in the Dungeon. He was breaking guys into the business to see who he could use for the show in September. A week or so before the show started he had whittled us down to two.... Night after night, I saw guys getting annihilated.... These were potent, powerful men. He just ate them up and spit them out. I saw guys screaming for their lives, turning colours I didn't think imaginable. I saw guys have bowel movements. I saw him choke guys out so bad that their eyeballs turned a brilliant red. Some guys ran out of the basement. Some crawled out, crying.... He was like a lion playing with his cubs and suddenly he'd eat one of his own."

Kroffat is one of the few Dungeon graduates who was never stretched, oddly enough. If he had been, he doesn't think he would have returned. "He trained me, taught me falls and stuff. But he never hurt me," Kroffat says. "Maybe he thought I had something. Maybe he thought I had a look he could use." But each time Kroffat returned to the Dungeon, he was convinced his time was coming. "Walking into that basement was terrifying," Kroffat says. "I could see the ghosts of so many who had come before me.... It was like walking into a war zone and knowing you could get killed, but for some reason, you stay.... The fear was driving me out the door but my desire outweighed that decision.... I wanted to be a wrestler so bad."

Chapter five

Pirates on the Prairies

"The whole thing was born, they say, in the late 1940s, when most ex-GIs wanted to get back to an orderly pattern: college, marriage, a job, children – all the peaceful extras that come with a sense of security. But not everybody felt that way.... There were thousands of veterans in 1945 who flatly rejected the idea of going back to their prewar pattern.... They wanted more action...." So wrote Hunter S. Thompson on the rise of American motorcycle gangs in *Hell's Angels: A Strange and Terrible Saga.*[1]

When Keith Hart spoke about his father's savage and eccentric gang, the 1950s stars of Big Time Wrestling, his words bring Thompson's to mind. Whether the ticket to freedom was a motorcycle or a wrestling ring, the sentiments were identical. "These old guys came out of the war era and they didn't want to punch a clock," Keith says. "These guys wanted to travel ... work their own hours. They wanted freedom.... Some of the most remarkable people I ever met were wrestlers.... I admired the class guys who were smart, like my father. Then you had guys who got into the business because it was a big ego trip and a slack way of life. You could make some money, sleep till noon, party all night."

Like the bikers, pro wrestlers found a way to live a sex, drugs, and rock 'n' roll lifestyle, before rock 'n' roll was even around. Decades later, when the likes of Vince McMahon Jr. and Bruce Hart made the connection between rock and wrestling, they were picking up on the primal elements, the kindred spirit the

Al "Mr. Murder" Mills, late 1940s or early '50s.

two forms share. The colourful, larger-than-life characters. The wild, liberating act of standing nearly naked in a spotlight, howling like a beast, thrashing a guitar, or an opponent, by the neck. The defiance of society's conventions. Most wrestlers were dropouts and thrill-seekers, rebels who had shunned the rat race to run away and join the circus. Living hard on the road, surviving from gig to gig, from skirt to skirt, in truck stops and cheap motels.

The early wrestlers – during the Great Depression and the World Wars – were often poor, lost souls, renegades trying to make their way in the harsh, uncertain world. John Dolin, director of the documentary *Wrestling with the Past*, sees the old school grapplers as Steinbeck figures: "They were like itinerant workers who went from one territory to another. They would harvest their popularity in one area and then they'd move on. They'd put thousands of miles on the road."

That was the case with Phil Klein, who grew up in Rocky Mountain House, Alberta, during the Depression. By the time he was fourteen, Klein was riding the rails in search of work and a better life outside the hard-luck Prairies. At one point, the schoolyard scrapper put his skills to the test in the boxing ring. "I think I made $5 a fight," recalls the eighty-eight year old with an endearingly gruff chuckle. "You'd do anything to make a dollar in them days." After he had his face flattened a couple of times, he decided boxing wasn't for him.

By the mid-1940s, Klein was married to a waitress and living in the basement of her parents' Calgary home, trying to support two children, one of them the future premier of Alberta, Ralph Klein. "I was working in construction, and in the winters you were basically laid off," he says. "But I never drew unemployment insurance a day in my life. I always found an alternate way of making a living."

For a bruiser of his size – Klein weighed about 270 pounds – wrestling was a natural choice. He was introduced to the game by Stu's old wrestling idol, Jack Taylor. After dominating the Canadian wrestling scene during the 1920s, Taylor, who "had a pair of forearms on him like a guy's thighs," according to wrestler Gene Kiniski, had retired.[2] When Klein met Taylor, he was working in Edmonton as a bouncer at an illicit gambling joint.

Through Taylor, Klein fell in with a clique of Alberta wrestlers, including Ray and Bud Osborne, Al and Tiny Mills, and Tiger Joe Tomasso. He began training, learning the ropes, and by the early 1950s he was wrestling for Stu as Phil "Killer" Klein. "I never made it too big, but I never really wanted to," says Klein, whose career lasted about eight years. "It was something to keep the wolf away from the door in the winter."

For a rough 'n' tumble free spirit like Klein, wrestling was a hoot. He remembers being in the ring with Ray Osborne one night when a blow landed for real. "I caught an elbow smash and it broke my nose," says Klein with a barrelling laugh. "I rolled out of the ring [covered in blood] and one of the fans said, 'Ah, it's just ketchup.' I took a handful of blood, wiped it across his face, and said, 'Try that on fer ketchup!'"

Such physical interactions with the fans were commonplace. The spectators would get so worked up at the matches that they frequently attacked the wrestlers. It came with the job. "You had to pick out the instigator and lay one on him good," Klein says. "That generally softened up the rest of 'em." Sometimes the fans got the better of the wrestlers. Klein remembers one grappler getting "knifed in the butt" by an overzealous army private in some B.C. town he's long forgotten. Another time an audience member snatched the ring bell and tried to crack open a wrestler's skull, a blow that cost the grappler a head full of stitches.

Sometimes, though, fan participation was encouraged, especially during the summer rodeo and carnival season, when many wrestlers worked as special attractions, performing feats of strength or challenging local toughs to pin them for prize money. Klein was working as a referee at one such event in Ponoka, Alberta, when a chuckwagon racer stepped into the ring with Tiger Joe Tomasso for a shot at the $100 purse. A short, scrappy Italian from Montreal, who Stu described as "an indestructible little bastard," Tomasso was surprised to find the ranchman almost too much for him. But he managed to pin the cowboy.

"The next night this guy came back and wanted a rematch," says Klein. "Of course, he brought all these cowboys with him. I said, 'Look, Tomasso, let this guy go over 'cause if you win, we're going to have to fight that whole gang.' Tiger took a fall that night! The cowboys were all happy. The guy got his hundred bucks and went home a hero."

Such circus gimmicks permeated the wrestling game in Klein's day. Wrestling with bears and tigers was not that unusual. One wrestler who passed through the Stampede territory from the late 1950s to the mid-'60s was the late Dave "Wildman" McKigney. He travelled from town to town with his famed wrestling bear, the seven-foot, 650-pound Terrible Ted. Those who dared to get in the ring were instructed to stay in tight and roll around with Ted. Keeping one's distance would result in a frustrated swipe of the paw levelled with enough force to break a man's neck. Nobody liked wrestling Ted in the spring, since the bear was bad tempered after hibernation.

McKigney lost control of the bear on a few occasions. Once, Ted fell out of the ring and stumbled, terrified and confused, into the panic-stricken crowd. It took a gang of wrestlers to pull Ted back into the ring, yanking on his chain and strangling the poor bear in the process. That enraged Ted and it took a full ten minutes for McKigney to soothe the growling, spitting beast.* "The fans were reluctant to take their seats again," recalls Stu's daughter, Diana Hart. "Little kids were still whimpering and the adults were all shaking."[3]

The shows with animals sometimes had disastrous consequences. While there are no reports of fans being eaten alive, one wrestler was nearly crushed. Calgary casino owner Frank Sisson, a close friend of Stu's, remembers strongman Paul Baillargeon returning to the West for a repeat performance of his famous horse-hoisting trick, which had been a sensation in 1952. But this time, some wise guy with a BB gun shot at the horse. The horse bucked violently and Baillargeon buckled, his leg muscles popping like balloons as he went down. "It took four or six wrestlers to get the horse off that man," Sisson says.

As for gimmicks, it was a safer bet to bring in midgets, women wrestlers, or a hypnotist such as Reveen the Impossiblist, who was a household name across Canada in the 1960s and '70s. In the early 1960s, Reveen hypnotized a wrestler, telling him that his body would become rigid "like a bar of steel." The man was laid on two chairs, his head on one and his heels on the other. When massive Mexican wrestler Jesse Ortega, known as the Mighty Ursus, came out and stood on the man's stomach, the wrestler didn't even buckle.[4] Another memorable trick came courtesy of Edmonton wrestler Reggie Parks, who once let someone drive a Volkswagen Bug over his "cast-iron stomach" for the entertainment of wrestling fans.[5]

Like Klein, Edmonton's notorious Osborne Brothers, Bud and Ray, who were stars in Stu's territory from the 1950s through to the '70s, found work on the carnival circuit. Hearty lads, the brothers got their start with Stu's Klondike Wrestling in 1950. Bud was twenty, his brother a year older. The brothers met Stu while working out at the Edmonton YMCA as teenagers. Stu noticed Bud when the young man out-bench-pressed him, lifting 480 pounds; Stu could move a mere 400. When Stu started up Klondike Wrestling, he was keen to bring the Osbornes on board as a tag team.

"I was big and kind of ugly," says Bud, who in his day was a bald brute

---

*McKigney would make headlines in July 1978 when another of his bears, Smokey, killed his girlfriend in their home, after the wrestler forgot to lock the bear's cage.

with a Fu Manchu–style moustache. "My brother was shorter, with dark curly hair. He'd come out and people would whoop and cheer. Then I'd come out right behind him and, Christ, they were threatening to kill me before I done anything…. Ray was a much better wrestler than me, so I raised all the raucous and he settled it down. We made a hell of a team."

Some of the earliest blood baths in the Stampede territory came as a result of Bud's fierceness. Bloodletting was a long-established trick of the wrestling trade, used to generate "heat," or excitement, among the fans. Most often the gore was planned. The wrestlers might have razor blades taped to their fingers or hidden in their boots. Some kept the blade in their mouths. At the right time, when they were in a position where the fans couldn't see what they were doing – buried beneath their opponents or writhing under the ring apron where they had been tossed – the wrestlers ran the blade across their foreheads. This was known as "getting juice." One or two minor cuts were usually all it took before they were bleeding like hogs at a slaughterhouse. They spread the blood across their faces and through their hair until it looked like their skulls had been cracked. Pandemonium ensued.

Not all the bloodletting was planned. In a 1954 match in Calgary, Bud's opponent broke his nose and stuck a thumb in his right eye, permanently impairing his vision by 20 percent. Bud retaliated by chomping off the end of his opponent's nose. "I can still feel my teeth going through," he told the *Edmonton Journal* in 1978. "Everybody wants to progress in the eyes of the promoter. If I figure I can better myself by bashing a guy and busting him open, I'll do it."[6]

Based in Alberta, Ray and Bud wrestled until 1979, when they finally said to hell with it and retired to concentrate on their thriving real estate business. Bud says the toughest man he ever faced was Stu Hart. "In the ring, he was the best. Mean as hell. None was meaner. He respected you if you had talent and fought back, but if he hated you and you had no visible skills, he'd tear you apart. On the mat, I was not his equal. Very few men were." Bud is quick to add that Stu never hurt him. "He knew good and well if he did any of that stuff, I'd take a club to him. Or a gun."

Dave Ruhl and Big Time Wrestling were a perfect fit for one another. A burly, bearded, meat-and-potatoes grappler who was billed as a pig farmer, Ruhl was popular with the legions of farmers, ranch hands, oil-patch workers, and rural folk who flocked to the wrestling matches along the circuit. He had an appeal tailor-made for the territory. His character was so Stampede-centric, in fact, that when he wrestled in other territories, such as the

Top: A gruff Dave Ruhl fixing to tear
Sweet Daddy Siki's face apart, late
1960s.

Bottom: The giant on the right is
Toronto's Sky Hi Lee, at a Stampede
Parade in the late 1950s. Unidenti-
fied wrestler on the left.

Maritimes and Arizona, he had to adopt other identities – the masked Hooded Wasp, for instance.

Of course, the pig farmer identity was a shtick. Ruhl was actually a grain and cattle farmer. Respectable enough. But portraying himself as a pig farmer really got the crowd rooting for Ruhl. Any hard-working joe had to love a man's man who, when he wasn't kicking ass in a wrestling ring, was up to his elbows in pig shit.

Ruhl was born in 1920 in Watts, Alberta, near the town of Hanna, 135 miles northeast of Calgary. His uncle, Ray Steele, who had forged a successful career as a wrestler, encouraged interest in the mat game. By the mid-'40s, Ruhl had broken into the business. At first, he was primarily a jobber, the guy who frequently loses to make the stars look spectacular. "He was the dutiful foot soldier," says Ruhl's son, Glenn. Ruhl worked his way up the card, eventually holding the Canadian Heavyweight and Stampede North American title belts.

Despite his powerful full nelson and technical wrestling skills, Ruhl's primary importance wasn't as a wrestler but as Stu's top booker and second-in-command on the road, jobs he took on in the late '50s. As the business, along with the Hart clan, rapidly expanded, Stu and Helen found that running the operation by themselves was becoming impossible. Stu began recruiting agents to take care of business in his major cities, booking arenas, acquiring licences, and handling publicity for the shows. This group included his old friend Al Oeming in Edmonton, journalist Ned Powers in Saskatoon, and Bob Leonard in Regina. Leonard worked for Stu as a referee and co-promoter, but he made his biggest impact as a photographer. His works captured the action and flavour of the wild western promotion for over three decades. When Oeming stepped down as a co-promoter in 1959, high school principal Mike Bulat took over the job.

But it was Dave Ruhl who was most integral to the action on the mat. In his role as a booker he was in charge of guiding storylines in the ring and developing the characters in Stu's theatre of chaos. His wacky angles leading to the big feuds were fun-filled and entertaining. "There was a French Canadian who they sold as an ex-Nazi," says Glenn Ruhl. "They called him Hans Hermann. My dad got him to tell the audience that he had this deadly grip that he could use to win any match. But dad coached him to say it in German. So he'd be telling everybody, 'I will use my *schysse grif!*' which in literal translation means 'shit grip.' My dad had a lot of laughs."

It was no mystery why Stu placed faith in Ruhl. They were both Prairie boys born of solid farm stock. Both well versed in the art of wrestling, always placing a value on that, never allowing it to be lost no matter how popular the gimmicks. Both loved being members of the wrestling brotherhood, being chiefs of that fraternity where only the toughest of the tough were allowed. They were staunch supporters of kayfabe – "kayfabe" being an old carnie code word that meant guarding the secrets of the industry. They would sooner be flogged than reveal things were rigged.

"If somebody was nosing around about something [the wrestlers] didn't want them to know about, [the wrestlers] would sort of give each other a nod or a wink and say 'kayfabe' to let each other know that the person they were talking to wasn't on the inside," says Glenn. "They kept things very tight." In those days, it was believed that if people saw through the facade of wrestling, it would be akin to a magician whose magic was exposed as mere trickery. Guys like Stu and Dave believed it would destroy the wrestling business. Kayfabe was serious stuff. Funnily enough, many people were on to the fact that the matches were predetermined but still loved them.

But Stu and Dave also had enormous differences. Stu was even-keeled, while Dave had a wild side. For him, the boy's club wasn't just about the blue-collar ballet that was the wrestling game. The camaraderie wasn't confined to the ring, the Dungeon, or Sunday dinner. Dave was a good ol' boy, a subscriber to the world of fun 'n' frolic. He liked to see the gang raise some hell. He liked to party. This made him popular among the pirates of the wrestling business.

Ruhl was notorious for his pranks. On one of countless road trips, Ruhl decided to play a rib on one of the rookies. "Boy, it sure is getting windy," he said as he drove the tour van, which was hauling the ring down the highway by a trailer hitch. Ruhl was nervously looking into the rear-view mirror. "That trailer is wobbling around an awful lot. I need about 200 pounds back there to stabilize it." Ruhl turned to the resident rookie and looked him up and down. "You're about two hundred, right? Do you think you can help us out?"

The next thing the poor sap knew, he was riding in the trailer, steadying a ring that didn't need steadying, his teeth chattering as the icy wind pounded his body. Inside the van, the wrestlers howled with glee.

Ruhl's popularity wasn't unanimous. Some saw their boss as a bully. Once in some dressing room dispute he even slapped the Mighty Ursus across the face, according to Ross Hart. But Glenn Ruhl remembers his dad, who died in 1988, as a good man who raised money for charities and children's sports teams. He was also more grounded than most wrestlers, Glenn says, because of his life as a farmer and family man, which he managed to keep separate from his wrestling. "My dad got married to my mother when he was nineteen and they stayed married for the rest of his life. He always came back to the farm. He knew how to separate the image from reality."

The gonzo cast who drifted in and out of Big Time Wrestling in the 1950s deserve to be immortalized. It is as if the richly drawn characters in a Charles Dickens's novel had been cross-bred with Hunter S. Thompson's Hell's Angels and the tragic circus geeks in the 1932 movie *Freaks*. Given how so many of them expertly milked political, racial, and ethnic stereotypes of the day – tweaking the sensibilities of the western audience – it's no wonder folks found them compelling.

The cast included the evil Commies, Ivan and Karol Kalmikoff. Entering the ring wearing boots to their knees and Cossack hats, ranting about Soviet superiority, this hated duo expertly played its Cold War-era audience. In reality, they were from Detroit and Oklahoma respectively, and not agents of Nikita Khrushchev sent to piss on the pure, God-loving people of Calgary. Either way, they often needed a police escort to get in and out of the venue in one piece.[7]

The legendary Montreal brute Maurice "Mad Dog" Vachon and his brother Paul "The Butcher" were billed as crazed Quebec lumberjacks when they worked for Stu in the late 1950s. Then, there were fightin' Irishmen like Tommy O'Toole, who lived up to the hard-drinking stereotype. He was pulled over by a young Mountie one night after a match. When O'Toole rolled down the window of his car, the smell of booze wafted out and the officer threatened to arrest the ring veteran. O'Toole, with his mean, bashed-up face, stared the Mountie straight in the eyes and told him in his whiskey-burned rasp, "You know, sonny, it'd be a good idea if you got your little yellow-striped ass back in your car and out on that highway before I open this door." The shaken cop took him up on his advice.

Sky Hi Lee, a seven-footer from Toronto, resembled a country bumpkin version of Jaws from the James Bond movies. "He was a hell of a heel," says Bob Leonard, "this great big, raw-boned guy who had the look of a corpse that had been left hanging around for a couple of days. He had long, shaggy hair. He was always unshaven. He wasn't all that fancy in the ring, but you remembered him. He was this monster who'd grab guys and start beating on them."

Sky Hi, born Robert Leedy, is remembered as much for his antics outside the ring as in them. Stories abound of him ordering shots of booze in bars and chewing the glasses when he was finished. He also liked to swallow light bulbs. "Sky did not exactly live clean," Leonard says. "His idea of breakfast in bed was a forty of whiskey. It was sort of like mouthwash and then he could get on with the day." Sky Hi eventually moved to Europe and either wrestled in England, where he wound up crippled, or joined a seedy Paris revue, where he played a brute who descended from a cave to abduct naked women. Either way, all stories about Sky Hi end with him drinking himself to death.

One of the biggest feuds of the era was the tag team matches between a pair of siblings. Dr. Bill Miller, a malicious, six-foot-six Ohio native teamed up with his real brother Dan, and sometimes his fake brother, Crazy Ed (Ed Albers) to torment the beloved tag team George and Sandy Scott from Hamilton, Ontario. When the heroes, adept at drop kicks and aerial moves, were dubbed the Flying Scotts, the Millers taunted them, calling them the Fleeing Scotts. It prompted a savage two-year feud in 1957 and '58. Up to six thousand people, George remembers, were turned away from one match at the Corral, which held only seven thousand.

George Scott, who often helped Stu with booking, went on to make a significant impact on the wrestling world as a booker. During the 1980s, he worked for Vince McMahon Jr. just as McMahon began his takeover of the wrestling world. Scott was instrumental in organizing the first two WrestleManias. He wasn't the only Big Time alumni who would have impact on the wrestling world. In fact, there's too many to list, but the standouts include Gino Marella, a six-foot-five Italian-American somewhere in the neighbourhood of 400 pounds, who showed up in the early 1960s. He became a star in the WWWF, both as a wrestler and a colour commentator, as Gorilla Monsoon.*

In 1953, Stu trained the young Texan Jack Adkisson, who was playing for the Edmonton Eskimos football team. Adkisson was reinvented as the postwar Nazi with the deadly "iron-claw grip," Fritz Von Erich. After a successful run in Stu's territory, Von Erich took his show on the road, becoming a sensation across the United States. By the early 1980s, Von Erich was the head of his own red-hot Texas-based territory, World Class Championship Wrestling, where he made his handsome, muscle-bound sons the stars, just as Stu's sons would be pushed as the stars of Stampede Wrestling.

In the mid-1950s, Big Time was terrorized by Johnny Valentine, one of the most notorious heels in wrestling history. Valentine was obsessed with making his matches look as real as possible, though, by many accounts, he really

*The WWWF, or World Wide Wrestling Federation, changed its name to the WWF, or World Wrestling Federation, when Vince McMahon Jr. took over the business from his father.

was sadistic and cruel. He liked to hurt his opponents and encouraged them to hurt him. His feud with Chet Wallick was so gory that a match in Regina on November 1, 1956, was stopped because of excessive bleeding.

"He had this icy persona," remembers Bob Leonard. "He walked into a ring and glared at people with that blond, blue-eyed iceberg look of his. He was almost unflappable and always so calm. His ring psychology was unbelievable ... but sometimes I think that was his real personality."

Valentine is revered in the wrestling industry, but many describe him as twisted. Journalist Ned Powers tells of a match in Saskatoon where Valentine inexplicably leapt out of the ring and sprinted out of the arena, despite below-freezing temperatures. Dripping with sweat and wearing only his boots and trunks, he tore down the block to his hotel, not to reappear for the remainder of the evening. Valentine was also known for his malignant sense of humour. Wrestler Freddie Blassie tells in his autobiography of Valentine taking an asthmatic wrestler's inhaler and filled it with lighter fluid, causing the grappler to violently puke up his guts when he went for a puff at the onset of an attack.[8]

Valentine's career was cut short in 1975 after a plane crash left him paralyzed. He died twenty-six years later at the age of seventy-two. His son, Greg "The Hammer" Valentine, went on to be a star in the WWF.

Like any promoter, Stu Hart liked the men who could make him money, but his personal favourites were those who could hold their own with him in the Dungeon. This elite group included Al "Mr. Murder" Mills, Rube Wright, Luther Lindsay, and George Gordienko. They were the shooters, genuine tough guys who could clean up when, occasionally, a work – a predetermined match – got out of hand and turned into a shoot – a legitimate fight. This was not uncommon. Maybe a punch isn't sufficiently pulled. Tempers flare. Egos get out of hand. Perhaps a champion doesn't want to lose the belt when the storyline demands it. At these times, matches derail, plans go south, and things get seriously ugly.

Most promotions had shooters: wrestlers who would take care of business for real should the situation call for it. If a blowhard with a chip on his shoulder decided to disobey the booker, he would find himself facing a shooter, who might break his leg if he didn't decide right then and there to be a team player.

Al Mills, raised Adolph Mittlestadt in Camrose, Alberta, was one of the most devastating shooters in the business, a top pupil of the great Jack Taylor, who trained him in the 1930s. So rugged and powerful was Mills that Phil Klein was afraid of getting on his bad side when the two of them stepped into the ring in the '50s. "I was watching myself," says Klein. "I didn't want to hit him too hard. He grabbed me in a headlock and whispered, 'Look, you throw those punches as if you mean 'em!' After that, I hit him hard. He said later, 'If you can't take a punch, you got no business bein' in the ring.'"

Al brought his little brother Henry into the business in 1948 as the brutish Tiny Mills. In the 1950s, the *Toronto Star* dubbed them "the most hated men in all of grappledom."[9]

Rube Wright from Phoenix, Arizona, was another competitor who meant business. According to Glenn Ruhl, "Rube was a guy who would go into the dressing room and say, 'Well, boys, tonight I think I'm going to win.' And nobody questioned him. That included Stu. He was the pièce de résistance."

But, as with many legitimate wrestlers, Rube's style in the ring wasn't flashy enough for the fans. His brother Jim "Riot Call" Wright was a bigger draw; he was the quintessential '50s villain with a nasty, rough-hewn face like Oil Can Harry's from Mighty Mouse cartoons, if Harry had his face walked on with a pair of cleats.

Winnipeg's George Gordienko, whose skills made Stu gush, was wrestling's rare Renaissance man. He debuted in 1946 at age eighteen. By the early '50s, Gordienko's career was stalled by Senator Joseph McCarthy's Communist witch hunt when it was discovered that the grappler had at one time joined the Communist Party of Canada. Blackballed in the United States, Gordienko was lured back to Western Canada to wrestle for Stu Hart. With his wrestling skills, good looks, and powerhouse build, Gordienko was a sensation. In 1976, he retired and went down a most unlikely path, moving to Italy and becoming a painter and poet.

Luther Goodall, or Luther Lindsay as he called himself in the ring, was Stu's best friend. Stu carried a picture of the African-American wrestler from Virginia in his wallet, where it stayed until Stu died. Wrestling gossip suggests that Stu's reverence for Lindsay began when Luther did the impossible and bested Stu in the Dungeon. Lindsay could apparently escape from Stu's best holds and slap them right back on him. He was said to have once locked Stu in such an agonizing submission hold that the King of Pain was, for once, the man screaming. Stu tried to fake Lindsay out, saying he heard the phone ringing and had to take the call. Lindsay told Stu he'd have to call whomever it was back.[10]

Keith Hart was backpacking through Europe in the summer of 1971 when Lindsay died of a heart attack in an Oregon wrestling ring. He got the news from his shaken father when he phoned home. "It really hit him," Keith says. "They were like brothers."

Put this gang of crazies together on an endless highway, add buckets of alcohol, and naturally it made for many a loco night out on the Canadian Prairies. Fuel that testosterone with the promise of a stacked sex-fiend with a taste for stud-bull wrestler blood, and there was no telling what might go down.

That was the idea behind the Mabel rib, spearheaded by Dave Ruhl and Al Oeming and notorious in wrestling circles around the world. This elaborate prank was played on a wrestler who was new to the territory and began with the boys swapping stories in front of him about their sexual conquests of Mabel. No ring rat, the mythical Mabel was a classy dame, a married woman whose husband, usually said to be a pilot, was always out of town, not fulfilling her needs. Voluptuous, sexy Mabel was insatiable. She craved large, virile men. That's why she was so hungry for the rock-hard wrestlers. The point was put across as a challenge: only the greatest of lovers could handle this goddess of erotica.

The newcomer begged to be set up and, eventually, one of the grapplers would tell the rookie that Mabel wanted to meet him. Mabel insisted on meeting at a discreet location, a farmhouse in the country. The wrestler was to bring a feast – steaks, seafood, champagne, only the best. Mabel also wanted the wrestler to bring one of his colleagues: she needed another stud for her friend.

Anticipation built throughout the week, Mabel's victim becoming a tightly wound libido bomb ready to explode. Finally, he arrived at the farmhouse to find, sure enough, a beautiful sexpot waiting for him. The other wrestler made an excuse to leave so that his buddy could be alone with Mabel. Just as the rookie was making his move, in burst Mabel's husband, insane with rage, screaming obscenities and waving a gun: he was on to his wife's infidelities. On cue, the wrestler's buddy charged in to help, and the husband fired a round into his chest, blood soaking his shirt. The wannabe lover would flee for his life.

That's when the party ensued. The dead man rose, pulling the rigged ketchup packet from inside his shirt as the other wrestlers emerged from hiding. Mabel and her husband joined the jackals, digging into the feast the victim had left, carousing into the night.

The Mabel made for many memorable moments over the years, always a great laugh for those in on the joke. One rookie was Mabelled as late as the early 1970s. "The RCMP found him covered in cow manure and totally frostbitten [after his dash through the farmer's field]," says Ross Hart. "He had lost one of his shoes and was totally panic stricken."

The most celebrated Mabelling involved a wrestler–circus sideshow called the Great Antonio. A Yugoslavian immigrant of Siberian descent who came to Canada in 1946, Antonio Barichievich lived in a Montreal scrapyard, sleeping in a broken-down bus. The 450-pounder soon discovered he was strong enough to pull his bus around the scrapyard, and he parlayed this into a career. A beast of a man, with a grizzly beard and greasy black hair that hung to the ground, making him look like Rasputin, Antonio made a name for himself in Montreal in the 1950s, hauling up to four packed buses at a time down city streets. In 1952, he made it into the *Guinness Book of World Records* by pulling a 433-tonne train 19.8 metres. He also famously braided and taped his coarse dreadlocks together, using his hair, bizarrely, as a golf club. Wrestling promoters from around the world sought to bring him into their territories, and Stu was no exception. Antonio arrived in Calgary for the first time in 1959.

According to Paul "The Butcher" Vachon, Dave Ruhl phoned Antonio one day pretending to be Mabel. "I just love your body," Ruhl said in a sultry voice. Antonio, who stunk horribly because he ate raw garlic every day, didn't receive many sexual propositions and went wild. Mabel told him, "I want you to bring Dave Ruhl and Mad Dog Vachon with you. I've got two girlfriends who want to meet them."

"No! No! I go by myself," Antonio said. "I take care of all of you!"

Eventually, Antonio agreed to Mabel's terms and that Saturday night the three wrestlers went to meet the temptress. When the insane husband showed up, he blasted Ruhl and Mad Dog. As he went down clutching his chest, Mad Dog turned to the Yugoslavian madman and cried, "Run, Antonio! Run!" The giant bolted out the door and into the pitch-black night, sprinting across the field, cutting himself on barbed-wire fences along the way. The wrestlers came out and partied hard on the beer and whiskey Antonio had brought with him to woo Mabel. By most accounts, Stu usually kept his distance from such debauchery, but on this particular night he too was in on the gag.

At seven the next morning, Antonio called Paul Vachon in his hotel room, ranting that Ruhl and Mad Dog had been shot and now the killer was out to get him. Vachon accused him of being drunk and hung up. Antonio went to the RCMP, who began an investigation. ("My mom wasn't too happy about that one," recalls Glenn Ruhl. "My dad got charged with public mischief.") The Vachon brothers showed up at the RCMP station and, after convincing the petrified behemoth that it was all a rib and that he wasn't going to be assassinated, got him in the car and back on the road. He would wrestle for Stu off and on until the 1970s.

Despite a career that brought him minor celebrity as an oddity – he appeared on such TV programs as *The Ed Sullivan Show* and Johnny Carson's *Tonight Show* – Antonio wound up a penniless eccentric on the streets of Montreal, selling postcards and brochures of his life story until he died of a heart attack in 2003. But in 1959, Antonio was one of Stu's soldiers and there was no time to lick his wounds after his hazing. There was an endless row of towns to hit along the circuit. There was hell to raise, and thousands of fans eager to fork out their hard-earned pay, addicted to the crazy, violent dramas that Stu and the boys cooked up week after week.

These were the pirates of the Prairies and this was their life.

Chapter six

TV, Slick Sammy, and a Jet Plane

The year 1956 brought changes to Big Time Wrestling that would raise the stakes forever. That was the year the Prairie wrestling promotion became more than a travelling circus of folk heroes. That's when it became a television show and its folk heroes became something infinitely more powerful and influential: TV stars.

It was not easy running a wrestling promotion in the Prairies. The endless road trips were brutal at the best of times, with every city and town on the circuit far apart, but in the winter, on those glare-ice highways, it could be downright terrifying. Plus, a wrestler generally couldn't make as much money in a smaller city such as Calgary as he could in the major centres of Toronto, Montreal, and New York. To come to Stu's territory meant one was remote, far from the hot spots. It was hard to get the big name draws in town.

But Stu was connected and respected in the wrestling business, and when he got the stars in Calgary, the action-hungry westerners responded by packing the arenas for weeks on end. Despite the challenges Stu faced, by the mid-1950s, the promotion was firmly entrenched as a Calgary institution.

But by 1956, the playing field had changed. Alberta had been starved for TV. Since its invention in 1929, the boob tube had been behind a cultural revolution, especially once it entered living rooms in the United States, in 1945. With the turn of a dial, every man, woman, and child now had access to world

Stan Stasiak is sent flying through the air by "Canada's Greatest Athlete," as Gene Kiniski referred to himself, late 1960s.

news, sporting events, and frivolous entertainment, available in an instant on the screen, bringing it all to life in a way radio never could.

In the early days of the medium, television signals reached only a hundred miles or so from the transmitter. This meant that southern Ontarians could pick up U.S. programming on their sets, but Albertans were out of luck. A survey taken in 1950 indicated that 61 percent of Ontarians could watch TV. On the Prairies, only 14 percent had experienced the new-fangled luxury.[1] On September 6, 1952, the Canadian Broadcasting Company stepped up to the plate, airing the first Canadian broadcast from its Montreal station. Two days later, Toronto followed suit. Ottawa, Vancouver, and Winnipeg got publicly owned CBC-TV outlets the following year, but Edmonton and Calgary were classified as secondary markets by the federal government and Albertans were deprived. The government did allow, however, for privately owned CBC affiliates to begin broadcasting on the Prairies. This paved the way for the launching of Calgary's CHCT-TV, on October 8, 1954.

Stu was keenly aware of the power of television when he saw what it did for Toronto promoter Frank Tunney. Tunney had begun televising his Maple Leaf Wrestling matches nationally on CBC-TV, and he was making men such as Whipper Billy Watson, Killer Kowalski, and even Edmonton's Gene Kiniski, who Stu helped develop, into household names. As any baby boomer will recall, these wrestlers were among the first major TV stars. As his audience grew via mass TV exposure, Tunney was selling out Toronto's Maple Leaf Gardens consistently, and his empire expanded throughout Quebec and Atlantic Canada. Because the CBC broadcasts were being seen in Alberta, Stu began negotiating to get Tunney's stars on his cards.

Having joined the National Wrestling Alliance (NWA) in 1951 helped his cause greatly. The NWA was an organization of wrestling promoters from across North America who were dedicated to working together while respecting each other's territorial boundaries. At annual conventions, the promoters drew from their collective talent pool to elect a world heavyweight champion. The champ toured from territory to territory, facing each promotion's top stars and attracting sellout crowds. As a member of the NWA, Stu was able to bring in the champions and trade top talent with other promoters.

Stu could see that the wrestling landscape was changing, becoming increasingly dependent on TV. When he was unable to book Tunney's TV stars for his shows, business slumped. Stu knew he had to get his show on TV, and so he began negotiating with CHCT-TV to get Big Time Wrestling on the local airwaves. By 1956, the deal was struck, and Stu found himself producing two programs. Both were shot live in the studio with a single camera and made cheaply (the average locally produced program at the time had a budget of about $5 per show).[2] The programs included a fifteen-minute *Meet the Wrestlers* spot, which aired Fridays at dinnertime to drum up excitement for that night's match on the Stampede grounds.

Meet the Wrestlers involved the grapplers cutting promos – in other words, being interviewed to hype their matches. This gave them a chance to bellow, issue threats, and develop their wacky identities for the audience. A guy like Wladek "Killer" Kowalski, from Windsor, Ontario, the son of Polish immigrants, was an instant star. Behind the scenes he was a good-natured if no-nonsense man, a vegetarian who frequently emptied a ten-gallon salad bowl at Hart House while gulping carrot juice by the jug-full. But his on-screen persona was different altogether. Frighteningly intense, he would glare like a maniac into the camera lens, all 300 pounds of him looming toward it, jabbing his finger menacingly at it – and viewers at home. Then there was the bully-faced Gene Kiniski, with his belligerent rants and insufferable boasts that he was "Canada's greatest athlete." Promos like these filled arenas week after week.

The flagship program was *Mat Time*, broadcast Saturdays and Sundays. This was filmed before a studio audience at the CHCT headquarters. The studio held 150 people, but on some weeks up to 1,000 would show up, hoping to get a seat. *Mat Time* included both wrestling matches and the scream 'n' yell shenanigans.

Around this time, Stu also produced a hokey radio spot called *Dear Wrestler*, an absurd forum where the various grapplers answered questions, supposedly sent in by the fans, that were better suited to a *Dear Abbey* column. The wrestlers answered in whatever outrageous fashion was appropriate to their characters. Helen Hart wrote many of these spots. "They'd be questions about anything," says Keith Hart. "Killer Kowalski would answer questions about etiquette. You'd have The Great Antonio on affairs of the heart. My mom got a big laugh writing those."

The real brain behind Stu's early success on TV was Sam Menacker. A superb ideas man and a first-rate hustler, Menacker was sharp and witty. He understood the wrestling business inside and out. He knew how to get the best from the wrestlers and how to work the fans, the marks. "Mark" was another old carnie term adopted by the wrestlers. It meant a sucker. Carnivals made their money off marks, or suckers, and so did the wrestlers, who sold an illusion to the fans. To Sam Menacker, the whole world was his mark.

A stout man, with dark, slicked-back hair and horn-rimmed glasses, Menacker hailed from New York City. He had been a wrestler himself before the

Gene Kiniski rampaged through Stampede territory once or twice a year during his days as the NWA World Heavyweight champion. Referee Bob Franks checks Kiniski before a match, mid-1960s.

Second World War; after the war, he returned to the business as a promoter and booker. Menacker was a fast, charismatic talker, and when TV became an important component of the wrestling business, he quickly found his voice as an announcer. He made a name for himself in Detroit, where he played the crusading TV commentator, morally outraged by the wicked antics of the perpetually cheating heels. Menacker was one of the first announcers to develop such a voice, and to this day it's an important element of pro wrestling broadcasts.

Stu had met Menacker in his New York days and had followed his exploits ever since. When he planned to get Big Time Wrestling on TV, Stu couldn't think of a better man to work with in the new medium. Stu's instincts were dead-on. "Sam was like a maestro conducting," says Keith Hart. "He was electric and he had everybody up. He made my dad more money than any other booker."

On TV, Menacker became the voice of Big Time Wrestling, resuming his Detroit shtick as the righteous commentator. Behind the scenes, he devised the format of the TV shows and developed angles that drove the fans wild. One such angle involved Czaya Nandor, who had been a freedom fighter during the Hungarian Revolution of 1956, when the country fought to break free of Communist control. When the uprising was crushed, Hungarians fled their homeland en masse. About thirty-seven thousand were admitted to Canada. Calgary, with its large Hungarian population, guaranteed Nandor a passionate following.

When Nandor got his Canadian citizenship papers, it was spun into a black comedy. The Hungarian community held a ceremony at a *Mat Time* taping to honour its hero. Nandor was presented with his papers and a white cream cake that an elderly Hungarian woman had baked for him. Suddenly Killer Kowalski came bolting into the studio, firing insults at Nandor. The Polish-Canadian villain attacked the Hungarian, smashing the cake into his face. Keith Hart will never forget the sight of the hero wiping cake from his face and crying on television, his fans sobbing along with him, devastated by this cruel turn of events. "It was the most heinous thing ever," Keith says, "and it must have sold out a million matches. Week after week the Corral was packed." It was a work of art.

Now that big time was on tv, the top wrestling stars in the world started hitting Calgary on a regular basis. These included Lou Thesz, thought by many to be the greatest wrestler of all time; the arrogant pretty boy, "Nature Boy" Buddy Rogers; and the Flying Frenchman, Edouard Carpentier, whose acrobatic moves dazzled fans. Toronto hero Whipper Billy Watson was another regular. Watson, the epitome of fair play and a man devoted to charity work, particularly for handicapped children, was worshipped in Canada.

Gorgeous George Wagner, billed as "the toast of the coast" and "the human orchid," was nearing the end of his career – and his life – at this point. On Christmas Eve, 1963, he died of a heart attack in his Hollywood apartment, having spent his final days destitute and battling alcoholism. But his Calgary appearances were spectacular.

Introduced by Menacker, the Gorgeous One fluttered his way to the ring, enraging the homophobic crowds, which hated the mere sight of his flowing robes and bleach-blond locks. George tossed rose pedals and golden hairpins – Georgie pins, he called them – at the rubes, and before he entered the ring, his beautiful female valet would spray it with sanitizer. George didn't want to catch any germs from the filthy wrestlers.

Of all the screaming mad heels to make a splash on *Mat Time*, Gene Kiniski may be the greatest. His ring persona was egotistical and cantankerous, "about as diplomatic as a punch in the face," as wrestling photographer Bob Leonard puts it. Kiniski's relationship with Stu outside the ring ran hot and cold over the years. Stu usually spoke highly of Gene, and the two of them did some co-promoting together in the early 1980s, but there was definitely friction between the two. In recent interviews, Kiniski has responded angrily to the suggestion that Stu trained him.[3]

Stu met Kiniski at the Edmonton YMCA when he was an amateur champion and Kiniski was just a teen. Kiniski asked Stu for his tutelage and Stu obliged. Eventually, Kiniski got into amateur wrestling and excelled, winning championships in both Alberta and at the University of Arizona. While in Arizona, Kiniski trained with professional wrestlers Dory Funk Sr. and Tony Morelli, and he credits them as his trainers. It was in Arizona that Kiniski wrestled his first professional match. But before he pursued wrestling seriously, Kiniski played football for the Edmonton Eskimos. In a 1952 game, he tore the cartilage in his knee. After going through a year of therapy for his injury, Kiniski launched his wrestling career full time, working for Stu.

Though Stu would later say he viewed Kiniski as a hot prospect, Phil Klein tells a different story, one that might account in part for Gene's animosity. He says Kiniski was working as a referee one night in Edmonton when Whipper Billy Watson was wrestling for Stu. "[Watson] said, 'Stu, what are you going to do with that kid?' Stu goes, 'Ehh, he's got a bad knee. He'll never make it as a wrestler.'" Watson asked Stu if he could use Kiniski and ended up taking the rookie to Toronto. Within a year, on the strength of his brutal, plowing style and big mouth that wouldn't quit, Gene was one of the top heels in North America. Kiniski would go on to be a world heavyweight champion, and his wrestling career would last forty years. "The Whip could see the potential in Gene," says Klein. "[Stu] never gave Kiniski a chance."

Despite his loud, bullish demeanour, Kiniski is a smart man and that has been a key to his phenomenal success. He always knew just how to offend the audience wherever he wrestled, to the point where crowds screamed for his blood. In a 1967 interview with the *Calgary Herald*, he belittled the beloved Calgary Stampede.[4] To Cowtown crowds, this alone was a hanging offence. Kiniski also had a way of putting people off with his relentless bragging. He used to begin his interviews with the line: "Hello out there in TV land. I'd like to welcome you as Canada's greatest athlete."

It wasn't a persona that Kiniski turned off when the lights went down, either. Sid McCoy, a former Saskatoon cab driver, remembers picking up Whipper Billy Watson one winter night at the wrestler's hotel and driving him to the airport. Watson left him a $3 tip. Later that day, McCoy picked up Kiniski, also headed for the airport. The driver mentioned that he had just dropped off Watson. Kiniski went into one of his trademark tirades and then growled, "How much of a tip did he leave you?" The driver lied and said that Watson had given him five bucks. Determined to outdo his enemy, Kiniski slapped a $10 bill into McCoy's hand before storming off.

Once Kiniski took off in Toronto, Stu had to pay top dollar to get him to wrestle in Alberta. He did, though, and "Big Thunder," as Gene called himself, would be in and out of Calgary for the next three decades, always a hot ticket, particularly during his epic battles with Watson, which Stu felt was one of the greatest feuds ever. "It was classic good against bad," Stu told the *Calgary Herald*. "While Kiniski was a noisy spokesman for the sport, Watson's delivery was calm and reasoned. They made a beautiful pair and promoters may never see that opportunity again."[5]

One can see why Stu felt that way. One night in Edmonton when Whipper and Kiniski were squaring off, twenty thousand fans were turned away at the gate after the arena sold out. A 1957 match between the two at the Corral grossed $25,000, one of the greatest paydays of the Big Time era.

Having joined the TV revolution, Big Time Wrestling was soon reaping the benefits of this new maximum exposure. Things were going so well financially that Menacker, a licensed pilot, was able to talk Stu into purchasing a plane for the promotion. Stu bought a Comanche 250 for $25,000.[6] It made good business sense. The expanding territory covered thousands of miles.

Stu was putting on shows as far away as Alaska. A plane would save valuable time. Stu could take care of business in person on the road and still have time to raise his family. It would also be good for morale, sparing the wrestlers the gruelling road trips. It was a lot easier to entice the likes of Watson, Kowalski, and Kiniski when they could jet from city to city like the stars they were.

According to George Scott, this made for a few scary moments. "Sam Menacker was a hell of a pilot, but he almost killed us a few times," he says. In one instance, Scott was airborne with Menacker, Stu, and Kiniski, flying home from a match in Montana. The plane ran into a blinding snowstorm and Menacker began to panic. "We're supposed to be over Calgary! We should be there by now!" he said in an increasingly shaky voice. "If it wasn't for Kiniski, I think we would've crashed," says Scott. The mouth that roared maintained a level head and talked Menacker through the crisis. "That's it, Sam," Kiniski said, "just take it down a little bit lower."

Close calls aside, business was so good in those first few TV years that Menacker strutted around Hart House boasting about the fantastic money they were going to draw from the big shows. He had a knack for predicting the gate to within a few dollars, writing his prophecies on the bathroom mirror with his wife's lipstick so Stu and Helen would find them later that evening.[7]

But all good things must come to an end. By the late 1950s and early '60s, a series of incidents conspired against Big Time. For one, Menacker jumped ship without notice in 1958. Letters to Stu and Helen from that time, while friendly, indicate he felt he was due a bigger piece of the pie for his innovative ideas. He was also dissatisfied with the production values at CHCT-TV and he threatened to sue the company, claiming he was owed royalties for his TV concepts. Furthermore, his wife, the world woman's champion June Byers, was injured in a Medicine Hat match when a fan threw a bottle, striking her in the eye. Menacker told Stu she might need an operation, citing this as another excuse for his not being able to work for Big Time. Menacker was the lynchpin of the TV production, and his leaving was greatly felt.

Meanwhile, the Calgary Boxing and Wrestling Commission, which would haunt Stu throughout his career, had been increasingly cracking down on the promotion, protesting against the violence and the wrestlers' unruly behaviour. It began issuing fines, such as the $50 levy handed to Riot Call Wright, who pummelled Stu while the promoter supposedly lay unconscious on the ring floor. Stu might have protested, telling the commission that it was a work, a planned happening, and that he wasn't really in jeopardy, but such admissions were taboo in those days. If news of that sort got out, the wrestlers believed it would kill their business.

One of the commissioners, Pat Sullivan, lived across the street from the CHCT-TV studio. Sullivan kicked up a fuss about the number of cars parked on his street every Saturday afternoon when fans flocked to the studio for the tapings. Sullivan took a petition signed by himself and other irate neighbours to City Hall, causing friction with CHCT.

In 1960, Iron Mike DiBiase, an American heel who was the stepfather of future WWF star Ted "Million Dollar Man" DiBiase, was on live TV when he loudly proclaimed: "If brains were dynamite, the people of Calgary wouldn't be able to blow their nose!"[8] The thought of it is laughable today when risqué and tasteless TV is the norm, but back then the statement was scandalous. The station was flooded with phone calls from outraged viewers and it pulled Stu's TV spots.

"We started to [operate] without television again and it was disastrous," says Ross Hart. "Without the TV coverage, there was no exposure, no interest, and that spread to all the other cities. Without TV, the promotion was doomed." It became more and more difficult for Stu to book the superstars, and the arenas were impossible to fill up without the TV hype and the big names. At certain points, Stu was losing up to $5,000 a week.[9]

Fortunately, there proved to be a quick fix. A second TV station, CFCN-TV, had started up in Calgary, and it was keen to have a wrestling program. CFCN's studio was built atop Broadcast Hill, just up the narrow dirt road from Hart House. When CFCN launched the one-hour weekly program *Big Time Wrestling*, it gave Stu's business a new lease on life. Slick Sammy came back to the fold for a time, promising Stu the world. In a letter he wrote in July 1961 and signed "Sad Sam Menacker," Sam promised Stu that within one year he would have a nationally televised wrestling show and the strongest territory in North America: "You will be banking thousands of dollars each week, with Sam Menacker following you to the bank, hoping you'll drop some of the filthy lucre his way." He even jokingly promised that Stu would have his own Rolls-Royce, with Sam as his chauffeur. Menacker closed off with the boast, "Have no fear, Sam is here!"

For a time, he made good on his promises. Media from this era suggest that *Big Time Wrestling* was a hit. A TV *Guide* article published in March 1963 says the show was syndicated in major Canadian cities, including Windsor, Ottawa, Montreal, and Halifax. It was also seen across the border, in Detroit and San Francisco. According to the article, Stu even received fan mail from New Yorkers who were able to pick up Montreal stations. A retired New York police officer was said to have forwarded Stu a pair of handcuffs to help him detain the bad guys who were always interfering in other wrestlers' matches on behalf of their rotten brethren.[10]

But *Big Time*'s CFCN years were plagued with problems. Sometime in 1962, Menacker was beaten up by Hamilton wrestler Mike Sharpe on live TV. "Sam was interviewing him and Mike hauled off and punched him right in the nose," recalls Ross Hart. After Menacker was hurt and humiliated by Sharpe, there was no appeasing him. He left town in the company airplane, claiming in a letter that it was half his and that Stu owed him money for travel expenses. Stu hired a lawyer to get the plane back, but the aircraft was registered in Menacker's name. There was nothing Stu could do.

Stu's brother-in-law Jock Osler sums up the Menacker experience. "They brought him in when the business wasn't doing very well and he was going to be the great saviour, the great rainmaker. He was going to be the salvation of everything.... He was an imaginative promoter and he did bring in some good guys.... But I think he took Stu for a lot of money."

Menacker's replacement was Ernie Roth, a former Ohio radio announcer. Small at about five-foot-seven and 130 pounds, Roth too was charismatic on TV, with a creative flair for the wrestling business that would eventually make him one of the biggest stars in the industry.

In the late 1960s, the Jewish Roth found fame in Detroit, assuming the identity of the weasel-like Arab Abdullah Farouk, manager of a bloodthirsty savage known as The Sheik. In the '70s, he began working for Vince McMahon Sr. in the WWWF, where he terrorized Madison Square Garden in loud polyester suits, a turban, and funky sunglasses, calling himself the Grand Wizard of Wrestling. As the despicable Grand Wizard, Roth managed Superstar Billy Graham, one of the biggest wrestling stars of that era.

But Roth, who died of a heart attack in 1983, never got the chance to develop his money-making ideas in Calgary. Roth had a secret which, if exposed, would have been scandalous. "He was a homosexual," says Ross Hart. "Back then, the two worst things you could be accused of being were a homosexual and a communist." Roth was careful to be discreet, but it was known among the wrestlers that he lived with a male hairdresser, a situation that was often treated as a joke behind Roth's back. Even Stu had fun with it. "Stu kind of laughed at [Roth]," says Osler. "There was a lot of wink-wink, nudge-nudge. Stu would say, 'He kind of minces his step.' But if there was a guy who seemed to be a homosexual who was flouncing around camping everything up, if that was good for business, it was fine with Stu. That's show biz."

Roth's brief tenure in Calgary ended soon after CFCN executives voiced concerns about his lifestyle. According to Ross Hart, the station managers were tipped off by a bitter Sam Menacker, who didn't like the idea that he could be replaced. Ross says Menacker launched a smear campaign against the new announcer, painting him to be a dangerous pervert. In the early 1960s, even in the most liberal centres – which Calgary certainly was not – homosexuality was something to be feared and despised. Roth was hurt by the untrue accusations and left the territory forever.

After Roth left, Stu took on popular sportscaster Henry Viney as his regular announcer. Viney, then head of the sports department for CFCN, was a pillar of the Calgary community. He had been one of the first announcers for Big Time Wrestling in the days before TV, and even after Menacker came along, Viney was the announcer for the Friday night matches at the Pavilion.

By all accounts, Viney was a character in his own right. On a few occasions, "the little man with the big cigar," as Stu used to refer to him, got carried away and tried to take out a few of the more villainous wrestlers himself. "Stu had to get in there and stop him," remembers casino owner Frank Sisson. "He'd say, 'Jesus, Hank, you're gonna get killed!'" But despite Viney's charisma and whatever success the TV show was having, the business was suffering considerably. Without his plane and the help he got both promotionally and creatively from Menacker and Roth, Stu was again struggling to fill the arenas.

To combat the problem, he made an arrangement with the new Vancouver-based promotion, All Star Wrestling. Vancouver being much bigger than Calgary, All Star had easier access to the biggest wrestling stars. Stu began co-promoting with All Star, sometimes running its show in his TV slot in exchange for the All Star wrestlers, who the promotion regularly sent to Calgary. Among them was Kiniski, the "Mormon Giant" Don Leo Jonathon, and the Fabulous Kangaroos, a popular team from Australia that entered the ring to the song "Waltzing Matilda" while throwing tiny boomerangs into the audience.

"Their show was terrible," says Ross. "[All Star promoter] Rod Fenton was a cheesy commentator and not that charismatic. My dad's announcers prior to that were really well received. They always spoke to the locals. Now we were getting this generic show out of Vancouver and people didn't relate to it…. This was even more of a disaster for my dad because he was flying in all these big names from Vancouver and paying their airfares and hotel bills, but business was plummeting. After about nine months, dad had to dissolve his relationship with Vancouver." CFCN continued to broadcast *All Star Wrestling*, but now Stu had no affiliation with it. Once again, he was left without a TV show.

By the fall of 1964, the business had hit rock bottom. Normally at that time of year, Stu and company were kicking off the wrestling season, trying to ensure it was booked to the hilt with matches all along the territory. But this was not to be in '64. "Stu had to stop promoting completely," says Ross. "He went out of business. He tried to get refinanced and had been turned down by several banks.... [Stu and Helen's] finances were very tight and they had eleven kids to support. My mom was expecting Owen then, too. The promotion was not going to survive unless Stu was able to get another TV contract.... Times were very tough."

Where once he bought a new Cadillac every year, by the early 1960s, Stu could barely afford to keep the old ones in operation, beaten up as they were from so many thousands of miles on the road. The Hart's backyard and the grassy fields surrounding the estate became a junkyard of run-down Caddies, most of them merely rusted-out shells.

When the coffers were overflowing, Stu began upgrading the house's front windows. After the financial problems set in, the work could not be completed, and for two or three winters in a row, the paneless windows were covered only with cardboard. Keeping clothes on the kids' backs was also a challenge. One winter, Stu had gone to a liquidating clothing store and bought red, down-filled hunting jackets for his kids, all in one size. For the older children, it wasn't the best fashion statement to be making. For the younger kids, the jackets fit them like tents.[11] The Harts were teased by their classmates about their "welfare rags." "Hart farts" was another familiar taunt. They often fought back, and protected each other fiercely on the school ground. There were plenty of schoolyard scraps, with the older brothers constantly defending their younger siblings.

Being one of the eldest Hart children, Keith was mature enough to understand how well off the family had been in the heyday of Big Time Wrestling. He felt the loss all the more as the Harts went from rags to riches in a few short years. When times were good, Stu had landscapers level the backyard to make room for a swimming pool. The greenhouse was torn down. The lush grass and the beautiful flower beds were ripped up. Stu planned to plant anew once the pool had been installed. "I was sad because I used to like the old yard," says Keith. "[Dad] took out all the old trees where we used to play hide and seek. He took away all the flowerbeds where we used to play with our little dinky trucks. One day [the tractors] came and uprooted those trees to put the pipes in for the swimming pool. That was in the summer. Then September came and the bottom dropped out."

A great hill of dirt remained in the Harts' yard, created when the pit for the swimming pool had been dug. Keith remembers watching it become a mound of weeds as the years progressed and the junky old Caddies multiplied. He describes the scene as something from John Steinbeck's *Grapes of Wrath*. "We went from the family that had everything, to the Joads almost overnight," Keith says. "I went through my formative years without a lawn, without trees. Nothing. It was just a fight to survive after that."[12]

Chapter seven

Uncle Ed and the Wildcats

Ed Whalen was the almighty voice of the Stampede territory. The promotion had a number of ringside announcers over the years, but none of them, not even Sam Menacker, had Whalen's monumental impact. Not only did he spend the most time on the job – working with Stu off and on for close to forty years – but he also came to define the show's spirit.

Whalen was the host and central personality of the TV show that would come to be known as *Stampede Wrestling*. Wrestlers would come and go, the program's quality would ebb and flow, but Whalen, along with Stu, was the foundation. By the mid-1960s, he was its star. He gave the show its continuity, injecting into the mix a sense of fun that was homespun and endearing. He guided fans through the bizarre twists in the storyline with his colour commentary, selling them the action like a ringmaster at the circus. When fans tuned in for their weekly wrestling fix, the one certainty was that Whalen would be there to greet them like an old friend.

It's strange then that as key as he was to the show's success, Whalen was in no way cut out for the world of professional wrestling. While he enjoyed the guerrilla theatre of the game, he was a tenderfoot who had no stomach for its brutal side, and he always did his best to suppress the ugly stuff the fans so craved, ordering the cameraman to stop filming when things got too bloody. Whalen was moralistic and too conservative in nature for the shock and awe tactics at the heart of the wrestling business.

Stoic Stu faces off against Archie "The Stomper" Gouldie in a war of words in which Gouldie looks ready and willing to get physical. Announcer Ed Whalen is sandwiched between the two. Calgary, late 1960s.

For the most part, Whalen held himself above wrestling and could even be condescending about it. A charismatic if corny sportscaster and a serious journalist whose idol was Walter Cronkite, Whalen seemed to partake in wrestling for little more than a lark. "You might ask what a journalist is doing associated with something you could call the Colgate Comedy Hour," he said with characteristic playfulness in one interview. "It's entertainment. There's more showmanship than sport. It's a modern-day version of the old western mellerdrammer, the good guys and the bad guys and everybody just loving it."[1]

In another interview, Whalen stated, "I've never considered [wrestling] a sport. Some of these 250-pounders object to that, but fortunately, Stu protects me. I have fun with it. If they asked me to do a serious show, I'd refuse. I'm not out to con anybody."[2]

Whalen's wife, Nomi Whalen, a marriage commissioner and a former Calgary alderwoman, says her husband was sometimes embarrassed by his association with wrestling when things got too lurid. "We had a similar view on it," she says. "I can appreciate good acting, but when you have to resort to putting a razor blade in your beard or whatever.... It offended me. It still does. I found the brutality disturbing, and also the fact that a lot of the fans believed what they were seeing was real.... Ed had a love-hate relationship with wrestling. He quit twice because of blood being drawn.... He said it was taking the phoney shit too far." It was only Whalen's close relationship with and respect for Stu that allowed him to return again and again.

Next to Stu, Whalen was arguably the most important figure in the history of the TV show. He gave the show a likable down-home voice, a distinctive identity that set the Calgary promotion apart from other, more powerful, wrestling groups in North America. Promotions in Toronto, Detroit, New York, and Los Angeles had weekly access to stars who Stu could afford to bring in only a few times a year. Those shows had better production values than the single-camera, low-budget program that came out of Calgary. And the Corral was no Maple Leaf Gardens. As for the Victoria Pavilion, which *Calgary Herald* columnist Johnny Hopkins once referred to as "a frontier Taj Mahal,"[3] it was little more than a glorified barn. But this stuff was part and parcel of the charm of *Stampede Wrestling*. It's what made the show so distinctly western Canadian, so special to fans in the region. Nobody drove this point home like Whalen. For everything other wrestling promotions had that Calgary was lacking, what they didn't have was Whalen.

When Whalen developed a rapport with the wrestlers, his cheeky back and forth with them made for hilariously funny moments. The Stampede bad guys had some of their most memorable battles not in physical confrontations with other wrestlers but in verbal sparring matches with Whalen.

When Tiger Joe Tomasso boasted about his sexual conquests, referring to his women as birds, Whalen dubbed him "Tweet Tweet" Tomasso. This enraged Tomasso, and he would lunge at Whalen, only to have the announcer brain him with the microphone, to the delight of the crowd. Sometimes Stu would come to Whalen's defence. A sharp slap to the head would send the gremlin-like Tomasso scampering away. It was sheer lunacy, like something out of a Three Stooges feature.

On one occasion, an interview Whalen was conducting broke down into a staged battle between several grapplers, the sort of wild rumble the wrestlers liked to call "a Pier-6 brawl." Whalen calmly dodged the clashing titans, looked into the camera, shrugged, and smoothly quipped like some prairie Rat Packer: "I wonder what my insurance agent is saying right now?"

"He played it tongue-in-cheek," says Nomi. "That's why there were grandmothers watching it with their grandkids. I don't know of any other sport, other than Don Cherry in hockey, where an announcer so owned the show.... Ed was a good actor, and that's why he was Stampede Wrestling."

Although that's an overstatement, there's no question that Whalen embodied the show's personality, bringing a refreshing comic relief to the table, coming across as everybody's favourite uncle. Today, when western Canadians look back fondly on Stampede Wrestling, Uncle Ed's catchphrases, or Whalenisms, replete with a kind of hokey western charm, are recalled as much if not more than the actual matches. A particularly wild bout was dubbed a "ring-a-ding-dong dandy." "Off those ropes!" he'd exclaim when a wrestler was bounced off the ring ropes and careened across the ring. Just before a human collision occurred, Whalen would bellow in his nasally voice, "Look out, Nellie!" The collision itself was called a "malfunction at the junction." When a wicked heel got his just desserts in the form of a sound thrashing, Whalen would cry out like an excited fan, "How suh-weet it is!" In Western Canada, his stock lingo became part of the pop culture lexicon.

Of course, there was the patented weekly sign-off, delivered by a chuckling Whalen with the same cool rhythm each week: "In the meantime, and in between time ... that's it ... for another edition ... of *Stampede Wrestling* ... Bye now." Then the credits rolled and the jaunty theme music, which sounded as if it had been plucked from a Bavarian beer hall, blared from TV sets across the West. It was a joyous experience, and Whalen's shtick was the biggest part of it.

Whalen's first major contribution to the Stampede territory was in 1965 when he used his considerable pull on Calgary television to get Stu's

Top: NWA World Junior Heavyweight champion Nelson Royal cuts a promo with Ed Whalen before putting his title up against the Dynamite Kid during Calgary Stampede Week, 1979.

Bottom: Tiger Joe Tomasso, or "Tweet Tweet" Tomasso as Whalen called him, rants before a match, as Ed looks on, late 1960s.

promotion back on the air, resuscitating it after it flatlined. But Whalen's association with Stu Hart far predated '65. The two men met in 1952 at a wrestling card in Saskatoon. Whalen was twenty-four years old, doing his pre-med degree at the University of Saskatchewan.

A meek youngster, Whalen grew up painfully shy, burdened with a sense of shame because two bouts of rheumatic fever had left him physically weak and because his father worked as a janitor at his high school. Smart and sensitive with a creative flair, Whalen found, as a performer and media personality, the confidence he had been lacking. During the Second World War, he had a gig as a singer in a swing band and acted in local theatre productions. To pay his way through university, he did on-air work at the local radio station, CFQC. The blossoming personality found another way to supplement his income in 1952, when Stu offered him work as a ring announcer once a week for the Big Time Wrestling shows at Saskatoon Arena.

Inevitably, Whalen's love of broadcasting won out over any aspirations he had to study medicine, and he dropped out of university to work full-time at the radio station. When TV arrived on the Prairies, Whalen was entranced by the medium and, by 1955, had worked his way to Calgary's CHCT-TV as the station's news and sports director. When Stu got on TV in 1956, he once again offered Whalen work. Menacker was the big man with Big Time at that point, but Whalen was often on hand, providing a second voice and filling in whenever needed. Watching an episode of *Mat Time* from about 1960, it's evident that Whalen had not yet come into his own as a wrestling announcer. His delivery was confident enough. There was even a trace of the wit that would later be his calling card as he described heel Tarzan Tourville as being "about as popular as a garbage sandwich." But he lacked the charming presence he later developed. His look wasn't as distinctive in those days either, his balding head and clean-shaven face barely resembled the toupee and moustache-wearing gent western Canadians would come to know and love.

Ed got a long break from the wrestling business in the early 1960s when Stu moved over to rival station CFCN. When that ill-fated venture went under, the Harts found themselves in dire straits. Stu was desperately trying to attract financing to relaunch the promotion but had been turned down by several banks. He was forced to take out a second mortgage on the Hart home. Even putting food on the table was a challenge. Finally, in 1965, after months of negotiating, Stu was able to return to his original TV haunt, CHCT, which had by then changed its call letters to CFAC. Whalen deserves much of the credit for this. He had clout at the TV station and when he backed Stu in his pitch for a new wrestling program, offering to be the full-time announcer for the show, it improved Stu's chances immeasurably.

Still, there was one more obstacle to overcome. Stu was required to pay a set-up fee of $1,000 to get the new show – to be shot every Friday at the Victoria Pavilion – up and running. It's a testament to how poor the Harts were at this time that Stu could not come up with the money. He was forced to borrow it from a friend. "That loan helped save our bacon," Stu later said.[4]

With the bacon saved, the Prairie wrestling promotion was reborn as Wildcat Wrestling. It was an appropriate name considering the cast of hellions who came on board.

The black Gorgeous George. That's how Stu described Sweet Daddy Siki, one of the great heels of the Wildcat era. It fit, as Siki's act was the jive talkin' equivalent of George Wagner's.

The 255-pound African-American, born Reginald Siki in Texas, entered the ring sporting sunglasses with sparkling frames, a long, pink cigarette holder in his mouth. He wore a sequined tux with tails, admiring himself all the while with not one but two handheld mirrors so he could capture every angle as he strutted before the fans. His most striking feature was his bleach-blond afro; his eyebrows, dyed the same colour, made for a sharp contrast with his chocolate-brown skin.

Siki was the epitome of arrogance, seldom making eye contact during his interviews with Whalen because he was too busy admiring himself in his mirrors. He declared himself "the sweetest dude in wrestling," as well as "the ladies' pet and the men's fret." There may have been some truth to that. Despite the similarities between Sweet Daddy and Gorgeous George, Siki's persona was never as fey as that of his white counterpart. Mr. Irresistible, as Siki used to call himself, bragged about his womanizing, telling people that the women he met in Montreal gave him the name Sweet Daddy.

As Keith Hart recalls it, Siki had a girlfriend at the time, the daughter of a prominent University of Calgary professor. "He drove around with her all over town. It was very flamboyant," Keith says. "You had the blond-haired black guy with this tall, leggy white girl with great big hair, eyelashes two inches long, and this super tight mini skirt. She looked like one of the Chiffons."

Siki's interviews were highlighted by his dismissal of the competition Stu had for him, saving his greatest ridicule and contempt for "that silly old pig farmer" Dave Ruhl – and riling up every farmer and farmer's son in the audience in the process. "He'd get everybody so angry, they were dying to see him lose," says Dave Ruhl's son, Glenn, "and who better for him to be defeated by than this down-to-earth grassroots hero?"

Inevitably, Ruhl would come out in his black suit and tie and polished cowboy boots to challenge Sweet Daddy in the name of good rural folk everywhere. Siki would sucker punch Ruhl and abuse him for a while, heaping on the humiliation. One week, he tied a dead chicken around Ruhl's neck. Even more grotesque, he later crowned his enemy with a pig's head. The resulting feud sold out the Corral for five weeks, and it continued to rage, off and on, until Siki left the territory in 1970.

"I remember them wrestling for a solid hour," wrote Bret Hart in the *Calgary Sun*. "You could smell the sweat and the cigarette smoke in the air and everyone was left hanging right to the last second. Sweet Daddy gave Ruhl three or four drop kicks in the dying seconds and just when Siki thought he had him right where he wanted him, Dave slapped that full nelson on and the house exploded."[5]

Siki had other memorable feuds in Western Canada, but they seldom matched the chemistry that he and Ruhl generated together. Bud Osborne remembers having a rough time with Mr. Irresistible. "Stu wanted me to put Siki over one night, and I agreed to," says Osborne. "But he was making me look a little too bad, and I took exception to it. So he was picking me up and I let go with a shot right in his sack." Stu was furious when Osborne got back in the dressing room. "He said, 'You son of a bitch! You bastard! Now I can't trust you.' He never raised his voice. Not ever. He just had this low guttural growl and when it got really low, you knew you were in trouble."

Both Ruhl and Siki were along for the ride in what was one of the great misadventures of that era, during one of the promotion's infrequent tours through Alaska. Accompanied by Stu, the stars of Wildcat Wrestling made the trek across the narrow, winding roads of the Alaska Highway, two thousand miles from Calgary. As in so many wrestling stories, with embellishment and the passage of time clouding memories, details of the trip are murky. Did the incident occur in Anchorage? Juno? Fairbanks? It's no longer clear, and it doesn't particularly matter. It's the craziness of the trip that earns it its immortality.

The drive was treacherous, and when the wrestlers finally reached their destination, testy as hell, they went to the hotel watering hole for a few cocktails. A woman in the bar patted midget wrestler Sky Low Low on the top of his head. Insulted, he leapt up and grabbed her by the throat. "That's it, the wrestlers are in town!" laughs Glenn Ruhl, whose father told him the story.

As Stu recalled, the three-foot-eight, eighty-six pounder went on a rampage, drop kicking both the woman and her husband. "Siki grabbed Sky Low Low under his arms and [Sky] was yelling at Sweet Daddy, 'Put me down! Put me down!' That little weasel tried to get away from Siki and everybody was laughing.... The people he had drop kicked got out of there, saying, 'This is a bunch of nuts here!' Sky was on fire.... He was such a short-tempered little devil."[6]

Such drunken, violent outbursts were not uncommon from the Montreal-born "Little Atlas." But Sky Low Low, whose bald head and tough face made him look like a pint-sized version of the man on the Mr. Clean container, was a big draw. Touring from territory to territory with his babyface nemesis, the mohawk-sporting Little Beaver, the midget stars used to command up to 15 percent of the gate at cards they appeared on.[7]

To Stu, they were worth it. Midgets were a novelty attraction back then, and Little Beaver and Sky in particular gave the fans plenty of action and belly laughs for their buck. When Beaver struck Sky, the bald midget toppled end-over-end cartoon style, coming to rest upside down, balanced on his head like a wobbly bowling pin.

The life of a midget wrestler was tough and often sad. Sky Low Low had a complex about his size that made him an angry fellow, especially when drunk. He was a full-time carouser, constantly chasing women, but he had his heart broken many times by girlfriends who made off with his money.[8] Despite his temper, Sky Low Low enjoyed cracking the boys up with his blunt sense of humour. On the notorious Alaska trip, Stu decided to take advantage of the kitchen in his hotel room and cook the men dinner. One thing the kitchen didn't have was a pot for Stu to mix the ground meat in. Ever industrious, the promoter emptied a trash can to use. Sky Low Low walked in, saw Stu's unsanitary methods and, taking a beer from the fridge, walked back to the party in the next room without saying a word.

That evening, as the wrestlers dug in to a feast of cabbage rolls, plenty of compliments were directed at Stu, until Sky piped up like a hardened Spanky from a *Little Rascals* episode: "Guys, these aren't cabbage rolls, they're garbage rolls!" The remark caused a stir, and much merriment, but the feast went on unabated. Such was life: weird, wild, and frequently unappetizing on the road.

Another wildcat star was "Mormon Giant," Don Leo Jonathon, who stood six-foot-six and weighed 340 pounds. Although he made better money in other territories, Jonathon loved Western Canada and returned to it a few times each year in the mid-1960s. He came from the prairies of southern Utah and felt at home on the plains. An avid hunter, he also loved "varmint shooting" in the region.

Trained by his father, Jonathon, born Don Heaton in 1931, had been grappling since the age of three. After a stint in the U.S. Navy, he decided to turn pro. He first appeared in Calgary in the early 1960s, an imposing figure with a mountainous frame and bushy, black mutton chops.

"Don Leo was one of my favourite men," Stu gushed in one interview. "That big man could do backflips and somersaults and nip-ups like a cat."[9]

Jonathon feuded with Dave Ruhl, Sweet Daddy Siki, and New Brunswick's Yvon Cormier, who wrestled as The Beast. But his biggest war was with a Quebec street fighter named George Stipich. That beef had legitimate roots. "Me and him go all the way back to Chicoutimi in northeastern Quebec," says Jonathon. "He had a little gang there and every week they used to come take potshots at the wrestlers. He was big and fast.... I'd already had a few run-ins with him, caught a few glancing blows. One night, one of the Frenchmen said, 'That kid is looking to clean your clock tonight. Watch for him 'cause he's gonna come in from the corner and blindside you.'"

Jonathon, on his guard after the match, was heading back to the dressing room when he saw the kid coming for him. "I pretended I didn't see him," says Jonathon, jolly at the memory of it. "I waited till he cocked his fist. When he swung, I ducked, threw an uppercut, and knocked him out cold. I set him up! I never seen him back at the matches after that."

The next time the Mormon Giant laid eyes on his attacker, the kid was in a Calgary dressing room, now a wrestler himself and going by the name Stan Stasiak. Getting knocked out by Jonathon had been a turning point for the brash youngster. "I'm surprised to see you here," said Jonathon. Stasiak replied in a bullish yet respectful tone, "After our last little run-in, I figured I better learn something, so I came to see Stu. I'm lucky you didn't kill me."

The two men had a laugh and started making plans to work together. Their feud was one of the hottest of the Wildcat era, with Jonathon's giant jungle cat moves pitted against Stasiak's mad bull approach and his deadly heart punch. The heart punch was exactly what it sounds like: a stiff shot to his opponent's chest, sold as if it could stop the organ from pumping were Stasiak to land his fist just right.*

Jonathon says that despite his love of the territory, Stu stopped booking him because of a rib that frightened the hell out of the usually unflappable

---

*Stasiak wound up in the wwwf, even holding the world heavyweight title for nine days in 1973.

promoter. One night on the merciless Stampede loop, six wrestlers, Stu included, were jammed into one of the promoter's clunky Cadillacs, making an overnight run back to Calgary. Stu drove while the boys gobbled sandwiches and downed beer. Soon everybody had fallen asleep, their heads and bellies full. Stu was exhausted and afraid he might nod off at the wheel. Jonathon offered to relieve him.

A couple of hours passed, and sleepiness was beginning to overcome Jonathon as well. He was fading fast, trying desperately to stay awake as he crossed the endless prairie. Off in the distance he saw the light of a train coming his way. There was a railroad crossing up ahead. Jonathon stuck the car in neutral and coasted toward the tracks. In a moment of devilish inspiration, he punched Stu in the arm and shouted, "Hey, Stu! Do you think I can make it?" As Stu awoke with a start, Jonathon stomped on the gas pedal, making the engine roar as if he were going to try to beat the train. Stu screamed like a man falling from a cliff, clawing at the roof of the car.

Jonathon coasted to the edge of the tracks before his passenger realized he was the victim of a gag. "Stu took over the driving after that," the big man says, "and you can better believe he was wide awake, too.... I didn't think it would scare everyone as bad as it did. But I sealed my fate then and there. After that, Stu never did call me."

Jonathon missed the territory greatly, and one day he talked to his old friend Stasiak about it. When Stasiak asked Stu why he hadn't booked Jonathon in such a long time, he was met with the grumbling, ornery reply: "Ehh, bastard likes to chase trains."

The name "Wildcat Wrestling" was changed to Stampede Wrestling in the fall of 1967. Wildcat had been a fine name, but the Stampede moniker captured the promotion's identity right down to its western roots. After all, since 1952, people had been flocking to Calgary's Stampede grounds every week to see this insane soap opera play out. There was a wild, woolly flavour to the show too, like a day at the rodeo, filmed as it was in that smoky old barn, the Victorian Pavilion. The show's Calgary-centric persona was further entrenched with Ed Whalen, one of the city's top TV personalities, as the program's sole host.

If the promotion was Calgary to the core, than what better title for it than Stampede Wrestling? Didn't the Calgary Stampede define this little western Canadian city in the eyes of the world? Attendance for the week-long party was fast approaching one million visitors a year. Wisely, Stu had long tried to run his promotion to complement the Stampede. Not only were the year's big angles and feuds brought to a climax during Stampede week in July, but it was also a time when Stu went all out, bringing in the top draws in the wrestling world – Andre the Giant and world champions such as Harley Race – to take on his stars. He would also bring in sports celebrities, usually retired boxing champions such as Rocky Marciano and Joe Louis, as guest referees. They'd be given the hero's welcome, introduced with much fanfare at the rodeo grandstand shows. It lent a world-class air to the Stampede, and it helped promote the week's wrestling cards.

"Professional wrestling has become a popular addition to the Stampede," trumpeted the Calgary Stampede's general manager Maurice Hartnett in the July 4, 1964, *Calgary Herald*. For his part, Stu said, "We're more than happy to be a part of Canada's biggest show."[10] Stu and Helen had also become a permanent fixture of one of the Stampede's exclusive wingdings, the Hays Breakfast. When such dignitaries as Prime Minister Pierre Trudeau and entertainer Bob Hope visited the Stampede, they invariably wound up at the Hays Breakfast, where they were introduced to the Harts, among Calgary's other elite.

Even the Hart children had become a part of the Stampede. The local media loved to catch Stu's brood taking part in the festivities. The cameras captured them posing with visiting celebrities, horsing around on the midway, and digging in to ears of corn. "The Harts never met a camera they didn't like," says Helen's brother-in-law Jock Osler.

From at least 1957 onward, the wrestling promotion played a big part in the spirited Stampede parade, which wound its way through downtown Calgary on the event's opening day. Every year, Stu and company joined the procession of colourful floats, usually atop a wrestling ring on wheels, bending and creaking under the weight of the rasslers. The eccentric cast rode through the city centre, posing and waving to happy parade-goers, or scowling at them, depending on their characters.

"Stu never hit a parade where he was fully prepared," laughs Stampede photographer Bob Leonard. For several parades, Stu stationed Leonard on the float with a microphone to hype the stars of Stampede Wrestling. "Most often the float was a wrestling ring with aircraft tires," Leonard says. "[To pull it] we used Cadillacs, pickup trucks, John Deere tractors…. Then you might have the world champion in a convertible with a big banner on it. But we always had our share of catastrophes."

Leonard chuckles remembering one year in which, one after another, three of the four tires blew beneath the ring. When the first and second tires went flat, the ring skewed sideways, limping along the parade route.

Stu ordered that the show go on. But when the third tire blew, the wrestling float ground to a halt, holding up the whole event in front of thousands of parade-goers and a national television crew. The parade marshall was furious. "Stu! Get that thing outta here!" he yelled, ranting that wrestling would never again be part of the Stampede parade. But every year, Stu and his crew showed up with another rolling disaster.

Ross Hart says it always ended up being a "colossal embarrassment. I'm amazed the Stampede people even let my dad enter [the parade] after a while."

Stu often used the parade as an excuse to fire up a feud while the world watched. In 1965, he tried to orchestrate a battle between the hated pseudo-Nazi Waldo Von Erich (actually a Toronto boy by the name of Wally Sieber) and retired boxing great Rocky Marciano while the two rode a float together. Von Erich did his best to provoke the sixty-one-year-old Marciano by pulling his cowboy hat down over his eyes. Stu was hoping the original Italian Stallion would swing a punch, setting up a match that could be finished in the ring. "We could've sold out the Corral the next week," Stu told *Saturday Night* magazine. "The place would burn up."

But Marciano refused to play along. "Just clench your fist, anything," Stu told him. "But Marciano didn't want any part of it," said Stu. "He was ... self-righteous or something. He thought all this wrestling stuff was comedy."[11]

Over the years, two of the larger-than-life parade favourites were the McGuire Twins, Benny and Billy, from North Carolina. Weighing 814 and 784 pounds respectively, the brothers, recognized as the world's heaviest twins in the *Guinness Book of World Records,* worked as wrestlers in the 1970s and, as a freak show attraction, they were a big draw come Stampede time.

In the parade they rode a pair of Honda mini-bikes, which they endorsed, riding the machines across the country, presumably to demonstrate the bikes' mettle. One of the bikes blew a tire on the parade route and the twin riding it had to waddle along for the remainder of his journey. It nearly killed the lumbering brute. "They had no stamina," remembers Ross Hart. "They were so heavy, they could barely walk from the Pavilion dressing room to the ring."

Because of their size, the McGuires couldn't attempt most wrestling moves. Their act consisted of choreographed spots, usually involving the wrestlers running into them and bouncing back as if they'd hit a fortress of blubber. The McGuires piled on top of their opponents, one on the other, squishing the man on the bottom. "I've had wrestlers poo-poo in their pants from the weight," Benny McGuire was quoted saying.[12]

Another eye-popping Stampede attraction, albeit in a completely different way, was exotic dancer Babette Bardot, a blond Swede whose

Babette Bardot chats with "Cowboy" Dan Kroffat, proudly holding a wrestling trophy won during a mid-1970s card at the Calgary Stampede, while midget star Little Beaver brandishes a sledgehammer, as if he's about to wreak havoc.

bountiful bosom was constantly threatening to burst loose from her low-cut, cleavage-baring tops. With measurements of 44-24-38, this over stuffed cheesecake, who claimed to be a second cousin of sex symbol Brigitte Bardot, had appeared on Johnny Carson's *Tonight Show* and *The Merv Griffin Show*. She began appearing in a Calgary hotel in the early 1970s as a nightclub singer and exotic dancer.

Bardot made a splash, attracting the wrestlers, who took in her act before the road trips. Recognizing an opportunity, in 1973 Stu crowned Bardot Miss Stampede Wrestling, and had her ride on the float during a number of Stampede parades over the years. She too got caught up in Stampede Wrestling's yearly disaster on the parade route when the wrestling float broke down, spooking the horse she was riding on. The horse bucked the scantily-clad Bardot to the road and she grew hysterical, her bust heaving in front of awestricken parade-goers and the drooling Hart boys.

For several consecutive summers, Miss Stampede Wrestling appeared on the *Stampede Wrestling* TV show as a celebrity guest, presenting awards such as outstanding wrestler or rookie of the year to various grapplers. She was also on hand to greet the world champion or a star such as Andre the Giant. Andre was said to have been smitten with Bardot, who gave him a peck on the cheek on TV. This infatuation was cute but at times troublesome. When Bardot was in town, Andre refused to wrestle anywhere she wasn't, even though Stu wanted him to make appearances all along the circuit.[13]

"The Eighth Wonder of the World," Andre the Giant, was the greatest of all the Stampede attractions. Until Hulk Hogan became a mainstream star in the mid-1980s, there was no bigger star in wrestling history. From Grenoble, France, Andre Rene Rousimoff was afflicted with acromegaly, a glandular disease that causes a chronic secretion of growth hormones in the body. But in 1964, when he began his wrestling career, at the age of eighteen, Andre was still lean, muscular, and agile. Things took off in 1970 when he moved to Montreal and began selling out the Montreal Forum repeatedly.

Eventually, Vince McMahon Sr. took over Andre's bookings and put the Giant on a permanent world tour, renting him out to promoters – from Canada and the United States to New Zealand and Japan – who knew having Andre on the card meant sold-out arenas. By the mid-'70s, the Giant had become a pop culture novelty, with appearances on *The Tonight Show* and *The Six Million Dollar Man*. In 1987, he had a role in the Rob Reiner movie *The Princess Bride*.

By the time he reached his prime, Andre stood at six-foot-eleven and tipped the scales at 350 pounds, a weight that eventually climbed to 550. When his height peaked, Andre's disease spread to his limbs and his skull grew to freakish proportions. If he grabbed an opponent by the face, the man's entire head would disappear within Andre's massive hand.

Andre was, for the most part, a friendly giant. He knew that he would not live long with his condition and was determined to eat, drink, and be merry. Because of his size, he could drink astonishing amounts of alcohol. Stories abound of Andre's consumption. It wasn't uncommon for him to drink a case of wine in one sitting. He could knock back fifty bottles of beer and walk away only slightly tipsy. Because drunken merry-making is the order of the day at Calgary's Stampede festivities, Andre loved wrestling for Stu during the event. It was written into his contract that four bottles of red wine be left in his dressing room, the contents of which would be swishing in his belly by the time he entered the ring.

Andre's greatest Stampede performance was in 1977, when he squared off against NWA champion Harley Race, a rugged grappler from Missouri who is recognized as one of the all-time greats of the wrestling biz. At 250 pounds, with steel plates in his forearm from a car accident – his death grip could supposedly snap a pair of pliers – Race was an awesome physical presence.[14] But he posed no threat whatsoever to Andre, who threw him twenty feet across the ring so hard that Race broke several of the wood planks beneath the mat. As per the storyline, Race hung on to his title that night, but only because the Giant played along.

He didn't have to. Bret Hart recalls fighting Andre and having the Giant step on his throat with his size twenty-two boot, making Bret's face turn blue. "At that moment, I understood why Andre did this to everyone he worked with," Bret wrote in the *Calgary Sun*. "It was his way of secretly letting me know he could kill me for real anytime he wanted."[15]

With disease spreading through his body, it was inevitable that Andre would meet a sad end. By the 1980s, he had grown to such proportions that his movements were stifled. Near the end of his career, he was bloated and in constant pain. This did little to thwart his popularity, and he made sports history in 1987 at WrestleMania III. The angle, pitting the colossus of the 1970s against the new giant, '80s icon Hulk Hogan, was a natural and played up beautifully. A record crowd of seventy-eight thousand fans poured into the Silverdome in Pontiac, Michigan, to watch Andre take on the Hulkster. It was wrestling's first live gate to shatter the million-dollar mark, grossing U.S.$1,599,000 plus $5.2 million in closed-circuit pay-per-view revenues.[16]

Andre's physical condition continued to deteriorate and by the time he wrestled his final matches in 1992, barely able to move in the ring, he had become a sad sight to even the most naive fans. He died in his sleep from heart failure on January 27, 1993.

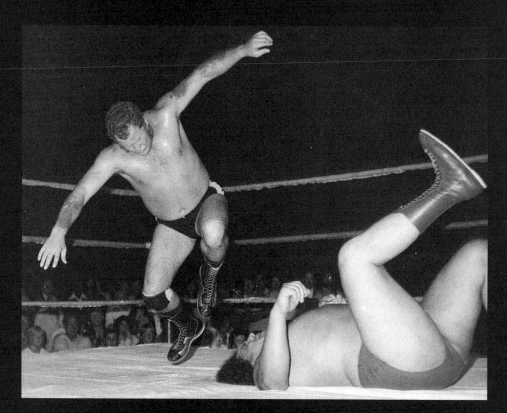

Top: Harley Race drops his knee on Andre the Giant's head, Edmonton, 1970s. Race defended his world title belt against Andre several times in Stampede Wrestling. During this particular match, Race lifted the Giant, bringing all 500 pounds down on the mat for a rumbling body slam – more than a decade before Hulk Hogan pulled off the feat at WrestleMania III.

Bottom: Helen Hart warmly embraces Andre the Giant in downtown Calgary during Stampede Week, mid-1970s.

The Harts didn't just do business with these bizarre characters, they also opened their homes to them. Helen was a creative sort with a literary flair, and there's no question she got a kick out of these pirates, carnies, and eccentrics who passed through her home. Every day, the Stampede Wrestling circus yielded new mind-boggling stories, new adventures, new extraordinary pictures for the scrapbook.

But running such a sideshow was a life of little stability, and over the years the pressure got to Helen. This was not the path she would have chosen. Wrestling was not her great passion as it was Stu's, and Helen found it hard to cope with the constant ups and downs of the business. Especially when they threatened to ruin her massive family, which had swelled to twelve children when Owen was born in 1965. Rich one day and in the poorhouse the next. It was too much to take, and at times she resented the wretched wrestling business.

Stu always took the hardships in stride, believing that no hurtle was insurmountable and that tomorrow would be a better day. Helen, on the other hand, worried herself sick. According to Diana Hart, the pressures drove her mother to drink. This is one of the most contentious points of Diana's autobiography, *Under the Mat*, and several of the Hart children vehemently deny it. But hints of the pattern Helen was developing are evident in "Harts and Cauliflowers," the autobiographical essay Helen wrote in the early 1970s.

On the stress of raising twelve children, Helen writes: "I am an anxiety-prone candidate for Snap City. With me, worrying is an art.... Almost from the very start, Stu and I were outnumbered and outmaneuvered, and this we accept, each coping in his own way. Stu drinks tea and often whistles, 'We shall overcome;' I turn to gin and tonic and, it being a big house, I hide a lot.... The other evening as Stu and I surveyed the downstairs disaster area we beheld the wall-to-wall children, clutter, pets, laughter, life. Eyes wet with emotion (and only partly attributable to that last gin and tonic), I murmured to him, 'Ah, look at them. When will they be like this again?'

'Tomorrow,' he said.'"[17]

Like most of her brothers and sisters, Alison Hart was stung that Diana exposed the family's private business. She acknowledges that at times her mother used alcohol as a crutch but stresses Helen was never anything other than perfectly poised in public. "I don't think that was a fair depiction," she says. "My mother was a very strong woman. She was a good parent ... a sweet, loving person ... and that was, unfortunately, her coping mechanism.... But to depict her as a raging alcoholic is a lie. It's not right."

Chapter eight

Butchers, Stompers, and Cheats

"Got to kick at the darkness till it bleeds daylight," sings Bruce Cockburn in his 1983 hit "Lovers in a Dangerous Time." Nothing else nails the coming of "The Stomper" so squarely on the head. Archie "The Stomper" Gouldie, hailing from a dairy farm in the sleepy Alberta town of Carbon, seventy-five miles northeast of Calgary, stomped away – with his size thirteen cowboy boots – the economic clouds that loomed over Stu's business for most of the 1960s. He ushered in a period of prosperity for Stampede Wrestling, and many of the promotion's key players, including Bret Hart and photographer Bob Leonard, consider him the single greatest heel to ever terrorize the territory.

Nobody saw such greatness in the teenager when he first appeared on the scene in the late '50s. He was just another tough guy, a townie who thought he had it in him to lick a wrestler. Gouldie had been coming to the wrestling matches for years, studying the proceedings intently.

In his early twenties, Gouldie moved to Calgary, where he managed a service station. The darkly tanned, husky kid with the burning glare was also venting his aggression, crushing gorilla-sized gladiators on the football field for the North Hill Colts. But his wrestling obsession had not faded. Gouldie dreamed of climbing into that ring, and the hunger to do so was burning a hole in his belly.

Finally, one night at the Pavilion, the fan decided to make his move. He marched up to the ringside, snatched Ed Whalen's mike, and hollered

Archie "The Stomper" Gouldie, scourge of the Stampede territory, lays a massive boot to former Hamilton Tiger-Cat Angelo "King Kong" Mosca, early 1970s.

murderous threats, challenging the formidable Mills Brothers as they made their way to the ring. They invited the brash young bruiser to come up and prove himself. Archie was about to when the police escorted him, barking at the grapplers like a mad dog, out of the building.[1]

In the weeks that followed, Gouldie was back, again trying to prove himself with the wrestlers. Stu warned him that he might be hurt if he stepped in the ring. Gouldie growled in reply, proclaiming that he was going to become a pro wrestler and he was willing to take his chances. "Don't take it lightly till you've tested it," Stu said. "Come on down to my house. I have a gym in the basement. If you can handle me, I'll give you some of my men."

Gouldie accepted the invitation. Stu, having lured a new victim to the Dungeon, stretched the young man without mercy. "I scared the hell out of him," Stu told the Glenbow Museum. "I really worked him over.... His forehead down on his belly button ... his face purple from trying to escape. You get panicky.... He was so fearful that he didn't come back for another three or four months." Nobody expected Gouldie to return after the shock of his Dungeon visit, but eventually he showed up at Stu's door. "Sir, I appreciate you tipping me off about how ugly wrestling is," Gouldie said politely, and implored Stu to train him. The stretchings continued.

Gouldie, his mother, and his wife lived about five miles from Hart House and, on some training days, the wannabe wrestler trudged through snow and freezing winds to be savagely tortured before limping back home. "I'd keep going – until he hurt me so bad, I couldn't go. I'd take a couple of days off and I'd go back," Gouldie recalls.[2] My mother used to shake her head and say, 'There's something wrong with you, boy.'"

Gouldie thought at times that he was dealing with a supernatural force. "I seen [Stu] walk outside in his bare feet with about a foot of snow on the ground," he says. "It was twenty below zero and a car drove into the yard. Stu walked out to talk to them. He stood out there with no shoes or socks for a good forty minutes."

Keith Hart has a vivid memory of The Stomper's days in the Dungeon. "I remember one time my dad heeled him in the nuts," Keith says matter-of-factly. "He put him in a double grapevine [a wrestling hold] and stuck his ankles in between Archie's legs to ride him down. It's just like spurring a horse. But he spurred him right in the balls." Keith, just a boy at the time, remembers Gouldie crawling to the bench, spent. "He looked at me and said, 'Hey kid, ever seen a swollen nut before? Look what your old man done to me.'" Archie pulled his trunks to the side and out popped his bruised testicle. "It was like a big coconut," Keith says.

Most men whither under such siege. Archie toughened up. A 1967 *Calgary Herald* article captured Gouldie's steely resolve to do whatever it took to make it in the wrestling business: "[If I have to] I'll carry Stu up to the highest peak at Banff," he said.[3]

Stu finally put Gouldie on the card in 1962, but not to wrestle the main-eventers Gouldie had been gunning for. Instead, he worked the preliminary matches, usually doing jobs, getting beat to make other grapplers look good. "Stu never put me over," Gouldie says. "You've got to prove yourself to him. You've got to prove that you can make the right moves and be the right kind of person." After a year on the bottom rung, though, Gouldie was fed up. He decided he had to venture out and start fresh in other territories. When he made his name away from home, Stu would have to give him his due.

The Stomper persona was born in Kansas City, Missouri. At first he was reinvented, oddly enough, as the Mongolian Stomper. "He was the only Scottish Mongolian I ever met," laughs Bob Leonard. It was former world champion Pat O'Connor, then a promoter in the territory, who came up with the character. O'Connor had Gouldie shave his head save for a patch of jet-black hair on the crown of his skull that hung a good ten inches long. He wore it in a ponytail, grew a thick Fu Manchu–style moustache, and came to the ring a vicious, mute Mongolian. In this guise, Gouldie became a top heel in the southern United States. He incensed fans to the point where one stabbed him, in San Francisco, opening a wound that required seventy-four stitches.

Suddenly Archie Gouldie was somebody. And Stu, struggling in 1967, looking for a character who could heat up his territory again, took notice.

When Gouldie returned to Stampede Wrestling, the mute bit of his persona was ditched, the ponytail shorn, and a full shock of close-cropped black hair grown. He wore a horseshoe emblem on his wrestling trunks and a big pair of cowboy boots, which assisted him in stomping his victims into a bloody paste. It made sense that Stampede Wrestling's premier villain should be an Albertan, a vicious cowboy with the intensity of Hang 'Em High Clint Eastwood, had Eastwood's character been totally psychotic.

And Gouldie finally got his turn at the microphone. A terrible tremor shook Stampede country to the core. As devastating as he was in the ring – and Archie Gouldie had become a bone-breaking, blood-taking machine – his interviews were the stuff of legend. A seething cauldron of rage, raving with a craziness that scared children and adults alike, Gouldie, his wild eyes flaming as he unleashed his horrible invectives, was unforgettable. Hunched over and glaring into the camera, his massive shoulder and neck muscles swelling up tight as if dragon wings were about to sprout from his back, it seemed as if Gouldie was going to burst through TV screens and stomp everyone watching to pieces in their living rooms. Even Whalen stood back and let Gouldie explode. What could anyone add to such a deranged symphony? "I love pain! I love it!" Gouldie would bellow, the veins in his temples bulging as if ready to burst.

Wrestling programs from the period read like previews of bad 1950s monster movies when describing Gouldie: "Here is a man who has absolutely no compassion! Sympathy is an unknown factor to him! Gouldie is like something from outer space ... something evil!"[4]

The Stomper tried his best to live up to the ruthless image, and his opponents were frequently carried out of the ring on stretchers. "Why not put wheels on the stretchers?" he suggested to Whalen with glee. "That would make it a lot easier for the fellows carrying them, and it would mean a smoother ride for the guys riding in them. And that is important to me. I may whip up a design for a stretcher with wheels and patent it. The use I could make of it! I'd be a millionaire."[5]

His black humour aside, Gouldie's temper was something to be reckoned with. A notorious tantrum occurred in 1969 when he fought English wrestler Billy Robinson. Robinson was thought to be one of the best legitimate wrestlers in the world. He had been an amateur champion in his younger days and was a star in Europe. When Robinson wanted to break into the North American scene, Stampede Wrestling was his first port of call. Even though he was no looker – his crossed eyes gave him a goony appearance – Robinson was clean-cut, a natural babyface. He was thrown into a program with Gouldie where the two scraped week after week for The Stomper's North American title belt. The storyline called for Gouldie to be the ultimate victor, putting him in line for the end-of-season blow-up at the Calgary Stampede, where he was to take on NWA World Champion Dory Funk Jr., from Texas.

But Gouldie and Robinson did not click. Robinson, said to be arrogant behind the scenes, was known for using shooter tactics on opponents he didn't like, tying up challengers in painful submission holds. Some wrestlers accused Robinson of deliberately trying to injure them in the ring. Robinson wouldn't sell his opponents' moves either. They'd throw their pulled punches at him and, rather than play the part, acting as if the blows hurt him, Robinson remained unfazed. It made a wrestler look weak and ineffective.

Robinson played such games with Gouldie in July 1969 and, after several nights of this, The Stomper was enraged. He stormed into the dressing room, threw his boots against the wall, and left the territory for the remainder of the year. Stu put Robinson up against the world champion in Gouldie's place.*

Gouldie was hard-nosed, too, when it came to business matters, with a no-nonsense approach to his job. A good angle was to be played out to the letter. He was impatient with the Harts' perpetual lack of organization. "He was a perfectionist, and he'd get frustrated because he was always on time and we were always late," says Keith Hart. "He was super organized. Always had a neat bag. His socks were always pure white. Always had a clean towel in his bag. Nothing was ever dirty or smelly."

Outside the ring, Gouldie had matured into a quiet, soft-spoken gentleman, a clean-living fitness enthusiast.** Those who knew him well say he had a warm, good-humoured side. Few saw it, though, because Gouldie was a loner, selective about who he befriended.

But for fans, who saw only his ring persona, Gouldie was frightening. Bret Hart, who spent his life surrounded by vicious villains, was particularly terrorized by The Stomper as a boy, even having nightmares about him. Bret was traumatized when Gouldie told Whalen he was going to tear Hart House down brick by brick until he found Stu, who he promised to rend limb from bloody limb. Not even Helen would be safe, The Stomper seethed, and he threatened to drag her out onto the interstate and pile-drive her on the road.

Eleven-year-old Bret was trembling with fear the next day, running for cover under the kitchen table, when he saw Gouldie walking up the driveway toward the house, a scowl on his face. Helen answered the door. "Hello dawling," she said in her New York accent and gave The Stomper a hug. That day Bret got an early lesson in the truth behind the family business.

The Stomper was just the monster Stu needed to put the fear of God back into the fans. People had never seen such a vicious beast – at least not since the days Kowalski scourged the territory – and week after week people flocked to the Pavilion, eager to see if Stu's knights could slay the dragon. Most nights, the dragon reigned supreme.

Archie stomped in an era that was outstanding and dynamic, as full of berserk fun as any period in the history of Stu's territory. To many fans, the late

---

*To Robinson's credit, the matches he had with Funk were incredible. The chemistry between them was so great that Funk returned to Calgary in September 1969 to work another series of sellouts with Robinson.

**He still is. Today, Gouldie, a retired prison guard in his late sixties, delights in biking up to a hundred miles a week near his Knoxville, Tennessee, home, hauling his grandchildren in a baby carriage behind him.

1960s and early '70s represents the promotion's golden age.

Certainly, *Stampede Wrestling* was a hit. TV ratings for 1970–71 reveal that in the Calgary-Lethbridge region a typical *Stampede Wrestling* broadcast drew 114,900 viewers. The show's popularity came close to that of *Hockey Night in Canada*, which drew on average 120,000 viewers.

With a hit TV show and packed houses all along the loop, the company coffers were flowing and healthy once again. The brand new Cadillacs were back. So too was the antique furniture, the tailored suits, and the snake-skin boots, even though Stu was just as comfortable in rags. The wrestlers used to joke that half the time Stu dressed like a hillbilly. Nevertheless, he loved to own the finest things. He even bought a twelve-passenger limousine, which he frequently packed with kids, dogs, and cats.

Not all the credit for the territory's miraculous turnaround is due Gouldie. It was a group effort by a colourful, motley cast that helped bring about the change. Ed Whalen, for one, was never better than in this era. This is where his catchphrases and slick patter began to take shape. This is where Whalen began asserting himself – sometimes to the chagrin of the wrestlers – as part of the show, which he often stole. A 1970 *Calgary Herald* article tells of Whalen climbing into the ring, taking off his glasses and, to the amusement of the crowd, handing them to the referee, who seemed to be the only one in the arena who didn't catch the heel's dirty tactics in the previous match.[6]

When Gouldie arrived, there was already an incredible roster on hand, including Tiger Joe Tomasso, Dave Ruhl, and Sweet Daddy Siki. The Stomper tore into this talent pool mercilessly, soon thumping Ruhl for the Canadian Heavyweight title.

Trying to create a more global image, a new title belt, the North American Heavyweight title was invented in 1968, introduced to western Canadian fans as a much-sought-after championship with a long, glorious history. In the days before the Internet and today's mass media culture, who knew any better? Gouldie's protege, Pat O'Connor, was the man who came to town wearing the belt, to drop it in an epic battle with The Stomper.

Now that the territory was red hot, news travelled fast across the grappling landscape. Soon, Stampede Wrestling was set upon by a mass of phenomenal talents, including the British stars Les Thornton and Geoff Portz, Canuck bruisers Gil Hayes and Big John Quinn, and Puerto Rican superstar Carlos Colon (then called Carlos Belafonte). There was also a young man from Nova Scotia named "Soulman" Rocky Johnson, a superb athlete whose marriage to a wrestling promoter's daughter in Hawaii would spawn Duane Johnson, better known today as wrestling and acting superstar The Rock.

By now Stu's Dungeon was widely celebrated, and wannabe wrestlers queued up to study under the master and work in his territory. Stampede Wrestling became something of an elite school, a stepping stone to wrestling stardom. Leo Burke from New Brunswick wrestling family the Cormiers came to Calgary to learn from Stu and break into the business, despite that he was already solidly trained by his established older brothers The Beast (Yvon Cormier) and Rudy Kay. Both of them had worked for Stu, and when their seventeen-year-old sibling said he wanted to follow in their footsteps, they sent him to the mean old man in Calgary for his final test.

It was the same with little Rick Martel from Quebec City. Rick's brother was the beret-wearing Michel "Mad Dog" Martel, and he too sent his teenage sibling to Stu in 1973. At the time, Rick was a gangly kid, a shy, pretty boy. Once he filled out, Martel went on to a massive career in which he won a world heavyweight title.

Stu also recruited a handful of football players for Stampede Wrestling in this golden era. Among them was Bob Lueck, who Stu pushed as a star attraction for a number of seasons. Lueck's career with Stampede ended around 1973 when his wife, leery of her husband being on the road all the time, issued an ultimatum. But Lueck says Stu always encouraged him to stay out of trouble. "He was a family man," says Lueck. "He lectured me all the time. 'Don't be out there with these fucking ring rats. Keep your nose clean.' I got that shit every day. It did me some good, but it didn't do all the good it should've done."

Another football player Stu recruited was Angelo Mosca, of the Hamilton Tiger-Cats. Mosca, a Canadian Football Hall of Famer, was thought to be one of the fiercest players in the CFL. The Italian-American, from Boston, Massachusetts, wrestled in the off-season, taking up wrestling full time when he retired from the CFL. Standing six-foot-five and weighing 265 pounds, "King Kong" Mosca, who had the ring style of a charging bull, went on to enjoy a successful career in territories all across Canada and the United States.

Today Mosca, sixty-eight, has mixed feelings about Stampede Wrestling. "Some guys liked to keep their thumb on ya," he says, referring to Dave Ruhl. Mosca feels Ruhl, who was the head booker at that time, never liked him and tried to keep him out of the main event matches. Despite his problems with Ruhl, Mosca says he enjoyed his time in Calgary. He made $500 a week, and the notoriety Stu's stars had in the territory came with fringe benefits. "I went through a divorce at that time and there was a lot of broads," he chuckles.

Mosca used to get a kick out of the Hart family, whom he found strange.

"They were the original Osbournes," he says, comparing the Harts to the crude MTV family of rocker Ozzy Osbourne. "[Helen] would say, 'Hello, Angelo. How are you today?' Then in the next breath it would be, 'Where is [Stu], that sonofabitch?'"

He remembers seeing the Hart boys hanging around the dressing room after the matches. "If Stu gave us lousy pay, I'd kick 'em in the ass! They'd go, 'What's that for?' I'd say 'Ahh, I'm gettin' even with your dad.'"

The former football star recalls having to struggle with Stu to get paid. Mosca worked the main event one night at the Pavilion and didn't feel he got his rightful share of the gate. The following week, he was again at the top of the card, and he held up the show, refusing to go to the ring until Stu ponied up. "I want my money for tonight and last week's fuckin' money," growled the Italian "King Kong." Desperate, Stu tried to write Mosca a cheque. "I don't want no fuckin' cheque. I want cash." Stu went to the box office to get the wrestler's money. "I took all that cash, put it in my trunks, and went to the ring," Mosca says.

The biggest fish Stu ever reeled in, in the words of Bret Hart, was Wayne Coleman, a bodybuilder from Paradise Valley, Arizona, who was being scouted by the Calgary Stampeders. Stu was always impressed by large, strong men, and he was bowled over when Coleman, sporting arms twenty-three inches around, approached him in 1969 about becoming a wrestler.

After lifting weights down in the Dungeon, where Stu was further astounded when he bench-pressed 600 pounds, the monstrous Coleman was given his first lesson in wrestling – and humility. "Let me see your head," Stu said to the unsuspecting bodybuilder. Before he knew it, the Hart papa had Coleman – who believed himself invincible – struggling for air in a front facelock, feeling as though his neck was about to snap.[7]

For Coleman's first match, Stu devised an angle in which the bodybuilder ran to the ring in a battle between Mosca and Lueck, interfering on behalf of Mosca. When Stu gave Coleman his instructions, however, Coleman refused to play along. He had nothing against Lueck. Why would he attack him? "I didn't know what was a work and what wasn't," Coleman told an interviewer.[8] Enraged, Stu grabbed his pupil by the throat and said, "You do what I tell you because I'm your boss."

For a time, Coleman and Mosca worked as tag team partners, but behind the scenes the Italian never liked the bodybuilder. "I had no respect for him. He was full of shit.... He didn't know a hammerlock from a padlock. He was a circus freak ... a big juice monkey. Coleman was one of the first guys I ever saw take Dianabol [steroids]."

After working in the Stampede territory for a short time, Coleman went to San Francisco and made the transformation to Superstar Billy Graham, the nickname taken from the rock opera *Jesus Christ Superstar* and the famous evangelist, Billy Graham. The Superstar's look and attitude – the enormous physique; colourful wardrobe; golden tan; long, bleach-blond hair; and fevered, jive-talking lingo – would be enormously influential in the wrestling business. Working for Vince McMahon Sr. in New York, Graham became a huge star in the wwwf, winning the world heavyweight title in 1977. Graham's influence was obvious in the way his look and style was so famously adopted by both Hulk Hogan and future governor of Minnesota Jesse "The Body" Ventura.

For all his positive influence in the wrestling business, Graham was also one of the first megastars to bring steroids into the game in a major way. The book *Sex, Lies, and Headlocks* by Shaun Assael and Mike Mooneyham, an exposé of the underbelly of the wrestling business, says Graham was one of the "most devoted spreaders of the steroid gospel." Graham claims he was the one who turned a young Hulk Hogan onto steroids.[9]

By the late 1980s, however, when his joints were destroyed and he was living in constant pain, Graham radically changed his tune on steroid use. His career ended, and he appeared on national talk shows speaking about rampant abuse of the drug within the wwf. (At the time, the wwf was embroiled in a steroid scandal which led to the U.S. federal government prosecuting Vince McMahon Jr. for distributing the illegal drugs to his wrestlers. McMahon was found not guilty.)[10]

In any case, even after he became the great Superstar Billy Graham, Wayne Coleman never forgot the man who gave him his start in the wrestling business. During Graham's New York peak in the 1970s, a heavy package was shipped to Hart House. It was a TV set, Graham's way of saying thanks. Stu was amused to find a Holiday Inn tag on the back of it.[11]

November 2, 2004. It's the night of the U.S. presidential election and the final counts are rolling in. It's also the night I finally track down Larry Shreeve after weeks of phone calls to his Atlanta, Georgia, restaurant.

"I'm sorry to disturb you on election night," I say to Shreeve, catching him on his cellphone as he leaves Abdullah the Butcher's House of Ribs and Chinese Food. "Were you out voting today?"

It turns out the man known as Abdullah the Butcher couldn't give the slightest damn about either George W. Bush or John Kerry. "Nah. Fuck dat shit," he says. "I gotta take care of my business."

By business he doesn't mean only his restaurant, where, according to the Atlanta Happenings website, he likes to wander around the dining area "smiling and answering questions in a sweet voice," thanking his patrons for choosing Abdullah's.[12] He also means the wrestling business, in which, at the age of sixty-nine, the 360-pound Butcher is still active. Within twenty-four hours of this interview, he'll be on his way to Puerto Rico. In the months to come, he's scheduled to wrestle in Montreal and do a tour of Japan.

He insists he's in great shape, but that's not the description that springs to mind when one sees the most recent pictures of him posted on various wrestling websites. Even in his 1970s prime, Abdullah was a karate-kicking, eye-gouging butterball. Now, as has been his look from the start, he wears loose-fitting karate pants to the ring, pulled up high to cover his massively bloated belly. The folds of his fat, in particular his hideously sagging breasts, fall over his waistband.

That said, he still cuts an imposing, fearsome figure. He looks like somebody who knows how to inflict hurt. Much of that is due to his forehead, which is mangled beyond belief. Abdullah's chopping block of a brow, which in the words of Keith Hart is so thick with scar tissue, "he needs a scimitar to cut through and find a vein," screams mean. That's what forty-three years of cutting will do. Abdullah has spent his life carving up his bald head. The bloodbath is his specialty. He was not the first wrestler to cut himself, to "get juice" for the fans. But he was one of the first to elevate the act to an art form of sorts. The typical Butcher bout consists of rivers of blood, flowing from both his and his opponent's heads – blood raised from forks, bottles, blunt objects, bites. An Abdullah match is designed to be a gory monster movie come to life.

Abdullah pioneered the bloody hardcore matches that are a staple of today's wrestling world. In the 1990s, the ECW (Extreme Championship Wrestling) promotion thrived, with an emphasis on extreme violence. For a time, the WWF established a Hardcore Championship title for such bouts, though few of those matched the raw intensity of Abdullah's ugliest confrontations.

"Sir, I started it all," The Butcher says, annoyed at being mentioned in the same breath as any of his imitators. "People thought they could do what I do, but they couldn't do it. They didn't know how. I am a professional. I know how to take care of business and draw people.... Sometimes it got carried away. I did hurt a lot of people everywhere I went. But I had to make the people believe in it. That's why they kept coming back."

Stu knew it well. Along with Gouldie, Abdullah was his top draw in the early 1970s. If The Stomper was King Kong, Abdullah was Godzilla.

Larry Shreeve, born and raised in Windsor, Ontario, began studying karate at age twelve. By the time he was in his twenties, he was a seventh-degree black belt, teaching martial arts to the local police. On the side he did maintenance at a gym, which is where he met wrestler Gino Brito. Brito convinced Shreeve he could make a lot of money in the mat game. By the late 1960s, Shreeve had developed the gimmick that would make Brito's prediction come true. Abdullah the Butcher was billed as the "Madman from the Sudan," a North African savage whose insatiable blood lust brought him to the world of wrestling, where he got his jollies feeding on young babyfaces.

When Stu brought Abdullah to Calgary in 1969, he knew right away he had found a cash cow. "I never had an empty house while he was with me," Stu told an interviewer. "On the coldest day of the year I had them lined up on 17th Avenue [outside the Stampede grounds] trying to get into the [Corral]."[3]

Behind the scenes, Stu and Helen welcomed Abdullah like he was family, even baking him a cake on his birthday. But when the TV cameras were on, it was a different matter. Stu, well into his fifties, was still wrestling every so often, and he had a feud with The Butcher. One Friday night, Abdullah threw pepper in Stu's eyes and tore into the promoter with such ferocity that it scared the younger Hart children, who watched their dad being slaughtered on TV. A few days later, The Butcher phoned Hart House to talk to Stu. Alison, about twelve at the time, answered. "'I'm not going to let you talk to my dad! Are you crazy? How dare you?'" she said, horrified. "I kept hanging up on him. Finally, he got his girlfriend to call and [not knowing her] I put her through. Then she put Abdullah on to my dad. He must've been calling for an hour." Later that day, Stu gently reprimanded his daughter: "The next time Abdullah calls, you might want to put him through. Don't worry about me. I can deal with him."

Being kept in the dark about the wrestling business must have played havoc on the minds of the Hart kids. One day, Stu was sharing a slice of cake with Abdullah the Butcher. The next day, the beast was butchering daddy before the eyes of the city. What were they supposed to think? Stu believed in the business so fervently that only insiders were let in on the secrets, and until they got into the business themselves, the kids were not confidants. It lent a sense of surrealism to the children's lives that had to have been troubling at times.

Even Ed Whalen got caught up in the insanity once in a while, forgetting it was all an act. That was easy to do when the heel was as overwhelming as

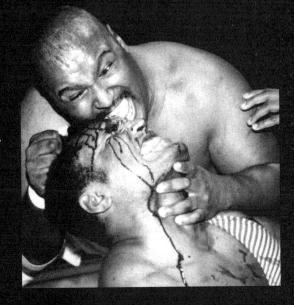

Top: Abdullah the Butcher launches his 300-pound frame across the ring, bringing a flying elbow drop down on another foe, early 1970s.

Bottom: The gruesome Abdullah the Butcher takes a bite out of the bloody forehead of Carlos Belafonte. Belafonte came to fame in his native Puerto Rico – and around the world – as Carlos Colon.

Abdullah. Once, Whalen was interviewing Billy Robinson in the ring when Abdullah came barging in and attacked the English wrestler. The madman snatched Whalen's microphone from his hand and began strangling Robinson with the cord, all according to the plans cooked up in the dressing room. But Whalen, who was not in on the twist, was a big fan of Robinson's. Furthermore, the mike belonged to Whalen, and he became incensed when the wrestlers grabbed it from him. Announcers in other territories typically cowered before the monster heels in their territory, selling the fearsomeness of the beasts. Not Whalen.

After a struggle, Whalen regained his mike and smashed Abdullah on the head with it, cutting open The Butcher's scalp. In retaliation, the brute clubbed Whalen, which the announcer later told people gave him an eighteen-month headache. A genuine battle was about to break out between the two men when Stu ran into the ring and got between them. Seeing red, Whalen tried to get around Stu to throw a punch at The Butcher. Stu's whispered warning brought the announcer to his senses. "If I let you go, you're dead."[14] Whalen had become a mark, just like the fans. It wouldn't be the last time.

Realizing he had lost his cool, Whalen felt badly, but he knew there was no apologizing to an angry Abdullah, whose head required seven stitches. A few weeks later, around Christmas time, Whalen was in the Calgary airport awaiting a flight when he saw The Butcher walking toward him, having just arrived from Japan. Whalen was petrified. He looked around in a panic but couldn't see a cop. He was already picturing the ambulance ride ahead of him. "Only my laundry man knows how scared I was, y'know what I mean?" Whalen would later say. But instead of attacking the announcer, Abdullah handed him a package. "Here," he grunted. "Open."

"I'll never forget it," Whalen said. "Three hundred pounds … and not much brains, bless his heart, and he looked at me and said, 'Whalen, when you get that look in your eye, you make me nervous.'" Then he walked away. In the package was a beautiful silk kimono. Abdullah respected Whalen for standing up to him, and he forgave the announcer for the mike to the head. What were a few more stitches, after all? The fight excited the fans, and when the fans were excited, money was made.

Naturally, Stu pitted his two greatest monsters against one another the first chance he got. Archie the Stomper versus Abdullah the Butcher was a dream match, a work of sublime violence, made all the more intense by the genuine dislike the two men had for one another. "They were jealous of each other," said Stu. "Abdullah, he'd make out that he couldn't remember Archie's name.... Archie would calmly refer to Abdullah as 'the black bastard.' Every time they came together, we had to turn people away."[5]

Abdullah admits there was animosity between him and Gouldie, but with so many years between them, he has respect for The Stomper. "The way we used to fight, it was real," says Abdullah. "He'd stomp on me and I'd stomp on him and we hit harder and harder. We didn't give a damn. But he's a gentleman and I like Archie. We made a lot of money together."

Bret Hart remembers the matches vividly. "Those were probably the biggest matches Stampede ever had," he says. "That was the fight of the century between those two." Keith Hart agrees. He says having fearsome heels such as Abdullah and Gouldie was the key to Stampede Wrestling's success. "If you don't have that feature attraction, it's like having a monster movie without the monster.... There were times when my dad couldn't get the top heels and you'd watch the business go under. We'd lose so much money. My mom would plead with my dad, 'Stu, let's get out of this business.' He'd say, 'If we can just get the right talent, we'll make money again.' It was a matter of getting guys like The Stomper and Abdullah to come back."

"You're costing me a lot of damn money on this telephone," says Abdullah about ten minutes into our chat. The man is exactly what he says he is, all business, and talking to a writer in Calgary, where he has neither a match nor a restaurant to promote, is of little interest to him. He answers a few questions, sometimes coolly and evasively, sometimes curtly and to the point. Then he cuts the interview short with a message to his fans: "Every so often, get on your hands and knees and pray."

But it's the men who have looked the "Madman from the Sudan" in the eye who provide a real feel of the Abdullah the Butcher experience. Like "Cowboy" Dan Kroffat, who credits Abdullah with spring-boarding his career from rookie status, perpetually doing jobs at the bottom of the cards, to a Stampede Wrestling main-eventer.

"One night Stu sent me in to do a job for Abdullah," Kroffat says. "[Before the match,] Abdullah took me aside and said, 'Kid, tonight we're gonna tear the house down.'" At first, the match went as did so many of Abdullah's matches, with The Butcher destroying his foe. Then, just before he went to drop his devastating flying elbow on Kroffat, he whispered, "Move." As Abdullah launched his elbow, Kroffat rolled out of the way in the nick of time. Abdullah crashed down so hard on the canvas, the building seemed to vibrate. The crowd went wild. Abdullah whispered again, "C'mon, kid. Make your comeback." Kroffat got to his feet, the brutal beating he suffered a mere moment before completely forgotten, and he laid into Abdullah with a bevy of drop kicks and chops to the chest.

Finally, Abdullah jumped up and fled the ring. "The crowd was ballistic," Kroffat says. "Ed Whalen almost had a hernia announcing it. Stu didn't even know that was coming. Abdullah just decided that was the night he was going to put me over. Stu looked at me and said, 'That bastard made you. You're made from here on in.'"

Abdullah gave a similar boost to former football player Bob Lueck. "I want to work with that kid," The Butcher told Stu. "He's a nice little white boy and we can get a lot of heat."

The first time Lueck was ever called on to blade in the ring, he was to be cut by Abdullah. "It was a tiny cut, but he hit a vein right on my forehead," Lueck says. "I had blood running down my pecs, my thighs. I said, 'Son of a bitch! I'm bleeding to death.' He whispered, 'Keep going, kid. We've got the heat!'"

Not even the Hart boys were safe from The Butcher. Keith Hart remembers being an eighteen-year-old kid selling programs for his father at the Pavilion. "I happened to stroll by Abdullah when he was getting into the ring," Keith says. "He grabbed me by the hair, put his arm around my throat, cut me, and started chewing on my forehead. He said to me [whispering], 'Sell it, kid. Sell it.' It wasn't planned at all. I've still got the scar...."

"He was the scariest thing."

Chapter nine

Overkill

"Cowboy" Dan Kroffat stood at the top of the teetering eight-foot stepladder in the centre of the Victoria Pavilion wrestling ring. Six feet tall, Kroffat strained to reach the Cellophane bag full of money, $1,000 hanging from the lights by a string.

The cool grand was just within his grasp when the ladder began to rock dangerously. The Japanese warlord Tor Kamata, a man built like a sumo wrestler, was tipping it over. Kroffat braced himself for a rude crash to the canvas that might break his neck. Some in the capacity crowd of two thousand held their breath, fearing the worst for their hero; others screamed as if they were going down with him.

It was September 1972 and those present were witness to the world's first ladder match. One of the most enduring and popular gimmicks in the wrestling business, the match typically involves a title belt or a bag of money suspended from the ceiling, which combatants compete for. The first one to snatch the prize wins. The objective is to beat one's opponent until he's lying in a broken heap, unable to create problems for the man climbing the ladder. As such battles ensue, wrestlers take nasty lumps, flying several feet in the air, crashing inside and outside the ring, sometimes onto the cement surrounding the ring, other times through ringside tables. Often the ladder itself becomes a weapon, the wrestlers using it as a battering ram on one another or snapping it shut on each others' limbs or heads.

Bret Hart, having begun wrestling for his father in 1978, had great

Tor Kamata comes over the ropes with a big karate chop on a bloodied Abdullah the Butcher, early 1970s.

success with ladder matches. Some of most riveting battles of his early career were fought atop ladders with Dynamite Kid and Bad News Allen. He liked the match so much that he introduced the idea to the WWF in the 1990s, where it became a huge attraction for wrestling fans the world over.

The original Stampede ladder match, invented by Dan Kroffat, was more than just a shock tactic. It was the pinnacle of a feud between Kroffat and Kamata that had been artfully orchestrated, built up week after week until it culminated in this epic confrontation like nothing the fans had ever seen before, held high above the ring.

"Tor kept running out of the ring on me," Kroffat says, sitting in the office of the successful Calgary car dealership he owns. "We were against each other in a bunch of matches.... He'd beat the shit out of me. Then, when I'd make my big comeback, he'd run away.... To get him to stay, I had to create a match where the fans believed he would want to stay. So I hung that bag of money over the ring, and it was his greed that made him stay. In order to get the money, he'd have to beat me down, climb that ladder, and pluck the bag."

Despite his fall from the ladder, Kroffat, then twenty-seven, the all-Canadian babyface, kept fighting. Kamata threw salt in Kroffat's eyes and cold-cocked him. His opponent down, Kamata struggled, huffing and puffing, to pull his 300-pound frame up the ladder. Then Kroffat rose and drop kicked the ladder. Kamata tumbled down like the fairytale giant from the beanstalk. Eventually, the two warriors met on top of the ladder, where they brawled furiously. In the end, good overcame evil. The Japanese warlord lay on the canvas defeated, while Kroffat jumped for joy, throwing $20 and $100 bills into the ecstatic crowd. The match was such a hit that Kamata and Kroffat took it around the circuit. Instead of money, they eventually hung the North American title from the ceiling, with the winner walking away the champion.

Kroffat had emerged as Stampede Wrestling's pre-eminent babyface in the early 1970s. He was beach-blond and hairy chested, with the natural, he-man build of an old-time movie hero. He wasn't packing sculpted bodybuild-er muscle but, rather, a solid, working-man's frame. He was a handsome fellow, too, and the warm smile he had for the kids in the audience won everybody's heart. Kroffat's personality – bright, charismatic, upbeat – sealed the deal. The fans in Stampede country loved the guy.

But Stu had more than just a superb babyface with Kroffat. He also had an excellent ideas man, and he gave the young wrestler booking duties. "I did well early in my career because I went to Stu and proposed to him that the business was about building ideas, like ladder matches," Kroffat says. "The big attraction for me was creating and selling personalities, building concepts, telling stories with the wrestling."

One of Kroffat's most inspired, elaborate angles involved Archie Gouldie, in 1973. Having returned to the territory after a several-month hiatus, The Stomper was mowing men down week after week, leading up to his inevitable collision with Kroffat. The week the two were to tussle, Kroffat was doing a pre-match interview in the ring with Ed Whalen when he was blindsided by Gouldie.

"I was wearing a nice suit and he tore it off, leaving me almost naked in the ring," Kroffat says, his eyes lighting up at the memory. "Then he gave me three of those big stomps to the head and my legs were twitching the whole time. On the final stomp, the twitching stopped. I wanted the crowd to think he'd almost killed me."

Kroffat was carried away on a stretcher. In the weeks that followed, Whalen told the crowd, with deep regret in his voice, that the cowboy's career was ended by the attack, that he was now slowly recovering in a Vancouver hospital. This made The Stomper look more ghoulish than ever as he boasted, "I'm bringing careers to an end!"

About a month later, Stu announced to the audience that the masked wrestler The Destroyer, who had a strong run in the territory in the 1960s, was returning to Stampede Wrestling to take out Gouldie. On the night of his debut, The Destroyer came to the ring for an interview with Whalen. "So you're in town to take on Archie Gouldie?" Whalen asked. "What are your chances?" The masked man said nothing. A bizarre two-minute silence ensued, the wrestler glaring at the camera menacingly. Finally, Whalen made a crack about that being a record for the least dialogue exchanged in any interview.

Later that evening, Gouldie and The Destroyer squared off, the masked man launching into The Stomper with a fury the villain was unprepared for. Stepping on Archie's throat, The Destroyer again glared into the camera and peeled off his mask, revealing himself to be none other than Dan Kroffat. The crowd roared with glee. So did Whalen, who was as shocked by the turn of events as anyone. The Stomper reacted as if an electric jolt had been sent through his body. No matter how mighty a bad guy might be, an unwritten rule for heels decrees that they are all cowards ultimately, masters of the cheap shot, all too willing to beg for mercy in a pinch. As such, Archie jumped to his feet and fled in terror. The stage was set for a series of sold-out matches between the two men in the Corral.

"I saw the business as entertainment," says Kroffat. "We were acting.... I

Top: Dan Kroffat developed into an exciting and explosive talent early in his career. One of his best weapons was a sky-high dropkick, like this one launched against Gil Hayes, early 1970s.

Bottom: "Cowboy" Dan Kroffat and Tor Kamata do battle in the world's first ladder match, Calgary, September 1972.

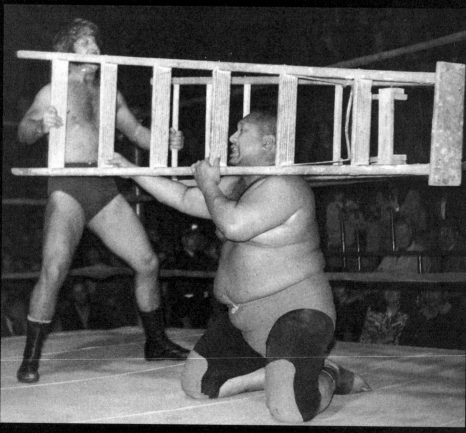

picked villains I could tell a story with, guys who would cooperate. I'd say, 'If you go along with me, we'll build up [a feud] for four or five weeks. It will be massive. You'll be a bigger heel than ever.'"

Kroffat certainly upped Kamata's value in Stampede Wrestling. Tor Kamata, born Ronald Kamaka in Hawaii, had been brought to the territory in 1971 by Stu, who was looking for another monster heel to put into the rotation. Gouldie and Abdullah were in demand worldwide and would stay in the territory for only a few months at a time.

Kamata had been working the pro circuit since the mid-1960s and had established himself as a hated villain in the southern states by billing himself as Japanese, capitalizing on the hatred that lingered in America from Pearl Harbor. In some arenas, the promoters had to sneak him in and out of the building for the matches. "I would've been killed," Kamata says. "In one city, somebody told the promoter, 'You bring that dirty, no-good Jap here, we're going to destroy the arena.'"

Kamata had a solid fighting background, having studied martial arts as a boy. He trained as an amateur wrestler in 1959 while in the air force. Later, he worked as a bouncer in a Honolulu restaurant frequented by professional wrestlers. They persuaded him to try his hand at the business. Kamaka was dubbed Tor Kamata, after Tomás de Torquemada, the grand inquisitor of the Spanish Inquisition.

Kamata hit Calgary in a suitably grisly fashion, thrown into a wild feud with Abdullah the Butcher. The pictures of the two behemoths at war, blood streaming down their anguished faces, speaks to the intensity of their clashes. For a time, Kamata was pushed as a top heel, but after a botched angle, he fell out of favour with Stu.

In the summer of 1972, world champion Dory Funk Jr. was headed to the territory for the Calgary Stampede, where Stu wanted him to face Kamata. In the week leading up to the match, Kamata was to fight Les Thornton and win, thus making him the number one contender for Funk's title. Instead, Kamata and Thornton wound up brawling outside the ring, where the referee had no choice but to count them out. Stu saw this as a disaster. There should have been a decisive winner in place to meet the champ. "Tor hadn't followed orders, and he let himself be manipulated by Thornton," says Ross Hart. "Stu was pissed."

Tor had lost his position and was gradually moving down the card. He would have been on his way out of the promotion if Kroffat hadn't chosen him for the ladder match. It resurrected Kamata's career in Stampede Wrestling.

Although he cut an ugly figure, Kamata was never as fierce as Abdullah or The Stomper. "He wasn't frightening enough," says Keith Hart. "He was more like a big Buddha. People sort of liked him." Because he had this light side, Kamata clicked with Ed Whalen, and his most entertaining Stampede feud was with the beloved announcer.

A devilish grin spreads across Kamata's face when he remembers the good old days with Whalen. "I gave him a bad time every week," Kamata says, now sixty-eight. "I'd run down the way he dressed.... It got to the point where people just wanted to listen to Ed and me." The rapport between the two men was comedic. Tor fancied himself a classy champion in his beautiful suits, alligator shoes, and diamond rings, and he flattered Whalen with promises of Geisha girls and fine silk suits from the Orient. Whalen inevitably scoffed at Kamata and chastised him for his cheating ways. Kamata denied all with a taunting, fiendish smile: "No-o-o-o-o chancee, Mr. Whalen!" The phrase also came in handy when Kamata trash-talked his opponents. "Everybody had no-o-o-o-o chancee when they'd wrestle me!" he says. This became such a popular phrase that in the early 1970s the Harts were selling T-shirts and pins with it printed on them.

Like Abdullah, Tor had success in the restaurant business, opening up the popular Calgary eatery Tor's Teriyaki. "I had a booth open at the Stampede matches, too," Kamata says. "My teriyaki sauce was so great, we were selling it by the gallon." Alas, it all ended in 1975 when Kamata and his wife split up. Kamata took his show on the road, finally retiring from the wrestling business in 1987 to open a restaurant and a shiatsu business in Saskatoon. He returned to Calgary in 2002.

It has been thirty years since Tor Kamata was a household name in Calgary, but it seems every other week he is approached on the street or in the supermarket by somebody pointing and grinning ear to ear. Kamata always knows what he's about to hear. "No-o-o-o-o chancee!"

Life in the asylum that was Hart House was never boring. Some years, however, were more tumultuous than others. The 1970s was a particularly wild time. The Hart kids were coming of age and making their first forays into the family business. Stu's brats, as some of the wrestlers viewed them, were going to make their presence felt in the territory for better or for worse, no matter who liked it. Including their old man.

It was also a time of major shifts in the Stampede Wrestling universe. On one level, things were just as nutty as they had always been. Alison Hart remembers walking into the kitchen and having Japanese wrestlers bow down to her. Then, she would step into her backyard – where Stu had added an outdoor wrestling ring for summer training – and watch sweaty behemoths screaming, torturing one another. She recalls her father being called to the old Regis Hotel one afternoon because a midget wrestler was drunk and doing handstands on the roof.

It was at the 1972 Calgary Stampede that her father fought a 600-pound tiger. Before putting the tiger on his TV show, Stu wanted to get to know it, to see if man and beast could click. Was the beast game for a wrestling match? "At first, the tiger had a real bad attitude," Alison says. "It lifted its leg and pissed all over the wall." But once Stu began playing with the big jungle cat, a bond was established. The Hart patriarch and the tiger wrestled to a draw on the July 1972 wrestling program, although even Stu would have been helpless had the big cat decided to get mean. Were the Hart kids ever frightened that their father might be mauled? "No," says Alison flatly. "We all sort of thought of him as Superman. We knew he'd be all right."

But as the business progressed, attracting a new generation of fans, Stu began to lose some of his oldest, most trusted colleagues. His best friend Luther Lindsay died of a heart attack in 1971. Stu's buddy, Jesse Ortega, The Mighty Ursus, who had wrestled for him since the early 1950s, also checked out in the '70s, dying of cancer in the later part of that decade.

Another tragedy of the era befell a new man, thirty-one-year-old Japanese grappler Yukihiro Sakeda, who wrestled as Tokyo Joe. On March 18, 1974, Joe and the boys were driving from a match in High River, Alberta, when they hit a patch of ice and spun into a ditch. A tow truck came to the rescue and Joe was aiding the driver when another vehicle spun out of control. Joe's legs were pinned between two vehicles. A tourniquet was tied to the wrestler's mangled leg Joe was rushed to the hospital. But nothing could be done. His right leg was amputated four inches above the knee. Joe stayed in Calgary where he remains to this day, training young wrestlers and recruiting them for the All Japan wrestling promotion in Tokyo.

Without a doubt, the most significant loss of the era came as the result of a road fight. The man downed was "Hanna pig farmer" Dave Ruhl, Stu's right-hand man almost from the start. The real story behind Ruhl's end has been blurred by the passage of time and endless trips around the rumour mill. It's certain that some sort of dispute between Ruhl and Carlos Colon turned violent on a road trip sometime around October 1972, as the wrestlers made the trek from Medicine Hat to Saskatoon. Ruhl, fifty-two, was behind the wheel of his Cadillac. Dan Kroffat was in the passenger's seat and Colon, twenty-seven, then wrestling under the name Carlos Belafonte, was in the backseat with his tag team partner Gino Caruso. Colon, a suave Puerto Rican who would go on to be a superstar wrestler and promoter in his homeland, was feeling ill.

As Kroffat remembers it, it was a cold, frosty night and Ruhl was puffing on a cigar. Colon was nauseated by the oppressive smoke that filled the car. He rolled down the window to get fresh air.

"Close the window, it's cold out," Ruhl growled.

"Then put the cigar out," Colon snapped. "I've got a headache."

"It's my car, and I'll do whatever the hell I want."

The exchange got increasingly ugly, insults and challenges being spat back and forth. Finally, Ruhl pulled the car over to the side of the road to settle the score. The two squared off, dancing around one another like boxers, each man waiting for an opening.

Ruhl always insisted he was never hit. Kroffat says Colon caught the older man with a hard slap to the side of his head. Whatever happened, Ruhl lost his footing on a patch of ice and fell backwards, cracking his head hard on the cement. "It clunked like a coconut," Kroffat says. "It knocked him right out." At that moment, another car full of wrestlers pulled up. Carlos and his partner got in with them and carried on toward Saskatoon. Kroffat dragged Ruhl's limp body over to his Caddie and laid the booker on the backseat, then also continued on to Saskatoon.

"I could hear him groaning in the back, and I wanted to take him to the hospital," Kroffat says. "By the time we got to Saskatoon, at the Executive Hotel, he was coherent but groggy." Kroffat asked Ruhl if he needed to go to the hospital. The older man was adamant that he did not, that he only needed a good night's sleep.

Keith Hart got a good look at Ruhl the next day. At the time, Keith was taking pre-law courses at the University of Saskatchewan and, to earn a bit of money, worked as a referee once a week when Stampede Wrestling came to the Saskatoon Arena. Keith had been to the arena earlier in the day and was surprised Ruhl was not there. Puzzled, Keith went to the hotel and found Ruhl unconscious in his room, lying in bed with blood on his pillow. At the hospital, he was diagnosed with a serious concussion.

Word among the wrestlers was that the fight between Ruhl and Colon had little to do with a rolled-down window. Instead, it was about a woman. As the story goes, after Sweet Daddy Siki left the territory, Ruhl moved in on the big-haired, long-legged professor's daughter his ring nemesis had been dating. After that, Ruhl's double life of wrestler and farmer became more divided than ever. On one hand was the salt-of-the-earth family man; on the other hand, the high-roller wrestling star squiring the young sexpot. "She rolled around with him to all the towns," says Keith. Perhaps Ruhl was going through a mid-life crisis. The girl, the flashy car, conflicts with the younger stars; he even took to dying his hair jet black. "It looked like he was using shoe polish," says Helen Hart's brother-in-law Jock Osler. "When he'd sweat, the die ran."

Allegedly, Ruhl's ego took a hit when his girlfriend got friendly with Colon on one of the road trips. Ruhl was infuriated that this young stud had moved in on his territory. By the time the two men stepped into the car together, on the night of the fight, there was already plenty of tension between them.

The consensus is that the head injury Dave Ruhl sustained ended his career. He attempted a comeback, but he was never the same man. His equilibrium was off. He could no longer maintain his balance when performing the standard wrestling stunts. The boisterous ring persona he adopted, the confidence he once exuded, that too was gone. He seemed subdued. Beaten.

Many of the wrestlers felt that Ruhl got what he deserved, that his power in the territory corrupted him and he needed to be knocked off his pedestal. But there was another camp that was sad to see him go. "I loved Dave," says wrestler Leo Burke, of New Brunswick's famed Cormier family. "When I came here, it was the first time I had been anywhere, and Dave was like a father to me. He really took me under his wing." Keith adds: "Most wrestlers by their very nature are in the business because they're individuals. They don't like the office. It doesn't matter how good the boss is, everybody turns on the man in charge."

Dave Ruhl's son, Glenn, defends his father's honour. He maintains his parents were happily married for forty-eight years. He denounces the story about Colon and his father fighting over a wrestling siren as "crap." He also disputes the notion that Dave's career was ended by his head injury. He says his father wrestled his last match in Japan that same year but was unable to finish his contract because of a kidney stone. Nevertheless, between the concussion and the other physical problems he faced, Ruhl had no choice but to hang up his wrestling boots. Ruhl held the Canadian Heavyweight title when he had his accident, and Stu decided to retire the belt along with the man. It was the symbol of an era gone by.

Ruhl did not find it easy adjusting to life outside the business. "It was ironic because when the accident happened ... he wasn't planning on wrestling that much longer," Glenn says. "But like most performers, he wanted to quit on his own terms. When he was forced to quit, that was problematic.... It gave him a lot of depression and witnessing that was really tough on my mother and me."

The same injuries that kept Dave out of the ring made farm work difficult. With neither farming nor wrestling putting food on the table, life became a struggle. "There's no pension plan in wrestling," says Glenn. "There's nothing to fall back on.... It was one thing for my dad to sell the farm on his own terms, but another thing to do it so [he and my mom] could live. It allowed them to have some quality of life. It would've been bad if he just had the wrestling."

Dave Ruhl died in 1988 at the age of sixty-eight. His funeral was held in Medicine Hat on a beastly cold December day. Highway reports deemed the three-and-a-half-hour trek from Calgary to Medicine Hat unsafe. "It took a brave soul to travel that day," says Glenn. Regardless, Stu Hart showed up, by himself, to say goodbye to his old friend and fellow road warrior. Another tie to his glorious past had been severed.

When Dave Ruhl walked away, an opening was left on the roster that Stu needed to fill. His third oldest son, Keith, then in his early twenties, stepped up to take the spot. Keith enjoyed wrestling but was not obsessed with it as some of his brothers would be. He got into the game mostly to help out his father.

Bruce Hart also became involved, and although he says wrestling was not his ambition at first, he soon became determined to one day fill his dad's shoes as head of the Hart empire.

Then there was Smith. Because he was the oldest, it is natural to assume he was the first to be considered for the top spot as Stu's heir. But from almost all accounts, Smith had been irresponsible from day one. He never seemed to take anything seriously – certainly not university – and Stu and Helen worried about him. What was to become of the kid? Stu and Helen had always said they would never turn the business over to anybody who didn't have a post-secondary education. They began bending their rule for Smith, as they would eventually bend all their rules for him. Maybe the wrestling game would motivate Smith, give him something to focus on. But too many times he would mess up when given a chance to work in the business.

Japanese wrestler Mr. Hito, a Stampede Wrestling mainstay in the 1970s and '80s, remembers Smith being in charge of one show in a small town in British Columbia. The gig was sold-out, and Hito, who was promised a percentage of the gate, expected a good payday. When Stu handed him a $100 bill, Hito, expecting a lot more, reacted angrily. Smith had told Stu the show was poorly attended and Stu had paid the boys accordingly. Hito says the incident led to Stu giving his eldest son a good stretching, making him scream. Smith, however, denies that such a scene ever took place.

But from the family's point of view, it soon became apparent that Smith was not responsible when it came to business matters. "He was neutered early on," says Bret Hart, "turned into a toothless hound. He never had much say in anything."

Smith, on the other hand, says he was an important player in the promotion at various times throughout the 1970s and '80s. He says he was his father's "troubleshooter" and, when he worked as a booker, he was a "matchmaking genius. Anything I did worked out well."

However, Keith, along with Bruce, did make an impact on the promotion. While a fine athlete, practical Keith was the least flashy of the Hart brothers in the ring – certainly not the showman his brothers turned out to be. His style was rooted in traditional wrestling, full of technical moves and submission holds. By today's standards – the average match moving at a speed metal pace – Keith's matches would be considered dull. Still, he was a good-looking, likable babyface, a straight arrow with a strong work ethic, and a solid moral centre, and the crowds got behind him.

"I wasn't the most flamboyant," Keith admits, "but nobody could see through my matches and that was the most important thing to my dad. He told me of all the boys, my matches were the most realistic, and I thought that was a compliment of the highest order. He was my boss, I respected everything about him, and I wrestled for him more than for the crowd."

When Keith had a good angle to work, he worked it well, as in the battle royal of 1977. In a typical battle royal, fifteen or so wrestlers climb into the ring at once and do battle in an every-man-for-himself war, seeking to eliminate the other wrestlers by tossing them from the ring. The last man in the ring is declared the winner. The twist in this battle royal was that a rope hung from the ceiling. At the top of it was the key to a Pontiac Trans Am Firebird. The first man to climb the rope won the match and the car. To do so, one had to eliminate or disable the competition. The match made for some daring high spots – a wrestler might pull himself twelve feet above the ring while another grappler grabbed hold of the rope, whipping it around until his nemesis came crashing down.

In the 1977 match, Keith climbed the rope as planned and plucked the keys as the sold-out Pavilion crowd went wild. It was a dandy of an angle as far as Keith was concerned. The car really was his for the keeping. Being a Hart kid on the Stampede Wrestling show had its benefits.

While Keith was a handsome jock, Bruce was more of a pretty boy. It's hard to imagine today, when his face has taken on such a scowl-bitten, world-weary look, but in his twenties, Bruce could have been mistaken for a member of a pop boy band. With his blue eyes, earnest smile, and soft blond curls, which he grew conservatively long, Bruce looked like the kind of boy mothers would want their daughters to bring home. At five-foot-nine and less than 200 pounds, he was dwarfed by the men he met in the ring, and this gave him an underdog status that he milked expertly. When he took a beating, he elicited sympathy from the crowd, selling every blow as though he were a suffering Tiny Tim. When he struck back, it was like wee David toppling Goliath.

In those baffling moments of pro wrestling injustice, when the bad guys boldly cheat – and everybody in the arena and in TV land sees it, but somehow the referee does not – Bruce embodied the fans' frustration, jumping and shouting, pointing and punching the ropes, and scratching his head so hard it looked as though he would tear his hair out. Bruce was actually being true to himself, according to Keith, who says his brother was spoiled, accustomed to throwing such temper tantrums in the house when he didn't get his way.

By the mid-'70s, Bruce and Keith were wrestling and taking on booking duties. Keith says Stu gave him the lion's share of the booking responsibilities at first. This chafed Bruce, a creative force who was always bursting with ideas for the promotion. But as Stu saw it, Bruce was a practitioner of "cheap heat." Matches he orchestrated were frequently bloody affairs, with heels using objects such as chains or brass knuckles and giving low blows, or "nut shots" as the Harts called them, to anger the fans. Stu believed such antics should be used sparingly, for maximum impact. Using such shock tactics regularly would cheapen the sport in the eyes of the fans – it would become a goon show with no connection to the athletic roots of the sport – and to Stu, that was a travesty. Wrestling, for all its theatrics, should be an athletic exhibition first and foremost, not some circus of depravity.

But perhaps, in the age-old way that a father can be too hard on his son, Stu was not being fair to Bruce. Stu had been letting men like Abdullah the Butcher take the business to unsettling extremes for years, so why then did he expect Bruce to be so squeaky clean? Part of it came down to pressure from the conservative Ed Whalen, who was becoming increasingly queasy with the direction the business was heading. As veteran wrestling journalist David Meltzer puts it, Whalen's idea of pro wrestling was mostly "scientific matches mixed with light-hearted and inoffensive comedy." The extreme stuff was hard enough to take coming from a pro like Abdullah, but Whalen wasn't about to tolerate it from one of Stu's upstart kids.

Keith, on the other hand, was a good boy, playing within his father's guidelines. "Bruce was a genius in a lot of ways," Keith says. "Everybody else, including me, was just so by the book. I was just trying to please my dad and give him realistic matches. I wasn't thinking outside the box.... But my dad didn't like a lot of Bruce's concepts. To him it was making a mockery of what he considered a true sport.... Maybe [Stu] was a dinosaur in that way. Maybe we should have gone completely farcical."

Either way, Keith says he had his dad's favour in the 1970s and was handed more creative control than Bruce. This is where Bruce – his mother's golden child since she almost lost him in the womb – began going to his mother to influence the business.

As booker, Keith had formed a tight working relationship with Leo Burke and Colorado's Larry Lane, just the sort of grapplers Stu liked: highly capable men in the ring but also straight-shooters who didn't rely on gimmicks. Together they painstakingly developed storylines to enact for the Friday night's TV taping. Then, when the night came, the rug would be pulled out from under their feet. The card had been changed.

"My dad always had the final veto on these things," Keith says. "But Smith and Bruce would be up in the office while I was on the road, and they'd pressure my mom until she'd say, 'Stu, we have to change [plans].' I'd come home and see Smith up there with his big bear feet, his toes wrapped around the edge of my mom's desk, harassing her. I knew [him and Bruce] had been up there all week. Then I'd open the program at the match and the card I put together was different."

Both Bruce and Smith harboured a grudge against Larry Lane because he had called them spoiled brats, Keith says. In retaliation, Bruce and Smith turned their mother against Lane. "That was total bullshit," Keith says. "But my dad might have promised Larry $500, and my mom.... wouldn't want to co-sign the cheque.... [This made my dad] lose respect with the wrestlers.... They'd say, 'What the hell, Stu? You promised me this.'"

"It was like Chinese water torture," Keith says of the way Bruce and Smith worked on their mother all week long to persuade their father to change plans. Because of this, Helen grew to hate Lane, even though she had little contact with him. Keith remembers talking to Lane under a veranda at Hart House. A large flowerpot was perched on the edge of the second-floor balcony. "It must have weighed fifty pounds," Keith says. "It was all [Helen] could do to move it. Well, one day she dumped it.... It landed at [Lane's] feet and he looked up. She said 'I'm sorry, Larry. It slipped.' That's what a rage [Smith and Bruce] had her in."

With the Hart kids on the scene, the territory had become a political minefield.

King Curtis Iaukea and Mark Lewin were brought in to save Stampede Wrestling in 1975. Stu hoped to repeat his success of the late 1960s when Abdullah the Butcher and Archie "The Stomper" Gouldie were brought in to save the lagging business. That era, in which Stu made up to $1 million a year,[2] was beginning to peter out. Gouldie and Abdullah had moved on, and because they could make more money in bigger cities, were returning less frequently.

Stu needed a new monster with the vicious intensity of his former stars. Texas bad boy Terry Funk, who had been in and out of Stampede over the years, recommended King Curtis. The brother of Dory Funk Jr. was beginning to develop a reputation for wild and bloody bouts, and Terry knew Curtis could equal Abdullah for sheer brutality. It was evident by the big man's forehead, which had the same mangled qualities as the Butcher's.

Iaukea, a bloated, bearded Hawaiian with a grimace of death, had been a star heel in Australia in the early 1970s. Working against Lewin, a wild man from Buffalo, New York, the two had a feud that was brimming with blood. The Australian territory flourished, so much so that promoters around the world, Stu included, began looking at Lewin and Iaukea with dollar signs in their eyes. They were the ultimate quick fix for any lagging territory.

But Lewin and King Curtis came with a catch-22 that most promoters ignored. "They'd go from territory to territory all over the world and get it red hot because they'd be doing more blood than any of these places had ever experienced," says wrestling journalist David Meltzer. "At the beginning it would be great, but they'd burn people out [with the non-stop gore] and then they'd move on to the next territory. That was their MO. The Australian territory never really recovered after those guys left."

Not long after the wrestlers arrived, with Lewin given creative control over their angles, Stu recruited another blood merchant, Big Bad John, a scruffy, leather-clad Texan. It was like having three Abdullah the Butchers in town at once. And three Abdullahs is two too many. It was overkill. Also, to Abdullah's credit, there was usually a great deal of ring psychology behind his violence. He bled buckets, but there was a method to his madness. His angles always told a compelling story. Critics of King Curtis and Lewin charged that they were all shock and no story.

"Why do soap operas on TV last for years and years?" asks Dan Kroffat. "They're propelled not through violence but through storytelling. Each week, they leave you with a cliff-hanger to bring you back. You got caught up with the characters.... Guys [like Curtis and Lewin] who told no story but went out and bled like pigs every night, can you bring them back week after week? Not really. Not for long."

There was a crude attempt at a storyline during the Curtis-Lewin era. Big Bad John was the general of a self-styled army, where the soldiers, who included Iaukea, Mr. Hito, and John Quinn, wore Nazi-style helmets and jackboots. At one point, this villainous army attacked sixty-year-old Stu in the ring, handcuffing him to the ropes and laying into him viciously. Dan Kroffat, Larry Lane, and Mark Lewin came to Stu's rescue, touching off the most graphic feud western Canadian audiences had ever seen.

"They set the promotion on fire at first, but it was far too radical," says Ross Hart. "They were [bleeding] every night, and the interviews were way over the top. King Curtis was talking about ripping people's entrails out.... Calgary had some hardcore stuff with Abdullah and Archie. That's what Stampede Wrestling was known for.... But this was so graphic. There were all these calls to the TV station complaining."

Stu and the offending wrestlers accrued hundreds of dollars in fines from the boxing and wrestling commissions in both Edmonton and Calgary. Stu also received a letter of warning from Calgary mayor Rod Sykes, letting him know that such reprehensible behaviour in the ring would not be tolerated.

Sykes's outrage spoke volumes. As mayor, he opposed the more offensive acts in the game. An article in the *Calgary Sun* on May 12, 1974, finds him expressing outrage at one wrestler who licked his opponent's blood off the canvas. But in the same piece, Sykes praised wrestling for providing "a healthy outlet for pent-up frustrations.... If it weren't for wrestling," Sykes jokes, "many of these women would go home and beat up their husbands." He continued: "In our society, the borders between right and wrong are so blurred that people become confused and alienated. Wrestling has the old-fashioned good-versus-evil theme very clearly defined. It's a healthy change."[3]

With the coming of Lewin and King Curtis, Sykes stopped defending wrestling and threatened to revoke Stu's licence to hold matches. Stu protested, and the matter was taken to City Hall in August 1975.[4]

Ed Whalen also took a stand against the direction the show was taking, and his complaints brought about terrible consequences for the promotion. After one particularly violent program in March 1975, the beloved announcer appeared on the six o'clock news denouncing the violence and threatening to leave the show if it did not stop. Whalen thought Stampede Wrestling should be good, clean, family entertainment. "He was not going to play blood, period," says Whalen's wife, Nomi. "He knew there were a lot of kids watching that show, and he cared about what was being taught.... He didn't believe in portraying violence in front of young people. It wasn't okay."

When it came to Whalen, Stu had a dilemma. Of course, Whalen was an extremely popular figure who gave the show its personality – his personality. Stu felt Stampede Wrestling couldn't continue without Whalen. Yet, the announcer often turned up his nose at the business, and he didn't have the stomach for its inherent violence.

Whalen also expressed concern that being associated with such a show would damage his credibility as the CFAC news director.[5] This created problems for Stampede Wrestling. David Meltzer summed up the situation best: "In pro wrestling, it is inherent that at some point you are going to have to check your dignity at the door. Whalen, because he had power due to his standing with the television station, had frequent moral objections to pro wrestling. Whenever there was a battle between Whalen's dignity and pro wrestling, it was never a contest."[6]

This time, however, Whalen's stand was vindicated because, ultimately, Lewin and Curtis were toxic for business. After an initial boost at the gates, people began to react negatively to the excessive violence, perhaps spurred on by Whalen's denunciation of it. By the end of Lewin and Iaukea's eight-month stay, attendance at the shows had dropped considerably. When the violence merchants left town, "they left us nothing but scorched earth," says Keith Hart. "Whalen was disgusted with us, and we had lost a lot of goodwill in the community."

Although the show was cleaned up, the bad taste in his mouth remained, and before the year was out, Whalen phased himself off it. Brian Dance, who worked CFAC's sports department, took over the announcer's role, but he was never an adequate replacement. "He just didn't have Ed's charisma," Ross says.

After the excess of 1975, Stu steered his ship away from the bloody waters that had gotten him in such trouble. For a time, he overcompensated for his past transgressions. A February 2, 1977, *Calgary Herald* piece titled "Wrestlers Turn Cheers to Snores" featured Rabbi Louis Ginsberg of the boxing and wrestling commission complaining, "The pendulum has swung the other way." Ginsberg claimed that the wrestling matches had become so tame that they were "putting the crowd to sleep."[7]

Just like that, the promotion was in its worst slump since the early 1960s. The Stomper, Abdullah, and Tor Kamata were gone. Dan Kroffat was beginning to move away from the wrestling business. With a dying promotion,

Stu once again had trouble bringing in the top talents.

One of Stampede's top stars in 1976 was Ripper Collins, from Hawaii. While he did have a distinct flair, with his bleach-blond hair, effeminate voice, and crowd-baiting skills, Collins was grotesque. Not in the dangerous way Abdullah was grotesque but in a pathetic way, with his small arms and grossly swollen belly. Collins's ring skills were poor, too. His crowning finishing move was a lousy knee to the groin.

Even though Collins was married to a former woman wrestler, Barbara Baker, his homosexuality was well known in the wrestling community. This wouldn't have mattered had Collins been discreet. According to Ross, Collins got in trouble with the law when he picked up a hitchhiker one night driving home from a gig in Dawson Creek, British Columbia. The young man wound up fleeing from the van with his clothes torn, scratches and bite marks covering his body. When he was picked up by the RCMP, he told them that Collins had tried to sexually assault him. Collins was arrested, and Stu's van was impounded as evidence.

Collins, free on bail, claimed innocence, saying the young man had attacked him. Stu was leery but kept the wrestler on the payroll for a while, awaiting the trial. He fired Collins not long afterward when the wrestler made profane gestures to a male fan. Collins left Calgary before his case went to court, Ross says. According to wrestling journalist Meltzer, Collins died of AIDS sometime in the 1990s.

Things were looking dismal for Stampede Wrestling. Not even the return of Ed Whalen in 1977 was sufficient to give business a boost. Stu seriously considered selling the promotion that year, getting out of the roller coaster of a business for good. He spoke of retirement, about spending his twilight years travelling with Helen, in peace. She wholeheartedly encouraged the idea.

For years, Stu had been fending off advances from Ray and Bud Osborne, who wanted to start their own wrestling promotion in Alberta, to run as direct competition to Stampede Wrestling. The Osborne brothers had run shows in rural areas across the Prairie provinces for years and had applied to both the Calgary and Edmonton boxing and wrestling commissions for licences to hold shows in those cities. As Stu saw it, he had been good to the Osbornes throughout their careers. Now they wanted to run against him? It was a stab in the back. "Hey, it's a free country," says Bud Osborne today, defending his ambitions.

Each time the Osbornes made a move into his Calgary stronghold, Stu managed to block them. The commission received letters from the likes of

Archie Gouldie and Little Beaver, siding with Stu and stating they would not work for a rival promotion. Stu himself wrote letters of protest. "Wherever there are two wrestling factions battling each other in the same area, they not only kill each other off, but they kill the sport for the fans and all those involved," he wrote to the Calgary commission on April 13, 1976.

But as business continued to plummet, Stu began to wonder what the hell he was fighting for. After negotiating with the Osbornes, plans were made for Stu to close up shop at the end of the 1977 Calgary Stampede, at which time the Osbornes would launch their promotion. Long involved in real estate, the Osbornes put up land as a non-refundable deposit.[8] It looked like a done deal. Stampede Wrestling was finished.

Chapter ten

The Age of Dynamite

When he first laid eyes on Dynamite Kid, Bruce Hart had a revelation. The blond Hart boy, disenchanted that the family business was going down the tubes, had signed on with England's Joint Promotions in 1977 for a six-week tour of the United Kingdom as "Bronco" Bruce Hart, a Stetson- and chaps-wearing cowboy. He was wrestling in the northwestern English town of Chester at a beer-soaked community hall when he saw the eighteen-year-old Tommy "Dynamite Kid" Billington fly into action.

Bruce had been around the world's greatest wrestlers all his life, but he had never seen anybody move like this kid. Dynamite was unbelievably fast, flying around the ring like a ping-pong ball, and, damn, he hit hard. He stung those fat bastards he was up against before they knew what hit them. As his ring name suggested, Dynamite was explosive, with an innate sense of timing. His wrestling skills were technically sound, too.

The thing that most excited Bruce was Dynamite Kid's size. In the five years he had been wrestling, Bruce had taken his share of derogatory cracks about his stature. Bud Osborne, who was about to buy his dad's business, was an early detractor. "He was too small," says Bud to this day. "Just a little tit. He was a conceited little bastard too, and he knew you couldn't hurt him [because of Stu]. If it hadn't been for his dad, he never would've stepped inside a ring."

Dynamite Kid was the man who was going to make those sons of bitches

A scrawny Tom "Dynamite Kid" Billington at about age 16 with his trainer, Ted Betley, circa 1975.

eat their words, Bruce thought. This scrawny kid was even smaller than he was. Dynamite was five-foot-eight and about 155 pounds, and yet he hit the ring like a tornado. The giants could not squash him.

Dynamite also had a good head on his shoulders for the business. Despite his awesome skills, he wasn't out there to glorify himself. He made his opponents look like a million bucks every night. They could give the kid a love tap and he'd fly across the ring as if struck by the hand of God. Wrestling Dynamite, grapplers would later say, was like playing with a balloon. It was the ultimate compliment.

Here was somebody Bruce's size who he could team up with, or feud with, and they would both come out stars. Dynamite Kid was going to save Stampede Wrestling and catapult the lagging promotion into the stratosphere. Dynamite Kid was the future.

After the night's match, Bronco Bruce approached Dynamite. At first, the lad was not friendly. Billington was a shy, defensive kid, with a scowl for strangers. He often had a cold, emotionless look in his eyes, like a shark. But he warmed up when Bruce began talking business. Dynamite claims Bruce offered him an all-expenses-paid trip to Canada to wrestle in Stu Hart's promotion, as well as a free car, an apartment, and $400 a week. Compared with where Billington came from, it sounded like paradise.

Dynamite Kid came from the bleak coal mining town of Golborne, near Wigan, between working-class Manchester and Liverpool, in northern England. "When I went there, I found it very depressing," says Dynamite Kid's ex-wife, Michelle Billington. "There was not much to do other than hard labour. You could aspire to make factory parts for appliances. I remember there was a toilet roll factory in the neighbourhood.... Tom was actually born in the room we stayed in. There was no heat. Just a little gas fireplace downstairs.... Later on, when Tom made money, he helped his dad fix the place up, but his dad was always so proud. [He'd say,] 'I don't need no central heating!'"

Bret Hart suggests Dynamite Kid's lineage can be traced back to a family of executioners who hung criminals in England around the turn of the nineteenth century. Historical records confirm there was such a Billington family, though it's not clear whether they're Dynamite's ancestors. What is clear is that Dynamite came by his hardened, two-fisted nature naturally. His grandfather, who lived a block from his grandson, was a bare-knuckles boxer and a bully. "Everybody feared him," says Michelle. "Nobody was even allowed to walk on the sidewalk in front of his house. He would come out and ... he was just ferocious." Dynamite's father, Billy, also boxed in his younger days, as did Dynamite's uncle, Eric, who was a ranked pro. Dynamite's father

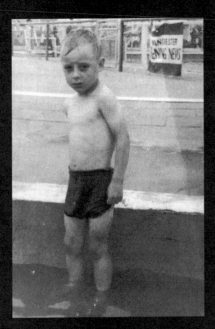

Top left: The man who would change wrestling: Dynamite Kid as a little boy. Top right:
A young and tough Dynamite Kid wears a fur jacket in Japan, early 1980s. "This was his
favourite picture," says his ex-wife Michelle Billington. "He thought he looked like Marlon
Brando." Bottom: Dynamite Kid (left) with his tag team partner Luke "Loch Ness Monster"
McMasters (right). Evil manager J.R. Foley is in the middle. Dynamite's speed and McMas-
ters' power led to the two winning the Stampede International Tag Team belts in 1980.

dreamed that his son would be a boxer and began training him when he was a little boy.

Billy was a harsh man. "If I did something wrong and he caught me, he'd crack me one straight in the face," writes Dynamite in his autobiography, *Pure Dynamite*. "No warning, he just did it. He broke my nose once."[1] But Dynamite never resented his father. Rather, he respected Billy and considered him a friend. Dynamite Kid's world was a world of hard-fighting men. That's all he knew. Even his autobiography is virtually female-free: his mother, two sisters, and even his two wives and daughters all get short shrift.

Dynamite had a mean streak and a wicked sense of humour that would manifest itself years later with the sadistic ribs he played on his fellow wrestlers. He gleefully recalls finding a doll his parents meant to give his sister for Christmas and painting it blue, ruining it.

Little Tommy hated school. He didn't like to read and was constantly in fights, which got him caned three or four times a week. The one class he did excel in was gym. He was a killer on the soccer and rugby fields. He was a natural gymnast, too, able to work the rings like an Olympic athlete. His coaches were convinced he could conquer any sport he chose. Billington's passion was wrestling.

Dynamite's mentor was the English wrestler Ted Betley, who fought in a mask and black cloak as Doctor Death. Retired, Betley was training young wrestlers when he met thirteen-year-old Tom Billington. Dynamite trained with Betley six days a week for the next three years. For part of his training, Betley took him to Riley's Gym, Wigan's version of the Hart's Dungeon, with its own fear-inspiring nickname, The Snake Pit. The Snake Pit had spawned such British wrestling legends as Billy Robinson and Karl Gotch. Like so many before him, Billington was inducted into the torturous world of submission wrestling. He was squeezed in leg locks until he screamed, thinking his legs would tear apart at the knee. But like Stu Hart, Dynamite was one of the boys who hung on, who kept coming back week after week.

At age fourteen, Billington dropped out of school, and at sixteen, christened Dynamite Kid by Betley, he began wrestling professionally. By the time he was eighteen, Dynamite held both the British Lightweight and European Welterweight titles. Still, he was not making what he was worth, promoter Max Crabtree paying him only twelve pounds a night. It's no wonder Bruce Hart's offer seemed so appealing. At first, though, Crabtree persuaded Dynamite to turn down Bruce's offer. If Dynamite left England, he would have to drop the belts he was so proud of. Crabtree also promised him a raise. That turned out to be one extra pound per match.

And on Bruce's end, too, there were impediments. Try as he might, he could not get his father excited about Dynamite. "Stu had a real obsession with size," Bruce says. "If you were under 240, he thought you were too small."

But the arrival of Dynamite was destined. In Alberta, the real estate market had collapsed, and the Osbornes were unable to buy Stu's territory. Meanwhile, Dynamite decided he didn't need Crabtree. Betley phoned Hart House and, talking to somebody he thought was Stu – though Billington insists it was one of the Hart boys pretending to be his dad – he scheduled Dynamite's Calgary trip.

Dynamite's cousin, Davey Boy Smith, four years his junior, came to watch The Kid's last wrestling match before leaving for Canada. Davey Boy worshiped his cousin. He was already following in Dynamite's footsteps, training hard with Betley. On April 27, 1978, nineteen-year-old Tommy Billington flew to Calgary with twenty pounds sterling in his pocket.[2]

"Ehh, you're a skinny little bastard," said Stu Hart the first time he laid eyes on Dynamite Kid at the Victoria Pavilion, prodding him like a disappointing cut of steak. The remark made Dynamite boil inside, but he managed to keep his cool. He was there to do business, and besides, he was about to show this Stu Hart what a skinny little bastard could do.

Dynamite fought his first Stampede match that night against Angel Acevedo, who wrestled as the Cuban Assassin. An inch shorter than Dynamite but a good sixty pounds heavier, the stocky Acevedo was the ultimate Cold War villain, his loco eyes, wild beard, and fatigues making him look like a crazed Fidel Castro.* Acevedo had a fast, heated rumble with Dynamite, the newcomer scoring the pin as per instructions. The crowd was sparse, but those who saw Dynamite Kid left the arena talking about him excitedly, and in the weeks to come they returned with friends.

After the match, Acevedo raved about Dynamite's skills, asking Stu if he could have a feud with the youngster. Already, the scrawny kid's stock had risen considerably with the Hart patriarch. But Acevedo didn't get his feud. Instead, Dynamite Kid, initially presented as one of the Harts' babyface friends, was thrown into a war with Australian heel Norman Frederick

---

*Born in Puerto Rico, raised in Cuba, and arriving in the United States in 1957 at the age of sixteen, Acevedo was a veteran of the mat game, having wrestled since the early 1960s. He settled in Calgary in 1976 and became a Stampede Wrestling mainstay for the next two decades. The fans loved to hate the wacky mongrel, who pulled all manner of foreign objects from the deep pockets of his army pants when the referees weren't looking.

Charles III. Bearded, heavily tattooed, and grizzled rotten, Charles seemed like a natural foe for young Dynamite, who was deceptively innocent looking.

Dynamite was a clean-living kid in the late 1970s. After the matches, he accompanied the wrestlers to the bar, but while they knocked back pint after pint of ale, he sipped glasses of orange juice. His only vice was smoking cigarettes. Dynamite also worked out obsessively, building a lean, muscular body.

Soon after he arrived in Calgary, Dynamite was furious to find Bruce Hart's promises – which Bruce denies having made – not kept. There was no car, no apartment, and $400 a week turned out to be $350.[3] He intended to go home after wrestling to the end of the six weeks he had committed to, but he soon found himself enjoying his Canadian adventure. Surprisingly, he and Bruce were becoming good friends. And to top if off, Dynamite was quickly becoming the biggest star of Stampede Wrestling. "Wrestling Dynamite Kid was like suddenly driving a Porsche, when we had been used to wrestling all these old slugs, which was more like driving a junky old stick shift," says Bruce.

Before long, the whole Hart clan embraced Dynamite as though he were a long-lost brother. He frequently visited Hart House for Sunday dinners, and Stu had no problem lending him any one of the Cadillacs. The boys took him camping and to parties, trying to introduce him to girls, but they quickly learned about his short fuse when he laid a few Calgarians out with his punch. Bret Hart would later say Dynamite was one of the few men he ever met who had a legitimate knockout punch. Big men crumbled like imploding buildings when the Kid landed a good one. "Tom had a vicious streak," says Ross Hart. "He had a thick Lancashire accent and could be quite insecure about it. He always thought people were mocking him. I remember we were at this old bar, the Scotch & Sirloin, and this guy came up to him and said, 'Oh, is that an English accent?' Tom knocked the guy out without hesitating. It happened so fast. The guy wasn't making fun of him."

In the wrestling world, though, such explosiveness was an asset. "He was a crazy dog, but he had a good side, too," says Bret Hart. "He was hard working and generally a straight shooter who was good for his word. He was very generous, and if he liked you, he'd give you the shirt off his back. He was the kind of guy you wanted on your team."

Even so, there was always a trace of malice lurking beneath the surface. In his autobiography, Dynamite writes about Bruce and Keith taking him to Banff to teach him to ski. As Dynamite tells it, he went up the mountain in only a T-shirt and jeans because the brothers had told him the sun would be shining. Keith insists they told him to dress warmly and not to wear denim, but stubbornly, Dynamite thought he knew better. Like all fledgling skiers, he tumbled down the mountain repeatedly and was soon soaking wet and freezing cold. He took off his skis and stomped down the mountain, waiting for the brothers below, sulking and trying to warm up with a cup of coffee. He seethed inside when Bruce and Keith laughed at him, convinced that the trip was a set-up to make him look the fool.

In the months that followed, Dynamite harboured deep resentment about the incident and gradually extracted his revenge. He tells of purposely knocking two of Keith's teeth loose in a match but pretending it was an accident. As for Bruce, Dynamite waited until his friend was taking a shower after a Dungeon workout, then turned off the cold water tap, which was on the outside of the shower stall. The blast of scalding water made Bruce yelp. "I'm sure he still has the marks on his head from the blisters," Dynamite writes.[4]

"He had a black heart," says Bret, who compares Dynamite Kid to Ty Cobb, the notoriously mean-spirited baseball player who dominated the sport in the early part of the twentieth century. "He was the Ty Cobb of wrestling, the kind of kid that grew up and liked to torture animals." Those are particularly harsh words from Bret. Of all the Hart boys, he was ultimately the closest to Dynamite. To this day he speaks of the wrestler with praise and admiration, citing the Brit as one of the greatest influences on his own career. He's often stated his opinion that, "pound for pound," Dynamite Kid was the greatest wrestler who ever lived.

Dynamite also formed a close relationship early on with Wayne Hart, the gangly Hart son whose love of the party life often put him at odds with his father. Wayne was working for Stampede Wrestling as a referee and living in Calgary's Ramsay area near the Stampede grounds. Wayne and Tom became roommates and eventually co-owners of a duplex in the rundown neighbourhood.

One Hart brother Dynamite had little respect for, even though he did get a kick out of him, was Smith. In October 1978, Dynamite, Bruce, and Keith were to go to Oktoberfest in Hannover, Germany, to represent Stampede Wrestling in an international wrestling tournament. When Keith was unable to make the trip, Stu sent Smith – who at the time was trying to break into the business – as a replacement.

It was a tradition of the tournament that after the matches, a parade took place where each of the wrestlers' names was called, along with the country they hailed from. Each wrestler then came to the ring and waved to the fans.

When Smith was called, he came out of the dressing room wearing a Hitler moustache and his boots on the wrong feet, which made him walk bow-legged. Smith goose-stepped his way to the ring, giving the Nazi salute to the shocked and offended fans. The crowd went silent, while the wrestlers cackled with laughter. When word got back to Stu, he was fuming.[5] Once again, his oldest boy had let him down.

Although Dynamite enjoyed the twisted prank, he wondered if Smith was half mad. Life with the Hart family, he surmised, was certainly going to be strange.

When Dynamite entered the picture, nearly all the Hart brothers had their hands in the family business – be it as wrestler, booker, referee, or producer – and they all wanted to steer the ship. But they seldom agreed on a direction. "Stu was the owner ... but most of the time it was his sons who seemed to be in control," writes Dynamite. "Too many chiefs and not enough Indians."[6]

Bruce and Bret were particularly assertive in the business. Both wrestling regularly and controlling their own storylines, they often clashed. Bret says Bruce wasn't organized enough: "He'd show up at the dressing room half an hour late, scratch his head, and figure out what he was going to do that night."

Bruce also couldn't keep his ego in check, Bret charges. He ran the show for his own amusement and to glorify himself, rather than for the greater good. If he was not involved with the main event, he undermined it with the matches he was orchestrating. Stu paid big money to bring in hot names such as Archie Gouldie or David Shults, a vicious Southern wrestler who distinguished himself in the early 1980s. They'd be booked for the main event in some wild angle – a cage match (fighting inside a steel cage) or a chain match (where two grapplers would be chained together), for instance. Bruce, Bret says, would spike his own match, earlier in the card, with a blood bath or some bizarre plot twist so that plans for the main event seemed anti-climactic.

"He'd howl and slap his leg ... but guys like The Stomper and Shults would be in the dressing room pulling their hair out," Bret says. "I remember both of them looking at my dad at different times and throwing their arms up: 'What now? What do you want me to do?' The guys who were pulling the wagon would just go crazy.... Bruce had no business running a dressing room. He couldn't control his own ego. He couldn't differentiate what was good for his own amusement and what was good for business."

This made Stu furious, Bret says, and Papa Hart often wanted to strip Bruce of his power, but Helen would come to her son's rescue. "My mom

Dynamite Kid flies off the ropes toward the menacing Bad News Allen, 1983.

babied Bruce so much, and she hated the business so much, that she wouldn't co-sign the cheques if Bruce wasn't kept in power. My dad had to appease my mom by keeping Bruce happy."

But some wrestlers feel Bruce's ideas were inspired. "Bruce was a genius booker," says Alison Hart's ex-husband, Ben Bassarab. "He was years ahead of his time, and what they're doing now in the WWF, he was doing twenty years ago." Wrestler Gama Singh agrees: "To me, he was the Vince McMahon of Stampede Wrestling."

Perhaps it was Bruce's egocentric quest to be a top man that led him to reconfigure the Stampede Wrestling game plan. But there's little doubt that approach revitalized the territory.

The first thing he did was turn Dynamite Kid bad. It was late in 1978 when Dynamite dramatically betrayed Bruce in the middle of a tag team match, attacking his partner from behind. "I got taken away in an ambulance, and people despised Dynamite from that moment on," Bruce says. "The hallmark of every great promotion was one really ass-kicking, awe-inspiring heel, and ours became Dynamite Kid."

The crux of the story, which Bruce devised, was that Dynamite had sold the beloved Harts out to ally himself with a fellow Brit, the corrupt million- aire manager John Foley. Like any good heel, Foley had no honour or sense of fair play, which made him the Harts' natural enemy. It was win at all costs for Foley and, with that philosophy, as well as his decadent, partying ways, he had supposedly seduced Dynamite, promising to make him a high-roll- ing champion.

Initially, Foley had come to Stampede Wrestling in 1976 at the end of a long career that had seen the Liverpool coal miner develop a reputation as one of the nastiest shooters in Britain. "He was a notorious tough guy," says Bret. "A real badass bully." Before arriving in Calgary, Foley had a stint wrestling in Kentucky for promoter Angelo Poffo. Foley had stretched Poffo's sons in the ring so viciously that the promoter warned him never to do it again. Foley didn't heed the warning, and the next time he was in the ring with Poffo's son Randy, he again set out to torture the rookie. Poffo ran into the ring with his other son Lanny and, in an act of frontier justice, the Poffo family kicked the hell out of Foley. John always prided himself that despite the beating he took, he never went down. Randy "Macho Man" Sav- age went on to be a one of the biggest WWF stars in the 1980s, while Foley migrated to Calgary.

Despite his toughness, Foley was no star when he came to Calgary. He was too short and too old, at least in his late fifties, with a flabby body, a drinking problem and, consequently, an unsightly beer gut. Brought in as a wrestler, he failed to excite western Canadian fans. "Stu thought it was maybe time to get rid of him," Bruce says. "But we kind of felt sorry for the old fart."

Bruce decided to reinvent John Foley. He had the old geezer come to the ring and announce to Ed Whalen that he had inherited several million dollars from a rich uncle. From here on in, he was going to use his wealth, his power, and his "number one boy" Dynamite Kid to foil the Hart family.

As the weeks went by, Bruce let his imagination and his twisted sense of humour run wild, with Foley as his canvas. The old drunk's character development was so absurd it was genius, and unique in the wrestling world. The most popular show on network TV at the time was *Dallas*, so, taking a cue from the evil J.R. Ewing, John was recast as J.R. Foley, coming to the ring in a suit and cowboy hat, with wads of money clenched in his fist. Sometimes he'd enter the ring wearing a sailor's hat, as if he were the captain of his own yacht. "Money talks, Ed," he'd say with his cockney accent, laughing in the announcer's face.

On one of the road tours, when Foley had drunkenly passed out in the back of the van, Dynamite shaved off part of his manager's handlebar moustache. When Foley sobered up, he was furious. Then Bruce got another one of his bizarre ideas. He had the veteran further shave his facial hair into a Hitler-style moustache. When he wasn't appearing as some sort of cowboy Adolf, Foley came to the ring as J.R. the General, wearing a army helmet and fatigues.

J.R. was clearly a fink, a kook of the first order, and Ed Whalen had fun mocking him for his eccentricities. But J.R. gave as good as he got, and weekly he taunted the announcer: "We're having a party tonight, Mr. Whalen, with the most beautiful women in all of Calgary. And you're not invited." Then he'd put his face inches from Whalen's so the announcer could look right into his bloodshot eyes and smell his boozy breath. "Let the good times roll, Mr. Whalen." That line became another enormously popular Stampede Wrestling catchphrase.

Bruce's eyes light up when he recalls such comedy. "We used to come up with that stuff riding around in a van twenty-five hundred miles a week," he says. "We were always rolling along having a few beers and that's when we'd hatch this stuff. We'd try to conjure up these mind-bending paradoxes just to screw with people's heads. We'd have Foley come to the ring looking like Hitler and quoting Winston Churchill. 'We will fight on the beaches, Ed Whalen …' I was always trying to incorporate all these bizarre contradictions."

Allied with Foley, Dynamite Kid became a character Tom Billington could own. "Tom liked being a heel," says Michelle Billington. "When he was a good guy, he had to smile all phoney and sign autographs. That wasn't his forte. He liked being bad so he could be rude and tell people to eff-off."

And so he did. The evil Dynamite Kid strutted around the ring like an arrogant peacock, boasting about how he beat his enemies fair and square, though everybody had seen him cheat his way to victory minutes before. He'd tell Whalen that he was "often imitated but never duplicated," and he would give spectators the middle finger salute. When a fan shoved him outside the ring, Dynamite leapt into the crowd, attacking the man. "Cut that out!" yelled an irate Whalen, pulling Dynamite away.

Dynamite Kid was such an effective villain that the entire territory shifted to better accommodate him. If the early 1970s was the golden age of Stampede Wrestling, the early '80s was the Dynamite Age. It was a time where the mid-heavyweight division became just as important as the heavyweight division. Two new title belts came into play, the World Mid-Heavyweight title and the Commonwealth Mid-Heavyweight title. This gave smaller men such as Bruce Hart a chance to shine, as well as impressive mid-heavyweights like Gama Singh and Billington's cousin Davey Boy Smith, who would soon enter the picture. Bret and Owen Hart also started their careers as mid-heavyweights.

Week after week, the struggle between Dynamite and the Harts became a game of cat and mouse. By hook or by crook, Dynamite would usually retain the World Mid-Heavyweight crown and weasel-like Foley would try to dodge the Harts, who were invariably the number one contenders. But Foley insisted that Dynamite defend the belt against hopeless jobbers, who never seemed to win a match. "The number one contender is Randy Webber," a straight-faced Foley would say to the TV cameras. "You Harts will 'ave to get t' the bottom of the line."

The fast, high-flying action of the Stampede Wrestling territory in the Dynamite Age eventually changed the face of wrestling. In the last decade, the giants of the industry, the WWF and WCW, featured megastars who launched their careers weighing less than 230 pounds. Chris Benoit, Chris Jericho, Brian Pillman, Rey Mysterio Jr., Shawn Michaels, Eddy Guerrero, Matt and Jeff Hardy – they all owe a debt to Dynamite Kid. Any time you see a smaller wrestler delivering flying headbutts and performing crazy acrobatics twenty feet in the air – commonplace today – you're seeing moves Dynamite Kid brought to North America. Also commonplace are the body-destroying bumps that today's wrestlers take. Crashing through ringside tables, falling from the top of steel cages, giving back-breaking suplexes off the top turnbuckles; it's all part of today's hardcore wrestling style, and Dynamite Kid was doing it when such things seemed akin to suicide.

The axis of evil that revolved around Dynamite Kid and his manager J.R. Foley set the tone of Stampede Wrestling for the next six years. They would be the wildest, weirdest years yet.

Chapter eleven

Married To the Hart Mafia

"I think Julie took one look at Bret and fell in love," says Michelle Billington of her older sister.

When the two sisters started working as security staff at the Regina Exhibition Grounds in 1978, they had no idea it was going to change their lives forever. Julie and Michelle Smadu were seventeen and fourteen years old respectively, living on their own, and already stuck in the lower gears of the socioeconomic machine. They spent their early years bouncing from their mother to their father to a foster home, living in welfare conditions, and it was Julie who took on the role of mother to Michelle.

Working security at the Tuesday night wrestling matches was going to be easy money and a bit of a laugh. The girls had watched Stampede Wrestling on TV a few times and thought it silly. But when Julie saw twenty-one-year-old Bret climb into the ring, she was smitten. Wrestling suddenly became a lot more appealing.

He was long and lean, six feet tall with a solid, manly frame he had yet to grow into, thick-boned with broad shoulders. He had a serious look about him, his dark brown eyes penetrating, but his baby-fat face and the thick brown hair that framed it gave him a handsome yet boyish quality that made Julie feel weak. His sexy smile sealed the deal. Work or no work, she became a regular at the wrestling matches from then on and gradually got to know her crush.

The handsome Hart family, late 1970s. Back row, left to right: Stu, Helen, Dean, Wayne, Bruce, Ross, Smith, Bret, Keith. Middle row, left to right: Alison, Diana, Georgia, Ellie. Front row: Owen.

After many months of flirting, Julie, a cute number herself with long brown hair, a ripe figure, and a sly grin, planted her first kiss on Bret on his twenty-second birthday, July 2, 1979. Things moved quickly from there. When Julie decided to move to Calgary to live with the wrestler that same year, her little sister was devastated. The only person who ever really looked out for her was slipping away. Before the year was up, Michelle dropped out of school and moved in with Bret and Julie. She took a job as a waitress at a dirty old hotel near the house Bret rented in the Ramsay Court area of town.

Michelle had seen Dynamite Kid wrestle a number of times, and she knew he was impressive. She also knew he was a creep, associated with the vile J.R. Foley, and she wasn't supposed to like him. That changed the day Bret sent her on an errand to his brother Wayne's house, two blocks away, to borrow a vacuum cleaner. Michelle rang the doorbell, expecting the Hart referee to answer. Instead, she found herself standing face to face with Dynamite Kid. What was he doing hanging around a Hart? She managed to stammer her request for the vacuum and was surprised at how pleasantly he responded. "He was very polite and sweet," she says. "Not like his ring persona at all. He was shy, not making much eye contact."

After that first meeting, Dynamite started coming out of the dressing room when Michelle was at the wrestling matches to make small talk with her. "I was always afraid Bret would see me talking to him," she says. "I didn't want to hurt his feelings by talking to the guy who had just beat him up." Although Michelle was unaware of what went on behind the scenes at the wrestling matches, there was in fact a real tension between Bret and Dynamite.

Like his father, Bret had been an excellent amateur wrestler, training since the age of nine. In his late teens, he won city and provincial championships and, while wrestling for Mount Royal College, where he was taking courses in film studies, he was encouraged to try for the Canadian team for the Commonwealth Games. But Bret was wrestling mostly to please his father. He didn't see a future in amateur wrestling and was losing his passion for it. "I started to realize there wasn't five cents in it," Bret says. "I thought if you pursued it, you'd just end up being an old amateur wrestling coach or phys-ed teacher at a high school, and I didn't want to do that."[1]

Bret was also blowing it at school and dropped out after one semester, intending to give it another try the following year. In the meantime, he needed a job and so began refereeing, all the while watching the wrestlers intently, wondering if he could do what they were doing. One day, the Japanese grappler Mr. Hito approached Bret and asked in his broken English, "You

Dynamite Kid is sent reeling by a flying
uppercut from Bret Hart, early 1980s.

biggest one [of Stu's sons]. How come you no wrestle?"[2] Hito and his tag team partner, Mr. Sakurada, offered to show Bret the ropes down in the Dungeon. Stu had taught Bret submission wrestling while he was growing up, but it was the Japanese wrestlers who introduced him to the art of pro wrestling. For the next five months, Bret learned how to take bumps – how to fall and protect himself – and, more importantly, how to protect his opponents in a wrestling match, all the while making the battle look so real and punishing that nobody could see through the facade.

After wrestling his first couple of pro bouts in towns along the Stampede loop, Bret was sent on a wrestling tour of Puerto Rico. This turned out to be more embarrassing than anything else, as the less-than-dedicated Smith was his tag team partner. When Bret returned, he was pushed into a feud with the freshly turned heel Dynamite. Perhaps because of the animosity between Bruce and Bret over creative direction, Dynamite, firmly entrenched with Bruce, wrestled a series of rough, uncooperative matches with Bret.

Dynamite says that Bret was not yet comfortable with the ways of the pros and initially "wrestled stiff as a brush." Dynamite found Bret "rigid and awkward," so he broke his nose with a forearm smash. "It did the trick – he wasn't rigid anymore," Billington writes. Back in the dressing room, Dynamite says Bret was so furious he tried to pick a fight, but Hito and Sakurada held him back.[3]

Bret's skills soon improved, and he and Dynamite learned how to work together beautifully. Their matches were among the best in Stampede Wrestling history. In the *Calgary Sun*, Bret wrote of a 1981 ladder match in Regina in epic tones. As Bret sets up the action, the two men had collided skull to skull after an ill-timed move. Dynamite's head was split open, and Bret had such a gash in his face he could poke his finger through a gaping hole in his nose. "I remember Dynamite jumping up high, gripping that heavy steel ladder, coming straight down on my head," Bret writes, noting that although the blow looked devastating to the fans, the ladder never actually hit him.[4]

"Dynamite began to climb to the top [of the ladder].... Suddenly, I jumped up, throwing a desperate dropkick, just like he asked me: 'Just barely touch the ladder with your toes. I'll control how I go over.'" Bret describes the ladder wobbling and tipping over, Dynamite Kid flying into the ropes, bouncing out of the ring on top of J.R. Foley. Both fighters went to the hospital together that night for stitches, too tired to say a word but full of respect for each other.

Business aside, the friction between Bret and Dynamite heated up when the English wrestler became interested in Michelle, whom Bret viewed as a little sister. Too insecure to ask her out, Dynamite lured Michelle over to the duplex he and Wayne shared with a spur-of-the-moment ploy. A ring rat had showed up on their doorstep; the woman had had an encounter with Dynamite somewhere along the Stampede loop and now she fancied herself his girlfriend. Dynamite wanted to get rid of her. He had Wayne phone Michelle and ask that she come over and pretend to be Dynamite's girlfriend. Michelle was only too happy to oblige.

When Dynamite answered the door, she threw her arms around him and kissed him. "Hi, honey," she said. The girl from the road was shamed and quickly made an excuse to leave. She was still packing her bags when Dynamite asked Michelle if she would like to go for a walk. "It was the most romantic walk I ever had," Michelle says. "The snow was fresh and it was crunching under our feet. He told me about his life in England. We walked around the block and he invited me in for a cup of tea. He was a real gentleman."

Dynamite was walking her back home when Bret screeched up beside them in his silver Ford El Dorado. The Hart boy was not happy. "What are you doing? Get in!" he snapped at Michelle. "I'll take it from here," he snarled at Dynamite as he drove away. On the way home, Michelle got a lecture from Bret on the evils of Dynamite. Bret told her how Dynamite "uses women and then hangs them up like his wrestling boots." He told her how The Kid disrespectfully booted the ring rats out of his room when he was finished with his business. He told her to stay away from him, lest she become just another ring rat. "I'm going to ask him what his intentions are!" Bret huffed.

Michelle hoped Dynamite's feelings were the same as hers, though deep down she didn't believe it possible. But Dynamite continued to treat Michelle like a princess, and Bret was unable to prevent the relationship from moving forward. By 1980, Michelle had moved in with Dynamite Kid. She was sixteen, he was twenty-one.

Dynamite's hair-trigger temper became evident early in the relationship. If any man gave her a second glance when they went out, Dynamite exploded. "I always missed it," Michelle says. "By the time I turned around, the guy would be lying on the ground with his teeth beside him. At the time I was flattered. It gave me a false sense of security. I was stupid." Dynamite's temper seemed far less attractive the first time he blew up on her, when she accidentally spilt an ashtray onto the carpet. Michelle doesn't elaborate on the encounter. She does say his fury was something to behold. "He was always so remorseful after [his rages]," Michelle says. "There's a switch that goes on in me head," Dynamite told her, "and I can't shut it off." Dynamite Kid came by his volatile temper naturally, but by this time there was something new in his life that was propelling his anger to code-red proportions.

Dynamite Kid was introduced to steroids in the summer of 1979 by a 280-pound wrestler named Sylvester Ritter. Stu had christened him Big Daddy Ritter, a white-womanizing black stud who angered the hell out of the men in the predominantly white audience. Ritter, who hailed from North Carolina, was not a great wrestler, but his cocky charisma riled up fans. Stu gave him a big push in Calgary, making him North American champion.

Despite his dedication to weightlifting, Dynamite was becoming increasingly frustrated that his bulk and muscle mass was not even close to that of the heavyweight wrestlers. He was a small-boned man, never meant to be over 200 pounds in Bret's estimation, and he had a complex about that. Dynamite could see that the wrestling business was changing. The days of the beer-bellied bruiser were coming to an end. Soon, even the smaller wrestlers would be required to be finely sculpted musclemen, and no one under 200 pounds would have a chance of making it big. When Dynamite vented his spleen to Ritter, the big man gave him a handful of his first Dianabol pills. The steroids would prove to be a much-appreciated gift. Within three years, Dynamite weighed about 215 pounds of solid muscle. He had Michelle inject the juice into his backside. "Sometimes there would be three needles in each cheek," she says.

Dynamite also discovered speed around this time. Jake Roberts, a wrestler from Georgia, brought in to feud with Ritter, gave him a Yellow Jacket before he climbed in the ring one night, during the 1979 Calgary Stampede. Dynamite wrestled a one-hour match that evening and walked away with energy to spare.[5] He was sold.

Both Roberts and Ritter went on to world fame in the 1980s while working for the WWF – Ritter as the Junkyard Dog and Roberts as Jake the Snake, a grappler who brought a twelve-foot python to the ring, draping it over his victims.

Another demon on Dynamite's shoulder was former wrestler Cedric Hathaway, an eccentric Englishman who Bruce brought to the territory as a loopy, high-strung referee bent on making life hell for the Harts. Hathaway was into the occult, and every time he got stinking drunk, which was pretty much every day, he ranted about witches, which spooked Michelle. When he first came to Calgary, Hathaway stayed with Dynamite and Michelle. "That's when Tom's orange juice became vodka and orange juice," Michelle says. She remembers the first time she saw Dynamite bombed. "He was about twenty-two, I think. I remember laughing because the first time I got drunk, I was probably about thirteen."

Living with Dynamite Kid made Michelle feel important and protected. Suddenly life, which once seemed so depressing, was thrilling. When talk turned to marriage, Michelle had never been happier. The plan was to tie the knot in Golborne, but Dynamite decided he didn't want to get married in front of his family. He didn't want anybody to hear him express his love. A show of emotion like that seemed weak to him and his pride wouldn't allow it. Instead, the two got hitched in Calgary on March 25, 1982, in front of a justice of the peace.

On the way to the courthouse, a homeless person asked Dynamite for money. "Get the fook out of here, you little yard dog," Dynamite snarled. Michelle started to cry. "I can't believe I'm marrying this mean man," she thought. Somehow she reconciled the matter in her heart, however, because when the judge arrived, she became Dynamite's bride. Bret and Julie were present as witnesses.

Bret must have been inspired by the moment, because he married Julie the same year, on his birthday, also in front of the justice of the peace. The couple entered holy matrimony without telling anyone. Helen was hurt that her son did not include the family in his wedding plans. But she would be throwing plenty of weddings in the years to come. The kids were growing up. The Hart mafia was fortifying their ranks.

J.R. Foley was constantly raving at Ed Whalen during interviews about his struggles with the all-powerful Hart mafia that made life a nightmare for him and his army of heels. The system was a sham, Foley blustered, with Stu mollycoddling and favouring his sons, keeping them on top. J.R. and his men had to resort to their rotten tactics to get ahead, Foley insinuated. When Whalen defended the Harts, demented banter ensued. It was just another storyline, but the Hart mafia wasn't entirely a figment of J.R.'s mind.

The Harts really did permeate every corner of the Stampede Wrestling territory in the 1980s. It wasn't just Stu and Helen, who controlled the money, or the boys, who had a hand in every aspect of the business. Now the Hart girls were getting in on the action, too, three of the four marrying wrestlers and the other one marrying a bodybuilder and sometimes wrestler.

Bradley Joseph Annis, known around Calgary as B.J., married Stu and Helen's daughter Georgia in 1975. Stu and Helen liked B.J. the first time they met him. The Boston native had served a tour of duty in Vietnam; had a degree in marine engineering from the prestigious Kings Point military academy, near Helen's childhood home of Long Beach, New York; and was a pilot. He had become heavily involved in competitive bodybuilding in Hawaii, where he opened up his first gym.

The cocksure B.J. began visiting Calgary for ski trips, accompanying a friend who played football with the Winnipeg Blue Bombers. Eventually, B.J. decided to open a gym in Calgary, a risky proposition in the days before the fitness craze swept North America.

Twenty-eight year-old B.J. met the Hart family during the 1975 Calgary Stampede, when the kids were setting up a wrestling ring on a flatbed truck in front of the building he was converting into a gym. Blond, blue-eyed Georgia, with her kind nature, caught his attention immediately. Before long, he was dating the nineteen year old, which was fine with Stu and Helen.

What was not fine was B.J. marrying their daughter in December of that year and keeping it a secret from them for five months. When the truth got out, Helen was furious and told Stu to apply some Dungeon-worthy damage to her new son-in-law. B.J. to this day is relieved that he managed to avoid a stretching by the Hart patriarch – the only son-in-law to have done so.[6] Within a year or two, though, B.J. got back into the good books with Georgia's parents. He was certainly the son-in-law who caused them the least grief over the years. Complete with a wrestling ring and state-of-the-art weight training equipment, which bettered by far the crude facilities of Stu's Dungeon, BJ's Gym became a popular haunt for wrestlers and bodybuilders.

Another son-in-law, Jim Neidhart, came into the picture in 1979 looking to be trained by Stu. Standing six feet tall and weighing about 280 pounds, with a rock-solid beer belly, the twenty-four-year-old was built like a little tank, and Stu was only too happy to test the young man's mettle.

Neidhart was a California boy raised mostly by his well-to-do father, an accountant who spoiled his son to compensate for his divorce from Jim's mother. Neidhart had been traumatized by his parents' split and went through an introverted phase before finding his confidence in the world of sports. From the start, he was outstanding on both the baseball diamond and the football field, displaying the power of a rhinoceros. Neidhart played football for both the Dallas Cowboys and the Oakland Raiders, but the sport he really excelled at was shot put, a talent that won him a scholarship to UCLA. Neidhart's goal was to compete in the 1980 Olympics in Moscow, a dream that was dashed when the United States boycotted the Games in response to the Soviet Union's invasion of Afghanistan. It was a disappointment Stu could relate to all too well – the Second World War had crushed his youthful Olympic hopes.

Unlike Stu, however, Neidhart was a man of many vices, a party boy who went wild in the halls of academia, running afoul of the university. Stu's biographer Marsha Erb refers to a May 1979 *Washington Post* article on drug use in sports in which Neidhart is cited as a cautionary tale. According to the report, in high school, Neidhart was popping uppers before every track meet. His drug intake became even more excessive in UCLA where, in 1976, fortified by a cocktail of amphetamines, tranquilizers, and alcohol, he went on a destructive rampage, destroying his hotel room and swinging like Tarzan from his fourth-floor balcony.[7]

This was the wild child who showed up at Stu's door looking to become a wrestler. Stu embraced the big hulk from the start. "My grandfather was almost infatuated with my dad," says Jim's daughter Nattie, today a promising rookie wrestler herself. "They would go down to the Dungeon and it was like two big rams butting heads. They would literally kick the shit out of each other. They wouldn't hold back.... I think beating my dad up were some of the happiest moments of my grandfather's life." Jim would snort and spit, turn beet red and holler in pain and frustration as Stu stretched him, but he seemed to enjoy his time in the Dungeon, and he always returned, ready for anything Stu had to give him.

Before long, Neidhart was featured on Stampede Wrestling cards. Sold as a hot-headed strongman, he was popular with the fans even if he was only a moderate star in the promotion. He had yet to develop the maniacal, orange-bearded, sunglasses-wearing "Anvil" persona that later rocketed him to fame in the WWF.

Neidhart became a fixture of the Hart family when he started dating Ellie. Short and cute, with dark eyes and olive skin, the family often compared Ellie to Helen's Greek mother, after whom Ellie was named. It was more than her appearance that earned such comparisons. Ellie had the same outspoken, spicy flair. She was fiercely proud of her family, never afraid to say what she was thinking, and open with her emotions. She had a warm, loving soul, though easily upset. Ellie also had a lot of insecurities.

"She had a real lack of confidence growing up," says Keith. "She didn't have an identity, other than being Stu Hart's daughter.... She was very defensive. She hated the girls at school who had the nice clothes. She hated the girls us boys went out with ... because Ellie felt awkward. Half the time she wore hand-me-downs from the boys when business was bad. She had one dress."

When Neidhart became smitten with Ellie, flirting with her and showering her with affection, she was overjoyed that such a man was interested in her. "All of a sudden, she's got this football star paying attention to her,"

Keith says. "Here was her chance to thumb her nose at all the girls she went to school with. She was so proud to have him as her beau."

It's easy to see why Ellie would be drawn to Jim. If you were on his team, Neidhart was a great guy to be around, even if he did tend to overindulge in the party favours. "Everybody liked Jim Neidhart, except Jim," says retired wrestler Leo Burke. "He would hurt himself with the stuff he was taking, but he was everybody's friend."

Ellie and Jim Neidhart married on December 26, 1979.

In May, 1983, Alison Hart married bodybuilder Ben Bassarab, a member of BJ's Gym who the Harts took under their wing and trained to be a wrestler. But of all Stu's sons-in-law, it was Dynamite Kid's cousin, Davey Boy Smith, who would make the biggest splash in Stampede Wrestling.

Diana, the youngest of Stu's daughters, had her first big crush in 1978 when she was fifteen, and it wasn't on any of the boys in her class. None of them held a candle to the young Dynamite Kid. She was so infatuated with Dynamite when he first arrived in Calgary that during her school lunch hours she went to the apartment building he lived in to eat her lunch in the stairwell.[8]

Her crush was understandable. Dynamite Kid was a star, and as he became more ingrained in the territory and more confident in himself, he got to be quite dashing, in a villainous way. In those days, before he became too hardened and beat up, Dynamite was a good-looking lad, with his upturned Brit nose and youthful features, framed within flowing, shoulder-length brown hair. He was tougher and more athletic than any boy she knew, including her brothers.

Diana was blossoming into a striking young woman with golden hair, a pretty smile, and long, statuesque legs. She was the most athletic of the Hart girls. When she was a kid, she and Owen practised backflips in front of visiting wrestlers. Stu called her his little blond palomino. But despite her looks, she was never able to get the attention she craved from Dynamite.

And she forgot about him, when eighteen-year-old Davey Boy Smith strutted into town, in 1981. To the Hart girls, Davey Boy represented a kinder, gentler Dynamite Kid. Dynamite was wild and rough around the edges, with a mean streak. He liked to walk into a room and be feared. Davey was a softer, sweeter version of his cousin; a naive kid eager to please and get along with people.

Davey's upbringing might account for his more affable demeanour. Although he came from a similarly rough neighbourhood, his household wasn't as harsh as Dynamite's. His mother, Joyce, Dynamite's dad's sister, was a loving woman, and Davey's father, Sid, never struck his son. Like Dynamite, Davey didn't take to schooling but, unlike his cousin, he wasn't a troublemaker.

Bruce met Davey Boy back in 1977 when he first spotted Dynamite, and even then he could see the young athlete's potential. Davey, who wanted to be just like his cousin, was already training with Ted Betley. Bruce never forgot about Davey and he kept tabs on his progress. By 1981, Bruce and Dynamite cooked up the angle. They wanted to bring in Davey Boy as a babyface and throw him into a feud with Dynamite. Davey Boy would be the Abel to Dynamite's Cain. Two fast, good-looking British lads, high-flying and tough, fighting to the death on Stampede soil. Bad seed Dynamite, J.R. Foley's number one cretin, versus pure-hearted Davey, friend of the Harts. It would sell out the arenas for weeks.

When Davey got off the plane in Calgary, Bruce was pleased. The kid was as scrawny as Dynamite had been when he first arrived, but his wiry body was cut with muscle. He was six feet tall, 180 pounds and growing, with boy-next-door features. The first time Dynamite cut that pretty head open the women would scream.

Smith moved in with his cousin and Michelle, and right away fell victim to Dynamite's malicious pranks. It seemed that each bite of food he took was spiked with either Valium or Ex-Lax, causing diarrhea attacks that sometimes lasted up to three days and were so harsh that his stomach clenched in pain. Dynamite, meanwhile, cackled outside the bathroom door.[9] Pranks aside, if Davey was going to have a feud with Dynamite, he couldn't be living with his cousin. If the fans found out, they would know the whole grudge was phoney. He soon moved in with Bret.

Smitten Diana taped a picture of Davey Boy to the inside of her school binder and began daydreaming about him. He was friendlier than Dynamite and more receptive to her flirting. Dynamite warned his cousin to stay away from Stu's daughters, telling him he would be sent home if he crossed the line. Even so, the two began dating, going to movies together. In October 1981, they took one of Stu's Caddies up to Scotchman's Hill, overlooking Elbow River, to watch the sunset. There, they made love for the first time.

From then on, Diana was ringside for every one of her boyfriend's matches, cheering him on in his epic battles with Dynamite Kid and Gama Singh, a mid-heavyweight from India who was billed as being from Pakistan. Amazingly, Diana was not wise to the workings of the business. Gama remembers humiliating Davey in a match, knocking the Brit out with his deadly Cobra hold and shaving him bald. "Diana was in tears," he says.

Top: Leo Burke, from New Brunswick's Cormier wrestling family, was a Stampede Wrestling regular from the late 1960s to the mid-'80s, holding the North American Heavyweight title on a number of occasions.

Bottom: "The Great" Gama Singh was one of the most reviled mid-heavyweights of the 1980s. Here he locks his cobra clutch hold on Japanese star Hiroshi Hase.

Davey Boy hadn't been in Calgary long before Dynamite introduced him to steroids. The first time he took a shot, it was part of another Dynamite rib. Davey Boy was gullible. He lacked his cousin's street smarts, and Dynamite delighted in making fun of him. When Davey went to his cousin looking for steroids, Dynamite told him to pull down his pants and then injected a white liquid, claiming it was Winstrol V, a water-based steroid. While on the road the next day, Davey wondered why his fellow wrestlers were laughing at him. More strangely, why were they making cow noises at him? Davey could only laugh sheepishly when he found out that Dynamite had injected him with milk.[10] Davey was on the real stuff soon enough, though, and within a couple of years had bulked up in a way his cousin never could, boasting one of the most daunting physiques in the territory. Like many of the wrestlers who went on the juice, Davey began experiencing 'roid rage. This was obvious on December 2, 1983, when the wrestlers were returning from a week on the circuit. They were driving southbound on Calgary's Macleod Trail in a bus Stu had purchased for the tours when a Pontiac Trans Am full of drunken men ran a red light. Wayne Hart, who was at the wheel, slammed on the brakes to avoid a collision. The Trans-Am stopped too, and the drunks threw beer bottles at the bus, shouting obscenities and trying to pick a fight. That's when Davey Boy leapt from the bus and sprinted toward the punks in full attack mode.

The men, realizing they had picked the wrong rumble, jumped back into the Trans Am and sped away, the bus in hot pursuit. A few blocks later, the Trans Am ran into a police checkstop. As the bus pulled up, Davey Boy burst through the door and tore toward the car like a frenzied pit bull. He pushed past the shocked officers and thrust a beefy arm through the open passenger's window. As a cloud of marijuana wafted from the car, Davey Boy yanked one of the drunks out and was about to land a punch when a constable put his flashlight across the wrestler's throat in a bid to stop the wildman. Davey Boy flipped the officer over his back, catapulting the 180-pound man twenty feet through the air.[11] Several other officers jumped Davey and subdued him as the drunks sped away, no doubt scared sober.

Stu was forced to hire a lawyer to keep one of his top stars out of jail. At first, Keith says, Stu was going to let Davey face the judge on his own. "Diana was Stu's little crown jewel, and Davey was paying too much attention," Keith says. "At first, my dad was thinking he'd either go to jail or screw off back to England and the problem would be solved. But Diana said if Davey was going back to England, she was going to go with him. Stu thought, 'Oh, oh. We'd better get him a good lawyer.'" Ultimately, Davey Boy paid a $500 fine and the Calgary media treated the case as a joke.

Davey and Diana set a wedding date of October 7, 1984. By this time, the ranks of the Hart mafia were swelling to burst. Ellie had given birth to three daughters. Georgia also had three children, with another on the way. Bret and Julie too had started a family, as had Dynamite and Michelle. Keith and Bruce were also married and having children.

On his off-time, when he wasn't booking and wrestling for Stampede Wrestling, Bruce substitute taught at a junior high, where he had met a pretty student named Andrea Redding. Later, when Bruce was no longer teaching at the school, he ran into Andrea again when she started coming to the wrestling matches. The Hart family was horrified when he began a relationship with the teenager. According to Keith, Stu and Helen were worried that the liaison might cause a scandal that could hurt Stampede Wrestling. The worrying was kicked up one hell of a notch when Andrea announced in early 1983 that she was pregnant. The couple married in June of that year. Andrea was sixteen, Bruce thirty-three.

Ross Hart defends his brother. "All of us were aware of the age difference, but they seemed to really love each other, and their marriage was quite sound.... We didn't publicize it ... but it wasn't any sort of scandal."

The wedding of Davey Boy Smith and Diana Hart, held at Hart House, did attract a lot of attention, which in this case the family welcomed. The *Calgary Sun* published a full-page spread on the "fairytale" wedding between the "British-born Hercules" and the gorgeous Hart daughter, who had posed as a Sunshine Girl the previous year. The report described giant men wearing ill-fitting suits; stoic Stu walking his teary-eyed daughter up the aisle; Davey Boy choking with emotion as he recited his vows; jolly Jim Neidhart making a sentimental toast to the bride and groom; and the whole place erupting into a party as Prince's "Let's Go Crazy" blared from massive speakers. [12]

Frenzied photographers from Japan snapped photos for the papers back home. Davey Boy, Bret, and Dynamite had been wrestling on Japanese tours for years and were huge stars in the country. Indeed, Dynamite's matches with a masked Japanese wrestler named Tiger Mask set a new standard for wrestling excellence in the junior heavyweight division. Diana recalls one of the Japanese paparazzi getting too close for Dynamite's liking. With a prime-rib bone in one hand and a beer in the other, he turned on the media man and snarled, "That's it, yard dog, I've 'ad enough of you. Now eff-off." [13]

Behind the scenes, the fairytale was not off to the wonderful start it appeared to be. Three weeks before the wedding, Davey Boy had come to Diana in tears, admitting to an ongoing dalliance with a ring rat in Edmonton who now claimed to be pregnant with his child. However, she had been with several wrestlers and there was a good chance the baby wasn't his. Diana was inconsolable, but she loved Davey, and he loved her. Fearing he was going to lose her, he was heaving with sobs. She accepted his promise that he would never cheat again and, for years, she didn't breathe a word of the incident to anyone. It ate her up inside, though, and she lost fifteen pounds in the week leading up to the wedding.[14]

In the assessment of most insiders, Davey Boy was a good man with a kind heart, but he had a tragic flaw. "He wasn't too smart and was easily misled," Keith Hart says. "He loved being one of the boys. He would die for the boys.... And he didn't think much about consequences."

Alison loved her brother-in-law dearly but agrees with Keith: "The thing about Davey was he always followed the group. He had to be the biggest and the best. But if the whole group was going to throw tomatoes, Davey was going to throw them the furthest. If the crowd was going to riot and pulverize you, he'd go along with that, too. He followed the pack."

Chapter twelve

Let the Good Times Roll

"J.R. Foley is like a father to me, Mr. Whalen," crowed Dynamite Kid in Stampede Wrestling interviews, his arm draped over his crooked manager's shoulder. It was another angle that closely mirrored reality. At first, Dynamite and J.R. Foley were simply drawn to one another as two Brits trying to make it, surrounded by Canucks on the frozen prairies. Then they became hardcore drinking buddies. Eventually, the connection between the two men became heartfelt. "They were almost like clones of one another," says Bret Hart. "It was the old beat-up bully and the young man on his way to being a beat-up bully."

When Foley came to Canada, he brought his wife and teenage daughter. After a while, he began to think of Dynamite as a son. It turned out to be as much a curse for old J.R. as it was a blessing. The road stories of Dynamite's ribs on Foley are as endless as they are deranged. Wrestler Bad News Allen remembers sitting next to Foley in the van on one road trip. Being drunk and goofy, J.R. was wearing a paper baker's hat. "Foley kept saying, 'Jesus Christ, it's hot in here,'" recalls Allen. "I took a look at him and damn! Dynamite had set his hat on fire. I said 'Man, Tommy, you're gonna kill this guy. What's wrong with you?'"

Alison Hart's ex-husband Ben Bassarab recalls Dynamite at one Saskatoon hotel filling J.R.'s toilet with lighter fluid, knowing that Foley liked to smoke a cigarette on the can. When Foley threw the smouldering butt between his legs into the toilet bowl, the resulting flash singed his privates.

A muscular Dynamite Kid poses while J.R. Foley mugs for the camera, looking like a cross between Hitler and a vagabond.

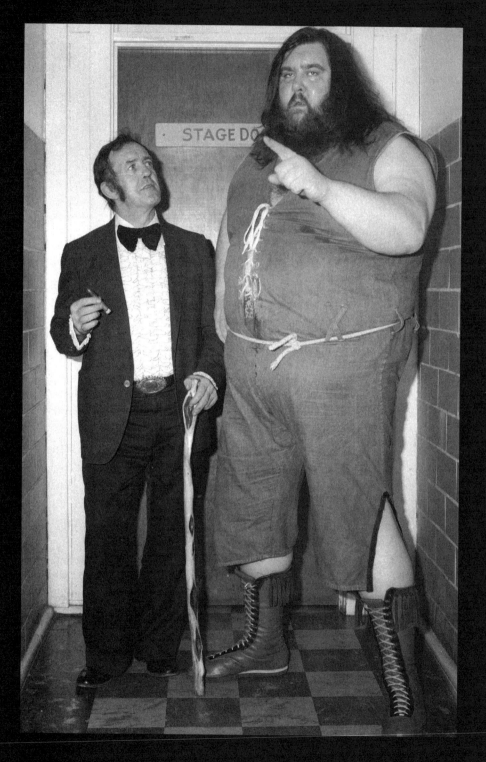

J.R. Foley looks up at his weapon against the Harts, the seven-foot, 685-pound Brit, The Loch Ness Monster.

On another Saskatoon stop, the "millionaire manager" arrived in town soused to the gills. His pockets empty, he couldn't afford a room even at the city's dumpiest hotel, where the carpets reeked of piss, tobacco, beer, and vomit. Dynamite and Bruce snuck the old grappler into their room by way of the fire escape and procured him a cot to pass out on.

"One night, we folded the cot up with him in it and stuck him in the elevator," says Bruce, relishing thoughts of the good ol' days. "We wheeled the old fart into the lobby. He woke up the next morning not even sure where he was, with two or three drunks staring at him."

"What the fook'er you lookin' at?" slurred Foley as he stumbled back to the room in his baggie underwear, scratching his balls and rubbing his beer gut.*

Foley's wife, Vera Lynn, resented the wrestling business, blaming the sport for leading her husband down such a pathetic path. She was also bitter that, as booker, Bruce transformed Foley, a respected wrestler in England, into the clownish J.R. character. "[The angle] rejuvenated an old guy who was washed up, and it made him into a bit of a celebrity," Keith says. "But I'm sure it was hard for Vera to look at it that way."

Foley didn't need Dynamite and Bruce to humiliate him, though. He did a fine job of it himself. Keith recalls the wrestlers sleeping on the bus one night on the way back to Calgary while referee Sandy Scott drove. "Piss call, Sandy," croaked J.R. from the back of the bus. The referee was slowing down by the side of the road when a woozy Foley opened the door and stepped off, tumbling into the ditch. Scott slammed on the brakes. "We all wake up and J.R.'s crawling back into the bus," Keith says. "He's pissed all over himself and he's dirty from the ditch. He sticks his head in the door and goes, 'What th' fook'r'ya doin', Sandy?'" Once again, the crew had big laughs at Foley's expense.

But the manager thrived on those laughs. He lived to party on the road trips. "There would be twelve guys in the van, [all these] monsters," Michelle Billington says, "and little [Dynamite] would go, 'Sing "On Top of Old Smokey," Johnny!' So he'd sing, and they'd be spraying shaving cream on top of his head, putting their smokes out in it. John was so drunk, he didn't know what was going on. When they got to Calgary, they'd walk him to his front door and ring the doorbell. They wanted to see [Vera's reaction]. He'd

---

*Saskatoon often brought out the worst in the wrestlers. The crowds were sparse because the arena was located on the seedy downtown strip, where parents didn't like their kids hanging out. To make matters worse, the building was unnaturally cold. "You'd be wrestling and steam would rise up off your back," Bruce recalls. "Guys would be huddled together in the dressing room.... King Kurtis used to refer to Saskatoon as 'the bitter end.'"

be trying to act sober, and she'd be saying, 'Don't drink anymore, John, or I'm leaving you!'"

It was male bonding at its most twisted but, through it all, J.R. and Dynamite had a real love for one another. Foley visited Dynamite at home, where the two would dive into the bottle. Once, Foley requested a haircut and Dynamite only too gleefully pulled out the electric razor. The cut was a horror, Foley's hair reduced to scattered clumps. "Looks fookin' great, Tommy," he said. "I knew ye' could do it." By that night's end, the fearsome Dynamite Kid was sitting on his surrogate dad's lap as J.R. drunkenly crooned the tune "Danny Boy." It was disturbing and touching all at once.

"I don't think Foley would've lived as long as he did if he wasn't around Dynamite," says Bad News Allen. "Just being around Dynamite, drinking and doing ribs. He really loved Tommy."

J.R.'s army was the most inspired concept of Stampede Wrestling's Dynamite Age. Instead of having one or two cretins wreaking havoc on the territory, there was an army of them under the comical tyrant J.R. Foley, locked in a mock epic struggle with the Hart dynasty. The ongoing saga gave Stampede Wrestling a fun flavour all its own. A number of J.R.'s goons are unforgettable.

Take "No Class" Bobby Bass, one of the best examples of Ed Whalen's influence in the territory. Dennis Baldock from Dartmouth, Nova Scotia, had long been wrestling under the Bobby Bass moniker when he came to Stampede Wrestling in 1980. Back then, the Maritimer was selling himself as a Texas outlaw. But Bass's name really took off the night he threw a midget so high into the air that the guy dinged the lamp hanging above the ring. Whalen was appalled and dubbed the heel "No Class" Bobby Bass. The name caught on and soon whole arenas were chanting it, united in their loathing of the midget-tosser.

Then there was bleach-blond Brit "Exotic" Adrian Street, who brought Gorgeous George's effeminate routine into the 1980s with a shock-rock blast. Street, all of five-foot-three, took the Gorgeous One's robes and rouge to the next level by wearing pigtails, pink boots, and a full-on makeup job that was part Alice Cooper and part transvestite. He frequently disoriented his opponents by planting a kiss on their lips. As the wrestlers jumped about, wiping their mouths in horror, Street would land some sort of dirty blow and win the match. Little boys in the audience could be heard chanting, "Fag-got! Fag-got!" until hoarse.

Stu wasn't comfortable with Street's gimmick, and he lasted in the territory only a month or so, in 1981. But his interviews remain hilarious. "My opponent had the audacity to cast aspersions on my manhood," Street seethes in true drama-queen fashion. "I'm a man! A real man! You Hart brothers, I'm going to show you what a man can do!"

Another bizarre character was Judas Rosenbloom, a crooked black pimp straight out of a blaxploitation flick. The "mind-bending paradox," as Bruce Hart cooked it up, was the Jewish name, black Jewish pimps being rare in the wrestling world – or any world for that matter.

"Champagne" Gerry Morrow from Martinique was a Stampede Wrestling mainstay for the better part of two decades starting in 1975. Morrow made a big splash with the Cuban Assassin as the Cuban Commandos. He called himself "Champagne" Gerry to allude to all the partying and womanizing he did. Whalen scoffed at such claims, referring to Morrow as "Rot Gut" Gerry.

No one who laid eyes on the 685-pound, nearly seven-foot behemoth known as the Loch Ness Monster would ever forget the sight. While he was not as charismatic or as skilled as Andre the Giant, Loch Ness was nevertheless a big attraction. People loved to watch him squash his opponents with his ring-rumbling body splashes. Loch Ness made an impression on his fellow wrestlers, too. "He was a big, stinky man," remembers Ben Bassarab. "He was so big he couldn't use a toilet in the hotels. He'd piss and shit in the tub and then try to make us rookies clean it up. I said, 'Nah, I ain't doing that.'"

One of the great tag teams of the period was "The Masters of Disaster," Duke Myers and Kerry Brown. Tattooed, bald, and beer-bellied, Myers, from Portland, Oregon, looked like a vicious sailor gone AWOL. He was notorious for the black glove he wore to the ring for each match, supposedly as a wrist brace on doctor's orders. The glove was loaded with a piece of lead, which helped him level many a babyface. Somehow, the referees never caught on to his trick.

Brown, from Winnipeg, was the nephew of grappling vet Bulldog Bob Brown, who also worked for Stu over the years. For a big man – Brown's rotund physique made Myers look trim – Kerry took some amazing bumps, constantly careening over the top ropes and into the audience. He also portrayed the smart-ass villain role with a humorous flair. "Bruce Hart, I saw you at the Eighth Avenue Mall at one of those burger stands, and you were standing on a crate because you could not see over the counter," he once lied in an interview. "You want a title match? You've got to be kidding."

But few bad guys had a way with words like Tennessee's Roy Wayne Ferris, who came to the territory in 1982 as a slick, sleazy Southern redneck by the name of Honky Tonk Wayne. Ferris developed the character – based on

Schneider, the oily janitor with the pencil-thin moustache on TV sitcom *One Day at a Time* – while wrestling in Florida. In Calgary, Wayne started slicking back his hair and wearing costume jewellery to the ring. He even wore an Elvis Presley jumpsuit a Florida fan had given him. Gradually, his character morphed into that of a sleazy Elvis impersonator. That transformation was complete in the late 1980s, when Vince McMahon recruited Wayne into the WWF as hated Elvis-wannabe Honky Tonk Man.

Wayne's physical skills in the ring were average at best, but on the microphone he was one of the greats, selling himself as an arrogant, fast-talking hillbilly with moonshine in his veins, a motor in his mouth, and a cheating heart. By the time he got to the WWF, he had the shtick down pat and, for a time, it made him a star.

"Dr. D" David Shults, the D standing for death, came to Stampede Wrestling in 1980 as another of Foley's minions. Hailing from Memphis, the six-foot-four, 270-pound grappler, a former solider in the U.S. Army, quickly distinguished himself as a fierce brawler and the most charismatic heel in the territory at the time.

Shults, who had a goatee and a shock of tightly curled blond hair, was also a master on the microphone, towering over Ed Whalen and making boastful proclamations in a style that was equal parts Wolfman Jack and Muhammad Ali. "Sheriff Shults has come to town, baby!" he'd rave. "The rich girl's lover and the poor girl's dream! Dr. D! King David! The Messiah of the Mat!" The fans loved to hate him and later, when he joined the good guys, they cheered him wildly.

David Shults was one of the all-time great Stampede Wrestling characters. But behind the scenes, many claim, Shults was not all that different from his Dr. D character. Laurie Mills, a member of the Calgary Boxing and Wrestling Commission, was leery of the Southern wrestler: "You never knew what he was going to do. He had his own ideas, and he could be hard to handle…. I never knew how much of [his persona] was made up, because he was a showman. But he was very nasty."

Certainly, Shults was a prickly individual who liked to intimidate people, his fellow wrestlers included. Some wrestlers were even scared to step in the ring with him because if they did something he didn't like, even accidentally, he'd deal with them harshly. As Ross says, "he was a bomb waiting to explode." "He had a temper and he could back it up, too," says Shults's friend Leo Burke, who considers his fights and tag matches with Dr. D among the best work of his career. "He was the kind of guy that [if he came after you,] you'd have to kill him to make him stop."

Dynamite recalls a match in which he briefly ran afoul of Shults after accidentally catching the Southern wrestler with a knee to the jaw. Shults stormed toward him in the dressing room: "Tahmmy, if you wanna play them kind of fuckin' games, I'll play them right back." Dynamite stood his ground. "Look, accidents do happen, Dave. What's the crack here? You get a little fucking love tap and you're upset over that? A man of your size?" Shults seemed surprised that Dynamite had stood up to him and said, "Tahmmy, we're friends. You're right. Anybody can make a mistake."[1]

Such a turn of events was typical for Shults, says Bad News Allen. "He was a gutless bully. If he knew he could beat someone, he'd go after them, but if he knew somebody could stand up to him, he would back down."

Shults was a loner. He refused to do the weekly circuit in Stu's beat-up vans and buses. Instead, he took his own cars, a Lincoln Continental and a black Ford LTD he called Midnight. He drove night and day. He was choosy as to who could ride with him. Leo Burke and the Cuban Assassin were among the chosen few. Bruce Hart was most certainly not.

In one match, when Shults was in the ring against Bruce, the Southerner felt Bruce tagged him with a couple of legitimate punches. In retaliation, Shults grabbed Bruce by his blond locks, threw him against the ropes, and smashed him square in the face. "He blew up Bruce's eye good." Keith says. "I thought he broke the socket. He didn't knock him out, but he sure as hell hurt him." Bruce angrily confronted Shults back in the dressing room. He never received much support over the incident from either his brothers or father. Honky Tonk claims Stu joked about the punch. Bret thinks his brother had it coming for being careless in the ring and hurting his opponent. "Bruce was used to everybody taking it because he was the promoter's kid, but Shults just drilled him," Bret says. "Shults was a hot-headed guy. One day he would be in a great mood, and the next day he would be bitchy and sour. But he was a great character and a hard worker. I liked him.... He had a short fuse ... but if you treated him professionally and dealt with him in a straight-up manner, he was pretty agreeable."

Shults achieved fame in 1984 when his friend Hulk Hogan helped get him booked in the WWF, where the two men wrestled against one another. But Shults's run in the big time was short-lived. On December 28, 1984, ABC-TV's news program 20/20 was shooting an exposé on pro wrestling and conducting interviews in the Madison Square Garden dressing room. Reporter John Stossel approached Dr. D and suggested that wrestling was phoney. "You think this is fake?" barked Shults, smacking the reporter in the ear and knocking him to his knees. The footage aired across North America. Stossel collected U.S.$425,000 in an out-of-court settlement with Titan Sports.[2]

Shults was finally cut loose in the lead up to the first WrestleMania, held March 31, 1985, when he tried to attack the actor Mr. T in an unscripted incident during a wwf show in Los Angeles.[3] Mr. T was part of the wrestling extravaganza's main event and, according to Hulk Hogan, Shults was angry he was not part of the angle.[4]

Shults wrestled for a few years after that incident, even returning to Stampede Wrestling for a while in 1986, when he nearly gave Jim Davies, a *Calgary Sun* columnist and ringside announcer, a heart attack. Davies had written a piece about the Stossel incident, which Shults didn't appreciate. He pinned Davies against the wall in the dressing room, screaming, "Are you trying to make a name for yourself at my expense?"[5]

By the late 1980s, Shults had retired from wrestling, reportedly finding work as a bounty hunter. I established contact with the reclusive ex-wrestler through his friend Bob Bryla, who sits on the screening board of the Professional Wrestling Hall of Fame in Schenectady, New York.

Bryla explained Shults is intensely private, not wanting anybody to know even where he lives, and he didn't think the wrestler would do an interview. After much back and forth, Bryla sent me an e-mail, passing on a message, supposedly from Dr. D: "Bob, tell Heath if he puts all the questions about me in true/false form, I will look at them. Let him know I am on a mission over in the Middle East area and it is top secret. Don't tell him who, what, where, or when."

The questions were sent off, and a few days later, the answers arrived. Shults answered "true" to punching out Bruce, being a loner, and working as a bounty hunter. He answered "false" to the suggestion that he was a hot-tempered sort who frightened his fellow wrestlers and tried to attack Mr. T. He also added a question of his own to the list: "There are many lies about the great DOCTOR D. True." In a parting message, Shults called himself "the greatest pro wrestler of all time" and claimed that lesser wrestlers like to spread lies about him out of envy. "Be very careful of what you hear and what you read," he warned.

Was the message really from him? It was certainly true to the character I had pieced together from so many sources. Even Dr. D's e-mails are intimidating.

With such a volatile mix of characters in the territory, not to mention the emergence of steroids in the business, it's no surprise that misadventures came fast and furious. After one particular evening of booze-fuelled mayhem in the early 1980s, the party carried on well after last call, ending up at the duplex where Dynamite and Wayne Hart lived. Duke Myers, who at the time rented one side of the property with his wife and children, was in on the revelry. Duke was a bad drunk. On this night, he lit a cigarette, flicking his match in Dynamite's face. The Kid swore at him, and Duke grabbed a baseball bat sitting by the door. "You wanna go, Tommy?" he screamed, swinging his club like a caveman.

"It was frightening," says Michelle Billington. "Nobody else did anything, but Tom stood up to him.... Duke was looking down on Tom, but if you were there, Tom looked bigger than Duke Myers, and Duke backed down. He was so fucked up ... but he still knew Tom could kick his ass." Realizing he was about to go toe to toe with Dynamite brought Myers to his senses, Michelle says. "[I think he thought,] 'What am I doing, calling on Dynamite? I won't have any teeth left.' He backed down and apologized."

As always, there were the road trips from hell. Perhaps the worst was a near fatal crash that occurred one winter night in early 1982 as Bruce Hart raced down the glare-ice highway in his father's brand new Cadillac Seville, trying to make a show in Lethbridge. Jim Neidhart was sucking back beers in the passenger's seat, while Mr. Hito, Gerry Morrow, and a road hand reclined in the back. Suddenly, a semi-trailer heading toward them turned into a gas station, veering into the wrestlers' path. Bruce pumped the brakes but the car skidded on the ice. Its hood folded like a squeezebox as the car slid into the semi's back tires. If the car had hit the side of the semi straight-on, the wrestlers would have been decapitated.

Bruce Hart sat for a moment, trembling. He let go his death grip on the steering wheel, realizing the steering column had broken off in his hands. In shock, he stepped out of the car into the icy night. But it wasn't the chill that jolted him back into reality; it was the third vehicle, a truck that careered past him, almost mowing him down. The truck collided into the same semi-trailer Bruce had hit.

The rest of the stunned wrestlers crawled from the car. They had taken a brutal beating inside the vehicle. Morrow had hurt his back and separated his shoulder. Hito, whose face was badly torn up, had broken his wrist and hip and dislocated his knee. But it was Neidhart who had been injured the worst. He stumbled toward the gas station bathroom, blood dripping onto his jacket, to inspect the damage. When he looked in the mirror, he shrieked. His nose was hanging by a thread of skin. He required plastic surgery, and about ninety stitches, to reattach it.

Despite such awful scenes, Bruce was at the top of his game in the early 1980s. As a creative force, he was a bolt of lightning, bringing fresh, entertaining concepts to the business. Regardless of what Bruce's detractors may say, he was taking Stampede Wrestling in a bold, influential direction that yielded some of the promotion's most unforgettable moments.

It wasn't only the way he and his spectacular recruits brought the mid-heavyweight division to main event status. Bruce was among the first North American bookers to use ring entrance music in a significant way, with major stars coming to the ring as signature tunes blared from the speakers. By the mid-1980s, this was a staple of WWF events. Today, Vince McMahon commissions rock and hip-hop artists to write theme songs for his stars. In the early '80s, Dynamite Kid arrogantly strutted down the aisle to the regal strains of British composer Edward Elgar's "Pomp and Circumstance." The Cuban Assassin made his entrance to "The Lonely Bull" by Herb Alpert and the Tijuana Brass. Heartthrobs Davey Boy Smith and Bruce Hart came out to Survivor's "Eye of the Tiger" and The Eagles' "Heartache Tonight" respectively, while David Shults's theme was the Mac Davis country hit "It's Hard to Be Humble," a perfect testament to his egomania.

A fine idea that never caught on in a big way was the penalty card system, inspired by German wrestling events. Each time a wrestler broke the rules, he was given a yellow card. A grappler was allowed two yellow cards in a match – which gave the heels two opportunities for cheating. On the third offence, a red card was issued, disqualifying the cheater. On major offences, the referee could hand out black cards, which meant a wrestler was suspended without pay from the territory.

This set the stage for Bruce's next innovation, the heel referee, the great abuser of power in the wrestling ring. The inept referee had long been a staple of the game and there had been angles involving corrupt referees in the past, but Bruce took the idea to a new level, where the evil referee became an integral part of the main event.*

Stampede Wrestling's ultimate referee-gone-bad was the lanky Scotsman, Sandy Scott. Week after week, Scott tormented the Harts, his bad decisions causing them to lose match after match. He always favoured J.R. Foley's army, and before long it became clear he was being paid off by the millionaire manager.

The Scott plot culminated in late 1980 when Scott levied an unfair suspension on Bruce. As the plot thickened, Bruce took the matter to officials of the

---

*The idea hit the world stage during the 1980s with dirty WWF officials such as Danny Davis, who conspired with the bad guys. The corrupt official angle was taken even farther in the 1990s when Vince McMahon became part of the storyline as the evil promoter, constantly trying to screw over fan favourites, including Stone Cold Steve Austin.

Top: Southern baddie "Dr. D" David Shults, one of the most vicious brawlers of the early 1980s, hammers a bloodied Bobby Burke to the mat.

Bottom: Looking like a crazed Fidel Castro, the Cuban Assassin was the ultimate Cold War villain. Here he is about to land a knee on some hapless opponent in the late 1970s. The referee is nineteen-year-old Bret Hart.

National Wrestling Alliance, who reinstated him. In a rage, Sandy attacked Bruce, pummelling the Hart boy with a cane, which Scott then gouged into the wrestler's windpipe. This led to a grudge match between the two on Boxing Day, which sold out the Pavilion that bitterly cold night.

But despite the good business this angle generated, Bruce got only resistance from his father. "My dad hated it," says Ross. "He thought [a heel referee] was taking the focus away from the villain wrestlers. But it made us money. People were packing the arenas every night to see Sandy Scott get killed. Conservative types like [photographer] Bob Leonard and [Edmonton co-promoter] Mike Bulat were saying, 'Stu, he's going to kill the promotion.' But people kept coming. People could really identify with the idea of the corrupt authority figure."

Ed Whalen was not a fan of Scott's either. As part of a storyline, Scott slapped Bruce in the face, Bruce supposedly powerless to defend himself lest he be suspended again. This riled up Whalen, who in turn slapped Scott. Scott grabbed Whalen by the throat and hissed, "Don't you fucking touch me, Whalen!" Whalen stormed off, promising that Scott would be fired. Once he had time to cool off, Whalen admitted he had crossed the line, but he held a grudge against Scott and began cutting the referee off in interviews. "Sometimes [Whalen] abused his power," Ross says.

Behind the scenes, Scott was the most ruthless womanizer on the road. "He was pretty good with the stick," Ross says. "He must have had a hundred women out there. He'd claim one in every town. Some of them went on to be wives and girlfriends of other wrestlers. He could be very smooth and elegant, really polite and charming." One of Scott's frequent conquests was an overweight ring rat in her fifties from Montana. Her name was Hazel, but the boys dubbed her "The White-Haired Tornado." She showed up at the matches when Stampede Wrestling came to town and pleasured the wrestlers in the dressing room. Sometimes her sad-sack husband came to the arena with her. Ross always thought the old guy knew what was going on but played dumb to save face.

Ross says he never understood the appeal of the White Tornado, who he estimates weighed around 225 pounds. Even so, she never had trouble collecting notches on her bedpost. Sometimes she accompanied the wrestlers on road trips, performing fellatio on the driver. "We'd pass by [on the highway] and you'd see her head pop up," Ross says. "The wrestler would be kind of embarrassed, but I guess it was hard for some of them to resist. Sandy [Scott] was serviced by her, too, but he was never shy about it. He didn't give a shit what anybody thought."

One evening, Dynamite played his Ex-Lax prank on the White Tornado, slipping an overdose of the laxative into the groupie's drink. She was sick for days. Not long afterward, when Scott was Ex-Laxed, he assumed Dynamite had done it. For days, Scott was overcome by diarrhea attacks and couldn't work, which angered Stu. Stu reprimanded Dynamite, who swore his innocence. Once Scott had recovered, he reported for work, showing up at a Mohawk gas station on Calgary's Edmonton Trail that had long been the weekly meeting place for the wrestlers to catch their rides and head out on the road. Scott was sitting in the van waiting to embark on the week's trek when Dynamite, still fuming at the accusation made against him and seeking revenge, punched him in the face. Scott jumped out of the van, announced he was quitting, and went to get his bag from the back of the van. It was gone. Dynamite had thrown it into a tree.

"Sandy was emotionally and physically wounded and he didn't work for another two weeks," Ross says. "Bruce patched it up, and Sandy did come back, but he was never the same after that. Tom had been a good friend of his, and to be attacked like that by him in front of all the boys.... He was pretty upset."

Ultimately, it was Scott's womanizing that did him in. He had been sleeping with a fifteen year old, Ross says, and the girl's mother was furious when she found out. She called the immigration board on Stampede's dirty referee. As luck would have it, Scott had allowed his visa to expire. He needed to leave the country – fast – and the next thing anybody knew, he was gone. The Harts never heard from their crooked official again.

Chapter thirteen

A Pop Culture Stampede

"We love stampede wrestling, We Love Stampede Wrestling," chimed the chorus of the happy Reggae tune, which Stu Hart was told was a hit song in Antigua. As far-fetched as it may sound, *Stampede Wrestling* was being broadcast in the Caribbean in the early 1980s, and the low-budget Western Canadian show had become a sensation in Antigua. It was such a hit that the prime minister of Antigua and Barbuda, as well as a senator and that country's minister of justice, paid Hart House an unexpected visit in 1982.

It was not the first visit Stu had received from Stampede Wrestling fans in faraway lands. At another point in the early 1980s, Hart House had been descended on by a busload of Swahili-speaking Kenyan missionaries who wanted to meet the Hart family.[1] But this time it was different. These Antiguan dignitaries had a business proposition. They wanted Stu to send his best talent, Ed Whalen included, to their country to put on a show. They offered to pay for the wrestlers' flights and all their expenses, the gate to be split with Stu. They played the Hart patriarch a tape of the hit song to impress upon him how popular Stampede Wrestling was in their country.[2] An Antiguan named Charles Buffong, who wrestled for Stu at the time, confirmed that his relatives watched the TV program and loved it: on Monday nights, when the show aired, the streets were empty because everybody was inside watching wrestling.

Reports vary as to whether Stu had been sending tapes of the show to the

The heels ride in the 1979 Stampede parade. At the far left is Sylvester Ritter, who would go on to become the famed Junkyard Dog in the WWF. Behind Ritter is Hercules Ayala, and Dynamite Kid is perched beside him. J.R. Foley sits in the front seat. The other man and the woman are unidentified.

174

Caribbean or if the tapes were bootlegs. Since the early 1970s, pirated copies of *Stampede Wrestling* had seeped into as many as thirty countries, many of them developing nations looking for free programming to broadcast from their ramshackle TV stations. Most of the time, the Harts knew where the show was being seen only once reports drifted back to them. Stu never saw a dime from any of it and never sued to rectify the matter. "My dad was fairly pragmatic about things," Keith says. "Maybe if he thought he had half a chance at collecting some of the dues, he would have."

As Laurie Mills, former chairman of the Calgary Boxing and Wrestling Commission, aptly puts it, "Pro wrestling is based on smoke and mirrors and bullshit," and often, as the stories make the rounds, facts get mixed up with fiction. No one can say with any certainty where and when the show aired, but without a doubt, it had wings and it flew around the world.

In a March 1981 wrestling program, Stu writes that *Stampede Wrestling* had been voted the most popular TV sports show in Saudi Arabia. It also had a devoted following in West Germany, Singapore, Bangkok, Nigeria, Tanzania, and Uganda. Ed Whalen, his wife Nomi says, received a letter in the 1970s from Idi Amin, the Ugandan dictator. Amin was such a *Stampede Wrestling* fan that he wanted to bring the show to his country and he invited the announcer to be a guest in his home. While Ed and Nomi were avid travellers, they "politely declined" the invitation, Nomi says.

Either way, Ed Whalen took great pleasure in telling people how recognized he was around the world as the host of Stampede Wrestling. "It's like the old cowboy ditty, 'I've Been Everywhere,'" Whalen wrote in the *Calgary Sun*. "I have been everywhere – like Europe, Japan, Australia, Singapore, the jungles of North Africa ... the list goes on and on. In places like Rome and Beijing, there's old Eddie, jabbering away in English, with subtitles at the bottom of the screen."[3]

Kevin Newans, a long-time sports director at Calgary's CFCN-TV, told the *Calgary Herald* he watched Stampede Wrestling in Seoul, Korea, while covering the 1988 Olympics. "I woke up at three in the morning ... flicked on the TV, and, believe it or not, there's Ed Whalen calling Stampede Wrestling.... I told our crew, if you've got insomnia or whatever, Eddie's on all night ... because they'd replay those shows over and over."[4]

Keith Hart got a taste of Stampede's global popularity in the most unexpected of places. In the 1970s, he and Bruce toured New Zealand, where they wrestled a pair of rough hometown boys, Butch Miller and Luke Williams. Butch and Luke had been wrestling for Stu off and on since the mid-'60s as a crazed team called The Kiwis. In Western Canada, they were cast as villains, but in their native country they were loved, and when Bruce and Keith arrived to wrestle them, the tables were turned. The Harts wrestled as villains, and, in the great heel tradition, they became a pair of no-good cheaters. Keith was shocked when an old woman in the front row chastised him for his conduct. "Your father and Ed Whalen wouldn't like this a bit," she said scoldingly. Keith later learned that *Stampede Wrestling* had been airing in that country.*

The popularity of Stampede Wrestling knew no bounds. Keith's doctor was travelling on a riverboat through Malaysia when one of the tour guides played a videotape of *Stampede Wrestling*. When the doctor told the Malaysians he knew the Hart family, they were incredulous and treated him like a dignitary for his connection to such greatness.

When the great Muhammad Ali passed through Calgary in 1976 for a promotional training tour – as he readied himself for his boxer versus wrestler match in Tokyo with Japanese star Antonio Inoki – the icon requested a meeting with Stu. Ali, always a wrestling fan, had heard the legends and wanted to meet the man himself. When they finally came face to face in the dressing room of the Corral, they engaged in a friendly verbal sparring match about the merits of their respective sports. They even got into a bit of playful shoving, pretending to go toe to toe for the cameras.

Without a doubt, when Stu decided to make the trek to Antigua with his stars in tow in the summer of 1982, his Western Canadian promotion had become a global phenomenon. The NHL's Calgary Flames was not quite two years old, and the Winter Olympics were six years away. Stampede Wrestling, in its many incarnations, had lasted more than three decades. Along with the Calgary Stampede, of which wrestling was a popular component, Stampede Wrestling had put Calgary on the international map.

Stampede-mania. That's the word that best describes exactly what the cast of Stampede Wrestling experienced when they got off the plane in Antigua that July.

In the days before "Hulkamania" exploded around the world, this was a reception no pro wrestler expected. Certainly not those on a Canuck prairie circuit. Whalen remembered the moment as surreal. A band played in greeting as thousands of screaming fans jammed the runways, smiling and waving at the stars.[5] As the wrestlers made their way to the arrivals area, they decided to give the buzzing crowd an impromptu show. The heels attacked

*Butch and Luke would go on to wrestle for the WWF in the 1980s as the clownish Sheepherders.

the babyfaces, and members of the frenzied crowd tried to get in on the action. The Antiguan prime minister had to dodge flying objects hurled at the heels as the police intervened.[6]

The shows, two held in Antigua and one in Guadeloupe, an island country just to the south, were a smash success, with twenty-thousand people showing up at the stadium on the first night. The wrestlers, who were treated like royalty, thought they had found heaven on earth. They ordered steak and caviar back at the hotel, and J.R. Foley drank several bottles of vintage wine. Nomi Whalen says the Antiguans even offered Ed a prostitute for the night, a perk he graciously declined.

But the Antiguan adventure was not without its problems. Smith's wife was from nearby Puerto Rico, so Stu took a chance on his often irresponsible eldest son and put him in charge of the show. If he was ever going to give Smith a chance to prove himself, this seemed like the time and the place to do so. But immediately after the shows, Ross Hart says the U.S.$25,000 profit collected went missing. The wrestlers were furious when they found out there was no money for them, Dynamite blaming it on Smith and demanding his head. Smith later told the family he took the money with him when he paid a visit to Puerto Rico. There, he gave it to a fellow wrestler for safekeeping, worried he would be robbed on the island. That wrestler took the money and went into hiding, claiming that Stu shortchanged him in the past and so owed him. The police were called and the wrestler was charged with theft, according to Ross. Smith recovered some of the money, but Stu wound up paying many of the boys out of his own pocket.

Stampede Wrestling was so popular in Antigua that the wrestlers were flown in for another show in October of that same year. This time, sixty-seven-year-old Stu came along. Clearly, the ship could not run without its captain.

Stampede Wrestling put Calgary on the international map, and the city was nothing short of revered in the world wrestling community. Letters poured in weekly from every corner of the globe – including Japan, Australia, Europe, and the United States – from wannabe grapplers hoping to work for Stu, who had developed a reputation as a promoter who would give young unknowns the chance to prove themselves. "My real ambition in wrestling is to work a territory such as Stampede full time," wrote a young New Yorker named Mick Foley in 1987. Though Foley never did work for Stu, he went on to be one of the WWF's biggest stars in the 1990s, notorious for his insane stunts, his ability to absorb punishment, and his fearlessness: the very style Stampede Wrestling helped birth.

Stampede was not a territory where wrestlers came to get rich or world famous, and there were no free rides – you either had to be tough or bursting with charisma – but if you could make it there, you had a leg up on grapplers from other territories. For serious students of the game, completing a tour of duty in Stampede was a badge of honour. You had paid dues that many a man could not pay.

"I had a T-shirt made up after my first run [in Stampede] that said, 'I survived Calgary,'" says wrestler Honky Tonk Wayne. "It was a test of a man's ability physically, mentally, socially, and emotionally. You had to deal with Stu, his children, all the other boys, the politics, the crazy ribs, the elements, and those long road trips. [Before I came to Stampede,] I had been wrestling in Florida, where our longest trip was maybe two hundred miles. For Stu, you'd cross the Prairies every week. It was difficult.... That's a fraternity not a whole lot of guys are a member of.... If the van broke down, well, it became a matter of survival. Y'all have to take care of each other.... Some guys would come and stay maybe two weeks, and they'd leave 'cause they couldn't take it. But if you stayed three months, six months, a year, that said something."

According to wrestling journalist David Meltzer, Calgary had become a sort of pro wrestling mecca. "In 1987, when I met [Japanese star] Chigusa Nagayo, at the time the most popular woman wrestler who ever lived, the first thing she wanted to know about North America was, 'Have you ever been to Calgary?' as opposed to a non-wrestling fan who would ask about Hollywood or New York," Meltzer writes. "To her, Calgary was a mythical wrestling paradise ... with real, hard-fought matches, no-nonsense competitors and the fastest paced style in North America."[7]

Because Stu was so open to global talent, Stampede Wrestling also became a melting pot of wrestling styles. There was the meat-and-potatoes Canadian style rooted in sound technical grappling, and the hard-shooting style of the Europeans. There were the Southern brawlers and the deadly Japanese, who kicked as if they were out to take heads off. There were the Sumo-fat heavyweights and the high-flying mid-heavyweights. Perhaps more than any other territory, Stampede had it all. It forced wrestlers to adapt to anything and everything. It ground out the weak and made the survivors hard.

Even the fans in Stampede country were tougher than those in other territories. Flashy gimmicks and fast talkers were fine, but not at the expense of hard-fought battles. "We had the miners, the lumberjacks, guys who wanted to see a very real style," says Bret. "When you walked out of the arena after a good show, everyone was buzzing. There was real tension in the matches.

When the work was bad, it didn't draw.... It was all about credibility. Next to Japan, [Stampede Wrestling] seemed the most real."[8]

Keith Hart seldom got into trouble. That's why he was so distressed in the winter of 1981 when he found himself behind bars in a Kalispell, Montana, jailhouse.

The incident erupted over a parking ticket. Keith had been skiing in nearby Whitefish with Smith's wife, Maria, and had an argument with the police when he returned to find them ticketing his Porsche. Maria exacerbated things by calling the police "pigs" and, as the situation escalated, the officers decided to throw Keith in the slammer for the night. When they tried to handcuff the wrestler, Keith resisted and a struggle ensued.

As Keith sat in jail with a drooling drunk as his cellmate, waiting to face a judge in the morning, he began to fret. "Oh, God, what am I doing here? How will I explain this to Dad? I'm supposed to be the commonsensical son. How did things get so out of whack?" To make matters worse, he had recently been hired by the Calgary Fire Department and was still on probation. He worried this incident might end his fledgling career.

Keith's fears were laid to rest the next day at the courthouse. "How's your dad doing?" asked the judge, who wore a bolo tie and steel-toed cowboy boots. "Where's Dave Ruhl these days?" The judge turned to the arresting officers and chastised them: "You guys be careful who you're arresting next time." Keith was speechless as the bitter authorities turned him loose.

Stampede Wrestling was a cult hit in the most unlikely pockets of the globe, but within the confines of its western Canadian territory – and the odd American state where the promotion's long arm reached – it was a full-fledged cultural institution. Grandfathers who had been following the action for decades sat and watched the show with their grandsons. Schoolboys followed the testosterone-fuelled soap opera religiously. They talked excitedly about the ongoing feuds. They spouted off Ed Whalen's catchphrases. They rough-housed at recess, playing Stampede Wrestling the same way they might play Cowboys and Indians or Star Wars.

Laurie Mills, sixty-six, a former CBC announcer and chairman of the Calgary Boxing and Wrestling Commission, remembers creeping through cattle pens at the Edmonton Exhibition Grounds and climbing up on the roof of the Sales Pavilion to sneak into the arena and watch the matches. A tall, skinny kid, Mills was picked on by bullies until he convinced them he was related to the fearsome Mills Brothers, Al and Tiny. Everyone in the schoolyard

A Keith Hart hip-toss sends Hubert Gallant
flying, early 1980s.

knew who they were and, once the rumour got around, nobody picked on little Laurie again.

Stampede Wrestling had become a long-standing tradition, a crucial part of the pop culture diet for generations of western Canadians. Every Saturday afternoon when the show aired, Helen Hart was up in the office fielding a steady stream of phone calls. "If a wrestler appears hurt, fans want to make sure he is okay," wrote a *Calgary Herald* columnist. "If the referee makes an unpopular decision, fans phone in to complain. Helen, in fact, seldom gets to see the show. All she sees is the business end of a telephone."[9]

The Hart boys were a big part of the show's appeal, helping develop a female following for the show, says Tonia Fanella of Calgary's Glenbow Museum. "My best friend had a crush on Keith Hart," she says. "The fact that Stu had very attractive sons that he put in wrestling tights definitely helped market the product, from the schoolgirls who had crushes on them to the groupies who I heard used to hang out at BJ's Gym."

Stu's contributions to the community were more than mere entertainment, however. He was also committed to charity work, raising thousands of dollars for charitable organizations, including the United Way, the Salvation Army, and the Alberta Children's Hospital.

Stampede Wrestling was part of the cultural fabric not only in the western cities. Stu never forgot the small towns. He knew they held a devoted section of Stampede Wrestling's fan base and that it was often difficult for the townsfolk to get to the cities. Whenever he could, Stu brought the show to them, constantly sending his circus to small towns and Indian reserves across the Prairies – places such as Swift Current, Camrose, Rosetown, Hobbema, Hanna, and Onion Lake.

The crew hit Drumheller, eighty miles northeast of Calgary, a few times year. A remote stretch of canyons and hoodoos known as the badlands, the area is famous as a rich reserve of dinosaur bones. On such visits, the older wrestlers would wind up the rookies, telling them that Stu was born in Drumheller and that the town had erected a statue in his honour. The young pups got out their cameras, eager to snap a photo of this rare monument to a wrestler. The boys would crack up when the van passed by the giant Tyrannosaurus Rex statue in the centre of the town. If that didn't look like an angry Stu, what did?[10]

"Stu and Helen helped build up these small town communities," says Alison Hart. "My mother would phone the mayor's office and say, 'We'd like to bring Stampede Wrestling in. If you let us perform in your arena, we'll give you a certain percentage of the gate.' If three hundred people came out, the town ended up with a fair bit of money."

The irony is that despite the valuable cultural contribution Stampede Wrestling and the Hart family made in the West, they rarely got their due, at least not until Bret and Owen found worldwide fame in the United States as part of the WWF. Stampede Wrestling may have been an institution, but it was not the sort of thing Calgary, an image-conscious city that was moving up in the world, necessarily wanted to trumpet.

Pro wrestling was never treated as a sport by most people. Hardcore fans may have lapped it up, but most serious, upstanding folks viewed it as a *Gong Show* put on by screaming, overgrown clowns. Even as entertainers, pro wrestlers were rarely afforded as much respect as strippers by the moral majority. Wrestling was seen as lowbrow entertainment, organized buffoonery, something to laugh at and little more.

"You had the mucky-muck types, and they tended to look down on it," says Stu's friend, casino owner Frank Sisson. "It was not the in thing to enjoy wrestling. It was thought of as an embarrassment. You would hear people say, 'I don't watch that stuff.' They could turn around and tell you about every match.... But they'd never admit it."

But wrestling wasn't just blue-collar entertainment. Local businessmen attended the shows regularly, though they tried to keep it under their hats, like a dirty little secret. "Wrestling always bordered on the seamy side of life," says Glenn Ruhl, son of wrestler Dave Ruhl. "It was an institution ... but it was only begrudgingly accepted. It was never quite respectable."

To hell with those mucky-mucks. There's no shortage of prominent Albertans who grew up weaned on Stampede Wrestling. Among them was Alberta premier Ralph Klein, son of wrestler Phil "Killer" Klein. When he was a boy, Ralph sold wrestling programs at the Edmonton matches. "My grandfather was a huge fan, absolutely, and so was my uncle, who was a good friend of Dave Ruhl's," Ralph says. "I used to watch it with them. [Stampede Wrestling] was synonymous with Alberta."

Another distinguished devotee was Ted Hellard, now president of the CFL's Calgary Stampeders. On Friday nights, he accompanied his father and brothers to the Pavilion for the wrestling matches. "Our family didn't have a lot of money," Hellard told the *Calgary Herald*. "If there had been a Calgary Flames then, we couldn't have afforded to go to the games. What we did do was go to Stampede Wrestling. My dad and I, we'd sit right down by the ring, scream and pound the mat while Dave Ruhl fought Archie Gouldie. It was so great.... It was something we could share together."[11]

Hellard, now fifty-one, has stated his prime inspiration for revamping the flagging football franchise is Stampede Wrestling. He wants Calgary Stampeders games to offer the same bonding family experience he had as a child at wrestling matches.

"I got caught up in the wrestling because it was theatre at its finest," says Hellard. "It was an honest form of entertainment.... [The wrestlers] were creating characters, of course, just like any actor, but it felt genuine."

Edmonton Journal sports editor Richard Helm watched *Stampede Wrestling* religiously every Saturday afternoon as a farm boy in Eston, Saskatchewan. "As a kid then you didn't have Xbox or a computer or the rich variety of TV programs that kids do today," Helm says. "But every Saturday afternoon, you had this incredible drama with comedy, violence, and heroics – as much as you could fit into a young person's life in an hour."

Gord Gillies, news anchor at Calgary's Global TV, remembers thinking that the wrestlers were part of the community. Gillies and his friends pestered Tor Kamata at the restaurant the villain opened near Gillies's childhood home: "We'd stick our heads in the door and say, 'No-o-o-o-o chancee!' Then we'd take off running."

For young Tony Spoletini, Stampede Wrestling was part of his Saturday ritual. "You got up, had breakfast, watched cartoons, and then it was Stampede Wrestling in the afternoon," says the former Calgary Stampeder and co-owner of Spolumbos, a trendy Cowtown deli. "It was part of our culture. It was just something we did.... Then, once high school hit, you'd go to the matches. Especially during Calgary Stampede time, when Stu brought in all the big cards. I don't think the Calgary Stampede ever had a better draw. Not even the chuckwagons. Stu brought people [to the Stampede grounds] probably more than any other event...."

"The Harts were like Calgary's version of the Royal Family."

Chapter fourteen

Bad News Rising

The crowd scattered in terror like the Japanese fleeing Godzilla. Women screamed and children cried as Bad News Allen leapt from the ring to destroy another wrestler. A fourteen-year-old girl who had been standing on her chair for a better view was knocked to the ground amid the scramble, tearing ligaments in her leg. Police officers on the scene declared it a "potentially dangerous situation" and called for backup as the sirens of an approaching ambulance wailed. Stampede Wrestling fans were used to wild, violent scenes. They were well accustomed to those moments where the action spilled from the ring, when the battle raged into the stands. But they had never experienced anything as out of control as this.

It was December 2, 1983, at the Victorian Pavilion. Fans knew they were in for a war when they flocked to the arena for the main event. It was a triple tag team match pitting Bret Hart; Davey Boy Smith; and the mohawk-sporting Iroquois Sonny Two Rivers against Archie "The Stomper" Gouldie, who had recently returned to the territory; his rookie son, Jeff; and the barbaric Bad News Allen. A bald, bearded black man who, in the words of one reporter, looked like "Mr. T's bigger, meaner brother,"[1] Allen had emerged in the previous year and a half as the most devastating heel in the territory, his style a mixture of wrestling, martial arts, and lawless street fighting.

As expected, the December 2 battle was vicious, with the babyface contingent taking a hellish beating. But this time, before they could launch their

Bad News Allen flies at a bloodied Bret Hart off the top turnbuckle like a bat out of hell, 1983.

inevitable comeback, a dark cloud fell over the arena. With the help of wrestler Kerry Brown and Allen's Japanese manager, the shrieking "Shogun warrior" K.Y. Wakamatsu, Bad News perpetrated a double cross on the Gouldies. The Stomper was beaten with Wakamtsu's kendo stick and calf-roped to the ring post while Bad News raked a fork across his head, opening up a gory gash. He then gave The Stomper's son a piledriver outside the ring, the young whelp's body driven like a nail headfirst into the concrete floor. Surely his neck would be broken.

An outraged elderly man burst from the crowd and punched Bad News in the ribs. "His hair was pure white, he must have been eighty years old, but I didn't see him and he almost doubled me over," Allen says. "I grabbed him by the hair and started shaking him."

"Listen, you old bastard!" Allen said. "Your ticket gives you the right to scream and yell at me, but it don't give you the right to put your hands on me! You do it again and I'll kill you!" To further punctuate his point, the six-foot-two, 265-pound wrestler grabbed the man's cane and tossed it into the bleachers. People fled in panic.

Horrified, Ed Whalen ordered the camera man to stop filming, as he often did when the bouts got too violent. When the filming resumed, however, chaos still reigned. The crowd had turned into a fearful mob, milling about frantically. Shouts flew, as did a few chairs, while Security held a rampaging Stomper at bay as he tried to rush the ring, where Bad News was being interviewed by a fuming Whalen.

"Take a look at this man!" raged Allen, pointing at The Stomper. "Take a look at his son. I crippled him! I broke his neck! I helped him die!" Again the filming stopped.

By the time filming had once more resumed, the Pavilion had cleared out. Following such high-pitched craziness, the silence in the arena was ominous. A shaken Whalen stood with The Stomper, whose head was bloody and bandaged. Gouldie was hunched over the ropes, his head bowed in shame, and he expressed regret at bringing his son into the wrestling business. "He begged me," The Stomper said sombrely, his eyes on the verge of tears. "He said, 'Dad, I wanna follow in your footsteps ... I wanna come wrestle in front of my gramma up in our home in Western Canada.' So I brought him up here. I'm not real proud of that, Ed."

Fans were used to Gouldie ranting like a madman. The contrast of his pained, sorrowful delivery on this night was riveting, then chilling, when he glared at the camera and vowed revenge. "It's time to get even. I'm going to get that man who hurt my son."

From the chaos of the audience turned mob to The Stomper's uncharacteristic vulnerability, everything about the show seemed to have derailed. Little boys across the Prairies watched Stampede Wrestling weekly, on the edge of their seats, assured by the grown-ups that the action was fake. But everything about this match deviated from the norm. Even the adults seemed disturbed by what they had witnessed. It all seemed so frighteningly real.

Then came the kicker. Whalen told viewers he refused to be part of such an ugly spectacle any longer and quit the show on the spot. He signed off for what he said would be the last time, hung his microphone over the ropes, and walked off camera. Uncle Ed, the Voice of Stampede Wrestling, was gone. Whalen had quit before, but never on the air like this. That settled it. It had to be real.

It wasn't. Bruce Hart had cooked up the twisted saga, designed to fill arenas across Western Canada for months to come. Jeff Gouldie's neck wasn't really broken. For that matter, he wasn't really Jeff Gouldie. This was no child of The Stomper. His real name was Tommy Dalton, and he was a nineteen-year-old rookie from Georgia.

The whole scene was a Hart creation – the set-up of what was to be the feud of the century – Archie the Stomper, terror of the 1970s versus Bad News Allen, the scourge of the '80s. It was a brilliant angle that the beasts sold with such brutal precision it backfired. Everybody, even the most jaded skeptics, bought into the drama. Including Whalen, who hadn't been in on the plot twist.

"The angle got so damn far over that people just went nuts," remembers Bruce Hart. "It became an Orson Welles's *War of the Worlds* type thing." Indeed. The mini-riot in the Pavilion was only the start of the promotion's troubles. The Calgary Boxing and Wrestling Commission suspended Stu's operating licence in the city for the remainder of the year and decreed that he would have to deposit a $10,000 performance bond before his permit was reissued in 1984. Bad News Allen was fined $1,000 and suspended from wrestling in Calgary indefinitely. During an Edmonton match the following evening, Allen's antics sparked another riot, and a pregnant woman in the audience was injured. Allen was banned from yet another city.

The Calgary incident was the talk of the town. Headlines in the *Calgary Herald* screamed, "Promoter Faces Suspension in War on Wrestling Violence" and "Bad News on the Wrestling Scene."[2] Glenbow Museum archivist Tonia Fanella, a student at the time, recalls the University of Calgary campus buzzing over the controversial match. Some fans even called Calgary hospitals to find out the condition of The Stomper's son. As no Jeff Gouldie was admitted anywhere, it was whispered in some circles that Stu hustled the boy out of town, not wanting a death in his territory.[3]

Despite the bedlam at the Pavilion, Keith doesn't think the controversy would have gotten so out of control had it not been for Whalen's reaction. Ed was a pillar of the community, people believed in him, and when he got spooked, so did the fans. "The whole city believed it, including Ed," Keith says. "Ed became a total mark.... He lost it. We probably should have taken him aside and told him, 'This is what we're going to do. Don't panic.' We figured he'd been doing it for so long, he wouldn't react that way. But he got hysterical. There was so much heat, and everybody just spun out off Ed's hysteria."

But Whalen, who was now also working as a play-by-play announcer for the Calgary Flames, stood by his decision. "I won't degrade myself anymore," he said the day after the riot. "It used to be fun announcing this show, but now it's obscenity. We're starting to scare the patrons with this violence outside the ring, and I will not be associated with it anymore. I feel sick."[4]

Stu, barred from staging any wrestling events in Calgary for the remainder of '83, had a boiling-hot grudge match on his stove and nowhere to serve it. His solution – to take the show to the Seven Chiefs Sportsplex on the Sarcee Indian Reserve, just outside Calgary – seemed resourceful. The reserve, as federal jurisdiction, was not bound by the rules of the city's boxing and wrestling commission.

But the Sarcee matches were a bust. Most fans didn't want to travel outside the city in the dead of winter. They were accustomed to the Stampede grounds. Stu organized a bus service to transport fans to the Sportsplex, but he still couldn't fill the venue. The Saturday night card, featuring Gouldie and Allen – joined at the wrist by a leather strap, which was used alternately as a whip and noose – was sparsely attended.

Another thing keeping people away was the absence of Ed Whalen. In a surprising turn of events, Stu patched up his differences with Sam Menacker, the announcer who had been such a boon to the business back in the 1950s. At first, given his track record, Stu and Helen had high hopes for Menacker. At Hart House, they presented him with a cake, the phrase "Play it again, Sam" written with icing.[5]

But the charismatic ideas man of yesteryear, now pushing seventy years old, was washed up. He had been out of the business for at least a decade and out of touch with the modern wrestling world. His commentating was lethargic, and he had trouble keeping up with the action in the ring. Half the time he couldn't remember the wrestlers' names. Only the oldest of fans remembered Menacker. The name meant nothing to the younger crowd, who missed Whalen.

The month of December was a disaster for Stampede Wrestling. Stu lost up to $300,000 because of the December 2 fiasco and the resulting fines and suspensions.[6]

Gouldie began to get antsy. His final run in Stampede Wrestling had been a wild one. The Stomper even got Stu, then sixty-nine, back into the ring in a tag team match in which Bret and his father faced off against Gouldie and J.R. Foley. Stu suffered cracked ribs when Foley stomped on him with his cowboy boots, but Bret says his dad loved it. "The glory was all coming back," he says with a grin. "Stu thought he was on the Ho Chi Minh Trail!" Even so, Gouldie felt he was on a sinking ship, and he turned in his notice, never to wrestle in the territory again.

Stu continued to fight the boxing and wrestling commission, arguing it was punishing his entire business for the actions of one rogue wrestler. "It's damn severe," he told reporters. "They've taken my livelihood from me." He publicly condemned Allen's actions. "I haven't officially kicked [Bad News] out yet, but I just can't abide this," Stu told the *Calgary Herald*.[7]

Privately, Stu blasted Allen too, but the irritable wrestler was having none of it. He says the entire Hart family supported the plot twist to "cripple" Stomper's son, including Stu. Allen had already been besieged by fines and suspensions in that year, and he claims he was reluctant to do the angle, thinking it would land him in the doghouse yet again. "Stu went to the press because he was the babyface promoter and he had to make it look like it was all my fault," Allen says. "But when I called him up and he started ranting and raving, I said, 'Listen, Stu, you were standing right next to me when I told those guys I didn't want to do this.'"

Stu grumbled, "I didn't hear it."

"Oh, all of a sudden you're deaf? I can see you doing this for the press, Stu, but don't you come down on me now. You know damn well it was your son Bruce who wanted to do this nonsense!"

Although Allen felt he was the scapegoat for the angle gone bad, behind the scenes it was Bruce who took most of the heat. Keith defends his brother: "My dad blamed Bruce for killing the business at that point. Bruce was the one who orchestrated the whole thing, but it could have saved Stampede Wrestling. They could've made enough money that Bruce might have earned my dad's respect. Then they could have turned the business over to him. Everybody would have lived happily ever after.... Instead, Ed quit and we got banished."

Spring 2004. I'm sitting in Bad News Allen's living room, face to face with the man who once decimated my childhood idols, Bret Hart and Dynamite Kid. Not an hour earlier, before I made my way across town for the interview, I joked to my wife, "If I'm not home in about three hours, call the police. Tell them I'm at this address." She looked at me as if I were a fool. But she doesn't understand the awesome presence this man once was – how for a whole generation of kids he was the ultimate symbol of tough and mean; pain and destruction; hell, all things nasty.

Of course, there's nothing to be intimidated by. That would be ridiculous. Allen Coage is not really the fierce killing machine I once watched on TV. Nevertheless, I sense it's best to tread carefully when interviewing him. I ask the tough questions, but I phrase them as politely as one possibly can when asking about bloodletting.

Allen is a serious man, cordial but not overly friendly. He has a hard, penetrating gaze and zero tolerance for BS. About three years before this interview, I was shocked when I pulled up to a gas bar and he filled my tank. When I told him I was a fan, he met me with a look that made it clear he didn't wish to talk to any fans. Now he is a security guard, teaching judo and wrestling on the side. He's still not interested in talking to fans. But a writer, that's a different story. If someone's going to be writing about Bad News Allen, he wants his say.

Allen walks with a limp. His knees were replaced a few years back after decades of pounding in the ring, but the arthritis in his joints still bothers him. Wrestling is no longer an option. There's a touch of grey in his beard, the odd wrinkle or two in his brow, but other than that the man has hardly aged. At sixty, he's solidly muscular, the last guy you'd want to bump into in a back alley. But it's when Allen begins his tale that he warms up considerably.

Although he was billed as a Harlem street fighter in the wrestling biz, Allen was raised in Queens. He didn't waste much time street fighting; from his early teens on, he devoted himself to the study of judo. It was his true love, and he dedicated about twenty years to the art, earning his fifth-degree black belt. He went on to win multiple championships, most significantly, two gold medals at the Pan American Games in 1967 and 1975 and a bronze medal at the 1976 Olympic Games in Montreal. By then, he was thirty-two years old and decided he had taken his judo career to its peak. "I filled my scrapbook," he says. "Now I was out to fill my bank book."

When his judo coach suggested he try his hand at pro wrestling, Allen bristled. "I don't wanna do that phoney stuff," he replied. But his coach wasn't talking about North American wrestling. He wanted to send Allen to Antonio Inoki's New Japan promotion. The Japanese style was far more serious than that of the Americans. They trained hard, they hit harder, and there was a greater emphasis on athleticism as opposed to showmanship. By late 1977, Allen was wrestling professionally throughout Japan.

In 1978, Allen went to the WWWF to wrestle for Vince McMahon Sr. He learned the value of showmanship by watching veteran wrestler Classy Freddie Blassie, whose catchphrase insult "pencil neck geek" was so hot that Blassie recorded a song titled after the phrase. "Freddie told me, if you wanna be remembered in this business, come up with a saying that nobody else uses," Allen says.

In his travels, Allen met the Hart boys and Dynamite Kid, appearing on the same cards as them in Japan and during a trip through the Middle East in 1982. Allen instantly disliked the way the Harts did business. "The Japanese are very punctual," he says. "If they say they're gonna be somewhere at five, they're there at four-thirty. But the Harts, they have no concept of time. They're always late. Keith and Bret used to make the Japanese so upset.... I'd say, 'Listen, you're really pissing the office off.' They didn't care."

It was Dynamite Kid who first approached Allen about working in Calgary. He saw potential in Allen's athleticism and intensity and recognized that a heel of his stature would do great business for Stampede Wrestling. Allen wasn't so sure. The New Japan office cautioned him about Stu's territory, about the erratic business and the crazy ribs the wrestlers played on one another. One of Allen's Japanese handlers phoned Stu and warned him that Allen would not take kindly to any nasty pranks. If anyone messed with Bad News they were sure to get hurt. Stu probably thought his territory could use such a man. He arranged to bring Bad News Allen in for the Calgary Stampede mega-card in July 1982. Allen was irked from the get-go: Stu picked him up at the airport half an hour late.

As Dynamite predicted, Bad News was good news for the territory – at least at first. He crushed the competition week after week, developing a loud, aggressive persona in interviews. Recalling the advice of Freddie Blassie, he invented his own catchphrase, an insult tailor-made for the Prairie audience: "Listen, you beer bellied sharecroppers...!" Another Stampede Wrestling expression entered the pop culture lexicon of the West.

Allen's first major Stampede feud was with Bret Hart. The two wrestlers had their share of knockdown, drag-out brawls that the fans loved, but Allen and Bret didn't see eye to eye on business. Allen's approach was in line with the punishing Japanese style of wrestling. When he hit, he hit hard.

The devastating power of Bad News Allen
and the aerial skills of Dynamite Kid is evident
here as Dynamite flies, shot through the air
by Bad News.

Bret didn't work that way. He too wanted the matches to look as legitimate as possible but believed the art of wrestling lay not in steamrolling one's opponent but in putting on an exciting exhibition where both men walked away looking like million-dollar warriors. That's what made the matches exciting for fans. He and Allen constantly clashed. "He would eat you alive," Bret says. "If you went in with him dressed as a nine, you came out a one. You never came out looking better than you did going in, and that's no way to build up a main event. Bad News Allen had no ring psychology.... He was a meat-chopper."

Wrestler Gama Singh remembers a match between the two in Regina where the story had Bret run into the ring and hit Bad News across the back with a kendo stick. Bret did as they had planned, but instead of acting as if the shot were devastating, Bad News snatched the stick away, threw Hart to the canvas, and pressed the bamboo shaft across his throat. Gama remembers Bret's bitter comment after the match: "I came in a rose and left smelling like a piece of shit."

Allen thought Bret was a prima donna, always having his hand raised in victory because he was the boss's brat. If Bret didn't like a storyline, Allen says, he'd sulk and refuse to cooperate. Allen recalls one angle where he stabbed Bret in the eye with a fork. To make it look real, Bret was supposed to wear the eye patch around town for a week. "He refused to do it," Allen says. "I said, 'Why'd we even do the damn [angle] then?' He was hard to do business with."

Given their relationship, Allen took pleasure in defying Bret every chance he got. Once, when Allen was holding the North American Heavyweight belt, he was to lose the title to Bret. Instead, he dropped it to Davey Boy Smith in some small town, when none of the Harts was present. Not even Davey knew it was coming. When he covered Allen for the pin, the wrestler was supposed to kick free but didn't. Before Davey knew what was going on, he had his arm raised in victory.

The next night, in Regina, Ross and Bret approached Allen, telling him he was to lose the belt that evening to Bret. "I started laughing and said, 'That's impossible. I'm not the champ anymore. Davey's the champ.'"

Allen grins from ear to ear remembering the moment. "Bret was marching around. Man, he was hot."

If Bret and Bad News couldn't work together, Dynamite Kid was queued up and ready. The trouble was, both men were heels. For a feud to really take off, one of them had to turn babyface.

Dynamite was the clear choice. By 1983, he looked like a comic book super-hero – 218 pounds of lean, steroid-pumped muscle in tights that seemed to fly across the ring at his foes. Occasionally, the fans would catch themselves cheering for him even though they weren't supposed to. But Dynamite's character was so irrevocably linked with the despicable J.R. Foley that casting him as a good guy was going to be tricky. The easy way out would have been to stage a dispute between Dynamite and Foley. Instead, Bruce found a way to make old J.R. vaguely sympathetic.

First, he introduced the shrieking Wakamatsu to the fold as J.R.'s lieutenant. A short Japanese man in a karate suit, Wakamatsu spoke barely a word of English, but his approach – a sneaky assassin, barking insanely in his native tongue – made the fans loathe him. As Wakamatsu became more wicked and lethal by the week, Foley increasingly became the comedy relief.

J.R.'s supposedly rich, spoiled son, Athol, was introduced to the fold around this time. A wimp, who constantly whined to his daddy about corruption in the Hart mafia, Athol – actually a very capable British wrestler named Bernie Wright – originally appeared as a younger clone of his father, complete with his own Hitler-style moustache. As his character developed, he grew a beard and cut his hair to look like Mr. T, the tough-talking muscleman of the hit TV series *The A-Team*. This looked asinine on a young Englishman. Enhancing his reputation as the village idiot were Athol's mixed-gender matches with female wrestler Wendy Richter, who beat and humiliated him.

Perhaps the cherry on top of the Athol sundae were the trunks he sometimes wore, which resembled a diaper. He became an object of ridicule for the fans, who gleefully chanted "Asshole! Asshole!" each time he came to the ring. This caused Athol to jump up and down and stamp his feet like a child throwing a tantrum. With J.R. dedicating his energies to Athol's progress, Wakamatsu, as per the story, established himself as the devious brain behind Bad News Allen.

Things came to a head one Friday night when Wakamatsu and Allen double-crossed Foley, laying into the old Englishman with a nasty beating. Dynamite Kid rushed to his friend's aid and banished the bad guys as the crowd pounded on the bleachers, chanting excitedly "Dy-na-mite! Dy-na-mite!" The Kid was a hero. The stage was set for a Dynamite–Bad News feud.

Although Bruce Hart is usually blamed for the bloody excesses of the 1980s, he had little to do with the Dynamite–Bad News feud, among the most controversial of the time. That's because Stu cut Bruce out of the action. According to Allen, Stu said, "You and Dynamite are professional enough

The Japanese warlord K.Y. Wakamatsu brings
his kendo stick down on a felled grappler
outside the ring.

that you can do your own matches. Don't listen to Bruce." Allen recalls that the first time Dynamite and Bad News clashed, in Regina, Bruce tried to orchestrate the match's finish, telling him he was to defeat Dynamite that evening. "We got two things going here," Allen snapped. "One, I ain't beating him. And two, get the hell out of here. We're in charge of our own matches. We don't need you."

In the ring, Bad News and Dynamite were of like mind. Bad News liked to play rough and so did Dynamite Kid. "That's the way Tommy and I approached it," Allen says. "He'd really lay in with the chops and the punches and I would do the same. When the audience saw it, they thought, 'This is the real thing.'"

Dynamite in particular paid little heed to safety, and his body suffered for it. "Tommy was more dangerous to himself than anybody else," says Gama Singh. "I remember one time he dove off the ring's top corner post onto the cement floor, where he gave Bruce a flying headbutt. The whole impact of the move was absorbed by his elbows, shoulders, and knees. There's no give on a cement floor. The next day, Tommy could barely walk. He was never afraid to do risky moves like that."

In Dynamite, Bad News had an opponent perfectly willing to take anything, and the former Olympian took full advantage of the situation. In one match, the brawl spilled out into the stands. Bad News smashed open the glass compartment encasing the fire extinguisher, pummelling Dynamite with the heavy metal object. Next, he slammed the blood-covered Dynamite onto a wooden ringside table and picked up a fire-axe. "I told him, 'Make sure you move, 'cause I ain't gonna stop with this thing.'" Dynamite remembers Bad News towering over him, brandishing the weapon, a maniacal look in his eyes. He rolled out of the way just as Allen buried the axe in the spot where he had laid. That was the first time the Calgary Boxing and Wrestling Commission suspended Bad News.

The feud between the two warriors spilled outside the ring one evening in Vancouver. The wrestlers were staying in a dive hotel off Granville Street. A wet T-shirt contest was being held in its bar. Surly Allen didn't drink and didn't like bars, but on this night an excited Wakamatsu convinced Allen to accompany him. Allen knew it was a mistake when he entered the bar and saw a group of wrestlers, including Dynamite, already drunk. He and Dynamite were wrestling in town as enemies, so it wouldn't do for them to be seen together at a bar. Allen turned to leave when Dynamite saw him and began hurling insults for the benefit of the barflies. Lit up on booze, Dynamite ran across the bar and shoved Allen. Allen grabbed Tommy and threw him, knocking over a table full of drinks. The next thing Allen knew, he and Waka-matsu were being jumped by a mob of drunken fans who thought they were rescuing Dynamite Kid. The two wrestlers were lucky to escape the bar in one piece.

The next day, Allen spotted a hungover Dynamite Kid crawling into the tour van. Allen grabbed him. "Listen, Tommy, the next time you pull a stunt like that I'm gonna beat your brains out," he said, seething. "You could've gotten me stabbed. What the hell's wrong with you?"

"I was just trying to drum up business," Dynamite replied groggily. Even he wasn't about to take on Allen for real.

With the Dynamite–Bad News war, Stu had box office gold on his hands and a suspension would not do. After much negotiating with the commission, the promoter managed to get the suspension lifted on the promise he would better control his wrestlers. But the violence only got worse. In one match, Allen gashed open Dynamite's head with a broken bottle. Again he was suspended.

Ed Whalen was becoming increasingly agitated at the direction the show was taking and the Calgary Boxing and Wrestling Commission began coming down on Stu for any infraction it could find. Fines and suspensions were issued on a weekly basis. Some of the commission's complaints were reasonable, such as those about fighting in the audience. What if a fan was hurt? But coming down on the wrestlers about the use of weapons in the ring and beating up referees was unreasonable. Although Stu would never go so far as to admit the violence was largely an act, he did tell the *Calgary Herald*, "You can't run wrestling on Olympic rules."[8] Most of the commission members were well aware that what they were seeing was entertainment rather than a straight-up sporting contest. Gordon Grayston, chairman of the Calgary Boxing and Wrestling Commission, certainly knew it, as he had worked as a Stampede Wrestling referee for years.

Grayston argued that the violence would have a negative influence on children, who might mimic what they saw on TV. But with that rationale, pro wrestling would have to be stopped altogether. Or, at least, all the dirty play would have to be taken out of the game, and that would rob the show of its drama, effectively neutering Stampede Wrestling.

Bruce Hart rebelled against the commission every chance he got. He went so far as to introduce a snivelling, dictatorial referee to the show who he named after Ron Hayter, the chairman of the Edmonton commission. Stu thought this was just asking for trouble and didn't want Bruce to introduce the angle. Bruce did it anyway.

In a letter sent to Calgary City Council on May 17, 1982, Stu protested the city's boxing and wrestling commission, arguing it was "openly hostile to [Stampede Wrestling]."[9] He told reporters the commission was trying to run him out of business. As Stu saw it, the root of his problem was Grayston. Stu and Gordon went all the way back to the navy, where Grayston had made a name for himself boxing, just as Stu had wrestling. According to Alison Hart, Grayston and Stu got into a fight on the base in Cornwallis, Nova Scotia, while Grayston was refereeing one of Stu's navy matches, and Stu knocked Grayston out cold. Stu always said that was the beginning of Grayston's deep-seated grudge against him.

In the 1960s, Grayston tried to start up a boxing promotion in Calgary. When that failed, Stu lent him money and hired him as a referee. Many of the Harts believe that Grayston was always envious of Stu's success. When he became chairman of the boxing and wrestling commission, he saw it as an opportunity to settle old scores.[10]

Former commission member Laurie Mills says he never saw any evidence that Grayston had such an agenda. He does admit that a few overly conservative people on the commission "wanted to prevent anything that would make wrestling work," but he maintains Grayston was not one of them.

The Harts weren't the only ones who had a problem with Grayston. In an interview with the *Calgary Herald* after the December 2, 1983, debacle, Bad News Allen accused the commission of discrimination, claiming that white wrestlers who used extreme violence were not punished as harshly as he was. Allen threatened to report it to the Alberta Human Rights Commission.[11]

"News would be the guy to pull that card," says Mills, adamant that Allen was in trouble for his actions, not the colour of his skin.

Around this time, Stu set up a meeting between Allen and Grayston to try to smooth things out. It only heightened tensions. "When I got there, [Grayston] said something and started pointing his finger at me. I told him to eff-off and walked out," Allen says. "After that, he tried to stick it to me every chance he got. He hated me with a passion."

There was similar animosity between Bad News and Whalen. Whalen so disapproved of Allen's style that he quit the show over it on December 2. As for Allen, he thought Whalen was bad for business. Whalen always got queasy at blood-soaked matches. He insisted that Ross Hart edit out anything Whalen deemed too nasty. It was common for highly anticipated matches to be cut off halfway through the action, the filming ordered stopped by Whalen. This often frustrated fans, as they missed the battles they were dying to see. It was especially hard for a grappler like Allen. Violence was his stock-in-trade, and Whalen was censoring his best work.

Allen also hated the way Whalen ran the show, cutting certain wrestlers off, not letting them say their piece in interviews. "The bad guy is supposed to get everybody hot for next week's match," Allen says. "But if you got the announcer saying, 'I'm not gonna listen to this' and walking off, you're killing the business.... I think if Ed worked in any other territory, they would have fired him for the things he did."

But despite the dissension behind the scenes, one common theme seemed to unite many of the key players in the game. And that was that Bruce Hart was trouble. Whalen and Grayston disliked him for his bloody matches and his risqué concepts. Allen said it was ludicrous that Bruce booked himself as one of the stars of the show when he didn't have the mat skills to back it up. Bret thought Bruce was too disorganized and his booking concepts ill-conceived. Keith hated the way his brother played politics in the dressing room. "Bruce was a very Machiavellian character," Keith says. "What really did him in was his duplicity. He'd blow smoke up one guy's ass and knock the next guy, then he'd go to the next guy [and say the opposite]. He thrived on controversy and conflict. He manipulated people and in a small territory eventually guys would compare notes and then he'd have everybody pissed off." In Bruce's defence, complaints like these against the booker are all too common in the wrestling business.

Stu too had reservations about his ambitious son. He hated the way Bruce defied orders and he thought his son's concepts often robbed the sport of the dignity Stu believed it had.

Many thought that as a manager Bruce was a disaster, which was a shame since his booking concepts were often spectacular. From the hardcore action to the fast-paced fliers to the absurd scenarios, Bruce, with a low budget, was moving in the direction that characterizes today's typical wrestling program. He really did envision the future.

But on December 2, 1983, Bruce lost control of the wheel. His crazy concepts seemed to be steering Stampede Wrestling right off the proverbial cliff.

Could rock 'n' roll save Stampede Wrestling's soul? In 1984, it looked like it might, and following the crisis of December '83, the promotion certainly was in need of saving. The wrestling business was becoming more competitive than ever. Vince McMahon Jr. had taken over his father's World Wrestling Federation in the spring of 1983 and was already using his financial clout to poach stars from other promotions. There was also much money to be made in Japan and in the booming American territories. To hang on to top stars like Dynamite Kid and Bad News Allen, Stu was paying them about $1,500 a week, plus picking up their expenses on the road. Furthermore, the Stampede Wrestling payroll was unnecessarily long for a small business. Most of Stu's kids, not to mention their spouses, were collecting a paycheque from the organization for a variety of menial tasks.

A valiant attempt had been made to boost business. Exciting new stars were introduced, including good-looking babyfaces Phil Lafleur from Montreal and Alison Hart's husband, Ben Bassarab; high-flying masked man The Cobra; the Mongolian giant, Killer Khan; and the Iroquois, Sonny Two Rivers, who was actually from Japan.* Southern scrapper "Rotten" Ron Starr, a former Vietnam veteran from Mobile, Alabama, was another hot addition to the roster. "[Starr] was a real slimeball," says Bret. "I remember the fans spitting at him and he'd catch the spit in his mouth, spit it back into the air, and catch it in his mouth again. It would just make you sick." Starr was an excellent heel and the fans longed to see his gruff, smug face covered in blood.

The wild feud between Dynamite and News was also resurrected. On a card in the spring, Dynamite's eight-month-pregnant wife, Michelle, was brought into the fray when the couple was honoured in the ring, announcer Sam Menacker presenting Michelle with a bouquet of flowers and gifts for the baby. Suddenly, depraved Bad News and his cronies showed up to offer congratulations of their own – a good stomping for Dynamite. Michelle seemed on the verge of a similar fate until she was rescued by the good guys. According to an outraged letter in the *Calgary Herald* screaming that "Bad News deserves the boot," Stu got in on the action, too, giving the villains "a few swift kicks in the butt."[12]

Despite such heady programming, TV ratings were down in Alberta and Saskatchewan. People missed Whalen – without him, the show had lost its flow – and, with all the negative publicity, there was significant ill will in the community toward Stampede Wrestling.

The show's saving grace was the invaluable beachhead that had been established in Vancouver thanks to Bruce Allen, a rock 'n' roll manager who had guided the stunningly successful careers of acts such as Bachman-Turner Overdrive and Loverboy. The aggressive Allen was only twenty-eight years old when he and his client, rising rock star Bryan Adams, first introduced

*"With that mohawk, he looked more like an Indian than an Indian did," says Bruce Hart of Two Rivers. "We'd go to all the reservations and the Indians loved him. They thought he was the real thing, oddly enough. In one place they even made him an honorary chief."

themselves to Davey Boy sometime in the fall of 1983 in the dressing room of Tokyo's Sumo Hall. *Stampede Wrestling* had been airing regularly in Vancouver for a couple of years at that point, and both men were fans. It was then that Allen first hinted he would be interested in doing promotions for Stampede Wrestling in Vancouver and Victoria.

For most of the 1970s, Stu stayed away from Vancouver, as that was the domain of All Star Wrestling, which Gene Kiniski had long co-promoted. But in 1977, Winnipeg wrestler Al Tomko bought into the promotion and Kiniski found himself with a partner he disliked.[13] Bitter, Gene quit the promotion, but not wanting to give up on his territory, approached Stu about co-promoting Stampede Wrestling in the heart of British Columbia. Stu was open to the idea, as All Star had been trying to establish a foothold in Calgary.

With its phenomenal roster, the *Stampede Wrestling* TV show was well received in Vancouver, the excitement of the Pavilion matches far outdoing All Star, which was recorded in front of a small studio audience. Stampede Wrestling cards were also doing fair business in Vancouver, although in a city of that size, Stu felt they should have done far better. Stu's men often felt demoralized, driving twelve hours to Vancouver for shows that were not well attended.

Bruce Allen thought Stampede Wrestling was far superior to All Star. Holding it back, he felt, was lack of promotion. The Harts, too, were dissatisfied with Kiniski's promoting efforts, which Ross claims usually amounted to a tiny advertisement in the newspaper.

Davey Boy passed Bruce Allen's message onto the Harts when he arrived back in Canada from Tokyo, and the rock manager met with Stu and Bruce. He offered to step in and promote two shows at his cost. He told the Harts that if there was no increase in attendance, he would walk away. If there was, he wanted to become a partner in the Vancouver-Victoria operations.

Bruce Allen was a tough businessman with a proven track record in the music industry. Still, Stu was leery. What did a rock manager know about wrestling? Allen's plans were promising, though, and he had media connections that couldn't be beat. Bruce saw the potential immediately and convinced Stu to give Allen a chance. Against Kiniski's wishes, Bruce Allen was cut into the action. He made a huge difference immediately. "It was incredible," says Ross. "He got a brewery as a sponsor and the rock radio station CFOX started doing on-air interviews with the wrestlers.... They hyped the matches and gave us an identity we didn't have before."

Under Bruce Allen, a Stampede Wrestling event took on the qualities of an arena rock concert, with music booming from the speakers and the house lights down save for a spotlight on the wrestlers as they made their dramatic entrances to the ring. Stampede Wrestling was exploring the rock 'n' wrestling connection a good year before Vince McMahon popularized the concept by promoting the inaugural WrestleMania on MTV and bringing pop star Cyndi Lauper into the ring briefly as a manager. "We flourished," says Ross. "Suddenly instead of drawing five hundred people [for the Vancouver shows], seven thousand fans would show up." And the wrestlers were treated like rock stars. Under Bruce Allen, they stayed in a finer class of hotels than they were used to and catered food awaited them in the dressing room.

When Bruce Allen turned the business around so radically in Vancouver, Kiniski grew even more sour, feeling squeezed out of the operation. Ross confirms the Hart kids wanted to "put Gene out to pasture" by buying him out. It was Stu who stuck up for his old colleague. He argued that he had a thirty-year-plus relationship with the veteran, and he refused to renege on their co-promoting deal.

Following a match shortly after Bruce Allen started promoting, Allen came into the dressing room and, according to Stu, Kiniski grabbed him and threw him down a flight of stairs. Stu caught him at the bottom. "He didn't want to [go] back up," Stu told the Glenbow Museum. "Gene said he'd boot the hell out of him if he did. I got a hold of Gene and said, 'This fella has connections with the sports departments on radio and television everywhere. For you to throw that kind of money down the stairs …'"

"I like my privacy," Gene barked.

"Bruce Allen was really upset with that," Ross says. "He said to my dad, 'Why do you need this guy around?'" Still, Stu remained loyal to Kiniski.

Meanwhile, the two Bruces struck up a wildly popular plot line when they brought notorious NHL bruiser Tiger Williams to the ring in August 1984. Williams, who had just been traded to the Detroit Red Wings from the Vancouver Canucks, was called on to act as a celebrity referee one night. "Rotten" Ron Starr got to the microphone and hurled insults at Williams. A tough guy on the ice, Williams was not one to take such abuse and challenged Starr to a match.*

The feud culminated in a tag team bout on August 29, 1984, at Vancouver's Pacific Coliseum, pitting Tiger and Bruce Hart against the Rotten One and Gama Singh. Between 4,500 and 6,000 fans showed up for the match. Hart and Tiger came to the ring accompanied by three burly bodyguards from the B.C. Lions football team. Starr and Gama entered to the malicious

*This did not please the Red Wings' head office, which pulled Tiger's NHL insurance. Bruce Allen countered the problem by insuring the hockey star himself at a cost of $9,000.

chant "Go home, Paki! Go home, Paki!" being directed at the turban-wearing Gama. The racial slur had long been a popular feature of Gama's matches. Starr then took over the microphone and questioned the sexual preference of the football players. Thirty seconds into the contest, all four combatants were brawling at once in the centre of the ring. The epic battle finally ended, after many dramatic twists and turns, when Gama took a hockey stick and cross-checked Williams.[14]

Bruce Hart was elated. "The promotion has been very innovative," he told the Vancouver *Province* in an article about wrestling's newfound hipness, which referred to the sex appeal of the modern wrestler. "We're getting a younger, more vibrant audience."[15] Bruce felt he was leading the family business to great new heights in the 1980s, bringing it to the MTV generation with a blast. He knew he was standing on the brink of something great, just like his father thirty-six years earlier when he started the promotion. He felt he was fulfilling the Hart legacy and the world was his for the taking.

Two days later, he arrived back in Calgary and turned on the six o'clock news, hoping they'd promote that night's card at the Pavilion. Just like that it all came crashing down. Stu had sold his territory to Vince McMahon.

The promoting rights. Gone. The TV spots. Gone. The new, creative direction that was going to revitalize the family business, not to mention the whole goddamn wrestling industry. Gone.

How much of his life had Bruce given up? How big a chunk did this game rip from his heart? The endless politicking with his family, the tyrannical commissions, and Whalen, not to mention all the crazies who constantly came and went – it seemed as though the last decade had been a constant struggle for Bruce to see his creative vision played out. And now, on the cusp of greatness, to have it pulled away from him. Bruce thought he was going to explode. He could barely speak. He wasn't even clear as to what had gone down. He rushed to the Pavilion, where the wrestlers had assembled in the dressing room, equally confused.[16]

Immediately, Bruce got to the bottom of it. It was already apparent that McMahon's WWF juggernaut was out to conquer the wrestling world. McMahon was running one North American territory after another out of business, going head to head with the various promotions by getting his program onto TV screens in their respective regions. Independent promotions found it impossible to compete with McMahon's big-budget, star-heavy production and the territories were gradually folding. In hindsight, it was inevitable that McMahon would covet the wrestling-loving audience of Western

Canada. Perhaps because Stampede Wrestling was such a cultural institution in the region, McMahon approached Stu with an offer to buy him out, rather than aggressively trying to run him off the game board.

When the initial call came from Jim Barnett, McMahon's right-hand man, it could not have caught Stu at a more vulnerable, weary moment. Between his financial woes, Whalen's departure, and the never-ending war with the boxing and wrestling commission, as well as his constant back and forth with Bruce and the mess with Kiniski, Stu felt like he was being torn apart, pulled in a dozen directions at once. At the age of sixty-nine, did he really want to take on the juggernaut that was the WWF? He had only to look to Helen to know the answer to that question. Stu's Tiger Belle, who he loved more than anyone in the world, who he had dragged into this business as a reluctant participant, had just been diagnosed with Type 2 diabetes. She would not fight any longer. She didn't have the strength.

"It was time to get off the treadmill," said Stu when news of the sale got out. "I owe it to my wife. She was on the treadmill, too. I'd hate to die knowing that I didn't get off."[7]

Stu and Helen knew Bruce would resist the sale every step of the way, so they kept him in the dark. Instead, they brought in Keith to help broker the deal. Bruce was on the road when Stu, Helen, and Keith met with George Scott, who had wrestled for Stu in the 1950s and '60s. Scott was now booking for McMahon and, given his history with Stu, it was natural that he be tapped to hammer out the deal. While Stu Hart's biography *Stu Hart: Lord of the Ring* states the deal was sealed on a handshake, a letter to Stu from Barnett indicates that an agreement was signed on August 24, 1984.

Vince would purchase the territory, including Stu's TV spots, for $1 million, to be paid off $100,000 a year, for ten years. Stu was also promised 10 percent of the gate from all house shows in Edmonton and Calgary. The agreement stipulated that Vince would hire Bret, Dynamite Kid, Davey Boy Smith, and Jim Neidhart.

Bruce would be given work too, as a booking agent, organizing WWF shows and lining up publicity in major cities such as Calgary, Edmonton, Vancouver, and Seattle. It was a prominent position, but as far as Bruce was concerned, it was table scraps. How dare they treat a man of his vision, the rightful heir to his father's throne, as a mere flunky? "Bruce was so incensed," Keith recalls. "He felt like he had the carpet pulled out from under him."

Ross agrees: "Bruce was unhappy. He wasn't offered a job as a wrestler [or a booker] … and I think he felt he was at the prime of his career. In reality, [at thirty-four] he was a little older than some of the others and maybe he just didn't have the size and weight the WWF was looking for.... I think Bruce felt kind of shunned."

When Stu arrived at the Pavilion dressing room on August 31, 1984, he faced his son's wrath but stood firm. "It's my promotion," he said. "I'll do what I want with it."[18]

More than twenty years later, Bruce remains bitter about the experience. "I basically got screwed on the whole deal," he says. "I wasn't told a damn thing about it. Between Stu and Keith, I never knew anything was cooking. The consensus was that if they called me I would've been pissed and I would've raised hell about it.... [Stampede Wrestling] at that time was pretty much my recipe ... and it was an awesome recipe. We could have taken it anywhere."

Chapter fifteen

Back In The Saddle

"The worst year of Stu's life was the year he didn't have wrestling to worry about," said Keith Hart to a reporter late in 1985.[1]

The wrestling game was in the Hart papa's blood. It was his obsession, and without it he was lost, stalking around his mansion in a huff, rambling about the glory days of his beloved sport.

Stu wasn't sure he liked the WWF's product, its slick *Maple Leaf Wrestling* program airing every Saturday afternoon on CFAC-TV in the old Stampede Wrestling time slot. But he looked forward to co-promoting the WWF events when they came to Calgary. It made him feel involved once more with the business he lived for.

Stu was as shocked as anybody when the first WWF shows failed to live up to expectations at the box office. In October and November of 1984, and in January 1985, the WWF came to the Calgary Saddledome, a new eighteen-thousand-seat arena on the Stampede grounds that was built as a home for the Calgary Flames and in anticipation of the 1988 Winter Olympics. Business was so disappointing at the Dome that, by February, the WWF had given up on the venue and moved to the seven-thousand-seat Stampede Corral across the street. But a February 27 show at the Corral was the WWF's worst yet, bringing in only about seven hundred fans.[2] It was startling, as the WWF was routinely selling out Madison Square Garden, Maple Leaf Gardens, and the Philadelphia Spectrum.

Wrestler Karl Moffatt as monster heel Jason the Terrible, a hockey-masked, axe-wielding knockoff of the teen slasher from the popular *Friday the 13th* movie series.

What the WWF failed to grasp was the extent to which the new brand was a slap in the face to western Canadian fans. Suddenly, Stu's most popular son, Bret, a main event hero of the region, was showing up at the bottom of the cards, either losing to McMahon's stars or fighting boring matches with bums that weren't of his calibre. A sulky Bruce Hart was relegated to the sidelines, while the devious J.R. Foley was being used as a referee.

It seemed as if the WWF was treating Calgary as a secondary market. While its cards featured a few grapplers of star quality, such as Andre the Giant, they were mostly filled with mediocre talent that failed to excite the audience. A column in the *Calgary Herald* griped, "The WWF wrestlers are bigger and faster and better built [than the stars of Stampede Wrestling] … but bland to the fans."[3]

When it came to rowdy fun, the WWF's TV show couldn't compare with that of Stampede Wrestling either. *Maple Leaf Wrestling* seldom featured the best matches the WWF had to offer. Instead, it was full of interviews with the wrestlers, who played up their cartoonish personas, and "squash-jobs," where stars would easily roll over a series of nobodies, jobbers who were there to make them look good. The show was little more than a teaser for the live events and a far cry from the wild battles that had been fought each week on *Stampede Wrestling*.

Suddenly, out of left field, a new player came into the game. A group of investors and long-time Stampede fans decided to start up their own wrestling organization, which would run head to head with the WWF in Alberta. The upstart company's name? Stampede Wrestling. Stu had never bothered to trademark the name of his business.

When advertisements began appearing proclaiming "Stampede Wrestling is back!" the Harts denounced the organization and made it clear they were in no way involved. "These guys have a lot of gall," Stu told the *Calgary Sun*. "Using the name Stampede Wrestling is in poor taste and misleading." In the same piece, Bruce stated that his family was dedicated to developing the WWF's interests in Alberta.[4]

One of the investors in the all-new Stampede Wrestling told *Alberta Report* he was heartbroken when Stu pulled the plug on Stampede, and he took swipes at the WWF. "Maple Leaf Wrestling is boring!" he said. "There's no action. It's just a bunch of big goons."[5] The new product was hyped as a return to the glory days and, on the surface, the new promoters seemed to have a good game plan. The new show would be aired every Friday in the familiar old Victoria Pavilion, featuring fan favourites such as Bad News Allen, Leo Burke, Duke Myers, and the Cuban Assassin.

But the reality failed to live up to the dream. Without the Harts' involvement, fans saw the new Stampede Wrestling as an impostor and when the show debuted at the Pavilion in February 1985, the attendance was dismal. Top names dropped out rapidly and by the end of the month the gigs were drawing pathetic crowds of about fifty fans a night. The March shows were cancelled. In the middle of that month, a group of wrestlers, including the Cuban Assassin and "No Class" Bobby Bass, descended on the Calgary Boxing and Wrestling Commission. "All we want is the wages we were promised," Bass roared.[6] More than twenty wrestlers had worked some three weeks for less than one week's pay. Many of them wound up broke and stranded in Calgary, living in the dumpy Regis Hotel, which took them in as a gesture of goodwill.

The unofficial Stampede Wrestling was officially dead.

According to Ross Hart, Bruce had been in talks with the upstart promotion when it first formulated its business plan late in 1984. Bruce was working with the WWF and hated it. He thought it had a sorry set of wrestlers and believed he could run the show better. Bruce wasn't afraid to voice those opinions either. But his voice wasn't being heard. He felt like his creativity was being stifled and hated being treated like a puppet in a territory where he once pulled the strings. Investors in the fledgling wrestling group appealed to Bruce's bruised ego and his belief that he was cheated out of his destiny. They approached him to be a part of their organization, promising him he would be the booker. Once again, Bruce would be pulling the strings.

Bruce wasn't the only one who planned to join the new venture. Dynamite Kid and Davey Boy Smith, who together Vince McMahon had dubbed The British Bulldogs, were less than thrilled with the way they were being used in the WWF and, on Bruce's encouragement, they too gave serious consideration to joining the new group. In one sense, it would make life easier, as they were both married and starting families in Calgary.

The British Bulldogs were rising up the ranks in the WWF. They were certainly not stuck at the bottom of the cards as Bret Hart and Jim Neidhart were. But Ross says the Bulldogs weren't comfortable with what they saw as an "American clique" in the WWF dressing room. They also preferred working in Japan, where their wages were guaranteed, as opposed to working in the WWF, where the paycheque depended on how healthy the gates were and how high one was on the card.[7]

Their relationship with the WWF was also strained when, while working in Japan, they left the New Japan wrestling group for rival All Japan. Financially it made sense. They were offered $20,000 each up front and $6,200 a week for the tour, which was a grand a week more than they were making with New Japan. But New Japan was working with the wwf, paying McMahon huge booking fees to send his top stars overseas. When the Bulldogs went to All Japan, McMahon was furious.

So was Stu. He too was working with McMahon, co-promoting in the West, and accustomed to doing business with New Japan. When Stampede Wrestling was active, Stu collected booking fees when his wrestlers went on Japanese tours. Ross says his father was in negotiations with New Japan to begin booking talent again when Dynamite and Davey jumped ship. "When this happened, [New Japan] thought my dad was behind it somehow … and they never worked with us again," Ross says.

"What the fuck did you two think you were doing, going to All Japan?" Stu growled when the boys returned to Calgary.

Dynamite answered, "Stu, that's my prerogative."

"Well you just cost me, you little bastard."[8]

Ultimately, the British Bulldogs were too hot a property to risk everything they had on a fledgling promotion in Calgary, and they backed out of talks to be part of the new Stampede Wrestling. This reflected poorly on Bruce, who said he could bring the Bulldogs in. Meanwhile, it was rumoured that Bad News Allen refused to work for the new operation if Bruce was in charge. Bad News was going to be one of the stars of the promotion and the investors didn't want to lose him. Bruce was demoted before the show even began. He was told he wouldn't be the booker.

"Bruce bowed out and it was kept a secret that he had been involved [with the new Stampede Wrestling] in any way," Ross says. "It was a tough pill for him to swallow…. My dad was quite upset with Bruce." However, Ross stresses, his brother never actually worked for the upstart organization, and he always did his job for the wwf, sending out press releases and promoting shows in the West. Even so, Keith says McMahon found out about Bruce's talks with the competition and used the knowledge to his advantage.

After the wwf's dismal showing in Calgary, McMahon wanted out of his agreement with Stu. He told the Hart godfather that he couldn't afford to pay him the promised $100,000 a year and that the Harts were free to renew operations in the territory if they wanted to. Could Stu have held McMahon to the original agreement? Not easily. For one thing, if Stu fought McMahon, he would likely be jeopardizing the careers of his family in the wwf. And, according to Keith, Bruce's talks with the competition were viewed by McMahon as a violation of the non-competition agreement McMahon had made with the Harts. McMahon may have used this as a reason to cancel their agreement.[9]

That damn Bruce. It was becoming increasingly apparent that he would never be happy unless he was running Stampede Wrestling. It was his obsession. And Stu could not deny that a big part of him missed it, too. Within a month, Stampede Wrestling, the genuine Hart article, was back in business.

The return of Ed Whalen cannot be underestimated when exploring Stu's motives for again jumping into the frying pan that was the wrestling business. Whalen, then fifty-eight, had scored his dream job working as an announcer for the Calgary Flames. Here he was, a renowned sportscaster associated with Canada's national pastime. He felt he was at the pinnacle of his career working with a respected organization such as the NHL. Gone were the days when he stewed over the antics of the wrestlers, when he had to constantly stand guard, worrying about what Bruce Hart was going to try to get away with. He no longer had to be the voice of reason and morality, constantly enforcing these things to wild men who had no sense for such matters. His dignity was no longer at stake.

So why did he go back? For that matter, why did he again use his clout with CFAC-TV to get Stu a new spot, airing after *Maple Leaf Wrestling* on Saturday afternoons? Without television, it is unlikely Stu could have revived the promotion, so why didn't Ed just leave well enough alone?

"Ed loved Stu," says Nomi Whalen. "He saw Stu's sweetness and his spirit.... When he walked away, he was walking away from the behaviour, not Stu." Now, Whalen saw his friend needed him and stepped in to help. He did so on one condition – that he have a certain level of creative control over the show. He returned to Stampede Wrestling, which resumed operations in October 1985, not only as an announcer but as executive producer. Whalen promised the public that the violence would be toned down.

One of his first orders of business was to tame Bad News Allen. If Allen was to return to the show, Whalen decreed he would be recast as a babyface. It was a poor fit. In an interview with Whalen, who jokingly introduced him as Good News Allen, Allen apologized to the announcer and to the viewers for his past conduct, saying that he had learned the error of his ways. The speech, delivered by the wrestler in a dapper three-piece suit, was awkwardly delivered. Allen wasn't comfortable playing the humble, repentant role. Rage and indignation came far more naturally to him. "It was bologna," says Allen. "People wanted to see me as a heel."

News could have left the territory – McMahon was trying to recruit him – but he was starting a family and didn't want to be far from home. Had Bad News softened? Not much. When crossed, he was as dangerous as ever, a fact his former tag team partner Angel Acevedo, the Cuban Assassin, can attest to. Acevedo and Allen had been best friends, with Acevedo the best man at Allen's wedding in 1985. But when their wives had a falling out, it led to a near fight to the death between the two men in a Denny's restaurant parking lot.

The chaos began when Allen's bride, Helen, slapped Acevedo's wife, Pat, for supposedly talking behind her back. Allen says that when he got home late that night, he received a call from Acevedo, who threatened to kill his wife. It's a charge Acevedo denies. The venomous exchange escalated and soon the two men and their wives were headed to the Denny's, close to Acevedo's apartment, to settle the score. Allen backhanded Acevedo across his shaggy face, cutting his lip. Acevedo pulled a hunting knife and came after Allen. Allen grabbed a baseball bat from the trunk of his car and began swinging. Somehow, in the struggle, Allen's wife was slashed. Pat fled in a panic and called the police. When the cops arrived on the scene, Acevedo was in his car, attempting to flee as Allen smashed the windshield with the bat. Neither man was charged.*

Allen remains resentful about the dispute, but not Acevedo. "I don't have enemies," says the bearded villain who today at age sixty-four works for Keith Hart's son as part of a house painting crew. "I only have friends all around the world."

The fiery nature of the wrestlers aside, Stu and Ed faced another hurdle when they put Stampede Wrestling back on the air. In a galling turn of events, the upstart group that tried to promote wrestling in the territory earlier that year using the name Stampede Wrestling filed a $1 million lawsuit against Stu, Whalen, and CFAC-TV in late 1985. It alleged that the defendants were benefiting from using another company's name. The claim was thrown out of court.

Now there was nothing to stop the show from rolling. But how far could it roll without Bret, Davey Boy, and Dynamite, three of its greatest stars?

Bad News Allen was not the only Stampede Wrestling star to return to the fold when the promotion relaunched in October 1985. Kerry Brown, Duke Myers, J.R. Foley, Leo Burke, The Great Gama, and "Rotten" Ron Starr all reappeared. With Bad News working as a good guy, Honky Tonk Wayne was

---

*The battle continued in the late 1980s in the WWF, when the two men ran into each other in a Tennessee dressing room. Allen was being pushed as a top star at the time, and Acevedo was trying out for a spot on the roster. When they saw each other, Acevedo pulled his knife and Allen grabbed a chair as wrestlers struggled to separate the former pals.

pushed as the top villain in the territory. While not a great wrestler, he was an exceptionally funny entertainer who played his southern slimeball shtick to the hilt. When the Harts challenged Honky Tonk and Ron Starr to be part of a six-man elimination tag team bout, his reply to Whalen was priceless. "They wanna six-man elimination? That's fine with the Memphis Mafia," he crowed with a cocky grin. "We like six. We had six eggs over easy for breakfast this morning. I got six old ladies. I got six Cadillacs and I got six diamond rings, Ed Whalen!"

But Honky Tonk was not happy in the territory. Keith Hart remembers him constantly complaining on the road and making calls to his friend Hulk Hogan in the WWF in the hopes that he would eventually be booked for the big time. By 1987, his wish would come true.

Occasionally, when they had time off from other commitments, Bret, Neidhart, Davey Boy, and Dynamite returned to wrestle on a few cards. On these instances, business boomed, as all four men had become massive stars in the WWF. When they came back to Calgary, they were treated as royalty.

Playing hard to get with McMahon had worked in the British Bulldogs' favour, and he cajoled them back to the promotion for WrestleMania II on April 7, 1986, where they became the WWF World Tag Team champions at Chicago's Rosemont Horizon. With their combined speed and agility, along with Dynamite's hard, reckless style and Davey Boy's superhuman strength, they were the greatest tag team in the world.

Bret managed to turn around his fortunes too, after a shaky start. Initially, the WWF created a rhinestone cowboy gimmick for Bret. He was supposed to enter the ring on a horse, wearing a cowboy hat, chaps, and a glittering sequined jacket. Bret hated the idea and resisted it every step of the way. He didn't even like country music, he argued, and he thought it would be an insult to the real cowboys in his hometown.[10] As an alternative, Bret suggested he form a heel tag team called the Hart Foundation with his bulky brother-in-law, Jim Neidhart. They could even use Jimmy Hart (no relation to the Hart family) as their manager. The "Mouth of the South" was one of the best heel managers in the business, a charismatic weasel who dressed flamboyantly and screamed taunts at the audience through a megaphone.

Rechristened Bret "The Hitman" Hart and Jim "The Anvil" Neidhart and dressed in gaudy pink-and-black tights, the Hart Foundation became hugely popular in the WWF. Their heroic personas in Stampede Wrestling were ditched as they revamped themselves as a pair of villainous sleazeballs. Neidhart played the maniac role, wearing sunglasses to the ring and tugging at his orange, pointy beard as he cackled away during his interviews.

Bret greased his long brown hair, giving it a permanent wet look, and wore wraparound shades, playing it cool and cocky. He based his evil persona, he says, on Dynamite Kid's during his days as a Stampede heel. In a *Calgary Sun* column he wrote, Bret aptly summed up the team's dynamic created by Neidhart's incredible brute strength and Bret's impeccable wrestling skills: "We were like a Porsche and a tank."[11]

But bringing back the old faces wasn't going to be enough to revive Stampede Wrestling. Competing with the flash and sizzle of the WWF required upgraded production values, far-out angles, and a new school of stars. And Stu didn't have a Vince McMahon budget. The revamp would have to be done at a grassroots level.

The old, bloodstained mat on the wrestling ring was replaced by a red, white, and blue canvas brandishing the Calgary Stampede logo. Jim Davies, the pint-sized, fedora-wearing *Calgary Sun* columnist, was brought into the picture as Whalen's cheeky sidekick. Yet what the promotion really needed was a fresh infusion of wrestling talent.

Fortunately, the Harts had one more star to unleash on the world. In a family of outstanding athletes, Owen Hart, youngest of the twelve siblings, was the best of the bunch. Stories abound in the wrestling world of grapplers passing through Stu's territory in the early 1970s and being amazed by the little blond boy doing flying backflips and executing difficult wrestling moves to perfection in Stu's backyard ring.

Owen was always a natural performer. He was a gifted mimic and loved making prank phone calls to his dad, pretending to be various wrestlers and weirdos, confounding Stu with absurd scenarios. When Stu realized it was Owen he would chuckle and say, "That little bastard got me again." Owen wasn't a genuine troublemaker, however. Growing up, he both feared and respected Stu, and he wanted nothing more than to make his dad proud. In high school, he played football and wrestled, winning city and provincial championships. He continued the sport while pursuing a degree in physical education at the University of Calgary. "I was living my dad's dream, being an amateur wrestler and going for the Olympics," Owen said. "But I hated it.... I always had this feeling: 'When I come home I want to please my dad....' I should have said, 'I don't want this.'"[12]

Owen was exposed to the craziness of the wrestling business at a young age. When he was fourteen, he accompanied Bruce and Keith to a gig in Honolulu, where they were attacked by rowdy fans. The youngest Hart jumped to their defence, coming out of the rumble with a black eye. He was only sixteen when he began wrestling in small towns along the Stampede circuit, wearing a mask to maintain his eligibility as an amateur, as professional wrestlers were not allowed to wrestle in the amateur ranks.[13]

Owen was handsome and likable. Having grown up studying the greats who passed through the promotion, he learned to brawl with the brawlers, fly with the fliers, and mix it up with just about anyone in a technical wrestling match. From a young age, he also understood a thing or two about ring psychology. He knew how to tell a story with his body, how to pace a match, how to read the fans and keep them on the edge of their seats. Bruce, who had formed a close bond with his youngest brother, was "salivating at his potential in the family business," writes Owen's widow, Martha, in her book, *Broken Harts*.[14]

But Owen didn't want a career as a professional wrestler. He wanted to be a teacher. His girlfriend Martha Patterson, a pretty but prudish blond from a struggling single-parent home, who he had been dating since high school, wanted that as well. She was repulsed by the wrestling world and made no bones about it. She recalls an incident where out of the blue Bret asked, "You want to wrestle, right Owen?"

"I jumped right in," writes Martha. "'Oh no, he's going to be a teacher....' Wrestling was out of the question."[15]

But by the spring of 1986, Stampede Wrestling needed a hero and, like most university students, Owen needed money. Bruce persuaded his little brother to give it a try, and Owen made his pro debut in May of that year. He was a sensation, incorporating Bret's impeccable technical skills with the high-flying stunts he picked up watching Dynamite Kid and Japan's Tiger Mask, whom he revered. Long-time Stampede fans had a special affection for the blue-eyed baby of the beloved Hart clan, and Owen played up to it perfectly.

Retired wrestler Mike Shaw, who worked in the business for twenty years, including a stint in the WWF, says that, in all his years, he never saw a wrestler who was as genuinely loved by the fans as Owen was in Stampede Wrestling. "We did an angle once where Owen had to wear an eye patch, and I stuck a fork inside the patch," Shaw says. "People were taken out of the Pavilion in tears. Girls and guys were in the front row crying. People loved him. He was the Hart baby, the hometown kid."

Although he had little desire to be in the business long term, Owen enjoyed wrestling. He liked showing off his skills and entertaining fans and was happy to help his father. Most importantly, he was making $500 a week, a salary that eventually doubled. He was already set on building a nest egg for his future with Martha, and where else could a twenty-one-year-old kid make that kind of money?

In his earliest matches, Owen teamed up with his brother-in-law Ben Bassarab, and the two feuded with the masked Viet Cong Express, a duo that included future Japanese legend Hiroshi Hase. The non-stop action of those mercurial bouts gained notoriety around the world, and it wasn't long before the Japanese were clamouring for Owen.

A few of the wrestlers were at first turned off by the rising Hart star. They thought him conceited, demanding a star push in his rookie year simply because of his family. But any arrogance Owen displayed early in his career was eventually outgrown. He was generally regarded as friendly and down-to-earth. The youngest Hart was in many ways the most mature. He was clean living and never swore. He saved his money and never lost sight of his dream to marry Martha and start a family. For Owen, wrestling was a means to an end.

Owen wasn't the only fresh face in the territory. In the mid-1980s, the Hart boys began actively recruiting and training a new crop of wrestlers down in the Dungeon, just as Stu had in previous decades. Under Bruce, Keith, and Ross, the harsh training regiment became known as The School of Hart Knocks, and it churned out some of the greatest stars in the business.

By the mid-'80s, the world was more aware of Stampede Wrestling than ever. The show scored a coup when it was broadcast across Canada on TSN (The Sports Network). Meanwhile, with tag teams the British Bulldogs and the Hart Foundation standing out among the WWF's most spectacular stars, word got around that they were products of Stampede Wrestling and fans began paying attention. American wrestling magazines, which usually ignored Canadian territories, began reporting on Stampede regularly.

Certainly the most successful of the newcomers in this era was Chris Benoit, who is one of the biggest stars in the WWE (formerly the WWF) today, having held the World Heavyweight title in 2004. Benoit was a withdrawn twelve year old when his family moved to Edmonton from Montreal in the late '70s. Benoit's life was changed when he saw Dynamite Kid wrestle at Edmonton's Sales Pavilion in 1979. "I looked up to him so much," Benoit says. "He was my Superman. His style was so aggressive, so believable, so technically sound." Dynamite made Benoit want to be a wrestler, and the boy told his idol as much the first time they met. Bret Hart remembers a teenage Benoit staring down at his feet, blushing as he spoke to Dynamite, telling him he hoped to one day follow in his footsteps.[16]

When Benoit graduated from high school in 1985, he joined The School of Hart Knocks. Weekdays he worked at his father's air infiltration business, but come the weekend, the skinny young man was on a Greyhound headed to Calgary for the brutal stretching and bump-taking in the Dungeon. Benoit was primarily trained by the brothers, but a few times seventy-year-old Stu came down to join in the fun. The old man's vice-like holds made Benoit scream. But he was never deterred. Benoit was serious-minded, firm in his goals, and if this was the road he had to take, he was ready.

By the end of the year, the kid was making his pro wrestling debut. Even when he was green, wrestlers and fans alike noticed similarities between Benoit's style and that of Dynamite Kid. But Benoit had a more rational head on his shoulders. He was not hindered by a hair-trigger temper, and he showed little interest in excessive partying. Mike Shaw calls him "Dynamite without the dark side." Bret would later write that he saw "the ghost of the Dynamite Kid" in the ring when he watched Benoit wrestle.[17] Dynamite saw it, too. Years later, he staggered to the ring after one of Benoit's matches and drunkenly hung his wrestling boots around the young man's neck. It was the greatest honour he could bestow.

Another star of the era was Brian Pillman. A rash, high-strung athlete raised in a Cincinnati suburb, Pillman at first pursued a career in football with the Cincinnati Bengals and then the Calgary Stampeders. When Pillman broke his ankle with the Stamps, he made a call to Keith Hart. He was invited to the Dungeon.

Standing only five-foot-nine but bulked up on steroids, Pillman was strong and agile. A womanizing jock with a curly golden-brown mullet, pretty face, and a wildman persona, the Harts knew he'd be an instant hit with female fans. After a few months of training, they rushed him to the ring where, as predicted, he became a crowd favourite. "Flyin'" Brian was an airborne warrior with a dramatic flair that worked crowds into a froth. Soon, Pillman was teamed up with his mentor Bruce Hart, as Badd Company, a leather jacket- and headband-wearing duo who relished their roles as a pair of beautiful bad boys.

Stampede Wrestling was also set upon by some of the finest Japanese wrestlers in the world at that time, including the Viet Cong Express and Jushin Liger. The bouts the Japanese wrestlers had with the likes of Owen Hart, Pillman, and Benoit changed the face of wrestling, taking aerial exhibitions to new heights.

Meanwhile, a corny but effective gimmick was cooked up when rookie wrestler Karl Moffat was put in a goalie mask and a pair of coveralls and

Flyin' Brian Pillman sails across the ring, bowling over "Champagne" Gerry Morrow with a flying clothesline.

named Jason the Terrible, after the teen-slashing monster in the popular *Friday the 13th* movie series. It was not a particularly inspired concept. What made it work – for a time, Jason was the territory's hottest heel – was the zaniness with which it was carried off. Accompanying the mute, axe-wielding beast to the ring was The Zodiak, an evil masked character who controlled Jason with the powers of the occult.

Cheesier still were the Zodiak-Jason promos, pretaped for the TV show. Zodiak's voice, warped through a distortion box, sounded vaguely demonic. He and Jason stood in front of a giant screen projecting the image of moving stars: viewers were to think that the interview was being broadcast from another dimension. Unfortunately, it came off as two goons trying, and failing, to be scary using cut-rate production not fit for the worst B-movie. The scenes were so bad, however, that they took on an endearing, kitschy quality.

Bruce Hart's taste for absurdities also came into play as The Zodiak prayed to a malicious deity he called The Almighty Luke and Jason writhed and twisted like a tormented beast, frequently lunging at the camera man in a state of bloodlust.*

The Harts also responded to the Hulk Hogan craze of this era when recruiting new wrestlers. Hulk Hogan was a steroid-pumped bodybuilder with limited wrestling skills and the Harts were convinced they too needed a few impossibly muscular mutants in their stable. Answering the call was Boston's Steve "The Strangler" DiSalvo, New Hampshire's Ted Arcidi, and Wisconsin's Bill Kazmaier. Unfortunately, none of these men came close to matching Hogan's awesome charisma.

Of the muscle brigade, only DiSalvo made any real impact on the territory, coming off as a loathsome villain. Kazmaier and Arcidi were two of the strongest men in the world but neither of them had any business in a ring. As Mike Shaw recalls, "Kazmaier and Arcidi wrestled each other and it was like watching two guys knee deep in wet cement."

The Karachi Vice was the last evil army the noble Harts would face in their hometown ring. From its earliest days, wrestling had exploited societal fears and racial stereotypes. The Karachi Vice – it's name inspired by TV's *Miami Vice* – played on the attitudes of some audience members toward immigrants. That attitude had been clear for years as chants of "Go home, Paki!" and "Paki shit!" rattled the rafters in every arena Gama Singh appeared in.

---

*As dorky as this gimmick was, the WWF recreated it in the 1990s with Kane, a mute beast who was also controlled by the occult powers of an evil handler.

Gama, who was East Indian, played a despicable character to be sure. His most vile tactic was throwing fireballs into the face of his enemies, an ancient trick from the homeland, or so the crowd was told. (In truth, he was using flash paper, as a magician uses, which flashes vividly and burns out instantly. It was relatively safe, though there were a few cases of singed eyebrows.) Gama got his biggest reaction when he fireballed Owen. As the Harts' baby boy lay sprawled on the canvas, writhing in pain, his supposedly charred face buried in his hands, the fans screamed for Gama's blood. "People called Stu's house saying they were going to throw acid on me at the next match," Gama remembers. "Stu really had to beef up security."

Gama says he never took issue with the racist chants rising from the audience. In fact, he fanned the flames. "All that heat meant I was doing my job," he says. "This was my bread and butter." So Gama was disappointed with Ed Whalen when the show began airing on TSN. As the crowd erupted into a hearty round of racist chants, Whalen got on the microphone and ordered them to stop. "Listen," he lectured. "This show is going nationwide and this is not the image we want to portray of Calgary."

"Without realizing it," Gama says, "Ed was killing my heat."

While Bruce takes credit for developing the Karachi Vice angle in 1986, Gama says it was his idea to partner up with Mike Shaw, a sweaty tub of blubber from Michigan with hair on his back to match the beard on his face. Shaw, who weighed in at 360 pounds, was a mid-card performer until the decision was made to put a turban on his head and rename him Makhan Singh. "We cooked up this contrived notion about Makhan being a born-again Pakistani, whatever the hell that meant," says Bruce with a laugh. "But it worked."

Overnight, the Karachi Vice became a cult sensation. Shaw remembers walking with his wife in downtown Calgary when a can of Coca-Cola whizzed by their heads. He turned around to see a carload of teens giving him the finger and shouting, "Karachi Vice sucks!" "I think taking a white guy and giving him an Indian name just drove people crazy," says Shaw.

If Shaw's gimmick riled up the audience, his sharp tongue worked them into a frenzy. In interviews with Whalen, he frequently belittled Calgary, rubbing it in when the Calgary Flames lost a game, mocking the Calgary Tower as a symbol of phallic inadequacy. Shaw claims that just before the 1988 Winter Olympics he received a letter from then mayor Ralph Klein. "It said they were trying to promote Calgary as being a kind, loving western city and they wanted me to hold off on my negative comments before the Olympics," Shaw says. "Of course, I got worse after that.... If anybody's going to believe what's said in a wrestling match and not come to Calgary, they couldn't be of sound mind anyway."

At the gimmick's height, around 1988, there was even a Karachi Vice fan club. While the Harts sold Karachi Vice T-shirts, fans often showed up wearing T-shirts of their own, bearing insulting slogans such as "Karachi Mice" and "Karachi Lice." A popular poster for sale at the matches featured Mike Shaw wearing a toilet seat on his head. This was appropriate, as the babyfaces had taken to calling him "The Toilet Bowl."*

While Shaw and Gama were the nucleus of Karachi Vice, at various times the group also included such creeps as Steve DiSalvo, Ron Starr, Kerry Brown, and frizzy-haired female wrestler Rhonda Singh. There was a plan to put the 260-pound woman in a bikini and have her come to the ring as The Karachi Queen, but it never materialized.

Karachi Vice made every effort to portray itself as a grotesque group of deviants, bragging to Whalen about their dressing room orgies with women who supposedly found them irresistible. On these decadent occasions, the Vice dined, they said, on zesty barbequed eel and Karachi Kooler, which, according to the wrestling programs, consisted of scotch and cream soda.

The Vice found themselves a manager in the form of Abu Wizal. Outside the ring, Wizal was Mlad Elzein from Beirut, a hardcore wrestling fan who moved to Calgary in 1970 at the age of ten. Standing just over five feet tall and weighing about 130 pounds, Elzein never imagined he would be a character in the Harts' roving circus until Bruce stuck him in Arab robes and dark sunglasses, dispatching him into the ring to cheat on behalf of the bad guys. The original plan was to call him Abu Nidal, after the Palestinian terrorist, but Whalen protested that it was tasteless. Instead, Elzein was introduced as Abu Wizal, financial adviser to the Karachi Vice. That twist tickles him to this day: "Between us all we probably didn't have a hundred bucks to rub together."

---

*A good portion of Shaw's career was built on gross-out gimmicks, as during his WWF stint in the 1990s when he was cast as the world's most repulsive slob, Bastion Booger. He also had a successful run in Ted Turner's WCW as a lovable mental patient named Norman the Lunatic.

Chapter sixteen

The Death of Stampede Wrestling

Behind-the-scenes anarchy had been a part of the Stampede Wrestling world from day one, but by the late 1980s the territory was in chaos. There was bedlam on the tracks at every turn and by the decade's end this would play a major factor in permanently derailing the wrestling promotion Stu had spent his life creating.

The old problems between father and son cropped up almost immediately when Stampede Wrestling relaunched, with Stu the traditionalist butting heads with Bruce and his batty concepts. A December 1985 article in the *Calgary Herald* captured the struggle perfectly: "The problem is ... Stu wants his sons to take over, but isn't willing to allow them the freedom to do so.... He's afraid to let go." Stu's rebuttal seemed to be aimed directly at Bruce: "You're always hoping that maybe your kids will take over the responsibility.... I'm hoping some of my boys will cut down on their wrestling and take care of the administration.... I don't want to see this business go down the drain."[1]

One of the symptoms of the territory's ills was the endless pranks that had become so destructive and mean-spirited they were driving wrestlers away. Of course, this was the region that had given birth to the legendary Mabel parties. Wild ribs were nothing new. But fuelled by a smorgasbord of drugs, the gags took on a new edge that could slice a man in half.

It wasn't all cruel. Owen, Bruce, and Ross frequently targeted Brian Pillman, who they treated like a brother. On a tour stop in Kelowna, British

Bruce Hart (left) and Brian Pillman made up one of the dominant Stampede Wrestling tag teams of the late 1980s. With their shades, headbands, and leather jackets, they presented themselves as a bad boy duo Badd Company.

Columbia, Bruce and Owen took in a wet, mangy dog they found roaming the hotel parking lot. As Pillman was out for the evening with one of the many paramours he seemed to have in every town, the Hart brothers took the dog to Flyin' Brian's room. They fed the mutt pizza, then dressed it in Pillman's jacket and sunglasses and tucked it away in the wrestler's bed. They also removed the light bulbs from the room. A few hours later, when Pillman arrived from his fling, fumbling for the lights, the sharp-dressed dog leapt off the bed in attack mode and chased him from the room.[2]

Even Bad News Allen, never known for his sense of humour, got in on the ribs. When Jason the Terrible, otherwise known as Karl Moffat, was a rookie, the boys convinced him that the best way to get on the good side of the surly Allen was to ask him about his son, who they claimed was a concert pianist. Moffat approached the ever intense Bad News sitting at the front of the tour bus with trepidation and asked, in his high-pitched voice, "Mr. Allen, may I talk to you?"

"Go ahead, Karl," Bad News said.

"I just want to congratulate you on your son and what a terrific pianist he is."

Allen stared at Moffat as the rookie continued to stammer words of praise. Suddenly he slammed Moffat into a seat and put a knife to his throat. "Are you making a joke about my kid?" Allen screamed. "My kid lost his fingers in a lawn mower accident. I should kill you!" Moffat burst into tears, realizing he had been humiliated in front of his fellow wrestlers.

Nobody suffered as much as the massive Bill Kazmaier. Most of the boys disliked "the world's strongest man" immensely. With his sixty-inch chest and twenty-three inch biceps, there was no question Kazmaier, who set a world record when he bench-pressed 661 pounds, was monstrous. But in the ring, he could barely execute the most basic moves. Nor could he grasp the business. Once, when Kazmaier thought he had won the North American title belt only to have it stripped from him in the course of some wacky angle, he phoned Stu in a rage. Stu had to explain to him how the game worked. Still, Kazmaier was arrogant and often told the boys it was only a matter of time before he was a big star in the wwf. Then, he said, he would leave this small-time territory and its small-time talents behind.

Kazmaier was also vehemently opposed to recreational drug use, which put him at odds with many of the boys on the roster. Seeing this as his weakness, the grapplers played with his head relentlessly. One afternoon on the road, Ben Bassarab and Brian Pillman had a bag of talcum powder they pretended was cocaine. Sitting in the van in front of Kazmaier, they plunged their faces into the bag, snorting voraciously, acting as if they were flying high. When they offered a snort to young John Hindley, a newcomer to the territory who was wrestling as Davey Boy's cousin, Johnny Smith, Kazmaier became enraged.

"Don't do it, Johnny!" he shouted. "It's the devil!"

Hindley, meanwhile, in on the rib, played his role as the innocent lamb being led to slaughter to perfection. "I wonder what it's like," he said.

The wrestlers took another dip, the tips of their noses white. "Woo! Try it baby!"

Kazmaier roared, his eyeballs bugging out of his head as if they too were muscles ready to explode. "Don't do it! You'll get hooked!"

In another instance, the crew in the van planned a sting on the powerhouse. Gerry Morrow was driving when Bassarab made a racist joke. "Hey! Don't you talk about black people like that!" yelled the man from Martinique.

"Sorry, Gerry," Bassarab replied. "You're my buddy. I didn't mean to talk that way about niggers."

Morrow pulled the van over and the two men staged a fight in the ditch, as only two pro wrestlers could. As planned, Winnipeg wrestler Ron Ritchie jumped into the fray and he and Bassarab started beating Morrow. Bassarab broke a beer bottle and slashed Champagne Gerry across the forehead, as in a wrestling match. Kazmaier watched, trembling. When the faux fight was broken up, Owen, who had been pretending to be asleep, "woke up," took a look at the mess, and demanded to know what had happened. Pillman blamed the scene on the innocent Kazmaier, who played into Pillman's hands when he proceeded to charge at him like an angry bull. Pillman had gotten the rise out of Kazmaier he was looking for and, to the wrestlers' amusement, he was soon running for his life down the highway, chased by a raging mountain of muscle.

Alison Hart never defied her father. The very thought of doing so pained her. But this time she knew he was wrong.

It had been apparent for a long time that she had to get away from her husband, Ben Bassarab. Although Stu had witnessed one of the couple's meltdowns, he refused to support any talks of their divorce. Marriage is a serious commitment, he said, one you honoured for life. When a couple had problems, no matter how severe, they worked it out, they carried on. Especially when children were involved. Alison took her father's words to heart for years. Besides, she had loved Ben.

He arrived on the scene in the early 1980s, a regular at BJ's Gym, where him and Davey Boy Smith became best friends. When he started dating Alison, Bassarab promised her he wouldn't pursue wrestling – she had always hated the sport – but, as Bassarab was a muscular jock, it was only natural that the family invited him to give the game a try. He did, and loved it. By the time he married Alison in May 1983, Ben's career path seemed set.

Alison was determined to make the marriage work, even after the night of Davey Boy's stag, back in 1984, when Ben had been so cruel. Alison was pregnant then with her and Ben's first child and had just been released from the hospital after having an ovarian cyst removed. She wanted Ben to take her straight home. Instead, he left her at Hart House while he headed to the coach house out back. The Neidharts lived there at the time, and Jim was throwing Davey his party.

Keith Hart, who was taking part in the merriment, recalls walking back to the mansion to grab party snacks, only to find his sister crying. "I just got out of the hospital and I want to go home," she sobbed. "Can you tell Ben to give me the car keys so I can go home?" Keith marched back to the coach house to get the keys and smarten up Alison's husband. Bassarab, anything but repentant, made a few foul comments about his pregnant wife that nearly sparked a fight on the spot.

The inevitable battle occurred later in the evening, down the road from Hart House. As Ben, enraged that his wife had pulled him from the party, climbed into the car to drive home, Keith jumped in the passenger's side and started throwing punches. He jammed Bassarab's head under the steering wheel and hammered him in the face as Bassarab tried to gouge out his eyes. Suddenly, Stu was on the scene, dragging Keith by his feet from the car.

Stu followed Alison and Ben home that night and tried to talk sense into the father-to-be as Bassarab, his face bruised and swollen, raged. Alison says she didn't want her dad to leave. Stu told her it was her responsibility to work out her problems with her husband and walked out.

Ben denies being cruel to Alison, but he doesn't refute that he was a wild one. He laughs when he thinks of the so-called villains in the Karachi Vice, Gama Singh and Mike Shaw, being family men, going straight to bed every night after the gigs, while he and his fellow babyfaces raised hell. "In the real world, the babyfaces were the bad guys," he says. "The bad guys were the nice ones, and the good guys, we were just devils."

Bassarab was constantly out drinking and getting into bar fights in his wrestling days. This nearly proved his undoing in late 1985 when he was stabbed through the liver by a man he had been chasing outside a Calgary nightclub. He returned to the ring a few months later, but his rapidly deteriorating relationship with Alison eventually cost him his job. "I ended up leaving my wife because ... it was a joke," Bassarab says over Baileys and coffee during a Saturday afternoon interview at his southwest Calgary home. "I'm supposed to be a father and a husband and I'm out wrestling every night on the road, with a girlfriend in basically every town. I thought, 'This is not fair to Alison. I'm not a husband or a father. Why pretend to be one once a week?' So I left her. Stu was not very happy.... He ended up firing me."

Bassarab says he protested, telling Stu he was living a lie, admitting his infidelities to the old man. Even then, he says, Stu was adamant that Ben and Alison get back together. "Do you think you're the first guy who ever had a relationship on the road?" Ben recalls Stu saying. "You have a family at home." Ben wouldn't budge. He says the WWF expressed interest in him around that time but Stu exerted his influence and convinced the federation not to hire his estranged son-in-law. "He put the block on me," Bassarab says bitterly. "He dangled the carrot and said, 'If you get back with Alison ...'"

For a long while, Alison says, she wanted her husband back and did everything to make it work, even though she knew Ben was seeing another woman. Finally, one day, Alison looked at her two daughters – one a toddler, the other a newborn – and realized she didn't want them to be raised by Ben, despite what her father said. That day, a trembling Alison Hart defied Stu and called her lawyer.

The British Bulldogs were wild when they left Stampede Wrestling for the WWF in 1984. But compared with the crazy dogs who returned to the promotion in the latter half of 1988, they seemed like a pair of rambunctious puppies in their younger days.

The team terrorized WWF dressing rooms relentlessly, slipping Ex-Lax, sleeping pills, and hallucinogenics into wrestlers' drinks, cutting up their clothes, shaving people's heads when they passed out, beating the hell out of them if they protested. Dynamite, in particular, seemed to be on an endless booze-fuelled 'roid rage. That he was in constant physical pain made matters only worse.

Unlike his cousin, Davey Boy, who was naturally bigger than him, Dynamite's modest frame was never meant to accommodate the 228 pounds of muscle he had amassed over the years. That body armour, combined with his reckless, high-impact wrestling style, was destroying his body. Years of snap-suplexes, flying headbutts from the top of steel cages, and crash-landing wipeouts on cement floors were breaking him down, though Dynamite

A young, lean Davey Boy Smith sends his cousin Dynamite Kid flying upside down off the top turnbuckle, early 1980s.

never admitted it. He simply popped painkillers, injected cortisone into his joints, and carried on.

On December 16, 1986, he couldn't ignore the pain any longer. He and Davey Boy were taking on Don Muraco and Bob Orton at Copps Coliseum in Hamilton, Ontario. In mid-match, Dynamite crumpled to the mat, sharp pains searing through his spine. The heels, not realizing he was hurt, kicked him and bashed him with a chair as he lay wracked with spasms. Dynamite tried to stop them but his words came out an agonized whisper, drowned by the audience's chants of "Phon-ey!" They couldn't understand why their hero had collapsed when he hadn't even been hit.[3]

On his return to Calgary, Dynamite was told that he had two ruptured discs in his back and extensive nerve damage. After undergoing emergency surgery, he was advised that his body could no longer withstand the punishment he was putting it through. "In my mind, it was like hammering a car till the shock absorbers go," he wrote. Nevertheless, he wasn't about to heed the advice of any doctor who dared recommend he retire at the age of twenty-eight. "Bollocks to that," Dynamite muttered under his breath.[4] As soon as he was able to move, he left the hospital against his doctor's orders. His wife, Michelle, remembers him crawling up the stairs into the house that day.

That's when the calls started coming in from Vince McMahon. The Bulldogs were still the tag team champions and, given Dynamite's condition, they would have to drop the belts as soon as possible. Dynamite told his boss that he needed more time, that he could barely get up off the couch, but McMahon continued to apply pressure. He wanted the Bulldogs to lose the titles to the Iron Sheik and Nikolai Volkoff. Dynamite refused, saying the only team he was willing to drop the belts to was the Hart Foundation. "They earn it every night," he said.

Dynamite returned to work on January 26, 1987, at the Sun Dome in Tampa, Florida. On the way to the ring, he was arm in arm with Davey Boy. It made him feel like a weakling, but it was the only way he could walk. As planned, Bret and Neidhart attacked the Bulldogs from behind. Dynamite was taken out quickly when Jimmy Hart smashed him in the head with his megaphone, supposedly knocking him out cold. Then Davey Boy was double-teamed and pinned. The Hart Foundation was the new World Tag Team champions. To this day, Bret praises Dynamite Kid for giving him the single biggest break of his career.[5]

Before long, the Bulldogs were back in action full time, but Dynamite's abilities were rapidly deteriorating. Every other week he was contending with a new injury. His knees were giving out. He had torn all the ligaments in his shoulders. Dynamite paid it no heed, pushing his body to the limit nightly. He never took shortcuts, always executing the moves the fans loved despite the blinding pain that cut him to the core. Stu used to rightly say that "Dynamite took more bumps in one match than half these goddamn guys took in their whole career." But Dynamite's style came with great sacrifice. "His passion took over from common sense," wrote Bret in the *Calgary Sun*. "He was the consummate wrestling artist and much like Beethoven, who wrote his most brilliant masterpieces while he was going deaf, the Dynamite Kid had some of his most incredible matches while his back was disintegrating."[6]

The more his body gave out on him, the more Dynamite became consumed with self-loathing. He felt he was letting down the team. Davey Boy was gradually becoming the star of the duo. While Dynamite was losing size and strength, Davey was hitting his peak. He was bigger and stronger than ever. Davey maintained his heartthrob good looks while Dynamite was becoming increasingly grizzled. It was Davey Boy who was scoring the pins; Davey Boy who brought the team's silly mascot, Matilda the bulldog, to the ring, which made the kids love him; Davey Boy who smiled and waved to the crowd while Dynamite winced and scowled, trying to block the pain.

To Dynamite, whose two-fisted pride was everything, this was more than he could bear. He began to lash out. While he respected Davey as the greatest partner he could have, he seemed incapable of showing his appreciation. Instead, he called his cousin a simpleton and treated him like his personal windup toy. It was implicit from the start that Dynamite was the leader. He would decide where they wrestled, who they wrestled, and how they wrestled. Even when it came to the ribs, Dynamite was the instigator and Davey the sidekick. Once he started to slip, however, Dynamite began to feel like a liability, and watching Davey thrive without him stung.

He also suspected Davey's wife, Diana, of fuelling the rivalry behind the scenes. It was the same garbage that she had been feeding Davey for years – that he was the star and Dynamite was jealous and overrated. The only difference now was that a deep, dark part of him felt she was right.

The Harts insist Davey was a good friend to Dynamite through his physical traumas, even Christmas shopping for him when he was bedridden at the end of 1986. Dynamite remembers it differently. He recalls his cousin becoming increasingly distant and ungrateful. Once, Dynamite lashed out: "I brought you to Canada, took you to Japan, got you in the WWF; you are nothing but a selfish bastard!"[7]

At work and play, though, the two put on a united front. One of their favourite ribs involved Jake "The Snake" Roberts's twelve-foot python,

Top: Hinting at the steroid-pumped strongman he would become in the WWF, Davey Boy Smith hoists the Cuban Assassin straight over his head, in 1984.

Bottom: Davey Boy Smith drop kicks Hubert Gallant, 1982.

Damien, which Roberts draped over his felled opponents after a match. In between shows, Roberts kept the snake backstage in a securely tied sack. While the snake was bound, the Bulldogs thought it funny to elbow drop the bag, stick their steroid needles in it, and pour hot coffee over it. When Roberts took the snake out of the bag during his match, the tortured creature was ferocious. On a couple of occasions, it wrapped itself around Roberts's neck and began choking him. Roberts would run to the dressing room and, out of the cameras' sight, fling the serpent across the room.

"They did a lot of mean-spirited things that I couldn't be associated with," says Bret, who neither joined in the revelry nor turned on his destructive brother-in-laws in the dressing room. "You learn in the business to mind your own space. If you get involved and try to be a sheriff in town, you're not going to last."

The Bulldogs' reign of terror in the WWF culminated with Jacques and Raymond Rougeau attacking Dynamite Kid during a TV taping in Fort Wayne, Indiana, punching out his teeth with a pair of brass knuckles. McMahon tried to patch things up, but the Bulldogs were soured on the organization and quit soon after. Those close to Dynamite say that while he recovered from the beating physically, he never got over it mentally. As ever, fierce pride was his worst enemy, and he couldn't stand having people think he lost a fight. It was a constant thorn in his side that he never managed to extricate.

By the time the Bulldogs returned to Stampede Wrestling Bruce Hart had fallen out of favour with Stu, blamed for the chaotic state of the business on his watch. Still, the decision to give in to Dynamite's demands and try him out as booker was one the Harts would come to regret.

"He did love his guns," says Michelle Billington of her ex-husband. Indeed, Dynamite's favoured hobby, when not wrestling, playing evil ribs, and drinking himself silly, was another sign of his increasingly rampant nature.

With money pouring in during his WWF days, Dynamite had purchased a $220,000 ranch outside Calgary where he intended to raise his kids, his second child due May 1988. In the meantime, he turned the twenty acres around his home into a killing field. His toys included a sawed-off shot gun, a 30-30 Winchester rifle, and a nine-millimetre semi-automatic pistol – an arsenal fit for a drug raid. Dynamite enjoyed driving around his acreage, accompanied by his bullmastiffs and his wrestling buddies, blowing gophers to bits. Davey Boy Smith and Duke Myers were frequent visitors, as was Brian Peters, a wannabe wrestler who the Harts were training. Peters worked as a strong-arm for cocaine dealers, a job that eventually got him killed in May 1987.[8]

Michelle recalls the mock earnestness with which the boys took to the gopher hunt, competing to see who could get the most kills. "Somebody would shoot one," she says, "and Tom would shout 'Kill check!' There was so many carcasses that the eagles hadn't eaten yet, so you'd have to check every kill and make sure it was warm. Maybe you were just shooting a dead one and making it fly, right?"

One mate Dynamite couldn't invite to the hunt, however, was J.R. Foley. Around the time Dynamite was returning to Stampede Wrestling in 1988, Foley died of throat cancer. At the so-called General's funeral, Foley's daughter asked Dynamite to open the casket and ensure J.R. was being laid to rest in his favourite pair of cowboy boots, as he had requested. Dynamite did so, and said a private goodbye to the surrogate father whom he had tormented for so many years.

Dynamite Kid's booking did little to improve business, which was severely lagging. Despite its initial poor showing in Alberta, by the decade's end the WWF had caught fire and was gradually running Stampede Wrestling into the ground, as it had done to nearly every independent promotion in North America.

WWF shows at the Calgary Saddledome, held every few months, were selling out, drawing roughly fourteen thousand fans per visit. Even a live broadcast of the March 1987 WrestleMania III, shown on the big screen, attracted twelve thousand fans. Meanwhile, Stampede Wrestling was failing to sellout the two-thousand-seat Pavilion.

Stu was coming to terms with this new reality. He told *Alberta Report* that with the fast-paced lifestyle of the modern age, people had less time and inclination to attend weekly wrestling shows. They preferred to get their wrestling fix on TV and lay down their money every few months when the WWF came to town. "It's hard for us to compete with the big money show the WWF can put on, with fancy camera shots and cartoon-style wrestlers," Stu said. "I'm unaware of any independent promotion that is making money presently."[9]

Dynamite Kid did his best to turn the tide, using his WWF connections to recruit disgruntled stars – Harley Race, Corporal Kirchner, and Don Muraco among them – from the big league promotion, but they seldom stuck around long enough to make a difference. One can see why. Muraco had come from wrestling main events with Hulk Hogan to a promotion where a small-timer like Bruce Hart would try to tell him what to do.[10] He went from the huge paydays of the WWF to a place where wrestlers were racing to the bank on payday, hoping their meagre cheques wouldn't bounce.[11]

Mlad Elzein, who says he worked for free for several months, remembers the day Muraco was handed a $150 cheque for a week's work. Dynamite was embarrassed and went to Stu to get more money for "Big Blue," as Muraco was known, but that didn't stop the wrestler from leaving the territory in a hurry.

Dynamite began to take his frustration with the promotion out on the Harts. Keith recalls a match where he and Bruce were teamed up against Dynamite and Johnny Smith. Keith was fighting Johnny when he was hit from behind with such force he was nearly knocked out cold. He reached behind his head and was startled by the bloody gash at his hairline. He later learned that Dynamite had struck him with the steel ring bell. "It was ruthless, gutless, and deliberate," Keith says, still bitter. "I thought we were friends ... but after that I had no use for him."

One angle that should have boosted business on Dynamite's watch was the breakup of the British Bulldogs. The storyline, which mirrored reality, saw the former partners lashing out at one other, each believing they were responsible for the duo's success. Dynamite was again a heel, teaming up with John Hindley, who played Davey Boy's rogue cousin Johnny Smith. Chris Benoit was brought in as Davey's partner. The feud, hyped as "The Dog Fight of the Decade," promised to be one of the greats, but it was stifled by a number of factors, and particularly by Ed Whalen, who was dead set against the breakup of the Bulldogs. Exercising his power as executive producer, he edited a good deal of the action out of the TV show. Meanwhile, Dynamite's injuries continued to force him to the sidelines and, on a couple of occasions, he and Davey left for a few weeks at a time to tour Japan.[12] Every time "the dog fight" started picking up speed, it hit a roadblock.

To make matters worse, Owen Hart jumped ship for the WWF in July 1988, and Brian Pillman left shortly after. Some blamed the latter on friction between Pillman and Dynamite: Dynamite saw Pillman as a cocky punk who hadn't paid his dues.

Ultimately, Ross says, Dynamite had to be demoted from his position as booker. He was too much of a loose canon to manage the men, he was absent much of the time, and his booking concepts were not igniting the fan interest the Harts had anticipated. Again, Bruce was made the booker. To Dynamite, whose ego had already taken a hiding, this was a slap in the face. His spiteful rebellion culminated in an outright mutiny against Bruce on the infamous Yellowknife-Hay River trek, where Dynamite broke his former friend's jaw and looked like he might have Helen Hart's golden child lynched.

As Owen and Martha became husband and wife at Hart House, Bruce standing as best man with his jaw wired shut, Dynamite Kid sat in a Calgary strip club, drunk and belligerent.

He had been on the guest list for the July 1, 1989, wedding but was uninvited after the Hay River incident. Bruce refused to show up if Dynamite was there. Ever the diplomat, Ross tactfully asked Dynamite to work that Saturday in Edmonton. Somebody was needed to run the show, after all, and obviously none of the Harts could be there. Dynamite agreed but opted for a piss-up instead. Stu called him to ask where he had been, and Dynamite made up a transparent excuse about his car breaking down. Stu didn't say another word about it.[13] By this point, it was just another day at the helm of the rambling wreck his promotion had become.

Dynamite was becoming increasingly unreliable. His physical abilities were deteriorating, and the man who used to wrestle electrifying sixty-minute matches was now lucky if he could muster ten minutes in the ring. On some nights, he was unable to pull off his old moves and was hitting the bottle ever more frequently to drown his frustrations. No-shows like the one he pulled the day of Owen's wedding were now commonplace for Dynamite.

It was a day after the wedding, Ross says, that the crew set off for a gig in the resort town of Jasper, Alberta. Ross was driving the rental van, Davey Boy in the passenger's seat. Sitting behind them were Chris Benoit and Karl "Jason the Terrible" Moffat. Although it was summer, the roads were icy through the mountains, and Ross admits he was speeding. While negotiating a sharp curve in the road, the van hydroplaned. For a brief, terrifying moment, the lads thought they were going to plunge off the mountain. Instead, they crashed into a station wagon travelling toward them.

Ross, who was wearing his seat belt, emerged unscathed. Instinctively, he had stuck out his arm and stopped Benoit, who otherwise might have been rocketed through the windshield. Moffat, struck by a spare tire that flew up from the back of the van, was sprawled on the backseat screaming that his leg was broken. But it was Davey Boy who caught the worst of it. His head hit the windshield, shattering the glass and leaving him unconscious in his seat, his face covered in blood. Ross was panicked and began picking glass shards from his brother-in-law's head.*

Diana Hart remembers the phone call she received from her brother. "Diana, I don't know how to tell you this, but there has been a really bad accident," Ross sobbed. "Davey is unconscious. We can't wake him up. I wish to

*The driver of the station wagon shattered his femur.

hell it was me, not him. I'd give anything if it was me." She could hear Moffat shrieking in the background, "Davey's dead! Oh God, he's dead!"[14]

Davey was not dead, but he was out of action for the next five months. Diana says he took 135 stitches in his forehead and suffered two herniated discs at the top of his spine.

For Stu, it was another calamity, another reason to close up shop. But he stuck it out for a little while longer. He did so mainly because Owen had returned to the promotion after less than a year in the wwf, disillusioned after being stuck with the humiliating Blue Blazer gimmick. Owen had hoped to be a Canadian version of Japan's Tiger Mask. Instead, the Blazer character came off as a big goof sporting a feathered cape. As Dynamite put it, "He looked like a bloody parrot."[5] Fans responded less than enthusiastically to the Blue Blazer and the amazingly talented Owen found himself near the bottom of the cards. When Owen returned to Stampede Wrestling, Stu held out a final hope that his youngest son could turn the business around. A feud between Dynamite and Owen did do well, but not well enough.

Since Stu had revived Stampede Wrestling in 1985, Keith says, his dad had lost over $1 million. He was headed for the poorhouse if he didn't pull out. Helen's health had continued to decline and she begged him to get out of the business once and for all. Bruce, of course, cajoled him to stick it out. "My dad blew everything he made in wrestling trying to sustain it, running against Vince McMahon," Keith says. "In the end, I don't think he was even interested in running it, except as a career for Bruce and some of the boys."

At the end of 1989, Stu's promoter's licence from the Calgary Boxing and Wrestling Commission expired, as did his $2-million public liability insurance policy.[16] He wasn't prepared to spend huge amounts of money renewing either of them. He didn't have huge amounts of money.

By the first week of January 1990, Stampede Wrestling was officially finished. "Free at last," sighed Helen in an interview with the *Calgary Herald*. Bret summed up the end of the era: "The small wrestling business is obsolete."[17]

Chapter seventeen

Afterburn

The wrestling world was shocked on October 12, 1992, when, in a non-televised bout in Saskatoon's Saskatchewan Place arena, thirty-five-year-old Bret Hart was crowned the WWF World champion. He beat forty-three-year-old "Nature Boy" Ric Flair for the title, slapping his trademark submission hold, the sharpshooter, on the bleach-blond from Minnesota, making him howl for mercy. It was an amazing coup. While Hulk Hogan was the biggest draw in wrestling history, within the industry Flair was widely considered the all-time great. At six-foot-one and about 240 pounds, Flair fought with a down-and-dirty style, and his ring psychology was among the best in the business. In a twenty-year career, the flamboyant grappler won the NWA World title a record nine times and since arriving in the WWF had won that world championship twice.

Bret, on the other hand, who had switched from a heel to a babyface persona in the late 1980s, was an old-fashioned John Wayne–style hero. While he was as boastful as any wrestler – dubbing himself "the excellence of execution" and proclaiming himself "the best there is, the best there was, and the best there ever will be" – he also carried himself with a noble, Everyman quality. He was a positive role model, a proud family man with a wife and four kids, and certainly not a whiskey-drinking peacock like Flair or a larger than life superhero like Hogan. Consequently, Bret's win was a surprise, because in the modern wrestling world – where

Bret Hart suplexes T.G. Stone in the early 1980s.

it seemed only the flashiest stars could be on top – Bret represented the triumph of the common man.

Bret's work in the 1990s was nothing short of spectacular. After the Hart Foundation broke up in 1991, there was a fear "The Hitman" would founder. Jim Neidhart certainly did. Without Bret in his corner, his star status was never the same. Some of that might have come down to Neidhart's excessive, self-destructive ways. Neidhart's wife Ellie alleged in court documents that he was a heavy drinker and drug abuser, allegations that were never proven. But whether he had a substance abuse problem or not, it's clear he had a frightening temper. In his *Calgary Sun* column, Bret recalls an incident when Neidhart hurled a TV monitor at one of Vince McMahon's top employees. He was soon shown the door, though McMahon eventually brought him back.[1]

Bret, however, found himself on the fast track to singles success. He won the prestigious Intercontinental title and feuded with such top names as Rowdy Roddy Piper, Curt Hennig, and his brother-in-law Davey Boy Smith, who made it back to the WWF in 1991. Bret's match with Davey, before nearly seventy-nine thousand fans at London's Wembley Stadium, remains a classic.

Bret also had some of the best matches of his career with Owen. After failing to get into the Calgary Fire Department, the youngest Hart returned to the WWF in late 1991 but again had a hard time finding his niche. Despite his outstanding talents, as a babyface Owen just seemed too plain for WWF fans. Ironically, the squeaky-clean family man finally clicked in 1994 when he became a heel.

The angle was brilliant and for a moment it felt like a Stampede Wrestling reunion, with Keith and Bruce making a brief WWF appearance, teaming up with their brothers against Shawn Michaels and three masked wrestlers. Even Stu, then seventy-nine years old, was part of the action, coaching his boys at ringside. The match ended with Owen, supposedly jealous of Bret's success, turning on the family. Helen hated this plot twist, uncomfortable seeing the family portrayed as being so dysfunctional and fractious.

The Owen-Bret feud lasted for close to a year, with both brothers shining. Owen excelled as a heel, playing a petulant brat whose nose was out of joint from years of living in his superstar brother's shadow. "I've always been better than you, Bret!" he'd rant in interviews, an exaggerated pout on his face. "Mom always loved you best!" In the course of their feud, Owen defeated Bret at WrestleMania X in Madison Square Garden. He also cost Bret the world title in a November 1994 match when he tricked Helen – somehow McMahon had got even her involved – into throwing in the towel during Bret's match with Bob Backlund.

Stu and Helen were incorporated into a few storylines in the 1990s, highlighted by heckling announcer Jerry "The King" Lawler. "You know, Stu Hart is so old, I told him to act his age and he dropped dead," Lawler told the audience. "And Helen Hart ... she's the only person I know with an autographed copy of the Bible." Helen thought Lawler was hilarious.

While Bret's talent was indisputable, he also happened to be in the right place at the right time. In the early 1990s, McMahon was coming under heavy fire from both the media and the U.S. government for rampant steroid abuse within his organization. In response, he pushed a clean-cut but cool athletic type as his star, rather than another steroid monster. Bret fit the role to a tee. As well, business was down for the WWF. People were tiring of the over-the-top elements of the Hogan era. Bret represented the organization putting the focus back on wrestlers and away from cartoonish characters.

Bret would go on to capture the WWF World title five times in the 1990s. Most wrestling historians agree he is the greatest Canadian wrestler ever; indeed, one of the world's greats. No other Canadian grappler has been as recognized or popular on a global scale. In 1991, *Alberta Report* declared Bret the most famous Albertan in the world.

Bret's critics point out that he was not a huge money-maker for the WWF in the way that Hulk Hogan or "Stone Cold" Steve Austin were, but he was extremely popular in foreign markets, getting mobbed when he toured Europe. He was the face of the WWF at a time when fifteen million Americans watched the show weekly and it was broadcast in forty countries. At his peak during the '90s, Bret was a pop culture icon, immortalized on *The Simpsons*, appearing on Howard Stern's radio show, and being invited to the White House three times.

"He's got a tremendous amount of charisma," said a WWF spokesperson in November 1992. "It's hard to put your finger on, but he's got something that turns people on and that goes a long way in this business. There's sex appeal there for the women, the adult males respect his athletic ability, and, the kids view him as the coolest thing on two feet."[2]

Bret's rise was the one bright light in a dark decade for the Hart family and many Stampede Wrestling graduates. While Bret's star rocketed into the heavens, Dynamite Kid's came crashing to earth just as dramatically, bringing him right back to the gloomy English coal mining town of his birth a broken man.

Dynamite was never an easy man to be married to. He had a mean streak, intensified by drugs, and for all his hard-man talk he had insecurities, which caused him to routinely lash out at Michelle. When she read in front of him, it reminded him that he had dropped out of school at the age of fourteen and he would shout at her that she was being rude.

Michelle didn't realize the chronic pain her husband was struggling with until his back gave out at the end of 1986. He had never acknowledged it: to do so would have been weak. She remembers having to change the bedsheets every morning, as they would be soaked in sweat. One day she asked Dynamite why he sweated so much in the night. He exploded. "Because I'm in pain, ya fookin' cow!"

Despite all the money Dynamite made, the Billingtons' bank account was depleting at an alarming rate. With Dynamite's fast lifestyle on the road, he spent cash as quickly as he earned it, and he was generous to a fault with people he liked, buying them leather jackets and expensive meals on a whim. He continued to do so even when he stopped working.

When Dynamite's doctor warned him he would wind up in a wheelchair if he kept wrestling, Michelle convinced her husband that they should sell their country estate, to put some money in the bank. "That means I'm a failure," he spat.

"No," Michelle replied. "It means you're cashing in on an investment."

She was right. The couple sold the property for $475,000, coming out of the deal a quarter of a million dollars richer. They purchased five acres near the town of Cochrane, just outside Calgary. Moving day was horrific. Dynamite, who just had his shoulder operated on, was supposed to be in the hospital when the movers came. Instead, wasted on painkillers, he showed up to oversee things, drinking all the while. Michelle is not certain what set him off, but she remembers Dynamite jerking his arm violently, trying to throw out his freshly operated-on shoulder in an impotent rage, just to upset her. When he calmed down, she pleaded with him, "You don't have to wrestle anymore. Our house is paid off. You could work at a gas station even. I'll get a job. We'll thrive." Tom would have none of it.

Living with the legend that was Dynamite Kid had become an around-the-clock nightmare. "He was in turmoil," Michelle says. "He'd sit at home getting drunk [and] watching all his old wrestling tapes." Sometimes Dynamite left the house, saying he was off to rent a movie or run some errand. He would disappear with the car and not return for a couple of days. It was winter, and his wife was left stranded out in the country with two children.

The hatred that mired Dynamite's heart thickened when at the last minute Davey Boy backed out of a lucrative Japanese tour the duo had planned for the end of 1990. His reason? Vince McMahon wanted the Bulldogs back.

Dynamite told McMahon off, according to Diana Hart, while Davey Boy jumped at the opportunity. Dynamite considered this a betrayal and had felt nothing but bitterness for Davey from then on.[3]

Michelle hoped that a visit from Dynamite's mother and younger brother would lift his spirits, but it made things worse. Mark Billington was sixteen and Dynamite dreamed of turning him into the new Dynamite Kid. He began training Mark, but Mark, who had a weak heart, did not have the stamina. "He's not got the mettle," Dynamite said later, disappointed.

Maybe Mark couldn't wrestle like his brother, but they did have some things in common, Michelle says. Soon, they were going to bars and strip clubs together, getting into fights and lapping up the booze and drugs diet so common in the wrestling world.

For Michelle, the breaking point came on New Year's Eve, 1990. Pregnant, she was at home watching a movie with six-year-old Bronwyne and two-year-old Marek Thomas when Dynamite came home. He had a bloody gash in his cheek, so deep that Michelle could see bone. "Git fookin' dressed," he commanded her. "We're going out." Michelle had always managed to shield the kids from their dad when he was drunk. Seeing her father drunk and bloody upset Bronwyne. "What's wrong with daddy?" she cried. "I fookin' fell down, little girl," Dynamite said. "That's all ye need to know."

The truth was that he had been in a fight at Cochrane's Texas Gate bar. The bouncers had asked Dynamite to pay a $5 cover charge and he refused. He bullied his way in, aggravating every soused cowboy in the joint. The real trouble began when someone made a crack about Dynamite wearing his sunglasses in the bar. He had been wearing his shades everywhere since he had started having violent seizures as a result of his drug binges. Before the seizures struck, Dynamite saw a flash of bright light. He thought that wearing sunglasses would ward off the light and protect him from the seizures. But the cowboys thought he was being arrogant. They took exception to everything about this loud asshole who had barged into their saloon. They took Dynamite down. A few boots to the face later, he was thrown out the door.

Undeterred, Dynamite decided to round up his wife, even though he knew she was five months pregnant and wanted to stay home. They were going to celebrate New Year's Eve whether she liked it or not. Michelle took the kids to a babysitter, Dynamite crudely taped up his face, and off they went to the Cochrane Hotel bar.

Dynamite and Michelle ushered in 1991 at each others' throats. What was he doing getting into fights? Why did he insist on getting his brother in fights night after night? "Oh, my God," Michelle screamed, in tears. "How are you going to raise my son?"

"Little Tommy'll be watchin' me fookin' back!" Dynamite snarled.

No. Never. Her son would not be raised like that. "I had been an enabler and an eggshell walker," says Michelle. "It was time for damage control."

The couple had $3,000 in their bank account in January 1991. Michelle spent $2,000 on a one-way ticket to England, which she left on the kitchen table for Dynamite. She refutes the claim made in his book that he left her $30,000. He took the ticket and left Calgary on January 10, 1991, with twenty pounds sterling in his pocket, the exact amount he had in it when he first came to Calgary as a skinny, clean-living kid nearly thirteen years earlier.

Terrified, Michelle had loaded up the kids and gone to seek refuge at a women's shelter, believing that Dynamite would hunt her down. "He always said he'd cut up my face so that no man would ever look at me," she says. "I thought he'd kill me." Her voice quivers a little and she hangs her head, adding, "There was a time when I thought of taking my life and my kid's lives, rather than thinking of a future with him."

Today, Michelle and her children live in a modest home in northwest Calgary. On the front doorstep sits a statuette of a bulldog. Fittingly, the thing is damaged, old, and faded. One ear is broken off. At twenty-one, Bronwyne, a striking blond, is an aspiring deejay. Marek, seventeen, is thin and studious. Michelle and Dynamite's youngest child, Amarys, who was born after Dynamite left Calgary, is the most like him. At fourteen, she's tough and athletic, just like the father she's never met. She loves going to the gym and even talks about becoming a wrestler. Bad News Allen has offered to train her. Her father would not be thrilled. "He never approved of lady wrestlers," Michelle says.

Michelle went to school after Dynamite left and got her bachelor of education degree. She is now a teacher and able to make ends meet, but there were years when she could not. Fortunately, her brother-in-law Bret was always there for her. He bought the kids clothes, paid the bills when the electricity was about to be cut off, even took the family on holidays.

In 1995, Bret flew Bronwyne and Marek to England to see their father. He was working as a security guard at a metal-scrap yard in Wigan, living with his girlfriend on the grounds. For the most part, it was a nice visit, with Dynamite making an effort to get to know his kids. The rekindled relationship would be a short one, however.

In December of that year, the Hart boys organized a tribute to Stu at the Corral in honour of his eightieth birthday. The Harts tried to get Dynamite to attend. Bruce had a plane ticket waiting for Dynamite at the airport in England.

The kids were excited, but when they went to pick their father up at the Calgary airport, he wasn't there. Later, over the phone, he told Michelle that he had lost too much muscle and was too embarrassed to come. "I don't think he's a bad person who doesn't want to see his kids," Michelle says. "It's pride. His pride has always been a crippling thing for him. It's his worst enemy."

Things would only get worse for Dynamite Kid. Much of his post-Calgary life is shrouded in mystery, but horror stories abound. In his autobiography, Dynamite says he was wrestling in some cut-rate English promotion in 1991, billed as the British Bulldog Dynamite Kid, when he was hassled by the Trade Descriptions Office for using the moniker. By that time, Davey Boy was being billed as the British Bulldog in the WWF, and Dynamite claims Davey had a problem with his former partner using the name. In 1994, Dynamite attended a British wrestling match where Davey Boy was topping the bill. He tried to storm the dressing room to pick a fight with his cousin but was forced out of the building by police.[4]

Tom kept trying to return to the ring, finally giving up in 1996 when he had a seizure and was hospitalized during a Japan tour. Dynamite also told Michelle that throughout the '90s he earned money as a garage fighter. "They'd put Tom and the toughest guy in town in someone's garage and shut the door," Michelle says. "When they opened it up whoever was still standing would win the money.... Men would place bets on them."

It all caught up with Dynamite in 1997 when he was finally confined to a wheelchair. He remarried at one point, but he's said to be divorced again and destitute. In 2004, news circulated that Dynamite had part of his leg amputated and was hospitalized. Michelle tried unsuccessfully to contact him. If she was to contact him, though, it's unlikely Billington would be repentant or show any regret for the life he's led. His autobiography, published in 2001, suggests he'll go down bulldogged and prideful to the end.

"I had no idea things would end up the way they did," he writes. "But I'd do it all again. I wouldn't change a thing. Which I know sounds strange coming from a guy whose wrestling career put him in a wheelchair, but it's true. Wrestling was my life, and I loved it. No regrets. I had a blast."[5]

On the surface, the early 1990s were a dream come true for Davey Boy Smith. For a time, he was one of the top wrestling stars in the world. It was everything he wanted.

But the decade also had its share of catastrophes for the British Bulldog. For him, the year after Stampede Wrestling closed was dark and dangerous. Davey was wrestling sporadically, not fully recovered from injuries suffered from his 1989 car accident, and he needed money badly. He had a mortgage to pay and a wife and two children to support. To do so, Diana Hart says, he borrowed money from a fearsome drug dealer named Hermesh Erach Austin. In return, Davey allowed Austin to store stolen vehicles in his yard, Diana alleges.[6]

Austin, a tattooed bodybuilder of Persian heritage, first entered the scene in the early 1980s while a teenager, working at the juice bar in BJ's Gym. At some point, Austin began dealing drugs, and in September 1990, both Austin and Alison Hart's ex-husband, Ben Bassarab, were charged with possession of steroids for the purpose of trafficking. Those charges were dropped, but both men were sentenced to eighteen months in prison for beating the man who burned them on a drug deal.

Kevin Sluth, an associate of Austin and Bassarab, had been holding over 450 grams of cocaine for his friends in the summer of 1990. He was snorting the drug in his apartment when he heard a knock at the door. In a coke-fuelled panic, he flushed $30,000 worth of cocaine down the toilet, only to find it was just a TV cable repairman at his door. Five days later, Bassarab and Austin pummelled Sluth in front of his terrified girlfriend. Sluth went to the police, who sent him back to the two sharks, this time fitted with a wiretap, which led to their conviction.[7]

Bassarab says he disassociated himself with Austin after completing his sentence. Diana Hart says she doesn't know the extent of her husband Davey's association with Austin, but she felt uneasy in the summer of 1990 when he began riding a Harley Davidson Soft Tail given to him by the drug dealer. According to Diana, when Austin was arrested he ordered Davey to sell the bike, as he needed money for his defence. "Davey did what he was told," Diana writes. "You didn't fool around with these guys."[8] In 1991, Davey also cut off his association with Austin when he hastily moved his family to Florida.

In January 1994, Austin, by then running a $2.5-million cocaine operation, was convicted of first-degree murder in the death of Gregory Kungel, who had gone missing in September 1990. The story that unfolded is as sinister as it is grisly.

Austin and his henchmen abducted Kungel, twenty-four, and tortured the man for a week, believing he had stolen more than $10,000 from Austin. Kungel was taken to a warehouse in southeast Calgary where, as he pled for his life, he was savagely beaten. His hands were crushed in a vice, his ears cut with scissors, and the soles of his feet burned with a blowtorch. Finally, Austin and his henchmen took Kungel to the outskirts of Calgary, where Austin slit his throat and shot him in the head. Kungel's body was then buried.

Two and a half years later, one of Austin's cronies went to the police. The evidence was sufficient to put Austin in prison with a life sentence.[9]

Associating with monsters wasn't Davey's only problem in the 1990s. On July 25, 1993, back in Calgary for a visit, he and Diana were partying at a rock bar called The Back Alley when Davey got into a fight that nearly landed him behind bars for up to fourteen years. Trouble began when a twenty-year-old student drunkenly approached Diana on the dance floor and made lewd comments. Eyewitness accounts differ dramatically. Some suggest that Davey picked the man up and spiked him head first into the concrete floor. Davey claimed that he put the troublemaker in a headlock and walked him over to the bouncers. When he let go, the man fell backwards and cracked his head on the floor. Either way, the man suffered brain damage, including memory loss, from the ordeal.[10]

At one point during the trial for assault, Davey tried to play down his strength, telling the court wrestling was fake. Wrestler Karl Moffat countered that claim, testifying that Davey was a powerhouse capable of throwing any normal-sized man like a rag doll.[11] Ultimately, however, the judge ruled in Davey's favour. But winning the case did not come cheap. According to Diana, it cost the family about U.S.$500,000 to defend the Bulldog.[12]

As the decade progressed, Davey's drug abuse began to spiral out of control, with a morphine addiction added to his usual menu of steroids and painkillers. The quality of the Bulldog's work began to deteriorate. His agility and ring finesse long gone, he had become just another musclehead in the ring.

In 1998, Davey was working for media mogul Ted Turner's World Championship Wrestling (wcw), which dominated the wrestling business at the time. Turner had the money to hire McMahon's top talents out from under him, the most notable of the bunch being Hulk Hogan. For a long time, the wwf floundered, its Monday night *Raw Is War* tv program getting creamed in the ratings by wcw's *Monday Nitro* for eighty-three straight weeks, from late 1996 to early 1998.

But behind the scenes, the wcw – as led by its president Eric Bischoff – was in a constant state of chaos. The notorious Bischoff had his clique of favourites, including Hogan, but others claim they were mismanaged and mistreated. Davey suffered the worst injury of his career in wcw when he was power-slammed onto a steel trapdoor underneath the canvas, which no one told him was there. He jarred his back on the door's handle. The injury put him out of action for several months, during which he sat idle at home, often driven to tears by the pain in his spine, which he compared to being stabbed with a knife.[13]

Facing such chronic agony, Davey fell even deeper into his addictions. He stumbled around the house, slurring his words. During Sunday dinners at Hart House he was barely able to feed himself. Diana brought a water pistol to the table and squirted her husband every time he dropped his fork, but he was too stoned to notice. Diana's sisters berated her for the way she was treating her husband. "Am I the only person here who notices he can't feed himself?" she protested.[14]

One night in despair, Diana tried to take her own life. As Davey lay on their bed, incapacitated, Diana screamed at him, "Look what you've done, you bastard…! I'm going to take your goddamn pills so you'll know what I put up with night and day. I want you to know what it's like to live with a vegetable." As she swallowed an entire bottle of Xanax, a drug used to counter anxiety, Davey mumbled at her in a daze, "Please don't." Diana regretted her actions almost immediately. Realizing she did not want to die, she managed to call 911 before passing out. When she woke up, a day later, she was in the hospital.[15]

"She's never been the same since," says Keith. "I don't know whether something snapped emotionally, or if it was the pills … but she's never had that same sparkle and confidence she used to have. She was a very poised, charming person with a lot of potential. Since then … I think things are a little bit out of focus for her."

Davey Boy checked himself into a seven-week rehabilitation program in Grande Prairie, Alberta, on Boxing Day, 1998. When Davey collapsed in the rehab centre, wracked by the hellfire burning in his spine, he was transferred to Calgary's Rockyview General Hospital. There, he was given a bone scan. It showed he had three crushed discs in his back that, having gone untreated, had developed a life-threatening infection. The next thing Davey knew, he was laid up in a cast from his waist to his neck. For weeks he lay there, drowning in misery. The bitterness was compounded when he received his termination notice from WCW.[16]

Davey could not accept that his wrestling career was coming to an end. As soon as he was out of the hospital he was back in the gym, back on the steroids, and in talks with McMahon about returning to the WWF. He also returned to painkillers and morphine. But the drugs weren't his greatest addiction. "I'm an addict to wrestling," he told a reporter. "I've been down but I've always returned to the ring. It's the only thing I know."[17]

Tragedy dogged the Hart family in the 1990s, dealing blow after devastating blow at an unrelenting pace. First there was the death of wild-child Dean Hart in November 1990, the fifth-born Hart son succumbing to a heart attack brought on by his kidney disease at the age of thirty-six. Then there was the horrific demise of Stu and Helen's thirteen-year-old grandson Matthew Annis in July 1996. Annis, the son of Georgia and B.J., was already dreaming of becoming a wrestler, training with his young cousins in the Harts' back-yard ring, when a minor injury left him unable to walk. At the hospital, it was discovered that Matthew had flesh-eating disease. "One day he was fine," says Nattie Neidhart, Jim and Ellie's daughter. "Twelve days later, he had thir-ty pounds of puss on his body and looked like a gorilla.... His blood had ris-en to the surface and his skin was like burnt wood." Crushed, the family ral-lied around Matthew's bedside. Owen promised to hand his nephew the keys to his 1967 Mustang when the kid recovered. Matthew died within two weeks, on July 14.

"We were all so tight then," says Alison. "I was so proud of my family. We pulled together. If somebody looked at the Harts then, they would have said 'God, these people are amazing.' We took care of each other."

Another death rocked the family and the wrestling world in October 1997. Brian Pillman was like a brother to the Hart children and his downward spi-ral was painful for them to watch. During a seven-year stint in wcw, Pillman had developed a loose-canon persona that caught on with the fans, making him a hot property. His friends worried about him, though, as his behaviour outside the ring was also becoming erratic.[18]

Pillman had always been a wild man, but in recent years things had gone off the deep end. After a nasty breakup with his cocaine-addicted girlfriend Rochelle, with whom he had a daughter, Pillman married a former Penthouse Pet, Melanie, and the couple sued for custody of Pillman's child and won. Depressed at her loss, Rochelle shot herself in the head while talking to her mother on the phone. Pillman, tortured with guilt, began drinking heavily and abusing his pain medication.

By 1996, Pillman was at the centre of a bidding war between Vince McMa-hon and Eric Bischoff. Pillman had been up for two days straight consid-ering both offers, which were around $400,000 a year, when he hopped in his Humvee, hoping a drive would clear his head. Instead, he fell asleep at the wheel and hit a tree. He later claimed that just before his eyes closed, he saw Rochelle's ghostly face in his rear-view mirror. The crash propelled him through the windshield, sending him flying forty feet into a field. He woke up in the hospital with four steel plates in his face and a crushed right ankle needing restructuring.[19]

Pillman lied to McMahon, whose offer he accepted, claiming that doc-tors told him he would recover completely. After surgery Pillman's ankle

Makhan Singh (Mike Shaw), who fans liked to call "The Toilet Bowl," applies a nerve pinch to heartthrob Brian Pillman.

fused into a walking position and he was never again able to perform to his past level. To even enter the ring he began to rely on dangerously heavy doses of painkillers.

Pillman's final days were chaos, with his wife Melanie filing for divorce and Pillman violating a restraining order, which got him thrown into court-mandated anger management classes. He and Melanie got back together, however, and she was at home cooking dinner for their children when she received news that Pillman had been found dead in a Minnesota hotel room. Heart failure was listed as the official cause of his October 6, 1996, death, with cocaine a contributing factor. Several bottles of painkillers and muscle relaxants were found near the body.[20]

Critics blasted McMahon when, during a broadcast of *Raw Is War* the following night, he featured a live interview with a teary-eyed Melanie Pillman from her home in Walton, Kentucky, guaranteeing huge ratings. The vicious war between the WWF and WCW had reached a mean-spirited low.

Was it the art of pro wrestling or was it just trash? It was getting harder to tell all the time and Bret Hart didn't like it.

By 1997, Vince McMahon had finally found a way to turn the tides in the war he had been losing against the WCW. The answer was simple. Turn up the sleaze.

There's no question the WWF had grown stale in the early part of the decade. The age-old good versus evil shtick didn't resonate with the new jaded generation of wrestling fans. These kids grew up on Guns 'N' Roses, gangsta rap, Mike Tyson, Beavis and Butthead, and blood-sport video games. Eminem, *South Park*, and Girls Gone Wild videos were just around the corner. The voyeuristic, lowbrow *Jerry Springer Show* was becoming the hottest talk show on TV. This was a world of strippers, violence, and anti-heroes.

Nobody wanted to see a humongous Boy Scout preaching to the kiddies, telling them to go to school and eat their vitamins, as Hulk Hogan had done. In fact, over in the WCW, Hogan had grown a black beard, told his fans to go to hell, and turned into the villainous Hollywood Hulk Hogan. As for the WWF's cartoonish aspects, even the kids knew how hokey and pandering the gimmicks were getting when the federation introduced an evil clown to the ring called Doink, who would be accompanied by his look-alike midget sidekick, Dink.

However, Bret was uncomfortable with the new breed of hero McMahon was developing. A guy like "The Heartbreak Kid" Shawn Michaels was number one on The Hitman's hitlist. Michael Shawn Hickenbottom, from Texas, was a superb performer – acrobatic, charismatic, and more than willing to risk his neck pulling off dangerous stunts. He was also a cocky prima donna, both in the dressing room and in the ring, where he took his rock 'n' roll sex symbol act to extremes, dancing like a stripper, spreading his legs and feigning an exaggerated karate chop to his genitals. "Suck it," he told the fans, young men lapping it up as if Michaels were the coolest dude on the planet.

When the two met at WrestleMania XII, on March 31, 1996, in Anaheim, California, their differences could not have been more pronounced. World champion Bret marched down the aisle, paused at ringside, took off his wraparound shades, and put them on his six-year-old son, Blade. Michaels, on the other hand, flew in from the rafters, sliding along on a high wire attached to a safety harness, amid fireworks and flashing lights. He wore a glittering, silvery tuxedo that fit him like a second skin and, once in the ring, he broke into a peacock strut.

The two warriors fought a dramatic sixty-two-minute bout that was dubbed an "iron man" match. These types of epic battles had mostly gone the way of the dinosaur in modern wrestling – the audience just didn't have the attention span for such contests in the post-MTV era – but Hart and Michaels had the talent and chemistry to make such a match work. The Hitman dropped the title to Michaels that night.

Bret didn't mind. He planned to pursue a career as an actor, having already appeared in the network TV western *Lonesome Dove*, accepting a full-time role in the coming season. Those dreams were shattered when the series was cancelled. Bret became the prize in a tug-of-war between WCW and WWF. The WCW offered Bret a contract in which he was guaranteed $3 million a year for three years, making him the highest paid wrestler in the world after Hulk Hogan. Bret was tempted but remained loyal to the company that had put him on top. Hart returned to the WWF, signing a twenty-year contract that stipulated he wrestle for the first three years, at $1.5 million a year, then move into a prominent management position.

Prodded by McMahon, Bret turned heel in 1997, adopting an American-bashing angle where he berated U.S. audiences for their declining moral values. He told the Americans their sick society should be flushed down the toilet. It enraged fans in the United States, but his popularity grew in Canada and around the world. Bret felt uneasy about the angle – his mother was an American – but he went along with the storyline, which included the formation of a new and improved Hart Foundation, this time with a whole gang that included Neidhart, Davey Boy, Owen, and Brian Pillman, not three months before Pillman died. As despised as they were south of the border, they were a dream team to fans of the old Stampede Wrestling.

At the 1997 Calgary Stampede, when the Hart Foundation faced off against a team of American wrestlers led by "Stone Cold" Steve Austin, the hometown crowd erupted with pride. Stu and Helen were ringside and, before the match, Bret stopped and placed his shades on his mother. After the Canadians thumped the Americans, three generations of the Hart family climbed into the ring to join the wrestlers. The show of love from the crowd was thunderous.

Bret's feud with Austin marked a turning point in wrestling history, as it brought about a radical shift in the dynamics of the business. Austin, a bald, goateed bruiser known as "The Texas Rattlesnake," had been developing an image that would have made him a surefire heel not ten years ago. He was a beer-guzzling, gun-toting, white trash bully. While he was originally pushed as a villain, the crowd, many of whom identified with Austin, began cheering him on.

To make him a full-fledged hero, McMahon put Austin up against Bret. The two fought an exciting submission match at WrestleMania XIII in March 1997, in which the only way one could win was by making his opponent cry uncle. The battle ended with Austin screaming in agony in the centre of the ring, locked in Bret's sharpshooter as blood flowed from his brow. Instead of quitting, Stone Cold clung to life, finally passing out from the pain as his legs were twisted like pretzels. Losing like that gave Austin a badge of honour in the eyes of the fans. He was now established as the "baddest sonofabitch" in the game, and his popularity skyrocketed. He became the WWF's hottest commodity since Hulk Hogan.

The new "attitude" era of professional wrestling was in full swing. Before long, the WWF was a sleazy circus dominated by grapplers who played porno stars and pimps. One wrestler, calling himself The Godfather, routinely led a "ho train" of scantily clad beauties to the ring with him, proudly proclaiming, "pimpin' ain't easy!" Suddenly, the profile of women wrestlers was higher than ever before, only most of them didn't know the first thing about wrestling. They were half-naked bimbos with silicon D-cups posing as wrestlers, fighting in giant Jello bowls and bra-and-panty matches. Co-announcer Jerry Lawler leered in the background, hoping the women would expose their "puppies." Old Ed Whalen would have been disgusted. In fact, he was, and spoke out against modern wrestling on radio shows and newspaper columns.

Media pundits and pop sociologists swarmed, denouncing the new wrestling as a destructive influence on children and another sign that society was in the doghouse. Bret, who shared his father's love for traditional wrestling, was feeling increasingly alienated in this world and he too slammed the new direction. "It's fine to have Jerry Springer or Howard Stern, but they don't cater to kids," he said. "[The WWF] has built their company on the backs of young kids.... It's really awful."[21]

It was never clearer that Bret no longer fit into McMahon's master plan than when McMahon told him the company was in financial peril and could no longer afford to pay him as per his contract. McMahon encouraged Bret to explore his options with wcw. Hurt, Bret did just that, and found that Turner's company was willing to put its original offer back on the table.

Meanwhile, Bret was again holding the WWF World Heavyweight title and was going to have to lose it before he left the company. When McMahon suggested he drop it to Shawn Michaels at the November 1997 Survivor Series in Montreal, Bret refused. Animosity between The Hitman and Heartbreak Kid was at a fever pitch. That June, Michaels crowed in an interview that while Bret held himself up as a role model, he didn't live up to the image on the road. He then made a crack about Hart seeing "a lot of sunny days lately." Wrestling fans and insiders understood that Michaels was referring to Tammy Lynn Sytch, better known as Sunny, a smouldering blond wrestling manager who had won a 1996 "Slammy Award" for Best Buns.

Backstage gossip had it that Bret and Sunny were having an affair, which Bret hotly denied. The rumours must have caused marital problems for Bret because he confronted Michaels in the dressing room and told him the personal comments were affecting his family life. Michaels lipped off. Before he knew it, Bret was on top of him, laying in the punches. When management dragged Bret off the now black-and-blue-faced Michaels, he took with him a fistful of the wrestler's long mane.

Bret's critics slam him for his refusal to drop the belt to Michaels when McMahon ordered him to do so. In one sense, this was prima donna behaviour on Bret's part, no different than if a Stampede wrestler defied one of Stu's orders back in the day. However, Stu would certainly not have handled the situation in the underhanded fashion that McMahon did, and, in Bret's defence, his contract gave him full creative control over his character for his last thirty days in the WWF. There was no way he was going to lose to that low-life Michaels – who had taken to wiping his crotch and blowing his nose with the Canadian flag – in a televised match in front of Canadian fans.[22]

Bret suggested that he drop the belt to Michaels on another night and came up with a finish where Michaels would put Bret in his signature sharpshooter hold which, after a painful struggle, Bret would break out of. Then, his Hart Foundation cronies would run to the ring and interfere. The match would end in a disqualification, and Bret would hang on to his title that night. In a conversation with McMahon, which Bret secretly taped for *Wrestling with Shadows*, the documentary that was being made on him, McMahon agreed to this scenario.

That's not the way it went down. Instead, Bret was the victim of "The Montreal Screw-job," the most notorious double-cross in wrestling history. At the end of a hard-fought match, Michaels slipped the sharpshooter on Bret as planned. Bret winced, clenched his fists, and gritted his teeth, working the fans into a froth by playing up his apparent pain. He was about to reverse the hold as planned when he heard a voice bark, "Ring the fucking bell." It was McMahon. The bell rang and referee Earl Hebner declared Michaels the winner, as if The Hitman had submitted. He hadn't.

Realizing that danger was imminent, Michaels grabbed the title and scurried away like a rodent with a mouthful of cheese. Bret appeared momentarily stunned, then shot a vicious glare McMahon's way. McMahon gave Bret a look of arrogant defiance. On camera, Bret spat in McMahon's face and proceeded to smash thousands of dollars' worth of TV monitors as the Montreal fans howled their approval. Owen, Davey Boy, and Neidhart ran to the ring and pulled Bret away.

Backstage, Bret confronted Shawn, who swore he wasn't in on the plan. McMahon had locked himself in his office. Mark "The Undertaker" Callaway knocked on the door and angrily told McMahon he owed Bret an apology. Accompanied by his beefy son, Shane, and two road agents, McMahon approached Bret, who was towelling off after a shower. McMahon tried to explain himself but Bret warned McMahon to leave before he got a "punch in the fucking mouth." McMahon stood his ground.[23]

"It was time for me to punch him or walk out of the room," Bret said later. "I walked out and then it hit me clear. I could never live with that. I ran back and punched him. One shot. I popped him like a cork and when he fell down, he actually collapsed on his own ankle. I think he sprained it. I broke my right hand in three places. But it was the best thing I ever did. No regrets at all...."[24] Bret later described the punch as "a Stu Hart judgement call."[25]

McMahon's son jumped on Bret's back and Davey Boy dragged him off. The fight was over. McMahon's goons hauled him to his feet as he grumbled incoherently, his lower lip swelling. "Get this motherfucker out of here, or I'll hurt him," Bret said, his voice cracking with emotion.

By most accounts, Owen Hart wanted out of the WWF after his brother was betrayed. According to Owen's widow, Martha, he went to McMahon and asked to be released from his contract, which paid him close to U.S.$300,000 a year.[26]

McMahon allowed Davey Boy to break his contract (Davey claimed he paid a $100,000 fine to do so), and Neidhart, who was working without one, was able to walk away with no restrictions.[27] They followed Bret to wcw, where, amid the nasty dressing room politics, their careers nose-dived, and Davey received the back injury that nearly ended his career permanently. Owen could have gone to the wcw just as easily, but McMahon would not allow it: McMahon had plans for him. "Owen felt like a prisoner," Martha writes, "caught between his love for his brother and his livelihood."[28]

At first, Bret was angry with Owen for staying, but soon he begrudgingly accepted that his little brother had a family to support. Meanwhile, McMahon tried to settle Owen's discontent by upping his contract to U.S.$400,000 a year. Even with the substantial raise, Owen struggled to find a place in the new wwf where he could excel without having to compromise himself. Martha writes that in one proposed angle, Owen was to wrestle a creepy, homoerotic wrestler called Goldust, who would put his hand on Owen's crotch during the match. Owen shot the idea down.[29]

Owen eventually partnered with wrestler Jeff Jarrett. The two men came to the ring accompanied by their valet, Debra Marshall, yet another busty blond wwf diva. For the hooting boys in the audience, Debra was the star of the team, stripping down to her bra and panties in every match. A storyline was cooked up in which Owen would have an affair with Debra, who was supposedly Jarrett's girlfriend, thus starting a feud between the two men. "It was sick," Martha writes. That idea too was vetoed.

Finally, the Blue Blazer gimmick that Owen hated so much in his first wwf stint was resurrected. Owen was back in the blue mask and feathery cape. This time, though, the Blazer was played for laughs. The character was a parody of the goody-two-shoes superheroes who had populated the wwf only a few years earlier. Goofing on Hulk Hogan, the Blazer would tell kids to say their prayers and eat their vitamins. This crowd, however, preferred to see Steve Austin guzzle a six-pack and stick his middle finger in Vince McMahon's face.*

Martha writes: "Wrestling fans had become so putrid and tainted thanks to the angry mob mentality bred by Vince McMahon, that Blue Blazer was spit upon and degraded on a nightly basis."[30] Martha's horror is understandable,

---

*McMahon skilfully capitalized on the hatred fans had for him after his falling out with Bret by making himself a character in the ongoing story: the evil, bullying boss. His war with the rebellious Austin was the biggest feud of 1998–1999.

but Owen was doing his job and doing it well, goading the fans as heels had from the earliest days of the game. Only now, the playing field had become a crueller place. Still, it was a game Owen chose to continue playing. But his reservations were apparent in an interview he did with TSN on December 1998. "We are pushing the risqué button," he said, measuring his words carefully. "It's getting violent and a little cruder than I want. I make sure what I do as a pro athlete both in and out of the ring is acceptable to my family and my friends."[31]

Meanwhile, Bret was having trouble adjusting to WCW. As if the dressing room politics weren't bad enough, there was also a lack of focus on the part of the booking committee. Rather than developing storylines for the characters, they engineered wacky angles, abandoning them after a week or two, moving onto the next nowhere plot twist. It became difficult to follow the story from one week to the next. For a wrestler like Bret, who relied not on gimmicks but on his skills in the ring, it was a situation in which he could not thrive.

Even if he wasn't realizing his potential in the WCW, Bret was still a massive star. On May 23, 1999, he was flying from Ottawa to Los Angeles, where he was scheduled to appear on *The Tonight Show* with Jay Leno. Mid-flight, he was handed a note from the pilot: Owen had been hurt during his match in Kansas City. Bret felt sick to his stomach but kept his composure. Wrestlers got hurt all the time and Owen was tough. Besides, this was pro wrestling. This was likely some angle that the fans and media bought hook, line, and sinker. Still, he planned to call his parents as soon as the plane touched down.

Arriving in Los Angeles, Bret soon learned the horrible truth. Owen was dead.

Chapter eighteen

The Death of Owen

Owen Hart felt uneasy about the stunt from the moment it was proposed to him. A popular wcw wrestler called Sting had been flying into the ring lately, gliding down from arena rafters attached to a cable and harness. It had become Sting's shtick, and McMahon wanted to mock it with the Blue Blazer, his very own parody of such superhero wrestlers.

Dressed as the Blazer, Owen would similarly fly down from the rafters in Kansas City's Kemper Arena, flapping his arms like a demented chicken, his feathery cape swooshing behind him. There were even plans to send the thirty-four-year-old wrestler on the eight-story vertical drop accompanied by a midget, also dressed in the goofy Blue Blazer regalia. That was scrapped when it was decided it complicated the stunt.[1]

It wasn't that Owen was scared of heights. He was a high flier in the ring who once wanted to be a firefighter. He had flown from the rafters once before, too, about six months earlier in St. Louis, Missouri. But everything about this ridiculous stunt made the youngest Hart boy wary. In St. Louis, his harness had been attached to the nylon cable that lowered him by a locking carabiner, a metal connector often used in mountain climbing. That time, when Owen touched down on the mat, he had had to fumble with the carabiner to detach himself from the cable. McMahon was allegedly not happy. He thought it looked awkward and stalled the all-important action in the ring. He wanted something with a quick release.[2]

Chris Benoit and Owen Hart: young guns in the late 1980s.

The sensational Owen Hart soars high to land
hard on the masked Viet Cong Express No. 1
during a tag-team bout in the mid-1980s.

What Vince wants, Vince gets, and so Owen was to be dangled seventy-eight feet above the ring attached to his lifeline by a quick-release snap shackle. Once he was lowered, he would simply tug on the release cord taped to the front of his harness and be freed from the rappelling line to move about the ring and get the show rolling. It took a mere six pounds of pressure to trigger the shackle's release, "roughly equivalent to the pressure required to pull the trigger of a gun," Martha Hart notes.[3] Owen liked the security of the locking carabiner. This quick-release mechanism made him nervous. To make matters worse, he had to wear that asinine Blue Blazer outfit and, the way he was strapped in the harness, hanging above the ring, his heavy cape tugged annoyingly at his neck.

Owen told several of his fellow wrestlers that he wasn't comfortable with the stunt, and he was seen pacing around the dressing room before his scheduled match, but he felt he might as well just get the nightmare over with. In the last year and a half, he had rejected so many ideas for his character on moral grounds. There were only so many schemes one could refuse without running afoul of McMahon.

Owen did not want to jeopardize his job. He needed it now more than ever, having just built the palatial home he and Martha had always dreamed of, on two acres in Calgary's posh Elbow Valley. Martha was packing up for the move that weekend. The couple looked forward to raising their two children, seven-year-old Oje and three-year-old Athena, in that house. They were also talking about having a third child. Martha says Owen wanted to work for a couple more years and make as much money as he could, then quit the business and dedicate himself to the family that meant everything to him. He hated being away from them.

The Blue Blazer's match with wrestler-pimp The Godfather was the third on the card on that Sunday evening, May 23, 1999. During the wrap-up of the second match, Owen was suspended over the ring waiting to make his descent. He could hear the more than sixteen thousand fans roaring beneath him at the mayhem in the ring.

At 7:41 PM, the lights dimmed and a forty-second profile of the Blue Blazer played on the Jumbotron. Owen made what appeared to be an adjustment to his cape. Then the three stunt riggers up in the rafters heard the click of the snap shackle being released. Several fans later said they heard Owen scream as he plunged at forty-five miles per hour toward the mat.[4]

The lights went up just as 229-pound Owen bounced violently off the ring ropes, narrowly missing the steel turnbuckle. The masked man crashed to the canvas and bounced into the corner on his back as the crowd cheered.

Most of the fans thought the violent entrance was part of the show. Others thought a crash test dummy had been dropped into the ring.

The impact shattered Owen's left arm and tore his aorta, the artery leading from his heart. As his lungs filled with blood, Stu and Helen's baby lifted his head a few inches off the mat as though grasping for survival. A moment later, Owen weakly dropped his head, his eyes staring blankly ahead.

Co-announcer Jerry Lawler left his post and ran to the ring, along with two security guards, one of whom began giving Owen chest compressions and mouth-to-mouth resuscitation. "We've got a big problem out here," said co-announcer Jim Ross, pale with fright. "This is a very serious situation," Ross told the audience. "This is not a part of the entertainment here tonight. This is as real as real can be."

Medics arrived and tended to the shattered Hart. He had no pulse and was changing colour rapidly, first turning white, then grey, then purple. His lips were blue. As he was rushed from the arena on a stretcher the crowd chanted "Owen! Owen!" Some fans were crying. One fan shouted, "This is fucking fake."

Owen was rushed to Truman Medical Center, four miles from the arena, where he was pronounced dead. Vince McMahon decreed that the show must go on. Owen's tag team partner Jeff Jarrett came to the ring next with a pained look on his face. His valet Debra was crying. The wrestlers backstage waited for their scheduled bouts in a state of turmoil. But the script was carried on almost to the letter through the rest of the evening, with "Stone Cold" Steve Austin, The Rock, and the rest of the cast doing their thing. One pretaped segment, featuring Vince McMahon supposedly breaking his ankle and being whisked away from Kemper Arena in an ambulance, ran as scheduled.

Owen's name was mentioned only once more, when Jim Ross informed the pay-per-view audience that Owen had died.[5] It was an ugly shot of reality that spoiled the twisted fantasy cooking in the ring. That would not do. After the announcement was made, it was swept aside and the show kept rolling.

After the show, McMahon was cornered by journalists, who grilled him about his "show must go on" decision. Ever the bully, McMahon stared down one reporter, saying, "Lady, I don't like your tone." He issued a statement to the media shortly after, saying, "Our thoughts and prayers are with Owen's family.... The highest tribute that we can pay is to go on entertaining the fans he loved so much."[6]

Martha Hart had felt strangely ill at ease all that day. She couldn't understand why. It should have been a happy time. The kids were playing outside, and she was getting ready for the family's move to their wonderful, new home. And yet, despair gnawed at her. She was fixing the kids' supper when she got the call from Vince McMahon.

"Owen has fallen from above the ring and he's hurt," McMahon told Martha solemnly.

"Is this is a serious call? Or is this part of your production?" Martha snapped, rattled, thinking she was being made a part of some tasteless angle. Nothing was below the WWF as far as she was concerned. McMahon assured her it was a deadly serious call. Panic rising from the pit of her stomach, Martha began firing questions at the wrestling kingpin about the accident and Owen's condition. Vince had too few answers for her.

"I know how much you and Owen meant to each other," he said ominously, and told Martha that medics worked on Owen before he was taken to the hospital.

"Are those real, qualified paramedics, or are they uncertified quack doctors that you have sit at ringside?" Martha said, panic rising in her voice. Now she was convinced that the accident was real.

"Someone will call you soon," McMahon said meekly, ending the conversation.[7]

Martha made a frantic call to Hart House. Much of Stu's brood was over for the weekly feast. They knew nothing and the panic in Martha's voice shook everybody up. Martha said she would call back when she heard more. Minutes later, Martha's phone rang again. It was a Kansas City doctor. Martha doubled over in tears as he gave her the horrible news. Then, mustering up all her strength, she called Hart House again. Helen answered. The family was filled with dread. Word about the accident was already spreading like wildfire and after Martha's initial call, others had followed. Friends, family members, they all wanted information. They wanted to tell the Harts what they had seen on TV. They wanted to pass on their prayers. But no prayers were going to bring back Owen.

The seventy-five-year-old Hart matriarch pleaded weakly, unable to accept what her daughter-in-law was saying. "No, not Owen, he can't be gone." Then, as if struck by the black reality, Helen dropped the phone and let out an anguished scream. "Owen's dead!"[8] For the first and only time in his life, Bruce saw tears pour from his father's eyes. "They were coming out like sweat," he later said. "But he never said a word."[9]

The next day, both Martha's house and the Hart mansion were besieged by visitors. The calls poured in from friends, fans, and celebrities alike, all offering their condolences. Alberta premier Ralph Klein, hockey hero Wayne Gretzky, members of the Calgary Stampeders and the Calgary Flames, future heavyweight boxing champion Lennox Lewis, Ed Whalen, stars and wannabes of the wrestling game – they all felt for the Hart family's loss.

Media from around the world descended on Calgary. In the days to come, *Good Morning America, Entertainment Tonight,* and *Larry King Live* all wanted a piece of the story. The *National Enquirer* offered Martha's sister Virginia U.S.$10,000 for any inside information she had, an offer she refused.[10]

Stu and Helen had an open door policy. The family that had grown up in the spotlight was willing to grieve publicly. Cameras snapped away as Bret, the star, arrived at the house on his motorcycle, embracing his sisters and his frail mother. Stu sat at the massive dinner table, his eyes now dry as stones but filled with pain, looking at pictures of Owen. Bret's eyes watered as he put his hand on his father's shoulder.

Almost the entire family was cordial to the media, answering any question they posed. At times, Helen seemed to be on autopilot, polite and charming to reporters. But when the questions about Owen came down to the nitty-gritty details, she trembled and teared up. "I used to have nightmares about one of my sons getting crippled from wrestling," she told one reporter. "But not this. I can't believe it.... He was my little baby, so clever and fun. He was the light of our lives."[11]

Stu, eighty-four, was hard to talk to at the best of times. He was hard of hearing and in conversations his mind tended to wander. Even the day after his son's death he went off on rambling tangents about wrestling's glory days. It frustrated reporters, which seemed to amuse family members. But even Stu was succinct about one thing. "I couldn't be more proud of a son," he said in a gruff but vulnerable voice.[12]

At first, Ellie condemned the wwF, though she would soon do an about-face. "Wrestling has gone too far," she said. "In their efforts to beat the wcw, the gimmicks and the dangerous stunts have gotten out of hand. Owen was a sacrifice to the ratings."[13] Bret also lashed out at the state of the wrestling business. "This is the kind of wild spectacle that sells wrestling these days," he said. "Wrestling fans have become like wild dogs and they just clamour for more."[14]

Most of the Hart family slammed the wwF for continuing the show after the accident. Davey Boy Smith, however, who was hoping to get back into the wrestling business, stuck up for McMahon. It was a harbinger of the family's growing division on the issue. "No one knew Owen's condition after it happened," Davey said. "No one knew if it was fatal. You get people saying it was in bad taste that Vince went on with the show, but if you didn't, you'd have [thousands] of pissed off fans who might riot."[5]

On May 24, in St. Louis, Missouri, McMahon turned Monday night's *Raw Is War*, televised in 120 countries, into a two-hour tribute to Owen. It featured short, tasteful matches with clean pro wrestling exhibitions and no crazy storylines. The grapplers wore black armbands with Owen's name on them. The majority of the show revolved around the traumatized wrestlers speaking about Owen. They talked about his clean lifestyle and devotion to his family. His sense of humour was a popular topic, one grappler recalling the day Owen dumped a bottle of hot sauce into a pot of chili made for the wrestlers. Mark Henry, a tank of a man known as "Sexual Chocolate," read a poem for Owen and sobbed heavily. Jeff Jarrett said that in a "cold, callous, selfish, self-serving and unrealistic business," Owen conducted himself with dignity. Vince McMahon did not speak on the show. Instead, his son, Shane, spoke on behalf of the company. Furious, Martha denounced the show as "a sick way to profit from her husband's death."[6]

McMahon deserves no sympathy in this situation, but to be fair to him, he was in a position where he was going to be crucified for anything he said or did in relation to Owen – condemned if he ignored the incident and condemned if he paid tribute. One can understand Martha's scathing stance. When she took her children to the funeral home, she watched as her scared, confused daughter begged Owen to wake up.[7]

The funeral was held on May 31. It was a grey, drizzly morning. The three hundred seats at the McInnis & Holloway Funeral Home in southwest Calgary were reserved for close friends and family, but about fifteen hundred fans showed up, gathered to pay their respects and hear the service, which was piped outside through speakers. The fans, many of them weeping, brought flowers and held signs that paid tribute to the Hart family and said goodbye to Owen. Some of them had driven all night from as far away as Spokane, Washington, to be there.

Three busloads of WWF wrestlers pulled up to the funeral home and filed into the service as fans flocked toward them, snapping pictures frantically. The Rock, The Undertaker, Gorilla Monsoon, Mick Foley, Hunter Hearst Helmsley and his girlfriend, the Amazonian Chyna – they were all there, along with referees and officials. WWF newcomer Chris Jericho, a rising young star whom the Harts had trained in the Dungeon a decade before, was there too. A few WCW stars showed up as well, including Chris Benoit and Hulk Hogan, who was wearing a black suit and sunglasses, his platinum hair poking out from under a black bandana. And, of course, old Stampede

Wrestlers such as Bad News Allen, Gama Singh, and Dan Kroffat attended.

Vince McMahon was accompanied by his wife and business partner, Linda, his son, Shane, and his daughter, Stephanie. They entered through a side door to escape the media glare.[18] Many criticized McMahon for attending the funeral, but Martha had invited him. In fact, she insisted he come. She wanted him to see Owen in his coffin. She wanted him to see her fatherless children. She wanted him to see the damage his twisted games had caused.[19]

Bret and   delivered heartfelt eulogies at the funeral. Bret's speech made the crowd laugh as he recalled his little brother's lifelong sense of humour, recounting how as a little boy Owen entertained his siblings by orchestrating wrestling matches between his stuffed toys and the family's cross-eyed cat, Heathcliff.

Martha's emotional eulogy contained the most important words of the day, and they were clearly directed at McMahon. "There will be a day of reckoning. This is my final promise to Owen," she said in a defiant tone. "I won't let him down."[20] Martha had declared war.

That day, sparks began to fly. At Queen's Park Cemetery in Calgary's northwest, where the funeral procession was led by a police motorcade, Martha ordered the removal of a heart-shaped floral arrangement sent by the WWF that included the company's logo shaped out flowers. "[McMahon] wanted credit for his transparent generosity and compassion," Martha writes. "It wasn't going to happen under my watch."[21]

With his brothers as pallbearers, the youngest Hart was taken to the gravesite, his heavy coffin draped with a Canadian flag. As a bugler played "The Last Soldier," the coffin was lowered into the ground. The dreadful finality of it all sunk in for Keith Hart. "I always thought Owen was the one guy who would escape the business unsoiled, unscathed," he says. "That's the irony.... He was a smart guy, looked after his money, took care of his family, he had all his priorities straight. He was totally immaculate, and this is the guy who dies in the ring. It's like the business [leaves] no survivors."

The wake was held that afternoon at Hart House. Wrestlers mingled with Calgary dignitaries in the backyard. Off in a secluded corner, Bret stood face to face with McMahon, who had asked to meet with him. Bret had already been warned by Martha's lawyers not to discuss the accident with McMahon. Later, McMahon would use this against The Hitman. "He mentioned Owen in one sentence and the rest of it was about Bret," McMahon told TSN. "I couldn't believe what I was hearing – I'd ruined his marriage, I'd ruined his career. All he wanted to talk about was himself.... It was like looking into the eyes of a skeleton.... It seemed like he wasn't human."[22]

Months later, in his *Calgary Sun* column, Bret responded, reiterating that he was not allowed to talk about Owen with McMahon. "As for him to say I was like a skeleton," Bret wrote, "considering my family ... [just buried] my younger brother, is that surprising?"[23]

That day, however, the McMahons tried to position themselves as allies of the Harts. "What we have here is one big family," Shane McMahon said. "There will always be a great bond between the Harts and the McMahons." Some of the Hart kids believed it to be so. Diana told a reporter: "Dad is like a father figure to Vince and Vince felt like Owen was one of his sons. It must have been really hard for Vince to see Owen's father in this situation."[24] Martha was disgusted when she saw Ellie and Diana hugging McMahon.

That was nothing, however, compared with the fury she felt later that evening when footage of the wrestlers attending Owen's funeral appeared on *Raw Is War*. Martha claims she had told McMahon the proceedings were not for his show. "I feel exploited and violated," she told a reporter.[25] In response, McMahon wrote a letter to the *Calgary Sun* claiming that Martha had agreed to the filming "so that Owen's fans could say goodbye."[26] The two also got into mudslinging over who paid for what at the funeral. McMahon claimed that he tried to pick up all the costs but Martha wouldn't allow it. He was quick to itemize exactly what he did pay for.

It seemed nasty, but it was only a hint of what was to come. "All we had been doing the last week was sizing one another up," Martha wrote. "Now it was clear the fight was on."[27]

Martha Hart hammered her fist on the podium in a Kansas City hotel room, flanked by Stu, Helen, and Bret. She announced to the media assembled and to the world that she was suing Vince McMahon and twelve others, including the riggers who set up the stunt and Kansas City, which owned Kemper Arena.

"Professional wrestling has become a showy display of graphic violence, sexual themes, and ever more dangerous stunts," she said. "When I found out the WWF continued the show ... I was outraged and repulsed. To me, this demonstrates the mindset of the WWF and Vince McMahon."[28]

The 118-page statement of claim asked for "fair and reasonable damages," to be determined by a Kansas City jury. The media speculated that if successful, she would be rewarded as much as U.S.$500 million.[29] The civil suit included allegations of wrongful death due to negligence, equipment failure, and conscious disregard for human safety.

At the suggestion of Martha's lawyers, Stu and Helen were included as co-plaintiffs in the lawsuit. Martha hesitated at first, fearing that some of the Hart kids would try to interfere in the case, but after a sleepless night she changed her mind. "Owen was always very protective of his parents," she writes, "and if they were entitled to something, I decided they should get it. That's what he would want."[30]

Kansas City police were conducting a criminal investigation into the equipment, its use, and whether Owen was properly trained to be using it. "I was thrilled at the news," Martha writes. "I was encouraged to hear those responsible could face jail time."[31] Ultimately, however, criminal charges were not laid. Still, the investigation conducted by Martha's lawyers uncovered some disturbing allegations.

In past flying stunts, the WWF had used Joe Branam, a Hollywood stunt rigger who had worked for the Rolling Stones, Elton John, and *NSYNC. Martha Hart alleged that Branam had been told McMahon wanted quick-release snap shackles for the WWF flying stunts rather than the locking carabiner. Branam refused to work with the quick-release shackle. Martha writes that he told WWF officials that it was dangerous.[32]

In May 1999, the WWF asked Branam for a quote on a stunt involving Owen. Branam asked for $5,000, which he claimed the WWF found too expensive. Branam knew the industry was rife with riggers who would have no problem using the quick-release shackle and he began to fear for Owen's safety. He asked his right-hand man, Randy Beckman, to contact the WWF and offer to rig the stunt for $3,000. According to Martha Hart, the WWF declined the offer. When Owen's "fly-in" was set up on May 23, 1999, the WWF used an independent rigger, Bobby Talbert.

"There was no doubt in my mind that the reason the WWF didn't use our company and chose an unknown rigger was to save money and to get someone who would use the snap shackle like the WWF wanted," said Beckman in a sworn affidavit.[33]

Martha's legal team claimed that the snap shackle used was manufactured by a British company for the quick release of sailboat masts. Martha's lawyers found a number of experts in the stunt industry who believed that the clip was inadequate for such a stunt. They claimed that the way its release was rigged, with the trip cord on the front of Owen's harness, the broadchested wrestler could have inadvertently released the shackle merely by making certain movements, including fiddling with his cumbersome cape while hanging above the ring.[34]

In the fall of 1999, the WWF launched a countersuit against Martha, for $75,000 plus the sum of its legal fees, claiming she had breached Owen's contract. While Martha had launched her suit in Missouri, Owen's WWF contract stated that any legal action taken against the company must be litigated in its home state of Connecticut – where punitive damages are not awarded, thus generally lessening the impact of lawsuits. It was a mean shot. The WWF was playing hardball. What made the countersuit seem even more repulsive to Martha was the WWF's insistence that it was looking out for her best interests. Linda McMahon told CNBC TV, "[the WWF] would love to be able to settle and work through this ordeal with Mrs. Hart ... in a way that will take care of her and her children for the rest of their lives."[35] Martha writes in *Broken Harts* that her lawyers had not received a settlement offer.

Bruce, on the other hand, claims that McMahon approached Stu after Owen's funeral and offered the family a U.S.$33 million settlement, "no strings attached." Stu was inclined to accept the offer. He was disgusted by how the accident occurred and devastated by the loss of his son, but he also believed Owen's death was an accident and so long as McMahon accepted responsibility and looked after Martha's family he didn't think it was necessary to the make the wrestling kingpin fry.[36]

Bruce agreed with his father. "From a booking perspective, he must have felt horrible," Bruce says. "I orchestrated a lot of [angles] and I know if I had organized something that went dreadfully wrong, where someone got killed, heaven forbid, I'm sure I'd feel devastated."

Stu was reluctant to join Martha's lawsuit against McMahon, Bruce says, especially as he was asked to sign away all control in the legal proceedings to Martha, even though he was helping pay the huge legal fees. Nevertheless, he wanted to support Owen's family and he stood by Martha.

The battle was on.

Chapter nineteen

Harts
Torn Apart

The moment the suit was filed, the family was violently torn in two. On one side was Martha. She wanted much more than money. She wanted accountability. She wanted Vince McMahon found at fault in a court of law, before the eyes of the world. Bret, Keith, and Alison wanted this too. On the other side were Bruce, Ellie, and Diana. They argued that their elderly parents' health was fading and the stress of litigation was destroying them, making their final years hell. If McMahon offered a settlement, the family should take it, they said.

The Martha camp accused them of being selfish, saying they were only worried that Stu and Helen would die before the case was settled. If that happened, the cash-strapped kids might not get any of the money their parents might gain from the lawsuit. Martha and Bret also thought the three were shamelessly sucking up to McMahon. Ellie and Diana had husbands whose careers were on a downward spiral and wanted to be able to work for McMahon. As for Bruce, in the last year, he and Ross had revived Stampede Wrestling. For a short time, the new show was running on the fledgling TV network A-Channel and, for an even shorter time, the promotion returned to the Victoria Pavilion, though it soon found itself holding its cards in dimly lit legion halls. The talent on the new show was for the most part third-rate, and fan interest was dismal. A few of the old names came back for a while,

Nattie Neidhart and her ailing grandfather, Stu. The wrestling legend died on October 16, 2003, shortly after this picture was taken.

including Bad News Allen – who as an announcer was one of the show's few bright lights – but the funds weren't sufficient to pay his salary. Bruce hoped to foster a relationship with the WWF, where Stampede Wrestling would become a farm team for the federation, scouting and training young talent for McMahon. With such a relationship, Bruce hoped he could occasionally have access to some of the WWF's big draws.

Ellie and Diana fired back with accusations of their own, suggesting the lawsuit was driven by Bret's obsession with destroying McMahon because of the infamous Montreal screw-job, when Bret left the WWF at war with his former boss.

Wayne kept his distance from the family, while Ross and Georgia tried to remain neutral. To Martha, however, the situation was black and white: it was either her way or no way, and she was angry with anyone who maintained ties to the siblings she viewed as the terrible trio.[1] As for Smith, according to Martha he approached her lawyers, claiming that he had lost an asset in Owen; presumably he was trying to get in on the legal action. Nobody took him seriously.[2] Owen's widow was becoming increasingly controlling, causing resentment from some of the Hart children, as her lawyers pressured them not to speak to the media about their brother or the case.

Meanwhile, Martha professed to hold no grudges against any wrestlers in the family who depended on McMahon to earn a living, but she sided with Bret in his disdain of Davey Boy Smith when Davey inked a new deal with the WWF in August 1999. Bret lashed out against his brother-in-law in his *Calgary Sun* column. "Saw a strange sight the other day," he wrote. "Dogs rolling in manure and loving every minute of it. For some reason it made me think of how the British Bulldog will do anything to work for the WWF."[3]

According to Diana's book, Bret phoned her in a rage: "Listen you, bitch," he allegedly said, "If I see you, I'll kill you. If I see you walking across the street, I'll run you down with my car. I'm going to tear you and Davey to shreds if I ever see you at mom's house!"[4] For Bret's part, he denounced the book as being filled with "gross distortions."

The real casualties of the family war were Stu and Helen. They supported Martha in the lawsuit, they loved her and their grandchildren, but they also loved Bruce, Ellie, and Diana and refused to take a hard stand against them, even as the trio nagged them to settle with McMahon. Martha's lawyers warned her that if her co-plaintiffs, Stu and Helen, did settle, it might weaken her own claims, thus threatening to derail her lawsuit.

The vicious screaming matches between the kids typically occurred at Hart House, with Stu and Helen caught in the crossfire. Watching their children rip into each other with such venom, nose to nose and snarling with fangs bared, was beating the Hart parents down physically and spiritually – not just Helen, who was becoming a nervous, teary-eyed shell of her former self but also the invincible Stu, who felt powerless to stop the bad blood. This was not a contrived grudge-match in a wrestling ring. The promoter couldn't snap his fingers and make it stop. This was pure, ugly hatred, eating away at his family like a cancer, and it was all because of his other great love, wrestling.

"You know what, Ellie? Owen thought you were a loser," Bret would seethe, according to Diana.[5] Ellie fired back, tears streaming down her face, accusing Bret of being a self-obsessed egomaniac, gunning for McMahon not for Owen's sake but for revenge.

In an attempt to end the dissension that threatened her case, Martha's lawyers put together an allocation agreement to be signed by all ten of the Hart siblings. This promised to preserve any share Stu and Helen would be entitled to if they died before the case was resolved, provided the children didn't help McMahon's lawyers or try to derail Martha's case. Seven of the ten children signed it. Bret signed to show his support but said he didn't want any of the money. Nor did he need it, unlike his siblings.

Bruce, Ellie, and Diana refused to sign. Perhaps, as Martha suggests, they saw greater benefits for themselves by continuing to side with McMahon.[6] Perhaps they were truly opposed to a long-drawn-out lawsuit that was taking its toll on their parents, despite the promise of cash dangled in front of them like a carrot.

Either way, the lawyers' plan backfired when, unbeknownst to her parents, Ellie made a copy of the allocation agreement and faxed it the wwf's lead counsel, Jerry McDevitt. Ellie later explained her actions to the *Calgary Herald*, saying her elderly parents were devastated by the ongoing lawsuit and Ellie wanted them to pursue a settlement with McMahon rather than have the case drag out in the courts. According to Ellie, the wwf lawyers told her they were trying to reach a settlement, something her parents were not told. "My dad's eighty-five years old and he needed to get on with his life," said Ellie. "All I ever wanted was for him to have peace of mind."[7]

Possession of the allocation agreement gave the wwf much needed ammunition, McMahon's lawyers contending that the document was designed to buy favourable testimony from the Hart children.[8] It amounted to witness tampering, the lawyers claimed. Again, the trial was held up as wwf lawyers began cross-examining select Harts, including Keith, Georgia, and Helen.

Three generations of the Hart family, in the Hart House living room, 1997. Two years later, Owen would die in a WWF wrestling ring and the clan would be torn apart.

In her deposition, Georgia said she did not condemn the WWF. Her oldest son, the brash Teddy Hart, then twenty, had been trying out for the organization, and Georgia stated she had no concerns with him being employed by McMahon. Martha later took a jab at Georgia for this, writing: "Being a mother myself, I was alarmed by such a stand. I wouldn't want my son working for a company that obviously had little regard for the safety of their employees."[9]

When Helen was cross-examined, her comments provided a clue as to Ellie's motives. "I believe that Ellie is suffering from serious domestic, personal and financial problems, which are adversely affecting her judgement," Helen said, adding that her daughter was trying to get Jim Neidhart work in the WWF.[10]

Ellie's life with The Anvil had been a nightmare. In Jim Neidhart's 1980s heyday, the family moved to Florida, but they returned to Calgary in 1995 because of their financial problems, moving into a home purchased by Stu. Jim and Ellie were to make the monthly mortgage payments. Ellie alleges in court documents that by the end of the 1990s, even though Jim was, she claims, earning about $30,000 a month as a wrestler, he stopped making payments on the house.[11]

In a series of sworn affidavits, Ellie alleges Neidhart was a chronic alcohol and drug abuser. She also claims she suffered years of physical abuse, such as a time in January 1999 when she says Jim threw her up a flight of stairs.[12] Ellie's allegations were never proven in court. Her children, Ellie states, were terrified of their father. Even Stu, who opposed divorce, supported Ellie in a letter he wrote to Jim on March 10, 1999, found amid court documents. The Neidharts' living arrangements at the time were confusing, with Jim living at the house sporadically, but Stu clearly had his daughter's protection in mind when he wrote: "I am advised by my daughter … that you and she have now separated and have not been living together. I am aware … that my daughter is fearful that you will cause her major physical harm if you continue to live together…. Because of this, I must ask that you leave the home which I purchased."[13] Although Ellie initiated divorce proceedings on many occasions, she never followed through with them – something that frustrates family members to this day.

Already feeling betrayed by the family dissension, Martha felt she was crossed yet again when Bruce and Ross planned a Stampede Wrestling tribute to Owen one year after his death. Martha was furious when told the brothers were planning on bringing in WWF wrestlers for the show. Bruce defended the idea, saying the event was a way of honouring his brother and that the WWF wrestlers were attending out of respect for Owen. Nevertheless, the show was cancelled in the wake of Martha's protests.

Martha once more expressed outrage when she learned that the WWF had planned a show at the Saddledome on May 27, close to the anniversary of Owen's death. But her protests were not enough to stop that event. As much as she would have loved to stop it, the WWF juggernaut would not stop rolling for her or anybody.

"When I lost my trial date, I almost lost my mind," writes Martha in her book, *Broken Harts*.[14] At the rate the lawsuit was going, it looked as though the legal wrangling could go on for years, and after the fiasco with the allocation agreement, Owen's widow feared she stood to lose everything. She finally agreed to settle. Stu was barred from the negotiation sessions. He had forgiven McMahon for what he saw as a mistake and the lawyers were afraid the old man would shake McMahon's hand in the boardroom, weakening their stance as they tried to play hardball in ironing out a deal.

It was another example of the ill-treatment Helen felt she and Stu had been subjected to by the legal team. She felt they were kept in the dark and patronized by the attorneys, who, in her opinion, were too free with the Harts' cash. They worked for Martha and didn't care how Stu and Helen felt about anything, it seemed.

When one of the meetings opened with Martha's now all too familiar rant against the WWF, Helen was filled with despair. She wondered if the nightmare would ever end. She told Stu's biographer Marsha Erb that McMahon's speech that day in the meeting was a great relief to her. As Helen recalled it, McMahon came clean and said he wanted to "do right by [Owen's] family." McMahon added: "I know that nothing can ever bring him back."[5]

When the meeting ended, Martha says, Helen tried to talk to McMahon at Bruce's behest. She was going to approach the wrestling kingpin for a job for her wrestling-obsessed son. Martha nipped that idea in the bud.[16]

The case was settled for U.S.$18 million in November 2000. Martha would receive $10 million, minus legal fees. Her children would receive $3 million each, while Stu and Helen would receive $1 million each, minus their share of the bills. Shockingly, once the attorneys were paid and the taxman took his piece of the pie, the parents came away with less than $700,000 each.

The deal done, Martha began speaking to the media. Her message had a mean-spirited edge. Bitter about her experience with the Harts during the lawsuit, she lashed out at them in public. Her words were unnecessary and unkind, not in keeping with the saintly image Martha tried to project.

"These people worked against me," she told the *Calgary Herald*. "I am removing myself and my children from the family. I carry the last name, but I'm not related to them anymore."[17] In the *Calgary Sun*, she stated that "people need to know that Owen was a white sheep in a black family."[18]

The words were an unjust slap in the face to the Harts who had stood by her – Bret, Keith, Alison, and, most importantly, Stu and Helen. The parents unquestionably failed to stand by Martha as firmly as she would have liked, torn as they were by their love for all their children, but they did not back out, despite pressure from some of their kids and their own doubts. They saw the ordeal with Martha through to the end.

Martha's hostility toward Bruce, Diana, and Ellie is understandable. She believed she was seeking justice for Owen and felt they betrayed her. But Martha did not have to make a point of smearing Owen's siblings in public; she might have been more understanding. Bruce, Ellie, and Diana were not wealthy as Bret was, and, as distasteful as Martha found it, they needed McMahon to get ahead in the wrestling business. And, although Martha worked at a women's shelter, she never seemed to acknowledge that Ellie's behaviour may have been the act of a desperate woman in need of help, given Ellie's allegations about her abusive marriage.

Part of the reason for Martha being so forthcoming with the media was that she was announcing her plans to start the Owen Hart Foundation, a charity to aid the working poor. She also funded an addition to Calgary's Rockyview General Hospital and established an Owen Hart Memorial fund at the Alberta Children's Hospital. This was the way she planned to put Vince McMahon's "dirty money" (as she viewed it) to good use. But, when she told the *Calgary Sun*, "I plan on doing a lot of good in this city and I want my name distinguished from that family,"[19] she was being unfair. Stu had raised thousands upon thousands of dollars for countless charities for decades.

As a reporter for the *Calgary Herald*, I spoke to Martha the day she announced her settlement to the media. I sought to balance the story by contacting one of the so-called "black" Harts. I wound up speaking to Ellie, who was crushed by what Martha had to say. She screamed defensively into the phone, wrenching sobs punctuating her words: "I asked my parents, 'Have you talked with Vince McMahon at all? Did you know they tried to settle?' They had no idea.... I had no idea Martha was going to sit there and bury us. There's no closure in our lives. It's a damn mess and I'm sick of our family being portrayed as these horrible bastards."[20]

That night, after the newspaper had gone to press, I received a call from Helen. She sounded shaken. Ellie had phoned her, hysterical, and Helen was worried sick about the way the family would be portrayed in the *Herald*. She was afraid the Harts would come off as embarrassingly dysfunctional yet again. She begged me not to run such a story. I tried to assure her that I spoke to Ellie simply to hear her side of the story, but I don't think Helen was convinced. There was an unmistakable helplessness in her voice. Helen Hart sounded utterly defeated.

On May 28, 2001, the WWF returned to Calgary's Saddledome for a televised Raw Is War card. McMahon invited Stu and Helen to attend the event and they accepted. When Martha heard about this, she publicly stated that any Hart who attended the show was disrespecting Owen's memory. Bret felt the same way and promised Martha his parents would not be attending. The day of the show, Bruce and Ellie took their father from the house before Bret arrived to intervene. Helen opted to stay behind to do her hair for the evening ahead. When Bret arrived at Hart House, he persuaded his mother not to attend the event.[21]

As the show was broadcast across the world that evening, the announcer told the capacity crowd of eighteen thousand that members of the first family of wrestling were in attendance. Stu, looking gaunt and sickly from the pneumonia and heart problems he had been battling in recent months, was helped to his feet by Bruce, who raised his father's hand proudly. Diana, Smith, Bruce, Ellie, and many of the grandkids stood by Stu as the adoring crowd chanted his name for close to ten minutes. With a sly grin on his face, Smith held up a sign for the cameras to zoom in on. It said, tauntingly, "Hi, Bret."[22]

Later in the evening, Dungeon graduates Chris Benoit and Chris Jericho offered a tribute. "Both of us owe a lot to one man, the father of the greatest wrestling family of all time," bellowed the charismatic Jericho. "I'm talking about Stu Hart!" The crowd went wild. "I'm not going to forget another member of the Hart family, our good friend, Owen Hart!" The camera zoomed in on Stu, looking bewildered, as if he didn't know where he was. At Jericho's speech, he lifted his hand skyward again, his eyes, so empty of late, lighting up proudly.

That evening, Martha phoned Hart House. "I am ashamed of all of you and you should be ashamed of yourselves! Go to hell!" she screamed at Helen before slamming down the phone.[23]

Martha was behaving like a tyrant. When she opposed the Harts' being friendly with the WWF during the lawsuit, she had a valid point. Now she was merely being a bully. Were the Harts not allowed to make their own decisions and form their own opinions when it came to McMahon? She herself writes that she came to believe McMahon was sorry for the accident. She also says he sent a cheque for more than $50,000 as a donation to the Alberta Children's Hospital in Owen's name.[24] Years later, Bret would also make his peace with McMahon.

Three days after Stu's WWF appearance, the Hart patriarch was flown to Ottawa's Rideau Hall. There, Governor General Adrienne Clarkson presented him – along with such highbrow luminaries as June Callwood and Mordecai Richler – with the prestigious Order of Canada. Accompanied by Helen, Stu was recognized not only for his work as a wrestling promoter but also for his commitment to the Calgary community and his support of more than thirty charities.

That was one of few bright lights in a dark year. Diana Hart released her tell-all autobiography, *Under the Mat,* in the fall of 2001. In it she cast most of her family in the worst possible light, portraying her mother as a weak, ineffectual alcoholic and Bret as an egomaniacal bully. She also dished dirt on Bruce, Smith, Ellie, Ed Whalen, and countless wrestlers. Some of her most scathing commentary was reserved for Martha and for her own husband, Davey Boy, with whom she was embroiled in vicious divorce proceedings.

Davey Boy's WWF comeback had been marred by his continued drug addiction, Diana writes. He was still using steroids, abusing painkillers, and shooting morphine, all of which reduced his work in the ring to a lethargic, pathetic shadow of the mighty British Bulldog he had once been. Finally, McMahon let him go.

After Diana filed for divorce, Davey Boy got back at her by having an affair with her long-time rival, Andrea Hart, wife of Bruce. This scandal became public when Davey was arrested for allegedly threatening to kill Diana and Ellie, charges that were ultimately dismissed. Throughout his trial for uttering threats, Davey came to the courthouse accompanied by Bruce's wife, the mother of five children. Andrea was beaming on the arm of her new man. Three days after the Bulldog was found innocent, he was again in trouble with the law, this time for uttering death threats to Bruce. Almost eleven months later, the Crown again dismissed the charges against the wrestler.

When Bruce's wife left him for his brother-in-law Davey Boy, it was a fiasco that made the Hart family look like white trash. This eccentric, talented brood who had once been the toast of Calgary now appeared fit for the *Jerry Springer Show* – exactly what Martha accuses them of.[25]

Many of the Harts remained close to Davey Boy throughout the ordeal, but Andrea became a pariah to most of the family. Bruce had been a devoted husband and a dedicated father, says his niece Nattie Neidhart. He was faithful to his wife and never abused drugs or alcohol. He doted on their son, Rhett, then nine years old, who was born with cerebral palsy. "I think Andrea always wanted Bruce to be more in wrestling and she had this little crush on Davey, because he was a big wrestling star," says Nattie. "When Davey started to sink, she moved in there.... [Davey] was in a very vulnerable position."

Embittered by the situation with Davey Boy, Diana wrote a book that is highly litigious. Poorly written, full of factual errors, and oozing with bile toward a number of people, one reviewer said the world according to Diana Hart made "*Mommy Dearest* look like a Hallmark Mother's Day card."[26] The book is compelling in a morbid way – reading it is akin to gawking at the gory aftermath of a car crash. Putting aside the skewed facts and low blows, it is the truth as an emotionally hurting Diana Hart sees it, and not a complete work of fiction as its detractors suggest.

Soon after the book's release, Martha issued a statement denouncing it as "distortions, misstatements and unjustified slurs" that threatened to destroy her reputation and "undermine the memory of Owen." When she threatened to sue the publisher, distributor, and authors, the book was pulled from the shelves. Diana fired back in the *National Post*, calling Martha a rich bully. "Martha has money to fight me on it and I don't," she said. "I know what I've written is true."[27]

Martha released her own book, *Broken Harts: The Life and Death of Owen Hart*, in September 2002. She had told the press that, unlike Diana's autobiography, her book would not be cruel.

Her book is well researched. It is full of love for Owen and infinitely classier than Diana's book. But the bitter jabs are there. While *Under the Mat* was all about down-and-dirty trash talk, prim and proper Martha took her digs while looking down her nose at the Hart clan. Much of the book had a shrill, sanctimonious tone to it as she attacks not only the wrestling business but also the family that was so ingrained in the sport.

Martha's outrage at the Harts who stood against her is understandable. But her sweeping condemnation of the family and everything they stand for is unfair. She's even hard on Stu and Helen. Many of the Hart children, including Bret, were put off the book for that reason. One comes away from *Broken Harts* with the distinct impression that Martha wants to deny the part of her husband that was a Hart and a wrestler. She sees shame in the wrestling business and seeks to bring a dignity to Owen's life that she feels he lost as a wrestler and part of a wrestling clan. She can't come to grips with this side of her husband's life. But this was a very real part of who Owen was. It's sad, because her prevailing love for Owen is unconditional. *Broken Harts* is a tale of a woman in pain.

Helen would have agonized over the Martha-Diana book war had she lived to see it play out, and been deeply hurt by what both women wrote. As it was, she had been tortured enough spending a lifetime in the wrestling business she often hated. But the family she loved so dearly always made those hardships worthwhile. When that family was destroyed by the business, it was more than she could bear.

On September 26, 2001, seventy-seven-year-old Helen returned from visiting her sister in California. With the intense security at the airport in the days following the September 11 terrorist attacks, Helen was held up for hours. During the commotion, the long-suffering diabetic's blood sugar levels went awry. When she finally arrived home, she went straight to bed. The next morning, when Stu couldn't wake her, she was rushed to a hospital, where she had diabetic seizures and fell into a coma.

Stu sat by her side day and night, family and friends filing in and out, everyone praying that she would rally. A week later, Helen did come out of her coma. Filled with hope, Stu read her poetry the two had enjoyed when he courted her all those years ago.

On November 4, when it was all too clear Helen was slipping away, Stu said to his Tiger Belle, "If you could smile for me one more time, it would mean everything to me." Helen laid her eyes on the love of her life and granted him his wish, smiling weakly.[28] Stu held her head up and kissed her on the face to say goodbye.

Alison remembers the family gathering at Hart House for Sunday dinner after her mother died. Stu sat down at the head of the table and cried in front of the family. He couldn't stop. Alison panicked and phoned Bret. "Dad's crying," she said, "and I can't stop it."

"Let him cry," Bret said. "He needs to let it out."

Alison realized her brother was right, but the sight of her mighty father reduced to tears shook her to the core. "He was so strong, and I needed him to be strong still," she says.

Helen's funeral was a dignified affair, with burly wrestlers on their best behaviour seated next to Helen's posh sisters and women from her jazzercise class. Bret, Bruce, Alberta premier Ralph Klein, and Ed Whalen paid touching tributes, but it was Stu's speech that made the biggest impact. With a clarity that was rare for him in his later years, Stu reminisced about the beauty he met on the New York beach over fifty years ago. Ever positive, he tried to focus on the good in their relationship. "I'm glad I had this much time with her," he said.[29] But his profound pain was evident. "I'll never get over this," he said solemnly. "I don't have enough time."[30]

Helen was Stu's princess among the pirates of Stampede Wrestling. Now she was gone, and he didn't know how to live without her. The superman of the Prairies was suddenly a mere mortal, dying of a broken heart.

The tragedies continued in the months to come, fate hammering the spiritually battered Hart family with cruel relentlessness.

After he spoke at Helen's funeral, Ed Whalen went on a vacation with his wife, Nomi, to Florida, where the seventy-four-year-old sportscaster had a heart attack. After three days in a coma, the voice of Stampede Wrestling was silenced on December 4, 2001. It was fitting that Ed and Helen would die in such close proximity to one another. "My mother and Ed Whalen were really the only class elements of the business," said Ross Hart. "They both added so much dignity to our company."

Among the many tributes to Whalen was a three-minute montage played on the Jumbotron at the Saddledome before a Calgary Flames game. On the Global News website, nearly sixteen thousand messages were posted from around the world by people who wanted to share their favourite Whalen memories.

On May 18, 2002, the Harts suffered another devastating loss when Davey Boy Smith died of a heart attack, at the age of thirty-nine, while vacationing at the Fairmont Hot Springs resort in British Columbia with his girlfriend, Bruce's estranged wife, Andrea. Andrea told the Calgary Herald that the couple went to bed in each other's arms on Friday night and when she awoke on Saturday, the British Bulldog was dead. The coroner's report said Davey died of natural causes but made a point of stating he had used anabolic steroids in the past. A bottle of trenbolone acetate, a steroid extracted from cattle, was found in Davey and Andrea's hotel room.

Davey had again been attempting to relaunch his career, wrestling his last match on May 11 at an indie show held in a Winnipeg community centre. His tag team partner for the bout was his sixteen-year-old son, Harry. Harry says his father was full of pride that he got to wrestle side by side with his son: "It was a dream come true for both us." Other people close to Davey say, too, that he seemed happy in his final days. Andrea claims the two were discussing marriage (even though, according to Nattie Neidhart, Davey was at Diana's house three days before he died trying to reconcile with her).

Again, stars in the wrestling world – including Hulk Hogan, Vince McMahon, and Chris Benoit – came from around the world to pay their respects to a fallen comrade. Two funeral services were held for Davey, one organized by Andrea, the other by the Hart family.

Nattie Neidhart says that despite his problems, Davey had a warm and kind heart. "He was always there for us," she says. "When there were big fights between my mom and dad, he would help us out financially [and] give us a place to stay."

At the Hart family service, Bret delivered a moving eulogy in which he referred to the Hart family's last few years as "a long, exhausting argument with God."[31] Bret's frustration would become even more poignant less than a month later when he suffered a stroke while riding his bike along Calgary's Bow River, on June 25, 2002.

Bret's career had ended prematurely in December 1999 while wrestling the monstrous Bill Goldberg, a former football player who was fast becoming the biggest star in the wcw. But Goldberg's skills in the ring weren't as impressive as his massive 285-pound frame and he accidentally kicked Bret in the head during a match. Soon after, Bret called it quits at the insistence of his doctor. The official announcement of his retirement was made in October 2000.

Even though Bret claimed he suffered his stroke as a result of a bike crash after hitting a pothole on the path, many speculated that his crash occurred because of the stroke, the aftermath of his head injuries from the infamous Goldberg bout. When Bret was unable to get up and back on his bike after the accident, he phoned his wife, Julie, on his cellphone. When she arrived, she was frightened by what she saw. "The pupil in my left eye was the size of a bowling ball and I was drooling," Bret told a reporter. "I had pain right up my left side. And my back felt like someone had slugged me and left his fist in me. I tried to walk and I just fell over."[32]

Bret spent a month in the hospital almost completely paralyzed, crying as he contemplated his fate. The man who was once an icon of strength now had to struggle to merely lift a finger. What had he done, what had his family done, to have been so cursed these last few years, he wondered, his thoughts thrashing angrily as he lay trapped in the prison his body had become. But Bret had always been a fighter and he was determined to battle his way out of this one. It was the toughest challenge he ever faced. Once able to lift a 300-pound wrestler, it now took every ounce of effort to stir a cup of tea. It was a long road to recovery but, one day at a time, he would make it.

His greatest triumph in the hospital came the day Stu arrived for a visit. Being able to walk a few metres to embrace his sad, ailing father brought tears to The Hitman's eyes.

Stu Hart died on October 16, 2003, at the age of eighty-eight. His health had been on the wane for the last decade, taking a serious turn for the worse after Helen died. His knees were ruined and he increasingly relied on a wheelchair to get around. He had bladder and prostate problems, arthritis, and diabetes, and he was showing early signs of Alzheimer disease. He was often confused and disoriented. His old wrestling buddies Phil "Killer" Klein and Les Thornton tell of visiting him and having conversations where Stu reminisced about the good old days with almost photographic recall. Invariably, Stu would be distracted or called away; when he returned a moment later, he had no memory of the conversation he had just had. He acted as though he were meeting his old chums for the first time that day.

But even when he could barely walk, Stu's grip was still vice-like, and he loved nothing more than locking men in his submission holds. Bob Lueck, the former Calgary Stampeder who wrestled for Stu in the early 1970s, visited the wrestling godfather a year before his death. Stu was joking around and grabbed Lueck's neck from behind as if he were going to slap a headlock on him.

"'Ahh, shit, don't do this, Stu,'" Lueck remembers saying. "Even at his age, he still had that spunk, that fire. That sucker was an animal."

Stu's granddaughters, Jenny and Nattie Neidhart, lived in the Hart's coach house and looked after him, keeping him company and giving him his insulin shots. At the beginning of October, they noticed that their grandfather's elbow, which he had cut in a fall days earlier, looked infected. Stu was taken to the hospital, where he was kept for a staph infection. During his stay there he developed pneumonia. Doctors told the family he would never be able to return to Hart House: he required round-the-clock care in a nursing home.

A week later, Stu's condition worsened and the family was warned he didn't have long to live. He fell in and out of consciousness as friends and family gathered around him in his hospital room. Frank Sisson tried to sneak his old pal deep-fried chicken fingers he had brought from his casino – Stu had always loved them. Dan Kroffat, who considered Stu his role model in life, came by and told the old man exactly how he felt about him. Sometimes Stu knew where he was and responded to people. Other times he wasn't as lucid and would call out for his Tiger Belle – something he had been doing during moments of confusion ever since she had died.

Stu died in his sleep with Bret, Bret's by then ex-wife Julie, and granddaughter Jenny Neidhart at his side. It was time. Everybody agreed he had been dying slowly since Helen's death. "I think he really anticipated being with my mom again," said Diana hours after her father died. "She was probably reaching out. That's what we really all like to think, my mom's calling for him."[33]

Stu's funeral was held on October 23 at the First Alliance Church in southwest Calgary. Over a thousand mourners came to pay their respects to the wrestling icon, including a huge cast of wrestlers, among them Harley Race and Chris Benoit, and a sombre Vince McMahon. The Hart clan filled half a dozen pews at the front of the church as Frank Sinatra's "My Way" and Johnny Cash's "We'll Meet Again" played. Despite the bitter and lasting divisions in the family, on that day the Hart children held hands and rested their heads on one another's shoulders. At one point, Bruce and Bret, the leaders of the warring factions, embraced in the aisle. Ross rose and extended his arm to his brothers.

Those delivering eulogies spoke of Stu's down-to-earth nature, his love for animals, his charitable heart, and his lifelong compassion for the downtrodden. Laughter accompanied tears as many recalled the bizarre and funny aspects of Stu's life. Ralph Klein recalled his days as mayor of Calgary, when Stu would storm into his office and gripe for hours about his troubles with the boxing and wrestling commission. Klein joked that he always listened patiently, lest he wind up in the Dungeon.

Stu, Klein went on to say, "embodied the best of the Alberta spirit" with his "drive, energy and ambition." Bret honoured his father as "a real man, a great man.... [who] touched people right here in Calgary and all around the world."[34]

Nattie cared for her grandfather every day near the end of his life and was crushed by his death but, always positive, she puts things into perspective: "In a way, it was kind of a relief. After my grandmother died, he was never really the same. He lost his reason to live. He had this big family but nobody could get in his bed at night and be my grandmother. That was a huge void for him. It's actually very touching that he never got over her."

For all its madness and mayhem, there's also a tragic beauty to the Stampede Wrestling story, one rooted in Stu Hart and his two great loves. "It's sort of an epic," says Keith. "In the centre of it all, you've got this remarkable romance between my mom and dad. They worshipped each other. My mom was critical of my dad, but to her, there was nothing he couldn't do. He was the ultimate man for her." But Stu's other great love was wrestling, and he could never let it go, even as it destroyed his wife.

John Helton, a former Calgary Stampeder who wrestled for a short time, went to visit Stu during his final days. "Even in those last days of his life when he was sleeping, I know he was dreaming of wrestling," Helton says. "If ever a person can have a passion in life and live it the whole way through ... well, Stu's the only man I've known to live like that. He had a passion you could see in his eyes.... His wife meant the world to him.... but there was nothing he wouldn't do to keep his finger in the wrestling."

Chapter twenty

Harts Go On

Stampede Wrestling lives. Barely. Some fifty years after Stu set up shop in Calgary, the city's wrestling fans can still take in the action nearly every Friday night. The scene today, however, is a lame-duck imitation of those wild evenings Papa Hart orchestrated in the Victoria Pavilion so long ago.

The blame for that does not fall solely on the wrestlers. True, there are many third-rate talents in the promotion: grapplers with soft bellies, zero muscle tone, and minimal charisma who put on awkward, unconvincing matches. There are a number of skinny kids in that ring, too. Not lean and awesomely impressive, like a young Dynamite Kid, but scrawny, with no hope it would seem of getting anywhere in the wrestling game. In today's world, where chiselled muscleheads, flying daredevils, and glitzy larger than life characters dominate the biz, this lot seems all the more forlorn.

But Bruce and Ross have also recruited their share of highly promising talents. Not surprisingly, a few Hart spawn are among them. Harry "Bulldog" Smith, the son of Davey Boy, is a budding young powerhouse in the tradition of his father. The kid, who wrestled his first pro match at age eleven, has been a giant since his teens. Now, at the age of twenty, the growth spurt continues. Standing six-foot-five and weighing in at 250 pounds, Prince Harry, as the family calls him, has toured with New Japan of late and wrestled a few undercard matches for the WWE.*

---

*WWF changed its name to WWE, for World Wrestling Entertainment, after losing a nine-year court battle with the World Wildlife Fund, which laid claim to the abbreviation WWF.

"Stampede Kid" T.J. Wilson, a standout of the new Stampede Wrestling roster, delivers a flying dropkick.

Teddy Hart, twenty-five, the son of Georgia and B.J. Annis, may just be one of the most fearless and agile fliers in the business, pulling off insane aerial assaults with names like the twisting moonsault, straightjacket jumping piledriver, and horizontal 360 corkscrew, which he refers to as "Open Hart Surgery." Teddy, who is small boned but muscular, thrives in the spotlight. He has a flamboyant streak both in and out of the ring. He was once seen strutting through a Calgary shopping mall with his black hair braided, wearing sunglasses and a pair of obnoxious, furry white pants that looked as if they came straight off a yak's back.

Teddy is his own worst enemy. Arrogant and hotheaded, he had a developmental contract with the WWF at the ripe age of eighteen but was released from the training camp because of "attitude problems." Similar complaints have been heard as Teddy worked with independent wrestling promotions, including Ring of Honor, based in Philadelphia, and his family's own Stampede Wrestling. One Friday night in Calgary, Teddy got on the mike at a Stampede Wrestling match and, indifferent to the children in the audience, tore into a fellow wrestler with a string of profanity. "My favourite nephew," Ross said, sarcastically.

"Teddy Hart's got all the talent in the world and he could go somewhere, but he's got to get his head together," says wrestling journalist Dave Meltzer, citing Teddy's reputation as "a loose cannon."

Nattie Neidhart, twenty-three, is the daughter of Jim "The Anvil" and Ellie. Even though her home life was tumultuous – her father often spiralling out of control on the excesses of the wrestling biz – Nattie is a sweet soul: courteous, warm, and friendly. She's proud of her Hart heritage and struggles to stay neutral in a family so harshly divided. She dearly loves both her uncle Bret and her mother, who can't be in the same room together. Still, Nattie retains a positive outlook.

Nattie in the ring, however, is another story. There, she's an ornery wildcat, not unlike her dad, constantly fuming, outraged by the antics of her enemies, whom she's itching to tear apart. She can do it, too. Neidhart, who used to model in her teens, is cute with long, bleach-blond hair and an attractive smile. But she's nothing like the fake-boobed bikini models the WWE tries to pass off as women wrestlers today. While she was waif-like in her modelling days, today Nattie is a squat ball of strength who, like The Anvil, is able to pick up male wrestlers weighing well over 200 pounds and slam them to the mat with as much force as the guys. In 2005, she toured Japan, taking on butch broads who had more in common with the woolly Cuban Assassin than any WWE diva.

Her boyfriend, the high-flying "Stampede Kid" T.J. Wilson, is another fine talent. So is the brutal, six-foot-eight Portuguese giant Karnage. Ravenous Randy Myers, billed as the nephew of '80s bruiser Duke Myers, supposedly hailing from Kalamazoo, Michigan (he's actually Calgary boy Theo Francon), is another one to watch. Inspired by punk rockers Rancid and the bizarre, confrontational comedy of Tom Green and Andy Kaufman, Randy brings a punk sensibility to his ring work. Complete with a bellowing persona, goofy dance moves, and hair that juts up in long spikes, Myers never fails to entertain the crowd.

The problem is there's never much of a crowd. The new Stampede Wrestling is held at the Ogden Legion Hall, or the Ogden Legion of Doom, as it's dubbed, in southeast Calgary. Bruce says the shows draw anywhere from fifty to five hundred fans. On the nights I attended there were never more than a hundred. On one particularly lousy night, it looked closer to twenty-five.

Many of the city's wrestling fans are not even aware that Stampede Wrestling has been revived. Aside from the odd flyer posted in gyms and dive bars around town, Bruce does little to promote the matches. Some of his wrestlers complain he's not willing to spend money on advertising and, consequently, they're faced with dead houses most nights. Bruce, on the other hand, blames the local media for not supporting the Calgary institution he keeps on life-support, but he seems unwilling to do the simplest things to help it. I told him I would include Stampede Wrestling in the weekly entertainment listings of the *Calgary Herald* if he e-mailed the details once a week. He agreed to do so, but the e-mails never came.

When I wrote an article in the *Calgary Herald* magazine *Swerve*, honouring the great villains of Stampede Wrestling past (including a plug for the present-day promotion), Bruce was annoyed: Why was I not focusing on the current product? But a truthful story about today's Stampede Wrestling would not be the promotional rocket boost Bruce clearly feels he's owed as the son of Stu.

The scene at the Ogden Legion is touching in a way, as members of the Hart family struggle to keep the family tradition alive. There's also much to be said for the young wannabe grapplers, killing themselves for pay that is beyond lousy (most of them are lucky if they earn fifteen bucks a night) in front of dismal crowds. But for the most part, the picture is a pathetic one, considering what Stampede Wrestling used to be.

Of the small group of regular attendees at the matches, many of them are family and friends of the wrestlers. Ellie is there most nights to cheer on Nattie. Alison's daughters, Lindsay, twenty, and Brooke, nineteen, who are dating Randy Myers and "Pistol" Pete Wilson respectively, also never miss a card. They sit with Randy's mother, a gruff art therapist who's consistently in the front row watching her charismatic son play the clown.

A few fathers regularly bring their kids, and a handful of crusty old-timers make it out most evenings. There's also the odd sloppy drunk in the crowd. One night, I spotted a fellow who could barely walk. He was tossed out the door by an overzealous meathead of a security guard, a scuffle that stole the thunder from the action in the ring.

For some reason, a large portion of the audience is made up of mentally challenged children. They are in their glory, jeering and cheering and chasing after the wrestlers in between matches, hoping to talk to them and get their autographs. A couple of them seem to have a crush on Nattie and, whenever she can, she tries to make time for them. One night, one of the boys in a wheelchair asked her for a hug. She gave him one and the kid lit up like he had just made it to heaven.

As the matches unfold, Bruce is in and out of the dressing room, often standing at the sidelines. He watches the action intently like a kooky movie director. Some of the wrestlers express frustration at his storylines, at the twists and turns he concocts. There's a poor sense of continuity from one week to the next, they complain. Too often, things don't make sense, like the night Nattie was felled by a low blow, which would not be as devastating to a woman wrestler as to a man. An inferior sound system in the legion hall also makes the stories tough to follow. When the wrestlers get on the microphone to make their boasts and threats – crucial business in moving the angles forward – it sounds like a muddled mess.

But occasionally, there's a glimmer of the twisted genius that fired the Stampede Wrestling of old. For several months, Randy Myers was teamed up with seventeen-year-old Dan Vander-Griendt, who wrestles as Dandy Myers. They came to the ring with a hefty redhead called Ma Myers, their shtick similar to that of TV's popular *Trailer Park Boys*.

Meanwhile, the villainous Karachi Vice is back with Gama Singh's son, Raj, trying to break into the wrestling business as Gama Singh Jr. He's accompanied by a friend who wrestles as "Tiger" Raj Singh Jr. Often Gama Sr. joins the boys at ringside as their manager. For a time, a large group of kids from Gama's neighbourhood, the predominantly East Indian Terra Vista, came to the matches to cheer on the Vice. "Gama! Gama!" they chanted, a sharp contrast to the days of "Go home, Paki!" The Vice were meant to be heels, but there was such overwhelming enthusiasm from the ethnic crowd that the kids began cheering for them too, jeering the cocky Teddy Hart, a babyface.

Teddy seemed flustered by this and, during one match, it looked as though a real fight was about to break out between him and one of the more vocal East Indian fans.

At some point, Dandy Myers betrayed Randy and joined the Karachi Vice. A "born-again Pakistani," he now wrestles as Mahatma Dhandi. This twist echoed the conversion of Mike Shaw to Makhan Singh back in the day, and there was grumbling behind the scenes about Bruce being stuck in the past. But wrestling's always been about recycling ideas.

Some of Bruce's directions are questionable. One night in January 2005, Dandy Myers bladed for the first time. Maybe he was overzealous with the blade, because he bled buckets. The match raged into the men's washroom in the Legion, a very real pool of the teen's "juice" being mopped up by a janitor minutes later. After the match, a white towel was found outside the dressing room, soaked red with the high schooler's blood.

Dandy is a shy kid, dedicated to wrestling. He's been training with the Harts since the age of fourteen and dreams of making it to the WWE someday. He says he can't remember exactly how much he paid to be part of Bruce's wrestling camp, but he figures it was around a couple grand. (Stu, on the other hand, didn't charge the wrestlers he trained.) Dandy's skills have improved vastly since the first time I saw him taking bumps in the Dungeon, back in 2003, but he still seems an inexperienced kid in the ring. He's lanky and awkward, like so many teenage boys, and he doesn't seem ready to be slicing his head open for fans. True, young men have been doing it for decades. Wrestling is a mean business and if you're not tough enough, you don't belong in the ring. But watching Dandy bleed, I couldn't help but feel he was being exploited.

After the match, Dandy came and spoke to Bruce, who praised him for a job well done. Dandy seemed shaken up. Later, I asked him if he was, and he said no. Rather, he was feeling light-headed on account of all the blood he lost. But he's said he's definitely up for another blading when the time comes.

One of the kids approached Bruce after the match and asked if Karnage, who had supposedly injured Dandy, was going to be suspended. "He should be suspended by his foreskin," Bruce answered sternly. I couldn't help but laugh. "I've got a million of 'em," Bruce told me.

But just as in the '80s, Bruce can't seem to take his ego out of the equation when he's running the show, and some say his pettiness is ruining what little business he has left. Young wannabe wrestlers join the Hart training camp hoping to learn the art of pro wrestling and eventually exploit the family's ties to WWE, New Japan, and indie wrestling promotions around the world. But some of the kids who have moved on to other promotions say they have been discouraged by Bruce. The new Stampede Wrestling has a shortage of capable stars and Bruce is not happy when they leave him.

In June 2005, Randy Myers had just returned from a wrestling tour of England. He was ready to resume his run in Stampede Wrestling when Bruce told him he would not be performing that night. According to those backstage (none of whom wanted to go on the record), Bruce was bitter that Randy had wrestled elsewhere and was barring him from the ring that night to teach him a lesson.

"Faaawwwkk!" yelled the mohawk-sporting wrestler as he burst from the dressing room throwing a plastic bottle of Gatorade across the hall as puzzled fans gawked at him. Alison's daughter Lindsay followed him close behind. "Fucking abortion wrestling!" she spat. At the time of this writing, Randy Myers said his affiliation with Stampede Wrestling was up in the air.

A couple of months earlier, Harry Smith told me, "I'm done with Bruce." Teddy Hart also seems finished with the promotion, and Nattie wasn't sure if her boyfriend T.J. would be returning when he finished his tour of Britain. Even Ross, who worked side by side with Bruce for so long, has had a problem with his brother, insiders say. These days, Bruce is in charge of the Ogden Legion shows while Ross handles the spot shows in small Alberta towns such as Hanna, Cochrane, and Didsbury. Morale is much better at those shows.

Some of the young grapplers feel Bruce doesn't respect them. There's also a strong sentiment that Stampede Wrestling is a sinking ship and their careers would be better off if they disembarked. Bad News Allen worked for the new Stampede Wrestling as an announcer when Bruce and Ross relaunched the show in 1999. He quit when it became obvious there was little money in the promotion in its current incarnation. "It's the same old thing with the Hart brothers," he said in an interview posted on the Slam Wrestling website. "They have no organization at all, everything's done haphazardly.... I can't see them succeeding."

Dan Kroffat has similar sentiments. "They're still pounding away, trying to make it fly, but it will never fly," he says. "If you want to run the Indianapolis 500, take your race to worthy tracks. Don't run it out of a garbage dump. To run it out of the legion hall you'll never attract people."

Even Hart brother Keith thinks Stampede Wrestling is a lost cause. "It's sad," he says. "It doesn't exist anymore, except what [Bruce] pretends. It's defunct but [he's] still going through the motions."

Nattie, ever stuck in the middle of family squabbles, understands the criticisms levelled against Stampede Wrestling. But she considers it her schooling for a career in wrestling. For the Harts who take part in the legacy, it offers a feeling of family unity that has otherwise been lost. When Nattie wrestles, she sees her mother, cousins, and uncles drawn together by that which is in the family's blood. The weekly wrestling matches make her feel closer to her grandfather, too, as in the days when the Hart clan gathered in the dining room for the Sunday dinners and listened to Stu's stories. "We don't have the Sunday dinners anymore," Nattie says. "Now all we have is the wrestling, and it's very special to us."

In 2004, Hart House was sold. The cost of maintaining the crumbling castle was high. The place needed restoration. That, combined with property taxes and the usual bills, forced the Harts' collective hand.

Of course, squabbles ensued over the fate of the mansion. Bruce wanted to keep the house in the family, as he was still using the Dungeon to train wrestlers. He dreamed of turning the place into a shrine, a wrestling museum open to the public – for a price. Smith was still living there and wanted to remain for the rest of his life. Other siblings argued that although the place was near and dear to all of them, it was time to be realistic. The costs were too great, and with all the divisions in the family, no one could agree on where the money should be spent. The place had to go.

In May 2004, the property Stu had bought fifty-three years earlier was sold to Calgary restaurateur Dario Berloni for $1.5 million. He was to take possession in late August. Immediately, the kids started fighting over ownership of certain items. The artwork, antique furniture, beautifully framed pictures, the old title belts and Stampede Wrestling memorabilia, Stu's collection of amateur medals, family heirlooms; who would get what? What would be sold? Keith claims items started disappearing from the house. Martha wanted a framed picture of Owen as a child and Keith promised she could have it. But when he went to the house for it, the picture was gone.

Coaxing fifty-five-year-old Smith out of the house was a comedic misadventure, as Keith tells it, though nobody found it funny at the time. As the siblings rushed to clear out the house for the new owner, Smith grasped at any excuse that kept him from vacating the premises. Smith had all but turned the place into a hostel, according to Keith. "He was charging street people to live there.... They had mattresses dragged in and they were eating old distressed food, frying it up. The place smelled. Smith had this old chunk

Top right: Jim "The Anvil" Neidhart being an affectionate uncle with Harry Smith, son of Davey Boy Smith and Diana Hart, late 1980s. Today, Harry is a star of the new Stampede Wrestling.

Middle: A few stars of the new Stampede Wrestling celebrate the relaunch of the promotion. An ailing Stu Hart is seated among them.

Bottom: Hart House, the base of Stampede Wrestling's operations since 1951—in the days when it was called Big Time Wrestling—was sold in 2004.

of fish he was going to cook while everybody was cleaning frantically around him…. I grabbed this dirty, sour fish and said, 'Forget it, Smith.'"

"What the hell?" Smith answered. "I belong here. You can't throw me out of my own domicile."

Keith raised his fist. "Get out of here or I'll drop you right now." He grabbed the fish and threw it into the dumpster sitting by the back porch. Smith stormed off, threatening legal action. The next day – closing day – Keith got a call from the Harts' lawyer, advising him to finish any last-minute cleanup at the mansion. If the house was not presentable, if Smith was not gone, the deal was off.

Keith arrived back at the mansion and, to his astonishment, his older brother was back, even though the windows were boarded up and the locks had been changed. Smith had climbed up the side of the house and gotten in through one of the balcony windows. "Get the hell out of here," Keith shouted, chasing his brother from the house.

Of the incident, Smith explains he had bought a set of swinging doors to separate the kitchen and dining room. Smith entered the house to remove the doors, to take back what was rightfully his, he says.

Even after Hart House was sold, the hubbub over its fate continued in the press when Berloni announced plans to build apartments and townhouses on the land surrounding the house. He needed to do so, he said, to generate the revenue required to restore the heritage building. He also suggested that the mansion might be turned into a duplex. Bruce blasted the new owner in the media, saying he had no respect for the heritage home. Other family members said they were saddened by the change to the land but realized that Berloni was free to do whatever he wanted with the mansion so long as he didn't tear it down, as was their agreement.

The money from the sale of Hart House was surely welcome by many of the children. Had it not been for that, and the settlement with the WWF after Owen's death, the estate coffers would have been empty. Despite the millions of dollars Stu and Helen made over the years running Stampede Wrestling, bad investments and the lifelong drain of many of their children had run the well dry. A copy of Stu's will shows he deducted six-figure sums from the money left most of his children because of advances he had given them over the years. Houses had been purchased for Bruce, Ellie, and Diana, while Smith, Alison, and Georgia had received substantial financial support. Ross, Wayne, and Keith were more independent. As for Bret, Stu included as part of his will the payment of over $66,000 for a debt he owed his famous son.

But the biggest drain on Stu and Helen's estate could not be deducted from any bequests Stu might have made in his will. That drain was Stampede Wrestling. Fighting the losing battle with Vince McMahon in the late 1980s depleted the Hart estate. Keith blames his brother Bruce for this, who just would not let the dream die. "In the interest of Bruce, my dad blew over a million," Keith says.

The Hart clan has not gotten over the tragedies of the last decade, says Alison. As blow after blow rained down on the family, they picked themselves up and tried to continue, but each hit left them a little more fragile.

"After Owen, our family was like a smile with a big front tooth missing," she says. "He was one of our shining stars. He was always able to make peace. 'Bret, mom and dad need this. Ellie, calm down.' When we lost him, we never got that back."

But the most devastating blow was the loss of Stu. Helen may have been the family's heart, but Stu was its spine. He was the stony pillar that kept the family structure standing, even after all that the Harts had endured. When Stu died, the building blocks crumbled. Several of her brothers and sisters, Alison says, are in flux, trying to carry on. Some of the children have floundered, others have tried to stay as busy as possible. Alison obsesses about the past, talking endlessly about Owen, Stu, and Helen and the unjust universe that plucked them away.

The Harts are a proud lot, and whether they were rich or poor, it was ingrained in the kids that they were special. Many them had a sense of entitlement. The Harts live on Hart time. They do so to the chagrin of nearly everybody they deal with, but that is just too bad. That is the Hart way. Alison talks about the Harts feeling as if they were above the law. They are, for the most part, good, lawful people, she explains, but they live by Hart laws. Stu, for example, felt it was okay to lock ordinary people up in torturous, terrifying submission holds. The Hart kids found no fault in that. They got a kick out of it. Alison even talks about Hart stock and its superior qualities.

This is a family that felt blessed and invincible. "We were raised with a belief in God," Alison says. "But sometimes I think our god was Stu. When I think about it, he's the closet thing I encountered to God in my life. He was not perfect, certainly, but his values were traditional and great."

As the tragedies mounted, and one family member after another died, Alison says her teenage daughters felt angry and cynical. Alison remembers driving to Hart House for Sunday dinner shortly before Stu died. Her daughters spotted a family filing into church. "There's no God," they scoffed.

Alison defended the church-goers. "We're no different," she said. "We're going to our church.... We'd go every Sunday and listen to my dad.... I always came out feeling invigorated and ready to face the week. [Hart House] was my religion. That place was sacred to me."

If Stu's death represented nothing less than the loss of God for some of the Hart children, you wonder if they will ever recover. And, as Alison sees it, if Stu is God, then Vince McMahon is the devil. "I hate Vince McMahon," she says. "I hate him as much as I love my father. He destroyed my family.... He came in and destroyed the territory. There was no more Stampede Wrestling. But he didn't stop at destroying the business. He went even further and had Bret and Davey wrestling each other and Bret and Owen wrestling each other. You're dealing with people with big egos and this caused dissension. It was too much for my dad to control.... [Vince was] the master puppeteer. In his sick, perverted mind ... he thrived on it. After Owen died, we just couldn't pull it together anymore."

But others in the family appear to be moving on. Keith and Ross are level-headed, with positive outlooks on life. Georgia seems to be the family's new mother figure, always bright and smiling, looking out for everybody.

Things looked bleak for Ellie, however, until recently, when a glimmer of hope seemed to enter her world. In a sworn affidavit filed in June 2004 in which Ellie was seeking exclusive possession of the Neidhart home, Ellie alleged that Jim Neidhart, unemployed, typically downed a can of beer each morning before heading to the gym. His first stop after the gym was usually the bar. When he came home, he was drunk and abusive, Ellie claimed. The allegations were never proven in court.

In the winter of 2005, a lawsuit was launched against both Jim and Ellie by a Calgary businessman who alleged the Neidharts went into his home and made off with over $9,000 worth of jewellery which he had to retrieve from a pawnshop.[2] By the time spring rolled around, the lawsuit had been dropped. Jim Neidhart told the *Calgary Sun* that the whole thing was a "misunderstanding between good friends." He explained that he, Ellie, and the man's wife pawned the jewellery to buy a car engine, fully intending to buy the jewellery back. Somehow things were patched up and the lawsuit disappeared. "I'm not the Pink Panther, a thief and a liar," said The Anvil.[3]

But the lawsuit humiliated Nattie, who made a point of defending her mother. "It has zero to do with her," she told me. "[My mom] wasn't even in town when it happened." Rather, she says, her mother was caught up in another one of her dad's scrapes, pulled in because she was the one with the inheritance money, thus the only one worth suing.

Once again, Nattie was tortured by her parents' tumultuous marriage. She struggled when talking about her father. She didn't want to make him angry; she didn't want to sever her relationship with him. "I love my dad," she said. "Part of me wants to honour him with the wrestling. I love going to the ring and doing his laugh and stuff.... Sometimes he really did try, but over the years his problems got out of control.... I feel sorry for the way his life has turned out."

But in June 2005, Nattie told a more hopeful story. When she came back from a successful two-month tour of Japan, her father seemed a changed man. He was trying hard to give up his vices, even cigarette smoking, and was studying to be a real estate agent. He said he was proud of her. He told her he loved her. Nattie had never heard that before. She feels her father is trying to make up for lost time. She says she forgives him for his mistakes and she's proud of him for trying to change his life. "I hope he can stay on this path," she says.

Nattie faces a hard road with the wrestling life she has chosen. She barely saw her boyfriend, T.J. Wilson, in the first half of 2005, as the two were constantly off wrestling in other countries. But she's confident they're going to make it work, and predicts they'll get married someday. She's known T.J. since they were children, when the scrawny latchkey kid hung around Hart House playing with the late Matt Annis. Davey Boy, in particular, took T.J. under his wing, Nattie says. He even let the kid train with him. Ellie says Wilson is one of the family. She compares him to Robert Duvall in the *Godfather* series, the Irish orphan taken in by the Corleones.

Nattie says she's not worried about going down the same dark path as her father and uncles. The new generation of Stampede Wrestlers are mostly a clean bunch, dedicated to their craft and put off by the excesses of the generation before them. When it comes to her and Harry Smith, Nattie says, they're scared of drugs and alcohol. They've seen first-hand the damage it can do.

Ever the family success story, Bret recovered sufficiently from his stroke in 2002 and has reinvented himself. In the Christmas season of 2004 he made his theatrical debut as the Genie of the Lamp in *Aladdin, The Magical Family Musical*, a pantomime production that played at Toronto's Elgin Theatre. Bret is also the voice of the Hooded Fang in the animated TV series *Jacob Two-Two*, based on Mordecai Richler's children's books.

When CBC-TV asked Canadians to nominate the greatest Canadian of all time for a November 2004 series, Bret came in at number thirty-nine, beating out the likes of Bryan Adams, Pamela Anderson, Gordie Howe,

Margaret Atwood, Joni Mitchell, and Sir Wilfred Laurier. The CBC also selected The Hitman as one of the program's celebrity hosts, having him lobby for Don Cherry – loud-mouthed hockey announcer and icon of political incorrectness – as the top Canadian. It was a tough position. Cherry was up against Pierre Elliott Trudeau, John A. Macdonald, and Wayne Gretzky for the top spot. Snooty media pundits argued that Cherry had no business being on the list, and the fact that a pro wrestler was in his corner only added to the mockery. Bret later admitted that in his heart he was rooting for Terry Fox.

At one point, the show involved a debate on the merits of the top ten Canadians, and Bret was outclassed by media know-it-alls Rex Murphy, George Stroumboulopoulos, and Evan Solomon. Still, he came off with dignity as a strong, silent type defending the underdog from the righteous liberal guard at the CBC. If he had done such a program five years earlier, he might have fared better. Insiders say Bret's stroke has slowed down his speech patterns, which put him at a disadvantage dealing with the quick-wits on the CBC panel.

According to family members and a production manager on the *Aladdin* set, the stroke made it difficult for Bret to remember things, including appointments. He also suffers from a stiffness on his left side that he is self-conscious about. He trains three days a week at BJ's Gym, but he'll never have but a fraction of the strength he once had. That depresses him.[4] When I sat down with Bret after one of his workouts, he was open, insightful, and pleasant, even good-humoured. But there was also a sadness about him as he recounted the aftermath of his stroke and the wrestling days that have passed him by.

Bret has talked and written fairly freely about Davey, Dynamite, and Neidhart, acknowledging the destructive choices they made in life that he didn't agree with. But to this day he loves them all dearly. He once wrote of his closest comrades: "I'd trust them to breathe for me. To pump my blood with their hearts."[5] He elaborates on this for me: "It's like joining the army. Once you've been in enough battles together, you bond, you become friends and you never lose that.... Only we understood the sacrifices we made and the price we paid to be who we were."

Some of Bret's siblings accuse him of being an egotist, so wrapped up in his Hitman persona that he's standoffish. They complain that when they want to speak with their own brother, they have to go through his publicist. Bret also tends to hold grudges and obsess over things. He remains incensed at ranking only fourteenth in wrestling historian Greg Oliver's book *The Pro*

Wrestling Hall of Fame: The Canadians, on the top Canadian wrestlers of all time. (Fair enough. The book is wildly Ontario-centric and Oliver even ranks Sky Low Low above Bret. Is he kidding?) And don't get The Hitman started about wrestler Ric Flair, who wrote in his own book that he didn't consider Bret to be one of wrestling's greats.

Bret acknowledges this obsessive, angry side of his personality, but he's trying to change. "I used to dwell on what happened to my brother Owen and all the other tragedies in my life," he told the *Toronto Star*. "In my own way I was carrying a big bag of rocks with a lot of grief inside. I had to pick it up every day, throw it over my back and carry it around. The day I got my stroke, I dropped that bag. I don't worry about the past anymore."[6]

No doubt aiding him in his quest for happiness is his new bride. In September 2004, Bret was married in Milan to a young Italian woman named Cinzia. It was months before he told anyone other than his kids that he had gotten married. Some members of the Hart family didn't find out until they read about it in the newspaper.

Bruce Hart is the Dorian Gray of the wrestling biz. That's how his brother Keith sees it. Like the character from the Oscar Wilde novel, Bruce was in love with his youthful image, the picture of himself as a handsome, valiant wrestling star. Like Dorian Gray, Bruce sought to freeze that image in time.

"Bruce is still substitute teaching and wearing his wrestling boots in the schools," Keith says with exasperation. "He's got those ... cowboy boots [which he wears over his pant legs] and he's got his Stampede Wrestling shirts. He's got his bleach-blond hair. He looks like he's about to cut a promo. He's still waiting for his big break."

Keith shakes his head. His fifty-five-year-old brother could have become a full-time teacher and gotten himself a nice pension, but he couldn't get over his obsession with wrestling, even after wrestling long since passed him by. Keith sees Bruce deluding himself into thinking he's still a young, glamorous wrestling star but, as in the story of Dorian Gray, he imagines there's a self-portrait hidden up in his brother's attic that reveals his true appearance. "He [sold] his soul to wrestling," Keith says, "and one day he'll have to look at that picture of Bruce Hart in the dark closet up in his attic and he'll see what he really looks like."

It's a harsh assessment, but Alison agrees that Bruce is stuck in the past. He even reunited with his wife, Andrea, after she had run off with Davey Boy Smith. "He hasn't moved on," she says. "He hasn't changed since 1980. You know that Bruce Springsteen song 'Glory Days'? That's Bruce. I don't blame him. That's when he was happy and cool. That's when he was on top of the world."

As Bruce sees it, he's simply fulfilling his legacy, carrying on the Hart family tradition. "I think I have an inherent obligation to preserve and perpetuate what wrestling once was.... I'm just an extension of Stu, anyway."

Keith hotly rejects this notion. "Bruce is not representative of my dad," he says. "He thinks he is, but my dad didn't appreciate Bruce's style of pro wrestling.... Bruce was not heroic in my dad's eyes, and that was the saddest thing, maybe for both of them. They both loved wrestling and Bruce was so determined. He loved my dad, but ... my dad never credited him as being anything.... He wasn't a tough guy. He never earned my dad's respect. I think that's the one thing he craved all his life and that's the one thing my dad never gave him. My dad gave him money, status, whatever, usually grudgingly, but he couldn't respect him."

January 2004. Bruce Hart and I sit down in a pub for a marathon three-hour interview over chicken wings and beer. I was there to find out if he would cooperate with me on a book on the history of Stampede Wrestling. He was there to get me to write a story about the new Stampede Wrestling. He tried to convince me that the current product is as dynamic as the wrestling I fell in love with in the early 1980s. "People don't even have a clue how good it is," he says. "It's probably the freshest form of actual wrestling anywhere on the planet."

Bruce is a fantastic storyteller: creative, smart, and funny, with a literary flair. My interviews with him were invaluable, each one uncovering new gems about the sport. But my time with him was limited. After a while, when I didn't write the glowing piece on the new Stampede Wrestling that he was looking for, Bruce cut me off. He stopped returning calls and when I showed up at the Ogden Legion one night to interview him, he ducked out a back exit to avoid me.

Bruce likes to preach, and he did just that while my tape was rolling at the pub that night. But much of what he said was valid. "When I see the garbage that is being construed as wrestling right now [in the WWE], I just think it's disgusting and pathetic," he says. "Vince doesn't want to acknowledge it, but the big problem they've got right now is so many of their guys can't wrestle. They can barely lace their stinking boots up, those muscle-bound misfits.... They might know how to crash through a table or hit each other with chairs, but they can't really wrestle, so they resort to all this other garbage. The tits and ass and the props.... The stuff that insults people's intelligence. All the implausible, ass-backwards storylines."

But wasn't Bruce pushing such boundaries back in his heyday, making Stu and Ed Whalen pull their hair out in frustration? Bruce admits as much, but that's not what made Stampede Wrestling special. "The beauty of Stampede was, it was almost all improvisational," he says, his eyes glittering like burning embers. "The secret of improv wrestling is constantly feeding into the crowd, and they feed that energy back to you. The crowd is supposed to be part of the ultimate product, but [in the WWE] they're not. Not when the wrestlers are going through these scripted, pre-rehearsed matches.... A great wrestler is like a Van Gogh or a Picasso. They have a vision of what they want to paint and then they creatively render their art. It's not paint-by-numbers. It's not scripted with little diagrams, every little move detailed."

If today's grapplers knew the true art of wrestling, it would save the sport, Bruce says. He's tried to make McMahon see this. For wrestling to survive, he's told McMahon, the wrestlers need to be trained. Stampede Wrestling could be the WWE's farm team, the official training ground. But McMahon doesn't take Bruce all that seriously, it seems.

But then, Bruce's ego still gets in the way when opportunities arise. A few years ago, he got a call from MTV. It had teamed up with the WWF to produce a reality TV series called *Tough Enough*, in which contestants competed for a position on the WWF roster. Did Bruce want to send any of his talent for the tryouts? Once again, Bruce felt the WWF was treating him like a flunky. "I sneered at them," he says. "This princess calling me from L.A. and making out like she's offering me some great opportunity. I said, 'The guys I have right now are ten times better than the misfits you're pretending with.'"

Bruce kept promising to show me a movie script he wrote in the mid-1980s. If it had been made, the movie would have been "better than *Rocky*," he says. Instead, the script sits in his home, collecting dust.

"It's about a small wrestling promotion that kind of gets screwed over by a big promotion," Bruce says. The little promotion keeps trudging along, though – even as the giant steals its best talent – and, eventually, the little wrestling group starts to hold its own in the business. "Finally, public sentiment starts turning against the bad guys and, in the end, it comes down to a big showdown in the ring, a shoot match where even the audience thinks there's no way the small guy can win." Of course, in Bruce's script, the small guy does win. The giant is vanquished.

For over twenty years, Bruce Hart has dreamed of writing that ending into his reality: of vanquishing the giant that stole his family's dream. He would love to be the David that takes down the Goliath that is Vince

McMahon. The reality is that he's getting older and rather than getting stronger, he's gotten weaker, while Goliath is more entrenched than ever.

But like Stu, who refused to give up on the business through all the dismal years, like his scrappy grandfather, Edward Hart, who forced his family to live in tents on the harsh, frozen Prairies during a standoff for his land, it's quite possible that Bruce will never give up. Although Bruce has decided to take a year off from Stampede Wrestling – having a family friend run the shows for a season – it's a safe bet that he will be back. He'll keep lobbing stones at Goliath until he's too weak to lift his arm. He'll keep dreaming, fighting, and obsessing until the day he dies, because wrestling is his life. It's the only life he's ever known.

Endnotes

1 Mutiny and the Sinking of Stampede Wrestling

1. David Meltzer, *Wrestling Observer Newsletter* 27 Oct. 2003: 5.

2. Tom Billington with Alison Coleman, *Pure Dynamite* (Etobicoke, ON: Stewart House, 2001), 97, 102, 117.
3. Ibid., 116.
4. Ibid., 121.
5. Ibid., 143.
6. Steve Simmons, "Promoters Grappling with Empty Seats," *Calgary Herald* 1 Mar. 1985.
7. Billington, *Pure Dynamite*, 163.

2 Superman of the Prairies: Young Stu Hart

1. Marsha Erb, *Stu Hart: Lord of the Ring* (Toronto: ECW Press, 2002), 31–41.
2. Ibid., 41.
3. Gyle Konotopetz, "King of Hearts: Eccentricity Reigns in Broadcast Hill Castle," *Calgary Herald* 7 Dec. 1991.
4. Greg Oliver, *The Pro Wrestling Hall of Fame: The Canadians* (Toronto: ECW Press, 2003), 63.
5. Gyle Konotopetz, *Calgary Herald* 7 Dec. 1991.
6. Erb, *Stu Hart*, 65–70.
7. Ibid., 82-3.
8. Stu Hart Interview, Tape 3, courtesy Glenbow Museum, Calgary, Alberta.
9. Erb, *Stu Hart*, 84.
10. Ibid., 85.
11. Gyle Konotopetz, *Calgary Herald* 7 Dec. 1991.

3 Raising Harts: the Early Years

1. Diana Hart with Kirstie McLellan, *Under the Mat: Inside Wrestling's Greatest Family* (Bolton, ON: Fenn, 2001), 22.
2. Erb, *Stu Hart*, 99.
3. bid., 101.
4. Mike Maunder, "A Metropolis Is Superimposed upon a Feisty Ranching Town," chap. 3 in *Leduc, Manning and the Age of Prosperity 1946-1963*, vol. 9,

Alberta in the 20th Century (Edmonton: United Western Communications, 2001), 244.

5. Erb, *Stu Hart*, 99.
6. Diana Hart, *Under the Mat*, 33–5.
7. Lisa Dempster, "Harts Battle for Custody of Boy," *Calgary Herald* 13 Mar. 1999: A1.
8. WWF *Magazine*, May 1993: 29.
9. Diana Hart, *Under the Mat*, 64; Erb, *Stu Hart*, 169.
10. Erb, *Stu Hart*, 223.
11. Ibid., 224–5.
12. Diana Hart, *Under the Mat*, 71.
13. Martha Hart with Eric Francis, *Broken Harts: The Life and Death of Owen Hart* (Toronto: Key Porter, 2002), 71–2.
14. As quoted in ibid., 34.
15. Erb, *Stu Hart*, 106.
16. Ibid., 108.
17. Bret Hart, *Calgary Sun* 1 Nov. 2003: S5.
18. Erb, *Stu Hart*, 167.
19. Helen Dolik, "End of An Era," *Calgary Herald* 14 Jan. 1990: F5.
20. Bret Hart, *Calgary Sun* 31 July 2004: S18.
21. Helen Hart, "Harts and Cauliflowers," unpublished personal essay, c. 1970–1.
22. Linda Curtis, "Why Husbands Clean House," *The Albertan* 2 Mar. 1977: 23.
23. WWF *Magazine* May 1993: 26.

4 The Dungeon
1. Diana Hart, *Under the Mat*, 57.
2. WWF *Magazine* May 1993: 28.
3. Bret Hart, *Calgary Sun* 30 Apr. 2003.
4. David Meltzer, *Wrestling Observer Newsletter* 27 Oct. 2003: 3.
5. Erb, *Stu Hart*, 137.
6. David Meltzer, *Wrestling Observer Newsletter* 27 Oct. 2003: 3.

5. Pirates on the Prairies
1. Hunter S. Thompson, *Hell's Angels* (New York: Ballantine Books, 1966), 81.
2. Oliver, *Pro Wrestling Hall of Fame*, 166.
3. Diana Hart, *Under the Mat*, 12.
4. Erb, *Stu Hart*, 133.
5. Oliver, *Pro Wrestling Hall of Fame*, 183.
6. James Adams, "Bud and Ray and Fritz and Otto May Cry 'Uncle,'" *Edmonton Journal* 31 Mar. 1978: B7.
7. Erb, *Stu Hart*, 132.
8. Freddie Blassie with Keith Elliot Greenberg. *Legends of Wrestling, "Classy" Freddie Blassie: Listen, You Pencil Neck Geeks* (New York: Pocket Books, 2003), 118.
9. Oliver, *Pro Wrestling Hall of Fame*, 172.
10. David Meltzer, *Wrestling Observer Newsletter* 27 Oct. 2003: 3.

6 TV, Slick Sammy, and a Jet Plane

1. Ric Dolphin, "The One-Eyed Monster Arrives – Notwithstanding Some Heavy Odds," chap. 2 in *Leduc, Manning and the Age of Prosperity 1946-1963*, vol. 9, *Alberta in the 20th Century* (Edmonton: United Western Communications, 2001), 142.
2. Mike Murphy, *Where* Sept. 2004.
3. Oliver, *Pro Wrestling Hall of Fame*, 25.
4. Hal Walker, *Calgary Herald* 12 July 1967: 41.
5. John Hopkins, *Calgary Herald* 8 Apr. 1978.
6. Erb, *Stu Hart*, 118.
7. Ibid., 115.
8. As quoted in *Wrestling Observer Newsletter* 27 Oct. 2003: 4.
9. Bob Tate, "Personality of the Week: For Calgary Wrestling Promoter Stu Hart, Athletics Have Been a Way of Life," *Herald Magazine* 31 Oct. 1969: 4.
10. "Half-nelsons in the Living Room," TV *Guide* 23 Mar. 1963: 14.
11. Erb, *Stu Hart*, 121.
12. Ibid., 150.

7 Uncle Ed and the Wildcats

1. Kate Dunn, "You Gotta Have Harts," *Calgary* June 1984: 30.
2. Bill Musselwhite, *Calgary Herald* 6 Jan. 1975.
3. Johnny Hopkins, "Full Nelson Fever," *Calgary Herald* 23 Sept. 1970.
4. As quoted in Erb, *Stu Hart*, 153.
5. Bret Hart, *Calgary Sun* 26 Jan. 2002: S6.
6. As quoted in Greg Oliver, "The Stu Hart Interview," *Slam! Sports: Wrestling* 26 Nov. 1997. www.slam.canoe.ca/slam/wrestling/home.html.
7. Oliver, *Pro Wrestling Hall of Fame*, 32–7.
8. Ibid.
9. Oliver, "The Stu Hart Interview."
10. *Calgary Herald* 4 July 1964: 14.
11. Gare Joyce, "Brawl in the Family," *Saturday Night* Feb. 1993. Reprinted in *Ottawa Citizen* 21 Sept. 1999: C4.
12. Oliver, Greg, "Benny McGuire Dead at 54," *Slam! Sports: Wrestling* 29 May 2001. www.canoe.ca/SlamWrestlingBios.
13. Diana Hart, *Under the Mat*, 10.
14. Bret Hart, *Calgary Sun* 10 July 2004: S24.
15. Bret Hart, *Calgary Sun* 5 July 2003: S16.
16. John F. Molinaro, *The Top 100 Pro Wrestlers of All Time* (Toronto: Stewart House, 2002), 35.
17. Helen Hart, "Harts and Cauliflowers."

8 Butchers, Stompers, and Cheats

1. Erb, *Stu Hart*, 131.
2. As quoted in Oliver, *Pro Wrestling Hall of Fame*, 55.
3. Hal Walker, *Calgary Herald* 28 Sept. 1967: 49.
4. *Body Press* (wrestling program), 28 Nov. 1967: vol. 8, no. 11.

5. As quoted in ibid.
6. *Calgary Herald* 23 Sept. 1970.
7. *Wrestling Observer Newsletter* 27 Oct. 2003: 3.
8. Ibid.
9. Shaun Assael and Mike Mooneyham, *Sex, Lies, and Headlocks* (New York: Crown Publishers, 2002), 85.
10. Ibid., 122–30.
11. *Wrestling Observer Newsletter* 27 Oct. 2003: 3.
12. atlantahappenings.creativeloafing.com.
13. Oliver, "The Stu Hart Interview."
14. As quoted in David Meltzer, *Wrestling Observer Newsletter* 17 Dec 2001: 6.
15. Oliver, "The Stu Hart Interview."

9 Overkill

1. David Meltzer, *Wrestling Observer Newsletter* 17 Dec. 2001 6.
2. Gare Joyce, *Saturday Night* Feb. 1993. Reprinted in *Ottawa Citizen* 21 Sept. 1999: C4.
3. Tomm Smith *Calgary Sun* 12 May 1974.
4. "Wrestlers' Grudges Taken to City Hall," *Calgary Herald* 19 Aug. 1975.
5. Bill Musselwhite, *Calgary Herald* 6 Jan. 1975.
6. *Wrestling Observer Newsletter* 17 Dec. 2001.
7. Bruce Patterson, *Calgary Herald* 2 Feb. 1977.
8. Erb, *Stu Hart*, 199.

10 The Age of Dynamite

1. Billington, *Pure Dynamite*, 4.
2. Ibid., 15.
3. Ibid., 17.
4. Ibid., 23.
5. Ibid., 24–5.
6. Ibid., 16.

11 Married to the Hart Mafia

1. Bret Hart with Perry Lefko, *Bret "Hitman" Hart: The Best There Is, The Best There Was, The Best There Ever Will Be* (Toronto: Balmur, 2000), 37.
2. Bret Hart, *Calgary Sun* 21 Feb. 2004: S6.
3. Billington, *Pure Dynamite*, 28.
4. Bret Hart, *Calgary Sun* 28 Oct. 2000: S11.
5. Billington, *Pure Dynamite*, 29.
6. Erb, *Stu Hart*, 186–92.
7. Ibid., 195.
8. Diana Hart, *Under the Mat*, 77.
9. Ibid., 101.
10. Billington, *Pure Dynamite*, 40.
11. Tom Fennell, "The Wrath of Davey Boy," *Alberta Report* 26 Mar. 1984: 34.
12. Alex Tadich, "Sunshine Girl Weds Wrestler: Hart to Heart," *Calgary Sun* 21 Oct. 1984: S3.

13. Diana Hart, *Under the Mat*, 109.
14. Ibid., 107–8.

12 Let the Good Times Roll
1. Billington, *Pure Dynamite*, 46–7.
2. Assael and Mooneyham, *Sex, Lies, and Headlocks*, 56. Also www.wrestlingclassics.com/wawli/Nos.437-445.html.
3. Assael and Mooneyham, *Sex, Lies, and Headlocks*, 56.
4. Hollywood Hulk Hogan. *Hollywood Hulk Hogan* (New York: Pocket Books, 2002), 138.
5. Jim Davies, "Confessions of a Ringside Announcer: Get Ready to Rumble; Is Wrestling Fake?" *Edmonton Journal* 18 Apr. 1999: B1.

13 A Pop Culture Stampede
1. Erb, *Stu Hart*, 197.
2. Ibid., 203.
3. Ed Whalen, "Wrestling with the Past: Ed Recalls Crazy Days of Popular TV Show," *Calgary Sun* 1 Mar. 1999: 6.
4. George Johnson, "Memories of a Friend: Wailin' Eddie Connected with People as Few Ever Did," *Calgary Herald* 5 Dec. 2001: E1.
5. Dunn, "You Gotta Have Harts": 31.
6. Erb, *Stu Hart*, 203–4.
7. David Meltzer, *Wrestling Observer Newsletter* 27 Oct. 2003: 2.
8. Ibid.
9. Bill Musselwhite, *Calgary Herald* 6 Jan. 1975.
10. Bret Hart, *Calgary Sun* 8 Aug. 2003: S9.
11. George Johnson, "Hellard Driving Force," *Calgary Herald* 13 Jan. 2005: D1.

14 Bad News Rising
1. Roman Cooney, "On the Ropes," *Calgary Herald* 10 Dec. 1983: A16.
2. Portia Priegert, "Promoter Faces Suspension in War on Wrestling Violence," *Calgary Herald* 6 Dec. 1983.
3. Erb, *Stu Hart*, 211.
4. Dunn, "You Gotta Have Harts": 28.
5. Erb, *Stu Hart*, 212.
6. Gyle Konotopetz, "Mr. Wrestling Slips Headlock: Bows to Titan," *Calgary Herald* 8 Sept. 1984.
7. Roman Cooney, *Calgary Herald* 6 Dec. 1983.
8. Peter Morton, "Promoter Tangles with Commission," *Calgary Herald* 15 Sept. 1983.
9. Letter from Stu Hart to Calgary City Council, 17 May 1982.
10. Erb, *Stu Hart*, 207.
11. Ashley Geddes, "Racism Fight Next on Card for Wrestler," *Calgary Herald* 12 Dec. 1983.
12. *Calgary Herald* 12 May 1984. Letters page.
13. Oliver, *Pro Wrestling Hall of Fame*, 208.
14. Scott McDonald, "Wily Wrestler Ices the Hockey Player," *Vancouver Sun* 30 Aug. 1984.

15. Sorelle Saidman, "Wrestling Roars Back," Vancouver *Province* 21 Aug. 1984.
16. Erb, *Stu Hart*, 213.
17. Gyle Konotopetz, *Calgary Herald* 8 Sept. 1984.
18. As quoted in Erb, *Stu Hart*, 213.

15 Back in the Saddle

1. Steve Simmons, "Portrait of a Promoter," *Herald Magazine* 1 Dec. 1985.
2. Steve Simmons, *Calgary Herald* 1 Mar. 1985.
3. Ibid.
4. Alex Tadich, "Wrestling's Big Fight Rages out of the Ring," *Calgary Sun* 20 Jan. 1985.
5. Barbara Henker, "Hello Stampede Wrestling," *Alberta Report* 4 Mar. 1985.
6. Bob Bergen, "Stranded Pro Wresters Fighting Mad Over Wages," *Calgary Herald* 14 Mar. 1985.
7. Billington, *Pure Dynamite*, 84.
8. Ibid., 79.
9. David Meltzer, *Wrestling Observer Newsletter* 27 Oct. 2003: 5.
10. Bret Hart, *Calgary Sun* 30 Sept. 2000: S16.
11. Bret Hart, *Calgary Sun* 16 Aug. 2003: S7.
12. As quoted in Martha Hart, *Broken Harts*, 40, 58.
13. Dave Meltzer, *Tributes* (Etobicoke, ON: Stewart House, 2001), 4–5.
14. Martha Hart, *Broken Harts*, 57.
15. Ibid., 55.
16. Bret Hart, *Calgary Sun* 10 Apr. 2004: S17.
17. Bret Hart, *Calgary Sun* 9 Oct. 1999: S20.

16 The Death of Stampede Wrestling

1. Simmons, "Portrait of a Promoter."
2. Erb, *Stu Hart*, 220–1.
3. Billington, *Pure Dynamite*, 108–9.
4. Ibid., 108–9.
5. Ibid., 111–2.
6. Bret Hart, *Calgary Sun* 9 Oct. 1999: S20.
7. Billington, *Pure Dynamite*, 113.
8. Mario Toneguzzi, "Kickboxer Can Taste Success," *Calgary Herald* 26 July 1991: C5.
9. David Burns, "Down for the Count," *Alberta Report* 29 Jan. 1990: 52.
10. Billington, *Pure Dynamite*, 156–7.
11. David Meltzer, *Wrestling Observer Newsletter* 27 Oct. 2003: 6.
12. Ibid.
13. Billington, *Pure Dynamite*, 164.
14. As quoted in Diana Hart, *Under the Mat*, 126.
15. Billington, *Pure Dynamite*, 150.
16. Burns, "Down for the Count": 52.
17. Helen Dolik, *Calgary Herald* 14 Jan. 1990.

17 Afterburn

1. Bret Hart, *Calgary Sun* 7 Oct. 2000: S17.
2. Mario Toneguzzi, "Hitman Hart: One of City's Most Recognizable Exports," *Calgary Herald* 22 Nov. 1992: A1.
3. Diana Hart, *Under the Mat*, 128.
4. Billington, *Pure Dynamite*, 185–6, 192–3.
5. Ibid., 201.
6. Diana Hart, *Under the Mat*, 91.
7. Kim Lunman, *Calgary Herald* 27 Sept. 1990, 28 Feb. 1991, 21 Mar. 1991.
8. Diana Hart, *Under the Mat*, 98–9.
9. Helen Dolik, *Calgary Herald* 7 Apr. 1993; 8–11 Dec. 1993; 11, 12, 13, 15, 18, 22, 26 Jan. 1994; 4 June 1994.
10. Bob Beaty, *Calgary Herald* 30–31 Jan. 1996; 1, 2, 6, 8, Feb. 1996.
11. Bob Beaty, *Calgary Herald* 6 Feb. 1996: B2.
12. Diana Hart, *Under the Mat*, 154.
13. Eric Francis, *Calgary Sun* 24 Mar. 1999: 7.
14. Diana Hart, *Under the Mat*, 179.
15. Ibid., 5.
16. Rick Bell, "He's Back: Davey Boy Determined to Reenter the Wrestling Ring," *Calgary Sun* July 4, 1999: 5.
17. Ibid.
18. Meltzer, *Tributes*, 15–27.
19. Assael and Mooneyham, *Sex, Lies, and Headlocks*, 167.
20. Meltzer, *Tributes*, 15–27.
21. Larry Pynn, "Wrestling's Many Rumbles," *Vancouver Sun* 10 Apr. 1999: D1.
22. David Meltzer, *Wrestling Observer Newsletter* 25 Aug. 2003: 10.
23. Assael and Mooneyham, *Sex, Lies, and Headlocks*, 193–4.
24. Larry Pynn, *Vancouver Sun* 10 Apr. 1999: D1.
25. Bret Hart with Perry Lefko, *Bret "Hitman" Hart*, 88.
26. Martha Hart, *Broken Harts*, 100.
27. David Meltzer, *Wrestling Observer Newsletter* 25 Aug. 2003: 11.
28. Martha Hart, *Broken Harts*, 100.
29. Ibid., 101.
30. Ibid., 104.
31. Ibid., 103.

18 The Death of Owen

1. Martha Hart, *Broken Harts*, 110.
2. Ibid., 108.
3. Ibid., 194.
4. Ibid., 116.
5. Meltzer, *Tributes*, 2.
6. As quoted in Martha Hart, *Broken Harts*, 160.
7. As quoted in ibid., 128–32.
8. As quoted in ibid., 132.
9. David Meltzer, *Wrestling Observer Newsletter* 27 Oct. 2003: 2.
10. Martha Hart, *Broken Harts*, 153–4.

11. Mark Miller, "Mom's Nightmare: Owen's Death Is Worst Fear Come True," *Calgary Sun* 24 May 1999: 10.
12. Ibid.
13. Heath McCoy and Jeff Adams, "Harts Call for Inquiry into Death: Sister Says Owen Was a Sacrifice to Ratings War," *Calgary Herald* 25 May 1999: A1.
14. Ibid.
15. Ibid.
16. Martha Hart, *Broken Harts*, 162.
17. Ibid., 170.
18. Suzanne Wilton, "Widow Vows Justice for Owen," *Calgary Herald* 1 June 1999: A1.
19. Martha Hart, *Broken Harts*, 170.
20. Ibid., 181.
21. Ibid., 184.
22. As quoted in Michael Platt, *Calgary Sun* 28 July 1999: 3.
23. Bret Hart, *Calgary Sun* 8 Apr. 2000: S23.
24. Heath McCoy and Kirstie McLellan, "Rival Wrestling Federations Unite in Grief: Vince McMahon Shares Memories of a Fallen Star," *Calgary Herald* 1 June 1999: A6.
25. Cameron Maxwell, "Widow Is 'Repulsed,'" *Calgary Sun* 2 June 1999: 5.
26. Mike D'Amour, "Letter Slammed; McMahon Did Not Have OK to Air Funeral," *Calgary Sun* 5 June 1999: 2.
27. Martha Hart, *Broken Harts*, 189.
28. Tom Keyser, "Hart Family Lawsuit Alleges Wrongful Death," *Calgary Herald* 16 June 1999: A1.
29. Martha Hart, *Broken Harts*, 195.
30. Ibid., 194.
31. Ibid., 198.
32. Ibid., 217–8.
33. As quoted in ibid., 219.
34. Ibid., 222–4.
35. As quoted in ibid., 210.
36. Erb, *Stu Hart*, 239–40.

19 Harts Torn Apart
1. Martha Hart, *Broken Harts*, 212.
2. Ibid., 204.
3. Ibid., 206.
4. Diana Hart, *Under the Mat*, 187.
5. Ibid., 188.
6. Martha Hart, *Broken Harts*, 213–4.
7. Heath McCoy, "Legal Battle Creates Rift in Hart Clan," *Calgary Herald* 9 Nov. 2000: A5.
8. Martha Hart, *Broken Harts*, 215.
9. Ibid., 213.
10. Ibid., 211.

11. 22 Nov. 1999, Court of Queen's Bench of Alberta documents. Sworn affidavit, Ellie Neidhart.
12. 10 Mar. 1999, Court of Queen's Bench of Alberta documents. Sworn affidavit, Ellie Neidhart.
13. Letter from Stu Hart to Jim Neidhart, 10 Mar. 1999. Exhibit B referred to in the affidavit of Ellie Neidhart.
14. Martha Hart, *Broken Harts*, 235.
15. As quoted in Erb, *Stu Hart*, 244–5.
16. Martha Hart, *Broken Harts*, 238.
17. Heath McCoy, *Calgary Herald* 9 Nov. 2000: A5.
18. Eric Francis, "Hart Family Feud; With wwf Suit Settled, Dead Wrestler's Widow Lashes out at In-laws," *Calgary Sun* 8 Nov. 2000: 10.
19. Ibid.
20. Heath McCoy, *Calgary Herald* 9 Nov. 2000: A5.
21. Erb, *Stu Hart*, 253–8.
22. Martha Hart, *Broken Harts*, 249.
23. Ibid., 249.
24. Ibid., 242–3.
25. Ibid., 70.
26. Maurice Tougas, "Wretched Family Saga Makes Us Want to Know Less About the Harts," *Edmonton Journal* 2 Dec. 2001: D12.
27. Robert Remington, "Wrestling Family Feud Continues with New Book," *National Post* 21 Nov. 2001: A8.
28. Erb, *Stu Hart*, 262–3.
29. As quoted in ibid., 265.
30. Bill Kaufmann, "Hart Glory Days Relived," *Calgary Sun* 24 Oct. 2003: 5.
31. Peter Smith, "Tears and Tributes Flow for the British Bulldog," *Calgary Sun* 29 May 2002: 5.
32. Kerry Williamson, "Hart Gets a Grip on Huge Challenge: Wrestling Icon Fights Back After Stroke," *Calgary Herald* 11 Aug. 2002: C1.
33. Scott Crowson and Sherri Zickefoose, He Had a Good Heart: Wrestling Icon Trained Giants of Business," *Calgary Herald* 17 Oct. 2003: A3.
34. Linda Slobodian, "Tears, Laughter Flow at Stu Hart's Funeral," *Calgary Herald* 24 Oct. 2003: A1.

20 Harts Go On

1. Jason Clevett, "'Attitude Problems' Continue to Plague Ted Hart," *Slam! Sports: Wrestling:* 3 Nov. 2003. www.slam.canoe.ca/Slam/Wrestling/2003.
2. Kevin Martin, "Wrestler Accused of Theft," *Calgary Sun* 5 Feb. 2005: 4.
3. Kevin Martin, "Wrestler Free from Suit's Hold," *Calgary Sun*, 2 Apr. 2005: 8.
4. J. Kelly Nestruck, "The Hitman's Art," *Calgary Herald* 6 Dec. 2004: E1.
5. Bret Hart, *Calgary Sun* 25 May 2002: S15.
6. Richard Ouzounian, "Genie from the Ring," *Toronto Star* 2 Dec. 2004: G1.

Photograph Sources

Photography by Bob Leonard

Front cover; back cover (top); xiv; 1; 47; 49; 52; 55; 60 (top); 70; 73; 83; 86; 95; 98 (top); 100; 111; 115; 118; 141; 148; 157; 161; 162; 171; 180; 184; 191; 194; 205; 216; 220; 225; 228; 234; 245; 253; 254

Photographs courtesy of Michelle Billington

6; 133; 135; 174

Photographs courtesy of Alison Hart

15; 18; 28; 32; 35; 44; 60 (bottom); 98 (bottom); 146; 267; 287 (bottom)

Photographs courtesy of Nattie Neidhart

264; 280; 287 (top, middle)

British Acclaim for Isla Dewar

"Isla Dewar's novels occupy a unique and instantly recognizable world. Her characters are warm and lovably eccentric. She is a fine observer of the nuances of family life. . . . She evokes atmosphere and place powerfully. . . . Throughout, the novel maintains an upbeat, gently satirical tone."
—*Scotland on Sunday*

"Crackling with wit, and shot through with sharp observations."
—*Woman & Home* magazine

"An accomplished and beautifully written novel." —*Real* magazine

"She writes with wit and perception . . . well crafted, humorous, and insightful."
—*Sunday Herald*

"The power of Dewar's highly visual imagination brings off this tender, uncompromising story with panache and feeling." —*The Herald* (Glasgow)

"Dewar has a great knack of taking ordinary people and situations and flipping them on their heads, and her characters are engagingly eccentric and complex. . . . A magical novel." —*Glamour*

"Tender-hearted and poignant . . . Romantic yet never awash with sentimentality, powerful without being overpowering, Dewar builds the story into a novel of considerable depth." —*The Scotsman*

"Remarkable . . . uplifting, sharp, and funny." —*Edinburgh Evening News*

"A wonderful story . . . Wit and wisdom in every chapter, a true understanding of women's lives." —*Sunday Mail*

"You will wish that this magical, poignant, and funny story never has to end."
—*Glasgow Evening Times*

"Refreshing and powerfully adept." —*Irish News*

"Uplifting." —*Mirror*

"Isla Dewar's new novel takes the everyday and gives it a twist to make it funny and heartfelt." —*Publishing News*

"Funny, sad, an   ... and childhood. . . . Isla D   ... hells and
such warmth i   ... *ing Press*

Also by Isla Dewar

Secrets of a Family Album
Dancing in a Distant Place

Giving Up On Ordinary

Isla Dewar

Thomas Dunne Books
St. Martin's Griffin ❧ New York

THOMAS DUNNE BOOKS.
An imprint of St. Martin's Press.

GIVING UP ON ORDINARY. Copyright © 1997 by Isla Dewar. All rights reserved. Printed in the United States of America. For information, address St. Martin's Press, 175 Fifth Avenue, New York, N.Y. 10010.

www.thomasdunnebooks.com
www.stmartins.com

Library of Congress Cataloging-in-Publication Data

Dewar, Isla.
    Giving up on ordinary / Isla Dewar. — 1st U.S. ed.
        p. cm.
    ISBN 978-0-312-56161-1
    1. Single mothers—Fiction. 2. Self-actualization (Psychology) in women—Fiction.
I. Title.
    PR6054.E933G58 2009
    823'.914—dc22

                                                                            2009029269

First published in Great Britain by Headline Review, an imprint of Hodder Headline

First U.S. Edition: October 2009

10 9 8 7 6 5 4 3 2 1

With love to Nick and Adam, for all the socks,
books and funny chewed plastic things they
selflessly left lying everywhere for me to pick up,
without which experience this book would
not have been possible.

Chapter One

'I belong on a train,' said Megs. Dreaming of movement, she shut her eyes, sank deep into her bath. It was the best bit of her day. Her life had become so routine that week to week, day to day – minute to minute almost – she knew what she'd be doing. There was, these days, a strict timetable to her existence: get up, get children up, feed children, feed dog, clatter, bang, wipe, sigh, go to work, come home from work, feed children, feed dog, clatter, bang, wipe, sigh, slump, go back to bed. Sleep. If you can.

It was a fight against grubbiness and clutter. She hated it. Still, at least she knew when the good bits in her day were coming round. She savoured and looked forward to them. Leaning back in the bath was one. After this, there was that moment when she spread herself, unfolded herself into bed, alone in the soothing dark, waiting for sleep. That was the best bit. She was the sort of person who saved the best till last It was a lifetime's habit.

Sleep to her was a perfect thing. But then, she wasn't very good at it. She cherished that moment of waking, realising she'd been dead to the world, tranquillised by tiredness, for a few hours. The only thing she regretted about sleeping was that she was not awake to enjoy it. She longed to relish it, like she relished anything she did not get enough of. She got through night after night in a series of two- or three-hour bouts. This made her regard with envy and wonder those people who managed a sweet eight to ten hours every time they hit the sack. Her children, for example, especially little Lizzy, who was four. Nights, Megs would stand looking at her daughter – head on pillow, eyes shut, lips pursed – breathing sweetly. Megs loved to watch her lying there, making sleep seem simple.

1

'Definitely a train. I do not belong in this dusty box I live in, surrounded by bits of paper – bills, half-read newspapers, wrappings, supermarket receipts – paraphernalia of a life I did not plan. Oh, bugger . . .' Cursing, she stiffly heaved on to one buttock and removed from underneath her bruised, raised cheek the cruelly sharp little white Corvette she'd just sat on. 'Bloody kids.' She idly sent it wheeling away from her, heading for the taps.

Lorraine, on the floor across from her, chin on knees, back against the wall, said nothing. She was used to her friend's flyaway declarations. Megs had always been this way. Megs's mother, Vivienne, worried about her. But her Aunty Betty said, 'Let her be. A bit of dreaming never did nobody no harm.' 'A bit, maybe.' Vivienne shook her head. 'But she goes too far. Everything she does, she goes too far.'

The room was thickly steamed, damp towels hung limp from the rail. There was a pile of magazines by the lavatory, an awesome row of fruit and herb shampoos, moisturisers and deodorants – avocado and glycerine, coconut and jojoba, papaya conditioner, camomile and marigold hair strengthener – on the shelf by the mirror. At the end of the bath was a multicoloured heap of sodden toys – a dumper truck, a beloved, balding one-eyed doll, a pull-along sheep. Shameless, the dog, was lying on the floor, head between his paws. He gave a single indolent flap of his tail whenever Megs spoke. She was his love.

Down the hall in the living room Megs's son, Jack, was sitting, legs draped over the arm of the chair, watching *Ren and Stimpy*. He drank Nescafé from a chipped A-Team mug that had been his and his alone since he was four, and that had survived Megs's umpteen attempts to see it off. It bounced on the kitchen floor whenever she accidentally dropped it. Till at last she gave up accidentally dropping it. 'This damn thing will survive the holocaust. I'll emerge after the blast toothless, balding and in rags, and what'll I see? This hideous thing spotless and untouched on top of a pile of rubble.'

Every time a shriek of laughter howled out of the bathroom Jack raised his eyes in horror. He was seventeen. Parents were embarrassing.

Megs and Lorraine were drinking white wine from a box. They were discussing their day and complaining about life. Recently it

2

seemed whenever they got together – and they got together most days – the conversation, when it wasn't about men, children or sandwich fillings, turned to, wait a minute, how did this happen? And, how did I get here? And, this wasn't what I planned.

'Oh yes.' Megs warmed to her theme. 'I belong on a train rushing across distant continents.' Rushing, she said. Rushing. She liked that. She lifted her arms, dripping camomile-and-lavender-foamed water, and made a train-like movement. 'Rushing,' she said again.

Lorraine tutted. 'You do not have one iota of sense in you.'

'Sense,' Megs scoffed. Throughout her growing years sense had been held up as a desirable goal. A virtue to be worked for and treasured. But now she was having doubts about it. 'Comes a time in your life when you have to abandon sense.' She turned on her side, causing a small, scented wave to sweep over the edge of the bath, soaking the floor, and indicated the room and the flat beyond with a dismissive flap of her hand. 'This is what sense gets you. A box that costs a fortune. A small cluster of undistinguished rooms that you fill with your consumer goods and your arguments. Sense got me an ex-husband and a small brood of children whose only accomplishments as far as I can see are growing and eating. Sense! Fuck sense.' With a deep, throaty sigh she leaned back in the water. 'I love baths. You can do some serious thinking in a bath.'

She had spent the afternoon washing Mrs Terribly-Clean Pearson's kitchen floor, waxing her coffee table and matching pine bedside cabinets, wiping down her stair banisters, hoovering, cleaning her bath, squishing blue stuff down her loo, polishing the windows, changing the beds and ironing half a dozen identical white shirts for Mr Terribly-Clean Pearson to wear to work. After all that effort the place looked exactly as it had when she arrived three hours before.

'I really deserve this. A glass of something alcoholic and a hot tub.'

'Maybe you just belong in a bath,' Lorraine offered. She drank her wine. 'God, this is vile.'

'Well, go buy a bottle of something better, then.'

'You go.'

'I can't. I'm in the bath.'

'Well, I can't be bothered. I'll just have to put up with this. Anyway

I don't feel so guilty about drinking this early in the day if I'm drinking something I don't really like.'

'Well, you've got to feel guilty about something. You're a woman, it's your job.'

Megs knew about guilt. She was good at it. Every night in bed she'd do a rerun of her day – what she'd eaten, things she'd said, what she'd done, what she'd not done. Tomorrow she'd make up for her failings. Tomorrow, always tomorrow, she'd exercise, first thing – fifty squats and a hundred sit-ups every morning as advised in the 'Gorgeous Thighs in a Fortnight' article she'd read in one of Just-Keep-It-Above-the-Dysentery-Line McGhee's magazines. Tomorrow she'd allow herself absolutely no chocolate or biscuits or anything in any way likely to do unkind things to her hips. Tomorrow she'd clean the kitchen floor and remove the decaying thing, whatever it was, that was lurking damply at the bottom of the fridge. Tomorrow she'd keep her cool and she would not bawl at her kids. She wouldn't stay up late, sitting bleary-eyed on the sofa, drinking too much coffee, watching dreadful old films on television, keeping her feet warm the while by shoving them under the dog. Oh yes, tomorrow she'd get her life in order. 'Sod guilt,' she said before slipping down under the water. She rose, soaked and gasping. 'I'm back on my train.'

'Rushing?' Lorraine asked, reaching for the box.

'Rushing.' Megs smiled. 'Over strange terrains, watching new colours, listening to wonderful languages that I shall never learn, and feeling always, always slightly afraid.'

Lorraine leaned through the steam to refill her glass. She was taller than Megs, thin-faced, dark-haired. 'Fear?' she said. 'You? You don't know the meaning . . .'

'Being slightly afraid isn't fear. It's wonderful. A certain uncontrollable trembling in the tummy. It's dealing with mystery, strange destinations, the unknown. Fear isn't like that. It's a sweat that reaches into your palms. It's knowing your knees aren't going to hold. It's a vile curdling in your stomach and it's humiliating.' Megs looked at her, dark eyes, mascara oozing in the heat and damp. She smiled, a perfect row of gleaming ceramic caps. A present from Megs to Megs on her thirty-sixth birthday. Time, an absurd diet that she inflicted on herself while insisting her children eat healthy veg

4

and pasta, and a bitter, tear-sodden fracas with her ex-husband had ruined her natural set.

Lorraine and Megs had met thirty-four years ago on their first day at school. They'd been best friends by lunch time, sharing a desk and, at break time, a KitKat and a bag of roast chicken crisps. In those days that was all it took. Bonding only needed a shared smallness in a vast and scary world and a mutual passion for American cream soda and raspberry ripple ice cream.

'Do you like American cream soda?' Megs asked.

Lorraine nodded enthusiastically. 'Yes, it's my favourite.' This was serious.

'Mine too,' Megs agreed. 'You can be my best friend.' She added, 'For ever and ever.' It seemed like a fine idea to Lorraine, who was looking for someone to be her partner in the line out to the playground. Years passed and shared experiences on the way to being grown-up – first boyfriends, first bras, first cigarettes, first sex, first love – deepened the relationship. Now, here they were, facing forty, still best mates, and not a drop of American cream soda had passed the lips of either for years and years and years.

Friendship was so simple then. The older Megs got the harder she found it to make new friends. If only she could ask some stranger she thought had pal potential what was her favourite drink – vodka and Coke? gin and tonic? wine? What was her favourite ice cream – pralines and cream or Belgian chocolate? Favourite sandwich filling? Favourite television programme? Favourite sexual position? If you could ask someone you fancied for a chum these things and found some common ground then maybe you could make new friends easily. As it was, though, meeting new people always involved small sorties into emotionally safe conversational ground: the weather, holidays, the infrequency of buses. No wonder folk were lonely.

Lorraine thought Megs the bravest person she knew. All those years ago, first day in class, their teacher had said, 'Hello, boys and girls. I've still got to learn all your names. But I'm Miss Watson and when you talk to me, you put your hand in the air. You only speak when I tell you to. And you call me Miss.' She leaned back brightly folding her hands on her desk. That was clear and simple, was it not?

Megs stuck her hand in the air. 'Why?' she said, eager to be told, little voice, shiny eyes. This was puzzling, putting your hand up, calling someone who plainly had a proper name Miss.

Miss was stumped. 'Because you do,' she said. 'It's the rule.'

Megs's hand shot up again. 'Why?' she asked.

'Because it is. We need rules, you know.'

Up went the hand again. 'Why?' Again.

'Because we do. Without them there would be anarchy. Absolute anarchy.' She shook her head at the thought of it.

'Miss.' Megs raised her hand. 'What's an . . . an . . . that thing you said?'

'I'll tell you later, when you're old enough to understand.'

'I'm old enough now. I'm big. I'm at school.'

'You are disrupting class.'

'No I'm not.'

'You are. And do you know what happens to people who disrupt class? They get put in the corner.' So, within an hour of starting her education, Megs, the budding anarchist, was put in the corner.

'There is always one,' said Miss.

Megs was the one. She was the one then. She was still the one. Her bravery went on and on, Lorraine thought. Christ, she hadn't the nerve to do half the things Megs did. The only braveish thing she'd ever done was to run away from her husband, Harry, with a poet she convinced herself was her one true love. The heated romance hadn't survived the poet's arrogant disregard for regular meals or the chill of his unheated squat. She took Megs's glass. 'Ready for a refill?'

'When am I not?' Megs said.

Megs drank too much. She knew it, worried about it and warned herself regularly that she ought to stop. But she never did. She tempered it, controlled it, recognised that moment when she should place one firm hand over the top of her glass and with the other wave away refills. But she still could not deny that longing, when faced with a glass of something alcoholic, to drown herself in it. She was in constant pursuit of that moment when the spirit took hold and her feelings lifted. A sip and she felt better. Another, even better. Then she would feel it – for it was a real thing to her – that moment when she didn't care. When she smiled and laughed and thought

6

perhaps she wasn't such a failure after all. That wonderful, alcohol-induced twinkling when she actually liked herself.

'You drink too much,' Vivienne, her mother, worried.

'Rubbish,' Megs countered.

'You should be ashamed of yourself. You sleep around and you drink all the time.'

'What a slut you must think I am. And you brought me up, too. Nothing out of ten there.'

'How dare you speak to me like that? I'm your mother.'

'I know, Mother,' Megs said. 'You certainly don't seem to think very much of me, do you? So who's failed – you or me?' Then before Vivienne could answer, Megs corrected her. 'Actually, you've got it wrong. I don't sleep around. Haven't ever, as a matter of fact. No, I drink around and sleep alone. It's the healthy option, don't you think?'

'No, I don't. I'm not so stupid as you think. I've seen a thing or two in my time. I'm sixty-three, you know.'

Hardly a day passed when Vivienne did not, in a fiercely indignant tone, tell somebody her age. Sixty-three, how dare that happen to her? Sixty-three years, and she'd spent the last thirty-nine of them watching her daughter career through a life that was not a planned, step-by-step journey to some sort of sane, safe destiny but was instead a set of furious impulses.

Megs had left school at seventeen and turned down a good university place to sing with a rock'n'roll band. When that had fallen through, when the dreams of stardom and riches did not materialise, Megs married and started a family. When the family needed money, Megs started work at a mail-order market garden. A job she loved and was good at. Then she'd succumbed to one of her outbursts. She'd been swept along by the undertow of rage that bubbled constantly just beneath the cheery façade she showed the world. The fury and frustration she felt at living a life she considered a failure came hollering out. Megs had lost that job, and now she cleaned.

Vivienne shook her head when she thought about it. Her son, who'd worked so hard at school, had gone to university, then, as soon as he graduated, or so it seemed, had gone to live in Australia. He'd married and now had two golden-haired, bronzed children whom she hadn't met and who called her their Scottish Granny Megson. Her beautiful daughter, who had bounced so gleefully in her morning cot, whose first tooth was wrapped in tissue in a tiny, dark-blue padded box in her dresser drawer, who'd fallen from a swing and broken her arm, who had worn a frilly pink frock covered with pale blue daisies to her first school party, who had won the local church talent contest singing 'People', 'Peepole, peepole who need peepole', when she was seven, who had brought home hand-made cards covered with hearts and stars every Mother's Day, who had handed over glowing school reports that said, 'Megs has a natural musical ability' and 'Megs's use of language is both imaginative and creative' – that daughter went into other people's houses and cleaned them. It broke Vivienne's heart. She grieved for her daughter's dreams and she grieved for her own.

Vivienne could never fully understand her daughter's lifestyle. It was the lack of a man that puzzled her. In my day, she'd think, for she knew better than to say this out loud, a man was what you wanted. You got married and that was that. But Megs got married and that plainly wasn't that. She got divorced. 'Men,' she'd say. Huffing the word out as part of a sigh. 'Men.' There was no derision in her tone. It wasn't men she didn't trust. It was the embroiled tangle of emotions that came with sharing her life with one that brought out the worst in her. She came from the Groucho Marx school of relationships. She didn't want to have a relationship with the sort of person who would have a relationship with her. 'Men,' she rasped, mostly to herself, 'you win some, you lose some, and some just stay to tea.'

Vivienne hated to imagine her life without a man in it. A man made her feel safe. She had to admit that her man, Walter, had banished himself to the garden shed when he couldn't cope with the depression she'd suffered after her hysterectomy, and had – it seemed to Vivienne, anyway – spent a deal of his life in there ever since. She wished Megs and Walter would become close. They couldn't make up their differences. There were no differences to make up. It was their isolation from each other they had to resolve. Walter hadn't bothered much with his daughter when she was small, preferring instead to dote on his son. Vivienne had taken charge of Megs's upbringing.

Before retiring, Walter had worked shifts on the railway, so

Vivienne hadn't seen much of him. But still, he was there most evenings, in the armchair on the opposite side of the fireplace from her armchair. He'd read the paper and smoke. Then, about nine o'clock, there would come from behind the paper a deep breathing, then a deeper breathing, then a snore. Round about eleven they'd have a cup of Ovaltine, then bed. Walter would never admit that he'd been sleeping.

'Thinking,' he'd protest night after night. 'Having a bit of a think.'

But his evening sleeps were an important part of his day. If for some reason he was denied his two or three hours slumped in his chair, he'd be grumpy all the next day.

Sometimes, when she was cleaning the living room, Vivienne would stare at the two chairs on either side of the fireplace. One day one of them would be empty. Either she or Walter would sit alone in the evenings. In the depth of the night she would reach out for Walter and put her hand on his chest, checking that it was still rising and falling softly with sleep. Checking he was still alive.

She was older than him, two years. He was seventy. She had been declaring she was sixty-three for almost a decade now and, funnily, nobody seemed to notice. If you say something firmly enough, she discovered, people will believe it. Perhaps if Megs dreamed with a little more conviction, she'd believe herself and make something happen.

Megs never abandoned her dreams. She added to them, elaborated them. Her enthusiasm seemed boundless. Only occasionally did she suffer uncontrollable bouts of reality. A running rush of truth. The grim reality of the life she led, the job she had would arrive in her head and refuse to go away. 'This is me,' she would say. 'Thundering towards forty, three living children, one not living any more, a cluttered, noisy flat with a view of the cluttered, noisy flat across the road, a mucky job that does nothing for my nails, a cantankerous car that does not love me, a cantankerous mother who does and wants too much of me, and . . . Oh God.'

It was all too much. If she got a gushing bout of truth when she was at home she'd pour herself a glass of cheap plonk and wish it away. If it hit her when she was at work then she'd shout out, 'Oh God, no.' Or, 'Sod all that.' It was whilst suffering one of these truth bouts that she lost her job at the market garden on the outskirts of town. But that was a bout that could be forgiven.

It was after Thomas died. Six years old, he suffered for his wild imagination and impulsiveness. He had not waited at the school gate for her to come and collect him and had set off for home alone. Swinging his purple and black canvas school bag and mumbling to himself, he walked to the crossroads. Without properly checking the traffic, he stepped from the pavement. He had not made it to the other side.

For months after the funeral Megs sat all day at home on the sofa, staring. She wasn't even aware of the silence that filled her life. Neither Lorraine nor Vivienne could get through to her. They felt they stood on the edge of her life, watching her from across the room, whispering concern. 'Has she eaten?' 'Did the doctor give her something to make her sleep?' 'Has she taken it?' After the initial flood of sympathy cards, friends stopped calling. The doorbell stopped ringing. The phone was lifeless. On the rare occasions she did go out, people crossed the road when they saw her coming. They did not know what to say to her. Her tragedy was beyond their conversational range.

The pain, it seemed, was always there. First thing in the morning it was there. Sometimes when she woke and grief was rumbling through her, as it had been all night, even when she slept, she'd think: Why do I feel like this? Then she'd remember and start sobbing and rolling her head back and forth on the pillow. 'Oh no. No. No. No.' For months and months the only relief she got was that small moment between waking and asking herself what it was that made her feel so bad.

She couldn't accept the child was dead. Couldn't say the word. She'd look at the clock. 'Ten past three,' she'd say. 'Time to go fetch Thomas.' Or she'd serve up four plates at supper time instead of just three. Hannah and Jack, her other children, would stare at the plates and say nothing. But neither would they eat.

The pain was physical. It made her stoop. At last she went to the doctor.

'I think there's something wrong with my heart,' she told him. 'I think I'm going to die.'

10

He listened to the pain, and touched her chest. Long fingers, cool hands.

'You're not going to die,' he said. 'I know you want to but you're not. I'm sorry, but you're not.'

For a moment she looked mildly surprised at him. 'Is that where my heart is?'

He nodded.

'I always thought it was lower down.'

He smiled. 'No, your heart is there and it's fine. It's doing well.'

'But it hurts. It really, really hurts.' She thought she was going to cope with this conversation, but lost control of her voice. It slipped off the rails into grief. Her throat blocked and she cried.

'You thought a broken heart was a metaphor, didn't you? It isn't. Sometimes people suffer real pain as if the heart was ruptured.' He looked at her. A healthy heart he knew would chunter on. Stomachs were different. Stomachs actually went pale with loss, bled with anger. 'Are you eating?' he asked.

'I should. Somehow I've forgotten how. Lost the knack of it.'

He gave her something to help her sleep. She refused anti-depressants and returned to her sofa.

Vivienne phoned Aunty Betty. 'She just sits. It's not right. She's got other children. I can't fetch and carry any more like I used to. I'm sixty-three, you know.' She and Lorraine had been taking care of Hannah and Jack between them. They worked out a routine. Lorraine dropped them off at school in the morning on her way to work. Vivienne brought them home. Lorraine shopped, Vivienne cooked.

'Leave her be,' Aunty Betty said. 'She'll come to herself.'

But in the end Vivienne did not leave Megs be. 'Snap out of this,' she said stiffly. 'You have other children. Remember them? They really need you. All you do is sit about all day in that old dressing gown. Moth-eaten thing.' She tugged at the sleeve of Megs's pink towelling robe.

'You may not have noticed, Mother,' Megs sighed. 'But the style police don't come round this neighbourhood.'

'I hate you in it. And you have the baby to think of.'

Megs stared at her. It was the first time either of them had

11

mentioned her pregnancy, though it was daily becoming more and more obvious. The baby was as yet a bulge. But it was a bulge that caused small signs of disapproval – stiffening of the shoulders, tightening of the lips – in everyone who observed it.

Vivienne did not ask who the baby's father was, and neither did Lorraine. They both knew. It was Mike, her ex. There was something about the shifty way he and Megs eyed each other whenever he came round to collect Hannah and Jack on Saturdays. He would cast a slow, shameful eye across her stomach, and she would sigh, that small, resigned sigh of hers. Fine mess you got me into now, sort of thing, Vivienne thought, watching her.

Four days after the funeral Mike had come to the flat. He wanted some pictures of Thomas. He wanted something that had been Thomas's – a toy, a drawing from school – something to treasure. And he wanted someone to talk to.

Denise, his new wife, tried to share his sorrow but she could not reach him. He was in a turmoil of bewilderment, rage and sorrow that was beyond anything she had experienced. She could not plumb the depths of his wretchedness. When she saw him go to Megs, she felt glad, guiltily glad. She could watch a soap or laugh at a sitcom without suffering any self-recrimination. After he left she settled down to indulge herself with a video, a gin and tonic and a few hours free of torment.

Mike and Megs sat side by side on the sofa, looking through a photograph album. He chose as a token of remembrance of a lost love a picture of Thomas, three years old, wearing his navy cord dungarees tucked into his shiny red wellies, and his little duffel coat, offering a lump of bread to some belligerent ducks in the park.

'That's Thomas. Nothing put him up nor down,' he said, putting the photo on the table beside one of Thomas's drawings from school, an illustrated list of his favourite things, a crayoned, childish scrawl. 'My favourite things are – Shameless, toffee pudding, purpl things, football, trees, my frend Brian and cartoons.' He'd drawn Shameless looking large and shapeless beside a tree – thin brown trunk and rounded fuzz of green leaves atop.

Megs held the slightly tattered bit of paper. 'We should have looked after this. It's precious. You never know. Never know.'

Mike put his arms round her. Held her, put his lips against the top of her head. They rocked together, a slow, woeful movement. Hannah and Jack were with Vivienne. She brushed his neck with her lips. There was solace in the way he gently stroked her back.

The sex they had started as a comfort. The nearest thing either of them had got to sucking their thumbs in years. They were two despairing souls momentarily losing their sorrow in each other. There was a moment when they each lost control, started to shake and cry out. Not an ecstatic howl, just an anguished shriek from within. When they were done, they were weeping. It was quickly over. Afterwards they sat like guilty teenagers, adjusting unbuttoned shirts, crumpled skirts and tousled hair.

'Oh God,' said Megs. 'What a thing to do.'

Mike said, 'Sorry.' Then he asked if she had anything to drink in the house and went to fetch some whisky and two glasses.

'I sometimes think that was the only thing we ever did well together,' Megs said.

Mike did not answer. He finished his drink, gathered his photo and drawing and left, saying sorry again. 'And sorry about the tooth. Sorry.'

On the day Thomas died Mike had come round deranged with grief. When he discovered that Megs had been late picking Thomas up from school he'd swung at her. And missed. Megs stepped back, lost her footing and hit her mouth on the sink on the way to the floor.

'Oh God,' Mike cried when he saw the blood streaming down her chin. 'Oh God, I didn't mean it.'

'It's all right,' Megs said. She felt she deserved a smack in the mouth. But the pain her collision with the sink brought did nothing to relieve the guilt she felt.

He apologised for swinging at her, and for the sex they had. Looking back, she thought that all he did during their marriage was alternate between acting aloof and apologising. She never could figure it out.

They were too guilty, too shamed to discuss their moment of tormented love, even when the evidence of it became obvious. Even when Denise called Megs a disgusting, thoughtless slut for becoming pregnant so soon after her son's death, Mike said nothing.

13

At last, at Vivienne's insistence, Megs took off her pink towelling robe, the moth-eaten thing, and returned to work. She only lasted a day.

She'd been asked to pot on some geraniums. When she got to the greenhouse the air was heady with their tart green smell. There were more small plastic tubs of tender, tiny geraniums than she'd ever seen in her life. If she put her eyes level with the table top they stretched to the horizon.

'Can't I have some help here?' she asked Mr Hammond, her boss.

He shook his head. 'No, we're short-staffed. I need Jean in the office. Lorna has deliveries, and Cara's on the winter-flowering pansies.'

Megs sighed and started work. She gently removed the seedlings from their tiny pots and put them into larger plastic pots where they would settle and grow into saleable, robust geraniums. She held the frail tendril roots, dipped them in lukewarm water, then trailed them a second in sand. That slight weight made them sink straight, undamaged, into the hole she'd made for them. 'There you go,' she whispered to them, from a place so deep in her, her lips moved but no sound came out.

At four o'clock she once again put her eyes level with the table top and decided that the acres of geraniums still stretched to the horizon. She'd made no progress at all. 'I'm no further forward with this,' she wailed.

'Oh,' said Mr Hammond casually. 'I put another couple of hundred pots down when you were at lunch.' He jingled his car keys as he spoke. Megs looked at him mournfully. Soon he'd be driving home in his BMW. She'd take the bus, almost an hour's journey back to her flat in Stockbridge, because her cantankerous car had decided to take the day off and refused to start. The bus driver would stare rudely at her nails as he took her fare. She could never get them properly clean till she got home to her own sink and her own nail brush. Her cantankerous mother would be in the flat when she got back and would be walking round and round the kitchen table telling the children to eat their supper. 'When I was your age we didn't have lovely things like frozen hamburgers, you know,' she'd be nagging. The house would smell of overheated insides of grill pan and the television would be roaring. If nobody had remembered to take the dog out, there would be a huge damp patch by the front door. And she'd be potting on geraniums for the rest of her life. She could pot on a geranium in the dark. She could do it whilst sleeping.

Her arrival back at work after almost five months' absence caused a ripple of gossip and surprise. She found it hard to live with the silence when she arrived in a room and the whisperings when she left. There was a look, she'd seen it first in the hospital where they'd taken Thomas. A slow movement of the eyes away from her eyes. It said, that look, that death has touched you and you must keep away. As if tragedy was infectious. It was, also, plain that nobody approved of her condition.

'I do not need this,' she muttered furiously to herself. 'I do not need this.'

Jack, her oldest, seemed recently to have absented himself from the world. He disappeared to school early, came home late and spent his time at home earphones on, lost in his own rhythmic space. Hannah, two years younger than Jack, had decided two weeks ago that she was a vegetarian and that the rest of the family were gross for eating meat. She wanted to eat on her own.

Now Megs's pregnancy was bulging, and she was dreading the time ahead when the baby came. She knew well the unavoidable, draining routine that came with babies. She hated herself for how she looked. She hated herself even more for not wanting the child she was expecting. All that, and Thomas would not be there. He would not come banging down the hall. He would not argue with the others about his television programme. Or rattle through the kitchen cupboards demanding food.

'I do not need all this,' Megs said. Louder now.

Mr Hammond, on his last key-jingling round, popped his head round the door.

'Nearly done?'

'No,' howled Megs. 'No way. God, what a question.' Then she gave a full-throated protest. 'I can't stand this,' she yelled.

Her voice, always one of her best features, carried well. She was heard throughout the five greenhouses, across the gardens, in the salesroom and office, and down the phones. Several customers asked

15

in alarm as they ordered their summer bedding plants – lobelia, dwarf marigolds, begonias – what was going on. Mr Hammond boomed that Megs may have gone through a hard time but she was here to work.

'Oh, bugger you,' Megs screamed. 'I hate this. It's too much to bear.'

'Well, if you want to work here, young woman, you'll just have to bear up like the rest of us.'

Megs always wondered how people got to be the way they were. How did this man turn into such an absurd bully in a suit? She would try to imagine people in authority as they might have been years and years ago in primary school. This patriarchal man had once been a spiky-haired, skinny-kneed boy who snivelled at the gate when his mummy let go of him. He had been a whisperer of tales to teacher and grubby rumours to his pals. Now here he was, a grandiose being in a suit who got irritated simply at her presence in the world, who could not even tolerate her relatively inconsequential refusal to do what he wished her to do. To pot on geraniums, smiling. And grieve politely.

'Oh, bugger you,' Megs spat.

'Just what are you going to do if you lose this job?' Mr Hammond wanted to know.

'I don't need you.' Megs was sure of this. She banged her chest defiantly with her fist. 'There are millions of things I can do,' she bawled. Remembering this moment would, for years and years afterwards, embarrass her. 'I can scrub floors,' she boasted.

'You said what?' Vivienne could not believe it when Megs told her. 'That was a good job you just threw away. And you in your condition.' She considered the absurdity of her daughter's outburst, and the state of her kitchen floor. 'You have never scrubbed a floor in your life.'

'I could learn. Don't tell me there's any great knack to scrubbing a floor. Any arse could do it.'

'In that case you qualify as a floor-scrubber.'

Next day, then, Megs put an ad in the local paper. 'Scrubber seeks floors. Will also wax, wipe, dust, launder, iron and polish. Well-greased elbow. Distance no object.'

A couple of months later she was waddling heavily through strange houses, watching new lifestyles. Cleaning suited her. Or at least the mindlessness of it, the repetitiveness of it suited her mood. She was in too much despair to want to do anything more taxing than wiping, dusting and ironing. She, who rarely lifted a finger in her own home, did not mind cleaning up after strangers. And her strangers did not mind her, her grief or her pregnancy.

Six weeks after Lizzy was born, Megs went back to work. The baby went with her. She cleaned for Mrs Terribly-Clean Pearson Wednesday afternoons and Monday and Friday mornings; Mrs Emotionally-Deranged Davis Tuesday mornings and Thursday afternoons; Ms Just-Keep-It-Above-the-Dysentery-Line McGhee Tuesday afternoons and Thursday mornings; and after today Hundred-Miles-An-Hour Wednesday mornings and Friday afternoons.

Megs moved her arms in the bath, making small ripples waft round her. 'I feel life returning,' she sighed. 'I'm beginning to think I may be human after all.' She soaped her arms and hummed a snatch of a song that had drifted into her head.

Lorraine drank and joined in. 'Brie and chopped apple,' she said, 'on a bed of shredded lettuce, with a light vinaigrette and a slice of crispy, maple-flavoured bacon.'

'That'd be nice.' Megs nodded dreamily. 'Chicken marinated in soy sauce and ginger, grilled and chopped, mixed with a lightly curried mayonnaise and bamboo shoots.'

'On a wheaten bun?' Lorraine was keen to get all details perfect.

'No, sesame. Sesame with chicken.' Megs thought. She returned to her tune. Then, 'We could call it the Dixie Queen.'

'I like that.' Lorraine nodded and hummed along. They were still dreaming of sandwiches. Their sandwich bar plans were endless. It made them happy.

Megs stopped humming, reached for a towel and heaved herself, dripping from the tub.

'Hey, guess who I'm cleaning for now.'

'Who?' said Lorraine.

'Hundred-Miles-An-Hour.'

'Really?' Lorraine was thrilled. 'Have you been to his house? What was it like?'

'Full of things,' Megs said. 'Walls covered with pictures. Books. Clutter. Staff your granny threw away. He's a messy bugger, though.'

'And have you been to his bathroom? Does he have a comb?'

'Lorraine, I just had a quick look round. We only spoke for about ten minutes.'

Everyone knew Hundred-Miles-An-Hour. He was famous about town, well, at least their bit of it. He cycled uphill to the university in the morning and downhill going home at night. Uphill in the morning the effort creased his face and shoved his hair towards the heavens. Downhill in the evening the force of the prevailing wind pushed his hair even more dramatically upwards. He never seemed to think to fix it. He had, then, a constant expression of surprise, hair swept back as if he were travelling at great speed. Hundred-Miles-An-Hour. Gilbert Christie he was, but people only called him that to his face.

'He's a bit professorish. Know what I mean? Distracted if you're being kind. Daft if you're not. He's not my type.' Then, changing the subject, for she did not enjoy talking about her work, 'Hey, Lorraine, pour us another before my mother comes home with Lizzy and Hannah.' She put on the towelling robe her mother hated so much, and considered without mercy her body. 'Christ. Look at me. All cellulite and flab. I'm drooping. Gravity is cruel.'

'Middle age,' said Lorraine. 'Soon you'll have to start walking around with your arms folded under your tits to keep them up. You'll be standing at the door gossiping with your tits propped on your forearms. And walking along the street the same way. And running for the bus.' She demonstrated. Folded her arms and ran up and down the room, though it took only four steps to get from one end to the other.

'That'll be me.' Megs folded her arms and went into the hall, where she would get a full six steps. Up and down she ran, and into the living room. 'Look at me.' She danced, arms folded, tits propped. 'It's the middle-aged woman's jig. Arms folded, tits ahoy, here we go.'

Jack sneered, aimed the remote at the screen, switched off the set and left the room. Lorraine joined in, sashaying up and down to bump folded arms, then back down the room again. Back up again and bump again. They giggled.

'The pair of you. What are you up to?' Vivienne said. They had been too busy dancing to notice her coming in.

'It's a jig,' said Megs. 'Arms folded, saving-tits-from-gravity sort of thing.' She stopped dancing and panted.

'Will the pair of you ever grow up?' Vivienne looked at them witheringly. She stormed across the room, put on the television and showed Hannah and little Lizzy the sofa. 'Sit,' she ordered. Then, rounding on the two drunken dancers, 'And you,' pointing at Megs, 'shouldn't you be ready? Isn't it Glass Bucket night? I'm here to baby-sit. And your father will be along in a couple of hours.'

Megs always thought her father came to see his grandchildren, not her. He was especially fond of Lizzy. He'd call her name and hoist her into the air. 'Where's my little girl then?'

Vivienne heaved in her breath and disappeared into the kitchen. 'Wait till I tell Aunty Betty about this. I have never seen the like in my life. And I'm sixty-three, you know.'

Chapter Two

Every Friday night Megs sang at the Glass Bucket. She sang the songs Aunty Betty taught her when she was little: 'Sippin' Soda', 'Paper Moon', 'I've Got a Crush on You', 'Manhattan'. She did all sorts of jigs and toe-tapping tunes, 'Marie's Wedding', 'Star of the County Down'. Everyone joined in. She sang songs from the sixties and seventies, 'Here Comes the Night', 'Honky Tonk Woman', 'Something In the Air'. And how the crowd loved that. They swayed in their seats, drank till the booze and noise they were making helped them forget all the things they had come to the Glass Bucket to forget.

As the night wore on and people clustered round their tables to drift into little worlds of sudden relationships, moods, sighs, tangy cheese Doritos and the small truths alcohol helped them disclose, Megs switched to the blues. She sang Bessie Smith, ''Tain't Nobody's Bizness If I Do' and 'My Sweetie Went Away'. But mostly she sang Billie Holiday, 'Good Morning Heartache' and 'Speak Low'. When she sang about heartache people nodded and drank: yes, they knew about heartache. They'd been there. And when she sang 'Speak Low' and moved her hips to its jazzy rhythms, pouted and smiled, they all knew what she meant. People would smile and reach out to touch knees, naked shoulders – whatever was available to touch. They were going to get lucky tonight. Megs's voice, once pure and clear, was cracked and frayed around the edges; time and grief had taken their toll. It fitted perfectly the songs she sang.

Round about eleven o'clock, when the air was thick with smoke and thrumming with chat, Megs always sang 'God Bless the Child'. Everything would stop. People stopped drinking, stopped buying chicken in a basket, stopped touching, hoping. The crack stopped, the laughter. There were only sad spirals of cigarette smoke and the slow movement of glass to lip. She sang it the way Billie did. She didn't sound the 'l' in help. 'Hep,' she sang. 'God hep the chile'.

After Thomas died, when Megs poured her despair out across the room, the silence that greeted that song, then, was the sort of silence a bar manager dreaded. The till did not chime. There was no rustle of notes, no chink of coins. Women burst out crying. So Dave Roberts, manager of the Glass Bucket, sacked her.

'You're no good for business,' he said, poking her with a stubby, nicotined finger. 'I can't afford you. People come out for a good time. They don't want you bringing them down.'

For three weeks Megs stayed away. Then she went back to the bar. She was wearing her snakeskin shirt and tight black jeans. On her feet silver strappy high-heel sandals. Her toenails were painted bright red. Her hair, long and bottle-blonde, moved across her face as she spoke. She thought she ought to get it cut. Stop bleaching it. 'I'm too old for my hair,' she told Lorraine. But she never did anything. Drastic hair changes were too taxing.

'I need to come back,' she said to Dave. 'I need the money. Hannah's got to have new shoes, Jack has grown out of his school trousers and people need to be fed. And I have a baby. If you don't take me back I'll go sing at the Black Bull and everyone'll go there.'

'You upset folk,' Dave protested. 'They get depressed.' He knew she had him. He knew she was right. He'd lose his customers.

'A bit of sadness goes a long way,' Megs said. 'Especially if it's someone else's. Mine. They all listen to me and think, thank Christ it's her and not me.'

'OK, Megs,' he said. 'But when they stop drinking, switch to something happy. Stop reminding people of what they're waking up to in the morning. He stuck his hands into his pockets and stared at her. That was his deal, no 'God Bless the Child'.

'Do some of those jigs, Irish songs Aunty Betty taught you. People clap and stamp, work up a thirst.' He clapped and stamped, a small, joyless demonstration. His jacket moved perfectly with him. He spent a fortune on clothes. A girlfriend once told him that women laughed at men's trousers because they smelled of stale fast food, petrol and God knows what else. So he changed his clothes at least twice a day, got discounts at the dry cleaners he was such a good customer.

'I will for a bonus,' she said. 'I need the money.'

He stared at her. 'I bet you do.'

She had three children and no man to take care of her. That was how he still saw relationships, at least the relationships of the people who drank at the Glass Bucket. Women had babies and men brought in money – usually in cash in brown pay packets. He knew this wasn't true. People got paid the same way he did – money transferred straight into his bank account – but he liked to think he was a cut above his customers. He knew he was a cut above Megs. As well as singing on Friday nights, she cleaned five days a week and waitressed for Clark's Catering, banquets and official functions, whenever she could.

'Tell you what,' he said, 'sing those jigs and I'll give you five per cent of the increase in the take.'

'Ten,' she said.

'OK. Ten.' He shrugged. He didn't care. He was planning to give her an extra twenty pounds whatever happened. How would she know what the increase was? Business was slower without her. Furthermore, customers were asking for her. He had not realised how popular she was.

The following Friday, Megs, wearing her favourite short black dress, was back on the little stage again. She held the mike close to her lips, shut her eyes and moved in time to her songs. The life she led – cleaning, cooking for her kids and worrying – this was the only time her mind emptied enough for her to find some contentment. It was when she did a little forgetting of her own. Once she'd been a singer in a band. Now it seemed long, long ago – such a distance she had travelled since then – a different time when she was a different person. Life had been – hopes, dreams and spangled lights – fleetingly like a fairytale. She could almost say it was once upon a time. 'Once upon a time I sang with First Degree Murder. Remember them?' To her enduring surprise some people – not many – actually did.

She knew, of course, that she was rewriting her history in her head. She was romanticising what had been a time of long, kidney-jarring journeys bundled and bumping in the back of a van with dubious suspension. It had been years of broken dreams, frustration, sore throats, chilblains, boredom, noise, quarrels that started as squabbles, ended with full-blown fisticuffs, frustration and cruelly suspicious carry-outs from nightmare fast-food joints that all ought to have been called House of Diarrhoea. She still thought about those days, sometimes she even sighed for them. And sometimes she heaved herself from the gilded depth of her romanticising and admitted the truth. 'Giving birth to four children and battering about in that bloody van for years have taken their toll on my bladder for ever.'

Mike, her ex, was bass guitarist and the driving force whose ambition took them bumping, clattering and dreaming through ten thousand Saturday nights (or so it seemed), over a million miles of motorway and neglected pot-holed roads to play in universities, pubs, village halls and theatres. He wore his hair long then, and smiled enigmatically to the crowd as he played. It had taken him years to master this easy, lazy disinterest.

He was skinny, then. Weren't they all? They had, all five of them, that late-hippie debauched look, dangerously saintly. She sometimes saw the other members of the band, and how was life for them?

Eddy drove long-distance. Fred had been called to the bar. Josh still gigged a little, one-night stands in pubs. He played guitar. He drank. She did what she could. She got by. And Mike? Mike got a Filofax, and now he had a personal organiser. Wasn't there a song like that? Hadn't Lou Reed written it? Or was it Iggy Pop?

After six years (three hundred and twelve Saturday nights, in fact) and too many disappointments to bear, they'd given up. It hadn't been an abrupt or bitter parting of the ways, just the slow fraying of relationships that came with the dawning that life was slipping by and realistic decisions about the future had to be taken.

Mike decided his future was in accountancy. Megs took a job at the mail-order market garden to help keep them whilst he went to college. He emerged a fully qualified accountant with short hair, a trimmed beard and initials after his name. She got broken nails and an astonishing knowledge of plants and herbs that she didn't know was in her head till someone asked, what was a good ground-spreading flower for a shady border? Or, what fertiliser do you put on basil? Or, what's nivalis really called?

'Snowdrops,' she'd say, surprising everybody, especially herself.

24

Then she'd had Jack, then Hannah and later Thomas. By the time Thomas arrived, she and Mike lived separate lives. She dressed in jeans and T-shirts, wore her hair long and spoke about plants, music, what the children did, what they ate and where they went today.

He got a job with an upmarket firm in Charlotte Square, and had a better relationship with his hairdresser than he had with her. He wore a suit and spoke about clients, expense accounts, deals and how he needed the right suits and shoes if he wanted to be taken at all seriously. He bought a mobile phone and the famous Filofax. She wanted a dishwasher. It was some time before they realised how deep was the gulf that had developed between them. They had stopped speaking to one another. All they did now was say things: 'It's your turn to take Jack to his swim class.' 'We're out of milk.' 'Is there anything decent on telly tonight?' Through these and a hundred other innocuous questions and remarks they managed to express the constant undertow of their dissatisfaction. 'Would you like some coffee?' Megs might ask. But there would be a movement of her lips, a shifting of tone that only Mike would notice. Only he would know the deal of resentment that went into that little question.

Mike found someone new. Denise shared his new enthusiasm. He and Megs parted. He got the car and the record collection. She got the children, the flat and Shameless, the dog – a large, hairy, absurdly friendly impulse buy that she had wanted to call Leroy. However, every time Megs saw him lying sprawled on his back in front of the fire, or guiltlessly licking his genitals or sticking his cold nose up passing skirts, mooching her children's cornflakes, or scratching, sniffing in the kitchen bin for tasty bits, sleeping at full stretch on Hannah's bed, or silently filling the room with sudden, putrid, yellowed air from his guileless, unabashed farting, she called him shameless. In the end that was the name that stuck.

Mike turned into a far better accountant than he was bass guitarist. Time and money were kind to him. Now he and Denise lived in a new house on a small, select estate. They had a new car, a new stereo system and a new daughter. Megs didn't know who he was any more. Still, when Mike came back to the flat to collect the children for the weekend, he would linger longer than necessary. Sitting in Megs's kitchen amidst the mess and music and banter he felt the tension round his neck and shoulders ease. He did not mean to hurt Megs when he casually mentioned that Denise bought Betty Jackson jackets, or that she went once a month to Glasgow to have her hair done at Vidal Sassoon. But he did. Megs did not mean to inflict on herself that emotional wince she felt when she pumped him for information about his new wife and her credit cards. But she did. She couldn't help it. She still wanted a dishwasher.

The Blue Boys backed her at the Glass Bucket. They didn't have the spiralling aspirations of her first band. They were a don't-give-up-the-day-job sort of a bunch. Not that any of them minded. They had long stopped dreaming. Stardom was something to be scoffed at. They were happy with the perks being in the band brought them: a little respect, some compliments that bordered on flattery, free drinks, cash the tax man didn't know about and, for Jim, the drummer, sex his wife didn't know about.

For years Megs had a numbing weekly routine. Weekdays she cleaned for a small group of clients whose lives she found fascinating. Friday nights Vivienne, her mother, would baby-sit whilst she sang at the Glass Bucket. She got by.

Recently, however, she'd been feeling that getting by wasn't enough. The hankering for something better had grown from being a small itchy longing to a festering discontent that kept her awake at nights and plagued her during the day if she did not drive it from her mind with songs she hummed as she furiously wiped other people's kitchens, dusted other people's mantelpieces and picture frames, scrubbed other people's lavatories, baths and showers, changed other people's beds and listened to the small shifts and clicks of other people's houses when they were not at home. She liked the silence of strangers' houses. It was not as disquieting as the silence of her own.

All her life Megs had plans that were really just well-honed dreams. Lorraine got sucked into them. There was something irresistible about Megs's dreams. They were so much juicier than life itself. There had been the starogram dream.

'I'll dress as old dead film stars. Mae West, Joan Crawford, Ginger Rogers sort of thing,' Megs enthused to Lorraine. 'And I'll go along to people's work, parties and pubs and sing, "Always True to You

Darlin' In My Fashion" or "I'm In the Money" or whatever, rip open my frock. Flash my tits. You man the phones.'

Phones, definitely phones, plural. They were going to get inundated with calls. 'We'll make a fortune.' Then, considering the demoralising effect life, its trials and temptations, its chocolate and vodka, had had on her body, Megs said, 'Perhaps not.' The starogram dream had been a five-minute flirtation with success and riches. Once it was spoken out, its flaws – both of them – became obvious. Megs's tits were not up to the challenge. So the starogram plan was abandoned and replaced with the plant shop plan.

'Huge clay pots of marguerites and geraniums on the pavement outside, glistening white and red into the afternoon, so iridescent the redness glows up into the air around them.' Megs had verbal energy. She painted her fancies perfectly, swept Lorraine along. 'A whole wall of herbs, scenting the air – thyme, rosemary, lovage. The blast of basil in the summer, huge succulent leaves and clusters of tiny white flowers, will make people dizzy. They'll just stand outside breathing and sighing. A large plain glass bowl of daisies fresh every morning on the counter . . .'

Now the big plan was the sandwich bar. It was to be called M & L's (Megs and Lorraine's) and it was to look like an early American drug store. 'Norman Rockwell would come by to drink coffee, spin out homey philosophies and observe folk. James Stewart in his younger days would work behind the counter wrapped in a huge white apron that tied round his middle, shyly tripping over his words. The décor will be simple and wholesome.'

'Stripped pine?' asked Lorraine.

'No.' Megs shook her head. 'A glass counter, chrome rails, bar seats with red leather cushions and a bar made of shiny walnut beaded with a dark-red border.' She had it all worked out.

There would be fabulous sandwiches all named after blues singers or famous songs. Irresistible fillings tailored to markets. 'A free-range egg fried in chilli oil – the Satchmo (because you'd really have to get your mouth round it) – for the building site people, or tomato and mozzarella with fresh basil for the women office workers.'

'What'll that be?' Lorraine wanted to know.

'Dunno yet.'

Megs had spent nights and nights sitting about with the band. As they smoked, drank and discussed gigs and how they would handle fame when it came – they were all, except her, convinced it would – she'd read the copious notes on the backs of their albums. The only thing that superseded her knowledge of plants was her knowledge of the blues and the people who played and sang them. 'What about the Lil Hardin? Satchmo's wife. One of them, anyway.'

Lorraine shrugged. 'Perhaps,' she said.

'The Lil Hardin,' Megs glowed, 'will be creamy cheese and ripe fresh tomatoes that explode in your mouth, all peppered and tangy with fresh basil. It'll sing to you.' She paused a moment, considering her dream. The Lil Hardin and the Satchmo were their first sandwiches. There would be others. 'It'll be wonderful.' Megs was sure of this. 'It'll be the making of us.' They stared at each other, slightly embarrassed. They both thought they were far too old to be clutching at daydreams. At their age they ought to be living comfortable, sorted-out lives. It was as if sanity and normality had somehow passed them by. And that was all they'd really wanted.

'What went wrong?' Lorraine asked. They knew each other so well now they had no need to explain the heart-searching that went behind such a gruelling question. They could any time, anywhere, without any sort of lead-in, start the what-went-wrong conversation.

'Dunno,' Megs said. 'How did this happen? How did I end up grubbing about for a living? This isn't what I planned.' She suffered from the sort of recurring angst she considered only chocolate and alcohol could soothe.

Chapter Three

The name Megs was a legacy from that infants' class, all those years ago where she'd first met Lorraine. Actually she was Nina. Nina Megson. As a child Megs hated her name. She considered Nina a name fit only for fat old ladies, and had, therefore, refused to answer to it. She sat at her school desk hands stiffly by her sides, jaw set, refusing to respond to any mention of the word Nina.

'Nina,' her teacher would say. 'Nina, it's your turn to feed the hamster.' Or, 'Nina, hand out the reading books.'

But young Nina would look pudgily defiant, stare out the window, little brow knit, lips puckered. This wasn't happening. Who was Nina? Not her. She would never be Nina, as long as she lived. No. No. No. There was no Nina. 'I'm Megs,' she said. 'Megsy to my friends.' It was another small show of defiance from the infant anarchist.

After she married, the name still stayed. She took Mike's last name, Williams. Nina was not allowed in her life. She became Megs Williams. Now the only person who called her Nina was her mother. And at that only when she wasn't speaking to her.

Megs was the name she'd used when she introduced herself to Hundred-Miles-An-Hour. He, of course, had no notion of his nickname. As far as he was concerned he was Gilbert Christie.

'This is it, then,' he said to her, indicating with a clumsy body swerve, hands firmly stuck in his trouser pockets, the mess his house was in. 'Um,' realising the extent of his untidiness, 'it's got a bit out of hand.'

'So I see,' Megs said, looking glumly round. This man is disgusting, she thought. There was a mouldering mountain of newspapers threatening to take over the sofa. A thick layer of fuzz lined the tops of his pictures and skirting boards. His kitchen floor was sticky. She felt the soles of her shoes rasping against it. She doubted he'd ever thought to wipe the front of his fridge or cooker. A week's dirty dishes were piled on the drainer. She suspected he'd left them as soon as he heard she was coming.

Just-Keep-It-Above-the-Dysentery-Line McGhee had recommended her at a dinner party when he'd complained about not being able to see through his windows. 'I'll send my cleaning lady round to you, Gilbert darling. She's just what you need. Mrs Williams. Megs. You'll love her.'

'You've no washing machine, then?' Megs asked, casting her eye grimly round. The waste bin overflowed. There was an impressive display of empty wine bottles on the floor by the sink.

'Heavens, no.' He looked alarmed at the suggestion. 'Bourgeois things.' Washing machines, dishwashers, videos all horrified him. He felt that if he let any of them into his life a fatuous middle-classness that he'd been rebelling against ever since he left home twenty-five years ago would creep over him. After the washing machine came fitted carpets with matching curtains, a cocktail cabinet with bottles of sherry. Then he'd be putting gaudy Van Gogh prints on the wall and a fluffy cover on the lavatory lid. He shuddered. 'Wouldn't give one house room.'

'Right,' she said, bemused. She only mentioned a washing machine, for heaven's sake.

'You can take my things to the launderette round the corner.'

'And use the bourgeois things there,' she said. 'Perhaps,' she asked, 'you'd prefer it if I took your washing down to the river and beat it against some stones?'

'Hardly,' he said. Was she mocking him? He didn't know. Mockery was hard to recognise, even harder to bear. Especially from a woman – a woman such as this.

He took her upstairs. His living room was worse. There were beer bottles on the floor, old shoes, books – books everywhere, small piles of them on every step of the stairs. 'I kind of let it go when I heard you were coming,' he confessed.

'Let it go,' she mused. This was more than let go. This was years of neglect. He seemed to think she could fix it all with a single wipe

30

with a damp cloth. 'I won't be able to do it in a day. It'll take a bit of cleaning.'

'Whatever,' he said. 'Just come and do it.' He had no interest in anything domestic.

'When?' asked Megs. She studied his face. Faces interested her. Without being too obvious she studied them, tried to see the people within. His was long and slightly forlorn. His eyebrows were on the verge of taking on a life of their own. There was a small scattering of tiny broken veins on his cheeks – he drank too much. She could see that his beard, should he ever grow one, would be flecked grey. She liked that. His eyes would one day be clouded and watery, stained with the reading he did. But for the moment they were clear and deep, brown pools. Taking the face as a whole, the expressions that crossed it naturally, the lines those expressions left – she concluded that Gilbert Christie was perplexed and lonely and confused. But then, wasn't she? 'When?' she asked again.

'Whenever.' He hardly looked at her.

'I can do Wednesday mornings,' she offered.

'Can't you come in twice a week?'

'The only other time I have is Friday afternoons and I like to keep them free. I work Friday night at the Glass Bucket.'

'I don't think a little light housework will interfere with your barkeeping,' he said. He hated himself. God, that was patronising.

'I don't work at the bar,' Megs corrected him. 'I sing.'

'Really?' He looked at her for the first time. It was the first time he showed any interest in her. He imagined her fronting jolly singalong evenings, winding up at the head of a long, weaving, drunken conga line. She'd be wearing a spangly coconut matting sort of a frock. He thought she'd be part of that crazy, hearty world of booze and abandonment he couldn't ever join in, that fascinated him and that scared the pants off him. 'What do you sing?' he asked.

'Whatever,' she said flatly. She didn't think she liked him. 'Will you be here Friday afternoons?'

'No.'

'Well, I'll come then.' She needed the money.

'Um . . . how will I pay you?'

'Money'll do nicely.' She did not meet his eye.

'Not a cheque then?'

She shook her head. 'I'm not a banking sort of person.'

'Ah,' he said. Looking at her closely now, he could see she was the grown-up version of the sort of girl he'd always lusted after from afar when he was at school. She would have worn fashionable clothes, and have dated the most popular boy in class. Not him, definitely not him. He felt, though, he had the measure of her; she cleaned, she avoided banks and she led conga lines. Righto, he could deal with that. He flattered himself he had the common touch. Ordinary people liked him. Look at the way they smiled when he cycled past. It never crossed his mind that the smiles were not for him, but his perpendicular hairstyle.

He showed her to the door, saying he'd look forward to seeing her Wednesday and it would be great to have the place cleaned up. She looked at him and imagined what Lorraine would say about him.

'What was he like?' she'd demand.

'OK,' Megs would say. 'A bit vague.'

'Oh.' Lorraine would swoon expansively, clutching her bosom. 'All he needs is the love of a good woman.'

Whenever they came up against boorish, disinterested or rude men – pushily flirtatious salesmen, obnoxiously rude gynaecologists, irate drivers flashing and tooting wildly at some minor motoring misdemeanour one of them had made – they'd clutch their hearts and cry, 'All he needs is the love of a good woman.' It was their joke, stemming back to when they were teenagers – stars in their eyes, hope in their hearts. Love, they had convinced themselves, would conquer all. They both believed they'd grow into the sort of good woman whose pure and passionate love would sort out wayward, disillusioned, broken-hearted men.

'Were we ever that dumb?' Megs said when that adolescent naïvety came to mind. Thinking about Lorraine's abandoned crowing, Megs fought to keep her face straight. She resisted the urge to put a comforting hand on his arm, gaze soulfully into his eyes and tell him what he needed. She felt a fit of giggles coming on and, staring down at her feet so that she could compose her face without him watching, she noticed the carpet. It was dusty and crumb-ridden. 'You do have a vacuum, don't you?' she anxiously asked.

'Ah now.' He lit up. 'That I do have.' Vacuums, apparently, were not bourgeois. With a grandiose sweep he opened the hall cupboard, giving her an actual view of the beast. Beast indeed. But not to him. He was enthused. 'Behold the vacuum!' he cried, almost embracing it.

It was older than they were. It was brown, vast and cumbersome with a long handle that had a fraying cord wound round and round it. Its large bag would, Megs knew, bloat up with air as soon as it was switched on. Its noise would deafen her. Heaving it from room to room would do nasty things to her back. She hated it.

'Isn't it wonderful?' He was truly excited. 'Got it at an auction a couple of years ago. The Big Hoover Nine Six One. They don't make them like that any more.'

'Well, that's something.'

'Look at the style and the lines. Straight, well defined, no clutter. It makes a real statement about what it is and what it does. It is unpretentious and functional and that gives it a beauty . . .'

'It's a vacuum,' she interrupted him. 'Does it suck up the dirt?'

He looked baffled. 'Haven't a clue,' he told her. 'I've never actually used it.'

Glumly noting the small, round-pinned, two-point plug, she realised he'd never switched it on. He'd bought it because he thought it added a certain utilitarian elegance to his cupboard. 'It says something about domesticity – something sturdy.' It had never occurred to him to clean the floor with it.

'But, dammit' – no cleaning woman was going to cast aspersions on his vacuum – 'they used this very model in stately homes and on ocean liners. *Queen Mary* and such.' Patting it now. 'These things were built to last. It has style.'

'There you go,' Megs sighed. 'A vacuum with style. I'll bring my own.'

She wondered how somebody who considered washing machines bourgeois and thought vacuums should have style actually earned a living. 'What is it you do?' she asked.

'I lecture on the history of design. Right now I'm working on a book about packaging in the twentieth century. *The Theme Pack.*' He'd been working on his book for the past eight years.

The urge to giggle had gone; she could look into his face once more. This time she knew what she saw. She saw a man past forty who, though still confused about his identity, was very precise about the day-to-day details of his life – no washing machine and a vacuum cleaner that didn't actually vacuum but made a statement about vacuuming.

'Just what I need,' she sighed as she made her way out through the main door, and along the quiet, tree-lined street to her car.

The following Wednesday morning he stayed late to let her into his house and give her a key. 'I don't expect we'll be seeing much of each other,' he said.

That's a mercy, she thought.

Then, indicating his home with a sweep of his arm, 'Let yourself in and help yourself to coffee. Make yourself at home.'

'Oh, lovely,' she said. 'I'll have a bath, drink your gin and phone my brother in Melbourne.' And cursed herself inwardly for her sarcasm.

He looked dismayed, didn't know what to make of her. He was used to speaking whilst others listened. In awe, he hoped. Was she making a fool of him? 'Pardon?' he said.

'Oh, don't mind me.' She dismissed herself. Then, instantly bored with seeking the pardon of someone who owned a vacuum with style, 'I've already had a bath, it's far too early for alcohol, and don't worry, I won't phone anybody.'

He looked desperate to get away from her. She knew she was prattling, but couldn't stop herself. It was cleaner's defence. She imagined she was vulnerable to all sorts of humiliation, so before it materialised she got in a swift spot of mockery.

He looked mildly demented, was running his fingers through his hair which was starting to rise, and he hadn't even cycled to work yet. She noted with interest that he started the morning with his hair flat. The trials of his day and his bike journeys made it stand on end. He wasn't looking his usual hundred-miles-an-hour self yet.

After he left she moved slowly from room to room, trailing her hand over his things, observing his life. She spent so much time clearing out the clutter and stains of other people's lives, she had become expert at observing them. Just-Keep-It-Above-the-Dysentery-Line McGhee was, for example, overdrawn at the bank. Megs recognised the letters and overdrawn slips. She got them regularly herself. This was why she preferred to be paid with cash. Money put into her bank account got lost in the vast hole that was her overdraft. Cathy McGhee, however, solved her financial problems by buying wines from South Africa and Australia, tasty things from the delicatessen that she did not eat, and shoes. Megs tried the wines if any was left in an opened bottle in the fridge, and had developed a taste she could not afford to indulge for Rosemount chardonnay. She nibbled sun-dried tomatoes, anchovy-stuffed olives, pastrami and rare cheeses, and tried on the shoes. The soft black leather medium-heeled ones with straps that wound round her ankles were her favourite.

Cathy McGhee took tranquillisers, had problems with her periods and had migraine tablets by her bed. She spent a deal of time watching television, reading magazines, drinking wine. Her CD collection included Paul Simon, Kurt Weill, Marvin Gaye and Joni Mitchell. Sometimes she intensified her pre-menstrual tension by playing Shostakovich. Hidden behind her sofa was a Reebok step and an exercise thing for reducing thighs. Cher's exercise video was amongst the pile of tapes under the television table. Cathy McGhee had a lover who came by at weekends. He had dark hair. Cathy's was auburn. But the man who slept in her bed during the week was grey. Megs knew these things.

The interesting thing about the Pearsons, on the other hand, was their blandness. They had beige rooms, beige walls – they didn't want them white, white was too bold, too bohemian.

'Colours are so – so, well, colourful,' Mrs Pearson said, looking apologetic. They wore beige or beigeish clothes. The carpets throughout the house were beige and immaculate. Their three-piece suite was beige. In the corner a lustrous cheese plant flourished, shinily, almost defiantly, green. Megs could see that its vibrancy pained Mrs Pearson. But there was nothing she could do to mute it down. The only other thing that stood out against all this blandness was their son, Frederick. Called, to his mother's deep displeasure, Freddy by his chums.

In the midst of all this blandness Fred, the teenager, was surprising. His jeans were ripped, ears and nose pierced, his hair hung down rasta-style in long ringlets past his shoulders. There was a tattoo on his left forearm and a ring through his eyebrow. His Doc Martens dug into the perfect carpeting. He seemed at odds with his surroundings, vivid against his plain backdrop. Yet Megs could tell from his diffident, slope-shouldered body movements, his slow, uncertain eye contact and slight, gentle voice that underneath this rebellious exterior a nice boy lurked. In a couple of years he'd be beige like his mummy and daddy. No, the only rebel in the Pearson household was the cheese plant.

Mummy and Daddy Pearson roused Megs's suspicions. She suspected all this beige was a front. They seethed and raged secretly and did not know what to do about it. They hid behind their safe furnishings. Their bland clothing was a camouflage so they'd blend into their living room and nobody would know the turmoil within.

Mrs Pearson washed a lot. Not that she was often around when Megs was there cleaning, but when she was, she washed. Every twenty minutes or so Megs would hear the rush of the bathroom tap and the watery rustle of hands lathering. Mrs Pearson did not like bars of soap. 'Other people have been using them.' She used the liquid sort, from a bottle, camomile-scented. She washed, dried and then carefully, slowly softened her hands with cream. Twice a day she changed the towels. She insisted Megs disinfect the bath, then polish it.

'Polish it?' Megs questioned the order. 'Will that not make it slippy?'

'I like things shiny,' Mrs Pearson insisted. 'I like things neat and clean and shiny.'

The house was numbingly silent. Moving through it, Megs could hear her feet on carpet, or her begrudging exhalations when she bent to wipe the skirting board or remove from the rug a thread that defied the vacuum. It made her nervous. The Pearsons had a busy phone. Megs had strict instructions to let it ring if no actual Pearson was around to attend to it. Often Mrs Pearson stood by as it rang and rang. She'd stare at it and then at Megs. It seemed as if the perfect cleanness and shininess was being polluted by the noisy, vibrating thing. Megs got the impression Mrs Pearson would like her to scrub and polish the air round the phone, to wipe it clean of the insistent *tring-tring*.

Sometimes, when the silence, the blandness and grim tidiness became overwhelming, Megs gave in to screaming and shouting. It was then she addressed the Pearsons' living room. 'Hello, room,' she would say. 'How can people live like this, room? A lifeless life. This is me. And look,' opening her shirt, 'here's all of me. Tits, room. Tits. Haven't seen the like of that before, have you?' She'd put on a favourite blues tape, brought with her specially, Howlin' Wolf, Muddy Waters or the Allman Brothers, and turn up the volume till the ornaments buzzed. 'Boogie,' she'd cry, shimmying over the carpet. 'People do this, room. In the world out there, where colours are allowed, people dance. They play loud music and show themselves to one another. Have that, room.'

'Mrs Pearson.' Megs shook her head, describing the woman to Lorraine. 'Now there's a woman who has never even got within spitting distance of an orgasm.'

'Do you think that's her problem?' Lorraine wanted to know. Other people, even those she hadn't met, fascinated her as much as they did Megs.

'Probably. I don't think she enjoys anything. It hasn't occurred to her that she could. That, and she spends her life walking carefully. She and Mr Pearson walk carefully round each other, calling each other Madge and Don, saying names whenever they can. Reminding each other that they're there. They're treading softly, scared of what they are inside. As if they've seen it once and can't bear it.'

Mrs Terribly-Clean Pearson was an insomniac. She sat up at the kitchen table drinking weak tea, eating digestive biscuits, and often as she sat alone in the silence and chill, she cried. Megs knew this because there were four cups to wash in the morning and only three Pearsons. And Mrs Pearson's dressing gown pocket always contained screwed-up tissues. Once there had been a book Mrs Pearson was reading left open on the table, with damp drops on the page. Besides, Megs knew the symptoms. Here she was facing forty and she couldn't remember when she had last seen it through the night. She sat up at the kitchen table, too. Watching strange night-time television programmes, too. Cried sometimes, too.

'Have you been sitting up half the night again?' Vivienne accused that morning when she popped in for a cup of tea. They were a popping-in sort of family.

'Yes,' said Megs. 'How did you know?'

'The state of you. Baggy-eyed and look at the cups. Do you have to use a fresh cup every time? Could you not just rinse out the one and fill it again?'

Megs shook her head. Staying up half the night was bad enough. Staying up and being tidy was unthinkable.

'Why do you do it anyway? Why can't you sleep?'

'I'm scared.'

'Scared? Nonsense. What are you scared of?'

'Life. Getting old. I'm getting on. I have no prospects and no pension scheme. What's going to happen to me? One day I'll be old. I'll have nobody. The children will be gone and I'll be alone. I'll wear the same baggy cardy day after day. I'll shuffle on my walking frame down to the corner shop for a couple of slices of ham. And I'll shuffle back with them and I'll sit at this table eating them with some peas. Chewing them with a shaky jaw. Staring at the wall. And the house will be silent, and when I'm done I'll wander through empty rooms. Furthermore, I hate peas.'

'Goodness' sake, Megs. Stop it. The rubbish you talk. Stop it,' Vivienne said. The description had set up a chill in her heart. A dread she had not examined, far less come to terms with. 'Old age doesn't have to be like that. You keep yourself busy. Like me . . . I'm sixty-three, you know. And you don't have to eat peas if you don't like them.'

Hundred-Miles-An-Hour had one thing in common with the Pearsons. He was honest. Like the Pearsons he did not hide his life from her. Just-Keep-It-Above-the-Dysentery-Line McGhee and Emotionally-Deranged Davis both shoved their mess, shame, secrets, truth – old shoes, underpants, dirty plates, carry-out trays, magazines, bank statements – their lives, in fact, behind the sofa before she came, as if she wouldn't find them there. As if she had not been hired to clean behind the sofa along with the rest of the house. They were out-of-sight-out-of-mind people.

The pile of dishes in Hundred-Miles-An-Hour's kitchen had grown since her first visit. She turned on the tap and sighed hugely. No hot water. She looked in his cupboards and under the sink. Another sigh. There was nothing to clean with. No cloths, no washing-up liquid, no polish, no scourers, nothing. 'No stuff.' She sighed again.

She went upstairs, lumbered upstairs, stamping as she went, arms dangling by her sides, heaving in her breath. Boring, boring, this was boring. She stripped his bed, gathered towels from the bathroom, shoved everything into a selection of carrier bags, switched on the water heater and went to the laundrette. Medium wash with conditioner, she'd come back to put everything in the drier. Meantime she bought some washing-up liquid, polish and other cleaning things and went to do his dishes.

She walked the long terrace back to Gilbert's house, watching her feet move over the paving slabs. The very pavement here was classier than the pavement outside her own flat. Russian vines thrust up from basement plant pots, waterfalled vibrantly over the railings. She could peek into ground-floor living rooms, elegant high-ceilinged places, and could not imagine anything ordinary happening in any of them. If she did not come to clean, she would never enter any of these rooms. She would be outside, in her old suede jacket, nose pressed against the window panes, watching the beautifully lit, mannerly doings of the people who lived here. If she lived here, she would not worry about Lizzy playing on the pavement outside. Then the Botannical Gardens were only a step away. They could go there, walk hand in hand, Lizzy and her, reading the names of plants, touching leaves. Birds sang. Magpies, long tails trailing, flew on missions to raid dustbins.

Gilbert's house was on two floors. It had a large, elegant drawing room on the upper floor, a study and two bedrooms. Downstairs there was his much-used messy living room, a third bedroom and a bathroom. All those rooms for just one person, and in a crescent where cars purred politely past. Megs envied him.

Three-quarters of an hour later she returned to the laundrette, moved his damp bundle of sheets and towels to the drier and went back to his house to clean his bath and hoover his floors with her own vacuum cleaner. Then grumpily back to the laundrette, collect stuff and back to the house to make up the bed and drape clean towels in the newly clean bathroom. After that she dusted, wiped, gathered newspapers into bundles, emptied the kitchen bin and made an attempt at the kitchen floor. It was after three. She phoned her mother.

'Could you collect Lizzy from the nursery? I won't make it. There's more to do than I thought. It's filthy here . . .'

Gilbert came home, and shutting the front door caught these last words. He walked stiffly past her down the hall, wheeling his bike, a slow tick, tick, tick, said nothing. His hair was sticking up.

She worked on for another hour. Before she left, she found Gilbert in his study.

'I'll be off then.'

'Oh, all right.' He did not turn to look at her.

'Do you want me to take your old newspapers to the dump? I pass it on the way home.'

His newspapers? How dare she? They were his. There was an article on the new Chinese cinema somewhere in that pile, and a piece about an exhibition of French landscape paintings that he hadn't yet got round to. 'There are things I want to read in them,' he huffed.

'Ah.' She nodded. 'You'll have been planning to read them for some time. Some of them are five years old.'

'Nonetheless.' Stiffer now. 'I've left your money in an envelope on the kitchen table.'

'Righto, then.'

Sniffing disdainfully, he said, 'You've made my house awfully smelly. It smells of chemicals in here. I don't like it at all.'

'It's cleaning stuff. Would you prefer I did everything with cold water and elbow grease?' Looking scathingly round, 'It'd take a while.'

'No, of course not. I would, however, prefer it if you didn't use my phone. You said you wouldn't do drastic things to my phone bill. I trust it wasn't your brother in Melbourne.'

'It was my mother. I had to get her to collect my daughter from nursery. It took longer than I thought to clean up here. I had to go to the laundrette and buy washing-up things. I didn't want Lizzy hanging about on her own.' She glared at him, hot red spots flushing on her cheeks.

'Oh.'

'I'll go then. You owe me for the laundrette and the chemicals,' that last said with stinging sarcasm. 'I'll get it next week.'

'Right,' quietly now.

She took her vacuum cleaner and left. She was the sort of person who bought a vacuum cleaner for function not design. She was the sort of person who scrubbed and polished and bustled. She made vulgar smells in his home – crass lemon-scented abrasive things. She felt insensitive. And foolish with it. He watched her carrying her cleaner down to the path to her car. He had not considered she had a child to care for. He felt he was a boor, an insensitive boor. And filthy with it.

Megs drove home staring vilely through the windscreen, repeating, 'Smelly. Smelly. Smelly.' Over and over. A fine bile and bitterness brewed within her. 'Smelly. Smelly. Stupid bugger.'

The things she should have said to him rattled round her head. She longed to drive back, hurtling through the traffic, screech to a halt at his door and burst in on him yelling, 'Ripe nappies. Mushy things at the bottom of the fridge. A decaying hamster corpse amongst training shoes under the bed. Smells. In your precious life you know nothing. I'll show you smells.'

When she got home she was seething and slammed the car keys down on the kitchen unit. Her children were seated round the table eating ham salad and chips her mother had prepared, and stopped to watch her.

'How did it go?' her mother asked.

'Awful,' Megs sulked.

'Awful? Can't be that bad. Can it?'

'He says I made his house smell.'

'Smell!' the children cried in unison. This was their sort of conversation.

'Smell?' Vivienne was horrified. 'Smell? You?'

As far as she was concerned there was nothing worse than smelling. In terms of vileness she ranked it alongside homicide and rape. A deal of her adult life had been devoted to the eradication of all sorts of dubious aromas. One of Megs's abiding childhood memories was of her mother standing in her living room looking manic, sniffing wildly first facing north, then wheeling round, facing south, saying grimly, 'There's a smell in here. A definite smell.' She could set small crowds of people guiltily heaving air deeply into their nostrils in unison, saying, 'Yes. Yes. You're right. Old fish, anchovies type thing.'

'Yes. I made it smell of chemicals. Vim, Flash – the stuff you use to clean with,' Megs confessed. Then, still enraged at her own ineffectualness in dealing with his absurd accusation, she wheeled round on her children, spread her arms and shouted, 'Stop listening. This has nothing to do with you. Eat, eat.'

'Stupid man,' Vivienne scoffed. 'What does he expect his house to smell like?'

'Oh.' Megs gave a cynical wave of her hand.

Her mother folded her arms, pursed her lips. Here she goes, she thought.

'He'd probably like it to smell of lavender polish blending gently with wafts of fresh dark coffee brewing and bread baking in the kitchen. He'd like his bathroom to smell of gentleman's lime cologne and his bedroom to smell of freshly ironed Irish linen. Just so long as he doesn't have to do any of the polishing, brewing, baking or ironing. Stupid shite.'

'There's no need to swear.' Vivienne swore regularly herself but felt it her duty to stop those around her from doing it too.

'There is every need to swear,' said Megs. Then, sharply, to Jack, Hannah and Lizzy, who were still ignoring their food, listening to her expound, 'Don't let that food get cold. Eat, I tell you.' Turning to her mother she continued, 'You should see him. His face is florid. Booze, I thought at first. But now I've got a look at it again, I can see it's flushed with privilege. He comes from generations of beef-eaters. His cheeks are coloured pinkish, and he is arrogant. Not like us pale, wan serfs. Our faces are white, and we are stunted from the thin gruel our forebears ate.' She picked up a chip from Lizzy's plate and wagged it at her mother before stuffing it into her mouth. 'We come from poor stock, our shoulders are hunched, our bones brittle and malformed . . .'

'I beg your pardon,' Vivienne barked. She was enraged. 'Cheek of you. Pale and wan. Years of eating thin gruel.' She pointed a furious accusing finger at Megs. 'You have never eaten gruel in your life. You should learn to watch your tongue, my lass. You always go too far.'

Megs shrugged. 'He's a meat-eater and arrogant.'

'You ate meat. Beef stew with parsley dumplings. Roast chicken. Burgers. Lamb on a Sunday. Or pork. There was nothing wrong with the way I fed you. Gruel indeed.' Incensed, she stormed from the room and started to clear up. Tidying shoes and papers. Taking coats from where they'd been abandoned draped on the back of the sofa and hanging them on the hall stand. Bustling in a furious, don't-meddle-with-me way.

'Bacon and eggs. Sausages. Apple crumble.' She appeared at the kitchen door. 'Jam sponge with custard.' She disappeared again. They could hear her moving about the house, clearing and wiping. Working up a rage.

'Look at what you've done,' Lizzy said. 'She's in a bad mood.'

Megs said nothing. Why didn't she watch what she said? She spoke then she thought. Wrong order. But then she thought no matter what she said she would anger her mother. Their relationship was edgy. Megs could not recall a time when it had been any other way. Megs always felt inadequate in her mother's presence. Her life was never organised enough. Her house was never quite clean enough, her standards never high enough whatever she was doing. Wiping the sink. 'That's never clean.' Naming the dog. 'Shameless. You can't call him that. Imagine standing in the park shouting, "Shameless. Shameless." You'd feel daft.' Choosing a husband. 'You're not marrying him, are you? No good will come of it.' Losing a husband. 'I won't say I told you so. But I told you so.' They seemed doomed to bicker and sigh at each other.

'Fish pie,' her mother yelled from the other room. 'Macaroni cheese with bacony bits in. You used to love that.'

Chapter Four

Dave Roberts's office at the Glass Bucket was small and claustrophobic. A little room at odds with itself. Plainly, the man and his vision of himself did not fit within these four walls. The immaculately cut, soft-shouldered suit, still in its dry cleaner's wrapping, hanging on the back of the door; the computer, fax and palm seemed uncomfortable against the plain, time-stained mushroom walls.

The newly acquired electrical goods sat uneasily on a table made reliable with a paperback copy of *The Day of the Triffids* shoved under one of the legs, and on his chipped metal desk with drawers that rumbled open, clanged shut, under the gruelling glow of a long, fluorescent tube. They were perfect, gleamy things waiting, like Dave was waiting, for this place to smarten itself up for them. Then their proper life could begin.

Backstage at the Glass Bucket was a corridor lined with empty crates and beer casks where the band sat eating carry-out curries before starting work. There was a small, mirrorless lavatory and washroom that on lucky days had actual hot water. So it was in Dave's office that Megs made last-minute repairs to her hair and make-up.

She propped a mirror on his filing cabinet and stared at herself a moment. Her make-up routine was always the same. Didn't take long. She'd worn the same face for years. She moussed her hair, layered on mascara and grey eye shadow and, pouting at her reflection, coloured her lips pale brown. She considered her profiles, left first, then right, and ran her fingers through her hair. 'There,' she said at last, 'that's her.' As if she had created a new person. As if the woman who sang Friday nights at the Glass Bucket was not the same woman who went out cleaning five days a week.

She turned to go and saw the letter lying on Dave's desk. Unusual – for he was an immaculate man who kept everything in its place. Every night, Dave filed all letters and invoices and locked his filing cabinet. He polished his desk, watered his palm, and ran a clean yellow duster over his beloved fax and computer. He emptied his blue plastic waste-paper bin. He kept his affairs, business and personal, in perfect order. So perhaps it was the strangeness of spotting a ripple of disorder from the immaculate one, a rare chance to catch an insight into Dave's life that made Megs pause on her way out the door and pick up and read the letter.

It was written on thick pale-buff paper with a dark-green embossed letterhead. It said expensive. It was from a firm of architects and interior decorators, Ian and Myra Donaldson and Partners.

Dear Dave,

A note to thank you informally for the contract. It means a lot to us. I can't tell you how excited we all are at the prospect of being involved in the revamping of the Glass Bucket. Doesn't the old place need a facelift?

I'm sure you won't regret your decision to go with us.

We'll have plans for the renovations, including the removal of the stage and installation of a disco unit, ready to submit to the council next week . . .

Megs's heart tumbled. She read no more. Replaced the letter and left. She walked down the corridor, saw Dave coming towards her. She knew her dismay was showing on her face and couldn't move her lips into a smile, couldn't hide her shock.

'Dave,' she said as they passed.

'Megs,' he replied. They looked at each other – a lingering bit of meaningful eye contact. He knows I know, she thought. Yet she could say nothing about it, for then she would give herself away. I have been snooping, she confessed to herself. She realised then that he'd left the letter out deliberately, knowing she'd look at it. Knowing she and the band would voluntarily leave rather than lose their jobs to a disco machine.

That's it, then, she thought. Soon I'll only be a cleaner. The singer's for the chop. And she had always sung, all her life.

'We are the last of the singers,' Aunty Betty would say when she and Megs were working in the kitchen of the Seaview Guest House. 'We sing for singing's sake. People don't do that any more. Not like they used to in the old days when the world was still in black and white. Then people sang things like "When the Red Red Robin Comes Bob Bob Bobbin' Along".' She sang, demonstrating, with expansive arm movements, the bobbin' of the robin. 'Now though,' she lamented, 'they sing recordings. Everything's in colour and everyone wants to be a star. They know the drinks stars drink, the clothes stars wear and the exercises stars do to take their bodies to stardom. So they sing like stars. They have pretend microphones, play air guitars, and when they sing they also do the backing. I can't get no satisfaction, doo, di, doo di doo doo. Not the same. There's no innocence there.'

Aunty Betty was keen on innocence. 'We were happy back then,' she'd say, 'in the golden days before hygiene and cholesterol.' An era she pined for. The world, according to Aunty Betty, was not what it once was. People were not as happy as they once were. They no longer sang out loud. Window-cleaners and milkmen no longer whistled in the street. She blamed this loss of happiness on what seemed to her, at least, society's sudden discovery of hygiene and cholesterol. 'We were perfectly happy and healthy when we didn't know about them,' she'd say. 'People sang. Women sang as they cleaned their houses. People sang at work.'

It was true, Megs thought. She remembered years ago, when she and Lorraine were Hannah's age, dreaming of Stevie Wonder. They sang his songs, 'You are the Sunshine of My Life' and 'Superstition', backing and all, arms linked, as they walked the small route through school from French to chemistry. A cappella teenage angst. Lovely.

Tonight, as she sang, she scanned the faces in the Glass Bucket. Over the years they had changed. Familiar faces appeared week after week, Friday after Friday. But some had disappeared. And new ones taken their place. Young faces. These fresh faces did not gather round the small raised platform where she performed, preferring instead to stay at the bar, chatting and drinking. They were young. They had money. They did not want to listen to her youth. They wanted to drink and flirt and do their Friday-night thing to their own sounds.

This noticing of changing faces and haircuts was not new to Megs. In those years of standing before crowds, styles changed. She'd noticed trousers narrow and hair shorten. The sound she heard pouring from passing cars and shopping malls, roaring in pubs, stopped being young and cheeky, became raw and angry. She loved it. Mike hated it.

'We should do stuff like that,' she said, excited by its primitive energy.

'It's rubbish,' Mike dismissed her. 'We wouldn't demean ourselves. It'd be the end of us.'

'It'll be the end of us if we don't,' she said.

'Crap,' he spat and walked off. Now she realised he hadn't changed because he couldn't. Change scared him then, and it still did.

She sang U2, 'With or Without You' and 'I Still Haven't Found What I'm Looking For'. Then, when in the middle of her Bryan Ferry version of 'Smoke Gets In Your Eyes', Frank, the sax player, stepped forward to do a solo, she danced.

When she was little Megs had an invisible friend, Lonnie. She knew exactly what he looked like – dark curly hair, blue eyes. He went everywhere with her, sat beside her at the dinner table, agreed with everything she said. Perfect friends, they rarely argued.

Now she danced with an air man, the perfect partner. She curved her arms round him and they moved in time to the song, dipping and twirling. She loved to dance with her air man. He would never let her down. Not like Dave Roberts with his letter.

She saw him standing at the bar, watching her. He'd changed into a fresh shirt and tie and the suit that had been hanging on the door of his office. She watched him pull his cuffs down the jacket sleeve and brush some imagined something from his trousers. Preening.

Look at him, thought Megs. Three hours ago he was spotless, creaseless. Not a wrinkle in his pants, knife-edge sleeves on his shirt. Now look at him, spotless, creaseless. Knife-edges on his sleeves. And look at me. Make-up melted, lipstick licked off, my skirt all wrinkly round the bum. I guess some people are born to be creaseless. We should simply lie in their shadow, let them pass. We are not worthy, creaseless one. She hated him.

'"God Bless The Child",' she said to the band.

'I don't think so,' said Frank. He was tired. He worked in a garage fixing cars, starting at eight in the morning till five in the evening. Then straight to the Glass Bucket to play till after eleven. He was tired. He wanted to go home.

'Oh yes. I think so,' said Megs.

'The boss won't like it.'

'Exactly,' said Megs. 'If you won't do it, I'll do it alone.'

She started to sing unaccompanied. Everything stopped. Even the new faces turned to watch and listen. Her voice cut through the smoke- and booze-laden room. The till did not chime. Silence. No clink of glasses, no hum of conversation. Dave glared at her, slowly drummed his stubby fingers on the bar, an elaborate gesture of irritation.

Now he really knows I know, Megs thought. And she cursed herself for her weakness. He knows I've been spying on his life, reading his mail. She soared easily into the second verse and the band came up behind her, drifting sorrow. When she'd done she ignored the applause. Dave came across the room and gallantly held out his hand to help her step from the stage. 'Two months,' he said. 'We close for renovations in two months.'

She met his eye. She would not let him see how afraid she was of losing her singing persona, of becoming just a cleaner. 'There you go, then,' she said brightly, as brightly as she could manage. 'Two months.' She turned and went to sit with Lorraine and her husband, Harry.

'What was that all about?' Lorraine asked.

'Oh, nothing,' said Megs.

Oh, nothing. Lorraine knew oh, nothing when she heard it. It meant oh, something. Usually something dire. Megs would bottle it up till she ached. When the ache became intolerable, that something dire would come tumbling furiously out. Meantime, she fixed Megs with a long, knowing stare.

Wincing, Megs stared back. 'Oh shut up,' she said.

'I never said anything,' said Lorraine.

'Shut up your thoughts.'

'If only I could,' Lorraine said quietly. 'If only any of us could. How happy we'd be.'

'Yes,' sighed Megs. 'I know. Let's get horribly drunk and do silly things.'

'Alternatively,' Harry joined in the conversation, 'let's not.' Obviously he had firm ideas on the subject of getting horribly drunk and silly, and the man was not for turning.

'OK,' agreed Lorraine. 'Let's not.' She smiled at him.

They are in love, thought Megs. How ghastly of them. She drank slowly, letting the ice cubes move past her lips and chink against her teeth. She watched Lorraine wrap her fingers around Harry's. They had been married for years. Years and years, Megs thought. I was bridesmaid.

'You two have been married forever,' she said. 'When was your wedding?'

'Don't ask.' Harry waved her question away. He looked down into his glass, refusing to meet Lorraine's tipsily adoring gaze. Megs noticed, and wondered if, perhaps, it was only Lorraine who was in love.

'Our wedding was back in the golden days before hygiene and cholesterol, as Aunty Betty would say,' Lorraine offered.

Megs put her elbow on the table, chin in cupped hand, and tried to chase her encroaching depression away with songs in her head. She hummed a little snatch of 'Maggie Mae'. A crass and unsubtle choice since it was about an affair between a boy and an older woman. The poet Lorraine had run off with, her one big adventure, had been sixteen years her junior.

'Sixteen years,' Megs said to her. 'Doesn't it shock you that you're old enough to have someone in the world functioning – smoking and drinking legally, having sex – who is sixteen years younger than you?'

'I love him,' Lorraine said. So she left Harry and her job and climbed into her poet's yellow Mini with its clutter of jackets and boots on the back seat and drove off into the sunset.

To Bristol actually. There they stayed in a squat with a rock musician, a mime artist and a girl called Tasmin who was studying astrotherapy. They lived on brown rice and Guinness. Or so it seemed to Lorraine.

'It was wonderful,' Lorraine sighed. Then, sensing Megs's disbelief. 'Well, at first. Then I got indigestion. I mean, how much brown rice can a person my age take? My system isn't up to it. I need things – wine, chocolate. You know. Prawns in garlic and lime butter, peppered steak, crispy duck in black bean sauce, red jelly with hundreds and thousands . . . um.'

'Chips?' suggested Megs.

'Chips,' Lorraine enthused. 'Those little crispy ones at the bottom of the bag all salty and vinegary. I mean . . .' realising she had enthused perhaps a little too loudly, too long, '. . . what's the damn use of being a poet, writing all that poetry, and never mentioning chips?'

'I've always wondered about that,' agreed Megs. 'All that stuff by Byron and Keats at school. Not a chip there.'

'Exactly.' Lorraine nodded. 'Brown rice indeed.' She envied her poet his youth and his digestive system. 'How could he? And there's proper beds with duvets, and chairs and carpets. A person gets to a certain age and needs certain things.'

After a month Harry had turned up at the door of the squat. 'I think it's time to come home,' he said. Lorraine did not argue. She packed her bags and within ten minutes was sitting by his side, leaning back in his Ford Sierra. After insisting he stop at a motorway caff for chicken, bacon and chips followed by apple pie and ice cream, she had slept and cried alternately all the way home.

From the sweet distance of her third vodka Megs watched them. Remembering how Harry had, at the time, forgiven Lorraine everything, and thinking now she could say something to salvage what looked like a floundering relationship, Megs said, 'You are a nice man, Harry. A really nice man.' She was thinking about her air man, dance partner. She thought if she had stuck with an air man things would have been fine for her. Then, she thought, why leave it at an air man? If she had an air mother and air children her life, her dilemma, would be so much more manageable.

'Time to go.' Harry stood up.

'Already?' Lorraine protested. 'Why?'

'Megs has just said I'm a nice man. She's going to get maudlin. Time to go.'

'It will be nice to get home,' said Megs. She was longing to lie down. To be alone in bed, horizontal and warm, in a darkened room, and consider her life. Better yet, to be horizontal and warm in a darkened room and not consider her life.

Chapter Five

At home, alone, she moved through, listening to, her darkened flat. The fridge hummed and clicked in the kitchen. If she stood in the hall she could hear her children sleep: Jack's flat snoring, Hannah's sighs and Lizzy's small moans and childish mumblings.

What will become of me? she thought. What have I done to myself to get to here? How did this happen? When she became a cleaner it never occurred to her that when people looked at her a cleaner would be all they saw. It isn't what I saw when I looked at me, she thought. What do I do? she asked herself. I bustle and crow. I fuss and boss. If I wipe the sink so hard my whole body shakes from elbow to bum with the vibrancy of my wipe, and if I shout the odds loud enough, boss my children hard enough, I can just about blot out the demons. The doubts and fears.

She went to the living room and switched on the television, sound down, and sat amidst its glimmer and flicker. On screen young people in absurd clothes were dancing. Every time they saw the camera watching them they pulled insane faces and waved. They were frantically going through the motions, putting on a show of having a good time. But they are only bustling and crowing, she thought.

Yet she had always been relatively happy with what went on in her head – her observations of other people and their lives, her knowledge of music and plants, her hopes and dreams for her children. But last week something happened. Such a little thing, but it stayed with Megs, rattling round and round inside her head with all the doubts, fears and guilts that kept her awake at night.

Mrs Emotionally-Deranged Davis published the details of her blustery life on a series of Post-It notes pinned to the fridge, her computer in the living room, the bathroom cabinet, the bedroom mirror and the headboards of the four children's beds, and anywhere else likely to catch the eye of those family members she was currently bossing.

'Veronica's veruca – 2.30 at the outpatients!' 'Clive's cello lesson cancelled this week. Doesn't mean you can stop working on the Dvorák.' 'Robert! We have dinner at Johnstones' on Friday, 8.00 sharp. Please remember the Shiraz gives her a headache.' 'Lucinda – that horrible boy phoned. Can't remember when.' 'The downstairs lavatory is not to be used – it's overflowing.' On the wine rack: 'Whoever has been drinking the South African white is grounded.' On the television: 'Not to be switched on till all homework is finished.' On the kitchen cupboard: 'I've counted the KitKats!' On the phone: 'Remember, children, I get details of the bill.' 'Sasha – tidy your room. Find your missing blue sock. Your piano lesson is on Tuesday this week. Your school report is diabolical.' 'Everybody! My PDK test was negative. We can breathe again.'

There it was, Mrs Emotionally-Deranged's autobiography written on yellow notes. The more deranged her life, the more strewn with yellow litter the house became. Julia Davis was a therapist. She was rarely home. Then again, she was omnipresent.

Last week when Megs was there, cleaning, Julia Davis was home supervising verbally. Lucinda was at the kitchen table working on her school project, the Russian Revolution.

'I have to write about Lenin,' she whined, sprawling across the table top, head lolling over her books. 'I don't want to. It's boring. I hate this.'

Mrs Emotionally-Deranged Davis slipped into parental preamble. Megs recognised it. She'd heard herself deliver similar ludicrous preachings when she felt her children were on the verge of failure and defeat. She noticed that her imaginings of her children as adults were two-dimensional. They would succeed or they would fail. They would live in gorgeous homes or they would embrace the gutter. She saw them grandly sweeping through cheering hordes to collect their Nobel prize, or she saw them in green stripy aprons grinning vacuously from behind a counter, asking customers if they wanted a happy hat today. When they did their homework it was glittering prizes here we come, when they sat sideways on armchairs, staring open-jawed at old Bugs Bunny cartoons, it was happy hats ahoy. They gave her hope and she feared for them.

'This isn't about the Russian Revolution.' Mrs Emotionally-Deranged Davis sounded pious. 'This is about you displaying your ability to amass and coherently relate information. This is about you moving forward and getting closer to achieving your goals. You get good grades for this and you are a step nearer to getting more good grades, which will eventually take you to the university you want, and the course you want, and, in time, the job you want, and the life you want. It starts here, at this kitchen table, doing this project.'

Oh, heavy, thought Megs. Emotionally-Deranged Davis was being plagued by images of her daughter dishing out happy hats. Megs did not have to look round. She knew Lucinda would be slumped, chewing gum, staring away from her mother, silently mouthing, 'Shut up. Shut up.'

'I hate Lenin,' Lucinda moaned. 'I hate him. Why did he have to go and start that sodding revolution? If he hadn't I wouldn't have to sit here doing this. Why do I have to know his real name? Difference does it make?'

'It was Ulyanov,' said Megs. She was quoting from Hannah's chewed, chocolate-stained picture book, *Twenty Men Who Changed the World*. She did not turn round or stop squishing lemon cleaner on the kitchen unit doors. 'Vladimir Ilyich Ulyanov. Born at Simbirsk, son of a maths and physics teacher.' She wiped furiously. 'He was the third of seven, though one died. Then again so did his older brother. He was hanged for taking part in a plot against the Tsar when Lenin was only seventeen. Changed his life.' She squished some more. Then paused. 'Lenin's,' she said. 'Not the brother's. Though it would his too, I suppose. On account of getting hung. But that's what got Lenin going. He'd had a comfortable middle-class life. No need to rebel, really. Then again, some might say every reason to rebel.'

She wiped more vigorously, aware of the squall of silence behind her. She knew they were pulling faces behind her back, exchanging astonished, well-fancy-that expressions.

'Goodness, Megs.' Emotionally-Deranged Davis made no effort

to hide her amazement. 'How did you know that?'

'Read it somewhere,' Megs said, not turning, wiping on.

During her singing years she'd sat in the back of the van and read endlessly – books, magazines, comics, the backs of cereal packets, the contents of a can of Coke, the instructions on Mike's condom packs, which she could quote verbatim to this day. She was not a discriminating reader. But information stuck.

Uninvited titbits of information still wormed their way into her brain. Her gleanings included tabloid newspapers, *National Geographic* magazines in the dentist's waiting room, her children's school books, battered cookbooks, old magazines, as well as the books her clients left lying around.

Incensed, she confided in Lorraine. 'It was so insulting. They just stood there gobsmacked. They didn't say, "Well, thanks for your help, Megs." And they just took the information, as if it was part of my job to give it. They seemed so surprised that I knew about Lenin. Why shouldn't I know? I get to know things. From my worm's-eye view from under my stone, I see things. It's allowed.' She knew she was starting to rant. 'Who do they think I am? Just the cleaner?'

Lorraine carefully put her mug of coffee down on the kitchen table and turned to look at Megs. 'Yes,' she said coldly. 'That's what they think. You are just the cleaner. They prefer not to really see you. Then when you show them there's more to you than they thought, it stops them in their tracks.' She tapped the table with a red-lacquered nail as she spoke. 'If you know stuff and cleaning's happened to you, then it could happen to them. They are not so safe as they think.'

'I am wedged in their minds as a small brown person who totes a yellow duster.' Megs winced at the thought, then heaved up her self-image, adding, 'They do not know they are dealing with the leader of the Bucketeers.'

For two years she'd been leader of the Bucketeers, the Glass Bucket quiz team. She regularly dazzled her children with the casual way she fielded questions on *Mastermind*. She mildly came up with answers from behind her newspaper or called them from the kitchen. They regularly came to her trailing homework notebooks.

'Hey, Ma. What was Schubert's first name?'

'Where's Zaire?'

'Who wrote *The Pit and the Pendulum*?'
She rarely let them down.
'You should be on television,' Lizzy said. Little squeaky pronouncement. 'Then you'd win a million pounds and I could have a rabbit.'
'A rabbit?' Her children always surprised Megs.
'Yes. If we had a million pounds I'd have a pair of red shoes and a rabbit.'
'We have nowhere to keep a rabbit,' Megs said. Stupidly.
'If we won a million pounds we could buy it a house.' Lizzy was scathing.
'Of course.' Megs conceded that housing rabbits was not a problem for millionaires.

So now she sat, three o'clock in the morning, staring glumly at the soundless flicker on television, feet tucked under the dog, and fought off her demons. Fear and guilt. She'd lost her singing job. She was just a cleaner. That was how people saw her. And she could not afford a rabbit.

She stumped through to her bedroom, and, on a whim, fetched her old shoebox full of photos from on top of the wardrobe. Clutching it, she slid into bed. She took out some photos of herself years ago and spread them on the duvet. There she was with the band, young, blonde and skinny. She was wearing jeans and a T-shirt with a marijuana leaf on the front. Mike was wearing a hat and grinning. She thought she looked desperate. At the time she'd been convinced she was smiling her best smile.

Wondering if she'd been giving off false signals all her life, she gathered up her memories and put them back in the box. Then she slid down under the covers. 'God, this is good. Prone is good. I was born to be prone, Shameless. Prone suits me.'

She tried to sleep, but ghosts haunted her. Dave Roberts with his perfect suit and his grim smile. He did not think much of her, she knew that. Mrs Emotionally-Deranged Davis and her surprise at Megs's small show of general knowledge. What did Julia Davis think of her? Plainly not a lot. Hundred-Miles-An-Hour, with his flushed face and his distaste for chemical smells. Him and his vacuum. They didn't think much of her.

'We are defined by how old we are, what we look like and where we live. Shite to the lot of you,' Megs called out, chasing off her ghosts. 'Megs is thirty-nine, looks like shite and lives in a second-floor four-roomed flat in Edinburgh. That's all, folks. Good night to you and good night to me. Sod you all. Sod you all. There's more to me than that. I just have to find out what it is.'

She turned over and pulled the duvet up over her head, hoping sleep would come to her. The dog lay on the floor, waiting till the sound of her breathing became heavy and rhythmic. Then he'd sneak on to the bed. In the morning she'd wake in a lather with small child pressed next to her and dog sprawled over her feet.

Chapter Six

'You were always an awkward beggar,' Vivienne said. She was sitting at Megs's kitchen table drinking tea. She meant bugger, but couldn't bring herself to swear in front of her daughter. 'Your father and me often say that.'

'Why?' Megs was indignant. It seemed her father's thoughts and opinions always came second-hand to her, through her mother. She had stopped communicating with him, but couldn't quite say exactly when. Now his wishes were passed on by Vivienne. 'Your father said.' 'Your father won't like this, you know.' 'Your father and me have decided.'

'First there was the business with your name,' Vivienne said. 'There is nothing wrong with Nina.' She shook her head as she spoke. 'Your father and I loved that name.'

Megs said nothing. Recently she'd been reconsidering her decision, taken all those years ago when she was five, not to answer to her given name. Nina was beginning to appeal to her, Megs was beginning to pall. She was feeling foolish for refusing to answer to a perfectly respectable name.

'Then,' Vivienne was warming to her theme, 'you went off with that daft band when you should have been studying. After that there was the cleaning job. And there have been lots of other things along the way, little things.'

'What?' asked Megs, knowing she shouldn't. Her mother's memory was long and horrifyingly accurate.

Vivienne leaned forward. 'There was that hat.'

Megs flinched inwardly. The memory she was dealing with was more than long and accurate, it was vicious. 'Hat?' She tried to sound innocent.

'That green-and-pink-striped hat I bought you when you'd had measles and were going back to school. It was January. It did you no good, no good at all, going out in the cold after the temperature you'd had. But oh no, you did not want to wear it. The fuss you made, crying and stamping your foot. Then you came home without it. It was a lovely hat, too.'

'I have no idea what you are talking about,' Megs lied.

Vivienne glared at her.

'For heaven's sake, you expect me to remember a hat? It was over thirty years ago,' Megs defended herself. She remembered it well. Who could forget such a hat – pink and green stripes with a pink bobble on top. She'd hated it. She could still recall the tantrum, lying on the floor drumming her heels, refusing to leave the house with it on. It was an object of derision. It lacked the sort of style a five-year-old needed to gain playground kudos. In such a hat she would be a mockery. And all her life Megs had known no mockery as fierce and furious as playground mockery.

Her mother had been adamant. 'The hat stays on,' she insisted. She dragged Megs, hat on head, to school. But as soon as she'd disappeared, Megs snatched the hated hat from her head and on the way home stuffed it up a drainpipe.

'Whatever happened to that hat, anyway?' Vivienne asked.

'Dunno,' shrugged Megs. 'Can't remember.'

'Oh yes you can. You can tell me now. What did you do with it?'

Megs looked distractedly out of the window. 'Lost it,' she mumbled.

'I don't believe you.' Vivienne looked at her indignantly. She always felt her good taste was threatened by Megs's rejection of the hat. 'I liked that hat. It was lovely.'

Megs was chagrined. She noticed she was staring at her feet and feeling vaguely sweaty with guilt. Her mother could still do that to her. She still couldn't own up about the loathsome hat. She changed the subject. 'I don't think I'm an awkward beggar.' They stared at each other, mother and daughter, across the chasm they'd created. They were separated by years, a hat and other lies.

Megs was twelve when Vivienne was diagnosed as having TB. In those days it meant a long stay in a sanatorium. Wrapped in a tartan dressing gown, Vivienne would lean on the huge windows, staring out at the grounds, longing for her daughter. The disease brought lines to her face early. She always thought of the hideous spores her breath might carry. She feared that kissing her family might have brought them danger. She rarely put her lips to theirs after she got home. Megs still remembered going to visit every Sunday, wearing her best coat and shiny black shoes with a buckle on the side. She walked the long drive holding her father's hand, huge and rough against hers. He did not say much.

When the disease was first diagnosed, Megs, her brother and father had to go for an X-ray, checking that their lungs were clear. The clinic was huge, chill and empty. Megs hadn't wanted to strip and stood huddled in her vest, clutching herself, refusing to remove it. Her father had smacked the back of her head. 'Get on with it. You're wasting the doctor's time.' It was the only time he ever hit her. It was years before Megs realised how distraught the man had been.

He could not afford to take time off work, so Megs was sent to stay with Aunty Betty. Her brother was old enough to stay home alone. It was summer, and there was a 'No Vacancies' notice in the window of the Seaview Guest House. It was a busy time.

Megs learned to love the smell of hotel breakfasts. She helped serve them. She would tour the tables, politely reciting the morning menu, porridge and kippers, bacon, egg and tomato, and nod with solemn approval of their choice. Cornflakes or krispies? Tea or coffee? Toast?

After breakfast she'd help wash up. As she dried plates and cups she listened to Aunty Betty's stories. There was no doubt in anybody's mind where Megs got her imagination and her vivid vocabulary. Aunty Betty spun tales of her youth. Those long-ago days seemed to her to be the golden age of Bakelite. She could recall vividly the glorious time people had in the years before cholesterol and hygiene. 'They could eat what they liked, no bother. Eggs, chips, butter. White sugar. There was nothing wrong with that stuff, then. And I can remember going to the newsagent's on the corner. There was a big black cat sat on the counter. On the rolls. We just lifted it up and took what we wanted and put it back again. There was no thought of us getting food poisoning. We'd have none of it.'

Every morning, before her breakfast recital, Megs would lie listening to the sea and the eiders that came round to coo on the rocks outside her bedroom window. After breakfast and washing-up she'd walk along the sands to the shows. There she'd stand breathing in the greasy air, chips and burgers, candy floss and hot dogs, listening to the Beatles booming out. Hits of the day. In the evenings she always wrote to Vivienne.

Dear Mum,
    I'm fine. The weather is lovely. Hope you're getting better. I'm enjoying being here. I help serve the meals. Aunty Betty says I'm a great help. Aunty Betty says there didn't used to be food poisoning in the olden days when she was young and butter was good for you then.

Vivienne did not see the letters as cheery nonsense from a lonely twelve-year-old. She read them from the depths, the blackness of the depression and anger, the fluctuating moods that came with her disease. Her daughter preferred her sister to her. But then everybody preferred Betty to her. Always had. Betty had always been taller, prettier, cleverer, more popular than her. Betty had the handsomest boyfriends. With a flick of her fingers, Betty could do interesting things with her hair. Betty chose the best clothes, and wore the reddest lipstick. Betty danced in her memories always laughing, always flirting. Vivienne sighed. She had always walked in her sister's shadow. She was small and would never be fabulous – like Betty.

Dear Mum,
    Aunty Betty lets me play her records. I like Duke Ellington best. And Ella Fitzgerald. When we do the dusting we sing stuff like 'With a Song In My Heart' and 'The Lady Is a Tramp'.

With a pang of jealousy Vivienne imagined Megs and her Aunty Betty in yellow frocks, flashing through the housework with an effortless waft of feather dusters, the sunny way Doris Day did – all freckly smiles and shiny songs. She thought they'd be having a wonderful time, and here was she, half a woman, with decaying lungs, in a blue-and-beige-striped winceyette nightie. Vivienne wept.

Dear Mum,
   Aunty Betty can dance. She can do the tango and the foxtrot. She says she and Uncle Ron used to be the champions at the Salutation Ballroom. Aunty Betty says that dancing isn't what it used to be. She says that when she and Uncle Ron took to the floor everyone clapped . . .

'Aunty Betty says. Aunty Betty says. Aunty Betty says,' cursed Vivienne. Her condition made her despair. She coughed and spat. Every morning she had to hawk into a stainless-steel tray, her sputum test. She cried hopelessly, and never realised she was reacting to illness and drugs.

Of course it was true. Betty and Ron moved across the floor of the Salutation Ballroom in perfect harmony. They dipped, bobbed and twirled. Ron would lean Betty back and they'd smile to the small line of observers standing at the edge of the floor, dazzled by the show and hindered by their inadequacy from grabbing a partner and joining in.

Aunty Betty's records were thick and broke if you sat on them. Aunty Betty had a huge gramophone that could stack eight LPs and play them one after another. But Megs preferred to put them on one at a time. She liked the business of taking one record off, wiping it, putting it carefully back in its sleeve and taking out another. Megs played Count Basie, Glen Miller and Duke Ellington, and one day she discovered Billie Holiday. 'God hep the chile,' she sang, and it cut through Megs's childhood. This was what she wanted. She wanted to sing like that. More than that. She was on the turn, moving towards being a woman, and, like any sickening adolescent, she'd discovered the joy of being sad.

She was far from home and wanted her mum, who she feared was going to die. Nobody said it like Billie. 'God hep the chile.' She was a chile and she wanted God to hep her. She sat listening to that song over and over. It stopped and she put it on again, lifting the arm, replacing the needle at the beginning of the track. Over and over that song hummed and sighed through the Seaview Guest House till Aunty Betty said that if she ever heard it again she'd scream. And all the summering guests, with their red and peeling faces, smiled grimly and said if they heard that bloody thing again they'd go somewhere else next year.

Dear Mum,
  Aunty Betty says I can have her Billie Holiday record. Can we get a record player? Please. When I come home. I'll pay for it. Well, you pay for it and I'll pay you back. I am going to be a singer when I grow up. So there's no need for me to bother at school. I am going to sing the blues and rooms will stop at the very sound of my voice. It will cut through the night and break hearts.

Even then, all those years ago, Megs could weave a dream.

When this declaration reached her, Vivienne was at her window, wheezing in air. Imagining its cleanness cutting through the filth in her lungs. She threw the letter across the room. That sudden passionate swing of her arm pained her. She thought she'd never feel better. She'd been reduced to a slow, hunched shuffle that had more to do with her state of mind than her condition. She thought she'd never move across rooms with her old determined stride. She annoyed herself. The smallest undertaking, tying her shoelaces, putting on her bra, reading a magazine, exhausted her. She ached to get home. The intensity of this ache and the frustration at not being able to put her daughter in her place made her weep. She'd listen to the radio on the ward, the disc jockey played jolly tunes, beamed out bass sincerity, and she'd cry. Relentless tears kept coming and coming without her being able to stop them. Her sadness seemed like a tangible thing that followed her from day room to ward, morning and night. All that and she knew for sure she was useless.

Walter came and went. The shifts he worked formed the rhythm of their lives – ten till six one week, six till two the next, two till ten the week after. Then back to ten till six again. Sometimes he slept in the visitor's chair beside her bed, whilst Vivienne cried. Sometimes he stood by watching not knowing what to do. He found her illness perturbing. It made her flushed and passionate.

'Can I bring you something?' he'd ask, his big hands dangling by his sides. 'Grapes?'

'No. No.' Vivienne dabbed her cheeks. 'Not grapes. Please not grapes.'

When he got home, Walter could not bear to be in the house. So he'd banish himself to his garden shed where he would, making a comforting whistling noise from between clamped teeth, sand things down, glue things together, tinker with things, arrange and rearrange his tools into neat rows and peer out of the window.

Vivienne had convinced herself that Megs preferred the swirling glee of the Seaview Guest House to the drab routine she offered her. When she came home Vivienne never told her daughter how she'd longed for her, and Megs never told her mother that she'd been afraid she would die.

Chapter Seven

'How long has my mother been saying she's sixty-three?' Megs asked. She put down the iron, stared into the distance, considering this,

'Oh God.' Lorraine thought about it too. 'Ages. Years and years.' She'd come round to tell Megs that Clark's Catering had phoned offering them both four hours' work, double time, tonight. 'Yes. Years and years. She's been sixty-three since goodness knows how long.'

'She's been lying.'

'That's not a lie. That's not lying about your age. That's making a legend out of it. We should take note. We should stay forty at least five years, then move on slowly from there.'

'Yes,' Megs agreed. She was ironing her waitress uniform – black skirt, white shirt, white apron – that had been lying crumpled and forgotten at the bottom of the clothes basket for the last two months. 'I don't know if I'll remember. You have to admire my mother for the blatancy of her deceit. Declaring the wrong age loudly by the day is magnificently upfront. She has risen in my estimation.'

'Your mother is OK,' Lorraine said. Then, idly, 'Pork sausages on wholewheat bread spread with mustard then topped with apple sauce. What do you think?'

'That's not bad. Sort of business lunch and workers' lunch at the same time. Yes.' She smoothed out the sleeve of her shirt. Added, 'My mother has her moments.' Admitting Vivienne had moments was as much praise as Megs was going to give. 'When do we have to be there?'

'Seven,' said Lorraine, bored already at the prospect of the evening ahead. 'It's a university dinner.'

'God. Hundred-Miles-An-Hour won't be there, will he?'

Last week Hundred-Miles-An-Hour had walked through his house, arms spread, looking beatific. 'This place is almost human.' He smiled at her. 'You really have made an improvement. I mean, look,' and he strode manfully across his living room, 'I can walk from place to place without tripping over things. And I can see out of the window. There's the garden.' He pointed in wonderment.

'Well,' Megs said. 'Sometimes there is only one way to go. Up. When things get really bad, improvement is all that's left.' She followed his gaze out to the garden. A small tangled area of dried overgrown aubretia and yellowed lawn. She had her eye on that garden.

'No. 'Course he won't be there,' Lorraine answered her. 'Anyway, it'll be over by eleven.' As if that automatically meant Gilbert Christie wouldn't go. As if he never stayed out as late as eleven.

'Home by twelve and up again tomorrow morning to go clean for Mrs Terribly-Clean Pearson. I can hardly wait.'

Across the room the television blared an early-evening quiz show. Hannah and Lizzy were at the kitchen table eating spaghetti, Hannah deftly twirling it round her fork, Lizzy sucking it strand by strand into her mouth, splattering herself with tomato sauce. Jack came in and handed Megs a shirt. 'Iron this, go on? I need it for school tomorrow.'

'What do you mean, iron your shirt? Iron your own shirt, why can't you? Who do you think I am, your mother?'

'Yes. I thought that was the deal.' Jack looked confused.

'Well, that's only because I gave birth to you. Ironing was not mentioned at the time. And, quite frankly, motherhood is not what it's cracked up to be. In fact, if you ask me motherhood is a ruse dreamed up by the Church of Scotland to stop women from . . . from . . .'

'From having orgasms,' Lorraine put in mildly.

Megs looked at her in astonishment. 'We are not in the habit of discussing orgasms at the dinner table,' she said.

'Might be more interesting than ironing,' said Jack.

'What's an orgasm?' Lizzy wanted to know.

'Lorraine will tell you,' Megs told her. She left them to it and went to sit heavily in front of the television, hoping something mindless was on. She got ten brainless minutes of game show before Lizzy came bawling into the room.

'The man at the shop told me to go away and never come back,' she was sobbing.

'Why on earth did he do that?' Megs asked, only mildly interested because across the room the game show host was smiling and asking the contestants if they wanted to stick with their thousand pounds, their colour television set, video and weekend for two in a luxury hotel or did they want to risk everything and go for the four-wheel-drive jeep with CD player, leather seats and electric sunroof. Megs looked at her semi-hysterical daughter, and thought she wouldn't risk anything, she'd take the cash, the electrical goodies and the holiday. Yes, she could do with some of that.

'Because he said I was cheeky. He said I was filthy rude and he's never going to serve me again.'

The game show players chose to risk everything for the jeep. Lizzy was hyperventilating, shuddering with shame. Megs kneeled down, put her arms round her and drew the child to her.

Lizzy threw herself on to her mother, sobbing and wailing. 'I'll never go there again. Where will I buy crisps? I'll have to walk for miles . . . and he didn't even give me the orgasms.'

'What?' said Megs.

'So for the thousand pounds, the television set, the video, the luxury weekend for two and the jeep, name these tunes . . .' The orchestra struck up 'Only the Lonely', 'Fly Me To the Moon' . . .

'"Only the Lonely", "Fly Me To the Moon",' said Megs, rocking the child. Then, 'Orgasms? You asked for orgasms?'

'Yes, Lorraine said they were sweeties with the yummiest filling ever, so I took the milk money from the tin in the kitchen to go buy some. I asked for half a pound of orgasms and the man chased me out. He said I was . . .' she sobbed, gathered her breath and howled, '. . . RUDE!'

The orchestra on the telly played 'Mountain Greenery', 'Dancing In the Dark' and 'Mack the Knife'.

'"Mountain Greenery", "Dancing In the Dark" and . . . Lorraine,' Megs shouted. She heard her friend rattling speedily down the hall. With child wrapped round her front, Megs ran after her. 'Lorraine

. . . LORRAINE!' The front door slammed shut. There was the desperate click of high-heel shoes taking the stairs at a dangerous pace. 'LORRAINE!' Megs yelled again. But her friend was gone. 'I'll get you for this,' Megs said softly. She walked back up the hall. The orchestra was playing 'Gone Fishing' then battered into 'Manhattan'.

'Oh,' cried Megs, still cradling the child and nursing the wounded ego, stroking the little head. Her shoulder was wet with tears. 'That's "Mack the Knife", "Gone Fishing" and "Manhattan". Aunty Betty used to love that.' She sang it, gently dancing across the room, moving back and forth. The child silenced. Thumb went into mouth, little eyes rolled up.

'I'll talk to Mr Hodges in the morning,' Megs whispered. 'It'll be all right.'

But Lizzy was sleeping.

'You got them all. You could have won all that.' Jack was impressed. 'A jeep you could've had. A new telly. A holiday. A thousand pounds. What would you do with it?' Cash always got him going.

'Dunno,' Megs said, sitting down, still cradling Lizzy.

'You could buy yourself pounds and pounds of orgasms with really yummy centres,' Jack mocked.

'Sod off,' Megs said, softly stroking her child's head. 'I'll get that Lorraine, I really will.' She clung to her baby. 'Did Lorraine let her go out alone? She never goes out alone. She's too young.'

Jack sighed, slumped his shoulders, exasperated with her. 'It's only yards. She won't get lost.'

'That's not the point. She had to cross the road. You know I don't like her crossing the road.'

'She has to do it sometime. You can't hang on to her forever.' Then into the heavy silence he said, 'She's not going to get run over.'

'She might,' Megs said quietly. She would never admit she was wrong.

'You have to let go,' Jack said.

'Sod off,' Megs sulked. 'It's bad enough ironing your shirts without you being smarter than me.'

'It's dead easy,' he told her.

'What is?'

'Being smarter than you. Especially when you hide from your

smartness.' He chewed gum as he spoke. Looked almost disinterested.

She didn't want to move. They hadn't spoke as much as this in months. 'What do you mean by that?' As if she didn't know.

He sighed. 'I mean you don't have to do the things you do. You're just punishing yourself for Thomas. You could do better than clean.'

She said nothing. If she wasn't so overwhelmed with pride that her son had turned out to be so astute, she might have smacked him on the mouth for his cheek. 'Maybe cleaning's all I deserve,' she said.

His young lip curled. He even stopped chewing. 'Crap,' he said. 'The only thing you ever taught me was that there was no such thing as deserve and no such thing as fair.'

'I taught you more than that.' Relieved to be changing the subject, 'I taught you to eat with a knife and fork. I taught you to tie your shoelaces. And to swim.'

'Anybody could've taught me that stuff – teachers, mates, mates' mums. Deserve and fair – that was you.'

They stared at each other. She knew he'd been thinking this for a long time and had been working up to saying it. He wanted more for her. Also, she suspected, he wanted more for himself than a cleaner for a mother. She searched his face to see if it was numb, like she thought hers had become. And she bit her lip lest she say something to him that would send him reeling into himself, never to be honest with her again.

He was taller than her. His face was forming, emerging a little more every day, it seemed, from its adolescent lumpenness. She had seen that face when it was tiny, tender, innocent, wrinkled and just minutes old. She had watched this boy develop. She could remember him at ten months old heaving himself upright by holding on to the sofa, one hand over the other. Then up, look at me. He'd turned to her. He was wearing little blue dungarees and a striped red and navy jumper. He'd smiled to her, wanting nothing more than her approval and touch. Arms outstretched he'd stepped towards her. His first step. She'd been there. She'd seen it. She wished she had a photograph. But no, she thought, she didn't need one. It was one of her moments, she had it clearly in her mind. It would stay there untouched, uncreased – perfect.

At last she broke the tension between them by handing Lizzy to him. 'Here. Look after your sister. I have to iron a shirt then go off to work. To work,' she said, 'to serve food to people who are all smarter than me.' She did not say that she knew he was right, and it was time she sorted herself out.

Chapter Eight

The tables were laid – starched gleamy-white cloths, glistening glass and polished cutlery. At the top of the hall, stretched broadside, was a long head table where the dignitaries and speakers would sit. It faced half a dozen more that stretched lengthwise to the door.

Megs was on table one. The nearest to the kitchen. Hundred-Miles-An-Hour sat halfway down, facing her as she served. Oh bugger, she thought, it's him. He stared hard at her, trying to place her. He was bad at recognising people out of context. Had Megs been wearing jeans and T-shirt and standing belligerently behind her vacuum, he would have known her immediately. He had come with a woman Megs didn't recognise and they sat opposite Just-Keep-It-Above-the-Dysentery-Line McGhee, who sat, back to Megs, with her weekday grey-haired man. They were ardently discussing design. Megs could hear the forceful thrust of their conversation above the babble and hum, chink and clatter of the other one hundred and ninety-six diners in the hall.

'Style has become incredibly important, almost absurdly so,' Dysentery McGhee said.

'Absolutely,' agreed Hundred-Miles-An-Hour.

Megs moved down the table, reciting, 'Lobster bisque? Melon with port? Terrine of fresh mushrooms?'

'Thing is,' the woman who was with Hundred-Miles-An-Hour said, 'we are so attuned to style statements we can at a glance make judgements on others just by noting the stripes, or lack of stripes, on the side of their training shoe.'

'Exactly,' said Dysentery McGhee.

Hundred-Miles-An-Hour watched Megs approach. Who was that?

How come he recognised a waitress? She seemed so familiar. Where had he seen her before?

'Lobster bisque? Melon with port? Terrine of fresh mushrooms?' chanted Megs.

'You become so aware of making the simplest of statements about yourself, even on ordinary trips to the supermarket,' the woman with Hundred-Miles-An-Hour said. 'One glance in my trolley and you know who I am. You know my demographic grouping. My class, my background, even, I suspect, my aspirations.'

Megs reached the group. 'Lobster bisque? Melon with port? Terrine of fresh mushrooms?'

Dysentery McGhee nodded furiously. 'Hmm. I'll have the bisque, please,' without turning. 'Porcini, anchovies, Chilean red, Pellegrino, spinach,' she enthused. 'Says it all.' She spread her hands at this revelation about herself. She was naked and unashamed. They all laughed. Ha. Ha. Ha. How many ways to tell a lie? With make-up. With clothes. With shopping trolley. Dysentery McGhee was master of them all. What a liar she was.

She may buy that stuff, but the woman lives on toast, yoghurt, microwaved Lean Cuisines and wine from a box, Megs thought. Oven chips, bumper size, she thought. Giant packs of cornflakes and toilet rolls – I dare not think what that says about me and my aspirations.

'Good design should be an integral part of all our lives. It should be everywhere.' Gilbert glowed. Several whiskies and half a bottle of Chablis before he left home, he was not as sober as he thought he was. 'We shouldn't even think about it. It should surround us. A spoon,' he pointed to the nearest object, 'for example is a spoon. We all have one. But why shouldn't it be a beautiful spoon? Consider the spoon.' His face reddened as he spoke. He felt enlightened. He was seeing a spoon for the first time in his life. 'In the culinary panoply it's almost a haiku in deconstructive utilitarian design. Its very ordinariness makes it beautiful.' He looked at his companions, making sure they were sharing his enthusiasm. 'Honed by centuries of usage into a simple shape. Like the blade of grass.' He leaned forward meaningfully. 'Who looks at the spoon?' He picked his up and looked at it. Saw himself reflected, club-nosed and concave. Hair sticking on end. Slammed it back on to the table. Why had nobody told him he looked like that?

'Lobster bisque? Melon with port? Terrine of mushrooms?' Megs broke, flat-toned, into his shock.

'Melon,' Gilbert said swiftly. Horrified by what he'd seen, he'd said the first thing he could remember her saying. He hated melon.

He noticed Megs looking at him. 'Who is that?' he asked Dysentery McGhee. 'I'm sure I've seen that waitress somewhere.'

Megs thought, I scrub his bath, change his sheets, wipe his sink and God knows what else, and the arse doesn't even recognise me.

Dysentery McGhee turned to see who he was talking about, but Megs had disappeared into the sweat, rattle and frenetic thrum of the kitchen.

The bisque came from vast catering cans, some rusting along the bottom. It was dolloped into pans, heated and ladled top-speed into bowls, wiped round the rim, decorated with a sworl of cream and hustled out to the tables. Melon was sliced wafer-thin – three slices each plate, one grape, one half-strawberry and one half-ladle port-flavoured fruit sauce spread in the curve of melon. The bisque was salty. Megs had sucked some off her thumb after carelessly grabbing a bowl. The mushroom terrines were not popular. Strange that, Megs thought, she'd had one and liked it. She would take some home to vegetarian Hannah, who, however, had protested foully when offered broccoli. 'I'm not a broccoli sort of vegetarian. I'm just a not-eating-sausages sort of vegetarian.'

Megs laid two melon plates on her arm, then one bisque in her hand, another in the other. Thus laden she headed for the door, kicked it open, held it with her bum and stepped backwards into the hall.

Dysentery McGhee had, at Gilbert's insistence, been watching for her. 'Megs!' she called. 'Good heavens, Megs. How wonderful. Come here and talk to us, Megs.'

Megs looked over and allowed a small smile to flicker across her lips. 'Hi,' she mouthed and with a nod of her head she indicated the top of the table where she was headed with her load.

'Of course, you can't come chat. You're carrying food. How gross of me,' Cathy McGhee scolded herself.

Megs noted sourly that she was wearing the favourite strappy shoes. Probably had a glass or three of that nice wine before she left, too.

'Bisque?' She looked brightly round.

'Here,' said somebody. 'I'm bisque, and she's a melon,' pointing to his companion.

What did I have? she grumped to herself. Lukewarm Nescafé, a wailing child, and a vague confrontation with my son. That he won. Something's not right. *I want to be happy* – the jolly song, transformed into a small dirge, moved uninvited through her brain.

Across the room, Lorraine was flirting outrageously with a mushroom terrine and a bisque. Megs could tell she had her eye on a bottle of South African white that was so far untouched. So had a couple of the wine waiters. But, Megs knew, against Lorraine they hadn't a chance. She and Lorraine would kill that bottle along with their mushroom terrines when they got home.

On her way back to the kitchen she gave Dysentery McGhee a passing wave, a ripple of fingers. She knew that when she took her bisque to her, Dysentery McGhee would take hold of her and patronise her. There was nothing she could do about it. She was doomed.

And she was right. As soon as the soup bowl hit the table, Dysentery McGhee turned and gripped Megs's hand in both of hers.

'How gorgeous,' she thrilled. 'Our very own waitress. You'll be able to advise us.' Then, seizing the opportunity, 'You'll be able to bring us extra-large portions.'

'Even better,' said Megs, 'I'll be able to bring you extra-small portions.'

Hundred-Miles-An-Hour smiled. Ah, Megs thought, didn't think he could do that. He thought he would welcome smaller portions. This melon was absurdly sweet.

Dysentery McGhee refilled her glass, did not bother with any of the others nearby, and drank deeply. Megs watched. Sometimes she thought Dysentery McGhee was even more screwed up than she was. And this puzzled her.

'You would think,' she said to Lorraine once when they were in Megs's kitchen, doing their Saturday-morning review of their week, 'that she has it all. A good job. A nice house. Furniture. Clothes. A car – a natty black two-seater. Lovers. Note the "s". More than one. No children. Still she's screwed up.'

'Maybe it's the no-children bit,' Lorraine offered. She couldn't conceive and always felt that was part of her own screwed-upness.

'No. She's the sort of person who thinks things through. If she hasn't children it's because she's thought about it and taken that decision. Me now, I never thought about it at all. I got all hormonal one night in bed. I was in the right place, and I had the means lying beside me. Nine months later, bingo, a baby. I never thought about it. That's my problem, I never think things through.'

'Well, you know women,' Lorraine said. 'Give us the perfect relationship, perfect home, perfect job, car, whatever, and we'll make a mess of it. If a woman has the perfect man, she'll wonder if some other man isn't more perfect. Or if life would be more exciting with someone less perfect. Or if she could hack it on her own without the perfect man. Or she'll discover she prefers women. Screwing up? Nothing to us. We can do it every time – speciality of the species.'

By the time Megs served the main course the conversation had turned to seriously considering trivia. Trivia, thought Megs, I'm good at that. Hundred-Miles-An-Hour, remembering his spoon eulogy, was squirming. The measure of his discomfort was showing in his flushed cheeks and sticking-up hair.

'Good heavens,' his companion was saying, 'we go over the top at nothing at all these days. Our sense of excellence is diminished. This is brilliant, that is wonderful. Soon they'll be handing out Pulitzer prizes for T-shirt slogans.'

'I know,' agreed Dysentery McGhee. Her weekday grey-haired man was looking groggy and working his way through a second bottle of red. Megs laid his glazed lamb before him and smiled. Not a lot of fun for Dysentery McGhee when she got home tonight.

As they ate the main course Megs stood with her back to the wall, a discreet sort of lean. She slipped her hot and aching foot from her shoe and pressed it into the cool tiled floor. The massed conversations of the diners merged into a frothing babble. She put her cooled foot back into its shoe, and gave her other foot a cooling on the tiles.

Blah. Blah. Blah, thought Megs. From deep within herself she watched these people. How they drank – you never saw them swig hugely from their glasses yet the wine went down, and down. How they ate – they did not launch themselves into their dinners. They raised their heads, and cooed, 'How lovely.' 'Oh, wicked.' 'Asparagus, I cannot resist asparagus. Mmmm.' Megs wondered if they tasted something she didn't.

'It's only a vegetable,' she said to Lorraine. 'And they're getting orgasms over it. What are they like in bed?'

They would cut things up neatly and put down their forks as they chewed. They looked deeply at whoever was talking and listened with apparent unshakeable interest to whatever was being said, no matter how boring. Mostly what was being said was boring. But women put elbow on table, chin in hand and looked riveted. How did they do that without yawning? Or saying, so what? Or, who cares? Megs wanted to know as she put hot foot number two into its shoe and gave hot foot number one another turn on the cool tiles.

Nobody spilled a drop on their posh frocks and nobody wondered what was number one in the charts this week or what had happened in any of the soaps. It was unreal. But who was she to criticise? They were all tucking into glazed roast lamb with dauphinoise potatoes, baby turnips, glazed carrots and petits pois. She was only here to serve the pudding. And a very fine pudding it was too. She'd already had a couple and there were three more in her bag to take to her children.

Gilbert leaned back in his seat, twirled his wine glass on the table and watched Megs. He thought that if he ever mustered the courage to give up his job, this day job of his, he would like to paint her. She had a comfortable face. It had done a deal of living, that face, expressions moved easily across it. He was beginning to like having Megs in his house. Mornings when she came to him, he would linger, pottering with his bike, filling, emptying, then refilling his battered briefcase before strapping it to the carrier behind his saddle. On Fridays he'd come home early. Hers was a calming presence, he liked to sit in his study and hear her moving quietly from room to room. If he came into the kitchen she would smile at him, and gently scold him for some domestic absurdity she'd discovered. 'I cleaned out that drawer on your kitchen unit. Do you know you had three hundred-and-seventy-five wine corks in it? You could lash them together, build a raft and sail off to France. Take them home.' Her tales revealed small glimpses of her home life. 'I averted a major domestic disaster yesterday. Jack was heating up a tin of tomato soup by putting it unopened in the oven. Could've blown us all up.' He was changing his mind about her, starting to like her.

There are sneezes and there are sneezes. Some sneezes are a long time coming and some take the body by storm. Hundred-Miles-An-Hour was listening to his companion, Annette, talking with passion about cultural renaissance. His hand was hovering at his forehead, fingers poised to run through his hair. And he sneezed. He had not known this horrific thing was going to happen. It was as if the sneeze was some external force that overwhelmed him.

'Aaaaah.' Head pushed back, mouth opened. 'Chooo.' Head flung forward. A single pea, still perfectly formed, burst from his mouth and bounced on to the table in front of him. He watched, horrified. Conversations stilled as diners followed the escapee pea's progress down the centre of the table.

Megs put hot foot number one back in its shoe and gave hot foot two its turn on the tiles. She looked at the floor. It did not do for waitresses to giggle. She sucked in her cheeks.

The table silenced. Gilbert Christie stared, mortified, at the pea that had come to a halt some way down the table. All eyes were on it. Round and ebulliently green against the pristine tablecloth. It shamed him. He did not know what to do about it. But he felt its glistening presence was an effrontery to the other diners. And he felt it was his responsibility, his pea. He rose, and muttering apologies to everyone he passed, he mumbled and grovelled his way towards it. 'Sorry. Sorry. 'Scuse me. Sorry.'

Megs watched. Gilbert reached the pea, and apologising profusely to the people directly in front of it, he stretched over and took it gently between finger and thumb. 'My pea,' he explained. Flustered, blushing deeply, he returned to his seat, where he continued to apologise as he wrapped the pea in his paper napkin and put it in his pocket. He was in hell. Megs knew a tortured soul when she saw one. Her heart went out to him.

Chapter Nine

'If only he'd eaten it,' Lorraine said. 'That'd've made my day.'

They were at the kitchen table finishing the procured South African white, eating mushroom terrines and discussing their evening. Shoes off, feet up.

'He'll be scared of peas for the rest of his life,' said Megs.

'Peaphobia,' Lorraine said.

'One day far from now,' Megs said, 'he'll get those trousers from his wardrobe and put them on. He'll put his hand in his pocket and feel the napkin. What's that? he'll think. And he'll draw it out. And there it'll be. The pea. He'll get all hot and bothered remembering. Poor soul.'

'Why poor soul?' Lorraine wanted to know. 'I thought you thought he was a snob. Face flushed with privilege, you said. You've gone soft on him.' She pointed an accusing finger.

'No. No. I haven't. I can sympathise. He was so embarrassed. I know what it's like when your body lets you down. I'd be fine if it wasn't for my body.'

Lorraine's face was unyielding. The accusation stood.

'Oh, come on.' Megs squirmed. 'He's not my type. Right now he'll be snuggled up with his woman.'

'You think?'

'Yes. And when I go to bed I've got Shameless.'

'You need a man. I think you secretly fancy Gilbert.'

'I do not.' Megs denied it.

'I think you fantasise about him. Actually, all that cycling he does. He's got a nice bum. Quite firm and nubby.' She made a bum-groping movement. 'What do you think he's like in bed?'

'I can't think. Probably sort of sweet and gentle.'

Lorraine thought about this. 'You don't think he's a secret spanker, then? His type often are.'

'How would you know?'

Lorraine looked into her glass. 'I just know. Some things you know. Some things I know.'

'And you know about spanking?'

'I know more about sex than you.'

'Well, I haven't had your affairs.'

'I just need to know I've still got what it takes. Oooh, did you see that waiter at table three?'

'No.'

'Yes you did. I saw you. I could do with some of him. You could do with some of that, too. Watch you don't become like Terribly-Clean Pearson.'

'I will not. I don't ever want another man. I wouldn't know what to do with one. I've left all that flirting and getting to know somebody and everything behind. I wouldn't even know where to start. Where would I meet somebody?'

'Advertise,' said Lorraine. 'In a lonely hearts column.'

Megs smiled. 'What would I say?'

'You're better at that sort of thing than me.'

'Those columns – they're all lies. I could tell the truth. "Lonely cleaner, three children and smelly dog, seeks uncritical lover to cook her meals, run her baths, massage her feet and split mortgage payments."'

'They'll be battering the door down.' Lorraine refilled their glasses.

Megs regularly read the soulmates column in Dysentery McGhee's paper. 'It's all people wanting other people to share theatre, walks and log fires with lots of wine and conversation. When do I ever get to chat to somebody? Or go to the theatre? Or lie in front of a log fire?' She smiled, sudden inspiration. 'Actually, I have thought what I would write. "Woman seeks chum. Any age, any sex, any size, any shape, any star sign, any colour. Simply must not use the word brill to describe anything. Ever. For any purpose."'

'That's not too much to ask,' Lorraine said. 'That's a brill advert.'

Aunty Betty always said that grief either ravaged women or it

82

graced them. Megs had been lucky. Or at least, in the light of her tragedy, her face had been. Her lips did not fall into a bitter slit, her eyes were not bagged and rendered tearless from too much crying. Her face fell into a soulful sulk when she forgot her front and thought nobody was watching her. She was sulking now.

'I feel,' she said, 'that I don't belong anywhere any more. I've lost my place in the world. I don't understand what's going on. Right now a telltale computer is keying up the fact that I'm three months behind with my credit card. Nobody asked me if it could do that. People are sitting in on courses looking at flip charts, getting the gen they need to sell me soap powders and shampoos I don't want, and to get me to sit down and watch TV shows I don't like. I don't know what's going on. Whilst I was busy with my back turned bringing up kids, doing my crap jobs, the world moved on and left me behind. I'm old and I'm fat and I don't belong any more.'

Lorraine looked at her glumly. Considered this a while. At last she said, 'You're not that fat.'

'Suppose,' said Megs.

Lorraine leaned over and touched her hand. 'C'mon, girl,' she said. 'You got to get on with things.'

Megs smiled. She was numb with exhaustion. Her innards felt as if they were already sleeping. It was two in the morning. Outside occasional cars rattled by. Shameless, under the table, snored and shifted. She felt she had been isolated, standing alone with her grief whilst all around her rushed on with their lives. Her children grew up. Her mother retired. Lorraine danced, laughed, teased her husband, had odd affairs and sometimes leaned across the kitchen table, touched her hand, sympathised. 'C'mon girl. You got to get on with things.'

'What things?'

'Life. You know.'

'No I don't. I don't do life. I've forgotten how. How do you meet someone new? How do you get to know someone? And if I do meet someone, how do you kiss for the first time again? And how do you get into bed with someone you don't know? I couldn't. I'm too old. Too flabby. I don't want a stranger looking at me.'

'Oh, come on. If it came to the bit you'd know what to do. Everybody does.'

'I'd be all right if it wasn't for my body. It lets me down. I fart in supermarket queues. I belch. I get hiccups. Intimacy seems terribly difficult. I'd drink too much and say something stupid. Oh no.' She hid her face in her hands, wallowing in her fear and inadequacy. 'I can't do it. I'll never do it again. I'll never have sex again. I'll never lie beside someone and feel his lips against my neck. Or hear him sleep beside me. I'll never wake with someone and we'll turn to each other, toasting warm, sleep still dripping from us, to enfold each other and love. Make love whilst thrushes gather outside on the lawn and distant buses rumble taking morning people to work. Sparrows chatter in the eaves and my hands are in his hair and down his back, and his cheek is rough against me. Never.' She was making herself cry.

'Stop it,' said Lorraine. 'Stop it. You're wallowing.' Megs's description had set up a longing in her. She wanted to rush home to Harry, to lie beside him. Then in the morning do all the things Megs had just said she would be denied for ever. 'Besides, you don't have a garden.'

'I do in my daydreams.'

'Oh, come on. You never know what treats and goodies are out there waiting for you.'

Lorraine was an optimist. Some people thought that life was something that happened to them. A set of occurrences, mostly miserable, that beset them on their bewildered journey from birth to death. But Lorraine believed that life was something wonderful waiting just outside her window for her to come to it. And this she did anew every day.

She was a receptionist with a large insurance company. She wore her hair piled up on her head. She applied careful make-up. All day she said, 'Will you hold?' And, 'That's Mr Makepeace for you now.' And, 'I'm sorry, Mr Harrower is in a meeting.' She painted her nails. She smiled lavishly at visitors. 'Can I help you?' She walked on perfect carpeting. She watered the plants. She got bored. She would lean into the small microphone on her desk and in a soft, confiding voice ask for Albert Einstein or Rolf Harris to report to front office, please. She had occasional affairs. 'It isn't passion,' she told Megs. 'It's curiosity. I want to know what other people are like. What other women have. It's exciting.'

84

Being a receptionist made Lorraine, in Megs's opinion, one of the glacé people. There was a time, Megs thought, when you could go to the dentist or hairdresser and meet folk. A whole range of human beings – fat, thin, shy, brassy – were out there in the world ripe for the meeting and chatting to. There were stories to be told. Now you went somewhere and there was behind the reception desk the same chirpy, glossily friendly person you met at the last reception desk. You met people who'd gone on courses to learn how to be people. They were frosted like glacé fruits. Who'd think a glacé cherry had once been a cherry, dark and red and succulent? Where had the cherry gone? Who'd think the woman behind the desk at the building society, who was interchangeable with the woman behind the desk at the hairdresser's, who was interchangeable with the woman behind the desk at the dentist, was in fact a live and functioning woman who cried at night, hated doing the washing-up and read her horoscope. She was a glacé person. Where, Megs wondered, had all the people gone? And where did the real Lorraine go during the day? What became of her? Sometimes she thought Lorraine only came out at night.

'I have to go,' Lorraine said now. 'Poor old Harry will be wondering where I've got to.' She reached for her coat. 'We could do a breakfast sandwich. Egg, bacon and tomato in a warm roll.'

Before she was a receptionist she worked at a make-up counter. One of those terrifying, over-made-up front-of-the-shop people who told you you needed a matt foundation 'for your skin, darling' and made you feel just terrible. Before that she sold cars. And before that something else and before that something else. She couldn't settle. Recently, though, the idea of a sandwich bar appealed to her. 'I'd be my own boss,' she told Harry. 'I could serve sandwiches in a French maid's outfit. That'd go down a treat.'

'No wife of mine . . .' started Harry. Lorraine held up her hand, shushed him. In the end they settled for jeans and a T-shirt. 'Scoop-necked,' said Lorraine, indicating with a sweep of her fingers across her tits the depth of the scoop she had in mind.

'Yes,' said Megs, stirring herself. If she didn't get up now, she'd be too tired to go to bed. 'And a date and cheese and apple might go well mid-morning. I'll never sleep with anyone again. It's over for me.'

'Rubbish. A smoked haddock with mayo and cayenne could go. People are into fish these days. Of course it isn't over for you. You'll find someone. I know you will.'

'Rubbish. Who'd want me? It's over I tell you. Smoked fish repeats on me.'

'Bet it isn't. You don't have to eat it, then.'

'How much?'

'Bet you a fiver.'

'You're on. A fiver that my sex life is over for ever and ever.'

On her way out the door Lorraine said, 'Actually, I don't know what you're on about. You're not fat at all.'

After Lorraine had gone, Megs stared glumly into the fridge. The only thing in there was a pack of bacon with one drying slice in it, a wrinkly tomato, a tiny lump of cheese and several ketchup bottles. She would have to shop tomorrow. She felt vaguely thankful that her diminished supplies saved her from her longing to eat and eat.

It was two-thirty, and Shameless was hovering by the front door, looking guilty. If she did not take him out he would, she knew, disgrace himself. Reluctantly she put on his leash and walked him to the small scrubland park at the end of the road. She hunched herself against her imagination. Muggers, thieves and rapists were about. Every distant step, rustle of wind, slow rattle of empty crisp bag drifting along pavement made her stop. Her stomach chilled. When she stopped, expecting something dreadful to happen, the silence was appalling.

She stood clutching her coat round her, shifting from foot to foot, waiting for Shameless to pee. 'Hurry up. Hurry up.' The dog ran gleefully, nose glued to the ground, tail waving. There were fresh scents, scurryings of urban wildlife on dewy grass. He was in no hurry to go home.

Right now, she thought, everyone I know is in bed curled against a fellow being. And I am alone in this park waiting to be mugged. Lorraine will be snuggling into Harry. Gilbert Hundred-Miles-An-Hour Christie will no doubt be hanging on to that woman, if the sneeze did not put her off for ever. Mrs Terribly-Clean Pearson will be sleeping sensibly next to Mr Terribly-Clean Pearson, both wearing safe, no-nonsense pyjamas. Emotionally-Deranged Davis will be heaving the bed clothes from Mr Emotionally-Deranged Davis, giving him a lecture on duvet sharing and whose bit of bed is whose. Dysentery McGhee will be zonked out next to her weekday grey-haired man. Mike will be lying spoonlike next to Denise. My mother will be lying with my father in the bed they've shared for over forty years. Even their teeth will be companionably soaking side by side in glasses in the bathroom. I'm alone. Alone, she thought. Too late for me. She stood perfectly still, listening to the night: lorries trundling on the main road and a wheezing, a vile snorting and hoarse breathing behind her.

Her stomach curdled. Blood crystallised in her veins. Her breath stopped in her throat. She thought to run, but knew it to be a mistake. Walk, she told herself. Walk naturally. Do not look round. She put Shameless on his leash and headed out of the park. The snorting and wheezing did not stop. It was there. It was real. She moved faster. Shameless, sensing something behind her, turned and lunged.

'Come on, dog,' she ordered. 'Home.'

The vile snufflings got closer. Oh God, she thought, I am going to die. Nobody will miss me. I'll be found in the morning. Savagely beaten, skirt wrapped round my waist and Shameless looming over me, breathing foully. The thing behind coughed and dragged its spluttered breath. How dare someone frighten her? How dare he do this? She should be able to take her dog out unmolested. Suddenly furious, she whirled round. 'Leave me alone.' Nothing. She glared back up the path. Where had he gone? The bastard. How dare he disappear? She was fired up with fury, and ready to berate him for scaring her. Shameless lunged again. She looked down. A hedgehog was shuffling and snorting, a wheezing waddle, making its flea-bitten way along the path.

Humbled, foolish and crying with relief, she ran all the way home, panting and turning, checking for muggers, thieves and rapists. Heart pounding.

Home and straight to bed. Clothes torn off and thrown to the floor. Covers over head, shivering in the dark. All I want is someone who will hold me and tell me I'm wonderful. Someone who will lie to me when I need it, she thought. But this is me – a loveless fool who faces up to hedgehogs.

Chapter Ten

It was summer when it happened. Megs was wearing a short red T-shirt dress, dark tights. She never wore that dress again. A Wednesday. Business was brisk seven days a week at the market garden. So for the gardening months, Megs worked Sundays for double pay and took Wednesdays off.

'I'll collect you from school,' she told Thomas. 'Don't you go setting off without me.'

She would curse herself for saying that. 'I shouldn't've said it. It was a challenge. He thought he would come home on his own and arrive saying, "Look at me. I did it without you." Children are like that. They spend their little lives proving they're not children.' She would agonise and reprimand herself for the rest of her life.

She left the house well after three. A little late, but no hurry really. The school was only ten minutes' walk away and it was such a good day. She'd take her time, a slow stroll through the heat. She bought him a can of Coca-Cola. He would come to her, as children did when set free at the end of the school day, tumbling and tearing across the playground like puppies spilling from their basket. He'd trail his bag along the ground. His school jersey would be tied by the sleeves round his waist. Shirt hanging out of trousers. Hands grubby and sweatily damp after an afternoon wrestling with pencils, paints and school glue.

'Anything to eat?' he'd say. She would hand him his drink and a chocolate bar. It was a routine they went through every Wednesday.

She met Josh. One of those long, slow encounters that last the length of the street. She saw him approach and couldn't decide who he was, or how she knew such a creature. He shambled towards her, smiling slightly. She frowned, chewed her gum – who was that?

'Hello, Megs,' he said. Smiling. Bad teeth.

'Hello,' she said. Trying not to smile too much. Trying to pass by. She stared at him. The features were familiar – where had she met him?

'You don't know me, do you?'

She felt it rude to admit it, but slowly shook her head. 'No. Sorry.'

'Josh,' he told her. 'Remember? With the band?' She could not hide her shock.

'Josh? Josh? Is that you?' This could not be him.

She remembered Josh beautiful. He used to shut his eyes when he played, his lips would move with some song only he knew. He had blond hair that flowed over his face when he leaned down, checking his fingers. Women would gather to watch him with blatant longing. They did not bother to flirt, they just wanted him. Now look at him. He'd spent too much of the five years since she'd last seen him in his head. It was not a pretty place to be. Loneliness, poverty and isolation had ruined him. He was in tatters. His jeans were threadbare and lifeless, raggy at the bottom. His left shoe was open at the tip and a single sad toe stuck grubbily into the daylight. He wore a greying T-shirt that had once been black. Over that a shirt, no buttons, threads hanging from the collar. The cuffs hung out from the sleeves of his denim jacket. His hair was long, tangled. Nicotined fingers, nails rimmed dirty. He hid them in his pockets. He smelled of old booze and cigarettes. Stubble on his chin. He spoke slowly, pausing to swallow every few words, as if he'd lost the knack of casual conversation. They communicated with silences and apologies.

'Sorry,' she said. 'I wasn't thinking about the band. I couldn't place you. You know how it is.' In the distance a siren sounded.

He smiled. 'Sorry,' he said. Indicating himself, all of him. He was a mess. 'Sorry. Things haven't been going so good. How are you? What are you doing?'

'Still at the market garden. Still potting geraniums.' She smiled. Shoved her head to one side. A little apology for not having a grand tale to tell. 'And you?' she asked. As if she needed to. His appearance said it all.

'This and that,' he said. 'I still play, you know.' He shuffled a little, scratched his head, apologising for the lie. 'Are you singing?'

'Friday nights down the Glass Bucket. Come see me. Actually, I quite like it. I do old Bessie Smith numbers and Billie. Stuff I couldn't do with the band. It's good.' She nodded. Yes, it was good. Really it was good.

'Um,' he said. He grinned embarrassment. Hand moving to scratch his head again. Apologising in advance for what he was about to do.

He's going to touch me for a fiver, thought Megs.

'Um.' Again. 'Don't suppose you've any money on you? Only I need a bit right now. Got to see someone about a job. And . . .'

She reached out to touch him, silence him. No need to apologise. When they were young they had sat side by side in the back of a van, day upon day. She had sat moving with the rumble of wheels on the road, sucking Strepsils, staring vacuously at her companions, the way people do when they have travelled too far together and there is nothing left to say.

'Ciggie?' He'd offer her a battered packet of Camels.

She would look at the pack and lift her lazy, empty eyes to his, shaking her head. 'Nope.' Silence again. That small piece of communication was all they could manage.

She remembered he always stood up for her in a way Mike didn't. Mike wanted to be one of the lads during the day and to come to her bed at night. Mike wanted everything. Once on the way from Inverness to Perth, travelling down the A9, they stopped to let her out to pee. Lately, she'd noticed she was always needing to pee.

'Again,' the others complained. She was beginning to suspect there was more to this recurring need to empty her bladder than the amount she'd drunk. Could she be pregnant?

Three o'clock in the morning and chilly. Shivering in the sudden cold, she stepped into the undergrowth, carefully placing her feet, afraid of what unseen ditches and tangled heather roots might do to her ankles. She wandered further than she planned. Outdoor peeing was the only time she ever suffered penis envy, no matter what Freud said. Men had it easy. Squatting in the undergrowth, bum shining white in the night, she worried about lurking strangers in bushes behind her, observing. Then, pulling up her knickers, she felt she'd captured half the insect population in them.

But when she'd done she relaxed and started to like the night. It was soft, sweet. She stood idly scratching her arse before making her way slowly back to the road, trailing her hand on the long grasses. Tiny moths sleepily rose at her touch, seeds and pollen spread. It was not dark, just the textured grey of northern summer. Distant mountains, thunderous, still as lions, shouldered the sky.

She did not want to go back. This silky, cold air was cleansing. . She lingered. Tugged up some heather to put on the front bumper of the van. Only when she got back to the road, it was gone. She looked after it, the way it must have gone, then started to slowly walk, sniffing her heather. They were playing a trick. They'd be just round the corner. Waiting. But they weren't. She walked on down the road. A little faster, she could not see the tail lights. She started to run. Alone in this place with nothing for miles and miles. Running, hearing her feet on the tarmac. She was wearing silly shoes – open-toed slingbacks. What had become of them? What could become of them in a few minutes in this place? A small dread started within her. She could feel it. Something had happened and they'd moved on without her. Something had happened to Mike. They were racing him to hospital. She still ran. Still clutching her heather.

They blasted the horn, put on the lights and flooded her with panic. They had been coming slowly behind all that time. Instead of pulling ahead they'd backed up round the corner. Then they followed her. The horn rasped again, they knocked on the windscreen and laughed. It seemed it was them against her. She turned to scream at them. Hated them seeing her like this. Crying because she was alone and afraid. 'Bastards,' she shouted. 'Bastards. Let me in.'

The van pulled past her and stopped. She reached the back door, stretched out for the handle and the van pulled away from her. She chased it. Reached the door, stretched for the handle and again the van moved away. She chased again, stretched again for the door and again they pulled away. She gave up. Let her arms drop miserably to her sides and slouched behind them. Her sweat chilled to goosebumps. 'Stop it. Stop it. Stop it.' They opened the door and called to her. She always remembered Mike's face. It was more than laughing. He was enjoying her pain. 'Let me in,' she said. 'Let me in.' Josh put a stop to it. 'Pack it in,' he called. And reaching out for her, pulled her into the van. 'Let her be.' She was crying, had thrown her precious heather to the side of the road. 'Bastards,' she said. Josh handed her a hankie, 'It was only a joke,' he said. 'We didn't mean nothing.' Three days later the band split up.

She took five pounds from her purse and handed it to him. Apologising. 'Sorry.' Sorry for having some money. For getting by. Sorry for not being true to my ambitions, for selling out. For surviving, when you obviously are not.

He took it. 'Sorry,' he said. 'You were the best.' Genuine admiration. 'It was you. We all knew it was you. Everyone said so. Did Mike ever get round to telling you about the bloke?'

'Bloke? What bloke?'

The distant sirens turned to hyper. A wild panic that clattered and vibrated the air. It became more than a sound. It was a hard and tangible thing that dinned and howled through the air, bouncing off walls, hollering above the rooftops. Clanging and foreboding. Face fraught with dread, she turned in the direction of the uproar. Thomas.

'I have to go,' she said. 'I've to pick up my son.' She turned and fled. Josh held the money up, thanking her. Then he went back to the pub.

Megs ran through the streets to the school. All the way, every step, she knew the sirens were for her. Urgency and horror were stamped on her face. People stepped aside, turned to watch her go. 'Oh no. Oh no. Oh no,' she wheezed. There was scarcely a breath left in her. She was rushing through the noise.

The child was already covered when she arrived. 'No,' was all she could say. 'No. No. No.' Police cars, an ambulance. Whirling lights. The policeman stepped aside to let her past. No need to explain, he could see who she was. She dropped to her knees on the road. Reached out and touched him. It was the last time she ever felt his little body. She leaned over him. Her mouth was open. Hand reaching out. She was gasping. When she looked up, two policemen and an ambulance nurse were standing over her, bending down to her to stop her from collapsing. She put her hand to her face. 'Oh,' she wailed out loud. 'Oh.'

That moment of coming into view, seeing him lying, the policeman holding his school satchel. The way everyone turned to her. That moment kept coming back to her, for years and years it returned. It arrived in her head, always uninvited. And always, always as vividly as it had been when it happened. There it was. Every time she'd look wildly round to find someone who might save her from drowning, from reeling and crying. But every time there was never anybody there.

If only. If only she hadn't met Josh. Or stopped to buy the Coke. Or thought she had lots of time. She would have arrived before school closed. She would have taken him home. He would have told her about his day. What he ate for lunch. The little story he'd written about Captain Scarlet, his hamster. She kept reconstructing that afternoon as it ought to have been. She would have held his hand all the way home. She would never have let it go.

In the evening she sat frozen in grief by the gas fire. It hissed warmth. Megs was cold though summer shimmered outside. People on telly dressed thinly in the heat, frolicked in fountains. Tonight's national news. Vivienne came to her. She carried a yellow plastic basin, warm water clouded with Dettol slapping against the sides. A smell of disinfectant.

'Your knees,' she said. 'I have to fix your knees.'

Megs looked without really seeing. There were two huge holes in her tights where she had dropped down beside Thomas. Her knees shone whitely through them. They were pitted with grit and dried blood. She hadn't noticed. Vivienne gently dipped cotton wool into the cloudy water, squeezed it and drew it across the open wounds. She'd thought her days of wiping and bathing were over. 'What a mess you've got yourself into,' she said.

Chapter Eleven

Gilbert was at home when Megs arrived, carrying her vacuum. He was looking his hundred-miles-an-hour self, hair on end and agitated. She was in good form. The thing about the late-night contretemps with the hedgehog was that it had set her up for a night's undisturbed sleep. Her first in years.

He skulked in his study but still the house was filled with the quiet rage he was working up imagining all the cruel things that were being said about him behind his back. Everybody he knew was laughing at him. He listened to Wagner, always a barometer of his despair. At the moment it was a gnawing drone. But by evening, when his angst reached full howl, it would be roaring, and his neighbours would all know that Gilbert was suffering.

Megs moved mouselike from room to room, going through her routine. She stripped his bed, trying not to notice that he'd slept alone last night. The pea from hell, she thought. He's going to let it ruin his life. The dark hum of German opera battered the walls. Getting louder. When she left for the laundrette she could hear it outside. When she came back she could hear it at the end of the road.

It filled the house as she polished and wiped. She thought that what she did was so mindless nothing could distract her. But she was wrong. There was nothing like Wagner blaring to put a person off life's little mundanities, such as cleaning the bath and doing someone else's pile of dirty dishes, a week's pile. She was in the kitchen, working through the clattering greasy mound, hands encased in pink rubber gloves, when he came in, scowling.

'Is there a cup?' he said. 'I want some coffee.'

She nodded at the neat row of cups in his cupboard. He took one. Put on the kettle and stood waiting for it to boil, hands deep in the pockets of his training pants, staring out at his back garden. Sometimes he switched his gaze back at the kettle. Occasionally he flapped his pants. He did not speak. How could someone fret so much over a small incident?

The kettle boiled. He took a paper filter from its pack, placed it on a jug, scooped out three spilling spoons of Colombian blend and poured boiling water over it. A thick, bitter smell of coffee flooded the room.

His nerves were catching. Megs could feel them round her throat and deep in her nostrils with the coffee. She felt that his nerves and this overwhelming smell of coffee were crowding her out of the room.

'Oh, for heaven's sake.' She could no longer contain herself. 'It was only a pea.'

He glared at her. Cup paused halfway to his lips. The cheek of the woman, scolding him. 'What do you know about peas?' he demanded. 'What do you know about sneezing?'

She snorted. 'A pea,' she said scathingly, 'valuable source of riboflavin, lactoflavin, pyridoxine and magnesium. A sneeze,' she said, 'involuntary expulsion of air from nose and mouth. Caused by cold, allergy and sometimes emotional tension.' She was quoting from *The Bumper Book of Home Medicines*, by Fanny Tryer. A huge, once scarlet but now faded pink, crumbling and extremely dubious reference tome that had been in her family for over fifty years. Vivienne had consulted it often during Megs's childhood. Between its pages old postcards were lovingly preserved and flowers pressed. The advice it offered, however, was dire. It recommended milk of magnesia or caster oil for everything from flu to sprained ankles and duodenal ulcers. The very sight of Vivienne slowly turing its wafer-thin pages was enough to make Megs declare herself cured of whatever had been ailing her. No illness was worse than the effects of a double dose of laxative.

'The longest recorded bout of sneezing,' Megs pushed past Gilbert, pulled a clean dishcloth from the drawer, flapped it open and started to dry his week's cups, 'was a woman in Hereford who sneezed more than two million times over a period of nine hundred and seventy-six days.' 'Startling Stories – Sensneezional', from the tabloid she'd used to line Terribly-Clean Pearson's bin a month ago. 'That's two thousand sneezes a day. Eighty-five an hour and over one a minute.' Hannah and Jack had worked it out with their calculator when she'd told them about it. It was the most interest in anything mathematical they'd ever shown. She dried as she spoke, shoving the red-and-white-striped towel down inside the cups, turning them briskly, squeaking dampness from them. 'Think about that. The mountain of peas you would have left if that had happened to you.' Reaching for another cup, her tenth, 'However bad it seems, it could be worse.' She wished she believed that.

He sipped coffee. Never thought to offer her some. Words formed on his mouth, but came to nothing. Melted instead into the wordless depths of his quandary. He thought he might never go out again.

'My goodness.' Megs was in full flow. An undisturbed night's sleep made her chatty and bossy with it. 'Last night I found myself shouting the odds at a hedgehog.'

'A hedgehog?'

'Yes. It was coming along behind me in the park and I thought it was a man. Snuffling and wheezing. You know, I was sure I was about to be murdered and raped.'

He wondered if that was the right order of ordeals.

'So I turned on him and told him to leave me alone. I really told him.'

'A hedgehog?'

'I thought it was a bloke. A murderer. A rapist.'

He wanted to say that not all blokes were murderers and rapists. He refilled his cup, cradled it between his palms and said nothing. He lived alone. He'd left behind long ago the need to communicate.

So she interpreted his silence for him. Decided what he was thinking. He'd made up his mind that she was a scatter-brain, prone to hysterical impulses. She knew she was a fool. Had rushed home along the street, dog scampering easily beside her as she moved, wheezing and leaden. Her black high heels clicked frantically on the pavement. Fleeing from the hedgehog.

'Well,' she excused herself, 'there you go. Silly me.'

He looked her way, gave her a small, watery smile.

'Good God,' she went on, 'can't you laugh at yourself? What's the good of all your books and your damn education if you can't even laugh at yourself?'

He did not know. He thought he should be working. 'Um,' he told her. 'Um. Help yourself to coffee.'

She turned to the jug, but it was empty.

She cleaned his house. She vacuumed and did not care about the din she made. When he came to her, she shoved the violent machine up and down between them. The great hooing wail a noisy wall to hide behind. He leaned down, switched it off. The silence made her vulnerable.

'Shouldn't you be going?' he asked. 'Isn't your little girl waiting?'

'My mother picks her up.'

'Your money's on the table.'

'Thank you.' She walked stiffly past him, unplugged the vacuum, then returned to the machine, pressed the button and the cord snaked across the room, rattled into the body of the vacuum.

'Goodness,' he said. 'How handy. You won't have the cord trailing.'

'Yes.' She was sarcastic now. 'They do that. Machines made since the nineteen-twenties do that.'

'Can I carry it to your car for you?' he said.

'I can manage.'

'I know. But I can do it for you. Save you.'

She wondered if it was surly of her to refuse. Didn't care if she was surly.

'I'm OK.'

'Only.' His hand moved to his hair, hovered a moment, then plunged in, ruffling it, pushing it upwards. She watched. Felt compelled to copy him. Clenched her fist lest she did.

'Only,' he said, 'I was wondering – what's the point of your damn lecture if you won't let a chap carry your vacuum for you?'

He did not bother with her consent. He lifted the machine and walked down the path, leaning awkwardly to one side against its small weight. Awkwardly, because it was an alien thing to him. He only ever carried books, a briefcase, and occasionally his bike – upside-down, slow wheel ticking round and round.

'Is this your car?' He thought he was hiding his dismay. But it showed. He had long lost the knack of controlling his facial expressions.

The car was fifteen years old and orange. His most hated colour. One of its many previous owners had put a sticker in the back window – WINDSURFERS DO IT STANDING UP. He read and was horrified.

'Dunno who put that there.' Megs read his face. 'I bought it with the car.'

'Ah.' He did not understand why she had not removed it the instant she got it home.

She opened the boot for him. He gently laid the vacuum in beside the vast accumulation of motoring rubbish: maps, welly boots, carrier bags, a selection of various-size anoraks and jerseys, a cracked thermos, towels, a dog bowl and spare leash. A cheap, brightly coloured Indian durry lay over the back seat. It was covered with toys, children's books, clothes, a pair of red canvas shoes and a big silver balloon. For a second he fancied being a child again, being driven in that car, sitting barefoot on that durry playing with the balloon. In a lavish bit of courteous behaviour he took her key and opened the driver's door for her. Paused only a moment to consider, surprise and confusion flickering over his face, the cans of diet Coke, the chocolate wrappers, discarded parking tickets, sunglasses, raincoat, battered copy of Vita Sackville-West, and spilling of cassettes pouring from the rack beside the gear stick on to the floor: Billie Holiday, Bessie Smith, Etta James, Janis Joplin.

'Thank you,' she said, getting in. Though she hated people seeing the inside of her car, she was only vaguely ashamed of the rubbish she carried back and forth daily through the city. She switched on the ignition. 'I'd Rather Go Blind.' Etta blared and soared. The blast widened their eyes.

'Sorry, sorry,' she said, unable to find the volume control for noise and guilt. 'I forgot I had it so loud.'

She calmed the din, shifted into first and smiled goodbye. 'See you next week.'

He stood, watching the car rattle and splutter down the street. She was his cleaning lady. He'd had only small glimpses of her life. Oh, he imagined her leading the conga line, singing jolly songs, or trailing a howling squall of thin-lipped, TV-eyed, pallid children. That was the sort of thing cleaning women did. Wasn't it? This one, however, had a book that had obviously been opened, music she listened to. And yes, he had started to find her domestic presence comforting. But now he was fascinated. Changing his opinion of her was hard work. He fantasised about laying his head on her breast. She would stroke his hair and sort out his turmoil. 'It's all right, Gilbert. It was only a pea, Gilbert.' He stared down the empty street, rearranging his thoughts. His hand moved slowly up to his hair, fingers raked through it, shoving it upwards.

Chapter Twelve

Gilbert was an only child. A precious boy with a silver lonestar gun and a red holster. He rode the range making clip-clop horsy noises on the back of the chesterfield in his daddy's study, alone. His father, a barrister, had died of a stroke when Gilbert was ten. Gilbert had no friends. His parents could find nobody suitable. Other children were too rough, or they had atrocious table manners, or they were too silly, too common or just generally not quite up to snuff. Children, Gilbert's mother noted in horror (and if she'd noted this in time she wouldn't have had one), picked their noses, fiddled with their genitals when they got nervous or excited, had grubby knees, asked silly questions, never sat still at dinner and spoke during *Gardeners' Question Time*. All his life, then, Gilbert had felt conspicuous and uncertain. He apologised when he entered rooms, and again when he left them, even if nobody else was there.

When he was four Gilbert was taken to his first opera – *The Marriage of Figaro*. He took a dislike to the Count, stood up pointing at the stage and screamed, 'I don't like that man.' His mother took his hand and yanked him from his seat and out of the theatre. Once in the street, round the corner and out of sight, she shook him viciously. 'We do not shout at Counts in the opera,' she hissed. Shake. Shake. For days afterwards she mourned that Gilbert was turning into quite an unsuitable sort of person.

When he was eight he was given a giant paintbox. It had a number three sable brush and one hundred colours, each one a tiny square: magenta, crimson, ochre, sepia. His favourite was midnight. A deep, fathomless blue that set up a longing in him. He never knew what it was he longed for. He felt he belonged in this endless blueness, he could plunge into it and be happy. He bought *The Junior World of Watercolours* with his pocket money and taught himself painting. He did washes, letting water then paint flood the page, dark at the top, paling, paling down. He watched the colour flow. He painted skies and hills, then moved on to flowers. When that started to bore him he turned to sketching.

He drew trees, the sea, horses, old buildings, walls covered with ivy in a series of sketch pads that with use grew battered and coated with a fine-powdered skim of charcoal. He taught himself the art of practical staring – he took in what he saw. Trees, he noted, had a rhythm and symmetry. No tip grew out further than the others. As they spread out into the sky, so they spread into the ground – roots reaching out as far below as branches above. He drew all this leaning into his little A5 books, perfectly honed, lovingly tended pencils scrutting over the page. His face twisting and contorting the while, reflecting the moments, passions, pleasures he was drawing. When he drew an old man smiling with unabashed joy, he smiled with unabashed joy. When he drew a tree he imagined to be wise and worn with weather and time, his eyebrows knit, his brow furrowed, mouth slid downwards at the corners, his face became wise and worn with weather and time.

His mother was proud. She turned the attic into a studio for Gilbert, where the boy could be alone and develop his talent. He had, at last, proved himself suitable to be her son.

Gilbert's mother, Muriel Christie, was tall, formidable. She pulled her hair severely from her face and tied it behind. A no-nonsense hairdo that intensified her imperiousness. She never walked. She strode, slapping one sensibly clad foot in front of the other, eyes fixed on the horizon. And when she spoke she threw her voice forward, a great welter of words that boomed across rooms, across shop floors, stations and doctors' surgeries. 'Gilbert has swollen nipples.' There were no secrets, only scarlet shame. She looked power-dressed in bathrobe and slippers.

By the time Gilbert was fourteen he had abandoned watercolours and sketching and turned to oils and acrylics. He worked alone in his cluttered attic, his private space. He painted his name on the door, 'Gilbert's Room – Keep Out'. He dreamed of going to art college when he left school. He would wear paint-splattered jeans and a black T-shirt or a round-neck sweater with the sleeves rolled up. He would grow his hair long, drink beer, talk about art and life and have, he hoped, a small, thin, blonde girlfriend who would sit close to him in the pub. He would keep his arm round her.

Now he painted on canvas that he carried to his loft in great rolls, cut out and stretched over wooden frames he built himself. Every new canvas he started was bigger than the one he'd just finished. He lost his fascination for trees and old men and became interested in surrealism. He bought books on Dali and Magritte. He painted a toad sitting on a roof gloating down at naked women-tadpole creatures dancing, leaping whilst a tall, phantom-like scowl – a severe hairdo, vast flat feet and in between nothing but a womb – stood apart, fearsome and disapproving. He painted that same phantom-scowl standing beside a bath full of naked women-toads, lathering and laughing. As he painted canvas after canvas the naked women-toads dropped their toadishness, became simply women, and larger and larger, whilst the scowl with the intense haircut got smaller and smaller till it was minuscule and hysterical beside the languorous ladies. Then it disappeared. The late works of Gilbert Christie, aged sixteen, showed only huge women, rolling and frolicking, leaping, dancing in rings, hair flying, thunderous thighs rippling. Sometimes they were writhing on a soft forest floor in bacchanalian glee. They were all stark naked. And they were always, always joyous.

Sometimes he was in his paintings, a tiny soul dwarfed between two vast, quivering snow-capped tits, or mountaineering his way along a huge stomach towards a dense forest of pubic hair. In one, an enormous woman was lying on her back, propped on her elbows, legs bent, open slightly. She was a bed – pillows, sheets, eiderdown on her vast, comfortable tummy. Gilbert was tucked up sweetly under the covers, head on pillow, eyes shut and smiling a little soft, smirky smile. Beside him lay another woman, one his own size. She also was smiling. This was to be his last painting.

One day Gilbert came home from school to find the house in turmoil. His mother was in a fury that was so intense he could sense it, feel it in his guts as he walked up the path. It was five o'clock, a summer afternoon in the suburbs. The air was vibrating rage. It came in black waves from the front door, stormed down the path, and the very pansies and lupins growing on the borders trembled. Gilbert stood, hand on door knob, contemplated running away, a notion that haunted him. He could run away. He could just turn now, down the path, out the gate and away. Away, away he could go, running faster and faster. Down the street, round the corner, away for ever. He could disappear in the city, live frugally in a bedsit, earn a crust working in cafés or delivering milk. Or he could find a cave on a hillside somewhere and live wild, eating berries, snaring rabbits. He would sleep on a bed of moss and bracken. He would be free, he had no need of paltry bourgeois comforts. He was an artist. He need never see his mother again.

He went in. She was standing in the hall, blocking the light, glowering the glower of an insane empress. Hands on hips.

'Come through here,' she said. Her voice was soft with menace. She was terrifying. He followed her into the living room. All his paintings were lined up, propped against the wall. All his laughing ladies looking wanton and voluptuous. Their frenzied frolicking made him feel foolish and guilty. His mother had the knack of making him feel smaller than he was. He felt his face slide into an expression of oily sycophancy. He hated himself. She always did that to him.

'I can explain,' he said.

'Explain!' His mother had abandoned the soft menace mode and reverted to her normal boom. 'No need to explain. There is nothing to explain. I do not want an explanation. I want this rubbish out of the house. NOW.' She pointed, arm quivering, finger stiff with intent. 'Burn them, Gilbert,' she demanded.

He should have refused. He should have stood his ground. Put himself defiantly between insane mother and paintings and protected them. All his life, in agonising reruns of that afternoon, he knew that was what he ought to have done. But he didn't. Perhaps if his father had been alive . . .? he wondered. But he wasn't. So Gilbert said nothing. He carried his beloved paintings, one by one, out into the garden, across the long lawn, round behind the hedge, past the vegetable plots to the bonfire patch. His arms were outstretched full width, only his fingertips curled round the edges of his masterworks. Every now and then he had to stop, put down the canvas he was carrying and adjust his grip. Then he would peek over the top, checking his route. Muriel Christie's garden was her passion. Stepping off her official paths across lawn and round edges of vegetable plots was a sin.

Trip after trip he made, placing the canvases one on top of the other. When he was done his mother fetched the old black paraffin can from the shed and grimly handed it to him. He emptied it on to the pile, and, glugging, paraffin rushed over the paint. She gave him a kitchen box of matches. He lit one, watched it fizz into flame, then threw it on to the pile. The fire shot up, a searing blue-yellow whoosh of heat higher than the hedges, spitting and splattering sparks. Gilbert felt his eyes widen, he stepped closer to it. For a moment he thought he might throw himself on to the pyre. But he didn't. He turned and walked back into the house, still saying nothing.

His silence enraged Muriel even more. She stood, hands on hips, glaring at the blaze, then she turned to stride after her son, shouting, 'Trees. Seascapes. Flowers. That's what you said you were doing. Not this . . . this . . .' She groped about in her mind for a word. 'Filth,' she said. She was searching for something to make her behaviour reasonable. Gilbert did not reply.

He went to his room, shut the door and sat on his bed. There would be no art college now. No paint-splattered jeans, no passionate talk of life and art. There would be no little blonde girlfriend who adored him. He could see that now. None of that was for him. How foolish he was to imagine that he could join in such a world. When he left school he studied art history, but found painful this association with art that did not involve him in actual painting. So he switched to studying the history of design. In time he gained a small, specialist, international reputation for his studies on packaging in the twentieth century.

During his last two years at home, Gilbert shut himself off from his mother. He felt shame in her presence. Their conversation was limited to passing comments in the hall. 'Excuse me.' 'Have you seen the evening paper?' 'Take your coat if you're going out, Gilbert. It looks like rain.'

Gilbert studied. His mother gardened. Every afternoon when he came home from school she was kneeling on the lawn, face close to the earth, trowelling, weeding, muttering to herself. She snipped and preened, watered and fertilised. Everything outside the house flourished in vast, spilling bursts of colour. In summer blue tits and chaffinches hopped on the lawns and moved in undulating flights from cherry tree to weeping willow to bird table to feed on the bacon strips and cake crumbs that were lovingly laid out for them. Tamed, they came to Muriel's call. 'Come on, birdies. Tweet, tweet,' raising that dictatorial boom an octave, softening it. 'Tea time.'

Standing at his bedroom window, hands in pockets, Gilbert would watch her. The house turned musty and dank. A thin coating of dust lay on the dressers and along the top of the picture frames. A milky film formed on the windows so that it was hard to see out. Then again, it was also hard to see in – swings and roundabouts. The fridge was empty, biscuits went soft in the tin with a picture of Buckingham Palace on the lid. Gilbert left school, toured France and Italy for six weeks and started university. He hardly ever went home.

It was 1971, the sixties were still buzzing. People wore fabulously silly clothes, headbands, flowered shirts, absurd trousers, Afghan coats. They were gloriously, noisily gaudy, except Gilbert. His sensible, no-nonsense outfit – tweed jacket, flannels and shiny brown brogues – made him conspicuous. It seemed to him that he moved joylessly through crowds of vibrant people arguing politics and feminism, listening to ostentatious music and dancing. When he was invited to join in, he couldn't. He stood on the edge looking on. What was it all about? He couldn't debate. He didn't understand the songs. And dance? He couldn't dance. His legs wouldn't do what his brain told them to do. They took on a life of their own, kicking, tripping people up, stepping on partners' toes. His knees jutted out. They did all their mischief at their own pace. No matter what music was playing, Gilbert always danced to his own clumsy tune.

Chapter Thirteen

It wasn't a good day. Mrs Emotionally-Deranged Davis ran out of money. Again. Mrs Emotionally-Deranged Davis only took her own money seriously. Amounts she owed to other people did not make it into her accounting system. Bills took her by surprise.

'Oh my goodness, Megs,' she said, breezing into the kitchen, stuffing her hand into her wallet, opening it wide, staring into it with affected consternation, 'I seem to have run out of cash. I'll see you next week.' She laid her hand, briskly, briefly on Megs's arm.

'That's what you said last week,' said Megs, looking grimly at the hand on her arm.

'Did I?'

Megs looked round. There were signs of financial frolicking everywhere. Julia Davis never arrived home from any sort of trip without bringing in yet another bag stuffed with some sort of consumer goods. Megs wondered that the house could continue to contain all that was brought into it week by week, day by day: CDs, books, bottles, clothes, cushions, plants – endless things. These people made affluence seem ordinary.

A bottle of wine with a small swilling left at the bottom stood on the kitchen table beside an overflowing fruit bowl. In Megs's house that fruit bowl would contain only stalks and a twiggish skeleton that had once been a bunch of grapes. Food in her house did not last. In this house half-empty packs of smoked chicken, dried up, white-spotted with age, were tossed into the bin. Exotic vegetables bought only out of mild interest and supermarket trolley upmanship were turning to decay in the fridge.

On the wall there was a framed photograph of the family on

holiday in Provence. They were sitting round a table on a veranda high up on a hillside, behind them slopes of vines and across the valley in the distance another château where another family was probably doing the same thing – being photographed drinking wine, wearing summer clothes and smiling.

It was the hand on her arm that did it. It was Emotionally-Deranged Davis's assumption that a small piece of physical contact was enough for her. A reassuring little pat would keep her going till next week. This woman plainly thought the small amount she paid Megs hardly worth bothering about. What did she know of managing? Megs had had enough.

'I'm beginning to think, the way you forget to pay me, that you don't think very much of me. Then again, the way you don't pay me, it occurs to me that I don't think much of you.' She fixed Emotionally-Deranged Davis with a furious glare. She was discovering that mutual dislike was liberating. 'Money,' she said. 'I want money. I do not clean your floor for love. I do it for money. I don't do it because I'm good at it. I don't want to be good at it. Money. That's all, money. You don't talk about money, you don't have to. You have it. I don't, so I do. If it offends you, disturbs your middle-class politeness, I'm sorry. There it is, money. MONEY. I want it.'

'It isn't everything.'

'So people like you would have people like me believe. But I don't go for that. There's money and love and music and beautiful things and honesty but without money – where are you? You want a roof over your head, food in your mouth, in your children's mouths. Money. You need money. And sex. You enjoy it. You can have orgasms aplenty because you are warm, comfortable and relatively secure. It's all money, isn't it?'

'I'll pay you next week.'

'I work for money. Do your bosses in the health centre where you work say they'll pay you next month? If they did, what would you say? And I know you love your work. Would you do it for nothing?' She looked desperately round. She was tempted to take the bulging supermarket bag from the kitchen unit, saying that would do instead. But didn't really dare. Besides, she suspected she didn't want anything it contained. She had the feeling she was being absurd. She didn't care. She wanted to shock this woman. She wanted to see the mildly patronising look replaced with one of horror. She hated this. 'Money,' she shrilled instead, shaking with indignation. 'Money. Money. Money.' She slapped a damp cloth helplessly on to the unit she was wiping.

'Well, Megs.' Mrs Emotionally-Deranged Davis slipped into her therapist persona. Dipping freely into skills picked up on courses, role plays with other therapists on training routines. She folded her arms, put her head to one side, deepened her voice, tried to catch the naughty eye of the recalcitrant. She spoke with charming authority. 'Well, Megs . . .'

'How dare you speak to me like that.' Megs picked up the cloth and threw it on the floor. 'How dare you use your cheap, quickie, sort-the-little-person-out routines on me. You don't write case notes on me. I'm your cleaner. You don't turn this situation around. You don't make *me* feel guilty. You *pay* me. And,' turning on the woman, 'furthermore, how dare you reduce me to this . . . this . . . effing fury. How buggery dare you do this to me.'

She did not look round, would not give Emotionally-Deranged Davis a chance to reply. She picked up her denim jacket, her bag and went out the back door. Slamming it. Stood. Still furious. She would have to borrow from her mother to get through the weekend. A lecture coming, there. 'I don't know what you do with your money, Megs.' And, 'If these people don't pay you, why do you work for them?'

She opened the door once again. 'Not enough. Not enough,' she screamed. Slammed the door again. A good slam this time. A satisfying slam. She heard the fruit bowl tumble from the table and smash on the floor. That was better. 'Yes,' she shouted, 'that's the sort of slam. That's what I mean by a slam.'

She walked round the side of the house, down the path, out through the front gate, along the street to the corner – all that way before remorse set in. That was it for sure. They wouldn't want her back. 'Damn and fart and shite,' she cursed, breathed the words out, feet hit the pavement. 'Fuck, sod it,' swearing and striding all the way to the bus stop. 'Bastard, bitch, shite.' The fool she was. She stopped. Stood, staring ahead, lips pursed. Should she go back and apologise? A bit of grovelling? She imagined herself wringing her hands and whingeing, creeping and cringing forward under Mrs Emotionally-Deranged's uppity glare. 'No. Won't. Won't do it,' she said aloud.

Fellow queuers turned away, stared, stiff with politeness, into the distance, pretending not to notice. They had seen and heard her approach. They would have no truck with the potentially unstable. Suddenly aware of how she must appear to her co-queuers, Megs fell silent, humiliated. It's my turn to be the loony on the bus, she thought.

She sat in her favourite place, window seat, halfway down the inside. She could stare at pavements and people, did not like watching cars. She put her head on the window and felt the grumbling whine of wheels drumming tarmac, through her. The vibrations rattled at her, eased the guilt she was now feeling at her outburst. Whenever she remembered her behaviour, her hand rushed to her face. 'Oh God.'

At the West End the bus, caught in the early evening traffic, shuddered and crawled. Megs yawned, felt safely removed from the world she was watching. A newspaper vendor was hollering his wares. A cracked voice, ruined, constantly extended beyond its range. Whatever it was he was actually shouting, it sounded like, 'Left leg. Left leg.'

A busker played guitar in a doorway. He was absurdly thin. His clothes, cheap to begin with, were lifeless now and useless against any kind of weather. His eyes were shut and his blond hair fell over his face. He was playing 'Spoonful' and playing it very well, quite lost in the sound he was making. A quivering sadness that broke through the mindless evening rumble, and soared. But that mastery was lost behind the throaty moanings he made. A deep drunken hum, singing out the music as the song made its way from brain to fingers. He was not aware he was doing it. People only saw a drunk with wild hair, broken shoes and dirty fingernails humming incomprehensively. They gave him a wide berth.

Megs liked people-spotting. It was, along with eavesdropping and staring, her hobby. She loved to look at people's clothes and the rhythm of their movements and speculate about the lives they led.

Years ago, she and Lorraine, on their way home from school,

played the underpants game. They'd pick, from afar, some unsuspecting man, poor soul, and guess what sort of underpants he was wearing. 'Huge flappers,' Megs would whisper, giggling, leaning her head against Lorraine's – two dirty little minds at work.

'Enormous Aertex with skid marks,' Lorraine would add. Lorraine always went further. They'd snort helplessly, eyes watering. They were young and thought the world wondrous and gloriously grubby. Memories. Megs grinned hugely.

The busker looked up and caught the grin. 'Megs!' he shouted, stepping forward to knock on the window where she sat. It was Josh. Oh, please God, no. She did not want to see him like this. She turned. What happened to someone that he could start out dreaming and end up playing exquisitely to commuters who noticed only his dereliction, not the fabulous noise he was making? She rummaged through her handbag, scarlet and mumbling, pretending not to see him. 'Hey, Megs,' he shouted. 'Look at me. Hey, come on out. "God Bless the Child", Megs. Come on.'

Megs did not respond. She was embarrassed to know him. She did not want her fellow passengers to know she mixed with people like this. She wanted their acceptance. She studied her ticket, wishing the bus would move, whisking her away from this moment. When it did she heard him call, surprise in his voice, 'Megs. Hey, Megs. It's me. Josh.' She did not look round, but knew he was standing at the edge of the pavement, watching the bus, and her, go. An apology would be moving on his lips. 'Sorry.'

So what was it that made him apologise when all he'd done was say hello? She remembered when the band broke up. After their last gig he had driven her home. Mike and the others were drinking, smoking some unusually fine dope (mostly they smoked home-grown) and dedicating themselves to getting very, very incomprehensible indeed. She was pregnant, eight weeks, and taking her duties to her unborn seriously. She'd given up alcohol and had stopped smoking. The end of the band depressed her. They were in Eddy's flat.

'That's it,' Mike said. He was enthused. Endings always made him happy. His greatest glories were when making a triumphant show of leaving. Moving on – what to made no matter – was exhilarating. The business of goodbyes thrilled him.

'That's it,' again, reaching out, snapping his fingers. 'Hit me again.' He took a bottle of Jack Daniels and drank. 'Yes. C'mon, Megsy. Have some. Stop being so superior. Are you enjoying sneering at us?'

'I'm not sneering. I'm just watching out for the baby.'

'Oooh,' mocked Mike. 'The baby.' Then, to the others, 'She's been eating lettuce and stuff and drinking milk.'

'Looks good on it.' Josh admired her.

'I've got to go,' Megs said. If she couldn't join in, she didn't want to stay. She fetched her coat, a white Afghan that in a few months would not meet in the middle. After Jack was born it still would not fasten properly. Never again. She came back into the room to say her goodbyes. To kiss everyone and promise to stay in touch. Though they didn't.

The window was open. Mike was standing on the ledge, grinning at her. The others were looking helpless, shuffling their feet. 'Fuck's sake, Mike. Come in. Stop this.'

'See me, Megsy,' Mike leered. 'I can fly too.'

Fly too? Megs looked up, stared quizzically at the driver's back at the front of the bus. What on earth had he meant by that?

'Watch me,' Mike shouted. He turned to watch her watching him. She wondered how it felt. The way he looked back, the expression on his face – a vague, almost bitter triumph about him.

'Look at me. I can do it. I fucking can.'

They were one floor up.

'Christ's sake, Mike,' someone called. 'You're drunk, man.'

He jumped. Or rather spread his arms and embraced the sky. He looked back at her, grinning wildly. Ablaze. Did he really think he could fly? Was there, perhaps, a moment's belief? A full second's rapture – just before the plummet?

They rushed to the window. He was standing on the scrub of lawn below, surrounded by the woman upstairs's washing and a tangle of line. 'See,' he bellowed at them, shaking his fist. 'See. Told you I could do it. I can fucking fly.' Then he fainted.

Eddy and Fred took Mike to hospital to spend the rest of the night waiting in casualty. Josh took her home because she'd been sick, leaning out of the window, on to the scattered laundry.

He did not leave her that night. He stayed, made her tea, sat on her sofa and talked. He was more scared than she was.

'Them others, Eddy, Fred and Mike, they're going to do other things. You can see that. But me, at my age.' He was thirty then, and the oldest among them. Old enough, unnerved enough by too much contact with the really young, to think he was really old. 'I can't do nothing. I'm no good for nothing except playing.'

'Most people would die to play like you,' Megs said.

He smiled and shook his head. 'It's over for me.'

When he left he touched her hair and made to kiss her, then thought better of it. 'Sorry,' he said. Apologising again. 'Sorry. You wouldn't. I mean me.' He scoffed at himself. 'Look at me.' He feebly indicated his worn jeans, once blue, now pale with a dying weave, and T-shirt.

'No.' She touched him. 'It's not that. It's just the baby. And Mike, you know.'

'I know. But we can be friends. We're mates, us.'

'Friends,' she said.

Hers was the next stop. She stood up and made her way, balancing against the movement of the bus, towards the entrance. Another passenger, a man who remembered her from the queue, shot her a mildly sympathetic look. Not a smile, a furtive flicker of the mouth, a gesture of acceptance. Now that she, too, had refused to acknowledge a loony, she was OK. She could join the safe and sane travellers. Megs shot him a hostile glare. What was up with her? She'd sought the acceptance of strangers. Looking for reassurance from transient, fleeting eye-contact relationships with people who sat near her on a bus, she had denied a friend. She was ashamed of herself.

Chapter Fourteen

Lorraine was drinking coffee at the kitchen table when Megs got home.

'Who let you in?'

'Jack. Why are you in such a foul mood?'

'What makes you think I'm in a foul mood?'

'The way you slammed the door. The way you threw your things down. Your face.'

'It's been a day. One of those days.' She opened a jar of Nescafé and gazed ponderously at the small amount of instant left. 'I'll have to shop. Christ.'

Lorraine said nothing.

'First of all Mrs Emotionally-Deranged Davis tells me she's got no money and I'll have to wait till next week. Like I had to wait till next week, which is now this week, last week. Then second of all I took a tantrum, and now third of all she'll probably sack me.'

'I don't think so,' Lorraine soothed her. 'First of all,' she held up a finger indicating number one, 'she's at fault and knows it and she's all liberal. She'll be guilty. And second of all,' another finger, 'finding a good cleaner isn't easy. And third of all . . .' Another finger. She stopped, looked vaguely at finger three, thinking about this. 'There is no third of all,' she said.

Megs brought her coffee across to the table and sat opposite Lorraine. 'My feet hurt, that could be third of all.' She took one of Lorraine's cigarettes from its packet, turned it over, looking at it, then put it back. 'I'm going to have to borrow from my mother. And you know what she'll say?'

Lorraine shook her head.

'She'll say, "I don't know why you need to be forever borrowing money, Megs." No, it'll be Nina. I'm always Nina when she's ticking me off. "I have never, ever borrowed as much as a penny. I have never been in debt my whole life. And . . ."'

'I'm sixty-three, you know.' They chanted Vivienne's catch-phrase in unison.

'You could scupper her argument by telling her you know she's older than that,' Lorraine offered.

'Nah.' Megs shook her head. 'It's all I have over her. I'm saving it for something big.'

'I'll lend you money for the supermarket.'

Megs shook her head. 'No. You need your money to fritter on rubbish. You'll get withdrawal symptoms if you don't squander cash.'

'Come on. Let me.'

'No. I'll get it from Mum. She'll nag and boss and tick me off. She'll complain that I take advantage of her, only go near her when I want a babysitter or some money. Then again, if I borrowed from someone else she'd be offended. You know families. It's all very complex.'

'Was it a good tantrum, then?' Lorraine wanted to know.

'Pretty good, as tantrums go. I didn't writhe about on the floor and drum my heels. You need to be three to get away with that. But I got rid of some steam. My fury swept me along all the way to the bus stop before I felt silly. Then on the way home I saw Josh busking and I pretended I didn't now him. So that's me. A shameful bitch and snobbish with it . . .'

'Who's a shameful bitch? Who's a snob?' Mike stood in the kitchen doorway, jingling his car keys. He stepped into the room, looking carefully round. For what? Megs wondered. Signs of prosperity? Signs of squalor? Signs of change? He sat at the table next to Lorraine, crossed his legs and brushed an imaginary bit of fluff from a grey-tweeded trouser leg. His brogues were brown and not too shiny. 'A gentleman,' he always insisted, 'does not overshine his shoes.' He knew such things.

'Me,' Megs confessed. 'I'm a shameful bitch and a snob.'

'Oh, you.' He knew her. Didn't want to talk about her. 'Any chance of some coffee?'

She levered herself sorely out of her seat and moved to the kettle. 'What brings you here? This isn't your day. Who let you in anyway?'

'The door wasn't locked. I came to tell you I won't be able to take Hannah on Saturday. We're going away for the weekend.'

'Right,' Megs said, stirring his coffee. Hannah will be pleased, she thought. It was getting increasingly difficult to get either Jack or Hannah to spend time with their father. Saturdays were too precious to them. They had grown from the little children who had spent weekends being spoilt by their daddy and his new wife, to being young adults with their own lives to lead. For years they had spent two weekends a month with Mike and Denise. Megs had at first fretted resentfully at home as her ex-husband and his new wife had given her children a glimpse of a lifestyle she could not possibly match. Not that she needed to bother. Mike forgot how young his children were, and expected them to appreciate his sophisticated new home. To his dismay, the only thing about his wealth that impressed his children was the size of the television set and the electric can-opener in the kitchen. They wanted only to behave at his house as they behaved in their own. Alternate Sunday mornings, then, Mike and Denise were irritably woken at dawn by the explosive sounds of children's television shows. It was not what either of them had planned. But in time Denise found she had learned a lot about a culture – music, television comedy, comics – that would otherwise have passed her by. Denise worked too hard at making friends with her stepchildren. She spent hours making them elaborate meals that they would not eat. At last, she gave in and bought them carry-out pizzas and Chinese. After that Megs complained that her children would start to expect such extravagances from her, and she could not afford them.

When Mike and Denise eventually had a child of their own, everyone worried. Would the children get along? Would Hannah and Jack take exception to the adoration poured on to the new daughter, Sara? Of course they didn't. They thought all the doting absurd. Sara lived an organised life. She had dancing lessons, piano lessons, a reproduction Victorian rocking horse, books and clothes. Before she was even in the world Sara's name was down for an expensive private school. Mike worried that his other children would resent Sara's privileges. But they didn't. Denise worried about the influence Jack and Hannah would have on Sara. She needn't have. Despite the odd dubious word Sara learned from Hannah, having older children around was good for her. Denise knew, though she never admitted, that the mockery Sara received from Jack and Hannah helped sort out a very spoiled child. At last, however, Jack and Hannah started to protest that the weekend visits to Mike and Denise were interrupting their own blossoming social rounds and often refused to go. It seemed to the three adults involved that no sooner had they got the hang of this divorcee-stepparent-children relationship thing than the two children grew up and moved the goalposts.

Megs put Mike's cup on the unit just, annoyingly, out of his reach. Then she leaned on the sink to chat from there. She did not return to her seat. Did not want to sit close to Mike. Recently she'd noticed that in herself. She did not like to get too close to her ex-husband. He was carefully tapping the key to his Audi on the melamine top of the kitchen table. She distracted herself from the niggle of resentment his suit and car keys set up in her by raking through the freezer.

He leaned back and sighed. He liked coming here. There was something easy about this home. No demands were made of him. He felt he could curl up and sleep. There was a huge pot of chrysanthemums on the kitchen windowsill, a smell of coffee and food, the phone rang a lot, in the living room was the bluish flicker and constant babble of television. Music played in the kitchen – Megs's blues, usually. He realised every time he came that he never, ever played his old records. That part of his life was gone for ever. His own home was a showcase of all the things he and Denise had chosen. Everything matched. Everything had its place. There was a well-worked, carefully planned design that somehow left no room for the simple business of hanging out. He could hang out here. The atmosphere was relaxed, uncritical.

Perhaps that was why he kept coming back. He did not mean to return week after week with tales of his new life, but he did. He told her about Denise's trip to New York (she was marketing manager of a whisky firm). He told her about Sara's piano prizes. He told her about Denise's Italian cookery course, and her herb garden. Megs

118

knew how much Mike had paid to have a conservatory built on to his kitchen. She knew, too, the huge amount Denise had inherited when her father died. Megs did not mean to keep hurting herself by probing the details of Mike's home life and the joint bank account he shared with Denise, but she did. She could, of course, have asked Mike for more money. But since most of their wealth came from Denise, this meant asking *her* for more money. Megs thought it enough that Denise had her husband – she would not take her pride as well.

'Well, that's *it*,' Mike said now, placing his hands, fingers spread, on the table.

An indication of how absolutely it *it* was.

Now we hear the real reason he dropped by, Megs thought. She was tempted not to ask what he was talking about. But, 'What's it?'

'I've done it,' Mike said. 'Always wanted to. And now I've done it.'

'What?' Lorraine sounded disinterested. Lorraine was disinterested. Mike bored her.

'I have booked a holiday in Italy. Two months. A villa in Umbria with swimming pool. I've always felt a fortnight is not enough. I'll really get into the mood of the place. Get to know the people. Really experience the life.'

'Oh, goody.' Megs spoke flatly. 'We'll have pizza to celebrate.' She took three flat boxes from the freezer. 'One pepperoni, one mushroom and garlic and one tomato and cheese. There we go.' She thumped them on the unit and turned to switch on the oven.

'Is there anything for eating?' Jack shuffled into the kitchen and looked round without acknowledging his father. 'I'm starving.'

'Pizza in about thirty minutes,' Megs told him.

'Great,' he said. Only someone of seventeen could say it with so little joy.

'Your father has just told us he's going to Italy for two months this summer.'

'Great,' said Jack again. Joylessly again.

'I'll make some salad,' Megs offered.

'Great,' said Jack. Then, 'Only if you're going to eat it yourself. I mean, what's the point of lettuce?'

'You let that boy get away with too much,' Mike criticised.

Megs threw a dish towel at him. 'Don't you come here in your suit, flashing your car keys and holidays and start on me. Do you want some pizza?'

He picked the towel off his head. 'Why not?'

'I saw a good sandwich the other day,' said Lorraine. 'Cream cheese and marmalade. It's sort of cheesecakey.'

'We could do it for a sweet. Then again, some women like sweet things. They'd just have it for lunch. Or it could be a mid-morning snack.'

'And cheese is nutritious.' Lorraine flicked her cigarette ash into the ashtray. A deft movement that added authority to her sandwich suggestion.

'I was thinking, if we could do some chargrilled burgers and chicken, that'd go well. And it'd smell out the place nicely.'

'Good thinking.' Lorraine nodded. 'I'll have to go. That pizza's reminded me, Harry needs feeding.'

The front door slammed. Vivienne complained all the way down the hall into the kitchen. 'Bloody traffic. And this child is getting too wild for me. I should be taking things easy at my age . . .'

'I'm sixty-three, you know,' Megs and Lorraine mouthed at each other.

'It's you.' Vivienne came into the kitchen and shot Mike a filthy look. Everything that had ever gone wrong in her daughter's life was the fault of this man. She loathed him, and let it show. Fact was, she rather enjoyed the display of foul temper she unleashed on him. She, too, had discovered how liberating mutual dislike could be. 'I'll have a cup of tea in the living room with my grandchildren,' she said. 'You won't be staying long, will you?' This was not so much a question as a command. Go away, she was saying.

Lizzy came into the room. Megs swept her up and kissed her. 'Well, hello you. How was this Thursday for you? Good? Did wonderful things happen? Did you ride on elephants in the park? Swing on stars? Play tambourines? Discover the meaning of life?'

Lizzy pushed her away. 'Don't be silly. Put me down. I want to watch telly with Gran. There's cartoons on.'

'The burgers should be garlicky,' said Lorraine. 'And what about smoked salmon on a bagel with cream cheese and watercress?'

'Good one,' said Megs, setting Lizzy down. She leaned once more on the kitchen unit to talk sandwiches and life with Lorraine, ignoring Mike. After an hour she looked round at the oven, alarmed. 'God. The pizzas.' The crisp brown smell of burnt crust filled the room.

'I definitely have to go.' Lorraine picked up her handbag, yanked her leather jacket from the back of her chair and headed into the hall, small steps. Her heels were too high. 'See ya,' she called, waving.

'Yes,' said Megs, opening the oven. A cloud of smoke billowed out.

In the hall Lorraine stopped, took five pounds from her purse and put it in the inside pocket of the old raincoat that always hung by the front door. It was here that Megs kept her secret, emergency funds. Tomorrow, Lorraine knew, she'd find it and think it was money she'd forgotten about.

Jack, Hannah and Lizzy drifted into the kitchen, Lizzy still staring back at the television. They sat round the table. Hannah fetched knives and forks. Jack filled glasses with milk. A silent routine they went through every mealtime.

'Do you two have to?' said Mike.

'What?' said Megs.

'Discuss sandwiches when you're serving food.' He waved his fork at her. 'Hamburgers that are chargrilled and garlicky. Smoked salmon, for chrissakes. And look what you give us. This . . .' he pointed at Hannah's plate, '. . . muck. Think about the children. Talking glowingly about food and serving this . . . what is it?'

'You are well aware of what it is. It started life as a pizza. Now it doesn't know. It's got a complex,' Megs said.

'That's what they'll all have.' He indicated the gathering at the table.

'Jack and Hannah don't care. They just want to eat and go.'

'And I love it,' said Hannah. 'I love pizza with a complex.'

'There you go,' said Megs. 'Do you want your food with or without?'

'With or without what?'

'A plate.' She had a slice of steaming burnt pizza poised in her hand, aimed at him.

'I won't bother.' Remembering her accuracy with the dish towel, he was worried about his suit. 'I'll go.'

She showed him out. 'If you're so damn worried about your children, why don't you make more of an effort to see them?'

'What do you mean? They don't like coming over for the weekend any more.'

'You know what I mean.' Right now she hated him. He was going to Italy. She could not remember when she had last been on holiday. But she recognised the pang his announcement had made. It was that same pang she got when she looked at the picture of the Emotionally-Deranged Davises on their veranda in Provence. It was jealousy. More than that. She hated that she could not provide the children with such exotic things as holidays abroad. Long summer afternoons in rarefied places, breathing in foreign scents, listening to the outlandish clatter of strange languages would not be part of Jack's or Hannah's or Lizzy's memories when they looked back on their childhoods. She was swamped by guilt and envy.

'If you care about Jack and Hannah that much why don't you take them with you? Why don't you give them a holiday of a lifetime too? You could do that instead of criticising me all the time.'

It was always the same. They started out trying to be amicable but their good intentions always dissolved into an acid mix of jealousy, disillusionment, guilt and pain. They could not look at one another without pain. Even for this small moment in the hall. She took a step back. She was standing too close. She found she hated being near him. He stared at her – a defensive grimace that turned to confusion.

You weren't there. It's all your fault. My child is dead, he didn't say.

You were never there. Not for any of his six years, she didn't say.

'All right,' he said, regretting it even as he spoke. 'I'll take them.' They stared some more. 'Hannah and Jack,' he said. 'I'll take them.'

'Too right,' she said. 'You're not getting Lizzy. She's mine.'

Megs went back to her kitchen, slumped into a chair.

Vivienne was making tea. 'You forgot about me.'

'Sorry.' She picked up a piece of pizza crust left untouched on Hannah's plate and chewed it. 'Can you lend me some money? Mrs

Davis didn't pay me again. I'll pay you back.'

Vivienne turned, teapot in hand. 'Why do you work for people if they don't pay you?'

'Good question.'

Vivienne silently poured the tea. Well, she didn't say, I have never borrowed as much as a penny. I have never been in debt my whole life. And I'm sixty-three, you know. 'There's money in my purse,' she said. 'How much do you need?'

'Enough to get me through the weekend,' Megs said. The doorbell rang and she rose to answer it. She returned five minutes later, staring into an envelope, counting the money it contained. 'That was Mrs Davis. She brought me the money she owed me. I must get stroppy more often. It pays off.'

Vivienne sipped her tea, watching Megs. You shouldn't get stroppy with people you work for. You could lose a job that you need, she didn't say. 'That was nice of your Mrs Davis to come all this way,' she said.

'Nice.' Megs was angry. 'What was nice? She didn't pay me, that wasn't nice. And look,' she waved the money, 'she must've had it all the time. Or she must've gone to the cash machine. She could have paid me. Don't tell me about nice. You always think things are nice.'

'What's wrong with nice?' Vivienne asked. 'Nice is all you could want. Ask for nice, and you're not likely to be disappointed.' She meant it. She'd thought about it a lot. Nice was almost her only adjective. They'd have a nice bit of roast on a Sunday. Some days were nice. Some weren't. She liked to have a nice time at her club on a Tuesday afternoon. Bruce Forsythe seemed like an awfully nice man. Nice. If, on her death bed, she considered her life and concluded that, for the most part, it had been nice, she'd die happy. 'What's wrong with you, anyway? You're grumpy today.'

Megs looked at her mother. She was wearing her beloved green tweed skirt that fell roomily over her thighs, though she was thin enough to get away with something a lot more stylish. She had other, smarter skirts, but kept coming back to her green. It offered no challenges. The bad veins on her legs were concealed by thick brown tights. On her feet she wore low-heeled cheap beige shoes. The sort of shoes that cost £10 for two pairs. The shoes of a woman of low self-esteem.

It seemed odd now that this woman had forced her to school in a hideous hat, and had unshakeable faith in the healing properties of milk of magnesia. She also made the best pancakes in the world. Winter evenings when Megs and her father were sitting by the fire, watching early-evening television programmes, *Top of the Pops* or *Tomorrow's World*, Vivienne would bustle in with a tray, cups of tea, and a plate of pancakes heaped and golden, the room filled with the soft, comforting waft of fresh baking. She would complain that nobody was taking any mind of her standing with a heavy tray when the table was covered with papers and Megs's homework jotters. Megs and her father would sheepishly clear the table, making room for the laden tray. Then Vivienne would sit back and secretly watch them indulge. 'Hmm,' they would enthuse, hot butter dripping on to their plates. 'Wonderful. Best pancakes in the world.'

'Nonsense.' Vivienne would dismiss this as an exaggeration. 'Rubbish. Just some leftover eggs I had to use up.'

Yet if they did not say it, did not heap her efforts with praise and make a huge show of enjoyment, she would sulk for days. 'Nobody appreciates me around here.'

They saw each other, Megs and her mother, every day. Lorraine came by most days. Mike called in at least once a week. In the next room she could hear her children bicker as they watched television. Soon their friends would come round. This was the place where her children's friends gathered. This flat was always noisy and always full of people.

'I'm lonely,' Megs said.

Vivienne snorted softly. It was easier than answering. Her sister Betty always criticised her for being too soft, too easy. Only wanting nice when there was so much more. Her husband came and went, pottered in his shed, read the paper in the evening and didn't say much. Her daughter was lost in mists of guilt, grief and regret. She always wanted someone, an easy-going chum, to fancy nice with. She was lonely too.

Chapter Fifteen

'You're going.' Megs thumped a packet of cereal on the kitchen table, and a cloud of krispies spewed from the box, scattered over the table and on to the floor. Lizzy raced the dog to eat them, squatting under the table. Mornings were wretched.

'She's got an identity problem,' Jack scorned, leaning down, looking at Lizzy. He was feeling foul, venomous. He'd been ordered off to Italy for the summer when he'd been looking forward to an indolent stay at home, sitting draped sideways on a chair watching his *Beavis and Butthead* tapes, drinking, eating bowls of cornflakes. And Sharon, he'd just met a girl called Sharon, and suddenly that name would never be the same . . . 'You going to the Glass Bucket tonight?' he asked Megs.

She nodded. 'I've still got a few Fridays left before they switch to disc jockeys.'

'Well, I can baby-sit.'

She looked at him suspiciously. 'Why? Are you planning to have mates in? Will I come home to find a writhing mass of naked sweaty flesh, the air thick with dope? People in the corner snorting forbidden things? And the place awash with beer, cans everywhere . . . music blaring . . .'

'No.' Her accusation made him hostile. 'I just want to stay home. That's all.'

'Fine,' she said, ashamed that she had shown such distrust. 'Why not.'

Hannah's world had ended. Two months with her father and her father's new wife and daughter in a country with a different language when she had a love life to organise and some serious partying, clubbing and gossiping to do. She stormed from the house swinging her bag of school books, wailing that the worst thing about mothers was that they never understood anything. She vowed never to come home again.

Megs phoned Lorraine.

'It's her age,' Lorraine said soothingly. 'Remember?'

'No.' Oh, but Megs did. She was nagging herself that when she was that age she'd been worse. But admitting it would mean understanding her mother, and she wasn't ready for that.

'I have to go,' Lorraine said. 'If I'm late for work one more time they'll fire me.'

Megs dialled her mother's number.

'What's wrong?' asked Vivienne.

'Nothing. What makes you think something's wrong?'

'Why else would you phone this early?'

'Perhaps I just wanted to say hello.'

'Do you?'

'No. Well, yes. But . . .' Why did her conversations with her mother always go like this? 'It's Hannah,' she said. 'She's making a dreadful fuss about going to Italy. She gets this fabulous opportunity to go abroad for two months and all she can do is shout about it. I don't know . . .'

'What did you expect?' asked Vivienne. 'You didn't honestly think a girl that age would want to be uprooted from her friends and banished to some foreign country, did you?'

'What do you mean, banished? Good grief. I wangle this trip for her and she complains.'

'Of course she complains. She wants to manage her own life. Why did you do it anyway?'

'I thought it'd be good for her to be with her father. She needs to know him better. She'd get a sense of family. They both would.'

'She has a family,' Vivienne protested. 'She has us. What more does she need?'

'A father. She might need that. She might find when she gets older that she wishes she'd had one. Then there's me. What about me?'

'What about you?'

'I need things too. I need time to spend by myself. When did I last get that?'

'Why do you need time to yourself? In my day you didn't want things like that. This is modern rubbish. What are you going to do with time to yourself?'

'Think.'

'Think! What do you want to do that for? No good will come of that. Thinking is not good for you. If you start thinking you'll just get unhappy. What are you going to think about?'

'Me. My life. Who I am. What's happened to me without my planning it. Getting my life back on track. What I want.'

'What is all that?' Vivienne was shocked. 'Life. Getting back on track. Wanting. What do you want, anyway?'

'I want,' said Megs. 'I want . . .' She searched desperately for what she wanted. That feeling of being part of something. Of not being completely on her own. Of moving forward with people on ventures, adventures. Life. 'I want . . .' She didn't know how to put it. 'I want to belong again.'

'What!' Vivienne's shock deepened.

Megs held the receiver away from her ear. Oh dear, she thought. Shouldn't have said that.

'What on earth do you mean by that? Belong again? You belong. You've got lots to belong to.' Vivienne rang off, offended. Later, preparing lunch, heating a small tin of mushroom soup, she leaned against the stove, feeling mournful. Gas seethed against the pot, one of her everyday noises. But when she was depressed, ordinary sounds got intrusive. She wants to belong again, Vivienne thought. Don't we all. Don't we bloody, bloody all.

In the Pearson house the discontent was almost tangible. The air was thick with it. Every time Megs went there, winter or summer, blisteringly hot or Arctic cold, she would open the windows. When she left she would, after closing the front door, hold her breath till she got to the gate. Then she'd open her mouth, allowing some cool air on to her tongue. Tasting it. Smelling it. 'I think,' she said to Lorraine once, 'I must hate the smell of perfection.' But as her cleaning years passed, she realised that what she hated was the smell of deceit. That sweet potpourri that poured into the air in every room was part of the great Pearson lie. It was only a pretend sweetness.

Megs knew that houses had smells: coffee, books, old carpet, washing, sickness, yesterday's supper. Her home smelled of feet and instant food, noise, constant laundry and wet dog, with an undertow of craziness that teenage children brought. They were always moving. Her flat smelled used. In Megs's home senses intertwined – smells and sounds, sights and textures. The smell of a child's sleepy head in the morning and the wild halloo of the seven-thirty DJ hollering banter, playing the banshee strummings of this week's hero. A plant, glistening health brimming from its clay pot, spreading exuberant growth down the wall to the old patterned carpet with its soft coating of dog hair.

There were no signs of life in the Pearson house. Cleaning it was boring and perturbing. Start at the top, beds, washing, dusting, clean the bathroom, then the kitchen, into the living room, wipe, clean inside of windows, finish by vacuuming the whole house from top to bottom. Vacuum all the way to front door, doing a backwards shuffle for the last few steps. Put machine in cupboard by front door, then leave. Change shoes in porch, Mrs Pearson didn't like shoes that stomped over pavements to tread her carpets. All the time, from when she opened the front door till when she finally walked through the gate, Megs clamped her lips. Don't breathe till you hit the street, she told herself. Keep this disquieting stench from your lungs.

'It's all so orderly,' Megs complained to Lorraine. 'Stultifyingly orderly. It's not natural. I swear one day that Mrs Pearson is going to start screaming and screaming and never stop.'

Today Mrs Pearson was in the house as Megs cleaned. She sat in the kitchen drinking tea, reading the newspaper and staring into the garden. Every now and then her hand moved to her neck, she would spread her fingers over her throat and mouth her worries over and over.

Megs wiped the sink. Then wiped the windowsill, carefully lifting the pot plant and washing-up liquid, wiping under them. Mrs Pearson watched. The silence between them was neither hostile nor companionable. It was sterile.

The garden beyond the kitchen window was immaculate. The lawn, Wimbledon trim, perfect mower-width stripes. Each shrub and plant was allocated its little bit of border, any insubordinate growing was cut back. The earth was properly brown and crumbly. The weeping willow at the foot of the lawn draped glumly towards the grass it would never be allowed to reach. Megs always imagined that the plants mutinied against their regimented life by growing when the Pearsons were not watching. She thought they'd wait till the first fortnight in August, when the Pearsons always went on holiday, to behave like naughty teenagers. They'd party, indulge in an orgy of growing and spreading, flowering and flourishing. Then when the Pearsons returned their plants would shrink back into the allotted space. It would be the pruning shears for them, punishment for two weeks' abandonment.

Megs watched a sparrow bounce across the lawn. There was nothing the Pearsons could do about the suburban bird life, though they tried. The sparrow cockily strutted across the grass, flew up into the drab little willow and declared himself. This is me. This is mine. A female appeared. The male joined her. Together they bounced on the lawn. Then he was on her. Chittering, flapping, fussing – feathered ecstasy. It lasted all of two seconds. Then the male bounced off. Boing, boing.

'Well,' said Megs. 'I don't think much of that. And from the looks of her neither does she.'

'Who?' Mrs Pearson half-stood and glared out into the garden. 'Is there somebody out there?'

'Only a couple of sparrows having it off on your lawn.' Megs surprised herself. She did not usually chat to Mrs Pearson. And speaking about anything vaguely sexual seemed taboo.

But Mrs Pearson came to join her at the window. 'Where?' she asked.

'There, look.' Megs pointed at the lovers on the lawn. 'Look at him. Shoving out his chest, strutting his stuff. "Hey, babe. How was that for you?"' Megs flapped her elbows, did a swift cock sparrow impersonation. 'And her, she's bewildered. She's looking round saying, "How was what for me? Did something happen?"' Megs looked round in fake innocence and bewilderment.

Mrs Pearson laughed. 'Poor thing,' she said.

Megs looked at her. Sympathy with an unfulfilled sparrow, she thought. There's hope for you, Mrs Pearson.

'When I was a girl,' Megs said, 'I was sent to my Aunty Betty's guest house to help out at holiday times – spring and summer. In April the eiders came round to the rocks outside my bedroom window. They were not like the sparrow bouncing on his little bird legs, chittering and overexcited about a two-second fuck. They made love. I used to hear them woo each other. They cooed and moaned and made love sound fabulous. When I was little I didn't know why they made this joyous noise. Later, when I understood, I always envied them their rapture.'

Mrs Pearson took a tissue from her cardigan pocket, blew her nose, sniffed and dabbed her eyes. Megs did not spot any tears.

Later, after Megs had left, Mrs Pearson went upstairs. She lifted an old shoebox from the shelf in her wardrobe, laid it on the bed and carefully opened it. The watches it contained never failed to give her pleasure. There were three Guccis, two Rolexes, a Breitling chronomat and an Ellesse sports watch. She took her favourite Gucci out and laid it on her wrist. It was a beautiful thing. Its presence in her life, in her shoebox, filled her with a confidence she'd never known before. She felt that she had something in common with the glittering people she read about in her Sunday newspaper. She felt nearer to them. In her drawer was an unworn Betty Jackson shirt and a Nicole Farhi wool rollneck sweater. There were jackets hanging up in the wardrobe, and coats. Hidden about the house, Mrs Pearson had over twenty thousand pounds' worth of clothes, sports equipment (and she did no sports) and jewellery Mr Pearson did not know about, bought with credit cards he did not know about. Buying things made her feel good. She snapped her plastic on the counter, said, 'Do you take these?' and felt thrilled, and wanted. 'Rapture.' She repeated Megs's words. 'Rapture.' Her head had been turned. Fancying a bit of rapture, she thought she might use some of the secret credit cards, and shop.

Megs changed her shoes at the front door, made her breathless way back to the street, gasping at the gate, 'Ah. That's it. Get some pollution into my system, lead in my lungs.' She gulped in a blast of car exhaust, and her recriminations started. Had she said 'fuck' to Mrs Pearson? Oh God, surely not. She had expounded at some length, she recalled, about the sex lives of sparrows and eider ducks. She shook her head, trying to dislodge the memory. 'I must stop speaking,' she promised herself.

She picked Lizzy up from the nursery. Took her home, fed her and dropped her off at Vivienne's for the afternoon whilst she went to Gilbert's.

He was in his living room, waiting for her, standing beside a new vacuum cleaner. He gestured at it with his hand, palm upwards. 'Look.' He was awfully proud of it. 'It's French,' he said. 'I love the colour. Pure Gauguin. And,' he awkwardly tried to open the top, 'when I get this open, it has all the tools inside. A thing for dusting up high and a long thing for . . .' He looked baffled. 'Whatever you use long things for.' He bustled round it. Hair on end. She watched him. He was, she thought, all ego and thumbs.

She noted a birthday card on his mantelpiece. It only took a slight lean to one side to read it. 'To Gilbert, love Annette.' That was all. Still, it was a tasteful card. Unlike the gaudy, glitter-encrusted ones her children sent her. She watched him fuss round his new acquisition. He was a Gemini. Damn, she thought, she did not want to know that. Now she would add him to her horoscope routine.

Megs had a regimented horoscope routine. First she read Vivienne's, then Lorraine's, Jack's, Hannah's, Lizzy's and Mike's. She always hoped Saturn was doing malicious things in Mike's stars, and always forgave herself the sliver of shame she felt when uplifted at any misfortunes the stars had headed his way. Then she read her own, saving the best till last.

Now she knew she would incorporate Gilbert's astrological chart into her routine. Sometimes she read Dysentery McGhee's or Emotionally-Deranged Davis's. She felt it gave her the drop on them. She knew vaguely what was going on in their lives – financial problems, imminent journeys or romantic adventures. The nonsense in all this, of course, was that she didn't believe any of it. 'Horoscopes are just nonsense,' she'd say. Only it mattered to her when some stargazing tabloid guru promised good things. It was a small source of hope – a back-door, black-market, easy-access optimism. Sometimes, that was just what she needed.

'Good, strong primary colours,' Gilbert was saying. 'That is what you need in terms of design of modern household implements. Simple

131

straight lines and bold, uncompromising use of reds or blues. It says function. It says strength.'

'It's a vacuum. Maybe all it says is, "I'm a vacuum",' Megs said. His enthusiasm bewildered her. A vacuum was a vacuum was a vacuum. You took it from its cupboard, plugged it in, switched it on, sucked up the dirt and put it back in its cupboard again. Design never occurred to her.

'Yes.' He stepped back from it. Stuck his hands deep into his pockets and vaguely flapped his trousers. 'Of course. I'm sorry. I'm whiffling. I'm sure it'll do the trick. You won't have to bring yours any more.'

'Oh, don't apologise. It's lovely. It's a beautiful colour.'

'Yes. I've never been fond of reds. But that's a good one. Burgundy, really. Blues and greens interest me more. Greens are endless. You just have to think of young summer lawns or old wooden sports pavilions or the soft melty inside of peppermint chocolate or the steamy brightness of broccoli – hot and crunchily ready to eat – or . . .'

'Lampposts in the rain?'

'Yes.' Bending his knees, clenching his fists with enthusiasm. 'That's green going into grey. An intrinsic grubbiness that's so alluring. It has atmosphere and you think about all the weather this green has seen and the passing hands that have touched it.' He stopped. Oh God, he was speaking too much. He was talking rubbish about greens. 'Sorry,' he said. Brilliant limes in the fruit shop, soft, gentle, translucent olive oil. His mind was buzzing with greens.

'Don't apologise,' Megs advised. Heavens, she thought, he talks so much. When he gets going, he's worse than me. 'Don't explain, don't justify, just get on with things, as my Aunt Betty always says.'

'I think I'd like your Aunt Betty.'

'You'd be joining a majority group.'

He smiled. A majority group, part of the crowd, that would be a first. 'Would you like some coffee before you start?'

'I'd love a cup,' she lied. She'd drunk two cups for lunch and felt awash with the stuff. But this was not a moment to squander. If she said no, he might never offer another. He was so offendable. And, really, she asked herself, if she was going to clean for somebody –

132

wasn't it best to be friends? So she accepted his cup of Colombian and his questions. How come she was called Megs?

'It's my maiden name.'

'Are you married?'

'Not any more.'

'Ah.'

'My name is Nina Megson, or was. Now it's Nina Williams. Only when I was little I hated Nina so I insisted I be called Megs, or Megsy. It was my playground name. It has stuck.' She shrugged. 'I thought Nina was a name for old ladies with a single wiry hair growing from their chins, and fat upper arms.'

'Nobody calls you Nina, then?'

'Only my mother when she's not speaking to me.'

Nina. He loved that name. It was a Russian princess, a dark-eyed woman in a long white fur, staring at him across a crowded railway platform, with that icy gleam of forbidden passion. It was a torch singer in a Paris nightclub, aching out songs of lost love and lonely nights . . .

'You sing.' He suddenly remembered their first meeting.

'Yes. At the Glass Bucket.' She winced to tell him. 'It has the name in italicised neon at the front with a top hat alongside. It's all in blue. Not the deepening sky at midnight blue but the blue you coloured the sea with your first paintbox when you were little.'

He raised a finger acknowledging the colour. 'Know it.' They exchanged a shy look, mutual childhoods, mutual silly colours from cheap paintboxes, a lifetime ago when they were innocent, knew nothing of shades and tarnishes and stains and thought the sky was always seaside blue and grass was perfect green. 'So what do you sing?' He knew now he was wrong about the spangly coconut matting sort of dress and the conga line.

'The blues. Mostly. Sixties favourites when the manager gets his way.'

'Sixties favourites.' His face fell. Nothing made him more glum than sixties favourites. Rows and rows of jolly-cheeked people, arms linked, a multicoloured human mass swaying, drinking Newcastle Brown Ale, singing 'Itchycoo Park' and reminiscing about old Herman's Hermits' hits. He closed his eyes, cast the vision out.

She noted the shudder. Could not help but take pride in having caused it. 'You can have fun with sixties songs,' she told him. 'If you sing them to a different beat than the one intended. "Let's Twist Again", for example. If you sing it really, really slowly, moronically, really glumly, with your face frozen and your arms dangling by your sides, it makes you laugh.'

She demonstrated. Stood in his kitchen looking chronically depressed, chanting 'Let's Twist Again' in a monotone. Barely an expression moved on his face as he watched. This monotonous singing of a stupid song defined exactly how he felt about the sixties. It started with everyone dancing in absurd clothes singing songs about twisting the night away and ended with people wearing wide-bottomed trousers doing drugs and seeing purple butterflies and love. He'd stood back with his arms dangling by his sides, looking moronic in his funny haircut, feeling vaguely flatulent because smoking anything did that to him. Air sucked in at one end battered through him and came embarrassingly, without any warning, out the other. This wasn't funny. This was painful.

'Gosh,' said Megs, registering his tormented expression. 'I never realised it was that bad. I'll get on.' She scurried from the kitchen to hide her chagrin behind the drone of the vacuum and the officious flap of busy duster.

He watched her from the place he retreated to inside himself when painful memories came visiting. They kept doing that. Kept coming when he wasn't expecting them. It seemed getting older only meant adding more and more painful memories to his already plentiful store. 'I'm sorry,' he said. 'I didn't mean . . .'

But she didn't hear him. One more moment to revisit later, wincing.

Chapter Sixteen

The Glass Bucket never was salubrious. It was conceived to satisfy a distant longing for a long-lost seedy glamour. It reeked of a forgotten long-ago when people went out drinking and played at being worldly-wise. Seen-it-all-and-done-it-all types, Robert Mitchum or Bette Davis in grainy black and white. Movie dreams that were too old, even, for rainy Sunday afternoons, and now played on television in the middle of the night, when only insomniacs and night-watchmen were up. It demanded nothing of its patrons other than that they paid for their drinks and took their fights outside to the car park. Nowadays, grown-ups going out to play went to better places than the Glass Bucket. Places where they wore their best clothes, sipped their drinks, looked around them and, for an hour or so, took pleasure in pretending to be a whole lot richer than they were.

People at the Glass Bucket wore second-best, never cast an eye this way or that – who cared if nobody was looking at them? – there was nobody here to impress. Here they leaned on the bar, or sat at the round glass-topped tables, and spoke with the authority only alcohol can induce about sport, soaps, what was on telly last night and the embroiled relationships of distant superstars, or the folks next door.

But there had always been live music at the Glass Bucket on a Friday night. The people who went would mostly rather have had Country and Western. But they'd grown used to Megs. During her first set anyway, her songs didn't stop the fervent crack. They just slowed it down. People would tap their fingers on their glasses, move their heads in time with the tunes they were hearing, without really noticing they were doing it. It was her second set, when she sang the blues, that set people drifting into little worlds of forgotten dreams and distant memories.

It was her second-last Friday. Megs was wearing her black jeans and white silk shirt. She'd spent more time than usual moussing her hair and putting on one of the lipsticks from Lorraine's vast collection. Never a week passed but Lorraine spent time trailing round make-up counters. She was on a lifetime's quest, a mission that she never abandoned – the search for the perfect lipstick. This would be a red that was too deep to look cheap. A pale brown that didn't turn pink after a couple of gins. It was out there somewhere, on some scented counter, waiting for her.

Megs was coming to the end of the sixties selection, singing 'Me and Bobby McGee', nodding to Lorraine and Harry that she'd be with them after the next chorus, when she saw Gilbert. He was standing at the bar wearing his junior Humphrey Bogart outfit.

He was enveloped in a long raincoat, collar up. People nearby had shifted aside and turned their backs to him. Stranger in our midst, their body language said. He was standing alone, back to the bar, looking down at the whisky in his glass. Every now and then he looked up and gazed sadly ahead. Awkward stranger, his body language said.

Megs watched him as he took the room in. What did a man with his acute sense of shape and colour make of the Glass Bucket? She smiled, imagining his mental turmoil as he surveyed the tartan carpet and walls. She saw him glance at the ceiling. And looked at it too. She hadn't noticed it before. All those years, and she hadn't once considered the ceiling. It was brown from a million or three nicotined exhalations. How long had the ceiling been that colour? And why had nobody ever remarked on it? People round here don't look up. What sort of brown was it, anyway? Sort of yellowed, a baby-diarrhoea brown. Oh God, he's got me at it, she screamed silently. Defining colours.

She stepped from the stage. A little step on to the tartan, she could feel beneath her feet the vague squelch of an industrial-strength twist that had seen too much. It was jaded, the nights, the passions that had been played out on it. The lager it had absorbed.

'This carpet is clapped out,' she said, crossing to Lorraine's table.

'It has to go. Like me.' She nodded towards Gilbert and, grinning sheepishly, moved through the Friday-night crowd to him.

Lorraine squirmed round in her seat. Her skirt and off-the-shoulder top did not allow for much more movement than squirming. 'Told you.' She leaned across to Harry, aglow with gossip. 'She's gone soft on him.'

'So,' said Megs, leaning folded arms on the bar, 'what do you think of the Glass Bucket?' His obvious discomfort amused her.

'Um,' said Gilbert. 'It's . . . um . . .' He could not think of anything tactful to say.

'It's life, Gilbert. But not as you know it.'

'Yes.' He gave her a fragile smile. 'That'd do it. That's what I think.' Then, apologising for himself, 'I just never thought of it.'

'Come meet Lorraine and Harry.' She took his hand, led him across the room in the practised, comfortingly bossy manner of a woman overly accustomed to dealing with children, who has forgotten the ways of adults. It was just what Gilbert needed.

He placed his whisky carefully on the table and sat before it. His hand moved through his hair as he nodded hello.

'What brings you here?' asked Lorraine. She did not like this. Megs was hers.

'I wondered . . . You know . . . I wanted to hear Megs sing.' It was the first time he'd said her name. He'd rather call her Nina. He looked across at her. It seemed so familiar to say someone's name when you hardly knew them. He was not good at familiar. He never usually called someone by name till the third or fourth meeting. It took a little juggling the conversation, but he'd become expert.

'What do you think, then?' Harry wanted to know.

'Wonderful.' His admiration was genuine. 'I've only heard a little. But wonderful.'

Megs finished her drink. 'Time to go fix myself.' She smiled at Gilbert, touched his arm. 'Hope you're going to wait till I'm done.'

'Oh yes.' He was keen. He was drinking with the singer in the band. For the first time in his life, he was in with the in-crowd.

Megs went backstage to reapply Lorraine's cast-off lipstick, Sahara Sundae, and fix her hair. She lingered a while, considering her reflection – the person she preferred to the person she was – the singer in the mirror.

She sang 'Mad about the Boy' and 'Georgia'. She did a little Wilson Pickett, 'Midnight Hour' and U2, 'With or Without You'. When she was halfway through 'I Put a Spell On You' the crowd drifted off into their little worlds of stolen moments and lost chances remembered. People touched, drained handfuls of peanuts into their mouths and allowed themselves a little dreaming. Gilbert forgot he was in the Glass Bucket. He was falling in love with a torch singer called Nina who had a lonely look and a tragic past.

Lorraine looked at Harry, who was looking across the bar at a girl, young, slim, in tight jeans and a shirt that showed her navel. It was the sort of navel that could stand a little showing-off. The girl was looking at Harry. They were smiling that small slip of a knowing smile that said everything. You bastard, Lorraine thought. You're having an affair. Harry, with his balding head, his droopy moustache, his cuddly little beer belly and his lovely liquid brown eyes, was shagging this young thing – how dare he? Lorraine put her hand on the inside of his thigh and looked across at her rival. He's mine. And the younger woman looked away, said something inane to the bartender and laughed gorgeously at her own joke. Her shoulders shook, she put her head on her hand, and turned to look back at Lorraine. Oh no he isn't. And Megs sang on. 'One For the Road'.

When she'd finished, Megs came back to the table. She sat next to Gilbert and took a long swig of the drink he'd bought her.

'You two want to go on somewhere?' Harry was feeling sociable.

Gilbert and Megs smiled they were willing. But Lorraine took Harry's hand and said she was tired. She needed to go home, needed her bed. She put her head on his shoulder and licked the lobe of his ear. Just a flicker of the tongue. She had plans for Harry. She gripped his arm and glanced towards the young, self-assured one sitting at the bar. No chance, girl. Her rival simply sniggered, turned her back. That's what you think, oh old and baggy one.

'He can see you home,' Lorraine told Megs, gesturing with her head to Gilbert. She, too, didn't use people's names. Not when she suspected them of stealing her best friend, anyway.

For a moment Megs imagined herself going home on the back of his bike, wobbling through back streets, legs splayed out, keeping her tights intact. But Gilbert had a car, a 1967 Jaguar.

'I don't use it much,' he explained. 'It keeps needing to be fixed. But it's the shape. I love it. The classic lines. Then the dash isn't cluttered. Nice round dials.' When he switched on the ignition, Schubert played on the cassette deck. He waved his arms as he spoke, as he drove. They hurtled wildly. And Megs worried. Should she invite him in? What would he make of her tasteless clutter? She couldn't relax and enjoy this stylish ride through familiar grey streets, she was having too many doubts about her lifestyle.

She sat back in her seat, reviewing the contents of her home. The fridge and surrounding area alone would bring him out in hives. For the design-conscious, it was six square feet of hell. On top of the fridge was a pale-blue plastic box full of things – an empty can of Mr Sheen, a curler (though nobody used them), some crumpled J-Cloths, a sock waiting for a partner, some postcards and an old Christmas card. Why did she have these useless things? Why hadn't she thrown them out? A tasteful, organised person would have. Next to the box was a pair of Lizzy's wellies, small, bright red, with a sock dangling from one. They were up high, safe from Shameless's chewings. She thought there was a small blue plastic spade next to the wellies. And in behind the frayed wire that snaked up to the electric point was a wad of mail, mostly junk.

'I should've chucked out all that stuff from *Reader's Digest*,' she said into the dark.

'Pardon?' said Gilbert.

'Oh, nothing. Just doing a spot of self-recriminating.'

'Oh, that. I do that in the car, too.'

Then there were the fridge door magnets – two pineapples, a strawberry, a pair of bright-pink plastic feet, a couple of ancient Mr Men, a fried egg, if she remembered correctly. Behind each magnet a note. From Jack: 'Get cornflakes.' From her to Jack: 'Get a job. Buy your own.' From Hannah: 'I hate my school shoes.' That message had been stuck behind the pink feet for the past six months. From Lizzy a series of squiggles and hieroglyphics because she was four and couldn't yet read or write. But she wanted to join in everything. Next to the fridge was a basket filled with filthy potatoes and carrots, because dirty veg were cheaper. Oh God . . . that was just one small area. She considered the rest of her house trying to come up with one item she'd chosen. Everything she now owned, it seemed, had been gifted or donated second-hand by friends or relatives – mostly Vivienne and Lorraine.

He stopped outside her door and switched off the engine. They sat facing ahead, looking through the windscreen, saying nothing. The warmth, Schubert, their vaguely comfortable silence – it was, Megs thought, the most intimate moment she'd had for years.

'Would you like to come up for some coffee?' she asked.

He leaned on the steering wheel, staring up at her building. 'Why not.'

'Only,' she launched into an apology, 'it's messy. Cluttered.'

'My house is cluttered. As you well know.'

'Ah, but you chose your clutter, mine was thrust upon me. Like my life.' She wished she hadn't said that.

The flat was nervily quiet. 'Where is everybody?' Megs looked round. Hannah was staying over with a friend. But there was no sign of Jack. The television was playing silently to an empty room. There was an empty cider bottle on its side by the sofa. Shameless, wagging his tail insanely, intimately sniffed Gilbert's crotch.

'Where's Jack?' Megs looked into the kitchen. Then she checked on Lizzy. The child was in bed, hair spread over the pillow, sleeping effortlessly.

'Jack?' asked Gilbert.

'My son,' said Megs, putting on the kettle, noticing Gilbert taking in, evaluating, her clutter. 'He's meant to be baby-sitting.'

The phone rang. Megs lifted the receiver. 'Hi,' she said.

'How're things?' whispered Lorraine.

'We're about to have coffee,' Megs said. Cupping her hand over the mouthpiece she mouthed, 'Lorraine,' to Gilbert.

He couldn't understand this. They'd parted only ten minutes before. What could they possibly have to say to each other?

'Listen,' Lorraine breathed, 'I can't tell you now, but Harry's having an affair. He's in the loo. I'll phone you tomorrow. I have to see about this.'

'Harry?' Megs didn't believe her. 'Your Harry? Don't be daft.'

'Yes, he is. I know. I saw him. The way he looked at that girl.'

'What girl?'

'At the bar. Ten years old, flat stomach, brainless. I have to go.'
She rang off.

'Lorraine,' Megs explained to Gilbert again, as if he would
understand why people so soon parted would want to talk. He didn't.
In his entire life he had never once phoned someone unless he had
something very definite to say.

The phone rang again.

'Hello, Mum,' said Megs before whoever it was on the other end
could say a word. 'How did I know it was you? Who else would it
be? Yes, everything's fine. No problems. Jack's fine. He's sitting
watching telly. Lizzy's fine, sound asleep.'

Gilbert listened to this expert and soothing weaving of truth and
lies.

'My mother,' said Megs, putting the phone down. 'If I told her
there was no sign of Jack her blood pressure would rocket. She'd
explode.' Megs handed him a mug of instant. 'Where is Jack?'

Gilbert shrugged. 'Perhaps he just slipped out for something.'

'He has nothing to slip out for.' Megs stood a moment, listening,
sniffing. She knew that smell. She realised she'd been aware of it
since she got in. It was one of the smells of her youth. That smell,
and the little excitement of entertaining a stranger, a male stranger,
had made her heady, and nostalgic with it. Booze, incense, cigarettes
and dope. Yes, dope. She stood sniffing violently, thinking: God, this
is what my mother does. This suspicious snorting the air. And bath
essence. Yes, there was bath essence in with those other decadent
scents.

'He's in the bath,' she said to Gilbert.

'There you are. Problem solved,' Gilbert said simply.

'He's in the bath, drinking and smoking.'

'I do that.' Gilbert was quite enthused.

'I'll kill him.' Megs stormed up the hall to the bathroom, stood at
the door. 'Jack. Jack. Are you in there?'

Panicked whisperings and tidal waves of splashings from within.

'Jack? What are you doing in there . . .' Megs rattled the door,
opening it.

Howls. 'Christ. Get out.'

'Don't tell me to get out.' Megs was furious. 'If you don't want people to come in, you should lock the door. No doubt you were too drunk to think about that.'

The room was dim, thickly fogged with steam, and candlelit. It took a second before Megs's eyes adjusted. A ghetto-blaster on the cistern was playing a mournful Oasis song. There were two strange people in her bath, two young faces frozen in raw stupefaction. The girl was sitting behind the boy, legs curled round his back. They were bald, both of them. Megs gripped the towel rail. Her knees were giving way. My God, Lizzy was sleeping alone in the flat and two bald intruders were having a bath.

'Who the hell are you?' she shouted. 'What the fuck are you doing in my bath? Jack? Jesus, Jack. What have you done?'

Gilbert stood staring vacantly at the fridge. He was not too upset by the yellings to fail to notice its ghastliness. He hated fridge magnets. He did not know what to do. Perhaps he should go. But then he did not like to disappear without saying goodbye. It wasn't polite. He sipped his coffee and waited for Megs.

'What are you smoking?' she was screaming. 'And your hair. My God, your hair.' Then a small, torrid silence. 'And Jesus Christ, Jack. Her hair. Jack, you arse.' Splashings and the squeak of naked flesh against bath enamel. 'Get bloody dressed,' Megs shouted.

Gilbert heard her slam the bathroom door. She reappeared in the kitchen tight-lipped, rabid with rage and still clutching their joint. 'The little bugger,' she said. 'He's in the bath, in candlelight, smoking dope, drinking cider and with Sharon Wallace from round the corner.'

Gilbert smiled wanly. 'Oh well. Teenagers . . .'

'And they're bald,' screamed Megs. 'Bald. The stupid bastards are in there shaving each other's heads. Bald.' She said it again. Couldn't believe it. 'Bald.'

'Bald,' Gilbert repeated.

'Both of them,' Megs said. 'What am I going to say to her mother?' She looked at the joint in her hand. She hadn't realised she'd taken it. Without thinking what she was doing she inhaled deeply on it. 'Two white heads gleaming in the dark.' She took another puff. 'There is something about newly shaven heads and pubes. They always

142

look surprised and sort of innocent. Know what I mean?'

Gilbert shrugged.

Megs felt the tension and strain drizzle from her. She relaxed against the wall. 'Bald,' she said. There was whimsy in her voice. 'See your children, they will always knock the legs from under you. You think you're liberated. But they'll find something. Bald. That'd do it. We were such a hairy generation.' She sat at the kitchen table, cupped her chin in her hand. 'And see parents. Some folks are natural-born parents. The rest of us feel as if our psyches have been taken by storm. The natural-born ones breeze through it. This is the time of their lives. They speak soothingly. I see them in parks, on buses – places. They tie laces, wipe assorted grubby bits on and off the body, make endless plates of custard with chopped banana and think nothing of it. But the rest of us spend the whole time from birth to empty-nest syndrome with surprised, agonised expressions on our faces. We look pale and fraught. Our hair is constantly on end with the strain of it all.'

Realising what she'd said, she looked shyly across at him. But he showed no sign of offence. He had no notion of his hairstyle.

Sounds of semi-hysterical giggling came from the bathroom. Shaking with the effort of trying to appear sane and sober, Jack padded into the kitchen. He wore a towel wrapped round his waist. Megs and Gilbert stared at his head.

'What?' Jack stroked his naked skull defensively. His face looked worn against the newly exposed skin on top. His eyebrows were suddenly huge.

'You know what,' said Megs, smoking freely now, gripping the remaining stub of roll-up between thumb and forefinger. 'Jack, Gilbert. Gilbert, Jack.' She nodded from one to the other, introducing them. Gilbert, reliably awkward, held out his hand. Jack looked at it apologetically. He had one hand on his head, the other gripped his towel. He didn't want to let go of either.

'Sorry,' he said.

Gilbert smiled. This boy spoke his language.

'God.' Voice soft, Megs looked up at Jack. 'There's your head. I haven't seen that in years. You were bald when you were born.'

Jack said, 'Christ, Mother.' And padded out of the room again.

'Are you going to see Sharon home?' Megs called into the hall. 'When did her mother say she had to be back?'

'An hour ago,' Jack confessed. He looked down at his feet, wriggled his toes.

'The woman will be worried. Phone her and explain.' Megs pointed at the phone.

Jack didn't move. 'Couldn't you?'

'Me? What's all this got to do with me? You're the one that's been stupid.'

Still Jack didn't move. He clung to his towel and kept his eyes fixed on his toes. 'Please.'

Megs relented. 'All right. I'll see her home as I'm taking Shameless out. But really, Jack, you should take responsibility. What on earth am I going to say to her mother?'

Jack shrugged.

Gilbert seized the moment. If there were exits being made, he could make one too. 'I should go.'

'Don't go,' said Megs. 'Have some coffee.'

'You already made me some.'

'That's right. I gave you the good cup. You being so tasteful I couldn't decide if I should give you the nice cup, which is dark blue – very Gauguin – but cracked. Or one of the crap cups, which are cheap seaside-resort yellow, but crack-free. In the end taste won.'

'Well, thank heavens for that. You certainly have the measure of me.' He wondered if he should kiss her. They stood feet from one another, making fleeting ducking movements, a choreographed shyness, that did not lead to anything physical. He swallowed. His hand, as if it made its own decisions, went to his hair, hovered a moment at his brow, before it took comfort in ploughing a small row of furrows across his scalp. 'I'll see you soon,' he said.

Chapter Seventeen

'Look at it this way,' said Lorraine. 'You'll laugh at it in years to come. It'll be a family joke.'

Saturday morning, Megs's kitchen table, where for years they'd done documentary reruns and critical reviews of their Friday nights.

'I doubt it,' said Megs.

'What did Sharon's mother say?'

'She seemed to think it was all my fault. Not firm enough with my children. Then, who knows what she said, the amount of brandy she took. Of course I didn't need brandy. I just smoked his dope.'

'Good for you. Was it any good?'

'The best. Wonder where he got it.'

They stared at each other a moment before sniggering wildly.

'Look on the bright side,' said Lorraine. 'It'll be a great saving on shampoo.' Then, because she had to say it, and didn't know how to approach the subject, 'Harry's left me.'

'He hasn't. I don't believe you. Not Harry.'

'Yes.' Lorraine nodded. 'He's gone off with Flat Stomach and Brainless.' The room filled with her despair. She lit a cigarette, snap of lighter, fizz of singeing tobacco. 'I thought I'd take him home. Pour him a glass of malt and give him the best blow-job of his life. Remind him of how good he had things. But, "A blow-job won't fix everything, Lorraine," he says. "You think it will. But not this time." So . . .' she flicked ash into the plant pot, '. . . there you go. A blow-job doesn't fix everything. And here's me thinking it did. More fool me.'

Megs didn't like to fetch an ashtray. This was too dire a moment to be prissy about plants. 'He's left?'

'Yes. He wants a baby. Says he's been thinking about it for a couple of years now. And that's what he really wants – children. Now there's something a blow-job really won't get you.' She moved her tongue across her teeth, clamped her lips. She didn't want to cry. Avoiding Megs's sympathetic gaze, she looked out of the window.

'Well.' Megs was shocked. 'I never thought Harry . . .' Then, reassuringly, 'He'll be back.'

'I don't think so. Flat Stomach and Brainless is two months gone.'

'My God.' Then, stiffly through the gloom, 'Well, brainless she may remain, but the flat stomach's soon to be but a memory.'

Lorraine meant to smile, only grimaced. 'There's that.'

The squeak and honk, rattle and bash of Saturday cartoons battered through from the living room. A tear slid down Lorraine's cheek. 'There you go.' She was resigned. 'Don't people always want the one thing you can't give them?' She'd fought a long, bitter, hormonal battle with her body, cursing its inability to conceive. She hated it. She hated herself. Sometimes she'd lie alone on her bed in the dark on her pink-patterned duvet, under the framed picture of puppies in a basket, quietly punching her stomach, punishment for blocked tubes. 'Damn you.'

For years her monthly cycle brought her out in craziness and rage. She'd sit on the toilet staring with sorrow at bloodied tissue. 'Damn you.' She'd run her fingers tenderly over newspaper pictures of abused children. 'I'd love you. I wouldn't do that.' Sitting, weekday television evenings, side by side on the sofa, Harry would look across at her and she'd be crying. He'd turn back to the screen. There was nothing he could say. Babies were all she thought about. Her obsession made him lonely. 'Pack it in, Lor.'

After a couple of years of precision lovemaking – passion on cue, according to the demands of charts, thermometers, and Lorraine lying frigid when her body wasn't ripe, 'No, no, we must save it for tomorrow. It's my time tomorrow' – Harry had insisted Lorraine get tested. He knew it couldn't be him. His last girlfriend had aborted his child. Now he discovered himself thinking about it. He rather fancied himself as a dad.

When they discovered Lorraine's tubes were blocked, Harry tore up the charts and graphs Lorraine had lovingly drawn up.

'That's my life you're tearing into pieces,' she cried.

'Our life starts now.' He was adamant. 'And while I'm at it . . .' He reached up and took down the puppy picture. 'I fucking hate this.' Lorraine re-hung the puppies and took out a personal loan to pay for IVF treatment. But Harry said, 'I'm not wanking in a cubicle surrounded by porno magazines.' So they applied to adopt.

Then, two days before their interview, Lorraine met her poet. Friday night at the Glass Bucket, there he was at the bar, looking gorgeous. It was chemistry at first sight. He took her back to his flat and Lorraine remembered what sex was about. That fevered fumble, helping him to help her out of her clothes and never getting close enough. She lay on his bed, one hand on his neck in his hair, the other on his bum, and she thought, 'This is me. This is what I am. Sex is what I do best.' She only cried a little bit.

Next day she and her poet and her personal loan took off across the country. They battered and crunched down the motorway, listening to old Neil Young tapes, singing along. 'Hey, hey, my, my . . .' And Lorraine wept buckets for lost years. 'I should've been doing this all along.'

They stopped at motorway caffs, drank foul coffee, ate burgers, listened to the banter of long-distance truckers. Lorraine felt the throb of wheels and the hum of a different life. She borrowed money for the jukebox, played hits, old songs from happy times past before she declared war on her tubes. She breathed greasy wafts of fast food and decadence and she thought, All this life was out here, while I was in my pink bedroom crying for children that would never be born. Hands on the jukebox, back to the room, she danced with herself.

Harry meantime cancelled the adoption interview. Next day, caught in a traffic jam opposite a park, he watched a father playing football with his infant son. The child, knee-high to a white plastic ball, ran with uncertain legs at it, kicked at it wildly, watched it move a full six inches. The father cried, 'Great shot,' and made an absurd display of losing a tiny tackle. Then he lifted his son and gently cast him into the air. 'Away we go.' The child, chuckling wildly, fell back towards his outstretched hands. That wholesome, infantile laughter rang clear through the rattle and irate honk of impatient drivers.

Harry watched, unaware that the snarled knot of traffic had unravelled and the cars in front of him had all moved off. He was smiling, though he didn't realise it. He had never felt such a pang of envy in his life. He wanted a child.

'I wouldn't mind,' Lorraine sniffed, turning to Megs, 'but the bitch looks like I did fifteen years ago. Younger than me. Better-looking than me. And pregnant. I feel like shit. And everybody must've known about it except me. They must all have been laughing at me.'

'No,' said Megs.

'Is this how you felt when you discovered Mike and Denise?'

'Yes. Sort of futile and a failure and betrayed. Tricked out in old, worn, child-stained clothes, with lank hair and no make-up.'

From through the house came the cry, 'Baldy! Baldy!' Something was thrown. Something crashed. 'Shut up, Lizzy.' Jack's voice. Lizzy howled.

'You two stop it through there,' Megs hollered, leaning as far back in her chair as she could so that she could look into the living room without actually getting up.

'They were in bed when I got back. I just stood there at the door, looking at them. I think I said something cryptic like, "Having fun?"'

'Were they actually doing it?' Lorraine wanted details, though she'd heard them all before. Nothing soothed like other people's wounds.

'No. They'd not long done, though. She was getting up. Her clothes were on the chair by the window, all folded nicely. His suit was hanging up on the back of the door.'

'Oh, the tidy bitch. I hate that. How was she?'

'Cellulite. Fat arse. Droopy tits. A grippable roll of fat.' They grinned. 'Nah,' said Megs, 'she's got a great body. Mike was lying back, smoking. She was at my side of the bed. I can still see it. And now I realise they'd been doing it for ages. They had a routine.'

'What did you say then?' Lorraine prompted.

'Nothing. I just stood there. I don't even think my mouth was moving, the way it does, with all the insults that your brain is too shocked to let go of. I was leaning on the doorpost and I think my face was all torn with hurt and betrayal. Denise was horrified. But Mike was just lying there. Know what I think? I think he planned it.

148

I think he wanted me to find them. Then he wouldn't have to tell me about the affair. He wouldn't have to say he was leaving me. I had to throw him out.'

'I wouldn't be surprised,' said Lorraine.

'Know what I did?' said Megs.

'No,' said Lorraine. But she did. Of course she did. She'd been through this story often.

'I stripped the bed. Even though they were still there. I stripped it, and I was going to wash the sheets. But I threw them out. I ran down to the bin at the back and stuffed them in whilst Mike and Denise were struggling to get dressed.' She rubbed her face, and yawned. 'Then of course I had to buy more sheets. We only had one set.'

Megs gathered their empty mugs and took them to the sink, rinsed them under the tap and pressed the button on the kettle. 'More?' she said, lifting the coffee jar.

Lorraine nodded, and lit another cigarette. 'Harry and Brainless did it at her flat.' She pursed her lips. Considered her new identity as a cuckold. 'I suppose I had it coming. The affairs I've had. What goes around comes around. You can't say I didn't deserve it.'

Megs didn't answer that. It was bad enough for Lorraine to admit the truth without someone agreeing with her. She switched back to her own vile moments. 'I didn't want to ever sleep in that bed again. But of course I couldn't afford to throw it out.'

The word 'afford' started fear in Lorraine. She would have to manage on her own. The whole world of alone was looming before her. One little chicken breast under the grill, one plate to wash. No obliging bum to warm her cold feet on in bed. Nobody to chat to. Nobody to turn to after a night slumped before the telly and say, 'Well, that wasn't worth watching.' She never found any solace in silence. It scared her. Then again, if being alone was her future, she thought she ought to go home, lock the door and get on with it.

The front door slammed, Hannah was home. Megs heard her go straight to her room, shut the door, then to the bathroom, rush of water, rattle of toothbrush, back to bedroom, shut door again. 'Signs of a guilty conscience,' she said to Lorraine. 'Remember all that?'

'Do I ever. God, scrubbing your teeth, sucking Polos, smiling dutifully through a stinking hangover. At least I don't have to lie like that any more.'

'Be back in a minute.' Megs reluctantly rose and went to speak to her daughter.

Hannah flushed, and hurriedly stuffed something under her duvet as Megs came into the room.

'Did you have a nice time?' Megs said.

'Great,' Hannah enthused. 'Brilliant.'

'Who was it you stayed with?'

'Chrissy.'

'It was Lisa when you went out last night.'

Hannah flushed deeper. Was it? She couldn't remember. She was so hungover last night's lie seemed a lifetime away. 'No,' she said weakly. 'Chrissy.'

'Who have you been with?' Megs said, sweeping back the duvet cover to reveal a crumpled heap of scanty black underwear. 'Who is he?'

'Chrissy.' Hannah wasn't giving up on her lie. 'These are Chrissy's.'

'I like that lie, it's in the true child-to-parent tradition. Your belief in it is touching. I used to lie like that to my parents. I had parents too. You know, a matching set. Evenings they sat either side of the fireplace reading the *Mail* and I came home to them and told them lies. You have not let the family down. Who is he?'

'David.'

'How old?'

'Twenty,' said with hope.

'How old?' Megs folded her arms. She wasn't moving till she got the truth.

'Twenty-eight.'

'And you're sixteen. It's not on, Hannah. We'll talk about this later.' Megs returned to the kitchen. 'Lorraine,' she sighed, sitting down, 'I do believe the girl is worse than you.'

'Surely not. God help her.'

'Someone has to. She's seeing a man almost twice her age.'

Lorraine raised her eyes. Sipped her coffee and said, 'You'll have to get Aunty Betty and her wooden spoon to him.'

Megs smiled. Years ago, when she'd worked at the Seaview Guest

House, a tattooed man had came into her bedroom, naked. It had taken Megs a minute to see his nakedness through the blaze of decorations all over his body. But when she had, she screamed. Aunty Betty rushed from the kitchen wielding the first thing that came to hand – a wooden spoon. But her fury made it seem like some fearsome cleaver. The interloper had fled, down the stairs and out the door, naked and ashamed. Hours later the police found him cowering on the beach and came to collect his clothes for him. He was too scared to come himself.

'Aunty Betty,' Megs said softly, 'we need you.'

She folded her arms on the table, laid her head on them. 'Lorraine,' she said, 'I don't know – what is it about parents and children that we deny all sexual activity to each other? As if that isn't how they got here in the first place. Parents have silent, stifled sex and children sit suddenly bolt upright and stare ahead in feigned innocence. And I, who just entered the room, pretend not to notice the fumblings and dishevelled hair and rumpled clothing. Sometimes it seems that's all we do to each other, parents and children, lie and lie and lie.'

Lizzy came through. 'I want a drink.' She handed Megs a pink plastic mug. Which was handed back half-filled with orange juice.

'There's nothing in the house,' said Megs. 'I'll have to shop.'

'I'll come with you,' offered Lorraine. She decided to put off being alone for an hour or so. In fact, for as long as possible. She turned in her seat to watch Lizzy in her dungarees and huge dog's-face slippers pad back to the living room, clutching her mug in both hands. She smiled when she heard Lizzy's full-throated roar, 'Get off my seat,' and Jack's huge, resigned sigh as he heaved himself from chair to sofa.

'That one will have no problems when she grows up. Nobody will dump her. Nobody would dare.' She adored the child.

'It's Jack who'll have trouble,' Megs sighed. 'His sisters run rings round him.'

'I'll have to buy him a new baseball cap.'

'Lorraine.' Megs put a mug of coffee in front of her. 'You can't afford to indulge my children any more. You have to watch your cash.'

'I know. I should look for a new job. But who'd have me? What can I do? What am I good at?' She lifted her mug to her lips, blew on it, decided against taking a sip and put it down again. 'Well, there's that.' She shoved her mouth into a wan little smile. 'But we know now that doesn't solve everything.'

'You could put it on your CV,' suggested Megs. '"Gives a great blow-job."'

'Harry said last night that Brainless was better. Better at that. Better at anything you can think of, in fact. He says she really, really loves him. And she listens to him. Which apparently is more than I ever do. He says she makes him feel good about himself for the first time in years.'

'People hurt each other. We always come to that.' Megs cupped her hands round her mug and stared across the kitchen. The crazed cartoon blather and stramash still ricocheted through the living room. The fridge purred. There was a thin haze of dirt on the fake tile lino. The unit was strewn with crumbs, dollops of marg and jam, cornflakes, drops of milk and a scattering of sugar. There was a pile of dirty dishes in the sink and a crumpled tea towel beside the kettle. She should clean up. All her best fights had taken place in this kitchen. The one with Mike when she first had him alone after discovering him with Denise. That night, long after the children were in bed, he appeared in the kitchen to pick up his things.

'You bastard,' she said. 'I've been going out to work, looking after the kids,' she waved her arms – her grievances were too many to list – 'and you were fucking that cow. You were coming home here, moaning at me. Nagging me. "Can't you make an effort, Megs?"' She imitated him, whiny voice. 'Being all nicey-nicey to the neighbours, "Good morning, Mrs Thing. Lovely day, Mr Whatsit." Ignoring your children and . . .' she ran to him, to hit him. But he caught her arm, so she kicked his ankle, '. . . me!' she yelled.

'Bitch,' he spat. Clenched his fist and raised it. His face was knotted with loathing. 'Cunt.' He said it as hard as he could, for he couldn't bring himself to land the blow.

She picked up a plate. Glaring at him, she threw it to the floor. It splattered, scattering china pieces across the kitchen. Years later she was to find bits under the fridge.

'That's right.' His lip curled in scorn. 'Take it out on the crockery.'

She threw a cup at him. Missed. It shattered against the wall and a flying fragment missiled into his cheek. He put his hand over the pain and blood.

'You sodding boor.' Her voice was lowered. She opened her mouth but was too overwhelmed to speak. Her lips and lower jaw were loose, shaking with hurt and fury. When at last she found her voice, it came trembling from her throat. 'You wear your sodding suit and you shut me out. I'm not good enough for you any more, am I? I wear this old stuff and you're ashamed of me, aren't you? But you dump on me. Take your frustrations and tensions out on me. I am so handy for that. You're charming at work and come home to snap at me. Bastard.' She kicked him again. He did not move. 'Behind every successful man is a woman. BOLLOCKS!' Her voice returned. She screamed at him, waving two fingers. 'You fuck,' she shouted. 'Arse.' She was screaming, leaning forward at him, shoving a single, stiff middle finger in his face. Her face was nasty, contorted with pain and shame and disgust. Eyes puffed, swollen with tears. What must I have looked like? she mused. 'I hate you. I hate you. I hate you,' she screamed till her voice cracked. Cords bulged in her throat. She rushed at him, kicking and slapping. 'Hate. Hate. Hate,' she cried. In some recessed layer of untapped feeling beneath the heaving surge of fury, she realised, oh, the relief it was to tell him her true feelings, at last. He did nothing. He stood still under the raining blows, letting her let go. His hand was raised, but not to protect himself from her beating. It was the vile rush of her saliva that he couldn't bear.

'Behind every successful man is a woman with a brush and shovel, cleaning up the shit he's too full of himself to notice. Bastard. Bastard. Bastard.' But now she was not kicking him. She was knocking her own sorry, unloved head on the doorpost and weeping. Choking. She turned. Jack and Hannah were standing watching her. They were hand in hand, wearing matching bright-red tracksuit pyjamas, and they were staring at her with huge, sleepless eyes. Hannah was clutching her favourite toy, an ancient duck called Harvey. They were absorbing everything they saw, every detail of the scene that confronted them. They had seen her fury. She had never felt so ashamed. She thought she had ruined their innocence.

Mike went through to the bedroom to pack. When he came back

into the kitchen to tell her he was finally going she noticed he'd taken her favourite case but thought better of mentioning it. Besides, she had cast around looking for something to use to wipe her face and blow her nose, and finding nothing she had lifted her T-shirt up. Now she'd exposed her stomach and grubby bra, and he pointedly noticed.

'I have to get the children back to bed,' she said.

'I never knew you could be so rude.' That glimpse of sagging underwear and flab had given him the upper hand. His stomach was still smooth and flat.

'Oh, for goodness' sake, Mike,' she scoffed. Her throat hurt – too much shouting. Her voice was still shaking – too much emotion. 'Everybody can be rude. I was always rude. I was just too polite to let it show.'

It was three months before they could communicate again. Divorce. Maintenance. Visiting rights. After Thomas died Mike drifted back, lingering in this kitchen. She could not look at him without noticing the scar on his cheek.

How she hated to remember that night, her loss of control. She still recoiled from that hideous moment when she realised that her children had seen it all. She wondered if they remembered it too, and if they secretly hated her for it. She covered her face with her hands, protecting herself from her memories.

In the living room Lizzy and Jack started to quarrel. 'Leave me. Leave me,' Lizzy shouted. Then, hollering above the television, 'That's mine.'

'Will you two stop it,' Megs said. 'Please.' She did not want to shout. She did not want to move. Though she knew she ought to get up and go through to check that nobody was actually getting beaten up. Lizzy bullied Jack horribly.

'I'm just trying to show her how to make her Lego into something other than a little gun.'

'Lizzy,' Megs ordered, 'let Jack show you how to build something out of the Lego.'

'Don't want him to,' Lizzy sulked.

'Yes you do,' Megs said. 'You want to build things, don't you?'

'No.' Little pouty voice from behind the sofa.

'Oh well. Don't, then. Stick with making little guns. Don't advance yourself. Don't expand your mind to greater and greater things. But don't come crying to me when you're thirty and are still sitting behind the sofa in your silly slippers making Lego guns when all your friends are doctors, lawyers, architects or proper bricklayers complete with bum cleavage.'

Lorraine tutted. 'You shouldn't speak to her like that.'

Jack laughed.

Lizzy relented. 'All right. Show me. You do it.'

'Chip butties,' Megs's eyes lit up. She sat straight in her seat, face brimming with glee. 'Chip butties,' she said again, leaning across the table, gripping Lorraine's arms. 'It came to me just now, when my brain emptied. That's when the best ideas come to you. When you're not doing anything specific with your brain. Forget all the marinated chicken, the tomatoes, ham, cheeses, all the fancy sandwiches. We could open the world's first chip butty bar. The only thing we'll serve is chip sandwiches. Fat chips, thin chips, little crispy chips – whatever you fancy. With a selection of sauces. We'll make a fortune. Days of heaven and cholesterol. Aunty Betty would be proud. Return to the golden fries of yesteryear.'

For a moment Lorraine joined the fantasy. 'Chiparama,' she glowed. 'Chips a-gogo. Don't ask what we can do with your fries, ask what our fries will do for you. Salt, vinegar, ketchup. Mayonnaise, even.' She spread her hands, pardoning already misguided customers who might make this choice. 'They'll come for miles.' Then the truth snuck up and hit her. She shouldn't be dreaming. She couldn't dream any more. She had her life to sort out. And she didn't think chip butties were the answer to her prayers. 'We'll smell of fat all the time. Our hair will go all greasy and lifeless. Our pores will open. Our skin will be grey and flaccid.'

'Don't tell me. The face that launched a thousand chips.'

Grinning, Lorraine said, 'That was very Big Bill Broonzy of you, shouting out like that.'

'God,' Megs shrieked, hands flying to face, shielding it as long-gone expressions from a forsaken slice of her life spread across it. 'I'd forgotten all about that.' Memories. She let them flow. 'God,' she whispered. 'Big Bill Broonzy.'

It was their last tour. They'd done Amsterdam, Copenhagen, Marseilles and Paris. Small, hazy, smoke-filled back-street clubs where people gathered late, drank and listened to the blues. Megs loved it. There was nothing she didn't enthuse about: the buildings, the coffee, the clothes, the beer, the food. 'There are even strange colours. Every morning smells of coffee and fresh baking. And nobody knows who I am. I love being a stranger. All around me I hear the rhythm of strange words. I don't understand what people are saying. If I'm doing something as simple as ordering a beer I have to think about what words to use.'

'You play at home, at least you get ripped off in English. You come over here and it happens to you in a language you don't speak. I just love that,' Mike complained.

Walking in Montmartre she gripped his arm. 'We could come live here. In Paris.'

'Don't be daft,' he said.

'We could,' she said. 'We could play small bars, just you and me. You playing, me singing. We wouldn't need much. I love you.' She didn't mean it. She meant, I love this place. I love this moment. He didn't answer.

'Think of the people who have been here. Lived here. Worked here. Hemingway. James Joyce. Nina Simone. Maybe one of them walked down this street. Maybe their feet . . .' She pointed at the worn paving slabs. She was young enough to be dreamy about fame. To indulge in thinking that if she stepped on the very ground where one of her heroes once trod some of his fabulous gift would seep up through her shoes, through her. She stopped, spread her arms, felt the Parisian air, shut her eyes. She imagined them all here, in this street, walking in a long row, arms linked. Though she knew their times in the city did not coincide. 'Louis Armstrong, T.S. Eliot, F. Scott Fitzgerald, Gertrude Stein, Django Reinhardt. And all those blues singers, sons and daughters of slaves who learned their songs in fields and in Southern bars with wonderful names like the Dreamland Café or Pete Lala's, like' – the name escaped her – 'thing.'

'Who?'

'You know. Tall guy. Deep voice. Swore he ate two pork chops and three fried eggs for his breakfast every morning. You know. Thing.'

'I haven't the vaguest idea who you are talking about.' He was envious of her vast knowledge of the blues, its singers and their biographies. Besides, this was to be his last tour. He'd decided. He was tired of being poor. He felt poor and shoddy in an increasingly gleamy world. He was starting to look with longing at expensive cars and electrical goods. He lingered over adverts in supplements that showed richer men than him lounging on extravagantly comfortable sofas with fabulous women, drinking smart drinks, laughing and looking cool. He wanted that. He'd signed up two months ago to start an accountancy course. He just didn't know how to tell the others.

They came home and returned to their reality, the round of small venues – village halls, pubs, greasy food and bladder-torturing hours heaped and crumpled in the van with the radio on. Miles and miles, with Megs dreaming of Paris every inch. Now and then she'd sit up, staring quizzically ahead. 'Who was that guy? What was his name? Big, handsome face. Oh, I can see it.' The others chipped in to her quandary, sometimes offering names from their smattering knowledge of blues men. 'Blind Lemon Jefferson?' 'Furry Lewis?' 'Scrapper Blackwell?' 'Leroy Carr?' But Megs always shook her head. 'Nah.'

June. They gigged in Aberdeen, boozed, and played old hippie songs – 'Spoonful' and 'Red Rooster' – to students and oil men. Next night Inverness, then up to Nairn and down the west coast, heading for Oban, chewing gum, smoking, drinking lager and Jack Daniels and hardly talking at all.

They took a detour to Gairloch. Eddy said the lobsters were worth the drive. But Megs thought the drive was worth the drive. Trundling down through pine forests, looking over treetops to the sea. The smell of fresh air, intoxicating peaty draughts, dark-green pine scents seeped through the rusting gaps and holes in their van, cut their cleansing way through the fug of smoke, joss sticks, musk, forgotten carry-outs, sweat and old farts.

They fell silent, gazing out at the distant swell of blue, distracted from their usual travelogue: easy tabloid crosswords, small bickerings about old *Bonanza* plots or discontinued chocolate bars, to a constant musical backdrop of Bruce Springsteen or Bob Seger. 'Night moves,' that nicotined, booze-raddled voice would cry. 'Night moves,' they'd join in, even if they only lipped the words. They didn't sing much and they no longer planned or wove dreams out of spangled, elaborated stories of other people's success that floated to them on the musicians' grapevine. They were disillusioned.

They drove to the small quay and decanted, blinking, into a blistering summer day. They'd forgotten the weather. It was for ever late February in the back of that gaudy painted van. People watched as they shuffled out of it, stretching and scratching. People always watched, and they always performed. They looked like a bunch of deranged plumbers. But they were a band. They acted cool. They didn't look at anybody.

They walked the length of the quay. Four blokes and a girl. Mike draped his arm round her. She was his. That was how they always walked together – until they got married. After that she was usually three paces behind him.

Of course, they did not get a lobster. They stood watching as two lorries piled high with them drove off the quay, and south. Then they bought corned beef, bread, crisps, biscuits and beer to eat on the beach.

One o'clock in the morning, Mike and Megs sat alone by the sea. The others, zipped into sleeping bags, slept drunkenly in the back of the van. Megs dug her toes into the sand. They had one last tin of Carlsberg that they handed back and forth between them – a swig apiece.

There was pink campion growing up the bank behind them. The breeze shoved through it. The tide crept towards them, sucking and sighing back, dragging shells and shingle. A late tern called – a scraping cry.

'We could live here,' Megs said. 'We could stop touring and live here. We could grow our own stuff and be self-sufficient.'

'Last week you were going to live in Paris.'

'That was that dream. This is this one.'

'I'm going to be an accountant,' he said. 'I'm giving up the band and going to college in October.'

She stared at him. Couldn't believe it. 'You never said.'

'I'm saying now.'

'But why?'

'Why! Why do you think? We've been doing this for years and we're nowhere. We're nothing. We have nothing. It costs as much as we earn to keep going. I'm going to end up an old man with no decent home, no car. Nothing. I'm getting out.'

'But . . .' was all she could say.

Seeing how shaken she was, he put his arm round her. 'Marry me,' he said. 'We'll have our own house done out the way we want it. Kids even. We'll stop all this touring. All this sitting in the van. I can't stand it any more. I can't stand having nothing. No money.'

She didn't answer. Marriage hadn't really occurred to her. She wanted to keep going. She didn't think it through – she never thought anything through – but somehow she believed if she kept on going all the things she wanted would come to her. It was just a matter of time.

He did not know what to make of her silence. So he kissed her. 'Marry me,' he said again. 'I'll make you happy. I'll make you so rich you'll never want for anything.'

She didn't think she was wanting for anything now. But she kissed him back and felt that flicker of his tongue against hers, and she wanted him. They made love on the sand, with the campion moving behind them and the sea sneaking nearer and nearer. She wrapped her legs round him, clung to him. And then, oh joy, it came to her. It came the way things that have been evading an overenquiring mind always come – at that sweet moment when the mind stops enquiring, when it idles and is vacant. Just when Mike was starting to moan, and rapture was on its way to him, Megs remembered the name she'd been seeking.

'BIG BILL BROONZY!' she screamed. 'That's the guy. Big Bill Broonzy.'

Mike's ardour wilted. 'What do you mean by that? Is that what you're thinking about?'

'No.' She knew she'd hurt him.

'Don't you think about me when we're doing it?' He withdrew from her. Sat up. Turned his back.

'Of course I do. I think about you all the time. I love you.' She

159

didn't but she thought she ought to say it. 'It was just that I've been trying to remember his name. Then when I relaxed it came to me. That's all.'

Mike huffed. He lit a cigarette. 'You don't really care about me. Do you?'

'I do. I do. I love you. I want to marry you. I really do.' Anything, anything. She would say anything to cover the fact that she was lying to him, and to hide from the fact that he might be lying to her, too.

'Do you?' He reached out to stroke her hair.

'Yes.' She met his eyes. 'Yes.' For a moment she just about believed it herself. She stripped off what little she was wearing. 'Let's celebrate with a swim.'

'Too cold,' said Mike. 'And I'm too drunk.'

She ran the few steps to the sea alone and tiptoed in, gasping as she went deeper, arms above her head. 'C'mon.'

Mike wouldn't move. So she swam alone. Slowly up and down past him. The night was soft on her face, a small breeze drifting over the surface ruffled against her, chill against her damp cheeks. She turned, eyes level with the water. The sea seemed endless. She thought she could swim out into the Atlantic and keep going and going and going. She turned on to her back, spread-eagled, and floated. She could feel the swell and drift of the water beneath her, and above a dusting of stars, summer constellations. She was truly happy. At the time she thought it was because Mike wanted to marry her. But thinking about it now, she realised it was because he was not with her.

'Betrayed,' she said softly. 'Talk about betrayed. Look what I did. I betrayed myself and Mike.'

'Why?' Lorraine couldn't believe this. 'What did you do?'

'I married him. I was afraid of having nothing. When he said he was going to be an accountant, I couldn't think what I would do next. So I married him. What a shit.'

'No you're not. Don't say that. Rubbish. You and Mike had been together for such a long time, everyone was tired of waiting for you to marry.'

'I didn't love him, though. Did I? I'd been part of something for so long, I was scared of being alone.'

'Ah, that,' said Lorraine. 'I know that. But it's not all your fault. You can't go blaming yourself.'

'Oh well, Big Bill Broonzy.' Megs smiled. 'Better blame him, then. It's all his fault. All of this. Everything.' A wave of her hand indicated the flat and all her past life.

'You gotta blame someone,' said Lorraine.

'It's as well Big Bill Broonzy as anyone.'

Lizzy came into the kitchen, teetering on her high heels, scraping them on the lino. Tiny, naked feet making big boats of her mother's size five shoes. 'Who is Big Bill Broonzy?'

'He was a singer. He's dead. I was just remembering something that happened years ago on a beach. That's all,' Megs told her.

'Did you know him?' Lizzy hobbled dangerously towards her.

'No. It was just something I said.'

'What did you say?'

'I said his name. I'd been trying to remember it. It was at Gairloch. Years and years ago.'

Lizzy considered this. Then her face lit up. 'I remember,' she said. 'I remember that.'

'You can't possibly,' Megs scolded. 'It was before you were born.'

'I was always born.' Lizzy couldn't bear to think of Megs doing anything without her. 'I was there. You just didn't see me. I was hiding.'

'Ah.' Megs softened. 'That'll be it.' She watched the child wobble across the kitchen and felt her expression change. The love she felt. Sometimes it shook her. Sometimes just seeing her daughter made something within her tremble. Her mother often accused her of loving Lizzy too much. But Megs doubted anyone could love someone so small too much. This love was the purest thing Megs had ever known, but still it made her guilty. She thought that Lizzy was a child who was never meant to be. If Thomas hadn't died, Lizzy would never have been born.

The child made her precarious way back to the living room. 'I'm going to have to wear these shoes if we're going out. I can't tie my laces.'

'What?' Megs acted incensed. 'How old are you?'

'Four.'

'Four and you can't tie your own laces. Good heavens, when I was four I had a milk round *and* I was offered a job as head of British Industry.'

'You shouldn't speak to her like that,' said Lorraine. 'You'll give her a complex.'

Lizzy turned and shot Megs a mocking look. 'It's not my fault I can't tie my laces,' she said.

'Whose fault is it, then?' Lorraine wanted to know.

Lizzy looked surprised she had to ask. 'Big Bill Broonzy's,' she said.

Chapter Eighteen

They ordered pizza, hired videos and drank too much wine. Lorraine decided she'd drunk too much to drive home, and stayed over. Drinking too much and staying over suited her. It not only delayed that moment of going home and facing the great alone, but for a while she actually forgot about it. But Megs worried that she would take up residence on the sofa. She couldn't blame her. All those years ago on that beach she had found herself agreeing to marry because she too was afraid of being alone.

They'd slept on the beach that night, squeezed side by side in their double sleeping bag, under the stars. Megs woke early, roused by the rustle of wind through the grasses and campion in the dunes behind them, and the white swish of restless seagulls floating in the half-dark, knowing that something was about to happen. Dawn was going to break. When the first light appeared, a searing glimmer along the horizon, the gulls rose, shrieking. A callous clamour resounding across the morning. The new day seemed to take them by storm, the din they made. Maybe, Megs thought, resentfully lifting herself on to one elbow, in their tiny seagull minds they'd forgotten that this same thing happened yesterday, and the day before, and every single day before that. Maybe each new day scared them stiff. They saw that distant glare in its moments of blinding whiteness before it glowed into reds and golds, and they decided the end had come. 'End of the world, end of the world,' they screamed, a wild, clanging cacophony. Their uproar didn't last long. But Megs was awake. She felt hungover and filthy. Sand lined the secret recesses of her body and made her scalp crawl. She went back into the sea, to cleanse herself.

It was even colder than last night, but when she had grown accustomed to the chill she spread herself into the water and started to swim towards the new light. When she turned, she was surprised at how far she'd come. There was a vast expanse of choppy water between her and the shore. The wind out here was harsh. She rolled in the water and swam again, out towards that white glare, tempted again to keep going. Fear made her stop. She looked down, could hardly see her legs waving in the deep keeping her afloat. 'I'm scared of this, and scared of that. Scared of everything.' Scared of the grey murk below her, scared of the new dawn and scared of life on her own. Years and years she'd gone everywhere, done her growing up as part of a group. She'd forgotten what it was like to be an individual. She was afraid the individual couldn't cope on her own. She didn't trust herself to manage without Mike. Now he'd decided to go off on his own, she wanted to know what was going to happen to her. She couldn't wait to let life happen naturally, so she'd manipulated her future. She'd agreed to marry Mike. 'End of the world. End of the world,' she'd sang to herself as she swam ashore. Remembering that now, Lorraine's reluctance to go home seemed trivial. Still, Megs worried that she'd lose what little privacy she had.

It was a handy worry that distracted her from her main worries – money, work, her children. She lay in the dark, at her feet Shameless fidgeted in his sleep, whiffing, whining, paws scurrying over dreamland parks, chasing dreamland rabbits. Lizzy, clutching a purple toy Transit van that dug into Megs's side, slept noisily, breathing chokily, snorting slightly. Had she been an old man and not her beautiful daughter, Megs would have been deeply irritated. Megs stroked her perfect cheek and said, 'Wonder what Gilbert is doing now?' She surprised herself. Until that moment she had not been aware of thinking about him.

Gilbert was in bed with Annette. They always slept together at his place on Saturday nights, at hers on Thursdays. She liked the right-hand side near the window and kept a pair of ivory silk pyjamas in the top right-hand drawer of the chest next to the bed. She had a toothbrush in the bathroom cabinet and insisted Gilbert kept baking soda toothpaste, for she liked no other. She brought free-range eggs and fresh orange juice for breakfast. They drank Colombian coffee –

black, no sugar. They read the *Sunday Times*, swapping supplements. They didn't speak much. They thought they had a perfect arrangement. A marriage that had no legal bindings, no bickering about who had drunk all the Earl Grey and who should buy the toilet roll. A commitment that did not involve anybody's bank account.

Saturday nights, if they did not go out, Gilbert cooked. Saturday mornings he shopped, cycling – hair on end – between delicatessen, fruit shop, Italian bakers and Oddbins, where he spent a happy half-hour selecting the wine with the most tasteful label.

In the afternoon, wearing a vast butcher's apron with ties that twice circled his waist and knotted over his tummy, he'd set to. He laid out his Sabatier knives, and his best pots, cookbook propped open. For the past three Saturdays he'd done saltimbocca alla romana. This week was no different. He had veal, fresh sage and ham – he was perfecting the dish. He splashed a great deal, drank a great deal, hummed snatches of Verdi and Puccini. The more he drank, the more he splashed, the louder he hummed. He was happy. His hair was flat. Not once did fretful fingers reach towards his scalp.

Annette usually sat, legs curled, on his sofa, watching videos – always with subtitles, often in black and white. She drank white wine. Sometimes she read. And sometimes she came, leaned on the doorpost, not quite entering the cook's domain. Wine in hand, little smile – was she being patronising? Gilbert wondered – she'd watch. 'I'm rubbish in the kitchen,' she told him.

Once a month she ate out with her chums. Over pasta, salad and white wine they'd discuss their lives. The more wine they ordered, the more deranged, gigglish and critical the conversation. Gilbert was a favourite topic. They all agreed Annette should take him in hand. 'Sort him out,' someone always said. 'Get him a decent haircut. And his trousers.' Giggles. Gilbert's trousers were not what he thought them to be.

'I know,' Annette would sigh. 'They're sort of flappy.' She'd make flappy movements with drunken hands. Gilbert's trousers, they unanimously decided, flapped where they ought to be snug, and were snug where a bit of flapping would be the thing. Poor Gilbert.

He invoked such criticism, and all he thought he was doing was living his life.

Today, after he'd bought his Italian rice, fresh Parmesan and porcini, and packed them carefully in his rucksack, he cycled miles out of his way to where Megs lived. He pedalled past her building, looking up at her window. What was she doing? he desperately wanted to know. She would be up there behind her window, answering the phone, fending off friends and admirers. People would be constantly ringing her up with invitations, or perhaps just to say hello. People did things like that to someone like Megs. But not, he knew, to him. Then again, he never phoned anybody just to say hello. He was scared they might be annoyed at him and not want to say hello back.

Megs fascinated him. He imagined her to be a lot wilder and bawdier than she actually was. Suddenly scared that she might throw open her window and lean out, tits pressed on folded arms, to make saucy comments to passers-by, like Melina Mercouri in *Never on a Sunday*, and notice him gazing fondly up at her, he took off. Wheels whirring, feet a blur, he felt a fool. A passing child, exuberantly cheeky, shouted, 'Burn rubber, baby.' Gilbert squirmed. He hadn't done anything like this since he was fourteen and wildly in love with Virginia Watson, who was a precocious thirteen, wildly sophisticated. She drank Pimm's, smoked black Sobranie cigarettes and had a twenty-year-old boyfriend, but she thought him sweet and called him Silly Gilly. God, what was happening to him? He hadn't thought about her in years.

Gilbert and Annette had made love every Saturday night since their routine started. It wasn't ever anything spectacular, just enjoyable and comforting. They both knew they'd slipped into having the sort of orderly sex life they mocked in other people, married people, but neither liked to say.

Annette rolled over to look at him. 'How long have you been sitting awake?'

'Not long.' It was two-thirty. He'd been staring at the end of the bed since before one.

'Are you worrying about your book?'

'No.' He was. Though this bout of sleeplessness was also spent thinking about Megs.

'How's it going?'

'Very well.' It wasn't. Until this moment he hadn't realised how easily he lied to her. He lied as easily as Megs had on the phone to her mother.

'You should go up to your cottage for the summer. You'll get on with it there.'

'Yes,' he said slowly, mulling this over. 'The cottage.' He turned to her. 'Will you come?'

'Gilbert,' she scolded. 'You know I'm going to America.'

'Oh yes,' he said slowly, turning this over. He'd forgotten she'd be away for the summer. 'Pity,' he said. But he felt a little tug of joy. He thought about Megs. What was she doing now? How was she coping with her shaven son, her absurdly friendly dog, her girls and her gossipy chum? Was she in that kitchen? And wasn't it interesting what happened when clutter turned into a home? How individual items, ghastly on their own, somehow collectively became endearing. Maybe they took on the identity of their owner. Who would have thought that this discerning heart would shudder and jolt at the thought of a pink-plastic-feet fridge magnet?

'If you shave off all your hair,' he asked Annette absently, 'how long does it take to grow in?'

'Weeks. Months. Depends. Why? Gilbert.' She sat up. 'You're not thinking of shaving your head, are you?'

'Heavens, no.' Gilbert cupped a protective hand over his head. 'Never,' he said. He lay down. Perfecting his sleeping position, he tugged his pillow round his shoulders, a nightly ritual that ensured draught-free slumber. He relaxed. 'Nina.' He said her name. It spilled, unexpected, from his lips, surprising him.

'What was that?' Annette wanted to know.

'Oh, nothing,' said Gilbert. 'I was just falling to sleep. Dunno what I said.' Then, 'Sorry,' he apologised. For just saying that name in Annette's presence, the feelings it stirred in him, was to betray her.

Chapter Nineteen

Megs was washing his dishes when Gilbert asked her out to dinner. He stood at the door of the kitchen, watching her from behind. The slight wiggle of her bustling body as she wiped cups and plates, scrubbed out dirty pots and placed them on the draining board pleased him. Watching her, he was filled with a joy he hadn't known before. He caught himself smiling. He hated that. It was something his face did when he was happy. He wished it wouldn't. It had a life of its own. She turned and saw the expression on the undisciplined face.

'Something's made you happy.' She smiled back at him.

Something extraordinary happened to him, an exultation within. A bursting of some sort of internal blessedness. He put his hand on his stomach to control it. You, he thought. You have made me happy. 'Can't imagine what,' he said. 'Nothing to be happy about.'

'You can say that again.'

'How are things with the hairless one?'

She laughed. 'Oh, fine. We've all got used to him now. And the first prickle of hair is starting to appear. I still get a shock every time I look at him. But among his friends he's a hero. Shaven heads are the thing, apparently.' She wiped her hands on a tea towel as she spoke.

He was silent a moment, working up some courage. 'Do you eat?'

'As a matter of fact, I do,' she told him. 'Actual food at least once a day.'

'What sort of food do you like?'

'Anything hot that I haven't cooked myself.'

'Do you like Italian? Only, there's a new place not far from here. A small family-run restaurant. I thought we might go. Try it out. Tonight.' It would have to be tonight. Tomorrow was Thursday, and Thursday was Annette. On Friday Megs sang at the Glass Bucket. What am I saying? he thought. We can't go out. What would we talk about?

'Me?' She pointed to herself. 'You want to go out with me? All right. Why not?' she said. I can't go out with you, she thought. What would we talk about?

They spoke about themselves, and Gauguin. They spoke about children, childhood and Billie Holiday. They spoke about music, movies, soap operas, bad habits, school days, mothers and food. They started speaking at eight o'clock when they first sat down and did not stop till eleven when they left. They confessed embarrassing moments and secret, junk-food cravings.

It was a small restaurant, very Italian. White tablecloths, lamps on tables, trellising on one wall, plastic grapes and framed pictures of Italian football teams. Well, thought Megs, looking round, he can hardly criticise the Glass Bucket if this is his sort of décor. Waiters in white aprons breezed past them, and every time one of them pushed open the door to the kitchen the room filled with the rush of Italian babble and banter, the aromas of garlic, olive oil, basil and fresh bread baking.

'Smells promising,' said Gilbert, sniffing deeply. 'What shall we order?'

She stared at the menu, realising how long it had been since she'd been out. She was no longer used to choices.

'What do you like?' he asked. He was wearing a denim shirt, open at the neck, black jacket. His hair was flattish, she noted. This outing mustn't have caused him too much angst. She considered his face anew, she saw things she hadn't seen on her first scrutiny. She saw kindness, uncertainty and a deeper unhappiness than she'd really realised. That underlying sadness was so obvious she could almost reach out and touch it.

'Seafood,' she said. 'I like anything seafoody.'

'Pasta con frutti di mare,' he told the waiter. Bursting, badly, into a strange language, whilst tweaking his fingers in the air in a certain flamboyant continental manner, did not bother him. 'And I'll have osso bucco with risotto alla milanese.' This was what he planned to master next. He was working through the classic Italian dishes. 'Garlic bread, a carafe of house white. And salad.' He handed back the menus and smiling, turned to her. He liked to eat. 'Some places in Venice do your seafood pasta with champagne and cream,' he told her. 'I'll cook it for you, sometime.'

'You cook?' she asked. She wished people wouldn't make promises they had no intention of keeping.

'Love it. I cook every Saturday. Spend hours in the kitchen. What about you?'

'I cook every day. Fish fingers, baked potatoes, spaghetti. I spent as little time in the kitchen as possible. I must say, though, that I do a mean bacon sandwich.' She was tempted to add that she'd cook it for him sometime, but felt there was something morningish about bacon which suggested something all-nightish would have to happen before he got it.

'You got here all right?' he asked. 'No problem with baby-sitters?' She shook her head. 'You remember Lorraine?'

He nodded.

'She and Harry have split up. She's staying with me for the moment. She can't face her empty house. She hates being alone.'

'I've lived alone for so long, I don't know how I'd take to having someone around. You get set in your ways.'

'I've been surrounded by children for so long I've forgotten any ways I might have liked to get set in.'

Lorraine stayed on Saturday night, then lingered all the next day. At eight o'clock on Sunday evening, Megs asked, 'Aren't you going home, then?' They were standing in the kitchen, Lorraine was wiping the draining board, making it cleaner than it had been in years. Guilt?

'Do I have to go home?' She did not look at Megs. 'I hate it there. It's empty.'

Megs did not have a chance to reply.

'I know. I know,' Lorraine protested against any criticism Megs might be about to offer. 'I was awful to Harry when I had him. And now I don't have him, I want him. All I do when I'm at home is sit in front of the television flicking from station to station because I can't concentrate on anything. I'm too sorry for myself. Then I eat biscuits.

I flick stations and I walk back and forward to the biscuit tin.' She stopped wiping and pointed an imaginary remote control at an imaginary television set. 'What's going to happen to me? How'm I going to get by? And that's another thing I do. I think. God, I hate doing that. Better to let life happen to you without thinking about what might happen.' She stopped flicking stations and returned to wiping. 'I mean,' she said, back to Megs, 'you think all the time. You're good at it. But me, I'm scared of thinking. You never know what awful thing you're going to find in your head.'

'Oh, stay,' Megs said. 'The sofa's yours for as long as you need it. I can't help you with what's going to happen to you – that sort of stuff. But my children won't put up with idle station-flicking when they're watching, and they eat everything that comes into the house. That'll solve your television and biscuit problems, anyway.' She made to go back into the living room. But stopped. 'Lorraine?' she said. 'You were only alone for one night. At that you got in after midnight and were here with me by ten in the morning. You've hardly had any time alone.'

'I know. But I stayed up all night, and it was awful.'

Megs went to tell her family that Lorraine would be staying for a few days.

'Thought so,' said Hannah.

'Yeah,' said Jack.

Now that Lorraine was part of her household, Megs saw those little ways she might have liked to develop slipping further and further from her. She sat across from Gilbert, each considering the other anew – the vast differences in their lives.

'Do you enjoy your job?' she asked.

'I used to. I've sort of gone off it. Recently, I must admit, I've been fascinated by Gauguin.'

'Why?'

'He did what he wanted, I suppose. I don't think I ever have.'

'Why not?'

To his surprise, he told her about his painting, his mother, the great bonfire. He had never told anyone about this before. Not even Annette. 'Do you get along with your mother?' he asked.

'Oh, goodness, don't ask that. We have mastered the art of quality

172

bickering. We don't see eye to eye on any subject under the sun, yet we see each other almost every day – you'd think we'd come up with something we could agree on. She's incredibly good to my children. I think she'd do anything for them. Will you ever draw again?'

He shook his head. 'No.' He didn't mean this. He always intended to start painting again one day. He secretly fancied he had talent.

It was near midnight when he drove her home. 'Do you want to come up?' Megs asked. 'Only I have to warn you, Lorraine's there and she'll quiz you.'

'What about?'

'Where you come from. What you do. How much you earn. What sort of underpants you wear. Just the business of being you.'

'She's a gossip?'

'Well, maybe. She's a woman. She's curious to know what makes different folk tick.'

Gilbert was keen to see Megs at home again. He wanted to know everything about her. 'OK. I'll risk it.'

Lorraine was curled up on the sofa, dunking a biscuit into a cup of hot chocolate. She, Jack and Hannah were watching television, and they turned as Gilbert came into the room. Hand on hair. He felt like an intruder. The room was small, painted white. On the walls, in clipframes, were pictures of blues singers – Robert Johnson, Bessie Smith and Ma Rainey, with her gorgeous smile and defiant dentistry. Plants dripped from bookshelves that were packed with battered second-hand paperbacks. There was a plastic box filled with toys beside the sofa, and beside each chair, shoes that had been kicked off.

The only light was a table lamp in the corner. But the dimness was scattered against flickering blue on the television. An advert for spaghetti hoops spilled into the room, a freckled wide-faced child, mouth smeared with tomato juices, scooped forkfuls from the plate as a gleeful acrylic family fussed round him.

Stepping towards the sofa, Gilbert tripped over the vacuum wire. He was a stranger here. He did not know the domestic obstacles. Megs constantly left her vacuum lying. Having cleaned, she found it too much effort to put it away. Shameless leaped and whirled, pattered his front paws and joyously threw himself at Megs. Gilbert

173

found it difficult to move. He felt overpowered by the heat and the prattle of television adverts. He could not sit down. Lizzy was lying sleeping under her Thomas the Tank Engine duvet.

'What's she doing here?' Megs asked.

'She wouldn't go to bed,' Lorraine told her. 'She wanted to sleep on the sofa like me.'

Megs scooped up child and duvet together and gestured Gilbert to sit in the space she'd just cleared. 'I'll just put Lizzy to bed, then I'll make you coffee.'

The adverts stopped, and the film came back on.

A fully clothed cop was leaning on a doorpost, drinking coffee and chatting to a woman in her underwear. 'You can't fool me, honey,' the cop was saying. 'I know all about you.'

'Oh, doesn't he make you sick,' Lorraine said. 'He's so full of himself.'

'I hate men like that,' Hannah said. She had a huge mug of hot chocolate too.

The cop put his coffee down on the kitchen unit and moved across the room to the woman in her underwear. 'Yeah. I know what you want.'

Megs looked into the room. 'I'll get your coffee now. Back in a sec.'

'Thanks,' said Gilbert.

'Leave me alone, Billy,' said the woman in the film. 'I don't want you.'

'Yes you do,' the cop told her.

Gilbert leaned forward, drummed the heel of his shoe. Idly stared at the screen.

'Did you have a nice time?' Lorraine asked him.

'Oh, yes,' Gilbert told her.

'Don't you touch me,' the woman in her underwear screamed.

Jack got up, walked to the window and looked into the street. 'Is that your car? The Jag?'

'Yes,' said Gilbert.

'Cool,' said Jack.

'It isn't really.' Gilbert casually dismissed the compliment. 'It regularly refuses to start.'

'Doesn't matter,' Jack said. 'That's seriously cool.'

Gilbert was secretly pleased. He had never been called cool before.

'Good meal?' Lorraine asked.

Gilbert nodded. 'Yes.'

Lorraine considered his answer. She'd seen adverts for the restaurant they'd been to. She thought he could have taken Megs somewhere a little more expensive for their first date. He should want to impress her. 'What did you have to eat?'

Gilbert told her.

'Not bad.' Lorraine nodded.

The cop lunged at the woman, ripped off her underwear. Her tits tumbled out. She screamed. The two fell on the floor, taking some crockery with them, smashing a chair. The woman struggled. The cop yanked off her scant panties.

'She's got great thighs,' Lorraine said mildly. 'Do you suppose she works out?'

'Yeah,' said Hannah. 'She'll never eat Toblerones.'

'It's all make-up,' said Jack. 'They've got stuff to cover the cellulite.'

Hannah and Lorraine nodded. They liked that theory.

The cop held the woman's hands over her head with one hand, unbuckled his trousers with the other. Then he fell on her, licking her nipples, whilst she beat his back, small, useless fists. At last, weeping, she gave in to him, her legs curled round him. Yielding, she said, 'Billy, Billy, you bastard.' Their sex was crude and noisy.

Gilbert, Lorraine, Jack and Hannah watched, silently bovine. Their faces were all without expression.

'What's this?' Megs came in with the coffee. 'What are you watching?' She crossed the room, switched off the set.

'I was enjoying that,' Hannah protested. 'You think you can come in and switch it off because you've got someone with you.'

'Yes,' said Megs. 'I do.'

Hannah got up and flung herself towards the door. She always did a good flounce, Megs thought. She seemed to propel herself forward with her shoulders and elbows rather than her legs.

'Don't mind her,' Jack told Gilbert. 'She's all premenstrual today.'

'Jack.' Megs frowned at him to be quiet.

'It's true.' Jack would not be silenced. 'She's been a cow all night. And she's drunk two mugs of chocolate and eaten a

175

whole Toblerone. Never gave me any.'

'True,' Lorraine said. 'She's been in good form. Vile.'

Drinking his coffee, Gilbert wondered if it would be flippant of him to say that he liked Toblerones too. 'I think I ought to go,' he said instead. 'It's late.' He got up. With a small foot shuffle, he awkwardly bade Lorraine and Jack good night. As he walked down the hall he called goodbye to Hannah.

''Bye,' she called tonelessly, as if indifference was an art form.

Gilbert flushed slightly. Megs watched. His discomfort surprised her. She'd thought that dealing with students all day he'd be more used to mild tantrums than he was.

She walked back to his car with him. He leaned against it. 'Thanks for coming. I enjoyed it.'

'Me too.' She nodded. 'Sorry about Hannah.'

'I like seeing you at home,' he told her. 'You have a real family. It's good. I like your kids.'

Megs looked at him. 'I doubt that.'

'No, really. They're honest. Like you.' He reached out and stroked her hair. When she didn't object, he kissed her. Or rather he leaned over and placed his lips on hers. 'Sorry,' he said when they pulled apart.

'Why sorry?'

'For kissing you.'

The wine had made her bold. 'That was not a kiss,' she said. 'This is a kiss.' She took his head in her hands and kissed him properly, deeply. Halfway through it, she doubted herself. He must think me a tart, she decided. 'Sorry,' she said when they'd done.

'Oh, don't be,' he said to her back as she headed for the main door of her building. 'Really, don't be.' He watched her go, sat staring at her window long after she'd disappeared. He imagined her up there in her flat amidst her gaudy clutter. She'd be making coffee, laughing with Lorraine, bossing her son, sorting out her premenstrual daughter. Her clutter, he realised, extended far beyond the messy area around her fridge. It spread throughout her whole life.

It delighted him, though he couldn't imagine why.

Hannah was back watching her awful film when Megs returned. 'Is that him?' she asked.

'What do you mean by that?' Megs wanted to know.

'I mean you should watch yourself with him. He's a man. You know nothing about men.'

'What?' Megs couldn't believe what she was hearing. 'You think you know more about men than me?'

'That's obvious.'

'Perhaps you should have asked him what his intentions were?' Megs offered.

'Well, someone has to.' Hannah was even sitting knees together, arms folded. So schoolmarmish, Megs wanted to laugh.

'She thinks she knows more about men than you,' Lorraine said. She patted the sofa eagerly. 'C'mon, tell us all about it. I liked his jacket.'

'Yes,' Hannah said. 'Shame about his hair.'

'Poor bloke.' Jack got up. 'I don't want to hear this. I'm off to bed.'

'Me too.' Megs followed him. 'I don't suppose anybody has taken Shameless out?'

Guilty silence. 'Oh, great,' said Megs. She put Shameless on his leash, shoved on her coat and left. She couldn't slam the door in a display of displeasure for fear of waking Lizzy. Wishing she'd changed into flat shoes, she stumbled clumsily down the stairs and down the main hall, yanked by Shameless, who had gone into hyperpant. She heaved open the main door and saw Gilbert. He was leaning out of his car, staring up at her window.

'Hello again.' She smiled.

He reddened, reached for his hair. 'Hello.'

'I have to take Shameless out,' she explained.

'I'll come with you. Protect you from hedgehogs.'

'That'll be a comfort.'

They walked side by side down the street, Shameless pulling her. The sky turned to sludge somewhere above the sodium lights. It was going to rain. A gritty wind worried round them, flapping their clothes, chilling their cheeks, pushing their hair at angles to their faces. They both shivered.

'It's a lovely night,' said Gilbert.

'Yes,' Megs agreed. 'Lovely.'

Chapter Twenty

Megs woke, stared at the sun-bleached curtains. Six o'clock on the morning of the Friday she'd been dreading for weeks. After tonight it's a lifetime of cleaning for me. She let dismay swim through her. I'll be forever picking up after all sorts of people. A professional picker-upper. It's the end for me. She did not spare herself any sorrow, embraced instead the full gloom ahead.

She imagined her descent into misery. Getting older and older, wider and wider, fat-ankled in thick, wrinkled stockings, she'd shuffle from home to home, nagging and wiping. 'You'll be needing that bathroom of yours done today, Mrs Pearshon,' she'd say, squeezing her 's' through ill-fitting National Health dentures. Shuffling fatly through the awful tidiness with a bottle of Domestos and a can of Jif bathroom mousse, 'Oh God, no,' she cried out loud, sitting up. Shameless raised a sleepy head and looked glumly round, ears only half pricked. It was far too early for him to start leaping, panting and being friendly.

Megs lay down again. It wasn't just her last night at the Glass Bucket that she was dreading. It was Gilbert. The loveliness of the evening she'd spent with him had worn off now that she was running through it. She remembered stupid things she'd said. What did he think of her, her home and her family? She'd come into the room and found him sitting with Lorraine, Jack and Hannah watching a noisily explicit sex scene. What had he made of that? And what had he made of Hannah's mini-tantrum? What would he make of one of the girl's major outbursts? How could she face him, clean for him when she'd so passionately kissed him? That was not a kiss, she'd said. This is a kiss. 'Oh God,' she cried out loud, covering her face. She chastised herself. I will never drink again, she vowed for the umpteenth time. She knew she didn't mean it.

Considering the day ahead, cleaning for Terribly-Clean Pearson seemed a breeze. But then, Terribly-Clean Pearson had been easier to get along with recently. Her hair was less demented. Not so much a helmet that topped her head, more loose, like actual hair, in fact, Megs thought. Then last week there had been some mess to clean up. There had been crumbs on the kitchen table, and a ring round the bath, cigarette stubs in the ashtrays, a newspaper read and badly folded. Signs of life. Anyway, it seemed to Megs that Mrs Pearson was on the road to recovery from whatever ailed her. Whatever sent her scurrying to hide behind that perfection of hers. Megs pulled the duvet over her head and rubbed her feet together. Bed was the place to be. But she had a dire afternoon and evening to get through before she got to come back to bed, and hide again.

Gilbert was waiting for her when she arrived. He was leaning on the wall by the front door, looking sheepish. His hair gave his mood away. It was on its way to upright. He had his hands thrust in the pockets of his old black training pants. His sweatshirt had 'University of Ohio' on the front and needed washing. He was doing his grinning thing. His face was smiling, and he was wishing it wouldn't. It kept giving him away.

'Well, hello,' he said. 'And how are you?'

'Fine,' she said.

'And how's the family?'

'Fine,' she said. First lie of the day, she thought. Thinking of Hannah.

He offered her coffee. She accepted. But looking round at the mess thought it best any sort of small talk be cut short. There was a lot to do. Whistling toothily, he moved about his kitchen. He made fresh coffee and laid some dark-chocolate ginger biscuits on a plate. She didn't sit down, drank the cup he gave her leaning against the sink.

'Thank you for the other night,' she said. 'I enjoyed it.' Considering this, she found it to be true.

'Good.' He smiled. 'Do it again? Soon?' He was keen.

She wanted to say no. But couldn't bring herself to. It seemed, somehow, rude.

'Good,' he said again. He stepped towards her, took her cup, laid it on the sink unit and kissed her. It was a spur-of-the-moment move. Had he planned it he might not have spilled her coffee, pressed the small of her back into the draining board and crushed her nose against his cheek so that she couldn't breathe. 'I messed that up.' He let go of her.

'No you didn't.' He looked so ashamed of himself, she stroked his cheek, repeated, 'You make me think you only did that to be polite, or something stupid like that.'

'Oh no. No, really.' He gripped her arms. 'I wanted to. I want to.' He held her to him. She looked over his shoulder at all that was to be done in the kitchen. Really she should get started.

She always thought that if he hadn't made such a mess of that kiss, if it hadn't been so chokingly clumsy, he wouldn't have made such a meal of saying sorry. 'Though, heaven's sake,' she said to Lorraine later, 'my nose got crushed, my back bruised.' Nonetheless, if he hadn't seemed so sorry for himself, she wouldn't have tried so hard to comfort him. Her sympathy extended all the way from his kitchen, through his living room, up the stairs to his bed.

She lay on the sheets she ought to be washing and made love to him. He tasted of coffee, smelled of cologne. She felt she smelled of all the chemicals he so hated, and couldn't relax. She kept chastising herself for what she was doing, or about to do. What would her mother say if she could see her?

His room was light, huge windows, level with the tops of the trees. There were books on the floor and books on the chest of drawers by his bed. An anglepoise lamp *circa* 1950 loomed over her head. It needed dusting, she noted. She turned to him. He touched her face, then trailed a slow hand up her thigh. He lured her from her guilt, till she wrapped herself round him, clung to him. Sweating sweetly, breathing his name, she moved with him into those few precious moments when she forgot about everything. Absolutely everything.

There had, of course, been others. There had been a woman – a cycling enthusiast – who worked at the bike shop, a barmaid from the pub where he drank after work, the wife of one of his postgrad students, his hairdresser. If his long-time love, Annette, was as uncommitted as he was, all of his lovers were caught up in the same intense, boiling family involvement as Megs.

'It wasn't joyous,' she told Lorraine, 'just sort of comforting, passionately comforting. I slept after. And it wasn't embarrassing getting my kit off. That came naturally enough. Getting it back on again, though, was awful. Still, it'll teach me not to go out with old underwear on.'

Lorraine looked unimpressed. 'You owe me a fiver,' she said.

Megs slept till four o'clock, when summer had settled into the day outside, heat filled the streets. She hated summer. 'Oh my,' she said, sitting bolt upright, flapping the duvet. 'Look at the time. And look at me. I have done nothing.' She leaped from the bed. Naked, she stood gazing helplessly round, raising and lowering her arms. 'I have to go to the laundrette. And the dishes – I haven't touched them. And,' she touched her throat, which had reddened, '. . . I have to get home.'

Aware of how she looked with nothing on, she reached for her clothes, bundled at the end of the bed. The elastic of her knickers was escaping from its seam, her bra was torn at the fasteners, and, though clean, it gave the impression of being tired, overly worn. Underwear was not high on her list of priorities, since she reckoned nobody but her would ever see it. She rushed to cover the body and underclothes she so disliked with her shirt and jeans. She rarely bought anything for herself. 'Oh God . . . oh God . . . oh God . . .' she said. 'I must . . . I shouldn't . . . this is wrong . . . I have to . . .' She was distraught, sentences flooded her mind – too many of them to finish one.

Hopping, she yanked on her shoes. She fled the bedroom with him, skipping and tripping, heaving himself into his training pants, running after her. She saw her envelope on the table and turned from it.

'Take it,' he insisted.

'I can't. How can I? I haven't done anything.' She wheeled round, arms spread, displaying openly the work she had not done. The mess intact. The wages she would not accept. 'If I took your money for what I've just done – what would that make me?'

He did not know what to say. Stood forlornly holding his envelope, neatly sealed with her name on the front in his best writing, watching her flee down the steps, two at a time, to her car. And she was so lovely to him. She held his head, kissed his cheek, licked his lobes, and said his name. He loved it when women said his name like that. It cut clean through his loneliness – all the way to his heart.

'It was that messed-up kiss,' Megs said to Lorraine. 'That's what did it.'

For if she'd cleaned and vacuumed and wiped as she ought to have done, she'd have taken his money. When she didn't, it alarmed him. He hadn't considered this. He was not used to honesty. He felt more guilty than ever.

'See,' Megs said to Lorraine during their Saturday-morning review of their lives, 'it was just down to one screwed-up moment. When I moved my face a fraction too far to the left, and he moved his a fraction too far to the right. And we missed. It's all down to that.'

She drove home. He sat considering, for the first time in his life, the full implications of his actions. She would not have enough money to feed her children. If she would not take his money, she would damn well take his food. He would go to the supermarket and shop for her. He would take her food.

She went home, cooked burgers and fed her family as she ran a bath. She washed, and changed into her singing clothes. 'Last night, tonight,' she said to Lorraine. 'I can't stand it. I won't be able to do it. I'll cry.'

'Well, cry,' said Lorraine. 'You're the best crier I know. You're almost as good as me.' Only this afternoon Lorraine had done some crying. She'd gone home to collect some things. She had shoved into a matching set of cases clothes, shoes, CDs, make-up, jewellery, a couple of photograph albums and a threadbare toy spaniel called Fluff that was almost as old as she was – he'd been with her since she was two, had seen her through affairs, her marriage, umpteen jobs, more affairs – her helter skelter life.

Vivienne came to baby-sit. On her way to the kitchen she stepped over Lorraine's luggage. This was not a good sign. She thought Megs's house overcrowded enough. They would egg each other on into mischief like they had when they were little. They were not to be trusted. They'd stay up all hours talking and giggling. Lorraine would set Megs off on wild dreams when she should be settling down. All that, and she wanted her daughter to herself. She went into the kitchen where Jack was doing the washing-up. Vivienne considered his gleaming head and sighed. 'There's your head. You were bald when you were born,' she said, a slight throb of longing for younger, easier times in her voice.

Lorraine and Megs left. Giggling, high heels clicking down the stairs, along the street, through the evening.

It was the best night ever at the Glass Bucket. It was so fine, takings so high, that Dave, the manager, wondered if he'd done the right thing cancelling the band. Megs sang 'God Bless the Child', did three encores, spread her arms, yelled, 'That's it, folks. It's over. Me and the band are going to catch up with Friday-night sitcoms on telly.' She jumped from the stage on to the squelchy tartan carpet and set about getting drunk.

'See,' she said to Lorraine when they were considering the long-term consequences of that blundered kiss, 'if it hadn't been my last night, I wouldn't have had so much to drink. I wouldn't have been so drunk when I got home. And if I hadn't been so drunk, I wouldn't have agreed to anything.' They'd stayed late at the Glass Bucket, drinking and saying goodbye. Round after round they bought and had bought for them. 'Goodbye,' Megs said over and over, tears in her eyes. She sang snatches of favourite songs, closing her eyes, concentrating, making her phrasing perfect, easily reaching notes that needed all her concentration, knowing they were coming, breathing for them in advance.

She told people she'd never seen before in her life that she loved them and they were her dearest friends. She had a lovely time. At last she understood the thrill Mike got from breaking up the band, from walking out on the marriage and from all the other goodbyes he'd said over the years together. All the hugging and promising to stay in touch. It wasn't the new beginning that excited him. The great triumph was simply in leaving.

They staggered, giggling, home sometime after two o'clock. Vivienne was sitting on the sofa chatting to Gilbert, who was in the armchair that Jack usually occupied. They were, to Megs's astonishment, discussing Gauguin.

'I'd have gone,' Vivienne was saying passionately. 'I wouldn't have let him walk out on my five children. I'd have gone. Five children! They need a father. He wouldn't have got away with that with me. Oh no.'

'No, sorry,' Gilbert was saying. He was no longer apologising for himself. Now he was apologising for Gauguin, as if he had some personal involvement in the man's decision to leave his wife and family to go painting in Tahiti. Gauguin interested him. He'd abandoned his career as a stockbroker to paint. Why, the man had been in his forties – the exact age Gilbert was now – when he finally left his wife. Still fancying he had some ability as an artist, he comforted himself with thoughts of Gauguin. Forty was not too late.

'And it would have been good for the kids.' Vivienne was beginning to enthuse. 'All that fruit. And it's quiet. You wouldn't have had to worry about them going off on their bikes.'

'What are you doing here?' Megs said, clutching the doorpost. She wanted to look like she could keep upright on her own. She hated her mother to see her drunk.

'We've been having a good old chat,' Vivienne told her. 'We've been talking about packaging. Gilbert's writing a book about it. Fancy, you'd never have thought there was enough in packaging to fill a whole book. I was telling him that in my day you went to the shops, and the grocer or whoever would pop your things in a paper bag and give it a twirl.' She held her arms out, demonstrating bag-twirling as performed in shops in the fifties, giving Megs a rerun of the conversation before the Gauguin conversation.

'I brought food,' Gilbert told her. 'In the kitchen.'

Megs went through to look. 'Goodness.' She could not hide her surprise. 'Look at this.' Laid across the units were packets of cereal (Gilbert, not knowing what her children would eat, had bought a selection), a variety of cheeses, loaves of bread, six bottles of wine, a bottle of whisky, biscuits, two chickens, steaks, pork chops, oven chips, pizzas, Coca-Cola, Evian, bags of apples, oranges, bananas, papayas, mangoes – fruit she couldn't afford to taste. There was Marmite, thick marmalade and strawberry jam, cocoa, coffee, a selection of teas, Ovaltine. Gilbert's indecision showed, and she could see that it had cost him three times what he would have paid her.

'You didn't need to do this,' she said.

'Oh, I think I did.' He'd been to the supermarket for her. Did he have to do anything else to prove his good intentions? He thought not. He took her hand. 'You didn't take your pay.'

'Look at this.' Lorraine held up some lollo rosso. 'Posh lettuce. And tomatoes on the vine.'

Vivienne did not look at the groceries. She had already cast her critical eye over them. She watched Gilbert and her daughter. 'Why didn't you take your pay?' she wanted to know.

'Because,' Megs confessed, 'I didn't clean his house. I slept with him. Didn't I?' She grinned alcoholicly at her mother. 'And I couldn't take any money for that, could I?'

Vivienne tutted. But not, as Megs imagined, with horror. More at her childish attempt to shock.

'See,' said Megs, 'I can't take your money. I can't work for you now.'

'Well, don't,' Gilbert said, taking her hand. 'Don't work for me. Come away with me for the summer. Come to my cottage. Be with me.' He was feeling wildly romantic.

'I can't do that,' Megs protested. 'I work.'

'Stop,' said Gilbert. 'You can't go on cleaning for people. There's more to you than that.'

'You tell her,' said Vivienne. 'She won't listen to me.'

Lorraine ripped a leaf from the lollo rosso, munched it, and watched.

'Come to my cottage. Be with me. It'll just be us. You and me.'

'Me?' Megs leaned on her unit for support. 'You can't just have me. I'm not me any more.' She considered her bustling life. There was Jack, Hannah, Lizzy, Shameless, Lorraine, Vivienne and Mike, who came to her kitchen trailing tales of his wife and new daughter. 'I'm not me any more,' Megs complained. 'I'm a crowd.'

'Come,' Gilbert insisted. 'All of you. Bring the gang.'

'Hannah and Jack are going to Italy with Mike for the summer,' Lorraine said.

Vivienne watched them. She watched Gilbert take Megs's hand, the expression on his face as he looked at her. 'I'd go,' she said. 'If a man asked me to go to his cottage, I'd go. There'd be no stopping me.'

Broken down, drunk, afraid of her future, Megs said, 'Yes. I'll come for the weekend at least.'

'See,' she said to Lorraine later, when they were running through the fine details of the nonsense that had taken place. 'It's a farce. My nose got crushed, my back ricked and I sympathised with him. "It's all right," I said. "I don't mind." If I'd said, "Get off. Leave me alone," I'd be fine. But that's me. That's my life. I go along being ordinary. Ordinary day following ordinary day, and now and then I have forays into tragedy or folly. That's me.'

Lorraine opened a packet of Penguins, chose a red one. 'What?' she said. She had no idea what Megs was talking about. 'I wouldn't mind a little stay in some remote cottage. Even if it was with Hundred-Miles-An-Hour. Seems fine to me.'

Chapter Twenty-One

It was after four when Megs left Edinburgh. She did not take journeys lightly. The boot of her car was packed, as if she was setting off to circumnavigate the globe.

'Just in case,' she said as she jammed in welly boots and jumpers. 'You never know,' she said as she folded up her best frock and laid it carefully on top of the heap of clothes in her suitcase. 'We might need these,' she said, adding anoraks and raincoats. 'Lizzy might get bored,' shoving in books, crayons and Lego. 'Gilbert might not have anything suitable,' putting in Shameless's bowls. 'You know Shameless. He's bound to let us down,' just managing to find space to squeeze in his towel and some extra toilet roll. She fetched Lizzy's duvet and pillow and put them on the back seat. 'She might sleep.' Megs hoped.

Lorraine and Vivienne stood side by side waving, watching them go. 'Don't know what she sees in him.' Lorraine sounded sour. Still, she made an effort. When Megs looked in the driving mirror, she saw Lorraine smiling.

'They're soulmates,' Vivienne offered.

'Lost souls.' Lorraine loved a romance.

'Floundering's the word I'd choose.' Vivienne had long left romance behind.

It took over an hour to get through the Friday-evening traffic to the Forth Bridge, and another hour up the motorway to Perth. 'Are we there yet?' Lizzy asked not long after they turned out of the street where they lived. She seemed to repeat the question at regular ten-minute intervals. But Megs was too thrilled by her journey north to be bothered. She played Roberta Flack, 'The First Time Ever I Saw

Your Face', and sang along. Gilbert had drawn a map and given Megs detailed instructions on the road to take after the Perth ring route. But Megs never could follow instructions. She always made up her own.

Lizzy was sleeping. The little roads that turned off the long, boring stretch Megs was driving and wound towards the blue and distant became irresistible. She knew Gilbert's cottage was up there somewhere in those hills and felt she was getting close to him, faster, when she was pointed towards them. Besides, she found the narrow roads, with their unkempt, burgeoning hedgerows, a delight. June, it seemed to her, was unashamedly yellow. 'Tawdry month, June,' she said. 'A bit brazen for me.' Rape shimmered in fields bounded by dry-stone dykes. Six o'clock pheasants croaked from pinewood copses, and Lizzy woke. She demanded Roberta Flack be replaced by Disney's greatest hits. So to the saccharine strains of 'Wish Upon a Star' they battered through Alyth. Across the bridge, up the hill and nearer to Gilbert, Megs thought.

'I need a pee,' Lizzy complained.

'Can't you wait?'

'No.' A protesting squeal.

They found a garage where a man with a black beret pulled low over his forehead gave them the key to the toilet, and, when Lizzy had done, sold them oil for the car, which needed to be topped up every couple of hundred miles. Lizzy also insisted on a tin of Pepsi, an apple, Smarties and a pack of assorted lollies. Megs looked round the shop. They sold everything here. Socks, newspapers, clothes pegs, homemade tablet, jam pot covers. 'Goodness.' Megs picked them up. 'Jam pot covers. You hardly see them these days.' A couple of miles down the road Megs opened the bag of goodies and found she'd been sold two packs.

She drove down endless tiny roads. Stopped to let Shameless out. He sniffed gleefully, peed, then rushed excitedly halfway across a field, starting up a hare. Yipping wildly, he took off after it, disappearing full hurtle into the field beyond. Hands hanging helplessly by her sides, Megs bellowed him to come back. She looked at her watch – seven o'clock. Gilbert was expecting her sometime after five. At last, realising the futility of hare-chasing, Shameless, ears pricked, sat mid-field, watched his quarry go, then turned and returned to Megs. She noted glumly that he had one of Lizzy's lollies, a green one, sticking to his back.

Back in the car they played 'Hi-Ho Hi-Ho It's Off To Work We Go', sped past fields, woods, cottages set back against the road. Tiny-windowed, they were cowering in a vast landscape against a huge sky. They pressed themselves into the roadside, letting tractors past. Megs scrunged behind the steering wheel, arms over her head. How to behave when mighty-wheeled tractors shoved you to the side of the road was not covered in the Highway Code – this seemed the sanest way to cope. Several times they passed signs that pointed to Alyth. Each sign they passed said that Alyth was in another direction. Sometimes it was ten miles away, sometimes only two. The third time they passed the jam pot garage, Megs admitted to herself that they were lost. The tremblings in her stomach were not in the least thrilling. 'Bare Necessities' had never been more irritating, and Lizzy was needing to pee again. They stopped once more at the jam pot garage. Returning the lavatory key to the man in the black beret, Megs asked directions.

'Thocht youze were lost,' he said, shoving the hat up slightly, revealing a deep red weal mid-forehead. 'Third time I seen ye pass I says to masel', "They're lost."' He demonstrated not so much with arm movements, more by leaning his whole body in the direction Megs ought to travel. 'Go this way,' leaning forward, 'an' keep turning this way,' leaning left. It worked. Following the directions, Megs began to notice, at last, the names recited to her by the leaner in the beret. Airlie, Lintrathen, Cortachy – she said the words out loud. They sounded romantic, historic, mystic to her. Ancient Celtic kings and Pictish storytellers wandering here centuries ago. 'King of the Swingers' blared on the tape deck.

Megs drove slowly. The car had climbed into the hills. Megs stared out across the valley. She could see the great gulfs and hollows that glaciers had left aeons ago. Lights shone in cottages miles away. She wondered what people who lived in them did. She wished Lorraine was with her. Lorraine would have a theory or two about how people in remote places passed the time. 'They're all smoking dope,' she'd say. Or, 'They're into bondage, or they're bank robbers hiding from the law.' Sometimes Megs thought Lorraine had no notion of ordinary.

'What do you suppose the people in these little houses all the way across the valley are doing?' she asked Lizzy.

Lizzy had no doubts. 'They're watching their television programmes.'

'Oh no,' cried Megs. 'Don't say it. Don't say it.'

But Lizzy said it. 'When are we going to get there?'

It was late evening. Change of day, a small wind chilled down from the peaks. Still not sure of the way, Megs wound up the window and leaned over the steering wheel. Hills covered with conifers folded out of each other, each one higher than the next, till in the distance – they were mountains. Greens and forest greys. The sun slid low, turned the sky a deeper blue that bleached white far away where the mountains rimmed the dusk. The road was narrow, wound and dipped suddenly and absurdly. A curlew called, shrilled a broken cry.

Lizzy dug small fists into Shameless and cried in anguish, 'When are we going to get there?'

'Soon,' said Megs. 'Very soon.' She stared up at the hills, breathed the night scents. She was on the right road, at last. That earlier fear, which hadn't been in the least thrilling at the time, now seemed exciting. Getting lost had been a small adventure. 'This is it,' she said. 'What I was on about. Where I belong. Watching new colours, listening to sounds I've never heard before. I'm slightly afraid. And if I wasn't in this damn car, I'd be rushing.'

They found the sign at last – Lisdon Cottage – and turned down a narrow track, deeply rutted at either side. The grasses that grew up the centre rattled against the exhaust, whilst Megs, Lizzy and Shameless were pitched from side to side as the car's suspension heaved against unseen pot-holes.

Gilbert heard them coming and came out to greet them – sliding his hand through his hair. He grinned. His face again, working on its own again. He wore his apron.

'Who's that?' Peering from the back of the car, Lizzy considered him with suspicion. She did not take kindly to new people.

'It's Gilbert,' said Megs. 'I've told you all about him.'

'He's got funny hair,' Lizzy said.

192

'Don't you dare tell him that.' Megs was also tempted to tell her daughter not to pester him, but felt she'd just be putting notions into the child's head.

Megs clambered from the car, and stood unkinking herself from her stiffened travelling position. She scratched her bum, working some circulation into it. 'Nice place,' she said, nodding to the cottage. It was two crumbling storeys, peeling window frames, huddled against a small, dense conifer wood. The smell of pines. A wave of honeysuckle swam up against and flooded a small wooden porch at the front door. The lawns, overgrown and daisied, grew right up to the wall. The kitchen looked like a lean-to afterthought, but the windows were lit against the dusk. Megs could see a huge scrubbed table, wine bottles, glasses and books. Yes, Gilbert lives here. A thin drift of smoke spiralled into the air, burning wood. The day turned deeper indigo, darkness getting granular against the trees. First bats flickered through the gloom.

'Good journey?' Gilbert asked.

'I enjoyed it. Shameless and Lizzy complained all the way. So did the car. Actually,' she confessed, 'we got lost.' Then, grinning, 'But no mind, here we are.'

Lizzy tumbled from the back seat and stood staring at Gilbert.

'This is Gilbert,' Megs told her again. 'Gilbert, this is Lizzy.'

'Pleased to meet you.' He bent to the child, extending his hand.

Gazing at him intently, Lizzy shook it. 'You've got funny hair,' she said.

'Lizzy!' Megs scolded.

'Have I?' Gilbert reached up to pat it into place. He looked pleadingly across at Megs.

'It's fine,' Megs lied. 'I'm sorry.' She nodded to the child, who was headed for the cottage door. All the excuses she knew she ought to offer spilled into her mind. Her brother died, and I fear for her. I let her get away with too much. She's become too precious. Precocious. She offered none of them, however. 'I don't know what gets into her,' she said.

'She's lovely,' said Gilbert. He meant it. 'Come on in. I've cooked a stew. Cutturiddi.' He raised enthusiastic fingers and snapped the air. He was very pleased with himself. 'Lamb, baby onions, chilli pepper, wine.' Then he glanced at Lizzy. 'Does she eat that sort of thing?'

'She hasn't had the chance,' Megs said, feeling mildly guilty about her child's limited diet.

But Lizzy ate everything she was given. She's playing at being good, Megs thought. Flirting with Gilbert. Little girls are all the same. Was I? She remembered Uncle Ron when she'd visit the Seaview Guest House, before his second fatal heart attack. She remembered how she'd unashamedly flaunt herself before him when Aunty Betty was clearing up the supper dishes. He'd grab her by the waist and thrust his rough, evening chin over her cheek till she squealed. Yes, she thought. I was the same. Uncle Ron would put her feet on his feet, size three stocking soles on his polished size ten brown brogues, and, arm round her, hands clasped high, he'd dance her round the room.

'This is a dance,' he'd say. 'Relax. I'm doing all the work.' But she never could let go and let him dance her. She giggled and wriggled. 'It's a waltz. Good old-fashioned dance.' They'd glide fabulously over the blue-and-pink-patterned carpet, past the red moquette sofa, sailing, twirling over to the cocktail cabinet with the lime-green interior that played 'The Banana Boat Song' when you opened the doors. 'Now when you get yourself a young man of your own, you'll be able to show him what to do.' Of course, she never did.

'Why are you smiling?' Gilbert asked. After Lizzy's comment on his hairstyle, he was ready to be offended. He might have other mockable idiosyncrasies that he hadn't noticed.

'Oh. I was just remembering my Aunty Betty's living room. Blue and pink carpet, red sofa, lime-green cocktail cabinet. I was imagining what you'd make of it.'

'I might've quite liked it. There is something comforting about bold bad taste. You know you're in the company of someone who doesn't doubt herself.'

'That's Aunt Betty,' said Megs. She poured them both some more wine. 'Do you dance, Gilbert?'

'No. I have never mastered dancing. I think there's a link missing between my brain and my feet. Why, do you?' Faint horror that she might drag him off to ballrooms and clubs to entwine themselves in some flamboyant tango with body-checks and head-tossing.

She shook her head. 'Always wanted to. But no, I can't. Well, I can jiggle to music. But actual dancing. No.' She continued shaking her head, reaffirming her failing.

She twirled her glass and looked out at the dark. The kitchen door was open, spreading light, attracting night-time insects that bruised themselves frantically against the window pane. Lizzy slid from her seat and went outside. Then came back in again. Out again. Stepping out on her own was more freedom than she'd ever known. The whole wide world was out there, she could see it – shapes in the darkness. But light and warmth and her mother were just a jump away – a small leap back into the kitchen.

She stood holding Shameless by the collar, taking in the night sounds and scents: an ineffectual wind pushing through the pines, the rattle of ivy leaves, a curlew's late whimpering, the insistent thud of rave music inside a car miles away up the glen – village boys with nothing to do but their Friday-night hurtle, driving up one side of the glen, down the other, passing the end of the road every two hours, thoom, thoom thoom – and honeysuckle, grass, pines and soft air blowing down from the peaks. It was a wonder to the child.

'It's the first time she's been able to come and go on her own,' Megs said, watching her. 'Living in a flat inhibits children. We should have a garden.' She wondered if this moment would stay in Lizzy's memory. There were, Megs realised, thousands of moments imprinted on her own memory. Some things were retained for obvious reasons – her mother in her blue and white winceyette nightie and tartan dressing gown standing by her bed in the sanatorium, waving a slow goodbye, galloping behind Aunty Betty through the house, waving a feather duster, singing 'Sipping Soda'. But some things slipped away and had to be forced back with vicious proddings from her mother. There was, in the family album, a photo of Megs and her brother standing ankle deep in the sea. She was wearing a skirted swimming costume that left little square marks on her bottom. He wore woolly trunks that sagged when wet. She had chubby knees. They were carrying buckets and spades and their faces were puckered against the sun.

'This is us on holiday at Southport, remember?' Vivienne said.

'No,' said Megs. 'I don't remember going to Southport.'

'Remember.' Vivienne was irritated. 'You had a crab in that bucket. And you got stung by a wasp. We bought you a big strawberry ice cream to stop you crying.'

'No.' Megs shook her head. 'I don't remember that.'

'We walked along the pier. We hired deckchairs. We went to see *Mary Poppins.*'

'Did we?'

'We stayed at a small guest house. The landlady had a cocker spaniel called Daniel.'

'A spaniel? A black one?'

'Yes.'

'Daniel the spaniel I do remember. Vaguely. But I don't remember that.' Pointing to the photograph.

Would Lizzy remember this? Or would this trip come back only as some trivial detail? A fleeting flashback of Gilbert's hair?

They went to bed as soon as Lizzy was sleeping. She had the room across the landing from Gilbert's. It had a sloping ceiling. Checked curtains moved against an open window. She lay clutching her purple transit van, Shameless at her feet.

Megs and Gilbert lay in his big cast-iron bedstead, patchwork quilt pulled over them. 'Do you remember your childhood, Gilbert? Or do you look at photos and find yourself forced to recall something long gone?' Megs asked. 'That weird feeling of having the evidence of your being somewhere but you can't remember a moment of it.'

'Yes. I suppose. I remember my teenage more.'

'I had a good teenage. I fell in love. The first time you hold a boy's hand. That first touch palm against palm – first thrill. That's the most romantic thing that ever happens to you. It's never like that again.' She reached for his hand under the covers. Her fingers entwined his. 'I remember the first time I ever got touched by someone a different sex from me that I wasn't related to. It was wonderful. It was Jimmy Sutherland. He had black hair that our English teacher kept telling him to get cut. He was a year older than me, fourteen. He took my hand on the way home from the cinema. Early-evening showing of *Alice's Restaurant.* His hand was dry and rough, chewed nails. Mine was all sweaty. We walked all the way home like that, neither of us

196

mentioned that my hand was in his. If we spoke about it, it would stop. The thrill of it spread from my palm all the way up my arm and right through me. Frankly, that simple handhold reached parts of me American cream soda and raspberry ripple ice cream never got to. Things happened in bits I didn't realise things could happen in. Secret places. God. I was overwhelmed by Jimmy Sutherland. I thought about him all the time. Couldn't sleep. Stopped eating Mars Bars. His name was all over my French jotter. Love, did you say? It lasted a full three weeks. Had to end, something that intense. It'll never be like that again.'

Gilbert felt helpless, quite upset that he would never rouse her to such peaks of ecstasy with a simple meeting of palms. He'd never put anybody off their Mars Bars. He was positive nobody had scrawled his name over a French jotter. He was suddenly insanely jealous of Jimmy Sutherland. Wherever he was, Gilbert hated him. His free hand came out from beneath the quilt, reached for his hair. By the time he'd come out of his jealous haze, Megs, overcome by her journey and the wine, was sleeping. He frowned, cursed himself for being so stupid. This wasn't what he'd planned.

Chapter Twenty-Two

The grumpiness that had befallen him when he fell asleep was still with him when he woke. He stared across at the empty pillow next to his, imagining sourly that she'd left. For a bewildering moment he thought he was alone again. But he realised that the humming sound that had brought him from his sleep was Lizzy driving her van across the floorboards, providing her own sound effects of crunching gears and screeching brakes. He propped himself on his elbows and watched her. 'Where's your mother?'

'In the garden,' Lizzy told him. She did not take her eyes from her van.

He felt irritated. This was definitely not what he'd planned. They would wake together, lie sleepily warm, make love again. He'd rise, go barefoot to cook breakfast – smoked fish, bacon, toast and fresh coffee – whilst she washed and dressed. This child had not been cast in his daydreams. Of course, he'd known Megs was bringing her daughter for the weekend. But when he imagined their time together he had not as much as given the child a walk-on part. Now here she was, vrooming a hideous vehicle on his polished floor, and he was desperate to get up. Last night's wine was heavy in his bladder, he ached to relieve himself. But he did not want to get out of bed letting Lizzy see him wearing nothing but his boxer shorts.

'Why don't you go find her?' he suggested.

'No,' said Lizzy.

'Pl-ee-se.' The word spilled pleadingly from him. He did not know he was going to say it. He was in pain. 'Oh God. Please go see her.'

Lizzy got up, looked mildly at him and left.

Ten minutes later, washed, dressed and relieved, he joined them.

Megs was sitting on the kitchen doorstep drinking coffee. His eyes skimmed the plate beside her. She'd made toast. This wasn't right.

'Sorry.' She smiled at him. 'I was starving after I took Shameless for his walk. I just made some toast. Shall I get you some?'

He shook his head. Walk? Toast? He felt more disgruntled than ever. She'd taken his Schubert from his kitchen tape deck, and some popular American-type music was playing. Definitely things were not going to plan. 'I'll get myself some coffee. Then we'll have to go to the village. I have things I must buy.' It was never like this with Annette.

With Annette he didn't have to discuss plans, they just fitted together without discussion. He'd get up and she'd yawn, stretch, turn over. 'Lovely, I've got the bed to myself. Make us some wonderful breakfast, there's a love.' He'd go rattle and bustle in the kitchen, listening to the news, or Schubert if he'd a mind. Then Annette would come, sit opposite him and read her paper. He'd read his. They were rarely together. And when they were they hardly spoke. No wonder they got along. Perfect relationship, he thought. Trouble with these people was they spoke, they touched, they mingled. Scary.

It was after eleven when they got to the village. Lizzy, in the back of the Jaguar, was sitting, hands folded in her lap, legs sticking straight out in front of her, playing, Megs thought uneasily, at being good. Shameless, to his dismay, was ordered to lie on the floor. Gilbert did not have to say what he felt about dogs on his leather upholstery. The state of his eyebrows – halfway up his forehead – said it all. When they arrived at the village, Shameless, Lizzy and Megs tumbled out on to the pavement and looked about them.

'I have one or two things I have to get,' Gilbert said. 'Do you want to explore and meet up in an hour?'

'Sounds fine to me,' said Megs. She extended her hand to Lizzy. 'Let's have a look round, shall we?'

Lizzy shook her head. 'I want to go with Gilbert. I want to see what he's going to buy.'

'You come with me,' Megs insisted. 'Let Gilbert shop on his own.'

'No.' Lizzy put her hands behind her back. They were not available for Megs to take, lead her off.

'Come on, Lizzy.' Megs dreaded a scene.

'She can come with me if she wants,' Gilbert said. Had he said that? He couldn't believe it. He didn't want Lizzy with him. He wasn't sure about children. They seemed unstable to him. It wasn't just their unrestrained emotional outbursts, there was the business of their bladders and bowels. Children, it seemed to him, had unreliable digestive systems. Lizzy, to his amazement, took his hand. She stepped forward, leading him away from Megs. Things were getting out of control.

'Do you mind?' Megs asked.

'No. No. Not at all,' he said. But I do mind, he thought. Help me.

'Well, I'll take Shameless,' Megs said. 'Nobody should be burdened with him. Don't let her boss you,' she warned Gilbert, nodding at Lizzy.

They parted. Gilbert and Lizzy headed across the square to the shops, Megs and Shameless wandered. She walked up old lanes, high crumbling walls dripping ivy and stock. High above the rush and squeal of swallows. She looked up, Shameless sniffed at doorways, found fascinating patches of ground that he would not be dragged from, peed on lampposts. From open windows Megs heard that same insane chatter and scream of Saturday-morning television as would, she knew, be going on in her own home.

Every lane, every wynd she walked down led back to the square. Not that she minded. The little shops tucked up the lanes sold mostly craftwork – hand-made spoons, plaques, pokerwork name plates and homilies on highly varnished slabs of wood. 'Never borrower or lender be.' 'Home sweet home.' No, the square was more interesting. No more than ten shops facing a tall market cross. A grocer's, where, no doubt, Lizzy was bossing Gilbert and choosing things he didn't want to buy. Do him good. Megs smiled, imagining it. A butcher's painted yellow, with FRESH MEAT in huge lettering on the window. Next to that the Sunset Boulevard video shop, with several posters of Fred Astaire in mid-swirl, tails flying, in the window. It was closed. A wool shop, a fruit-and-veg shop, an ironmonger's, a sweet shop, a newsagent's and post office, an antique shop and the Blue Kettle bakery and café which had, propped on the pavement by the front door, a lopsided painting of a blue kettle. TEAS, the sign said.

Megs could not resist it. She crossed the square and stared in the window. What an array of vibrant cakes, such abandoned use of cochineal. These cakes looked like they'd been crayoned by children in primary school – there was no subtlety here. Megs bent forward to peer into the café. It seemed to be full of women, and it looked like they were all laughing. In years to come, when Megs thought back to the Blue Kettle Café, she would remember it to be filled with women in thick tweed suits – no matter what the weather – twin sets and pearls. They would all be fat-kneed, laughing and toothless. Of course it wasn't true. It was a fleeting first impression that would last forever.

She had to pull herself away from that window. She left these guffawing, hooting women and shyly stuck her head into the butcher's. 'Is it all right to come in here?'

The butcher, in his white overall and blue-and-white apron, sharpening a knife with wide arm movements, said above the rasp of steel on steel, 'Are you thinking of buying something?'

'Oh yes, eggs. It's just the dog. It's not very hygienic to bring him in.'

'Are you a health inspector?' the butcher wanted to know. He was bald, red-cheeked and chubby. He looked like a beef-eating man.

'No.'

'Well, come on in then.' The knife sliced air as he waved her inside. 'We'll forget about the hygiene.'

'Just want a dozen eggs,' Megs excused herself.

'The lad'll get them for you.' He leaned back and hollered into the back shop, 'BILLY!'

Billy appeared, knotting his apron. He was small, thinning hair pasted to his scalp, nervous, definitely past fifty. 'Yes?'

'A dozen eggs,' Megs said again.

The lad flapped open a couple of egg boxes and deftly filled them, lifting eggs four at a time from the basket in the window. 'You'll not mind a few feathers, will you?'

'Oh no. In fact I'd be disappointed if I didn't get a few.'

'Well, I'll pop in a few more.' He lifted some extra and let them sail the small distance from his fingertips to the box. 'There you go. New here? Just passing through?'

'Staying the weekend with a friend.'

'Who's that?'

The curiosity was so finely tuned, the question fired with such precision, it didn't occur to Megs not to answer it.

'Gilbert Christie.'

The lad frowned. 'There's nobody of that name here.' Aha, he'd caught her out.

'He has a cottage up the glen. Lisdon?'

'Him. The professor.' He turned to his boss, who was serving a woman, an obvious Blue Kettle regular. Not that he needed to. They were openly eavesdropping. They lived here, they had a right to know who was who. 'She's staying with pork chops and *Fitzcarraldo*,' he told them.

'Ah.' They nodded in unison. Now they knew about her.

'Say when,' the butcher said to his customer, holding his knife on a large fillet. 'You want thick steaks, or are you not giving your man much this week?'

'Oh,' said the Blue Kettle woman. 'He gets plenty. Ha ha. Make them thick, Kynoch.'

Kynoch. Megs looked at him. A good name for a butcher, she thought. And, indeed, he was robust, assured. Being addressed by his last name suited him. 'Pork chops and *Fitzcarraldo*?' she repeated, bemused.

'I do the video shop evenings and Sundays. If you want a film delivered I can bring it with your meat.' The lad nodded to the pile of videos by the door. Each had a slip showing membership number, film and meat order. Member 52, *Diehard*, 1 lb stew steak, ½ sweet-cure bacon. Member 44, *Three Colours Red*, venison sausages, 3 lb shoulder lamb, 1 doz eggs.

'I miss the old days. Before videos, the Sunset Boulevard used to be our picture house. It was always a good night out at the movies,' Kynoch lamented.

'You got a cup of tea, proper in a china cup, a sandwich and a film. *Song of the South, From Here To Eternity, The Philadelphia Story* – you don't get them like that any more.' The Blue Kettle lady joined him.

'You got a lot more than that if you sat in the golden divans,' Kynoch remembered.

They all drifted into a minute's silence in respectful memory of old movies, sandwiches, tea in real china cups and juicy adventures on the golden divans. Megs took her eggs and left them to it.

Gilbert and Lizzy were standing beside the car, waiting for her. 'I got eggs,' she told them. 'And I had a peek at the Blue Kettle Café.' She was enthused.

Gilbert wasn't. 'I can't go in there.' He imagined Annette bursting in and finding him ensconced at a plastic table, munching a bright-red coconut-encrusted cake with a glacé cherry on top. 'Good heavens. Gilbert. What are you doing?'

'Why not? It's wonderful.'

'No.' Gilbert was adamant. 'We'll go to the Stag and have a beer and sandwich.'

'It's that painting of the blue kettle, isn't it? It offends your fine-tuned artistic sensibilities.'

'No,' he lied. 'I just feel like a beer.'

'It's the women. All that screeching laughter. And the cakes. They're too vivid for you. Seaside-promenade yellow, fifties-lipstick red.'

'Nonsense.' He squirmed.

How could she know the ghosts that were with him? He imagined Annette's astonished sneer should she, in her Jasper Conran, appear at the door of the Blue Kettle Café, and spot him sitting with Megs and child, laughing loudly at some inane but naughty comment, mouth agape, flaunting a half-chewed gaudy cake. 'Gilbert?' She'd raise her prescription Calvin Kleins, peering at him, making sure her eyes didn't deceive her. 'Gilbert? Is that you?'

Oh God, he shuddered.

They went to the Stag, where, despite the heat outside, the fire was lit, Barry Manilow was playing on the jukebox and the landlord called Megs 'lass'. She could see it had its merits, but her heart was with the steaming ladies in the Blue Kettle.

They got back to the cottage after two. Megs watched as Gilbert unpacked the shopping and put on his green apron – his cottage cooking outfit.

'Chicken tonight,' he said. 'Chicken stuffed with soft cheese and herbs. Tomato and olive salad and some potatoes baked with rosemary and garlic.' He spread things out, putting corn-fed chicken, cheese, milk, herbs, tomatoes, olive oil, garlic in easy reach order. He considered a bottle of South African wine with a giraffe on the label. It was not his usual taste in wine labels, but Lizzy had insisted, and he didn't know how to refuse her.

One of his basic life rules was to avoid confrontations, yet every decade or so they came up. A confrontation with a child, however, was unthinkable. Sensing this weakness, Lizzy had come out of their shopping trip with some M&Ms, four white chocolate puddings, a packet of animal biscuits and a kite. This last Gilbert didn't mind at all. It was a traditional-shaped kite, blue and green with a long flagged tail. He imagined himself flying it, standing on some lush, mildly breezy meadow, cowslips at his feet, holding the string, Megs and Lizzy at his side. All of them watching the sky. The wine, however, was something else. He didn't trust it. He had no intention of drinking it.

Whilst he cooked, Megs, Lizzy and Shameless went for a walk through the woods at the back of the house. Gently kneading the chicken, easing the skin away from the breast, so that he could stuff the gap between loosened skin and bird with a soft paste of cheese, basil, oregano and sage, he realised that in his kite vision, Lizzy had been dressed in button boots and leggings. She'd had a straw bonnet on her head. She wasn't saying a word. The dog had been given a shampoo and blow-dry. Behind them was a field of lavender, fusing into the distance, muted indigo. It was, he realised, pure Merchant-Ivory. Standing stooped over the kitchen table, hands, encrusted with cheesy paste, stuffed up the chicken, staring straight ahead, he was horror-struck. Reining in his imagination, he realised that in his kite picture Annette had been leaning on the gate watching them, slightly approving, and more than slightly envious.

Megs, Lizzy and Shameless went carefully along the narrow path in the woods, avoiding the nettles, ignoring rusting cans, empty crisp bags, the abandoned bits of car and barbed wire and the furious spilling of brambles that engulfed them. Once through the woods, they waded waist deep through bracken to the river, staining their clothes. Burrs in Shameless's coat.

It was well after three o'clock. They started to wander, walking slowly along the river bank, staring down at the water, looking for movement – fish, frogs, otters. 'Anything living would please us city folks,' said Megs. They saw nothing, nobody. The river, sometimes a trickle, sometimes deep enough, wide enough to allow a small swim, ran the length of the glen.

Megs felt the silence, rubbed her arms against the chill she imagined it brought. The day was warm. Lizzy carefully ate her sweets, biting off the thick coating so that the soft chocolate centre was left. It stickied her hands, which she wiped on her T-shirt, smearing chocolate. She swore she saw a giant eel. Shameless rolled in a cowpat and came running to them, smelling foul. 'Oh well,' said Megs. 'You two are happy.' She knew there was misery in store – they'd walked too far and for too long. Had, therefore, to go all the way back again.

At the top of the glen, a small hump-backed bridge crossed the river. They climbed up the verge and through the fence to walk over it, to lean on the parapet, watch the water from above. Across the bridge, on the other side of the road, was a small hotel, next to that a hall. It was a wooden building with notices in the window. SCOUT MEETING 7.00 THIS THURSDAY. And ROAD IMPROVEMENT COMMITTEE MEETING, 8.00 TUES, TEA AND SANDWICHES. And DOES ANYONE WANT A KITTEN? OLAF HAS HAD SIX, FREE TO GOOD HOMES. IN FACT, FREE TO ANY HOME. And JEAN WATSON'S APPLE AND DATE CHUTNEY IS NOW SOLD OUT. A BATCH OF PEAR AND RED WINE JELLY IS NOW READY, CALL AT THE CREGGANS'. ALL PROFITS TO NEW HALL FUND.

There were more, Megs did not read them. It would be dark soon. A lone crow rasped from the telegraph wire. A grim call that heightened her worry. She thought to go into the hotel to buy Lizzy a drink and phone Gilbert, ask him to come get them, but she realised she hadn't brought her purse. City folks didn't go into hotels with empty pockets, especially when they were torn by brambles, blackened by bracken, reeking of cow dung and smeared with chocolate. She turned to walk down the road.

It took only a few steps on tarmac before Lizzy realised she was miserable. She dragged her feet, complained of the heat and hunger. Every two or three yards she sat on the verge, crying. Wiped her eyes with filthy fingers, grubbied her cheeks. Megs lifted her on to her back, and set off down the road again. 'Soon be there. Not far to go.' The lie was to soothe herself as much as her daughter.

When the van slowed up beside them, Megs ignored it. It did not do to encourage strangers, far less get into their vans. She strode ahead, refusing to give its occupant a glance. So it crawled beside them for a few yards before the butcher's boy rolled down the window and yelled, 'Are ye not speaking?' Megs turned, recognised a familiar face and smiled. 'Oh, sorry. I didn't realise it was you. Only, you know, a stranger in a car. You have to be careful these days.'

He leaned out of the window, teeth clenched, thinking about this. He was not a man to let clichés slide past him. 'Seems to me, if you're away from home, strangers are all you've got.'

'That's true,' Megs agreed.

'So,' he asked, 'are you wanting a lift or not?'

'Yes please. Very much. I do want a lift. We all want a lift.'

He leaned over to open the passenger door, then gathered some movie magazines and put them behind him, clearing the seat for Megs. She climbed in, sat Lizzy on her knee and put Shameless at her feet. 'Oh bliss,' she said. 'I'll never walk anywhere again. Have you been delivering?'

'Four steak pies, fillet steaks, bacon and *It's a Wonderful Life* and *Presumed Innocent* to the hotel.'

'Interesting,' she said.

'Your dog's smelly,' he said.

'I know, he rolled in some cow dung.'

'That's a dog for you. They'll do that.'

They had nothing more to say to each other. Megs was too tired to speak, and he was not in the habit of speaking for speaking's sake. They drove in silence till they got to the end of the track leading to Lisdon cottage. 'This'll be you,' he said.

'Yes. Thank you very much. You saved my life.'

'Aye, well. Sitting's better than walking. Usually anyway.'

She climbed out, thanked him again. He raised his hand, dismissing her gratitude, then drove off. Nothing more to say.

The air on the way down the track to the cottage was heavily succulent with wafts of Gilbert's cooking. When at last Megs entered his kitchen, she saw the table he'd prepared. A glass stand filled with fruit, dripping grapes in the centre, wine bottles, gleaming glasses, chicken cooked golden, a bowl of green salad, a white linen tablecloth. With a single flickering candle holding off the dusk, it was perfect.

'Good God,' he cried when he saw her. 'Where have you been? I was worried.'

'We walked to the top of the glen. Up the river to the hotel.'

'But that's miles.'

'I know.' She sank on to a chair.

He'd been worried about her. For the last hour, as he basted his chicken and prodded his potatoes, he'd imagined her lying at the foot of a ravine, both legs broken, unable to move. Or perhaps they'd wandered from the path and were lost, were plunging wildly through the heather, unable to find their way back, panicking and crying. Should he call Mountain Rescue? He thought not, best wait till she'd been missing for longer than sixty minutes. Instead, he fretted.

Emerging now from his worry, he saw how tired and filthy they were. He caught a whiff of Shameless. Annette, he knew, would be wearing spotless jeans, Italian canvas deck shoes – probably navy – and a linen shirt, with a cashmere sweater draped over her shoulders. What she would make of these smelly, bracken-blackened, chocolate- and tear-smeared guests – interlopers bruising his perfection – he didn't dare think.

He pushed his hand through his hair, making it stick up. His shirt was splattered with olive oil and cheesy paste. A thick sweat spread over him. His face glowed from working in his hot, low-ceilinged kitchen and a surfeit of wine. The knackered and grubby, then, congregated to worship the glistening glamour of Gilbert's efforts. Gilbert, meantime, looked sheepishly across at the chair where his imagined, impeccable ghost, Annette, sat hardly able to contain her disdain. He shrugged an apology to her.

'My goodness, Gilbert.' Megs broke into his despairing reverie. 'What a fabulous meal. And doesn't it all look wonderful? And look at us. The mess we're in. Will it wait till we go make ourselves presentable?'

'I think,' Gilbert said, 'it's going to have to.'

She put Shameless out into the garden, threw a bucket of water over him and put his dish, filled with dog food, at the door. Then she took Lizzy upstairs to the bathroom, where they stripped and climbed into the shower together. Gilbert, on his way to put on a fresh shirt, paused by the door to listen to them giggling and lathering one another. He wasn't sure about such intimacy. It made him feel squeamish. Yet it was Megs in his shower having fun, and he could not help the rush of envy that swept through him.

They reappeared half an hour later, looking clean and, in Lizzy's case, shiny. Megs, Gilbert noted approvingly, wore black jeans with a plain white cotton shirt. Her toenails were painted a soft pink-brown. She came to his table barefoot. She smelled of vanilla.

He was not used to such eating. His meals were normally savoured rather than devoured. But his guests tonight were ravenous. They ate. They saved the conversation for afters, with coffee.

'This is wonderful,' Megs enthused. 'Where did you learn to cook like this?'

'In the kitchen.' Gilbert was modest about his achievements. But he nodded towards the cooking area of the room, which was in chaos. The crazed debris of the enthusiastic amateur cook.

When Lizzy had eaten, the trials and physical efforts of her day caught up with her. She climbed on to her mother and fell asleep. Megs carried her upstairs to bed. When she came back Gilbert had opened a second bottle of wine and refilled their glasses.

She sank sighing into her seat. 'Oh, lovely,' she said. 'Peace.' She drank. 'Your wine is lovely. It's a one-glasser, your wine.'

'What do you mean by that?'

'I mean it only takes one glass, one sip, and you know it's good stuff. I buy three-glasser wine. You take a drink and you feel it scrape the back of your throat and corrode your tooth enamel. You make a face, a grimace. The sort of look you make when countering a force-nine gale.' She contorted her face into a post-swig-of-nasty-plonk grimace. 'Like this.'

'Right,' he said, leaning towards her. Making the face too.

'One glass you make the face and say, "This is vile." So you have another. 'Cos you're human and you have to check, also it's probably all you have. Second glass and your throat is already coated with the stuff and your system knows what's coming, so you say, "It's not that bad." So you have another glass and you say, "This is quite nice." My wine takes three glasses.'

'Ah.' He smiled. 'I've had wine like that.' He poured her some more of his one-glasser wine. It made her loosen up. He liked her when she loosened up. 'Tell me about you,' he said, chastising himself as he spoke. He thought he sounded like some stereotype Lothario working on his seduction technique.

'I live such a brittle life,' she said. 'I'm constantly waiting for something awful to happen. I drive to the supermarket in my car and all the way there I'm filled with a small fear that it is going to break down. I hear some jangle and I think, "That's it. Something's wrong. Huge bill for me." Then I realise it's only a sound effect on some song on the radio. But for a moment, my heart reels. That's my mood these days – trepidation. Then I get to the supermarket and I'm obsessed with parking as near to the door as I can. I eye other drivers lest they steal a place I'm after. That's me now, trepidation and competition. And I'm only shopping.

'What does a supermarket look like? Some Middle Eastern hacienda sort of building with a vast car park and a filling station. It smells of bread baking. But that's not bread – it's only a contrived smell. Now what have we?' She spread out her fingers to count her feelings. 'Trepidation, competition, cynicism. That's me these days. Not just on Saturday mornings at the supermarket. But all the time, really.' She poured another glass. Drank it.

'Do you think we've lost our sensuality, Gilbert? Do you ever do anything completely and utterly with all of you? Smell, taste, touch? When I was little, Aunty Betty used to send me out to the greenhouse for tomatoes. I'd go barefoot across the lawn, and I could feel and smell the grass. I could hear birds in the hedge. The greenhouse old and wooden, peeling faded paint. You had to lean on the door to open it. It creaked when it moved. You could hear it scrape on the terracotta tiles. Every summer they planted tomatoes in that greenhouse. Huge plants.' She lifted her hands above her head. A demonstration of hugeness. 'It was full of them. I could stand and feel cracks in the warm tiles on the soles of my feet. And I could smell that green, tangy, tomatoey smell. I was bathed in heat and scent. I could hold a tomato to my nose and breathe it in. I could bite into one and the sweetness of it burst into me. They were ripe and red. And they grew as the sun touched them. No one was a clone of the other. Not like supermarket tomatoes. They are cosmetic tomatoes. Red as red can be, every one perfect. "Look at me," they say. "I'm a tomato." Tomatoes with attitude. Not like real tomatoes in Aunty Betty's greenhouse.' She sprawled on the table, fully wined and slightly crazy.

Gilbert could only drink and listen. He'd had no idea she was so verbose.

'And sex.' Megs was at full steam now. 'In the cinema, I sit in the dark, one hand in my popcorn box, and I watch two people fuck. I sit amidst absolute strangers, and I watch amazing intimacies with them. Things we might do in the dark when we get home. Or not in the dark. Or not at all. It's perfect, cinema sex. Cosmeticised sex. Oooh and ahhs and choreographed rolling on top of each other. Shapely, well-lit bums in the glamorous dark. She never cries, "Get off, get off. I can't breathe." Or, "You're stopping the circulation in my arm." He never gets cramp. They never turn to find a little person, eyes level with the top of the mattress, saying, "What are you two doing?" Too perfect.' She scoffed, 'I do not trust perfection.' She lifted a slice of tomato from the salad dish, held it to her nose a moment, then to her lips. 'This is not a tomato,' she said. 'And that stuff on the screen. That's not sex.' She drank some more. Put down her glass. 'Do you fancy shagging me? Do you fancy having sex with me? All of me. All of you. Everything. Do you fancy the feel of me? The sight of me across the pillow? Would you put your tongue in me, taste me? Would you like to do that together, Gilbert Christie? Would you like to smell the soapy cleanness of the sheets and the breeze on the curtains coming down from the hills across the room, and the salty scent of what we're doing? Would you like to hear my breath in your ear and the sounds outside of grass moving and bushes shoving against each other in the wind? And the call of some late bird through the dark? And our cries when we come? Would you like to feel all over you our mutual sweatiness, and my hands on you, and . . . ?'

He reached over and took her hand. He could hardly bear his

urgency. He felt the warmth of her palm pressing against his. 'Yes,' he said. 'Yes.' Again. When he looked across the room, his ghost, Annette, had gone.

Chapter Twenty-Three

He woke. It was raining, bells were ringing far away. Sunday, and some folks in the glen were going to church. But he was lathered in sweat, and some small, irritatingly insistent hissing noise had pierced his dreams, brought him to consciousness. He did not want to open his eyes. He resisted the light. He reached across for Megs. She was not there. That did it. He lifted himself on to one elbow and looked around, trying to take in what he saw.

Shameless was lying sprawled at the foot of the bed, pinning down the eiderdown, causing his sweat. Lizzy was next to him, squishing mousse from a can. She had already plastered quite a handful on to his head.

'There,' she said, fussing over him. 'That's better. Your hair's always sticking up. I've fixed it. Look.'

Before he could stop her, she held up a mirror. This was not what he wanted to see first thing. He was glazed, looking, he thought, insane. His face was flushed, and his hair was glued to his skull. 'Oh God,' he said. 'Where's Megs?'

'In the kitchen. Washing the dishes.' She got bolder. She sat on top of him, smoothing down his hair. Little hands busy on his head. 'There. You look pretty now.'

'Shall we go find her?' he said, sliding clumsily into his boxer shorts under the covers.

She nodded, and as he climbed from the bed, reached up to take his hand. She led him downstairs. 'Here's Gilbert,' she told Megs, entering the kitchen. 'He's awake now.' Then, to Gilbert, 'Can we fly the kite now?'

He did not know how to refuse her. It was not in his nature to refuse anybody anything.

'Let him get dressed and have some coffee before you start nagging, Lizzy,' Megs intervened. Turning to Gilbert, she scolded, 'Don't let her bully you.'

'I'm not used to children. I never know what to say to them,' he excused himself. 'Goodness, this kitchen's clean. You shouldn't've bothered.'

She shrugged. 'It didn't take long. I'm used to it.'

It was the first time she'd referred to the beginnings of their affair, and the routine she was about to go back to. He was a university lecturer, and she was his cleaner. He didn't think he was comfortable with that. What would his friends say? Gilbert looked across the kitchen. Annette was back.

They walked in silence the way down the track to the field, open enough, breezy enough to fly the kite. Still saying nothing, they climbed the gate, whilst Shameless wriggled through the lower spars.

The kite staggered into the wind, taking slowly to the sky. Gilbert showed Lizzy how to tug the string. 'Play the wind,' he said, squatting beside her, so that her face was close to his. He could see her small lips pulled tight, concentrating. 'You can feel the wind on the end of the string. You can feel the gusts and thermals up there.' He let her hold the kite, stood watching till she could manage it before he sat down on the grass beside Megs.

'She picks things up quickly.' He admired the child.

'Which isn't always a good thing,' she said.

He smiled. 'Were you a smart kid?'

'I suspect I was a pain in the arse. I insisted on being called Megs. I never did what anybody told me. You?'

'I always did what I was told.' Realising he'd hung his head as he said that, he played with a daisy. This wasn't a small movement of shame. He was interested in the ground.

'Your mother was a tyrant?'

'She made me give up painting. She had some idea of respectability she couldn't properly pass on except by inflicting silences and spreading a thick atmosphere of disapproval. You could breathe it.'

They looked over at Lizzy, tugging her kite, watching it jiggle and shake ten feet high.

'I often wonder,' Megs said, 'how people get to be the way they are. I had a boss once, at a market garden where I worked, who was a bully and a loud-mouth in a suit. I'm sure when he was six he must've wanted to be a train driver or an astronaut. How did that happen to him? I'm sure your mother never planned to be the way she was.'

He shrugged. 'She's dead now. I'll never be able to ask her.'

'Yes. That's the thing about death. It's the only thing that lasts and lasts. I remember when Thomas died I thought: this will go on for ever, this death, this never seeing him again.' It was her turn to study the daisies. 'I kept seeing him places. You know, in parks playing, or walking along the street. My heart would stop – literally stop. That's Thomas, I'd think, though I knew it couldn't possibly be.'

A week after the funeral she was passing the park on a bus. Sitting looking out of the window, her face frozen in an expression of grief that staved off fellow passengers. The bus was full, but nobody would sit beside her. Staring across the park at a group of boys kicking a ball about, she saw Thomas. 'That's him.' She was sure she had shouted it out. She got up, struggled up the aisle, past the strap-hangers, and jumped from the platform, though the bus was travelling at some speed.

She ran back to the park gate, then across the grass, waving wildly, shouting, 'Thomas. Thomas.' The children stopped playing, turned to stare at her. Their mothers, standing in a group nearby, did so too. The boys, young and tactless, made faces, screwed their fingers into the side of their foreheads. 'A loony,' they called. The mothers moved instinctively nearer to their children. You never knew with folks these days. Seeing this, reading the language of the bodies, emotional semaphore, Megs stopped running. Stopped waving. Stopped smiling. 'Sorry,' she said. 'I thought I saw somebody I knew.' She walked quickly away, feeling foolish and desolate.

'After my mother died,' Gilbert told her, 'I kept seeing her on the tube. I was in London doing some research. I'd be standing on the platform, and she'd be on a train hurtling past me. Then, sometimes, it was the other way round.'

215

Gilbert remembered standing on the tube, halfway up the aisle, five o'clock Friday night, no seats available. The train was leaving Piccadilly Circus, gathering speed, when he saw his mother standing on the platform. She was wearing her old tweed coat and black leather gloves and was carrying her brown shopping bag with her handbag tucked inside it for safety. She looked surprised. Gilbert stopped gripping the rail overhead and reached for her. 'My God,' he said out loud. People nearby pretended they did not hear him. He ran his fingers through his hair. 'A ghost,' he said. 'The ghost of my mother is waiting on that platform for the train to Kensington.' People about him pretended even harder not to notice him. The only person who looked ghostly was Gilbert.

'I'd better get my things,' Megs said. 'I want to get back before dark.'

'Must you go?' He reached for her hand. 'Why don't you stay longer?'

'I have to get home. I've work in the morning. Terribly-Clean Pearson.' She was adamant.

'Who?'

'Terribly-Clean Pearson. I clean for her. I have names for people I clean for. It's part of my survival. Terribly-Clean Pearson, Dysentery McGhee and Emotionally-Deranged Davis.'

'Do you have a name for me?'

'No,' she said, considering the daisies rather than meet his eye. He didn't believe her.

Lizzy screamed. Her kite had escaped and was soaring away from her. By the time Megs and Gilbert reached her, it was above the trees at the top of the field and heading for the hills. A multicoloured blob.

'You get it,' Lizzy commanded Megs.

'I can't,' Megs said.

'You get it.' Lizzy turned to Gilbert.

'I can't either.' He felt just awful about this.

'I want my kite.' The child clenched her fists, threw back her head and howled.

'Well, it's gone. Nobody can reach it. We'll get you another,' Megs said.

'I want that one.'

'That one's gone. C'mon.' Megs picked Lizzy up and headed towards the gate. 'Time to go.'

'Will you come back?' Gilbert sounded desperate.

They climbed back over the gate. Halfway down, Lizzy got stuck and refused to climb any further.

'I can't get down,' she wailed.

'I'll lift you,' Megs said.

'No.' Lizzy shook her head. 'Not you. I want Gilbert to lift me.'

Feeling absurdly pleased at being the preferred one, Gilbert swept Lizzy from the gate, whirled her high in the air before putting her down. 'There you go.'

'I think she's jealous of the attention you're giving me,' Megs told him.

'Right,' said Gilbert. 'I never thought. I'm not used to children. I haven't learned their little ways.'

Megs watched him as he took Lizzy's hand and headed home. So whose little ways have you learned, Gilbert? she thought. Who is it you are thinking of when you gaze into the distance, the way you do? And will you ever accept my little ways?

It was after seven when she got home. 'Are you still here?' she said to Lorraine, who was lying on the sofa reading the horoscopes on Teletext.

'Seems like it,' said Lorraine. 'You are going to have a shock tomorrow, it says here.'

'Well, thanks for that. Is everything fine here?'

'Nothing to report. Jack's hair is growing. Hannah's still in love. And your mother has phoned twice to see if you're back.'

'Everything's normal, then.'

'Yes. Did you have a good time? What did you do?'

'I'll never tell you.'

'That good, eh? You are looking healthy. Skin's smooth. Fresh air, food and sex, though not necessarily in that order, I'll bet.'

'Bet away. Make us some coffee, that'd be useful.' Megs sat on the armchair. Rose again. 'Jack has ruined this. You have to be under twenty with a teenagy flexible spine, to get comfortable on it. It's become a Beavis and Butthead chair.' She moved on to the sofa.

The phone rang. Megs picked it up. She knew who it was. 'Hello, Mum.'

'How did it go? Did you get back all right? How was the traffic? I don't like you going about in that car of yours.'

'I'm back. Traffic wasn't bad. The car's fine. Lizzy had a good time. She flew a kite. Shameless was, as ever, shameless. And I had a long walk and got a lift back from the butcher's boy. Gilbert cooked a lovely meal. That's all you need to know.'

'That's all I'm getting to know, anyway. Are you going back?'

'He wants me to.'

'You should go. It'll do you good. A man like that, with his education, could bring you to your senses.'

'What do you mean by that?'

'I mean he could show you that there's more to life than cleaning.'

'I already know that.'

'He could make you do something about it.'

'Are you coming round tomorrow?' Megs changed the subject.

'If you want me to.'

'I want you to. You can nag me then, in person, face to face.'

'I will. Good night.'

'Good night.'

Lorraine brought them coffee. 'Don't tell me. That was your mother.'

'She approves of Gilbert.'

'Goodness. As far as you're concerned, that's the worst thing that could happen to Gilbert.'

Megs smiled. 'Maybe not this time.'

Chapter Twenty-Four

A weekend away made it harder than ever to get up and face the day. Megs lay glumly staring at the ceiling. She wondered what Gilbert was doing. Did he have the kitchen door open, letting the soft hill air mix with the smell of brewing coffee? Was he sitting at that kitchen table she'd sat at, and was he mildly staring at today's batch of junk mail? How odd that the red postie's van moved through that exquisite landscape bearing the same rubbish that clattered daily through her own letter box – urgently gushing offers from the *Reader's Digest*, pension plan and loan fliers, breathlessly sincere firms proposing to develop two rolls of films for the price of one.

She could hear Lorraine moving about, switching on the radio, making coffee, before she disappeared pasty-faced and lank-haired in a faded blue dressing gown and reappeared half an hour later, glowing, mincing down the hall in high heels, shirt and tight skirt. A different woman. As soon as she vacated the bathroom, Jack would barge in, leaving Hannah to bang on the door shouting that she had to get in. Then Jack would appear washed and splashed, in multi-reek mode – aftershave, gel (when he had hair to gel), deodorant. After that, Hannah would go in to spray and mousse and fuss.

'It's seven-thirty,' Megs said to Shameless. 'All over the world people are listening to insanity on the radio, pushing mousse through their hair, making the first-sip-of-coffee-in-the-morning face as they hold the cup to their lips. And here's me. As ever, desperate for a pee and wishing I was somewhere else.'

But things were moving on. Now she knew where she wished she was.

She arrived late at the Pearsons'. Hurrying down the path, she did not notice that the front room curtains were still drawn. Had she seen this small break from the norm on the outside, she might have been prepared for the devastation inside.

The mess spread down the hall, strewn torn books, clothes and drifting squalls of feathers coming from the bedroom. Making her careful way to what had been the centre of the storm, Megs peered into the bedroom. The wardrobe was on its side, the dresser had been yanked apart – drawers pulled out, contents spilled on to the floor, make-up, hairspray, jewellery had been thrown at the mirror, which was smashed. The mattress was upturned on the bed, and the duvet slashed, hence the feathers, which billowed and spread in the smallest breeze. But the devastation reached full, catastrophic proportions in the living room and kitchen. Furniture was broken, food furiously splattered against walls, the fridge door swung open, dishes were smashed on the floor. The walls were scarred with the force of hurled crockery and cutlery. The hi-fi was in bits, and CDs, out of their cases, lay covered with coffee and tea poured from their glass storage jars. Tupperware and its contents – lentils, biscuits, flour, rice – spilled everywhere. The vast shiny rebel plant was uprooted, lay centre stage, wilting.

Terribly-Clean was sitting on the sofa. When she looked up, Megs could see her face was bloodied, bruised and swollen. Her eyes were red with more than sobbing – hysteria.

'Good God.' Megs couldn't take in what she was seeing. 'What happened here? Shall I call the police?'

'No. Please don't.' Mrs Pearson's swollen face hurt with every emotion that flickered across it. She raised a hand in protest rather than risk having to use her lips any more.

'Who did this?'

'My husband.' Terribly-Clean put her hand to her mouth.

'Your husband? Did this?' Megs looked round. 'But why?'

Mrs Pearson got up and went through to the bathroom. She returned holding a cloth soaked in cold water to her face. 'I suppose I should tell you. I've got us into terrible debt. He found out about it. He saw me with my credit card. He was on his way back to the office after a business lunch, and he saw me in the jeweller's buying a watch. Another Gucci, I'm afraid. I already have three. But I like them best. I have a thing about watches.'

'You?'

'Yes. Perhaps if he'd done something when he saw me, it wouldn't have been so bad. As it was . . .' she nodded at the room, 'he waited. He waited and checked up n me. He found out about my credit cards. He's known about the debt for a fortnight.' She turned to meet Megs's gaze. 'I have ten credit cards. I owe over twenty thousand pounds.'

'You?' Megs said again. It was all she could think to say.

'Well, last night Access phoned to ask when I was going to make a payment. I'm three months behind with them. And that was it. It set him off.' She blew air into her aching cheeks. 'He went berserk. He hit me in the face with the phone. And then . . . this. I just stood as he wrecked the house. He tore our lives apart. He destroyed everything.' She went back to the bathroom to soak her cloth in cold water again. 'It was awful.' She returned to slump on the sofa, sat back soothed by the chill against her face. 'I had no idea he had such passion. He said he'd worked all those years doing a job he hated just to support us. And I'd blown it all away. We're going to have to sell the house. He went on the rampage, ripping things apart, yelling about his wasted life.'

'Shall I make you a cup of tea?' Megs suggested.

'Yes please. I think the tea bags landed on the floor beside the washing machine. A place for everything and everything in its place. I did a domestic science course. That was one of the first things I learned.'

When Megs brought the tea through from the kitchen, Terribly-Clean Pearson was standing in the debris, crying.

'Never mind the mess for the moment,' Megs said. 'Sit down, drink this. Have you been here all night?'

'I was on the sofa for hours and hours, just staring. It must have been all night. Yes. He stormed out of the house. I haven't heard from him since.'

'He'll be all right, I'm sure.'

'I don't know if I care. I never knew he had such rage.' She looked slowly round at the mess. 'This, of course, is about more than my spending. It's about how bored he's been. Do you know? I think he was jealous that I'd been spending and not him.' She snorted. 'I had given up, you know. Then that day you started to speak about ducks, about rapture, I felt so desolate I got my card and hit the shops. That's when Mr Pearson saw me.'

'So it's all my fault?'

Mrs Pearson put out her hand to touch Megs's. 'Oh no. I didn't mean that. It would've come out one way or another.'

'You need some sleep.'

'How do I do that?'

'Normally I wouldn't be able to tell you. But in your case I think if you just lay down it'd come to you.'

'All those years,' Terribly-Clean said, 'and he's been utterly miserable. If only he'd said. I've been miserable too. I mean, I clean. I cook. I teach part-time, domestic science, showing young people how to cook. How many first-year pupils have I taught to make macaroni and cheese? God.' Then, really thinking about it, 'Probably thousands. I hate macaroni and cheese. Then I come home here and go through little lifeless routines. I make supper, he washes up. We watch television. At eleven we get ready for bed. I make a cup of tea and a digestive biscuit. We were doing all this and we were both utterly unhappy. What liars we were.' She sipped her tea. And winced. 'I have been sitting in this house whilst the whole world happened outside. Not like you, Megs. I don't have a fabulous life like you. I don't sing. I don't do the things you do. I don't wear dark colours.'

'What things?'

Mrs Pearson had no idea. She just imagined things. She hadn't even come to grips with what her imaginings were. 'Just things,' she said.

'I don't have a fabulous life,' Megs protested.

'Oh, I bet you have lovers.' The distressed creases in Mrs Pearson's face dispersed a moment as she imagined Megs's lovers. Her passion.

'I don't have lovers. I haven't had a lover for years and years. I sleep with my daughter and my dog,' Megs confessed. 'You are making up a life for me.'

'You haven't had a lover for years?'

'Well, not until last weekend.'

222

'Now you have one. Who is it?' The eagerness to know swooned out of her.

'He's someone I met.'

'What does he do?'

'He's a lecturer. He's writing a book at the moment.'

'There you go. He must be so interesting. So clever.'

'He's clever.' Megs nodded, musing. 'But he's not wise. He only knows what he knows. He has no intuition. People puzzle him. Life puzzles him.'

'The creative type.'

Megs wanted to laugh. 'Hmm. Perhaps. If he's creative he hasn't let go enough to create anything interesting yet.'

Mrs Pearson would not be dissuaded. She was convinced Megs led a complex, outré life. 'I bet you have lots of friends, though.'

'No.' Megs shook her head. 'Only Lorraine. I see quite a bit of my mother. Otherwise it's just odd folks at the Glass Bucket, though I won't be seeing them any more. And the band.'

'The band. That sounds interesting.'

'Believe me, they're not. They play Friday nights to make ends meet. Like me. They're ordinary, ordinary, ordinary.' There, that should convince her.

'Not as ordinary as me, as I've been all these years. It's what I wanted to be, nothing fancy, safe and ordinary.'

'Daft when you think about it,' said Megs. 'I think ordinary makes women cry more than lost love, being dumped, silent phones or any of that stuff. Women sit alone in absurdly clean living rooms, crying because they're ordinary. And they can't blame anyone but themselves, because it's what they thought they wanted.'

'Yes,' said Mrs Pearson.

'Yes,' Megs agreed with herself. 'Ordinary ain't what it's cut up to be. Still.' She looked round. 'You seem to have rather given up on ordinary,' she said.

'What am I going to do?'

'Drink your tea. Start cleaning up.'

'Yes.' Terribly-Clean Pearson nodded reluctantly.

But they did not move. They sat side by side, quietly companionable. A blackbird shrilled in the garden. Megs looked idly round. 'What a mess,' she said. 'What a lot of stuff we gather. If we didn't buy half the stuff we have, we wouldn't notice we didn't have it.'

'Exactly,' agreed Terribly-Clean. 'See that chicken brick that's smashed in bits over by the television, or what used to be the television. Well, I really wanted that. Used it twice.'

'I have a sandwich toaster – same thing,' Megs said. 'We really should make a start,' she nagged herself.

'Yes. We should,' Terribly-Clean agreed dreamily. 'We could have another cup of tea first.'

'Yes, that'd get us going.'

Still they sat. There was some mutual relief at seeing such a loveless life so passionately wrecked. They sighed. Megs began to idly sing. 'Gimme money. That's what I want,' she sang. Without really noticing she was doing it. She had the knack of plucking totally inappropriate songs from her repertoire.

'Oh, I never really liked that one,' Terribly-Clean Pearson said, taking no offence at all. 'Tell you what I used to love. "Dock of the Bay". Do you know that?'

'Oh, I love that.'

So they sang it.

'Do you know any old Rod Stewart numbers? I had a crush on him.'

Megs sang 'Tonight's the Night', getting into it. Moving and shaking on the sofa. Though not actually standing up. Terribly-Clean joined in the chorus. When they'd finished that one, they started on 'Every Picture Tells a Story'. And when they'd demolished that, Megs said, '"Mandolin Wind", God, remember that one?' So they tore into 'Mandolin Wind'. They bawled, hands waving over their heads.

Passers on the pavement looked mildly bemused at the crescendo blasting from the house at the end of the perfect garden path.

'. . . ah luv ya . . . oooh . . . hooo.'

Chapter Twenty-Five

Vivienne could hardly contain her glee when she heard about Terribly-Clean Pearson. When Megs told her, she got up from her seat by the fire (for such good news made sitting still impossible) and strode into the kitchen. 'Yes,' she said, jubilantly switching on the kettle. 'Yes,' again. Then, keeping her voice under control, 'You'll be wanting a cup of tea, then?'

'Suppose,' said Megs. Though she had a hankering for something stronger.

'You won't be working there any more, then?' Vivienne hoped the question sounded more mildly interested than celebratory.

'Nope,' said Megs. 'They're selling the house. They can't afford me.'

'So what are you going to do?'

'Worry. Gilbert wants me to spend the whole summer with him in his cottage. But I'll have to spend it looking for a job.'

'Go. Why don't you? It'd do you good.'

'I have to find work. I have kids to feed.'

'Your kids will be away all summer. At least two of them will be.'

Megs said, 'I have a mortgage to pay. At least half of one. Mike pays the other half.'

'Let Lorraine chip in. She's living with you. She's got more money than you. She ought to pay her way. Goodness, you haven't had a holiday in years. When you come back you'll be charged up. You'll find a job no problem.' Vivienne had high hopes of Gilbert. She thought he was the best thing that had ever happened to Megs. He would, she was sure, rescue her daughter from this nonsensical life she led and set her on the right track.

Megs said, 'Hmm . . .' And nothing else. She knew she'd reached a point when decisions had to be taken. She'd recently read an advert for business courses for women. She'd thought of applying. But hadn't. She worried that all the other women would be shoulder-padded in business suits, and she'd just be a cleaner.

Still, Vivienne took her noncommittal answer as a good sign. It was not, after all, a downright no.

Megs left her mother's in time to walk to the nursery to pick up Lizzy. It was a perfect day. Too good, Megs thought, to spend clearing up other people's debris. She stepped out to the hum of her worries. They stopped being tangible thoughts, became, instead, a mood she was in. A certain despair that, she realised, had been with her, unacknowledged, for some time now.

She tried to empty her mind, to listen to her feet on the pavement instead. She was unaware that she was walking towards Josh.

He stuck his head in front of hers. 'Are you not speaking?'

'Oh, sorry.' She started. 'I didn't see you. I was miles away.'

'Where are you going?'

'I have to pick up Lizzy.'

'Well, I'll not keep you.'

She started to walk away from him, but he turned, came with her. 'What are you doing now?' he wanted to know.

'Worrying, mostly.'

'I do that.' He considered his feet. Watched them moving over the ground. He was looking worse than ever. Tired, filthy, underfed and longing for a drink. Megs tried to disown him. She didn't know how to politely ask him not to walk beside her. She breathed her discomfort. 'Look. Don't ask me for money. I just don't have any.'

'I wasn't going to.' They walked on in silence. Megs tried to outpace him. But he kept up. 'I know it was my fault,' he said at last. 'I've been feeling guilty about it for years.'

'What was your fault?'

'Your wee lad. The one that died. I shouldn't've kept you talking.'

'It wasn't your fault, Josh. Don't blame yourself. It was my fault. I should have been there.'

'Have you stopped singing, then?'

'Yes, Josh.' It sighed out of her. 'I have.'

'So Mike never told you about that deal, then.'

'What deal?'

'Remember the night we slept on the beach at Gairloch? Remember that night? The night before at Inverness there was a bloke came to see you.'

That night at Gairloch had been a turning point in her life. She'd hollered Big Bill Broonzy in the middle of lovemaking. Mike had asked her to marry him. And, consumed with shame and guilt, she'd accepted. She'd swum as far out into the sea as she dared, circling gulls screamed, 'End of the world! End of the world!' How could she forget that night? It was a night that had the makings of magic, but she'd turned it to nonsense.

'He thought you had potential,' Josh told her. 'He wanted to build you a career.'

'I don't believe you,' Megs said.

'It wasn't much. He wasn't any big shakes. I think he wanted you to sing adverts. You know, like for chocolate and that. Well,' reconsidering this, 'maybe more double-glazing sort of thing. You had a selling voice.'

'It would have been better than cleaning.' Megs felt bitter.

'Is that what you do now?' he said. Not without sadness. 'We all knew and nobody told you. Mike said he'd do it. But he never did.'

'No,' said Megs. Staring glumly at the pavement. 'He didn't. And now I'm ordinary.' She wallowed. 'Bruised and ordinary.' She turned and ran.

'Oh no,' Josh called after her. 'You're not that. You're never that.'

For days after that conversation with Josh, Megs carried on her normal life. She went to work. She made supper. She watched television. She phoned her mother and nagged Lorraine about leaving dirty cups lying on the floor and folding towels in the bathroom and burning the dresser in the bedroom when she left her curling tongs on – all as if nothing had happened, as if there wasn't that little bomb of knowledge ticking inside her waiting to explode. She thought she was in control. But she wasn't really a bottling-things-up sort of a person.

She was in the living room, drinking coffee with Lorraine, talking, as they did, about nothing in particular with endless ease. Vivienne and Jack were watching the early-evening news, Vivienne saying the while that she ought to be going. Megs started to cry. Small tears at first that nobody noticed. She sniffed, pulled a pink tissue from the box on the television shelf, dabbed her eyes and wiped her nose.

'Are you crying?' Lorraine looked worried.

'Me? Oh, no. I'm just catching a bit of a cold.' Megs wiped her nose ostentatiously, demonstrating her ailment.

Vivienne looked round, eyed her suspiciously. 'Looks like tears to me,' she said.

'Oh, no,' Megs protested. Crying, her? She denied the charge. But more tears spilled over. She gulped, took a deep breath. No use. The tears kept coming till she was howling, sobbing, shuddering with sorrow. She covered her face with her hands.

'What's wrong?' Lorraine moved across the room to put her arm round her.

'Nothing,' Megs sobbed.

'Doesn't look like nothing to me.' Vivienne could spot a broken heart a mile away. 'Gilbert hasn't dumped you, has he?'

Megs shook her head. 'No. It isn't him,' she choked as she scrubbed at her nose with her sodden tissue.

'What is it then?'

'It's Mike.'

'Mike?' Lorraine and Vivienne cried in unison.

'Yes, Mike. Seems when we were in the band some bloke tried to sign me. He wanted to mould my career. Mike never, ever told me.' She slumped back, gasping and sniffing. 'Who knows what could have happened.' She gazed ahead, letting what might have been drift through her. 'He's all right. He got his nice job, his nice house in that nice scheme, his nice daughter and his nice car. Look at me – I scrub floors and I could have been a star.' The truth blistered out. 'A star,' she wailed.

'A star?' The word caught Jack's interest. 'You couldn't be a star. You're my mother.'

'Mothers can be stars,' Megs protested. 'Besides, I wasn't always your mother. There was life before you were born.'

He snorted. He doubted that.

'The bastard,' said Lorraine. 'The absolute bastard.' She patted

Megs. 'What a terrible thing to find out. It's awful.'

'I know, awful,' Megs sobbed. 'Years and years. Floors and baths I've wiped. Things I've put up with, and I had a chance I didn't even know about. A star. I could have been a star.'

Vivienne had been silent a long time. 'You don't know that,' she said. 'You don't know what might have happened. What did this person want you to do, exactly?'

'Sing.' Megs's voice moved up a note or two. She wasn't comfortable with this line of questioning.

'What sort of singing?' Vivienne persisted, watching Megs carefully.

'Adverts and that,' Megs said.

'Ah,' Vivienne scoffed. 'Adverts. Well, there you are.'

'What does that mean? "Well, there you are." People make lots of money singing adverts.'

'What sort of adverts?'

'Who knows?' Megs knew better than to confess to double-glazing. 'I would have been a star.' She was convinced. 'I'd have had fabulous clothes. Shoes made exclusively for me in Italy. A Mercedes. Not one of those big ones, one of those small two-seater convertibles.'

'Where would we have sat?' asked Jack.

She was indignant. 'What makes you think you're getting into my Mercedes? I'd have a big family people-carrier VW thing for you folks to follow me around in. It'd have "Friends and Family of Megs" on the side in swirling purple lettering.'

'She's got it all mapped out then,' Vivienne said. 'We're all cramped up in the smelly van whilst she's swanning in front in the flash car.'

'I'd have houses in London, Monte Carlo and San Francisco, and a flat in New York. Plastic surgery on the bags under my eyes, tits lifted, bum sorted.' Megs sighed.

'Nina Megson, superstar.' Vivienne folded her arms. This took some coming to terms with.

'Nina Megson,' Megs scoffed. 'Nina Megson. I wouldn't be Nina Megson. You know I hate my name. I'd be Roberta Bennett, or . . . or . . . Mamie Smith.' Softly she corrected herself. 'No, there's been a Mamie Smith. Josephine Sinatra . . .' she mused.

'I think someone's beaten you to Sinatra,' Lorraine said. 'Just a hunch, but I think so.'

'Well, I'd be incredibly sexy, a woman of mystery who the nation loves. A woman with a tragic past, whose romances come to nothing, who can't find love but is adored by her fans.'

'Oh, good,' said Vivienne. 'I'm glad there's some compensation for your messed-up love life. Of course, you have the car, the houses, the plastic surgery, not forgetting the van.'

Megs ignored her. 'I'd pick some sort of name that implies innocence, even though my image is of passion and longing for true love . . .'

'She's got it all worked out,' Vivienne went on.

'Victoria,' Megs suggested. 'Victoria . . .'

'Cross?' Lorraine offered. She didn't mean to be sarcastic. It just popped into her head, so she said it out loud. Then regretted it.

'Oh, funny,' Megs countered. 'Very witty – Victoria Cross, star of stage and screen.'

'What about Pearl Barley?' Vivienne joined in. 'Or Penny Farthing?'

'Iona Bike.' Lorraine started to giggle.

'Nan Bread,' Jack offered.

'Isla Alcatraz.' Vivienne screamed with laughter. Lorraine and Jack joined in, falling about.

'Oh, very funny. Very funny.' Megs was incensed. How dare they laugh at her? 'I lose my big chance in life, I could have been somebody, and all you do is mock. Huh. What do any of you know anyway?' She stumped through to the kitchen. Chastised, Jack, Lorraine and Vivienne stared shamefaced at each other a moment.

Then Lorraine shouted, 'Rosie Cheeks.'

Vivienne howled.

In the kitchen, Megs wiped her nose on her beef stroganoff recipe dish towel and thought, Oh, pathetic, pathetic.

'It could be worse than all that.' Lorraine teetered into the kitchen after her. She'd had a new vile thought she was anxious to share. 'You might've been a one-hit wonder and ended up as a question on Trivial Pursuit.'

That remark stopped Megs mid-dream. She looked up from the tea towel. 'Oh God, no,' she said. 'The horror. The horror.' Then, tossing the towel into the washing machine, 'Tell you what, Lorraine,' she said. 'If you're going to stay here, how would you like to pay your way? How do you feel about chipping in towards the mortgage? Let me get away for a few weeks.'

'Don't mind.' Lorraine shrugged. 'Where are you going?'

'I thought I might go live with Gilbert for the summer. Of course, you'd be alone here. And I know you hate being on your own.'

'I don't mind being alone in your house. I just mind it in my house.' There was such life in Megs's home, Lorraine never felt alone. In fact she began to relish having it to herself, then she could really enjoy it uninterrupted. 'Are you taking Lizzy?'

'Naturally. And Shameless. You'd only have yourself to bother about. And you know my mother will still come by to check on you. You're never alone with a Vivienne. Anyway, it'd only be for six weeks. Two months tops. No longer. Then I'd be back, and . . . There's gas, electricity, insurance. All my standing orders. I can't go.' The savage truth of her finances crept up on her.

'Go.' Lorraine stopped her. She waved Megs off in the direction she imagined would lead to Gilbert. 'You deserve a holiday. Need one.' She was enjoying being generous, she warmed towards herself. She was quite likeable, really. This surprised her. 'I'll pay your half of the mortgage. I was going to anyway. We can work out the rest. Go. For God's sake, go. You couldn't stop me if I had the chance. Shag yourselves to a standstill. Rip your clothes off and run through the heather.'

'A bit nippy, that,' said Megs.

'Well, roll about in front of blazing log fires, drinking vintage port and listening to old Billie Holiday songs. Get all sweaty and rude.'

'Right now,' said Megs, 'I feel like all I'll do when I get there is sleep. I'll sleep and sleep for weeks.'

Gilbert was thinking of Megs. It was better than thinking about his book, which was not going well. When he'd conceived it he'd been sure it would be a masterpiece. A minor masterpiece, perhaps, but a masterpiece nonetheless. He was working on chapter ten and had a sinking feeling that he was repeating himself. In fact, he thought he'd said all he had to say in the first chapter.

What would Megs be doing? He wished he could phone her, but he had nothing in particular to say. He envied Megs her family. He wanted to belong in that deep, entrenched way he thought Megs belonged. She was part of a family that folded round her. He knew now why she phoned her mother when there was nothing to say. She was keeping in touch, firming her bonds. It came naturally to her. It never occurred to her that she was phoning with nothing to say. Saying something was of no importance at all. It was the phoning that mattered, speaking, a voice down the line. He thought he could never do that. Yet tonight, sitting by his fire, tapping blandly at his laptop, he could no longer bear just thinking about Megs. He'd been thinking about her all week since she left, now he wanted to hear her.

He dialled her number and fretted. What if she wasn't in? What if she was busy with her family and they were all gathered round the kitchen table laughing and joking and she didn't want to be bothered with him? The phone rang. He almost replaced the receiver. Megs answered.

'Hello, Megs.' Gilbert said her name shyly.

'Gilbert.' She sounded joyous to hear him.

'Yes. I just wondered how you were.'

'I'm fine.'

He could hear laughter in the background, imagined her sitting with Lorraine and family drinking tea out of blue-and-white-striped mugs, eating thick slices of bread and jam, cosily bonded. He nearly put the phone down. He was intruding. She didn't want him.

'Listen, Gilbert,' Megs said. 'Do you still want me to come and stay for the summer?'

'Of course I do.'

'Then I've decided. It'll do me good. I'd love to come.'

In the living room, Vivienne smirked and silently thanked Josh. He'd made Megs angry and reckless. Now she'd go to her fancy man, and maybe even marry him. Vivienne had a deep-rooted belief in educated people. She thought teachers, doctors and lawyers to be in control of their lives and beyond ordinary dilemmas. They would not get overdrawn at the bank or drink too much and act silly like Megs did with Lorraine. Vivienne was convinced that this new man of Megs's would help her climb from her wrecked life and start afresh. He'd take her in hand. She'd become a mature student, then a teacher, or possibly a lawyer. The way she ran off at the mouth, she'd be good at that. Yes, Vivienne thought, things were working out fine.

Chapter Twenty-Six

Over the next two weeks, as she prepared to go off for what she now thought of as her summer idyll, Megs indulged in dreams of revenge on Mike. She imagined small scenarios where she emerged the triumphant, misunderstood, hard-working mother and he was exposed as the self-seeking father.

She thought she might phone Denise and tell her who Lizzy's father really was. No, better, she would hand her over to him at the airport when she was seeing Hannah and Jack off, telling him to look after the daughter he would not own up to for a moment. Naturally, this would be within Denise's earshot. Then, again, she could just arrange for Lizzy to stand close to Mike – the resemblance said it all.

In the end, though, her scheming came to nothing. She wandered over to the bookshop at the airport, looking for something for Hannah to read. Mike joined her flicking through paperbacks.

'I don't feel comfortable buying anything for Hannah these days,' said Megs.

'Teenagers have such precise ideas of what they like and what they don't. It's hard. You were the same when you were her age.'

'Hmm,' said Megs. She felt he had no right to criticise. 'I know all about that bloke who wanted to sign me, you know.' She needed to confront him and couldn't wait to manoeuvre the conversation into an argument.

'What bloke?'

'You know fine what bloke.'

'Oh, that.' He'd been feeling mildly guilty about this for years. 'He was a chancer. Not nice. He just wanted you to sing jingles for double-glazing companies, carpet warehouses and such. Local advertising. It was beneath you.'

'And cleaning isn't?'

He said nothing.

'It was my decision whether or not to do it. Nothing to do with you.'

'I know. I know.' Then, to her astonishment, 'I'm sorry.'

'I've been plotting my revenge,' she confessed without lifting her eyes from the book she wasn't reading. 'I planned to tell Denise about Lizzy.'

'She already knows. It's a bit obvious, isn't it?'

'She doesn't mind?'

'Minding doesn't come into it. She understands, that's all.'

'Goodness. I believe, Mike, the woman loves you.'

'Yes.' Mike nodded. 'She does. And I love her.'

Megs felt unbearably peeved at this. 'Did you ever love me? You didn't ever love me, did you?' she said.

'Of course I did,' said Mike. No, he thought, I don't think I did. 'Did you love me?'

She pursed her lips. She longed to kick him, to slap him. She wanted to yell that he'd ruined her life, stolen her best chance. Yet here she was in the airport bookshop being stiflingly polite. 'Yes,' she lied.

After they'd boarded the plane, she stood holding Lizzy's hand, waving goodbye, wishing them well. At least she wished Hannah and Jack well, and she hoped they'd behave normally – smoke a little dope, fall in love with revoltingly unsuitable people, disappear just before meal times, have dubious bits of their bodies pierced – which would, at least, give Mike a glimpse of all the angst he'd missed over the years.

She put Lizzy in the back of the car with Shameless and set off to Lisdon Cottage, to Gilbert. Lizzy said nothing. Mile after mile she said nothing. At last Megs asked, 'You don't mind Jack and Hannah going off in an aeroplane without you?'

'I don't want Jack and Hannah to go in an aeroplane. I'm never going in an aeroplane,' Lizzy told her. 'I don't want to get smaller and smaller.'

'What do you mean, smaller and smaller?'

'I've seen planes when they're in the sky. They're teeny. I don't want Jack and Hannah to get teeny. Will they get big again?' She started to cry.

Megs pulled in to the side of the road. Turned round to take the child to her. 'They don't get smaller and smaller. They stay the same size. The aeroplane just looks small because it's so far away. High, high in the sky.' She had the feeling Lizzy wasn't convinced. She pointed to trees and houses in the distance. 'Look at them. You know how big a tree is, and how big a house is. They're not little. They're just far away. Remember the people at the airport? Some of them had just got off a plane. They weren't teeny. They were the same size they were when they got on.'

Lizzy stared solemnly out at trees on the mountainside.

'We're going on our own holiday. We're going to stay with Gilbert. We'll walk up the glen and play in the garden and . . .'

'Get all sweaty and rude?'

Megs put Lizzy back beside Shameless. 'You shouldn't eavesdrop,' she said.

She drove to Gilbert, to her summer idyll. Actually, when she closely examined it, she had no idea what anybody on an idyll did. She imagined it entailed a lot of wafting in and out of the cottage in a long frock. She did not know how long she could waft without becoming totally bored. Ten minutes max, she thought.

Gilbert was standing by the door waiting for her when she arrived. He was wearing his cottage apron and waving. Though waving made him sheepish, and he stopped as soon as he found himself doing it. 'It's wonderful to see you.' He smiled. Then, 'Why not pop your car round the side, out of sight.' He didn't want any friends dropping by and finding a car at his door with a nodding dog and WINDSURFERS DO IT STANDING UP in the back window. Megs obliged.

She came into his living room, dropped her cases on the floor, flopped into the sofa with the tartan throw and said, 'Well, Gilbert, here I am.'

He smiled. 'Good to see you.' He meant it. 'Really good.' They beamed at each other. Let the idyll begin, thought Megs.

'Have you thought about what you are going to do whilst I'm working?' Gilbert asked, bringing her a cup of coffee.

'I shall walk. I shall garden. I shall spend time with my daughter. I shall enjoy myself.'

'Sounds good to me.'

At first it worked. They were delighted with each other. It took a week for their differences to emerge. It started to seem to Megs that it wasn't just her children who were experiencing a whole new culture. She and Lizzy were too.

They moved into little routines. In the morning she rose first, tuned the radio to a rock station whilst she made instant coffee for herself, and a boiled egg for Lizzy. He got up after her, couldn't bear the noise coming from his radio, retuned to Radio Four. Whilst Lizzy played under the table, bossing Shameless, running her purple van over his paws, Gilbert would listen to the news and read the morning paper. Every now and then, if some feature that interested him came on, he'd stop reading and gaze at the radio whilst listening.

Megs, however, joined in. She'd expound. 'Oh, I don't agree with that.' Or, 'What a pompous arse he is.' She repeated things he'd heard, just to make sure he'd heard them. 'Did you hear that, Gilbert? It's going to be fine all day. But rain coming in from the west this evening. That'll do the garden good.'

'I heard.' He was irritated that her opinions and quotations drowned out the broadcast. He was not used to other voices in his life.

Once or twice a week they'd drive to the village to shop. He went to the grocer's to buy extra virgin olive oil, fresh parmesan, espresso coffee, focaccia bread. She went to Tesco and loaded her trolley with rice krispies, tins of beans, Jammy Dodgers and Coca-Cola for Lizzy, and Pedigree Chum for Shameless. The vivid presence of these things in his careful larder made him wince. Food for him was part of his lifestyle statement. Food for her was what you produced at regular times in vast quantities because fed children were easier to cope with than hungry ones.

Every evening Megs would clear the supper dishes, remove the linen tablecloth from Gilbert's table, toss the crumbs she'd swept into her cupped hand out the door for the birds and place the fruit bowl dead centre. Every day Gilbert would tactfully move it slightly to the left. Dead centre was, he considered, tacky. He was constantly rearranging the little groupings of his *objets trouvés* that Megs would dust and put back wrongly. The seventeenth-century green glass wine flask went next to the two candles, not – good heavens, did the woman see nothing? – in between them.

Then there was the gardening. In his dream of Megs gardening, Gilbert had her in full waft, wandering about the lawn in a long white floaty thing, carrying a trug basket filled with lupins. Megs wore jeans. Megs dug. She yanked out weeds, freed tangled shrubs, she filled her watering can at the kitchen sink and carried it slopping water out the door. She got messy, sweaty. Lizzy busied after her, chatting, taking the trowel to dig little holes. She took the watering can, spilling pools on to the kitchen floor, and outside she watered the plants, the path, the clothes poles, the sun dial, Shameless, everything. There was mud under both Megs's and Lizzy's nails.

Gilbert had no experience of children. He understood that Lizzy had to eat, and tried not to mind seeing the odd hardened bean on his kitchen table, or finding half-eaten, slightly soggy chocolate biscuits lying on the arm of the sofa. He knew her clothes had to be washed daily and hung out to dry, and, on rainy days, draped over the heater in the kitchen. Still, he found it hard to come to terms with the clutter and noise a child brought into his house. Then there was the dog. Shameless stole his socks from the laundry basket and gathered them in a secret hoard under the bed. Gilbert swore foully to himself as he squeezed and stretched to get them. The dog, always delighted to find a face level with his own, licked him mercilessly.

No matter how much they were irritated by each other's habits, Gilbert and Megs worked hard at avoiding confrontation. Neither of them wanted to argue.

'Shall I switch the station?' she asked when he came into the living room and found her watching her favourite soap. 'Only I know you hate this.'

'No. Please don't.' Though he found the programme offensive. 'I've never watched this before. It's interesting.'

At times like this a look came over Gilbert. He seemed blank, bemused, bewildered. His arms would hang by his sides and he would turn, checking, Megs always thought, that there was nobody else in the room. Megs had no idea who he was looking out for, but whoever it was, it was a she. And Gilbert was hers.

Once they walked down to the river and sat on the bank whilst Lizzy tried to catch sticklebacks. They watched the flies on the water. Flitting, leaping, skating the surface, teasing the fish.

'I'll never dance like that,' Megs said. 'I'd like to dance.'

'I don't ever dance. But these flies only live for a day. They've got to do something.' He was level-headed. He did not long to be dancing on water.

'They've got a nice day for it, then.'

'For what?'

'Their lives. If you've only got a day, this'd be a good one. What sort of a day has it been for you? For your life?'

He did not know what to say. He did not usually field questions like this. He hated this sort of esoteric talk. Had not the gumption to take her hand and tell her the sun had come out. 'Fine, I suppose.'

'I've had a lot of freezing fog, cloud and drizzle. But I'm hoping for a ridge of high pressure – lots of wiggly lines.' She smiled at him. At last he smiled back.

After this, they started to enjoy each other. Gilbert slowly stopped minding all the attention he was denied whilst Megs looked after Lizzy, and started to love watching her face as she leaned close to the child, helping her out of her clothes, coming into the room with Lizzy, freshly soaped and bathed, enveloped in one of his huge bath towels. It amused him that she had a dog that looked blank when told to sit or stay – normal canine commands – but responded eagerly to the words cuddle or chocolate. 'Children,' Megs would shrug by way of an explanation. The idyll started to come together. They'd be sitting by the fire, window open, and the night scents – honeysuckle, wood smoke, pine trees, peaty mountain air – drifted in. They'd talk.

'Gilbert,' Megs said, 'you tell a better class of lie than me. I tell ordinary lies.'

'What do you mean by that?'

'All that stuff you buy. Focaccia bread and that. All this stuff you have, the groupings of objects, the way you like things, the fear you have of people discovering me here. Common as muck, me. It's part of the lie you tell. I'm not ordinary, you say. You don't have to work so hard at it. Nobody thinks you are. Not like me.'

'You're not ordinary.' He came across the room to her. Stroked her hair. 'Ordinary is the last thing you are.' They kissed.

In bed she clung to him. Wrapped herself round him. Pulled him into her. She pressed her cheek against his unshaven cheek, tasted him. 'I love you,' she said.

When they'd done he said, 'Don't love me. I don't want you to love me.'

'Don't worry about it, Gilbert. It's just something I say to someone who happens to be in bed with me, lying on top of me with my legs curled round his waist. Don't read anything into it.'

Once, in his kitchen, she found a little piece of ginger with a thick green shoot sprouting from it.

'Gilbert, I shall plant this for you and put it on your windowsill. Then, whenever you look at it, you'll think of me.'

'I'll think of you anyway.'

'You'll see it and think of me when she comes back.'

'Who?'

'The ghost that lives with us. The woman you fear will discover you with me.'

'My love?' He was scornful.

'No. I'm your love. But she'll get you in the end.' Megs touched his cheek. Then stood up on tiptoe and kissed him.

She went out to walk along the track. The night was soft on her arms; far away a curlew called. The moon was waxing, had soft circles round it. A harvest moon. A white owl behind her broke from the trees and flew, silent as snow, down the field where, only weeks ago, Lizzy had lost her kite. She watched it swoop and glide. She thought perhaps she ought to be upset that Gilbert did not deny the ghost he glanced at. But she wasn't. Shameless stuck his nose down a small hole he'd found – some tiny creature's nest – and snorted in excitement. 'What are you doing?' she asked fondly. The dog looked at her, bright brown eyes. Megs reached for him, scratched his head. She rather liked this new woman she was, who was not going to allow herself to get broken-hearted. Who was wise enough not to let a little bit of melancholy ruin an exquisite night.

In her time with Gilbert, Megs had felt her face unfold, relax. The muscles that grief and worry had knotted eased. She shut her eyes. She had the feeling that she'd been running very fast, very hard for a long time, and now it was over. She could stop. 'It's over,' she said to herself. 'It's over and I'm all right.' She went back down the track to Gilbert, to his bed, to let her tongue linger with his tongue, to move her fingers through the greying hair on his chest, to run her hand over his soft stomach and feel him next to her, in her.

When Gilbert felt Megs and her radio rock'n'roll too much for him, or when his work knotted him up, and words froze in his brain, he walked. Megs watched him go. He'll be back, she'd think. He'll be back with an apology on his lips. But Lizzy was not used to letting people go. She was little and liked everyone to be together. When Gilbert strode out, she strode after him. At first she stalked behind him, in her denim dungarees and striped T-shirt, imitating his walk. Gilbert always knew she was there and tried to ignore her. Eventually, however, Lizzy was allowed to stride alongside him. She'd try to take huge steps and would, from time to time, look up at him for approval. He could not resist her. After a while she was allowed to hold his hand. Gilbert was not used to physical contact and hated the feel of her soft and innocent palm against his, mostly because it made his hand feel huge and rough. But after a while he came to love that little hand. He'd squeeze it and look down smiling at her small, serious face as she tried to match his strides. Chatting to her, he visited conversations he had left far behind him in his childhood.

'What's your favourite thing to eat, Gilbert? Is it chips dipped in bean juice?'

'Bean juice?'

'You know, the sauce beans come in. Or is it pizza?'

'Um . . .' Gilbert pretended to think. 'Pizza.'

'Yes,' Lizzy agreed, nodding. 'Pizza's my favourite, too.'

'Look, Lizzy.' Gilbert pointed up at a plane tree. 'Look at the leaves. The dark shapes they make against the sky.'

Lizzy stared. 'How do you know it's the leaves making the shape? How do you know it isn't the sky? The sky is peeping through the leaves. It's watching us.'

He looked again. Why hadn't he thought of that? She saw more than he did. He stood gazing at the light shimmering through the trees. For days he thought about it, shapes and light. He started to draw again.

Chapter Twenty-Seven

After three weeks together they relaxed. Gilbert no longer glared spikily at Megs's gross additions to his gourmet kitchen. He found himself solemnly dunking a chocolate Hobnob in his coffee whilst humming along with Sting on the radio's Golden Oldie spot. 'Roxanne, you don't have to . . . dum . . . dum . . . any more. I like that one.' Megs no longer deliberately put the fruit bowl in the middle of Gilbert's round dining table then stood back watching him sigh and cross the room to place it left of centre. They started to trust each other enough to turn their small confidences and confessions into jokes and banter.

He bought her an art nouveau dragonfly pendant he found in one of the village craft shops. 'There,' he said, putting it round her neck, 'for you. If you don't like it you can always shove it up the drainpipe to keep your green and pink hat company.'

The garden started to flourish. It no longer looked as if it was recovering from the ravages of some cruel barber. Lunch times they picnicked on the lawn. After twenty minutes Gilbert always started to fidget and look worriedly across at the living room window. His desk and laptop were in there, waiting for him. *The Theme Pack* beckoned.

Megs reached over and stroked his ear with a blade of grass. 'You have no concept of sloth, Gilbert.'

Slapping away the irritating tickle at his ear, 'I don't think that's true.' He could hardly believe this. He was defending himself. He hated loafing about.

'I have never seen you sitting about doing nothing,' she accused.

'I often do nothing,' he said hotly. 'I sleep.'

'Sleeping isn't doing nothing,' she scoffed. 'Sleep's important. You rest. You dream. It's restorative. No.' He wasn't getting away with this. 'Sleeping doesn't count.'

'I watch television. I read,' he whined.

'That's being entertained, that's gathering information. That's not sloth.'

'Even if it's a programme I hate, or it's information I don't want?' The worst sort of information as far as he was concerned. Unwanted information somehow always stuck.

'No.' She was adamant. 'Being slothful, truly slothful, is lying prone on a chair, legs splayed, large tummy openly on view, arms dangling and not a constructive thought in your head. I've never seen you do that. You're always anxious about your work.'

'I could do that.' It was a challenge, and he never could resist a challenge.

'No you couldn't. You couldn't just sit and watch drivel on television, eating crisps.'

'I hate crisps. I'd have pork crackling. I'd have a flask of coffee to save me getting up to make more when my cup was empty. I'd wear two pairs of socks to keep my feet warm.'

'Ugh, not coffee from a flask. It's horrible from a flask. Pork crackling – how vile.'

He felt gleeful that he'd disgusted her. He'd broken down his defences, allowed a little trivia into his life. He'd won a point or two here, though he didn't really understand how. He continued, 'Of course I'd not wear any trousers. No trousers, luxury. I'd pull a travelling rug over my knees to protect myself from crackling crumbs and hot coffee spillages.'

'Gross,' she cried.

He felt oddly triumphant. It made her mediocre television programme and crisps seem polite and tame. He'd always considered himself to be the polite and tame one. 'There, how's that for sloth?'

'I feel sick thinking about it.' She made a sour face.

He matched her expression. He felt quite sickened by his slothfulness too. But he lay down beside her. 'Maybe you're right. I'll lie here. It's quite good, isn't it? Doing nothing. I could get into sloth.'

'There you go. See, I've taught you something.'

Every night after supper, they walked together across the field in front of the cottage. The summer grass was high and lush. There were wild lilies growing in the damp of the ditch, and campion. The hawthorn bloomed. Megs watched him walk in front of her. He wore corduroy trousers and walking boots, carried Lizzy on his shoulders. She felt a rush of love for him.

On the way back to the cottage, Lizzy curled into Gilbert's shoulders, put her face on his head and slept.

Megs reached out and steadied her as they walked. 'See me,' she said as they walked. 'My life is full of nonsense. I used to think stuff and nonsense. But the other day I decided it was more grief and nonsense.'

'What do you mean by that?'

'Well, I've had the most dreadful things happen to me. But they're matched by some utterly nonsensical, embarrassing things.'

'Like running over the park to the boys playing, looking for your son?'

'Yeah. Sort of.' Then, checking Lizzy was sleeping, she continued, lowering her voice. 'I never wanted Lizzy. I denied my pregnancy for the whole nine months. I went to the clinic. But I sort of hid it from myself. As if it would go away. Then when she was born I told them to take her away. I didn't want her. I wanted Thomas back. I felt she was pushing Thomas out. So I lay looking at her as she bawled her head off.'

The ward sister had come by. 'Baby's crying, Mum.'

'Who is Mum?' Megs asked bleakly. 'Don't call me Mum. I'm not your mother.'

Gilbert adjusted her sleeping child on his shoulders. 'But you obviously love her now.'

'Oh yes.' Megs nodded. 'That was the grief bit. Now for the nonsense. It was just before Christmas. She was weeks old, still in her carrying basket, and we were at the supermarket. I was unloading my trolley into the car. I didn't put her on the back seat. I just popped her on the roof as I put all my stuff in the boot. Then I got in and drove off with her still on there. I forgot about her. People in the car park flashed their lights and tooted their horns. People pointed and shouted and I thought, Look at these silly people. What's all the fuss about? I thought they were after my parking place, it was so busy. Bastards, I thought, can't wait. Then someone ran after me and banged on the car window. So I stopped. And that's when I discovered her.'

'So she wasn't hurt?'

Megs remembered the silhouetted figures in the car park, running through the dark waving and yelling. When she discovered what she'd done she felt shamed and foolish. 'No, she was fine. But I got such a shock. I could hardly drive home I was shaking so much. I nearly lost her, too. It was close.'

'Your life is a tragi-comedy,' he said gently.

'Yes.' She liked that.

Next day it rained. Gilbert wanted to cook a loin of pork in milk. 'Maiale al latte,' he said. 'I need white wine vinegar for my marinade. And we're out of coffee, garlic and those hideous jam biscuits that you buy.'

Megs agreed to drive to the village to shop whilst Gilbert would stay home, work and look after Lizzy. He enjoyed having the child to himself. Her quiet, deliberate presence pleased him. She would sit on the floor by his desk with a pile of his A4 paper and some crayons, drawing whilst he frowned at his screen, fretting over his book.

It was the first time Megs had been alone since she'd come to Gilbert's cottage. She relished it. She had decided to go to the Blue Kettle Café. She had longed to go there ever since her first visit, but whenever she mentioned it, Gilbert could hardly contain his scorn. Now, at last, she could go without him. She would shop first, then go. She would, as always, save the best till last. She bought Gilbert's wine vinegar and some sage. Then to the butcher's, where she ordered a chicken and asked Billy to deliver two videos for the weekend.

She always walked slowly past the Blue Kettle Café, longing to go in. The windows steamed, and laughter poured out into the street. There were cake stands in the window and cakes sat fatly on perfect doilies. Bright-red tower-shaped cakes covered with coconut, with cherries on top, meringues, Belgian biscuits and marzipan-covered Battenbergs – she didn't care which one she had. It wasn't the cake really. It was the steamy atmosphere, thick with cigarette smoke and gossip.

At last she went in. Waitresses bustled and prattled, far too busy laying out cakes and making sandwiches to bother with customers, especially ones they didn't know. Megs ordered tea and watched as it was poured from a vast stainless-steel teapot into a thick white cup. She took that, a cheese sandwich and a red coconut cake to a far corner, where she sat at a fake wood Formica table, hoping she'd go unnoticed. She looked round at the bad perms and anoraks, thinking that there was a lot of water being retained in the Blue Kettle Café today.

She sat with the fat-kneed ladies amidst their swelling laughter and prepared herself for a homey treat. The sort of gooey cakes Aunty Betty used to bake. But the tea was dishwater vile, the cake musty and tired and the sandwich was a slice of supermarket bread thick with marg, two flaccid tomatoes and a glum, lumpen slice of cheese. It was a loveless thing. A that'll-do thing. The waitress had smacked the bread down, beefily slapped it with marg, shoved on the cheese. That'll do. It was how they did things. That'll do. No need for fancy.

The longed-for gossip almost broke her heart. 'Has anyone seen Ina?' someone said.

'No,' someone else said. 'I saw her yesterday but I haven't seen her today.'

Was that it? Where was the steamy talk of love and death? The bawdy exchanges? Megs couldn't remember when she'd last been so disappointed. This'll do for a conversation. This'll do for a cake. This'll do for a life. She left her tea and food and never went back. She walked, hunched against the rain, back to her car, trying not to think that she was the same as the fat-kneed Blue Kettle ladies. She lived a this'll-do life.

She drove slowly home, too saddened by the café experience to play the radio. The doleful creak of her windscreen wipers was soundtrack enough for her disappointment. She almost drove past the butcher's van. It was parked by the side of the road, indicators flashing, hood up, with the boy peering glumly in at the engine.

She pulled over. 'Anything wrong?' she asked, winding down her window.

'She's broke.' The boy patted the van. 'Don't know anything about car innards, do you?'

Megs shook her head. 'They're a mystery to me. Can I take you anywhere? Back to the village? I owe you a lift.'

'You could take me to the hotel. I have to deliver these steaks, lamb chops and *Mad Dog and Glory* and *Casino*. I like a bit of Robert de Niro, don't you?'

'Yes,' she agreed.

'Then I can phone the garage from there and they'll come and get me.'

'I could bring you back.'

'Nah. I can get stuck up there and have a pint.'

He transferred his meat and videos into her boot and got in beside her. 'You think this is just a glen, don't you?'

She shrugged. Didn't know what to answer.

'But it's different to me. See that wall.' Pointing to a long, smashed dry-stone dyke. 'That's Will's wall. Every Friday he'd drive home drunk and miss this corner and drive into that wall. So they stopped fixin' it. Better to leave it broken. Then his car would just crash into the gap. Safer.' Then, a few miles further on, 'That's the lay-by where the dentist killed himself. He borrowed the farmer's shotgun and drove here. Blew his brains out.'

'Why?'

'Fed up looking at folk's teeth, probably. That, and his wife left him. See that cottage.' He leaned over, pointing at a damp and dilapidated cottage on the hillside. 'I was brought up there. Lived there with my father till he died over forty years ago, now. Yes.' He drifted off, remembering. 'My father died in that cottage forty-four years ago yesterday.'

She was so engrossed leaning over the steering wheel, staring up at the cottage, she almost did not notice the pheasant. Yards ahead a female pheasant craned out of the undergrowth, cast a beady and vaguely insane eye around and decided now was the time to make a dash to the other side of the road. She hurtled, startled and squawking, a wild hen's run in front of the car, and behind her came two crazed babies. Two tiny fist-sized balls of golden-brown fluff, squeaking hysterically, shot out in front of the car.

'Babies,' screamed Megs. 'Oh no. Babies.' She stamped on the brakes. The car screeched forward, wheels locked. 'Babies, babies,' Megs yelled. 'Watch out, babies.'

The car behind, a red Volvo that Megs had not noticed till now, braked furiously too and the driver put his fist on the horn – a rude, glaring wall of noise.

'Babies,' Megs yelled, turning in her seat, enraged at the tooting. But one foul toot did not satisfy the Volvo driver's rage. He blasted again and again.

'Babies,' Megs screamed, waving at the now empty road in front. The Volvo continued its furious honking. Blast. Blast. Blast. That was it. Megs got out of the car, leaving her passenger to heave himself upright from his sudden jolt forward.

'Babies,' Megs yelled at the driver behind. 'Didn't you see them?'

'Oh, I saw them,' the insane tooter called. 'I saw them before you did. Christ! You nearly killed us all! When something runs out like that you have to keep going.'

'That's just like a man. Squish everything in sight. Mow them down. Let me past. Out of the way. Mr Toad coming through in his shiny red automobile with the really loud horn. Fucking kill everything. Arse,' she bawled. 'Arse. Arse. Arse. You don't give a fucking fart about fucking life, do you? Just kill. Kill. Babies, they were babies.'

Two pressed and pristine children in the back of the Volvo palely peered at her through tinted windows. The driver touched the side of his forehead with his finger, gesturing that he thought her too insane to bother communicating with, put his car into gear and drove slowly past. Megs responded with another finger gesture, a single defiant digit raised aloft against all Mr Toads in all red automobiles everywhere.

'Arse,' she shouted after him. 'Arse. Arse. Arse.' Then, returning to her car, 'Did you see him? The arse he is. Going to squish the babies. What a fuck. What an absolute fuck.'

She sat gripping the wheel, sighing, not breathing. At last, realising the fool she'd made of herself, she turned to the butcher's boy. 'I'm sorry,' she apologised. 'You must think me terrible.' She sighed again. 'My little boy was run over. Just when I think I'm getting over it, something happens and I realise I'm not.' She put her hand to her mouth. 'Thing is,' she didn't know why she was telling him this, 'I always thought it was my fault. I was late picking him up from school and he set off alone. I should have been there.'

He did not answer. He sat staring at the cottage on the hill till they turned a bend and it was lost from sight. 'Aye,' he said then. 'Guilt'll do that to you.'

'Do what?' Megs asked.

'Make you daft.'

She was late getting back. She thought Gilbert would be standing anxiously at the door, gazing up the track. But he wasn't. He was inside, sitting on the floor with a sketch pad on his knees. He was surrounded by drawings of Lizzy. Lizzy drawing. Lizzy drinking orange juice. Lizzy with a ball. Lizzy twirling round and round on his chair. 'She won't keep still,' he complained. His hair was on end.

'She's still enough now.' Megs nodded at the child, who was curled on the sofa, sound asleep and covered with chocolate.

'I had to give her four chocolate puddings to get her to sleep.'

'Wonderful,' said Megs, not even trying to hide her sarcasm. She picked up his sketch pad and looked at the drawing of Lizzy sleeping. 'This is good, though; I have to admit. You really have caught her. The way she sleeps.'

'Yes,' looking at his drawing. 'She pouts, and she's got a little double chin.'

No matter how good Megs thought his drawings, Gilbert knew they were that most dreadful of things – mediocre. It was years since he'd drawn anything. Most of those years had been spent appraising and criticising artists more skilful than he was. Now he had a better idea of how good he was. He was not as good as he'd thought he was all those years ago, when his mother had made him set fire to his work. He felt furious at his failing. It was, after all, such a simple failing. He could not place the lines he was drawing exactly where he wanted them. The shapes he made on the page were not the shapes he saw, either out here in the room, or in his head. His frustration showed in his hairstyle.

'She's good at sleeping, isn't she?' Megs said.

'Yes.' Gilbert nodded. They stood watching Lizzy lying there, doing her childish trick that Megs so envied – making sleep seem simple.

'So where have you been all this time?' he asked.

'Don't ask. I had one of those traumatic shopping trips where you set out to buy something ordinary and end up having one of those pivotal life experiences that changes your destiny. Know what I mean?'

'No,' he said. Sometimes she made him feel so shallow.

'Well,' she sighed, 'I got a guided tour of the glen from the butcher's boy. And . . .'

'And?'

'I went to the Blue Kettle. You were right. It was awful. You and your damn gourmet cooking, you've spoilt me for the rubbish I used to like. You've ruined my punter's palate.'

'Ruined? I thought I'd developed it.'

'Sometimes a person gets nostalgic for food they've left in their past. Cake stands vividly laden, an egg chopped with butter in a cup. You think you can bite into such things and be whisked back to the magic summers of your youth. But all you taste is lard. It'll have to be the Manilow and Coal Scuttle from now on.'

'The what?'

'The hotel we usually go to. The first is always playing on the jukebox and the second is always right in the middle of the floor where people will trip over it.'

'All right,' he said, punching the air. 'It's the Manilow and Coal Scuttle for us.'

A couple of days later they went. They had game pie and Guinness and sang Lizzy's version of the song on the jukebox all the way home. 'The Copabanana'.

Chapter Twenty-Eight

It was inevitable that someone would show up and disturb the drifting calm of their perfect summer. The interloper was Lorraine. She arrived, mincing and squealing, wearing sling-back shoes and a skirt that scarcely covered her bum. She had come to show off her new toy, Jason, who sheepishly shadowed her. He was nineteen. He seemed to regard Megs and Gilbert as grown-ups, and, therefore, felt uncomfortable with them. Every time someone asked him to do something – sit down, carry some glasses from kitchen to living room – he politely did what he was told, which made the grown-ups uncomfortable around him.

'Isn't he gorgeous?' said Lorraine, linking arms with him. Leaning over to kiss him.

If he hadn't been standing two feet away, Megs would have said, 'No.' But he was, so she shrugged a reply instead. 'Is he staying with you?' she asked. As if Jason wasn't standing next to her.

'Yes.' Lorraine drooled, thinking of it. The juicy nights she'd had.
'At my house?'

'Well, yes.' Lorraine seemed shifty. 'But only because we can't go to his house. He still lives with his mum.'

Megs and Gilbert exchanged God-help-us looks.

'I'll be home next Friday,' said Megs. 'Normal life resumes on Monday. Know what I mean, Lorraine?'

'Yes.' A flat reply.

'Is there no chance of you going back to your own house?' Megs pleaded.

'Harry's moved back with his girlfriend. He's going to buy my half of the house from me. When the money comes through I'll get

253

my own place.' She squeezed Jason's arm, thinking of it.

'Well,' said Megs. 'We can make room for you. But not for your love life. I do not want any of my children to come across you frolicking in some abandoned fashion in the living room. They frolic enough as it is without you encouraging them.' She opened a bottle of wine and took them through to the living room, where they sat side by side on the sofa like two children visiting their aunty, being good.

'Good heavens,' said Lorraine, looking round. 'This place is full of drawings.' She picked one up. 'This is of you, Megs. And you've nothing on. That's not very nice.'

'Well, thanks for that.' Megs never expected tact from Lorraine.

Now that Gilbert had started drawing, it seemed he couldn't stop. Megs had spent the last few nights naked. She lay on the sofa trying to remember to keep her tummy hauled in, and pressing the soles of her feet against some cushions. She did not want him to draw them, for she feared they were filthy. Their intimacy worked only when they were alone together. It did not stand up to Lorraine's squealing interest, which made it seem, somehow, silly. Silly and chilly.

Gilbert had become obsessed with his art. He was a man possessed. His inability – that he kept private – to put the things he had in his head on paper made him bad-tempered. 'Don't move,' he'd snap. 'Put your hand up to your face. Turn into the light. Straighten your fingers, they look like a pound of sausages.' Then he'd throw down his sketch pad, pace about a bit, run his fingers through his hair, pour some whisky and come back. 'You've moved.'

'Of course I've moved. You went off to pout and flounce. Don't I get any whisky?'

'Not till I've finished.' She hadn't known he could be so bossy.

'Ooh.' Lorraine gripped Megs's elbow. 'Weren't you cold? He didn't draw your goosebumps. So, apart from sitting around in the buff, what've you been doing, anyway?' she wanted to know.

'Walking. Talking. Eating. Drinking wine. Staring at things. We go to the village now and then. I have slept all night for the last three weeks.'

'You look well on it. The food, the sleep. The sex more like.' Lorraine knew what it took to get a good night's sleep. 'See me, since

Jason. I haven't given Harry a thought. And sleep. God . . . well . . . you can imagine.'

'Yes.' Megs nodded.

Lorraine leaned closer. 'Is he any good, then?'

Megs looked towards the kitchen door. Gilbert was hovering, eavesdropping, running his fingers through his hair. 'Mind your own business,' she said.

'Oh well.' Then, 'I'll get it out of you. You know I will.'

Megs snorted. She knew she would.

After a plate of pasta, two bottles of wine and a whingeing stagger along the path complaining about the likelihood of encountering weasels and bats, Lorraine left.

Her exit was as intrusively noisy as her arrival. Jason opened the car door for her and watched as she squeezed, giggling, into his passenger seat – a deep-sided racing seat. Lorraine got in but her left leg, long, thin, mud-splattered, complete with red patent shoe, let her down. She somehow couldn't manage to wedge it in. Jason helped scoop her into place.

Megs leaned forward to say goodbye and caught a glimpse of the car's customised interior. It seemed to be completely velour. My God, she thought, a pimpmobile. Lorraine, chewing gum vigorously, caught her expression and grinned.

'Great spot,' Jason said shyly, indicating with a slight movement of his head the garden and glen beyond. 'Peaceful,' he said, walking round to the driver's seat. He got in, switched on the engine, a deep macho growl of tuned engine roaring through twin carbs, and leaned out the open window, obviously politely thanking them for the food, wine and peace. Neither Megs nor Gilbert could make out a word. The car's tape deck started with the ignition, a raging techno howl erupted. Jason turned up the volume. The louder the music the wilder Lorraine's gum-chewing. The car shuddered and slithered on fat wheels down the track, both Jason and Lorraine concealed behind blackened windows. But the noise they made lingered long after they were out of sight. Their rave and thump sounded round the glen.

'Do you think it will last?' Megs asked Gilbert when at last they could speak. Birds started to sing again.

'I have no idea,' Gilbert said. 'Does she really like all that stuff? That car? That music?'

'I don't expect so. You just won't get her to admit it.'

After Lizzy was sleeping, Megs and Gilbert stood outside in the garden. The night was at a standstill. She felt as if she was at the very edge of it, under huge static clouds, breathing in the drifting scent of woodsmoke.

'I feel as if I have been invaded,' he said, starting to walk towards the woods.

'You don't like my friends.' She walked with him.

'I have never actively sought the company of women who are all thigh and no brain, who talk about the doings in soap operas as if they're real life. I get confused.'

'Gilbert, how scathing. Actually, she'd be quite chuffed. She takes care of her thighs. Her brain makes its own way.'

'I feel she's criticising me.'

'She's not. She just cares about me.'

'Is that why she asked what I was like in bed?'

'Oh, don't mind about that.'

'But I do.'

'I didn't reply.'

'No. But you will.'

'Then I'll tell her you're a stud. Is that OK?'

He said nothing.

'Please don't fight. I have to go home in a few days. I don't want to argue with you now. Please. I don't want to hear what you think of Lorraine. She's my friend.' Megs leaned against a tree. Avoiding Gilbert's gaze, she looked up through the trees. The wood was like a cathedral tonight. A huge harvest moon was floating up towards mid-heaven. Long, long shafts of light filtered down through the dense weaving of boughs high above. They could smell musk. Deer had been here, minutes before. They would have raised their heads, ears twitching, when they heard Megs and Gilbert approach. 'Please,' said Megs. 'Please, I don't want to argue.'

It was by unspoken mutual consent that they made love. They seemed to fall into one another, sinking down on to the moss. Even the initial clumsy fumbling with underwear and zips seemed natural and joyous. Neither of them said sorry, or wait a minute, my arm's trapped. No buttons got stuck in their needy clamour to feel each other's skin. They moved against each other, trying to get closer and closer, to get to the core of one another. Megs clung to him, tasted him – she wanted to climb into his skin. She smelled the moss and ancient wood. She smelled him, his lime cologne and the carbonara he'd made for Lorraine. She did not say the word love. Whispered his name instead, 'Gilbert.' He lay on her, his lips on her ear, and said, 'Megs.' The sound of her name on his breath thrilled her. She realised how rarely he ever said it.

There was a moment afterwards when she was still beneath him, breathing in the darkness and damp of the ground they lay on. She had her fingers in his hair and her other arm spread. 'Oh God,' she said. 'Wonderful.' Then she remembered Lizzy alone in the house. She wrestled him from her, grabbed her clothes and stumbled away from him, still half naked. 'Lizzy. Lizzy,' she cried. 'What if she wakes and I'm not there? What if something happens?'

'No, wait,' Gilbert called, reaching for her. Shyly watching her white bum and thighs clumsily disappearing through the dense greenness. 'Wait. Lizzy will be all right. I want you. I think . . . I love . . .' but he didn't finish what he wanted to say. Besides, Megs was too far away to hear. Besides, he didn't really want to say it.

On the day that Megs left to go home, Gilbert got a letter from America.

Well, hello, Gilbert, Annette wrote. Her script was curved and polite. *How are you? And how's the book? Progressing in leaps and bounds, I'll bet.*

Gilbert glanced guiltily at his desk and at the drawings that now crowded his little living room.

My research is going well. I've been invited to stay for another few months, till the end of December, in fact. I will be back in the New Year. Looking forward enormously to seeing you then, and to reading the work in progress.

Fondly,

Annette

'Who's your letter from?' Megs said.

'Nobody,' said Gilbert, stuffing it into his back pocket. 'Just work. It's not important.'

Megs shrugged. She wished she didn't know he was lying.

Chapter Twenty-Nine

Megs returned, unwillingly, to her old routine. She hadn't much liked her life before her stay with Gilbert. Now that she'd had a glimpse of something better, it was harder to live than ever.

Gilbert wasn't home, and therefore did not need a cleaner. Terribly-Clean Pearson had parted from her husband, put her house on the market and was teaching full-time. She not only couldn't afford a cleaner, she didn't want one. She was enjoying being messy. It was, she told Megs on the phone, a phase she'd missed whilst growing up. She was making up for it now. 'I teach kids hygiene and neatness. I tell them how to have a balanced diet, then I come home, smoke a couple of fags, make a nice long gin and tonic, heat up something quick and hopefully nasty and eat in front of the telly. Freddy' – calling her son by the name she used to loathe – 'cleans up.'

Now that there was only Dysentery McGhee and Emotionally-Deranged Davis to clean for, Megs made up the difference in her earnings working nights, waitressing at private functions.

She'd come home, smelling, she suspected, of sweat and cooking fat. She'd slump on the sofa, too tired to take off her coat and kick her shoes on to the pile of assorted kicked-off shoes on the other side of the room – Jack's, Hannah's, Lizzy's and Lorraine's. 'Oh God,' she'd say, 'this has got to stop. What do you think, Lor? How do we sort out our lives? Failing that, how do we sort out that pile of shoes?'

The day after Megs got home from her stay with Gilbert, Jack and Hannah arrived back from Italy. Mike dropped them off on his way home. They were all delighted to see one another. How long, Megs wondered, would this delight last? Reunions were lovely, though.

Jack and Hannah crowded into the kitchen, looking tanned, slightly taller and older than when they'd left. Or maybe, Megs thought, they'd just got stuck in her memory as smaller, younger and paler than they actually were. 'How was it?' she asked, trying not to fuss round them. 'I want to hear all about it.'

'It was fine,' said Jack. 'Great.' He laid out the olive oil and wine he'd brought with him. 'Here's some Italian stuff.' Clutching a small parcel, he edged towards the door. 'I'll just go see if Sharon's in.' He disappeared.

Hannah brought Megs a red silk shirt.

'You shouldn't have,' said Megs, holding it up. 'This must have taken all your money.'

'Mike helped.' Hannah shrugged.

'How did you all get on?' Megs wanted to know.

'All right.' Small silence. 'In the end.'

'Did you and Denise hit it off?' Megs was hoping for a no.

'Yeah.' Hannah seemed surprised when she thought about it. 'She's OK, Denise.' She looked around. 'This is nice, isn't it?'

'What is?' Megs looked round, wondering what she meant. What precisely was nice?

'Here. Home. This kitchen. It's good.' She looked round at the morning cereal bowls propped on the draining board, the clothes half-hauled out of the tumble-drier, the overflowing bin. The sunlight caught in relief the crumbs scattered beside the bread bin. Music rattled from the radio. 'It's really nice. Isn't it?'

Megs didn't know what to say. In terms of describing her kitchen, nice had never occurred to her. She put the kettle on. 'I want to hear all about it? Tell me all the things you got up to.'

'There's lots to tell,' said Hannah. 'I just can't remember any of it now. I'll tell you bits when I think of them. Actually, Sarah's expecting me. I phoned her last night.'

'Well go,' said Megs. 'We'll have a proper chat later tonight.'

'I've got a date tonight.'

'Well, tomorrow.'

'Fine. Um . . . can I borrow that shirt?'

'Which shirt?'

'The one I bought you. Only I've got nothing to wear. Everything's dirty.'

'Go on then.' Megs handed the red shirt over.

Hannah smiled. On her way out, looking gorgeous, she asked if Megs could possibly wash some clothes. 'Everything's dirty,' she explained again.

When Vivienne arrived to see her grandchildren, they were long gone. 'Where are they?'

'Gone out,' said Megs. 'Come and gone.' She pointed to the teapot. 'There's tea if you want it.'

Vivienne poured herself a cup. 'So did they enjoy themselves?'

'Seemed to,' Megs said.

'And what about you? What about your stay with Gilbert? What did you get up to?'

Megs looked into the cup. She raked through her memories of the past weeks, trying to find something she could actually tell her mother about. It wasn't as if she'd done anything particularly naughty, but when she leafed through her days with Gilbert, all she could remember was being in bed with him, or having conversations with him that she could not pass on to Vivienne. She wondered if this was how, just half an hour ago, Hannah had felt when she'd been asked the same question. 'Do you know,' she said suddenly, 'it's lovely to see them both again. I missed them. I didn't realise how much till I saw them. Fleetingly, I admit. But there you go, I missed them. And I missed you.' She saw the surprise in Vivienne's face. 'No, really. I missed you. And I missed them. And I missed Lorraine. I missed everybody. It's good to be back.'

The family settled back into their routine. Hannah complained about the coffee. 'Denise has bought an actual espresso machine,' she told Megs. 'She brought it back with her. It's got a long handle that you pull.'

'That's what you'd do with a handle,' Megs said. 'Perhaps we should all go round for a cup. Denise would love that. Hannah, I can't afford an espresso machine. When you're out in the world making a fortune, buy me one.'

'OK,' Hannah said brightly. 'I will.'

'That girl is becoming likeable,' Megs told Lorraine. 'Do you suppose she's got some terrible secret she's working up to telling me? Or is this a lull? She'll get back to being her normal unsufferable self soon.'

'She's always been likeable,' said Lorraine. 'You just had to spend time away from her before you noticed.'

The bustling return of Megs and family bothered Lorraine. She had enjoyed having Megs's house to herself. She and Jason had stretched on the sofa watching films on telly. Then, when that wasn't quite comfortable enough, they'd moved the television into Megs's bedroom to watch it whilst lying, semi-clothed, on Megs's bed. Lorraine was missing that bed. 'I'm taking badly to sleeping on the sofa,' she said. 'There's no privacy. Your children wander to and from the kitchen all hours. Then I wake with Lizzy sleeping at the other end of the sofa. At my feet. I need a bed to myself,' she decided.

'Hold that thought,' Megs said. 'And expand it. You need a bed to yourself. What about a lavatory to yourself. A kitchen to yourself. A living room to yourself. In fact, what about a whole flat to yourself?'

'I know. I know.' Unable to meet Megs's eye, Lorraine made an elaborate play of stubbing out her cigarette. 'Shut up,' she said.

'Shut up what? I never said anything.'

'Speaking is just a technicality. I can see what you're thinking. You're thinking that I'm in the way. My stuff is taking over the place. My clothes are pushing yours out of your wardrobe. I'm always in the bath. Or hogging the bathroom one way or another. My moisturisers and toners and make-up have taken over the bathroom shelf. I never fold the towels. The backlog of laundry for five people is horrendous. Nobody can get into the living room to watch telly, 'cos I'm always there. When I bring food in, I always buy the wrong things. And I'm always making coffee. I use it all up, and I never bring back the cups. You are always going on cup hunts, finding my little cache of them beside the sofa . . .'

Lizzy came in. 'Can I have a biscuit?'

'Ask Lorraine,' Megs told her. 'She knows what I'm thinking.'

Lizzy looked at Lorraine. 'Can I have a biscuit?'

'It's nearly time for lunch.' Lorraine would normally have given the child what she wanted, but thought it time to be sensible. 'You don't want to spoil your appetite.'

'That was what I was thinking,' Megs congratulated her. 'As for the rest. Yes, you are the messiest person in the world. But I don't mind.' Then, 'Well, I do mind. But since it's you, be messy. Stay. But please bring your cups back to the kitchen. Oh, and fold a towel. Just one. Just once. So I don't have to.'

Lizzy returned. 'Shameless wants a biscuit,' she told Lorraine. Megs watched.

'Does he?' Lorraine made an elaborate show of fetching the pack of dog biscuits.

'No,' said Lizzy. 'He doesn't want one of them. He's gone off them. He wants a chocolate biscuit. He told me.'

'Did he?' Lorraine smiled. 'What did he say?'

'He said, "Fetch us a biscuit, Lizzy. Be a pal." He said he wanted an animal-shaped one. So's he could lick off the chocolate, then eat the biscuit.'

Lorraine brought the animal-shaped biscuits from the cupboard. Handed Lizzy a lion one.

'No,' Lizzy protested. 'He wants a elephant. Elephants are best.' Then, realising she must have overplayed her ruse, 'Shameless thinks so, anyway.'

'Righto.' Lorraine couldn't resist the girl. 'An elephant for Shameless. Shall I give it to him?'

'No.' Lizzy kept her cool. 'He wants me to do it.' She took the elephant and left. After a small while, from behind the door, 'Shameless wants another one.'

In unison Megs and Lorraine shouted, 'No.'

Lizzy said, 'Oh, bugger.'

'What did you say?' Megs called.

'Shameless said it, Shameless said it.' Lizzy was repentant. 'Shameless, you're a bad boy saying bad words.'

'Lorraine, my daughter is picking up your language,' Megs accused.

'I know. Sorry.' Lorraine put the animal biscuits beside the dog biscuits on the kitchen unit, boiled the kettle, took the last mug, made coffee and disappeared to sit with Lizzy and Shameless.

'Well, thanks for this,' Megs said. She put both packs of biscuits away. Then emptied Lorraine's ashtray. There were no cups left. Sighing, she went through to the living room to find one. 'And you leave overflowing ashtrays everywhere,' she said to Lorraine as she gathered half a dozen assorted cups and mugs from down the side of the sofa.

'Sorry,' said Lorraine.

'You're not really,' Megs said.

'I know,' Lorraine agreed. 'Sorry about that.'

In the middle of all the cleaning and domestic clutter and small family squabbles, Megs got offered a lifeline. Late one Friday night Josh turned up at her door.

'Hi, Megs,' shuffling a little. He was here to ask a favour. Megs knew that shuffle well.

'Josh.' She smiled. 'Come in.'

They went into the kitchen. 'I'll make you some coffee,' she told him. 'You could do with some the way you're shaking.'

'Oh, it's not the drink,' Josh said. 'I'm off the drink. I want a favour. I want a huge favour. And I hate asking for things.'

'What do you want?' She leaned against the sink, waiting for the kettle to boil. In the living room the sounds of Friday-night television nonsense went quiet. Lorraine and Hannah were listening in.

Josh's hands were deep in the pockets of his reefer jacket. A new jacket, Megs noted. He is sorting himself out.

'Will you come sing with me?' Josh asked. He did not look at her. 'There's a new place started up, a blues club, and I play there. I do at least one night a week. But if you came, I'd get two nights. I've asked the guys from the old band. They're thinking about it. They will if you will.'

'What is this place?'

'Yazoo City. It's after a place in the South where Robert Johnson played. He played a place called Inverness, too. Did y'know that? 'Course, not our Inverness.'

'No,' said Megs. 'Fancy.' She made coffee. Handed Josh a cup.

'Cheers.' He nodded thanks at the cup, couldn't look at Megs.

'I think I'd love that, Josh. I think that would just about save my life right now.'

So on Thursday nights Megs sang the blues again. She got out her black jeans and her white silk shirt and stood before a small crowd who drank Miller's and Rolling Rock and looked at her with the longing of people who wished they could do what she could do. She sang Etta James, 'Mad About the Boy', and she sang Robert Johnson, 'Rambling On My Mind'. She sang Bessie Smith, 'Kitchen Man' and 'I'm Wild About That Thing'. 'Ya-da, ya-da,' she almost shouted it. Smiling. Flashing those perfect ceramic caps. She sang 'Gimme a Pigfoot' and 'A Good Man Is Hard to Find'.

'Ain't that the truth,' Lorraine called, holding up a bottle of Bud. 'You tell 'em.'

Whenever she could, Megs spent time with Gilbert. It seemed that without missing a beat, they resumed their little world together. He would hear her car clanking down the path and come out to greet her, waving and smiling. He did not even make that small movement of his head as he looked round, checking he was not being observed being childishly excited. She would come into his living room, the smells of the night, cold and the city, clinging to her coat. The older the year got, the more the journey north pleased her. It coloured yellows and ochre. The trees got stark. Farmers burnt the corn stubble. Flames and spiralling smoke under a mellow moon.

They moved closer to each other. Keeping out the cold, she thought. They made a small ritual of building log fires, constructing them carefully, discussing which log to put on next, and where to lie it on the embers for best effect. They spoke about anything to ward off any actual discussions about themselves and their future together. The bedroom window would not shut properly, they'd wake to find a crusting of frost on the eiderdown. In this cold, the icy air burned down their throats and it hurt to breathe. In the chill and the dark, three in the morning, she heard mice scratching at the walls and deer moving about the garden. Megs and Lizzy spent their mornings in bed, keeping warm, hardly daring to creep out into the chill, whilst Gilbert moved about downstairs, making breakfast and lighting the fire in the living room.

Sometimes she ached to wake him, asking what they were going to do. What was to become of them? Yet she felt if she asked this, he'd feel pressured to answer. She didn't think she wanted to hear what he had to say. If only he was a better liar. Then again, were he to ask her about their future together, what would she say to him? She suspected he would not like to hear her reply to that question either. She was beginning to realise she didn't want commitment. Being loved a little, pampered a lot was more than enough.

She wore Gilbert's navy fisherman's sweater, as none of her clothes were made to combat the kind of cold she met here. 'It'll get worse,' the butcher's boy told her when she went into the village for bacon and free-range eggs. 'Febrerry's the worst. Ten feet of snow. You'll see real weather then, Megs.'

Gilbert resented these conversations. He was jealous of Megs's success in the village and at the hotel at the top of the Glen. Everyone called her Megs, or Megsy. He was still that professory guy in the cottage. He envied how Megs could burst into a room, oozing friendliness. Like a puppy, she'd come to people whilst he stood back, shifting slightly from foot to foot, trying to make his smile seem spontaneous. Smiling, he felt, didn't work for him.

'Hi, Megs,' the barman at the Manilow and Coal Scuttle would call. 'Back again? Can't keep away, can you? Vodka and tonic, is it?'

'That's me,' she'd say, collecting empty glasses from a table and bringing them to the bar. 'Look, am I not good to you, saving you a trip?'

Gilbert couldn't do that. He'd take glasses over, saying, 'Um . . . glasses.' The barman would look at him as if he was insane. But Megs's friendships seemed seamless. Gilbert could not remember when everyone started calling her by name, though nobody seemed to know, or care, what he was called.

'What are you doing for Christmas?' he asked Megs. They were sitting on the floor by his fire. He knew she'd be too embroiled with her family to come see him.

'The usual. Spending money I have not got. Standing in shops looking at Argyle pattern socks whilst listening to some musak version of "Jeśu, Joy of Man's Desiring". Then come the day getting woken in the pre-dawn gloom by one overexcited child, whilst two underexcited teenage children pretend not to be bothered. Then my folks will come round and we'll eat too much, drink too much, steam the windows getting hot and fall asleep in front of the telly. What are you doing?'

'Oh, I'll be here. I'll probably cook a steak or maybe some pheasant. Drink some claret and listen to some Schubert.'

'Don't stay on your own. Come to us.'

He didn't need to consider this. 'I can't,' he said. 'Not really. I like being on my own.' He couldn't go to her house. Lorraine would be there and she terrified him. 'Will you come for New Year, then?' he asked.

'I don't know if I can. My mother usually has a party, and anyone who doesn't go doesn't get spoken to till next New Year. It's a traumatic time. I'll come for the weekend in between Christmas and New Year. I'll leave Lizzy with Lorraine. It'll be just us and Shameless. I can't leave him, people forget to take him out. But us, we'll drink too much and do naughty things to each other.'

Chapter Thirty

December the 28th she arrived, teeth chittering. The heater in her car wasn't working. The cold stiffened her bones, gnawed her fingers and toes. She could not wait to get warm, stood in the kitchen complaining shrilly, stamping her feet and rubbing her arms. 'Oh God. Freezing. Freezing.'

He fussed round her, lacing her coffee with brandy, edging her towards the fire. 'It might snow.'

'Too cold for snow,' she told him. 'That's the verdict in the butcher's shop.'

He felt a stupid stab of anger that she should have stopped and spoken to other people on the way to him. He fancied her sitting in her car, pale face behind the windscreen, clutching the wheel, rushing through the cold and dark to get to him.

She laid his Christmas gift on the kitchen table. It was carefully wrapped (by Lorraine – wrapping gifts was not one of Megs's skills) in dark-blue paper with a multi-looped red bow. He eyed it.

'Oh no. After we eat. We'll sit by the fire and exchange gifts properly. I want the full love-nest treat. I've seen it in the movies. We drink wine from huge glasses, lie in front of a roasting fire, wearing comfy jerseys and exchange gifts. I want that. My Christmases have always been a rammy – noisy children, noisy toys, noisy relatives, noisy shows on the telly. I want a bit of class.'

She had bought him a checked cashmere scarf, chosen from Lorraine's catalogue. It cost her £45 – thirty-six weeks at £1.50 a week – that she couldn't afford. She was aware that £1.50 for thirty-six weeks worked out at £54. But that was how it was. Not having enough money cost more money.

He'd bought her a huge black rollneck sweater, a battered copy of Paul Oliver's *Blues Fell This Morning* that he'd found in a second-hand bookshop months ago, and a box set of *La Traviata*. 'I know. I know – opera. Not your scene. But give it a go. You'll love it.'

They lay on the floor, staring into 'he fire, drinking. The night outside was jagged and chill. The freeze crept in under the door, round the window frame, till Megs and Gilbert found they were sitting, joints stiffened and locked against the cold. Megs rubbed her nose. 'We'd be warmer in bed.' They ran upstairs, ripping off their clothes, shivering and eager to get under the covers. They clung to one another, complaining and giggling about each other's frozen feet and bum.

Megs pulled the eiderdown over her head, drummed her heels and cried out, 'Oh God, cold . . . cold . . . cold.' She took Gilbert's hand. 'Dance with me.'

'I don't dance.'

'Come on. We're under the eiderdown. There's nobody for miles. Dance with me. I won't tell a soul.'

But Gilbert wouldn't. He couldn't, even then, let go. Megs didn't care. The wine, the food – she was all sorts of drunk. She did an on-the-mattress strut. Waving her hands. Shameless joined in, jumping on the bed, nuzzling her. Gilbert felt his face go out of control – he was smiling wildly.

Her hangover woke Megs. 'Oh God, champagne. Never again.' Her head was in a throbbing cloud. She longed for someone to bring her a bucket filled with iced orange juice. She felt foul and she fretted about Lizzy. It was the first time they'd been apart.

Six in the morning, she wandered the cottage wearing only Gilbert's old jersey. She pressed her face on the window and stared out into the garden that had taken up so much of her time in hotter days. Her breath steamed the glass, and every so often she had to slip the sleeve of the jersey over her hand and rub it clean again. She remembered Lizzy out there on that lawn, struggling with the watering can, bossing the pansies. 'You're not getting any more. You'll get a sore tummy.' She wondered if Lorraine would be really mad, or only irritated, if she phoned to ask how they were. She dialled the number.

'Hello. Um . . .' She heard Lorraine's sleep-soaked voice. 'Time is it? Who's this phoning?'

'It's me,' Megs said.

'What are you doing? It's the middle of the night.'

'It's six in the morning.'

'That's what I said. The middle of the night. Why are you phoning? Is everything OK? Are you all right?'

'Yes. 'Course. I was just up. And thinking about Lizzy. How is she?'

'Sleeping. In your bed with me. She's fine. She had a great day. We went to the zoo.'

'The zoo?'

'Yes. It's great in winter. There's nobody about. We had a good time. We took a flask of soup.'

'Soup.' Megs repeated it slowly, peevishly. She felt jealous. She wished she'd taken Lizzy to the zoo. 'What else have you been doing?'

'Oh. I sat about with Hannah, talking about things. Stuff. You know. You, mostly. We spoke about you.'

'Me?' Megs didn't like this. She wanted to be home having a heart-to-heart with Hannah. 'What did you say about me?'

'Oh, just what a tough time you've had. How you've managed. How you deserve this time to yourself, to be with Gilbert. Hannah's decided she'll be nice to him in future.'

'Oh.' Megs still did not like the thought of her best friend and daughter discussing her.

'Then,' Lorraine went on, 'Hannah went out. She borrowed my red top.'

'Not your red top. That's a bit low-cut, isn't it? There's hardly anything of it. She's still young, you know.'

'She looked great,' Lorraine soothed her. 'Then Jack came home early to watch football. But he got cross with me because I kept saying things about the players' thighs and bums. So he went off to bed.'

'What are you meant to watch in football if not the blokes' bums?' Megs asked.

'Dunno.'

'I mean,' said Megs, 'if it was women running about the field in shorts, would men be watching the match?'

"Zactly.' Lorraine lit a cigarette. Megs could hear the snap of her lighter. She imagined her in the kitchen, leaning on the fridge, flicking her ash into the bin. Missing.

'Wipe up your flicked ash, will you.'

'What ash?'

'The ash you'll flick into the bin and miss.'

'If you emptied your bin occasionally, I wouldn't miss.'

'Where was Jason through all this going to the zoo and having heart-to-heart chats?'

'We've split up.'

'Oh, Lorraine, I'm sorry. What happened? Was his life too fast and loud for you? He wanted to go clubbing, and you wanted to stay home and behave like the sedate lady you secretly are.'

'No,' said Lorraine. 'No, wrong. He wanted to stay in. He wanted to watch telly and settle down sort of thing. But I've done that. I wasn't very good at it. I wanted something else. I want to go out clubbing and have a good time. So we split up.'

'Sorry about that. How are you? Are you upset?'

'Nah. Well, a bit. But not really. We hadn't a lot to say to each other.'

'I didn't think speaking was part of your relationship.'

'It wasn't at first. But when we at last got round to it, we realised we had nothing to say to each other. His mother hated me. Said I was mutton dressed as lamb.'

'Cheek. What does she look like? Mutton dressed as mutton?'

'Ha, ha. I'll remember that if I see her again.'

Megs got up from the rush-seated chair she was on. She scratched her bum, which was deeply marked, rush-seated. 'Oooh, my bum's gone all funny. It's imprinted with the chair. It's freezing here. I'm starting to shiver. I better go back to bed. See you soon.'

'OK,' said Lorraine. 'Phone you tomorrow, eh? Or today more like. It is today.'

'Yeah, it's today now. Phone you today.' Megs put down the receiver. She longed to be home having serious chats to Hannah, watching football with Jack, and taking Lizzy to the zoo with a flask of soup. 'Dammit,' she said out loud. 'They're having a fine time without me.'

The cold drove her back to bed. She ran up the stairs, Shameless running ahead of her. They both bounced on to the bed, waking Gilbert. 'Cuddle me,' she said. 'I miss Lizzy.'

He turned to her, took her to him.

'I can tell,' she said, 'this is developing into more than a cuddle.'

They spent most of that day in bed. Megs got up to take Shameless round the garden and came rushing in, bent and bundled, complaining about the weather. A slow wind started and shifted round the cottage.

'I think the temperature's gone up,' Megs said, stamping in through the door. 'I think I can smell snow coming.' She breathed in. Outside in the garden she'd sipped some air, tested it on her tongue. Dampness made it heavy. Snow, she thought. The air tasted dirty with approaching snow.

'You could be right.'

'Good time for you to get cooking, then. What're we getting?'

'Steaks and salad and Australian red.' They were city-born and bred, both of them. The dire implications of snow didn't occur to them.

They ate by the fire. And, lulled by too much wine, they went to bed to sleep some more, and sweat some more in each other's arms.

The light woke Megs. The light and the silence. A new grey translucence filled the room, a damp film of white coated the windowsill. Megs rose and looked out. The garden had been sculpted – the shrubs and trees were reshaped with snow. It was white out there, endlessly, endlessly white. 'Snow,' said Megs. 'Hey, Gilbert, it's snowed.'

Gilbert moved, lumpen, into a new sleeping position, yanked the eiderdown over his head, and said, 'Uh. Good.'

'No, Gilbert.' Megs came over to the bed and shook him. 'It has seriously snowed.'

He rose, pulled the duvet from the bed and wrapped them both in it before moving to the window. 'Christ. So it has.'

Outside the sky had cleared, turned indigo. Small, strident stars gleamed.

'Christ,' Gilbert breathed. 'It's beautiful. I've never seen it so beautiful.'

They stood side by side, gazing out. He thought they were like a couple of wide-eyed babes in a fairy story.

'Do you think I'll get home?' Megs asked.

'No problem.' Gilbert was sure of this. 'Snow never lasts.'

Later in the morning they walked, snow squeaking beneath their feet, to the end of the track. Shameless plunged ahead. Every few yards he would stop and roll joyously. There was something thrilling about all this sudden white. Megs stooped against the cold, hands deep in her pockets. The morning was icy against her cheeks. 'Isn't this beautiful?' she said, sticking her tongue out into the air. 'I have never tasted anything so pure, so clean.' She took some snow from the top of the dyke and put it to her lips. 'When you were little, Gilbert, did you eat snow?'

'No.'

'It still tastes the same as it did when I was little, which is more than you can say for American cream soda or Heinz Sandwich Spread or . . .'

'What does it taste of?' Gilbert lifted a handful and carefully licked it.

'Of being white and cold. It tastes snowy.'

'Yes.' He gave a gourmet's verdict. 'Snowy.' He turned, considering the world in wonder. 'Isn't it marvellous? It changes everything. You see everything anew. Reshaped as the snow hit it. Look, small layers along the wire fence, and the branches. It's amazing.'

Megs scooped up a fistful of snow that she moulded in numbing hands into a ball to hurl at Gilbert. She missed. It fell, disappeared into a drift. Shameless bounded after it, then stood looking vacantly round. Where had it gone? Megs made another and threw it for him. Then Gilbert. They had a small flurry of a fight, throwing armfuls of snow at each other. Iced and damp, they reached the road, stood in the chill and the silence, looked up, then down. There was not a tyre track to be seen.

'It's Sunday,' Gilbert said. 'Nobody goes out on Sundays. Well, not this time of year. It's too good on telly. You'll get home tomorrow, no trouble.' His breath spanned out in verbal bursts, his face glowed. He stuck his hands in his pockets. The cold was a deeper chill than he'd ever known. 'Oh yes,' he said. 'No trouble.' His voice trailed into disbelief.

Megs watched him. The glorious sparkle, the glittering morning had turned bitter. She shivered, not a lowering-of-temperature ripple, but a whole shaking of her body. Her teeth clattered. Her nose was running, she sniffed. Her clothes were acrylic. There was not a lot between her and the weather. 'I think I'd prefer to observe this gorgeousness from inside.'

They passed the day by the fire. Every now and then one of them would wander to the window to stare out. They watched the new world turn into evening. That glimmer gleamed against the evening, and took on the night. It didn't quite get dark.

It thawed in the morning. Ice on the guttering turned watery, dripped, leaving huge pockmarks in the snow below. On the lawn they could see where deer had wandered, looking for food, and a small scuttly track – little feet and a traily tail – a mouse out and about.

'I have to go,' Megs said over breakfast. 'I should leave before it ices over.'

'Stay.' He wanted to beg, but didn't dare.

'I want to. You know that. But it's New Year's Eve. I have to be home. I must bring in the New Year with my family. My mother will never speak to me again if I'm not there. It's traditional, we go to her house. Come with me, why don't you?'

'No.' He shook his head, emphasising his refusal. He felt awkward with her family.

She shrugged. 'Well, don't think you're not welcome.'

Driving, slithering slowly, down the glen, she could see mountainous clouds, heavy-bellied with snow, moving in, but ignored them. Calamities for her were bank statements, broken appliances, bruised children, an empty fridge. Weather never occurred to her.

The usual twenty-minute journey from Gilbert's cottage to the village took her over an hour. It was after midday when she got there, and snowing. She stopped at the butcher's shop to buy some steaks for New Year's Day dinner.

'You'd better get on home.' Billy, the butcher's boy, appeared from the back shop. 'Else you'll be stuck.'

'I was going back to town.'

'Not today you're not. Road's closed.'

'But . . .' protested Megs, as if this man behind the counter was in some way responsible. As if a nod from him would make the ten-foot drifts passable.

'If you don't hurry, you'll not even get back up the glen.'

'But . . .' Megs said again. 'It's New Year. I go to my mother's. I always go.'

He leaned on the counter. 'This year you'll just have to go to the party in the glen hall.'

She wanted to say that she didn't want to go to the party in the glen hall. She wanted home. She wanted to see Lizzy. She wanted to stamp her foot and cry. 'I better head back.' She sighed. 'I actually came in to buy some steaks to take home. I'll take something up to Gilbert. Is that a goose?' Megs pointed at a huge bird, plucked and glistening beneath the glass counter.

'It is that,' said Billy. 'This goose, this goose,' slapping it bitterly, 'this goose was ordered by Lady Morven herself. Wanted it for Hogmanay. I took it out this morning on my bike.'

'Bike?' Megs turned towards the weather. Snow, fat, freezing, penny-size flakes, freewheeled and blew past the window. She could not see across to the other side of the road. Gears crunching, cars crawled past, moving into the grey, lights on. 'Bike?' she said again.

'Aye. Ten mile. Five here an' five back again. Ten mile an' she said she'd changed her mind. Didn't want the bloody goose.' He pointed furiously at the beast as if it was all its fault. Well, it couldn't possibly be Lady Morven's, could it? She was a lady. She lived in the big house at the foot of the glen.

This morning, at seven, before the shop opened, he had put on his enormous brown slab-shouldered, double-breasted herringbone tweed coat. Wrapped his checked scarf round and round his neck, shoved the goose into the huge basket on the front of his delivery bike and set off. Saddle creaking, pedalling slowly. Contemplating the chill. He moved painfully into a bitter wind that left him gasping and turned his throat raw. His breath heaved and steamed before him, misting his glasses as he went. Grunting with effort. 'Too old for this. Too bleddy old for this.'

He was three miles out of the village, on the road cleared by the plough, when the snow started. Small, scudding flakes at first. He did not stop. 'Be there before it really comes down,' he promised himself. Wading ancient cycle through the morning. He did not look at the sky that bulged above him. It was pouring down when he reached Morven Hall. He banged the huge knocker. Moving it slowly against the door, staring at his feet. The Lady herself answered the door.

'Brought the goose,' said Billy.

'Goose?' Lady Morven withered. 'Goose? I didn't say anything about a goose.'

'Ordered one, three weeks ago. Wanted it for Hogmanay,' he pleadingly reminded her.

'No I didn't.'

'Did,' said Billy. 'Answered the phone myself. Said I'd bring it out. And here it is.'

'Well, I don't want it now. Take it away.' Lady Morven slammed the door.

Sadly, and without complaint, Billy turned. Trudged down the steps back to his bike, put the goose back in the basket and slowly, slowly pedalled back. By now the sky was emptying. It took him two hours of monotonous, deliberate pedalling to get back. The bike swished slowly over whitened roads. From the little battery a wan, wavering yellow light glimmered into the sheeting grey-blue weather. When he got back he was white. White like an iced man. There were tiny drops of ice clinging to his eyebrows. Snow formed layers on his trousers and filled the turn-ups. Snow lined the creases in his scarf, and caked his coat, melted and ran down the back of his neck. He moved one stiff, frozen leg at a time, like a robot into the shop, the goose straddling his spread arms that he held as if they were still gripping a pair of handlebars. Everyone stopped. Ignoring them, he continued his chilled shuffle through to the back and laid the goose on the table. 'Didn't want it,' he said. Then, 'Still, she answered the door herself. Her very self. Must've fallen on hard times.' He didn't actually know what the gentry did. But they certainly did not answer their own doors. 'I have had enough.'

'Enough of what?' Kynoch, his boss, asked.

'Enough of everything. Delivering geese. Being me.' Looking glumly down at his frozen coat, holding his hands, stiff fingers iced into the clench with which he grasped his bike, over the buttons. 'Undo me, someone,' he said slowly. For speaking was tricky. 'I'm froze.'

'I'll buy the goose,' Megs offered. 'If nobody else wants it.'

Kynoch wrapped it, smiling pleasantly. He thought he was going to be stuck with the thing. Hated goose.

'Um,' said Megs. 'Do you know how I cook it?'

Billy stepped forward. 'Rub it with salt.'

'Billy'll keep you right,' Kynoch said, nodding. 'He's right fond of cooking.'

'Prick it all over with a fork. Let the fat out. Then stand it on some sort of grill and put grill and goose into a baking tray. Keep it out of the fat. Don't want the bugger swimming in fat as it cooks,' Billy said, patting the beast softly as he spoke. Must've bonded on the long bike ride, thought Megs.

So with goose on passenger seat, safe from Shameless, she drove back. Gripping the steering wheel and hunched over till her face was close to the windscreen, she inched her way up the glen. Every now and then she'd rub a small viewing hole on the steamy windscreen with the back of her glove. Then she'd drag the same damp glove across her eyes, wiping her tears.

'I hate this,' she told the goose. 'I hate it.' She could not see the way ahead. The unending whiteness covered road and verge, filled ditches. The car whined forward in third gear. If she moved up into fourth, she felt it slip out of control, skate on frozen snow. 'It's all right for you, goose. You're already dead.'

The journey back took even longer than the journey down. Three hours after setting out, she opened the door and found Gilbert sitting at his kitchen table, head in hands.

'I'm back,' she said. 'And I've brought a goose.'

Chapter Thirty-One

Gilbert jumped when she burst in. He'd been agonising, confronting himself with some difficult truths and trying to come to a decision. There were three things in life that Gilbert wasn't good at – dancing, emotions and decisions.

In the time Megs had been slithering on ice-packed roads, Annette had phoned.

'I'll be back on the fifth of January,' she said. 'Can't wait. How are you, anyway?'

'Oh, fine.'

'And how's the book?'

'Um.'

'Oh, for heaven's sake, Gilbert, don't tell me you've been tucked away at your cottage all these months and haven't finished it.'

'Well.'

'What have you been doing?'

'Actually, I've started to paint again.'

'Really? That's wonderful. That is such good news, Gilbert.'

'Yes,' weakly said.

'I can hardly wait to see what you've done. Oh, I'm so glad.'

'Yes. I find it very soothing, calming just manipulating, juxtaposing light and shape. It's done me a lot of good. I've come to terms with myself.'

He had spent hours and hours drawing, then painting Megs. What he saw as the simple business of laying down the lines where he wanted them to go evaded him. He only knew the line was wrong when it was in place, so he'd redraw it. Still it wasn't right. Again and again he tried. He could never get his drawings on paper to match the vision in his head. His frustration became an ache. He drank. He threw his pencil, then his brush across the room. He ran both hands at once through his hair. In other words, as he tried to explain it to Annette, his paintings weren't as good as he thought they'd be. He was not the artist he'd always thought he was. His secret conceit had floundered.

A long pause. 'Well, that's reassuring. A term of self-discovery, eh?' Annette sighed down the line.

He could imagine that little wry smile of hers. It annoyed him that there never was any fooling her. 'I enjoy,' he said, trying to convince her, and enjoying also the first chance to expound pretentiously in months, 'the tiny nuances involved in artistic honesty. Searching for some kind of technical perfection is humbling. I feel I am finding a new humility. The actual act of laying on paint . . .'

'Gilbert,' she interrupted him, 'I have to go. I have a meeting. Will you pick me up at the airport? I get in at four o'clock on the afternoon of the fifth.'

'Yes,' he said, meekly.

After she'd rung off, Gilbert sat at the kitchen table, head in hands. He didn't know what to do. He did not want to lose Annette. The companionable life they'd built over the years suited him. Yet there was Megs. She intrigued and excited him. Then again, he felt that if his friends and colleagues knew he was having an affair with his cleaner, they'd laugh at him.

He imagined them all in the pub, drinking and discussing him. 'Oh no,' he cried, burying his face in his folded arms. There was also the business of his sketches and paintings. People would want to see them. Not only would they see who he'd been sketching and painting, they would see that he was not the undiscovered talent he'd quietly given the impression he was. Burn them, he thought. Yes. People would just think he was a poor tortured soul. Which, when he thought about it, he was.

Then Megs burst in, frozen stiff and carrying a goose. She could hardly move for Shameless leaping, eager to investigate the beast in her arms. 'I can't get home,' she wailed. 'The road's closed. I want to go home.' She dumped the goose on the table. 'I want to see Lizzy. I want to be there at midnight.'

His heart went out to her. He went to hold her. 'Phone home. Tell them what's happened. They'll be worried.'

'I wanted to be there. I'm always there for New Year.'

'Well, this year you'll be with me.'

She just stopped herself saying that she didn't want to be with him. She wanted her family.

'We'll go to the dance at the village hall.' He tried to enthuse. He was saying this for her. He knew he'd hate it. 'We'll boogie.' And he danced. He hadn't done such a thing since he was ten. He'd turned up at a birthday party wearing shiny shoes, pants with immaculate creases, white shirt and velvet bow tie. Everyone else was John Lennon. That afternoon he'd done the twist. So that was what he did now, a slow, clumsy hip-swivel. The dance of a man who did not dance. His body moved, but his clothes stayed still. Megs watched him in dismay.

She phoned home, but Vivienne was out panic-buying bread because the shops would be shut for the next two days. Lorraine thought it wildly romantic that Megs was snowed in with Gilbert. 'Just like *Doctor Zhivago*,' she swooned. 'That snowy bit with Omar Sharif and Julie Christie. You lucky bugger.' Lizzy, however, when she eventually got to the phone, was not as impressed as Lorraine and wanted to speak to Shameless. She missed him. Megs dutifully held the receiver to Shameless's ear whilst Lizzy spoke to him. Then she told Lizzy that Shameless was missing her too, and had said she should be good.

At ten-thirty they left Shameless locked in the cottage and set out for the glen hall. It had stopped snowing.

'It's Good King Wenceslas snow,' said Megs, stamping tracks in the pristine white. 'Deep and crisp and even.'

The cars that had gone ahead of them had rutted the road. Gilbert slid into a track and grimly crawled forward. Rubbled snow, churned by earlier travellers, gleamed in the headlights. Gilbert gripped the wheel, trying not to complain or let his fear of ice show. He didn't think terror manly.

They heard the party long before they got to it. The hooch and skirl of abandon echoed across the frozen evening. It cheered Megs up and added to Gilbert's terror.

The hall inside was wood-lined, overly lit. Ancient chairs with concave seats long carved into the shape of the thousands of bums that had descended on them lined the walls. On the stage at the far end the Purple Haze Trio – a Hammond organ, drums and a guitar – played something Jimmy Shand-ish. Everyone danced. The Purple Haze Trio were wearing their yellow-sequinned jackets, that's how folks knew who they were tonight. Wednesday nights, when they played the Manilow and Coal Scuttle, they wore tartan jackets. Then they were the Tartan Trio.

The guitar player stepped forward to the mike. 'Gonney change the mood now with something a wee bit more up-to-date.' They plodded into something that sounded deliberate and familiar to Megs, though she couldn't place it. She stood, head to one side, gazing quizzically ahead. 'My God, Gilbert, they're playing "Dark Star". Oh, I love it. All the way up here, Jerry Garcia in the middle of nowhere. Don't you love it?' She dipped her knees, did a little jiggle. Something familiar, she felt better already. Though she noted she was the only one moving. Older people did not want anything a wee bit more up-to-date. Younger people had a younger idea of up-to-date.

'No, I do not love it,' said Gilbert. He'd never heard of Jerry Garcia. He hated this already. He'd only suggested coming to make Megs happy and now he was regretting it. He spotted a lone chair by the door and resolved to spend the evening there. He fetched them both a drink, then settled into his hideaway spot. Megs left him to be sour and unsociable and joined the fray.

She danced with a man who beamed hello to her. It was New Year, everyone had come to party, locals and incomers. Megs slowly recognised the man she was dancing with. She'd seen him often driving his tractor on the cottage track. Then he would nod brusquely before ignoring her. He crossed the dance floor with that same furrow-straddling stride he used to cross fields. It took her a moment or two to recognise him without his bonnet. His face below the bonnet-line was ruddy, weathered. Above the bonnet-line, it was pasty white, sweat-beaded. Every now and then he would nervously slap it. It was obviously part of his body that he felt he'd rather keep to himself.

From his shy little corner, Gilbert watched and surreptitiously consulted his watch. Half past eleven, how long before they could politely leave? If another person came up to him and beamed, 'Smile, it might never happen,' he thought he might go insane. The friendliness was overwhelming. Strangers, stooped with concern, would lean into Megs, face inches from her face. 'Is yer glass empty? Sees it here. I'll get ye another.' Her glass would be whisked from her hand, and brought back refilled with whisky, advocaat, vodka or rum and coke – whatever the solicitous one thought she ought to be drinking. Megs knew she was getting absurdly drunk, but was sucked in. This party was infectious. The band played jigs and reels, old Beatles medleys, George Gershwin and anything that was requested. Megs, breathless from dancing, sank on to Gilbert's knee. 'This band has the repertoire from hell,' she said.

At midnight they reached new peaks in abandon. There was frenzied hugging and kissing and weeping. People linked hands, singing, 'Auld Lang Syne'. They clutched each other, saying one another's names with passion.

By now Megs was, to everybody present, Megs. But Gilbert, to his resentment, was still That Professorish Bloke Who Has the Cottage at the End of the Track. Despite that, several strange women lunged at him and wetly kissed him. Men slapped his shoulder and shook his hand.

'They don't like me,' he complained to Megs, who had fought through the sway to kiss him as the clock struck twelve.

'It seems to them that you don't like them,' she told him. 'You are being a tad stand-offish.'

'It's not my sort of do.' He fetched another drink and settled into his chair once more. 'When are we going?'

'Oh, come on, Gilbert. It's not long past midnight. The party's just hotting up.'

'Hotting up?' he cried, dismayed. 'I thought it already was as hot as it could get. I want to go home.'

'I don't.' She left him to be miserable.

She went out into the foyer to cool off. Stood pressing a cold beer can to her cheeks.

'Hot, isn't it?' The butcher's boy came to stand beside her. He wore an ancient, carefully tended tuxedo, starched shirt and black bow tie.

'My goodness, Billy.' Megs smiled to him. 'Aren't you smart?'

'I like to dress up. I wear an apron all day.'

'Yes.' Megs wondered if she'd been patronising him.

'So how do you like New Year all the way up here?'

'I think it's wonderful. I'm having a wonderful time.'

'It's different. Year after year it changes. Year after year there's more newcomers taking over the glen. As the locals leave to find work, strangers move into their cottages. They buy them as holiday homes. Or they come live here. The old school's a home now. New folk. They try to fit in, you have to hand it to them. Look at them.' He pointed back into the hall. A moving sway of dancers, whirling and hooching. 'They even do the dances better than we do. They've been to classes.'

Megs remembered her school days, thundering about the gym whilst Mrs Leadbetter, the teacher, bawled instructions. 'Skip, change of step, gels. Link arms with the person to your right and dance into the middle, then back.' She remembered them barging into one another, tripping and hysterical with giggles.

'Aye,' Billy said. 'You best change yoursel' before change changes ye. If y'see what I mean. So,' he said, suspecting he was depressing her, 'are you not dancing with your man?'

'It's not his sort of thing.'

'Right.'

They stood in silence, drinking and cooling off.

'Dunno what you see in him,' the butcher's boy said. 'He's not your type.'

Megs looked at him. She was tempted to tell him to mind his own business, but defended Gilbert instead. 'He makes me see a bit of myself I actually like. I feel less guilty when I'm round him.'

'Guilty? What've you got to be guilty about?' He was, she realised, terribly drunk.

'My little boy,' she said. 'Remember I told you? He was run over when I should've been there to bring him home. I was late.'

He shook his head. 'I'll tell you guilt. I killed my father. There's guilt.'

Megs felt a chill creeping over her scalp. 'I don't believe you.'

'Oh, it's true. My father was not a nice man.' He said the words carefully, sounding each one. 'He beat me. Used anything that came to hand. He hit me for nothin'. Couldn't find a match to light the gas, so I got it.' He did a drunken punch at the air that would have been ineffectual, but for the venom in his face. He rolled up his sleeve, showed a cluster of round white scars. 'Stubbed his fags out on me.' He hated these arms of his, stained as they were with parental rage. 'He had a look that came over his face. It started with his lips. The way he moved them. An' you knew what was coming. It's only these past couple of years I realised it wasn't me he hated. It was hisself. Only he couldn't hit hisself, could he?' He leaned into her again. She watched his face, deeply etched lines round his eyes, round his mouth. This face had been a long time miserable. 'I peed the bed every night till I was twelve. That's when I killed him. There, that's terrible. That's guilt.'

Megs didn't know what to say. 'I don't believe you did that,' she said when at last words came to her. 'How did you do that?'

'He took a heart attack.' He sniffed, swigged his whisky. 'He was in the living room. He just gripped his chest and fell down. He was gaspin' with pain. He lay on the floor and told me to go to the farm. Phone the doctor. His face was all twisted, and he couldn't hardly speak. He said to hurry up.' Billy looked at Megs, piercing, honest eyes. 'But when I got out the door I dawdled. Don't know why. It was a lovely afternoon and I felt so peaceful. I don't think I took him seriously.'

That afternoon forty-four years ago would never leave him. Every colour: the soft purples on the hill hazing into sunlit distance, the dank green moss on the damp at the foot of the wall of the cottage. Every scent: the blast of manure passing the byre, the sour curdle of dairy cows. He'd been a stick of a boy, refugee thin. His hair was heartlessly barbered, shaved up the sides and back, leaving a tuft atop. His face, white with mistrust, looked wizened, childishly wizened. The smattering of freckles over his nose and cheeks looked odd against his permanently worried expression. Puny pale legs stuck out from hand-me-down school shorts, two sizes too big. Scabbed knees. He wore a grey shirt, huge tails stuck into grubby underpants. His shoes, scuffed toes, had metal segs in the heels. He'd been an underfed sparrow of a child. He had not known he appeared like a starved fledgling to others. He'd thought that was how things were.

Hands in pockets, he'd taken two hours to walk the fifty yards from the cottage he shared with his father to the farm. He'd stopped to pick moss from the dyke with his grubby, chewed nails. He'd found a centipede and watched it scurry into a crack. He'd kicked at a stone embedded in the dried mud till it came loose. Then he'd overturned it and squatted, watching the wildlife beneath scatter and wriggle in the sudden flooding of light. He'd picked up a stick and dragged it after him. At last he'd knocked on the back door of the farmhouse. 'My father's ill. He asked me to get you to phone the doctor. He's lyin' on the floor.' After that, he'd been shoved aside whilst grown-ups took over. The farmer's wife had phoned for an ambulance, then run up the path to the cottage.

'But when she got there my father was dead.'

'Where was your mother?'

'She walked out years before.'

Megs shook. 'I'd like to say I don't believe you. But I think I do.'

'So after that Kynoch took me in. I was meant to go to a home, but I just stayed with him. Now I still work for him. I was the butcher's boy then, still am. So don't talk to me about guilt. Guilt'll make y'daft.' He walked to the door and stared out into the bitter dark.

'Why are you telling me this?' Megs asked.

'Always wanted to tell somebody. And you're the only person I know that I don't know. You can't pass it on to anybody local.'

'Why didn't you leave?'

'I belong here. I get excused here.'

'Excused?'

'For day-dreamin' my life away. It's not the thing to do, y'know. Folk'll take advantage. You'll end up tired and cold, standing in the snow with a goose and a door slammed in your face.'

'What do you day-dream about?' Megs touched his arm.

'Freddy. Freddy Stair. He would've danced with you, not like old misery guts back there.'

She stared at him. Then it came to her. 'Fred Astaire.' She glowed.

'Aye, him. He's dead, you know.'

'Yes.' She joined him at the door. The air was frosty clear. The sky deep and starry. The frost purified the air, every scent came to them.

Someone somewhere nearby was smoking dope. Megs wished she had some.

'When my boy was run down, when I kneeled beside him, I heard this awful noise. A terrible, terrible wailing. Demented. The noise was coming from me. I was making it. Do you think we all have a noise like that inside?'

'Aye.' The word came out on an inward breath.

'There.' Megs put her head next to his. 'I've told you something I have never told anybody else. I have always been horrified at that noise I made. And I don't think you killed your father. If he went quickly, it's unlikely an ambulance would have arrived in time. Then there's the trip to hospital. That would've taken over an hour. Don't blame yourself.'

He looked up, nodding. 'Sometimes I hate they stars. They're so buggery belligerent. All they do is shine.' He took her hand. 'C'mon inside.' A brusque order. 'I'll give you a dance.'

They took to the floor. Him with one hand on her waist, the other holding hers aloft. As the band ached out a drunken rendition of 'Hotel California' they waltzed. All her life Megs had dreamed of her perfect partner. Someone who would take her dipping and twirling across the dance floor. A man who could dance like Freddy Stair. Now here it was happening to her. She hated it. She felt controlled, manoeuvred into doing things she didn't want to do. Her feet weren't up to the task. Twirling, she was, beyond her abilities.

Chapter Thirty-Two

Megs and Gilbert got home after four. Megs was drunk. Gilbert was grumpy. On the drive back to the cottage he'd asked Megs why she had spent so long talking to the bloke who worked in the butcher's shop, and she had accused him of being jealous.

'Me?' Hand flying from steering wheel to point to himself. 'Jealous? I don't think so.'

They stopped speaking. Their silence thickened when they got in and found Shameless chewing Gilbert's briefcase. Shameless had had a busy night. He had climbed on to the kitchen table and eaten a bowl of olives and a packet of New York Cheddar crisps. He'd spilled a carton of milk and what contents he hadn't lapped up dripped on to the kitchen floor. He'd found the pheasant Gilbert was planning for his New Year Day dinner and eaten enough of it to ruin it. Then the olives, crisps, milk and pheasant had taken their toll. The mess was beside the door. He'd left the goose untouched.

In the living room Shameless had sought comfort by chewing a pair of Megs's shoes. Then he'd dragged a pair of Gilbert's boxer shorts from the laundry basket and lain on them as he chewed his briefcase. The contents, his book, *The Theme Pack*, were spread across the floor.

'Christ,' said Gilbert. He spoke with no emotion. He was too tired for emotion. 'Now I remember why I never wanted a dog.' He stared at the regurgitated pheasant carcass. 'Now we'll have to have the goose.' He hated goose, but hadn't liked to mention it to Megs. He went to bed.

What a sobering for Megs, cleaning up. She cleaned up the turds and sick, wiped and disinfected the floor. She gathered Gilbert's notes and put them on his work table. She put her dismembered shoes in the bin with the pheasant, milk carton, broken olive bowl and crisp bag. She picked up Gilbert's stolen underpants, thought to wash them, then said, 'Oh, stuff him, grumpy bastard.' And put them back with the clean laundry. It was five-thirty when she'd finished. She was no longer tired, and took Shameless out into the garden. He was too ashamed to bound ahead of her, walked instead at her heel, head down. 'It's a bit late to put on a show of good behaviour,' she told him. 'You have surpassed yourself. The New Year situation is now beyond redemption.' Still, when she, at last, flopped into bed beside Gilbert, she made sure the dog was at her feet. It was the only comfort either of them was going to get.

Next morning they moved stiffly round each other, each making deliberate movements, hoping the other would notice they weren't being spoken to. At last Gilbert broke the hostilities.

'What *were* you doing talking to the butcher's boy for such a long time?'

Megs shrugged. 'We were just talking about what it's like to live here all the time. He says it's not so nice as it looks.' She had no intention of telling him the truth. It had left her feeling depressed and raw. Then she was still tired from cleaning up after Shameless.

Gilbert made a testy sound, 'Nymph,' and disappeared into the kitchen to wrestle with the goose. Megs sat by the fire, reading the same page of a book over and over. During the afternoon and evening they drank too much. But alcohol did not mellow them. They were just boozily irritated with each other. The goose did not cook well; perhaps it was too travelled. Now they both had indigestion. They made odd, sharp exchanges whilst trying not to fart, hiccup or belch.

'I think the sprouts were a bit underdone,' Megs said.

'Well, you should've cooked them yourself.'

'Do you think I'll get down the road tomorrow?' she asked later.

'Should do.' He hoped his disgruntled tone hid how much he really wanted her to stay. He was too proud to end the argument. Besides, he still hadn't forgiven Shameless.

They went to bed early, still tired from the night before. Megs hadn't followed her usual habit of clearing up the kitchen after him. They left the sink piled with dirty dishes, the hob splattered with grease. The table was cluttered with dishes, wine-stained glasses and a half-demolished goose.

They slept sweatily, as deep as their exhausted digestive systems would let them. Voices, ringing shrill from the snowy garden, woke them. They lay a moment listening to footsteps crunching on the path outside and the quizzical surprise of people examining her car.

'Good heavens, whose is this?'

'It isn't Gilbert's.'

'No. That's his over there.'

'There must be someone with him.'

There was rapping at the door and window. 'Coo-hoo Gilbert.' They could hear someone rattling the letterbox.

He squirmed. Clambered from bed, and in his red nightshirt (his Wee Willie Winkie outfit, Megs thought) went to the window. 'Oh Christ. Oh Christ, no.'

'Who is it?' Megs sat up.

'Cathy McGhee.'

'Dysentery?'

'Yes,' he snapped. 'Dysentery McGhee is here. Outside. Wanting in.' He stared in horror at Cathy McGhee in jeans, boots and flying jacket, hopping about outside clutching a couple of bottles of wine. This was the moment he'd dreaded. 'She'll definitely be wanting in.'

'Gilbert,' came the voice from outside. 'I see you, Gilbert. Let us in. It's bloody freezing out here.'

'She's been looking at your car.' Gilbert looked at Megs crossly. 'Why didn't I get you to move it round the corner?'

'Ashamed of it, are you?' said Megs flatly. As if she hadn't always known that.

But Gilbert didn't hear her. He was in misery. 'Oh my God,' he moaned. 'Oh God. Oh God. Oh God.' He rushed downstairs.

Megs could hear him thundering about the living room as she pulled on her jeans and a sweater. When she got into the kitchen, Gilbert still hadn't opened the door, so she let Cathy McGhee and her boyfriend in.

'Megs,' Cathy cried when at last the door opened. 'Megs. What are you doing here?'

Megs could see that for a full two seconds Cathy thought she was here to clean for Gilbert. Then the truth dawned.

'Megs?' Knowingly said, finger moving between Megs and an imaginary Gilbert. 'Are you and Gilbert . . . ? My goodness.'

Megs could tell that Cathy McGhee desperately wanted to turn and drive immediately back to town to phone round with this snippet of gossip. Instead she burst past her into the kitchen, calling, 'Gilbert. Gilbert. Show yourself. We've brought goodies. And want fed.'

She found him by the fire in the living room, still in his Wee Willie Winkie outfit, looking shifty. The devastation of last night's meal was still untouched, but he'd cleared the room of all his drawings and paintings. Megs looked at him sharply, said nothing, thought, so that's what you think of me.

She went upstairs to shower. Still dripping, wrapped in a towel, she stopped on the landing on her way to the bedroom. She stood listening to the cries and guffaws as Gilbert, in his red nightshirt, held court.

'C'mon, Gilbert. Get into the kitchen, do your magic. We're famished.'

'In a second. I'm not quite ready. The culinary muse isn't on me this time in the morning.'

'It's half past eleven. What's this you've been eating last night, anyway?'

'Goose.'

'Well, you can rustle us up something. I'm sure a man of your abilities must know a million things to do with an old goose. Ha, ha.'

They started to talk about people Megs didn't know.

'Martin and Lucy are expecting again.'

'For heaven's sake, don't they know when to stop?' Gilbert boomed sanctimoniously. 'How many sprogs is that they've brought into the world?'

Sprogs, Megs thought. There was something dismissive about the word. It was a description of children from people who didn't have any. Did Gilbert think Lizzy was a sprog?

'So, Gilbert,' Cathy McGhee's companion said, 'how's the book?'

'Ha, don't ask.' Gilbert sighed. 'Actually, I put it aside and started to paint again.'

'That's wonderful.' Cathy's voice. 'Anything you can let us see?'

'No. Not yet.' Gilbert was defensive. 'It's not what I'm painting that matters. It's the actual act of doing it that's so exciting. The small technical decisions as you move through the canvas, trying to achieve some sort of perfection that's in the end exhilarating and humbling. I paint and I think about nothing else but the job in hand. There's a purity in that sort of concentration that's cleansing.'

Megs heard the snap of a lighter and the small fizz of flame licking cigarette end. 'I know what you mean. I feel the same when I work on my novel.'

'Right. You'd know,' said Gilbert. The sound of a whisky bottle being opened, glasses laid out on the table and filled. 'Water?'

'Hmm, please.' Voice lowered, but not lowered enough. 'So, Gilbert, what's this with you and Megs?'

'Oh, it's just . . .' Gilbert stopped. Megs knew he'd be looking vaguely round, running his fingers through his hair.

'A dalliance?' Cathy's boyfriend asked.

'Ha, ha. A pleasant dalliance?' Cathy pursued him.

Megs could tell Gilbert was squirming. 'Pleasant . . .' His voice drifted. 'Yes, pleasant.'

Megs went into the bedroom to finish drying herself, dress and pack. Ten minutes later she stood leaning slightly on the living room doorpost. 'I'll be off then, Gilbert.'

He looked shocked. 'You're not going, are you?'

'Looks like it.'

Cathy McGhee smiled and said, 'You're not leaving on account of us, are you?'

Megs shook her head. 'I have to get back. If you got here it must mean the roads are clear. We've been snowed in for the last few days.'

'How wildly romantic.' Cathy beamed.

Megs moved her lips into what should have been a smile. But she only grimaced. 'You could say that.'

'Wait till I get something on,' Gilbert pleaded. He ran upstairs.

By the time he'd yanked on a pair of pants, socks and boots, Megs had thrown her case in the boot, put Shameless in the back seat and was letting the engine idle.

'I don't want you to go like this,' Gilbert said.

'How do you want me to go?'

'Not like this.'

'I heard you, Gilbert. You denied me. I'm a dalliance, am I?' She could not hide her hurt.

'No. No. I just didn't know what to say. You know how it is.'

'No. No, I don't.' She pressed the accelerator and moved slowly towards the track.

He grabbed the car, ran alongside it. 'Oh please, please. Don't be like this.'

'How am I meant to be? Would you like me to bustle, clean up and smile whilst you and your friends hoot loudly and drink?'

'No.' His hand went to his hair. 'No. Really no.'

'You're ashamed of me, aren't you?'

He shook his head. 'Of course I'm not. I . . .' He couldn't tell her how much he cared. 'Megs, please don't be like this.'

His hurt, his pleading made her feel powerful. It eased her pain. 'You are so clever, Gilbert. You know so much about things I'll never understand. But sometimes, when it comes to people, I think you're just God's gift to stupid.' She pressed the accelerator. 'I'll let you get back to your friends. Go. Go back to your ghost woman. The one you think about and secretly glance at. Her. I won't bother you any more. Don't worry, when the phone rings it won't be me.'

Nightshirt flapping, he stood in the middle of the track, watching her car slip and shove towards the road.

She drove off. All the way home, driving over wet black roads, great dirty cliffs of drifts either side of her, she cried, wishing her parting words to him had been kinder.

Chapter Thirty-Three

When Megs got home Lorraine was curled up on the sofa watching television, drinking vodka and Coke. 'You're back,' she said.

'You always had a knack with the obvious,' Megs told her. 'Where is everybody?'

'Lizzy's with your folks. Hannah with one of her friends, forgotten which one. Jack is having dinner with Sharon's parents.'

'Goodness,' said Megs. 'They have forgiven the haircut, then?'

'Seems like,' said Lorraine. 'Wasn't expecting you till tomorrow. How was it being snowed up?'

'Don't ask.' Megs hung up her coat, kicked off her shoes, and walked through to the kitchen. Lorraine said nothing. Megs wheeled round, reappeared waving her arms. 'All right then, ask.'

'OK. How was it being snowed up?'

'Awful,' said Megs. 'We argued. We went to the dance up the glen. I got horribly drunk, spent too long talking to Billy who works in the butcher's. Then when we got home Shameless had wrecked the cottage. Then Dysentery McGhee turned up and I overheard them talking and I realised I didn't belong with them. So I came home. That was it.'

Lorraine said, 'Do you want a drink? Or a cup of tea?'

'A drink,' said Megs. 'Though the hangover I had after that dance, I was never going to touch alcohol again.'

'So what were you talking to the butcher's boy about?' Lorraine handed her a glass of vodka and Coke.

'Why did you pinpoint that?'

'Just call it instinct. I watched your face.'

'We spoke about guilt,' Megs told her. 'He has this terrible idea that because he took too long to go fetch help when his father had a heart attack, he killed him.'

'That's awful. Do you think he did?'

'No. He was just being a kid. That's all.' Megs lay back on the sofa, forcing Lorraine on to the chair. 'But it was horrible. I looked at him, at his weary old face, and he's only in his fifties, and I saw myself. I saw me in a few years, racked with pain and grief and guilt. Know what I was thinking all the time he spoke? I thought what a waste. What a waste of a person, waste of a life.' She put her glass on her forehead. 'Why do we do it?'

'Everyone feels guilty. You can't be blamed.' Lorraine spoke gently.

'No,' said Megs. 'Lie back and put your glass on your forehead.'

'Because you're daft?' suggested Lorraine.

'That'll be it. Sometimes doing something completely moronic is sort of soothing. Then when your mind's empty you realise you have to fix your life. But what can I do? Sing? Haven't made money doing that.'

'You can make sandwiches,' Lorraine said. 'We could open your sandwich bar. Of all your daft schemes, that's my favourite. My money from Harry came through,' she said.

'When?' Megs asked.

'The other day. We could do it, we really could.'

'Yes,' Megs said. Though the idea made her nervous. 'I'd rather just spend my life lying here on this sofa with a glass of something on my forehead. But I don't suppose it'd work out.' Then, after a while, she asked, 'Do you think my forehead's huge and flat?'

The room got dark, the television flickered silently. Their conversation roamed over past times, old loves, distant memories. Every now and then they tentatively explored the sandwich bar notion.

'I suppose,' said Lorraine, 'we're going to have to do it.'

'Scary though,' said Megs. 'There's only one thing scarier than doing it.'

'What's that?'

'Not doing it,' said Megs.

They were still exchanging reminiscences, anecdotes, snippets of their different New Year celebrations when Gilbert phoned. Megs picked up the receiver.

'Hello.' Gilbert sounded apologetic. 'Did you get home all right?'

'Yes,' said Megs. 'The roads were fine. And once I got on the motorway there was no sign of snow. There's nothing here in town.'

'Good,' said Gilbert. 'I'm coming home on the fifth. I've got to see someone.' He wasn't going to own up to Annette. 'And then a couple of days later I go back to work. My sabbatical's over.'

'Life goes on, eh?'

'Yes.' He sounded sad. 'I'm so sorry if I insulted you. I didn't mean anything I said to Cathy. I was trying to impress them. I was awful.'

She knew he'd been reliving this morning, and had been hard on himself. 'Gilbert.' She said his name softly. 'Don't blame yourself. I was as bad. I just stormed out. I should have come down and chatted. But I felt suddenly out of place. Know what I mean?'

'I know. That's how I felt at that dance.'

'You had the courage not to hide it, too.'

'Will . . . ? Are you . . . ?'

'We'll see each other again, Gilbert. You can bet on that. And no, Gilbert, I won't be cleaning for you any more. Not a good idea. I don't think I'll be cleaning for anybody soon enough, anyway.'

'Good for you,' he said. 'Is there anything I can do? Is there anything you want? Anything.'

She wished she could think of something. It would make them both feel better, she thought. 'If ever there's anything you can do, I'll let you know. Bet on it,' she said.

After she'd rung off, Gilbert sat alone. He had thought that once Cathy McGhee left to go home he would take all his sketches and paintings of Megs out into the garden and burn them. But now the moment had come, he couldn't do it. Instead he bundled them together and put them in his loft. When he'd done he poured himself a drink. He thought the silence in the cottage was hideous. It was filled with his longing.

Megs went back into the living room. Lorraine was lying on the sofa, glass on forehead. 'It is good,' she agreed. 'Putting a glass on your forehead. It's sort of mindless.'

Megs decided. 'I will start a sandwich bar. If you will.'

297

'I'm for it. I'll go for that.'

'We'll have to get our act together. We have to know what we're doing. Go on courses. Accountancy, hygiene and that.'

'You do accountancy. I'll do hygiene,' Lorraine offered.

'No, you do accountancy. You passed maths. I failed miserably. I got English and music.'

'I don't want to do accountancy.'

'Into every life,' Megs said wisely, 'a little accountancy must fall. See that box of wine we just finished? If you take the bag out and squeeze it, there's a glass in there. You do accountancy and you can have it.'

'OK,' said Lorraine. It seemed like a fair deal to her. 'But I want to work behind the counter. I want to look at the customers and flirt with the men.'

'Of course you can do that. I'll be in the back making sandwiches. Bacon, lettuce and tomato and such.'

'I like flirting,' said Lorraine. 'It's friendly. And flattering. It's good for you.' Then, wistfully, 'There'll be young boys. First job. Wearing their new suits, looking all shiny-faced and eager to please.'

'A good old-fashioned cheese sandwich,' said Megs. 'Thick bread, and chutney.'

'Or flirty men from building sites who call you darlin' and take their shirts off on hot days.'

'Nuts are good. Though some people are allergic to them. Chicken and walnuts. Or toasted pine kernels. Gilbert used to put them through things. Salads.'

'Older men, with comfy faces that have done a lot of laughing. With grey bits at the side of their hair. Who get drunk and sing to you. Romantic songs like "Fly Me To the Moon". Who take your hand and pat it and tell you you're lovely.'

'Yes,' said Megs. 'I like them. Next man I have, I'll have one like that.'

When Vivienne arrived with Lizzy she found Megs and Lorraine lying at each end of the sofa, each with a glass on her forehead, still talking about sandwiches and men. Mostly men.

'What are you two doing?' she asked.

'Being silly,' said Megs. 'How are you? Did you have a good New Year? And did you miss me?'

'Yes on both counts, as it happens.' Vivienne collected their glasses. 'I think you two could do with some coffee.'

Lizzy came into the room. 'You're back.' She posed dramatically a moment before rushing across the room, arms wide. For a moment Megs thought, goodness, the welcome I deserve, at last. But Lizzy passed her, fell on her knees. 'Shameless, my best friend. You're back.'

And Megs said, 'Oh well.'

Chapter Thirty-Four

On the fifth of January, the day Gilbert collected Annette from the airport, Aunty Betty died.

'She just drifted out of living in the middle of the night,' Vivienne said. 'According to the doctor she never felt a thing.'

The day after the funeral she and Megs went to clear out Aunty Betty's house. They collected her clothes into bundles suitable for Oxfam and bundles to be thrown out. They stripped her bed. Collected what they wanted to keep, and what was to be sent to auction. They sat at her kitchen table, looking through old family photos.

'Look,' Megs said. 'Here's one of me taken that summer when you were in the sanatorium.'

'Don't you look miserable?'

'I was miserable. Some of the time anyway. I was homesick.'

'I never knew that. I always thought . . .' Vivienne didn't finish the sentence. She always thought Megs preferred being with Aunty Betty to her.

'Look, here's one of her in the tracksuit after she took up jogging.'

'What, after the hysterectomy?'

They giggled.

Aunty Betty's hysterectomy was a family legend. It turned her from interesting relative to heroine. She did not suffer gynaecologists gladly. Constant bleeding, sore breasts, tiredness had sent her to her doctor, who had passed her to a consultant. As soon as she sat in his room, before he even laid a chilled hand on her, or pulled on the dread surgical gloves, he said, 'I think we'll have to give you a wee hysterectomy.'

'You do them in sizes?' Aunty Betty asked. 'You have hysterectomies in trial packs and large economy?'

The consultant raised his hand, dismissing this. Nobody, patients especially, questioned his judgement. 'We can remove just the womb, or we can whip out the works. At your age you'll hardly be needing it.'

'It has always been my intention,' Aunty Betty said, 'to part this world with everything I came into it with. Teeth and all.' She shot him a revealing smile. Sixty and still a perfect shiny set.

Nonetheless, the bleeding persisted. Eventually Aunty Betty gave in to medical pressure and ended up labelled, shaved and tranquillised, lying on a trolley in a corridor leading to the operating theatre of the local hospital. She was wearing a backless gown, a cap and large white socks. Her gynaecologist passed by and patted her arm, 'Soon be done,' he said briskly. 'You're third up this afternoon.'

'Sod this,' said Aunty Betty. She lay watching a small piece of afternoon through the little window opposite where her trolley was parked. She thought about her life. The children she always meant to have. Dancing on Friday nights, loves she'd known. Kisses. Nobody would kiss her again. And that moment in bed when you turned to someone you loved and he turned to you. 'That's a grand moment,' she cried out. Two passing nurses giggled. 'Now my face is chewed with time and worry and too much port and lemon.' She lay. The afternoon still drifted past. She watched it. Two doctors passed, talking about a boat they shared. 'Took her up the Sound of Jura. Lovely sailing. Drinks on the deck. That's the life.'

It seemed to Aunty Betty that the wombs of sorry women, lying on trolleys with bald pubes, paid for such treats. 'Sod this,' she cried. And got up. In fabulous, backless hospital wear she wandered down the corridor. Nobody said a word. She walked back to the ward, fished her shoes from the locker. Then, fearing someone might find her and force her into the operating theatre, she stole a coat from the back of a visitor's chair. And left.

She walked out of the hospital, down to the local taxi office, and arrived at the Seaview Guest House at four-thirty, just when afternoon tea was being cleared off the tables and dinner started in the kitchen.

'Bastards,' she cried, throwing off the stolen coat, revealing her bum through the diabolical hospital outfit to a gobsmacked clientele. The cap and white socks had been left at the hospital. 'Bastards,' she cried again. 'Shaved my privates. Were going to cut me up. I look like Telly Savalas down there. Buggers.' She thundered to the drinks cabinet, poured a huge whisky. Knocked it back. Went to bed and slept for two days.

She took up jogging. In a pink tracksuit she stumped daily along the beach at low tide. She started to eat broccoli and spinach and swore that greens and exercise were her salvation, along with whisky and port and lemon. She never went to the doctor again.

'There was nobody like her,' said Megs.

'No,' said Vivienne. 'She was a one-off.' Then, taking advantage of this moment of mutual mellowness, 'What happened between you and that man of yours? He was the best thing that ever happened to you. Why did you dump him?'

'I don't think either of us did any dumping. But I think we both knew it would have to end. Our lives were too far apart. He was so different from me.' She leaned over, touched Vivienne's arm. Smiling hugely, she said, 'He told a better class of lie than me. His bullshit was class.'

Vivienne tutted. 'Don't know what you mean.'

They moved to empty the food cupboards.

'Oh God,' Megs squealed, taking out a jar of Heinz Sandwich Spread. 'Sandwich Spread, I used to love that. You never bought it. I always vowed that when I grew up I would buy jars and jars of it and eat it all myself. Then I grew up, and it wasn't the same. I didn't like it any more.'

Vivienne objected to any criticism of her mothering skills. 'So that's why you ended up the way you did. I never bought you Sandwich Spread.'

'That'll be it,' said Megs.

'I never heard the like in my life. And I'm sixty-three, you know.'

Megs's heart turned over. She had to look away lest her mother saw her smile. Well, hello, old lie, she thought, haven't heard you in ages.

'You were always so obstinate,' Vivienne said. 'Not liking your name. Saying things like, "I didn't ask to be born." You were a trial.

Then there was that hat.' Vivienne still felt bitter about the hat.

'What hat?' Megs hoped she sounded innocent.

'That lovely pink and green hat I knitted you for school. You came home without it. What happened to that hat?'

Megs looked at her, swallowed and said, 'I lost it.'

'No you didn't, you stuffed it up a drainpipe,' Vivienne snorted.

Megs burst out laughing. 'I didn't know you knew that.'

'I know lots of things.'

'What do you know?'

'I know that if you open that sandwich bar of yours – and it looks like you actually will – you'll need as much money as you can get.'

'I know that too.'

'Your father and me will give you some. We'll match what Lorraine puts in.'

'I can't take your money. You'll need it for your old age.'

'This is my old age. And it'd be going a lot better if I saw you settled. Take the money. For my grandchildren, if nothing else. Your father and me want to chip in. We want to be part of it. A new lease of life. And after all Lorraine's done, it's the least we can do.'

Lorraine went on the accountancy course. It lasted three weeks, long enough for her to master bookkeeping, basic computing, the language of business plans, and, as she put it, the body language of someone who actually believed all this bloody business-speak – projected figures, meetings, business plans. 'That's mostly what business is about. Being cocky,' she told Megs. 'That and having a good jacket when you need it.'

Megs enrolled on a course learning hygiene standards. 'Aunty Betty would not approve.' Whilst she learned the importance of wearing a hairnet, keeping raw and cooked food separately, sterilising work surfaces and knives, Lorraine found a property just up from Stockbridge. 'On the edge of the business belt,' she enthused. 'We'll get the business trade, and the local trade too. We'll make squillions of pounds. I'll have a huge flat with high ceilings, a flash kitchen.'

'With an espresso machine with a handle,' Megs said.

'Two of them.' Lorraine was going to spare no expense. 'And a jacuzzi.'

When they found that Lorraine's money, with the money Megs's parents put up, was not quite enough, Lorraine went to see the bank manager. She bought a navy suit, borrowed Megs's white shirt and Mike's briefcase and promised not to giggle. 'I won't giggle,' she protested, hurt at the accusation that she might. 'I am actually starting to believe this is going to happen.'

She managed the interview well. 'Of course I'm sure it's a paying proposition,' she enthused. 'There's no competition around. Not everybody wants to walk miles for some lunch. A lot of people just send out. Then we plan to stay open late for folks who work late and folks who live round about. Look at this bank.' She waved her arms. 'How many people have you got working here?' And before she got a reply, 'Thirty?' she suggested. 'Well, if thirty people bought a sandwich costing say one pound fifty, that'd be . . .' she removed her calculator from Mike's briefcase, tapped the buttons with polished nails, 'Forty-five pounds a day. Two hundred and twenty-five pounds a week, which is . . .' she thought about this, '. . . not enough to run a business. But,' dismissing this failing, 'we can build on that.' Her energy and enthusiasm got her a loan and a promise of an overdraft facility when they knew how much they might need.

Lorraine emerged triumphantly from the bank, waving to Megs, who had been waiting across the road, because their raising-cash-and-meeting-people budget wouldn't run to two suits.

'We got it. We got it,' Lorraine screamed. She did a small knee-dip, fists clenched. 'Five grand.' She ran down the pavement, shouting, 'Five grand. Five grand. Five grand.'

She and Megs held each other, bouncing round and round. 'Let's get drunk,' said Lorraine. 'We've got five grand. We can spend a little of it. He wants to meet you, though.'

'Will he notice I'm wearing the same suit?'

'Nah, they all wear suits like this.'

'I know,' said Megs. 'Sod work, sod families, sod guilt, let's take the money and run away.'

'Ooh, tempting,' said Lorraine.

Chapter Thirty-Five

A week later, Megs phoned Emotionally-Deranged Davis to tell her she would not be back. The conversation was swift and polite.

'We're sorry to see you go, Megs.'

'Thank you.'

'Best of luck with your new venture.'

'Thank you.'

She went to see Dysentery McGhee personally.

'I thought this was coming,' Dysentery said. 'Is it me? Were we horrible to you at New Year?'

'No. It's nothing to do with that. Actually, I rather think I was horrible to Gilbert.'

'He is sweet really. He's actually a really nice man.'

'I know,' Megs said. 'You don't have to tell me. No, I just won't be cleaning any more. Not for him, or you, or Emotionally-Deranged Davis.'

'Who?'

'Emotionally-Deranged Davis. Julia Davis. That's what I call her. I found it easier to clean for people if they had nicknames. It's less personal.'

'So what did you call Gilbert?'

'Hundred-Miles-An-Hour, on account of his hair.'

'Oh yes. Very good. I like that. And,' lighting a cigarette, 'what did you call me?'

Megs looked away. 'Dysentery McGhee.'

'What! Why?'

'You said, "Just keep it above the dysentery line." So you became Dysentery McGhee.'

'I sound like something out of a bad Western. Dysentery McGhee. Actually I quite like that. It's a bit of rough. So, what are you going to do now, Megs?'

'Open a sandwich bar. I've been working it out with my friend.'

'I like that. I've always wanted to do something like that. Something that requires movement and meeting people.'

Megs looked round. 'You always seem to have the perfect life to me.'

'There you go. You never know what people are thinking,' said Cathy. 'Would you like some coffee?'

Megs nodded.

'What I always fancied,' said Cathy, bringing two cups to the table, 'was being a barmaid. You know, one of those lovable and worldly-wise women who lean on the bar. Big tits.' She indicated the size of tit she fancied, considerably larger than what was actually there. 'I'd lean on the bar and people would tell me their worries, and I'd say, "Never mind, my love. Here's your gin and tonic," or whisky or whatever. I'm just not the sort of woman who can call strangers love, or darling. You are.'

'Me? I have never called anybody I don't know darling.'

'You could.'

'I haven't got the tits for it either,' said Megs, pulling out her T-shirt and surveying her inadequacies.

'Yours are better than mine.' Cathy McGhee pulled out her T-shirt too, and looked at the failings within.

'Will you come for a sandwich?' said Megs.

'Try and keep me away. Do me a favour,' still looking, double-chinned, down her T-shirt.

'Sure. What?'

'Give me a shot at serving. Will you have aprons? And little hats? Let me try calling folk darling.'

'We're going to have matching T-shirts. Lorraine wants them low-cut. She's got the equipment to call people my love and darling, though.'

'I hate her already.' Cathy smiled. 'Go on, let me serve sandwiches sometime, please.'

'OK.' Megs laughed. 'Why not.'

When she left, Cathy kissed her. 'Take care, Megs. Best of luck. And keep in touch. Oh, and phone Gilbert sometime. I know he thinks about you a lot.'

That evening, when Lizzy was sleeping and Lorraine was poring over her projected figures, Megs phoned Gilbert. 'Just wondered how you are,' she said.

'I'm fine. Back to work. Quite enjoying it.'

'Still cycling back and forth.'

'Still cycling.'

'I'm going into business with Lorraine,' she told him. 'We're opening a sandwich bar.'

'I heard, Dysentery McGhee told me,' he said. 'And she told me about Hundred-Miles-An-Hour. Guess what? I've had a haircut. Not as drastic as your Jack's, but you can't call me that any more.'

'Pity. You suited it.'

She heard a woman's voice in the background call his name. 'Gilbert, who's that you're speaking to?'

That's her, Megs thought. The ghost in the corner.

'I have to go,' Gilbert said. 'I'll see you.'

'Yes,' said Megs. 'See you. Will you come for a sandwich?'

'Of course I will.'

But Megs knew he wouldn't.

After Gilbert had rung off, Annette quizzed him. 'Who was that on the phone?'

'Nobody.' He shrugged, not meeting her eye. 'Nothing. Just work. It's not important.' He was ashamed of himself. Looked apologetically across the room to his new ghost in the corner. Annette trailed her gaze after his. He kept doing that these days, looking across the room as if somebody was there, somebody he was saying sorry to.

Chapter Thirty-Six

They called it the Dreamland Café, after the café where Louis Armstrong first played. They spent the spring fitting out the bar and kitchen. They opened for business at the beginning of July. They called their sandwiches after blues singers and tunes. They had never been so tired in their lives. Megs's hands were raw from wiping surfaces and cutting up lettuce, tomatoes and onions. 'I never knew grating cheese could be so draining.' But by the end of the month they'd made more than their projected figure and were wildly pleased with themselves.

'I'll soon be able to afford a place of my own,' said Lorraine. 'Big flat, jacuzzi, here I come.'

It was late August, early evening. Lizzy, in her new school outfit, was home with Vivienne, who regularly came in to help, to boss and to tell customers she was sixty-three, you know. Megs and Lorraine had just locked the door and were walking down the hill towards Stockbridge. Laughing.

Gilbert and Annette were in a taxi, going back to Annette's, where she would cook a light supper before they went to the Filmhouse.

'We'll just have some smoked duck and a tomato salad before we go,' Annette said.

Gilbert reached into her supermarket bag, pulled out a tomato and held it to his nose. 'Fine.' He saw Megs and Lorraine walking down the hill, heard their laughter cannon up the street. 'Oh God,' he said. He knew he'd bump into her one day.

Seeing his expression, Annette followed his gaze. 'That's her, isn't it?'

Gilbert said nothing.

'I know there was someone, Gilbert,' Annette said. 'And I know she wasn't the first.' She fixed him with a look. One of her looks.

The taxi passed the two as they walked.

'Thank heavens,' Gilbert said.

The taxi stopped at the lights. 'Oh, change. Change, please.' Gilbert silently pleaded.

Megs and Lorraine drew level, turned to cross the road. For the first time in months, Megs and Gilbert were face to face.

She did not know what to do. Smile? Look away? Stick out her tongue? Oh no, not that. He had, in the end, denied her. But then he only got there first. How long would it have been before she denied him? He'd been good for her. Perhaps she'd even been good for him. She remembered summer evenings, things they'd done. They'd walked across the field. Him with Lizzy on his shoulders, her hand in his. Shameless running ahead. They'd sat together on the kitchen doorstep long after midnight, talking, rambling conversations. She'd told him some of her secrets. These things she'd done with him were favourite memories. Pictures she'd keep in her head.

She grinned at him. Leaned forward, knocked at the taxi window. Shook a scolding finger. 'Hey, Gilbert. That is *not* a tomato.'